The Best Book of
HIT SINGLES
Ever!

The Best Book of
HIT SINGLES
Ever!

All the Top 20 Charts
for 45 years

COMPILED BY DAVE McALEER

CARLTON

CONTENTS

INTRODUCTION

The only way to get a real feel of the UK pop scene at any given moment is from the pop charts, as they instantly transport you back to the time concerned. There is also no better way to judge a record than in the context of its contemporaries and no other book makes these nostalgia trips easier or more interesting. The simple aim of this book is to put the 6,000 plus biggest UK hits of the last five decades into some kind of perspective, and to help you follow the careers of the 2,500 acts that put these singles into the Top 20.

Many musical changes have occurred in the last 45 years, and they are all chronicled in these pages. Indeed, it could be said that the only constants during the period were the fact most parents didn't appreciate their children's music, a good "novelty" record usually found a ready UK audience and there was always a handful of "wannabe" teen idols waiting to dethrone the current crop of pop stars.

The major happening was, of course, the arrival and rise of Rock music: the hybrid of US R&B, Pop and C&W that was first heard in Britain in 1954. Rock has, of course, changed its direction and sound many times over the years, but even as the millennium dawns it is still the nucleus of pop music.

From a British point of view, the most important change to the music scene during this period was the upsurge of interest in UK recording artists. In the 1950s, few British acts could equal their American peers' worldwide popularity, and most of them simply recorded cover versions of US hits for the British market. After the Beatles broke down the barriers, countless other UK artists became internationally successful and for the last 35 years the influence of British artists and the UK chart has been felt right around the globe.

CHARTS USED. The chart positions used for compiling the monthly Top 20s were those accepted at the time as the most accurate. The NME charts have been used for the first 10 years, and after that the information came from the UK record industry bible, Record Retailer, later known as Music Week.

CHART FILES. The Top 20 charts are compiled by means of a complex and comprehensive system, which considers not only a record's weekly chart placings and peak position, but also the number of weeks it spent in the Top 10 and Top 20, its weeks at No. 1 (if applicable) and its performance on other major charts.

Apart from normal chart features these Top 20s also show:
(a) The total number of weeks a record spent in the Top 20 during that chart run.
(b) Whether it was the artist's (or the first named artist in the case of duos) first (F) or most recent (L) Top 20 entry.
(c) Whether it sold a million (G) or over two million (P) copies.

LISTING BY ARTISTS NAME. This easy-to-check index lists an artist's hits in alphabetical order and shows the month the hit entered this book's UK Top 20. Therefore, it is a simple matter to check the charts concerned for more information about the record. This index also shows the nationality of the act concerned and indicates if the record was a re-issue or re-mix of a previous Top 20 hit (*), or whether the act was a shared hit (<). If it was a shared hit, the main entry is under the artist first named on the label but the song is also listed under the second or other names.

LISTING BY SONG TITLE. An alphabetical listing of all song titles in this book with the artist's name.

TOP ALL TIME ARTISTS

TOP 100 ACTS & RECORD These Top 100s are chart rather than sales-related. Therefore, records with long chart stays, or more than one Top 20 run, benefit most. Singles which sold vast quantities during relatively short chart stays, such as Elton John's 'Candle In The Wind 1997' (which is 109th) fare less well. The charts are based on a points system that takes into consideration each record's weekly Top 20 position, its peak position and weeks in the Top 10 and Top 20. If a record has been re-issued or re-mixed then points are added together. If a record has been re-recorded, it is counted separately.

1	Elvis Presley	56	97
2	Cliff Richard	58	95
3	Madonna	84	98
4	Beatles	63	96
5	Michael Jackson	72	97
6	Rod Stewart	71	97
7	Queen	74	98
8	Elton John	71	98
9	David Bowie	69	97
10	Rolling Stones	63	95
11	Paul Mccartney	71	97
12	Abba	74	92
13	Status Quo	68	90
14	Stevie Wonder	66	97
15	Bee Gees	67	97
16	Kylie Minogue	88	98
17	Shadows	60	80
18	Lonnie Donegan	56	62
19	Pet Shop Boys	85	97
20	Slade	71	84
21	Everly Brothers	57	65
22	Hollies	63	88
23	George Michael	84	97
24	Shakin' Stevens	80	90
25	Tom Jones	65	94
26	Frank Sinatra	54	86
27	Diana Ross	70	96
28	U2	83	97
29	UB40	80	97
30	Erasure	86	95
31	Pat Boone	55	62
32	Madness	79	92
33	Whitney Houston	85	97
34	Prince	84	97
35	Roy Orbison	60	66
36	Take That	92	96
37	Perry Como	53	73
38	T. Rex	70	91
39	Wet Wet Wet	87	97
40	Phil Collins	81	96
41	Hot Chocolate	70	98
42	Supremes	64	72
43	Kinks	64	83
44	Adam Faith	59	64
45	Manfred Mann	64	73
46	Connie Francis	58	62
47	Duran Duran	81	95
48	Electric Light Orchestra	72	83
49	Janet Jackson	86	97
50	Frankie Vaughan	54	67
51	Bill Haley	54	74
52	Beach Boys	64	87
53	Petula Clark	54	88
54	Police	79	97
55	Blondie	78	95
56	Olivia Newton-John	71	90
57	Depeche Mode	81	97
58	Donna Summer	76	96
59	Shirley Bassey	57	97
60	Gary Glitter	72	84
61	Johnnie Ray	52	57
62	Four Tops	66	88
63	Mariah Carey	90	97
64	Frankie Laine	52	59
65	Showaddywaddy	74	79
66	Who	65	81
67	Mud	73	76
68	Celine Dion	92	97
69	Adam Ant	80	90
70	Iron Maiden	82	98
71	East 17	92	97
72	Wham!	82	86
73	Dean Martin	53	69
74	Cilla Black	64	71
75	Herman's Hermits	64	70
76	Sweet	71	78
77	Bon Jovi	86	96
78	Billy Fury	59	65
79	Dusty Springfield	63	89
80	Jason Donovan	88	91
81	Jam	77	82
82	Roxy Music	72	82
83	John Lennon	69	84
84	Engelbert Humperdinck	67	72
85	Boney M	77	92
86	David Essex	73	83
87	Eternal	93	97
88	Duane Eddy	58	86
89	Gene Pitney	63	68
90	Bay City Rollers	71	77
91	Boyzone	94	97
92	Oasis	94	98
93	Jacksons/Jackson Five	70	88
94	10cc	72	78
95	Spandau Ballet	80	86
96	Dickie Valentine	54	59
97	Bananarama	82	91
98	Simply Red	85	97
99	Human League	81	95
100	David Whitfield	53	58

TOP 100 SINGLES

1. Rock Around The Clock
   Bill Haley & His Comets
2. Bohemian Rhapsody
   Queen
3. You've Lost That Lovin'
   Feeling
   Righteous Brothers
4. Relax
   Frankie Goes To Hollywood
5. Holiday
   Madonna
6. (Everything I Do) I Do It
   For You
   Bryan Adams
7. Sailing
   Rod Stewart
8. Let's Twist Again
   Chubby Checker
9. Do They Know It's Christmas
   Band Aid
10. Take My Breath Away
    Berlin
11. Albatross
    Fleetwood Mac
12. Love Is All Around
    Wet Wet Wet
13. Reet Petite
    Jackie Wilson
14. You Sexy Thing
    Hot Chocolate
15. I Will Survive
    Gloria Gaynor
16. Young Girl
    Gary Puckett & The Union
    Gap
17. Blue Monday
    New Order
18. He Ain't Heavy,
    He's My Brother
    Hollies
19. Secret Love
    Doris Day
20. Imagine
    John Lennon
21. You To Me Are Everything
    Real Thing
22. Two Tribes
    Frankie Goes To Hollywood
23. Cara Mia
    David Whitfield
24. Space Oddity
    David Bowie
25. Tainted Love
    Soft Cell
26. Mary's Boy Child
    Harry Belafonte
27. All Right Now
    Free

28. Leader Of The Pack
    Shangri-Las
29. When I Fall In Love
    Nat 'King' Cole
30. Rose Marie
    Slim Whitman
31. Young At Heart
    Bluebells
32. I Heard It Through
    The Grapevine
    Marvin Gaye
33. Crazy For You
    Madonna
34. I Feel Love
    Donna Summer
35. A Whiter Shade Of Pale
    Procol Harum
36. Diana
    Paul Anka
37. I Will Always Love You
    Whitney Houston
38. She Loves You
    Beatles
39. Give Me Your Word
    Tennessee Ernie Ford
40. When A Man Loves
    A Woman
    Percy Sledge
41. You're The One That I Want
    John Travolta &
    Olivia Newton-John
42. Dancing Queen
    Abba
43. Temptation
    Heaven 17
44. Unchained Melody
    Righteous Brothers
45. In The Air Tonight
    Phil Collins
46. Think Twice
    Celine Dion
47. Reach Out I'll Be There
    Four Tops
48. Y.M.C.A.
    Village People
49. Wonderful Land
    Shadows
50. I Remember You
    Frank Ifield
51. Happy Xmas (War Is Over)
    John & Yoko & The
    Plastic Ono Band
52. Sugar Sugar
    Archies
53. All I Have To Do Is
    Dream/Claudette
    Everly Brothers

54. Cars
    Gary Numan
55. It's Now Or Never
    Elvis Presley
56. Cathy's Clown
    Everly Brothers
57. Mull Of Kintyre/Girls'
    School
    Paul Mccartney
58. All Shook Up
    Elvis Presley
59. Heartbreak Hotel
    Elvis Presley
60. Hey Jude
    Beatles
61. Don't You Want Me
    Human League
62. Last Christmas/
    Everything She Wants
    Wham!
63. Magic Moments
    Perry Como
64. Just Walkin' In The Rain
    Johnnie Ray
65. Who's Sorry Now
    Connie Francis
66. Rivers Of Babylon/Brown
    Girl In The Ring
    Boney M
67. Living Doll
    Cliff Richard
68. Stay
    Shakespear's Sister
69. Can't Get By Without You
    Real Thing
70. I'll Be There For You
    Rembrandts
71. You Got The Love
    Source Featuring
    Candi Staton
72. Young Love
    Tab Hunter
73. What Do You Want To Make
    Those Eyes At Me For
    Emile Ford &
    The Checkmates
74. Whatever Will Be Will Be
    Doris Day
75. The Israelites
    Desmond Dekker &
    The Aces
76. Have You Seen Her
    Chi-Lites
77. Side Saddle
    Russ Conway
78. I'll Do Anything For Love
    (But I Won't Do That)
    Meat Loaf

79. Tears
    Ken Dodd
80. Baby Love
    Supremes
81. I'll Be Home
    Pat Boone
82. Hold My Hand
    Don Cornell
83. Green Green Grass
    Of Home
    Tom Jones
84. Heart Of Glass
    Blondie
85. Let's Dance
    Chris Montez
86. Telstar
    Tornados
87. The Last Waltz
    Engelbert Humperdinck
88. Cherry Pink And Apple
    Blossom White
    Eddie Calvert
89. The Best Things In Life
    Are Free
    Luther Vandross &
    Janet Jackson
90. Drive
    Cars
91. Carolina Moon/
    Stupid Cupid
    Connie Francis
92. Wannabe
    Spice Girls
93. I See The Moon
    Stargazers
94. Rhythm Is A Dancer
    Snap
95. I'll Be Missing You
    Puff Daddy & Faith Evans
96. Things Can Only
    Get Better
    D:Ream
97. I Want You Back
    Jackson Five
98. In The Summertime
    Mungo Jerry
99. Apache
    Shadows
100. Softly Softly
     Ruby Murray

1954

This Mnth	Prev Mnth	Title	Artist	Label	Wks	(US 20 Pos)	
1	12	**Oh Mein Papa**	Eddie Calvert	Columbia	21	(9)	F
2	1	**Answer Me**	Frankie Laine	Philips	17		
3	4	**Let's Have A Party**	Winifred Atwell	Philips	9		
4	3	**Swedish Rhapsody**	Mantovani	Decca	18		
5	15	**Cloud Lucky Seven**	Guy Mitchell	Philips	15		
6	-	**Blowing Wild**	Frankie Laine	Philips	12		
7	-	**Rags To Riches**	David Whitfield	Decca	11		
8	6	**Chika Boom**	Guy Mitchell	Philips	15		
9	2	**Answer Me**	David Whitfield	Decca	14		
10	18	**Ricochet**	Joan Regan	Decca	5		F
11	10	**Poppa Piccolino**	Diana Decker	Columbia	10		F L
12	-	**Happy Wanderer**	Obernkirchen Children's Choir	Parlophone	26		F L
13	-	**That's Amore**	Dean Martin	Capitol	11	(2)	
14	11	**Crying In The Chapel**	Lee Lawrence	Decca	6		F
15	-	**The Creep**	Ken Mackintosh	HMV	2		F
16	7	**Swedish Rhapsody**	Ray Martin	Columbia	4		L
17	8	**I Saw Mommy Kissing Santa Claus**	Beverley Sisters	Philips	5		F
18	5	**I Saw Mommy Kissing Santa Claus**	Jimmy Boyd	Columbia	6	(1)	F L
19	-	**Oh! My Pa-Pa**	Eddie Fisher	HMV	3	(1)	
20	16	**Dragnet**	Ray Anthony	Capitol	2	(3)	F L

1	1	**Oh Mein Papa**	Eddie Calvert	Columbia	21	(9)	F
2	6	**Blowing Wild**	Frankie Laine	Philips	12		
3	5	**Cloud Lucky Seven**	Guy Mitchell	Philips	16		
4	13	**That's Amore**	Dean Martin	Capitol	11	(2)	
5	7	**Rags To Riches**	David Whitfield	Decca	11		
6	-	**Tennessee Wig Walk**	Bonnie Lou	Parlophone	10		F
7	12	**Happy Wanderer**	Obernkirchen Children's Choir	Parlophone	26		F
8	-	**Woman (Uh-Huh)**	Jose Ferrer	Philips	5	(18)	F
9	2	**Answer Me**	Frankie Laine	Philips	17		
10	4	**Swedish Rhapsody**	Mantovani	Decca	18		
11		**Skin Deep**	Ted Heath	Decca	3		
12	8	**Chika Boom**	Guy Mitchell	Philips	15		
13	-	**Don't Laugh At Me**	Norman Wisdom	Columbia	15		F
14	-	**The Book**	David Whitfield	Decca	15		
15	-	**I See The Moon**	Stargazers	Decca	15		
16	-	**Ebb Tide**	Frank Chacksfield	Decca	2	(2)	
17	19	**Oh! My Pa-Pa**	Eddie Fisher	HMV	4	(1)	
18	-	**Cuff Of My Shirt**	Guy Mitchell	Philips	3		
19	-	**Sippin' Soda**	Guy Mitchell	Philips	1		
20	-	**Dragnet**	Ted Heath	Decca	5		

◆ Swiss song 'Oh Mein Papa' (aka 'Oh! My Pa-Pa') was the top transatlantic hit. In the USA Eddie Fisher's vocal topped the chart with British-based trumpeter Eddie Calvert's version runner-up. In Britain the roles were reversed.

◆ American songwriter Joe Darion had a hot winter with his compositions 'Changing Partners' (Patti Page, Kay Starr, Bing Crosby) and 'Ricochet' (Teresa Brewer, Joan Regan) hitting on both sides of the Atlantic.

March 1954

This Mnth	Prev Mnth	Title	Artist	Label	Wks	(US 20 Pos)	
1	15	I See The Moon	Stargazers	Decca	15		
2	1	Oh Mein Papa	Eddie Calvert	Columbia	21	(9)	F
3	7	Happy Wanderer	Obernkirchen Children's Choir	Parlophone	26		F
4	6	Tennessee Wig Walk	Bonnie Lou	Parlophone	10		F
5	13	Don't Laugh At Me	Norman Wisdom	Columbia	15		F
6	4	That's Amore	Dean Martin	Capitol	11	(2)	
7	14	The Book	David Whitfield	Decca	15		
8	2	Blowing Wild	Frankie Laine	Philips	12		
9	3	Cloud Lucky Seven	Guy Mitchell	Philips	16		
10	-	Skin Deep	Duke Ellington	Philips	3		F
11	-	Changing Partners	Kay Starr	Capitol	14	(13)	
12	-	Bell Bottom Blues	Alma Cogan	HMV	9		F
13	5	Rags To Riches	David Whitfield	Decca	11		
14	-	Changing Partners	Bing Crosby	Brunswick	3	(17)	
15	-	Granada	Frankie Laine	Philips	2		
16	8	Woman (Uh-Huh)	Jose Ferrer	Philips	5	(18)	F
17	17	Oh! My Pa-Pa	Eddie Fisher	HMV	4	(1)	
18	18	Cuff Of My Shirt	Guy Mitchell	Philips	3		
19	-	Moonlight Serenade	Glenn Miller	HMV	1		F
20	-	From Here To Eternity	Frank Sinatra	Capitol	9		

April 1954

		Title	Artist	Label	Wks	(US 20 Pos)	
1	1	I See The Moon	Stargazers	Decca	15		
2	3	Happy Wanderer	Obernkirchen Children's Choir	Parlophone	26		F L
3	-	Secret Love	Doris Day	Philips	29	(1)	
4	10	Changing Partners	Kay Starr	Capitol	14	(13)	
5	5	Don't Laugh At Me	Norman Wisdom	Columbia	15		F
6	12	Bell Bottom Blues	Alma Cogan	HMV	9		F
7	2	Oh Mein Papa	Eddie Calvert	Columbia	21	(9)	F
8	-	Such A Night	Johnnie Ray	Philips	18		
9	7	The Book	David Whitfield	Decca	15		
10	-	The Kid's Last Fight	Frankie Laine	Philips	10		
11	-	Bimbo	Ruby Wright	Parlophone	5		F
12	4	Tennessee Wig Walk	Bonnie Lou	Parlophone	10		F L
13	15	Changing Partners	Bing Crosby	Brunswick	3	(17)	
14	6	That's Amore	Dean Martin	Capitol	11	(2)	
15	-	Dime And A Dollar	Guy Mitchell	Philips	5		
16	16	Granada	Frankie Laine	Philips	2		
17	-	Tenderly	Nat 'King' Cole	Capitol	1		
18	18	Cuff Of My Shirt	Guy Mitchell	Philips	3		
19	-	Friends And Neighbours	Billy Cotton & His Band	Decca	12		L
20	-	Happy Wanderer	Stargazers	Decca	1		

◆ Mixed quintet The Stargazers became the first British group to rack up two No. 1s; a feat that was not repeated until 1963 by The Beatles. The former group were produced by Dick Rowe, the Decca A&R man who turned down The Beatles.

◆ Al Martino was one of several American singers who covered US hits just for the British market. His own version of 'Wanted' sold just as well as original hitmaker Perry Como's recording in the UK.

1954

◆ British songstress Petula Clark made her UK chart debut with the French song, 'The Little Shoemaker'. This foot-tapping composition also gave The Gaylords their biggest American hit.

◆ American heart-throbs Frankie Laine, Guy Mitchell and Johnnie Ray had British hits with records that failed in their homeland. Among these was Ray's No. 1 'Such A Night', banned by the BBC for being too suggestive.

July 1954

This Mnth	Prev Mnth	Title	Artist	Label	Wks	(US 20 Pos)	
1	11	**Cara Mia**	David Whitfield	Decca	25	(10)	
2	1	**Secret Love**	Doris Day	Philips	29	(1)	
3	-	**Little Things Mean A Lot**	Kitty Kallen	Brunswick	23	(1)	F L
4	15	**Idle Gossip**	Perry Como	HMV	15		
5	12	**Wanted**	Al Martino	Capitol	15		
6	7	**Wanted**	Perry Como	HMV	15	(1)	
7	2	**Such A Night**	Johnnie Ray	Philips	18		
8	14	**The Little Shoemaker**	Petula Clark	Polygon	10		F
9	6	**I Get So Lonely**	Four Knights	Capitol	11	(3)	F L
10	3	**Friends And Neighbours**	Billy Cotton & His Band	Decca	12		L
11	-	**Three Coins In The Fountain**	Frank Sinatra	Capitol	19	(7)	
12	4	**Happy Wanderer**	Obernkirchen Children's Choir	Parlophone	26		F L
13	-	**The Story Of Three Loves**	Winifred Atwell	Decca	9		
14	-	**Three Coins In The Fountain**	Four Aces	Brunswick	6	(2)	F
15	5	**Someone Else's Roses**	Joan Regan	Decca	8		
16	8	**Heart Of My Heart**	Max Bygraves	HMV	8		
17	-	**Young-At-Heart**	Frank Sinatra	Capitol	1	(2)	F
18	-	**Never Never Land**	Frank Weir	Decca	13		
19	-	**Charleston**	Winifred Atwell	Decca	8		
20	-	**The Little Shoemaker**	Frank Weir	Decca	4		

August 1954

This Mnth	Prev Mnth	Title	Artist	Label	Wks	(US 20 Pos)	
1	1	**Cara Mia**	David Whitfield	Decca	25	(10)	
2	3	**Little Things Mean A Lot**	Kitty Kallen	Brunswick	23	(1)	F L
3	11	**Three Coins In The Fountain**	Frank Sinatra	Capitol	19	(7)	
4	4	**Idle Gossip**	Perry Como	HMV	15		
5	2	**Secret Love**	Doris Day	Philips	29	(1)	
6	5	**Wanted**	Al Martino	Capitol	15		
7	14	**Three Coins In The Fountain**	Four Aces	Brunswick	6	(2)	F
8	6	**Wanted**	Perry Como	HMV	15	(1)	
9	-	**My Friend**	Frankie Laine	Philips	15		
10	13	**The Story Of Three Loves**	Winifred Atwell	Decca	9		
11	8	**The Little Shoemaker**	Petula Clark	Polygon	10		F
12	9	**I Get So Lonely**	Four Knights	Capitol	11	(3)	F L
13	-	**Black Hills Of Dakota**	Doris Day	Philips	7		
14	-	**Little Things Mean A Lot**	Alma Cogan	HMV	5		
15	7	**Such A Night**	Johnnie Ray	Philips	18		
16	18	**Never Never Land**	Frank Weir	Decca	13		
17	-	**Midnight**	Eddie Calvert	Columbia	7		
18	-	**Three Coins In The Fountain**	Tony Brent	Columbia	6		
19	-	**Destiny**	Johnnie Ray	Columbia	4		
20	19	**Charleston**	Winifred Atwell	Decca	8		

◆ British balladeer David Whitfield had his biggest hit, 'Cara Mia'. It not only topped the UK chart but also reached the US Top 10, earning him a gold disc.

◆ Many US pop acts covered R&B hits: The McGuire Sisters scored with The Spaniels' 'Goodnight, Sweet-heart, Goodnight', June Valli's 'I Understand' joined the original by The Four Tunes on the American chart, and Canadian quartet The Crew-Cuts had a US No. 1 with The Chords' scat smash, 'Sh-Boom'. The latter becoming the first rock-related hit in Britain.

1954

This Mnth	Prev Mnth	Title	Artist	Label	Wks	(US 20 Pos)	
1	3	Three Coins In The Fountain	Frank Sinatra	Capitol	19	(7)	
2	1	Cara Mia	David Whitfield	Decca	25	(10)	
3	2	Little Things Mean A Lot	Kitty Kallen	Brunswick	23	(1)	F L
4	9	My Friend	Frankie Laine	Philips	15		
5	-	Hold My Hand	Don Cornell	Vogue	21	(5)	F
6	4	Idle Gossip	Perry Como	HMV	15		
7	5	Secret Love	Doris Day	Philips	29	(1)	
8	-	Smile	Nat 'King' Cole	Capitol	14	(14)	
9	13	Black Hills Of Dakota	Doris Day	Philips	7		
10	-	Gilly Gilly Ossenfeffer Katzenellen Bogen By The Sea	Max Bygraves	HMV	8		
11	-	West Of Zanzibar	Anthony Steel & The Radio Revellers	Polygon	6		F L
12	6	Wanted	Al Martino	Capitol	15		
13	10	The Story Of Three Loves	Winifred Atwell	Decca	9		
14	14	Little Things Mean A Lot	Alma Cogan	HMV	5		
15	8	Wanted	Perry Como	HMV	15	(1)	
16	-	Story Of Tina	Ronnie Harris	Columbia	2		F
17	-	Some Day	Frankie Laine	Columbia	3	(18)	
18	16	Never Never Land	Frank Weir	Decca	13		
19	-	Dixieland	Winifred Atwell	Decca	4		
20	-	Little Things Mean A Lot	Jimmy Young	Decca	2		

This Mnth	Prev Mnth	Title	Artist	Label	Wks	(US 20 Pos)	
1	5	Hold My Hand	Don Cornell	Vogue	21	(5)	F
2	8	Smile	Nat 'King' Cole	Capitol	14	(14)	
3	1	Three Coins In The Fountain	Frank Sinatra	Capitol	19	(7)	
4	4	My Friend	Frankie Laine	Philips	15		
5	3	Little Things Mean A Lot	Kitty Kallen	Brunswick	23	(1)	F
6	2	Cara Mia	David Whitfield	Decca	25	(10)	
7	-	If I Give My Heart To You	Doris Day	Philips	11	(4)	
8	-	Sway	Dean Martin	Capitol	7	(15)	
9	-	My Son My Son	Vera Lynn	Decca	14		
10	-	The Story Of Tina	Al Martino	Capitol	8		
11	-	This Ole House	Rosemary Clooney	Philips	18	(1)	
12	-	This Old House	Billie Anthony	Columbia	15		F
13	-	There Must Be A Reason	Frankie Laine	Philips	9		
14	-	Sh-Boom	Crew-Cuts	Mercury	9	(1)	F
15	10	Gilly Gilly Ossenfeffer Katzenellen Bogen By The Sea	MaxBygraves	HMV	8		
16	9	Black Hills Of Dakota	Doris Day	Philips	8		
17	7	Secret Love	Doris Day	Philips	29	(1)	
18	-	Rain Rain Rain	Frankie Laine	Philips	16	(30)	
19	16	The Story Of Tina	Ronnie Harris	Columbia	3		F
20	-	If I Give My Heart To You	Joan Regan	Decca	11		

◆ American vocalist Kitty Kallen failed to chart again after hitting the top.

◆ Both of West Indian pianist Winifred Atwell's Christmas hits, 'Let's Have A Party' and 'Let's Have Another Party', sold over a million copies worldwide.

1954

November 1954

This Mnth	Prev Mnth	Title	Artist	Label	Wks	(US 20 Pos)	
1	9	My Son My Son	Vera Lynn	Decca	14		
2	11	This Ole House	Rosemary Clooney	Philips	18	(1)	
3	1	Hold My Hand	Don Cornell	Vogue	21	(5)	F
4	20	If I Give My Heart To You	Joan Regan	Decca	11		
5	2	Smile	Nat 'King' Cole	Capitol	14	(14)	
6	7	If I Give My Heart To You	Doris Day	Philips	11	(4)	
7	12	This Old House	Billie Anthony	Columbia	15		F
8	18	Rain Rain Rain	Frankie Laine	Philips	16	(30)	
9	6	Cara Mia	David Whitfield	Decca	25	(10)	
10	5	Little Things Mean A Lot	Kitty Kallen	Brunswick	23	(1)	F
11	4	My Friend	Frankie Laine	Philips	15		
12	-	Santo Natale	David Whitfield	Decca	10		
13	-	No One But You	Billy Eckstine	MGM	17		F
14	13	There Must Be A Reason	Frankie Laine	Philips	9		
15	3	Three Coins In The Fountain	Frank Sinatra	Capitol	19	(7)	
16	14	Sh-Boom	Crew-Cuts	Mercury	9	(1)	F
17	-	I Need You Now	Eddie Fisher	HMV	10	(1)	
18	-	Let's Have Another Party	Winifred Atwell	Decca	8		
19	8	Sway	Dean Martin	Capitol	7	(15)	
20	-	Sh-Boom	Stan Freberg	Capitol	2		F

December 1954

This	Prev	Title	Artist	Label	Wks	(US)	
1	18	Let's Have Another Party	Winifred Atwell	Decca	8		
2	12	Santo Natale	David Whitfield	Decca	10		
3	29	This Ole House	Rosemary Clooney	Philips	18	(1)	
4	13	No One But You	Billy Eckstine	MGM	17		F
5	-	I Still Believe	Ronnie Hilton	HMV	14		F
6	1	My Son My Son	Vera Lynn	Decca	14		
7	3	Hold My Hand	Don Cornell	Vogue	21	(5)	F
8	8	Rain Rain Rain	Frankie Laine	Philips	16		
9	7	This Ole House	Billie Anthony	Columbia	15		F
10	4	If I Give My Heart To You	Joan Regan	Decca	11		
11	-	Heartbeat	Ruby Murray	Columbia	16		F
12	-	Let's Get Together No. 1	Big Ben Banjo Band	Columbia	4		F
13	-	Finger Of Suspicion	Dickie Valentine	Decca	15		
14	17	I Need You Now	Eddie Fisher	HMV	10	(1)	
15	-	I Can't Tell A Waltz From A Tango	Alma Cogan	HMV	11		
16	5	Smile	Nat 'King' Cole	Capitol	14	(14)	
17	-	Shake, Rattle And Roll	Bill Haley & His Comets	Brunswick	14	(7)	
18	6	If I Give My Heart To You	Doris Day	Philips	10	(4)	
19	-	Veni Vidi Vici	Ronnie Hilton	HMV	8		
20	-	Let's Have A Party	Winifred Atwell	Philips	6		

◆ Elvis Presley, who had yet to have a UK release, was voted eighth Most Promising New C&W Singer in *Billboard's* US DJ poll – Tommy Collins took the crown.

◆ The flagging dance hall business on both sides of the Atlantic was revitalized firstly by the growth in interest in Latin American dances like the tango and mambo, and secondly by rock'n'roll. The latter was just starting to make an impression in the UK thanks to records like 'Sh-Boom' by The Crew-Cuts and 'Shake, Rattle And Roll' by Bill Haley & The Comets.

1955

This Mnth	Prev Mnth	Title	Artist	Label	Wks	(US 20 Pos)	
1	13	Finger Of Suspicion	Dickie Valentine	Decca	15		
2	-	Mambo Italiano	Rosemary Clooney	Philips	16	(10)	
3	4	No One But You	Billy Eckstine	MGM	17		F
4	5	I Still Believe	Ronnie Hilton	HMV	14		F
5	11	Heartbeat	Ruby Murray	Columbia	16		F
6	17	Shake, Rattle And Roll	Bill Haley & His Comets	Brunswick	14	(7)	
7	-	Mr. Sandman	Dickie Valentine	Decca	12		
8	15	I Can't Tell A Waltz From A Tango	Alma Cogan	HMV	11		
9	-	Mr. Sandman	Chordettes	Columbia	9	(1)	F
10	8	Rain Rain Rain	Frankie Laine	Philips	16		
11	-	Mr. Sandman	Four Aces	Brunswick	5	(10)	
12	3	This Ole House	Rosemary Clooney	Philips	18	(1)	
13	1	Let's Have Another Party	Winifred Atwell	Decca	8		
14	2	Santo Natale	David Whitfield	Decca	10		
15	7	Hold My Hand	Don Cornell	Vogue	21	(5)	F
16	-	Give Me Your Word	Tennessee Ernie Ford	Capitol	24		F
17	-	Count Your Blessings	Bing Crosby	Brunswick	3		
18	19	Veni Vidi Vici	Ronnie Hilton	HMV	8		
19	-	Softly Softly	Ruby Murray	Columbia	23		
20	9	This Ole House	Billie Anthony	Columbia	15		F

		Title	Artist	Label	Wks	(US 20 Pos)	
1	19	Softly Softly	Ruby Murray	Columbia	23		
2	2	Mambo Italiano	Rosemary Clooney	Philips	16	(10)	
3	1	Finger Of Suspicion	Dickie Valentine	Decca	15		
4	16	Give Me Your Word	Tennessee Ernie Ford	Capitol	24		F
5	5	Heartbeat	Ruby Murray	Columbia	16		F
6	6	Shake, Rattle And Roll	Bill Haley & His Comets	Brunswick	14	(7)	
7	-	Naughty Lady Of Shady Lane	Dean Martin	Capitol	10		
8	-	The Naughty Lady Of Shady Lane	Ames Brothers	HMV	6	(3)	F L
9	3	No One But You	Billy Eckstine	MGM	17		F
10	7	Mr. Sandman	Dickie Valentine	Decca	12		
11	-	Happy Days And Lonely Nights	Ruby Murray	Columbia	8		
12	-	Let Me Go, Lover	Teresa Brewer	Vogue/Coral	10	(8)	F
13	-	Beyond The Stars	David Whitfield	Decca	9		
14	4	I Still Believe	Ronnie Hilton	HMV	14		F
15	-	Mobile	Ray Burns	Columbia	13		F
16	-	A Blossom Fell	Dickie Valentine	Decca	10		
17	-	Happy Days And Lonely Nights	Frankie Vaughan	HMV	3		
18	-	Majorca	Petula Clark	Polygon	5		
19	-	Mambo Italiano	Dean Martin	Capitol	2		
20	-	Drinking Song	Mario Lanza	HMV	1		

◆ Bill Haley's 'Rock Around The Clock' had a two-week chart run in Britain. In the US, it became the theme to the controversial film, *The Blackboard Jungle*.

◆ Not only were several versions of 'Let Me Go Lover' and 'Mr. Sandman' battling it out, but there were also two hit recordings of 'Mambo Italiano', 'This Ole House', 'Naughty Lady Of Shady Lane', and 'A Blossom Fell'.

1955

March 1955

This Mnth	Prev Mnth	Title	Artist	Label	Wks	(US 20 Pos)	
1	4	Give Me Your Word	Tennessee Ernie Ford	Capitol	24		F
2	1	Softly Softly	Ruby Murray	Columbia	23		
3	-	Let Me Go, Lover	Dean Martin	Capitol	9		
4	2	Mambo Italiano	Rosemary Clooney	Philips	16	(10)	
5	-	A Blossom Fell	Nat 'King' Cole	Capitol	10	(2)	
6	15	Mobile	Ray Burns	Columbia	13		F
7	7	Naughty Lady Of Shady Lane	Dean Martin	Capitol	10		
8	3	Finger Of Suspicion	Dickie Valentine	Decca	15		
9	5	Heartbeat	Ruby Murray	Columbia	16		F
10	-	Let Me Go, Lover	Ruby Murray	Columbia	7		
11	13	Beyond The Stars	David Whitfield	Decca	9		
12	12	Let Me Go, Lover	Teresa Brewer	Vogue/Coral	10	(8)	F
13	11	Happy Days And Lonely Nights	Ruby Murray	Columbia	8		
14	16	A Blossom Fell	Dickie Valentine	Decca	10		
15	-	Tomorrow	Johnny Brandon	Polygon	8		F
16	-	Wedding Bells	Eddie Fisher	HMV	11		
17	18	Majorca	Petula Clark	Polygon	5		
18	-	If Anyone Finds This I Love You	Ruby Murray	Columbia	11		
19	8	The Naughty Lady Of Shady Lane	Ames Brothers	HMV	6	(3)	F L
20	6	Shake, Rattle And Roll	Bill Haley & His Comets	Brunswick	14	(7)	

April 1955

This Mnth	Prev Mnth	Title	Artist	Label	Wks	(US 20 Pos)	
1	1	Give Me Your Word	Tennessee Ernie Ford	Capitol	24		F
2	-	Cherry Pink And Apple Blossom White	Perez Prado	HMV	17	(1)	F
3	2	Softly Softly	Ruby Murray	Columbia	23		
4	18	If Anyone Finds This I Love You	Ruby Murray	Columbia	11		
5	16	Wedding Bells	Eddie Fisher	HMV	11		
6	-	Under The Bridges Of Paris	Dean Martin	Capitol	8		
7	-	Cherry Pink And Apple Blossom White	Eddie Calvert	Columbia	21		
8	6	Mobile	Ray Burns	Columbia	13		F
9	-	Prize Of Gold	Joan Regan	Decca	8	(55)	
10	5	A Blossom Fell	Nat 'King' Cole	Capitol	10	(2)	
11	-	Under The Bridges Of Paris	Eartha Kitt	HMV	10		F L
12	-	Stranger In Paradise	Tony Bennett	Philips	16	(2)	F
13	-	Ready Willing And Able	Doris Day	Philips	9		
14	3	Let Me Go, Lover	Dean Martin	Capitol	9		
15	-	Earth Angel	Crew-Cuts	Mercury	20	(8)	L
16	-	Stranger In Paradise	Tony Martin	HMV	13	(10)	F
17	15	Tomorrow	Johnny Brandon	Polygon	8		F
18	14	A Blossom Fell	Dickie Valentine	Decca	10	'	
19	-	A Blossom Fell	Ronnie Hilton	HMV	5		
20	10	Let Me Go, Lover	Ruby Murray	Columbia	7		

◆ 'Give Me Your Word', which was the B-side of Tennessee Ernie Ford's minor US success, 'River Of No Return', surprised many people by topping the British chart.

◆ Less than four months after making her chart debut, distinctive Irish vocalist Ruby Murray had a record five singles simultaneously on the UK chart.

1955

This Mnth	Prev Mnth	Title	Artist	Label	Wks	(US 20 Pos)	
1	12	Stranger In Paradise	Tony Bennett	Philips	16	(2)	F
2	2	Cherry Pink And Apple Blossom White	Perez Prado	HMV	17	(1)	F
3	7	Cherry Pink And Apple Blossom White	Eddie Calvert	Columbia	21		
4	1	Give Me Your Word	Tennessee Ernie Ford	Capitol	24		F
5	15	Earth Angel	Crew-Cuts	Mercury	20	(8)	L
6	16	Stranger In Paradise	Tony Martin	HMV	13	(10)	F
7	3	Softly Softly	Ruby Murray	Columbia	23		
8	-	Unchained Melody	Al Hibbler	Brunswick	17	(5)	F L
9	5	Wedding Bells	Eddie Fisher	HMV	11		
10	-	Unchained Melody	Jimmy Young	Decca	19		
11	-	If You Believe	Johnnie Ray	Philips	11		
12	4	If Anyone Finds This I Love You	Ruby Murray	Columbia	11		
13	13	Ready Willing And Able	Doris Day	Philips	9		
14	11	Under The Bridges Of Paris	Eartha Kitt	HMV	10		F L
15	-	Unchained Melody	Les Baxter	Capitol	9	(2)	F L
16	-	Melody Of Love	Ink Spots	Parlophone	4		F L
17	-	Stranger In Paradise	Four Aces	Brunswick	6	(5)	
18	6	Under The Bridges Of Paris	Dean Martin	Capitol	8		
19	-	Stranger In Paradise	Eddie Calvert	Columbia	4		
20	-	Where Will The Baby's Dimple Be	Rosemary Clooney	Philips	13		

1	3	Cherry Pink And Apple Blossom White	Eddie Calvert	Columbia	21		
2	8	Unchained Melody	Al Hibbler	Brunswick	17	(5)	F L
3	10	Unchained Melody	Jimmy Young	Decca	19		
4	1	Stranger In Paradise	Tony Bennett	Philips	16	(2)	F
5	5	Earth Angel	Crew-Cuts	Mercury	20	(8)	L
6	2	Cherry Pink And Apple Blossom White	Perez Prado	HMV	17	(1)	F
7	-	Dreamboat	Alma Cogan	HMV	16		
8	6	Stranger In Paradise	Tony Martin	HMV	13	(10)	F
9	20	Where Will The Baby's Dimple Be	Rosemary Clooney	Philips	13		
10	11	If You Believe	Johnnie Ray	Philips	11		
11	17	Stranger In Paradise	Four Aces	Brunswick	6	(5)	
12	4	Give Me Your Word	Tennessee Ernie Ford	Capitol	24		F
13	15	Unchained Melody	Les Baxter	Capitol	9	(2)	F L
14	-	I Wonder	Dickie Valentine	Decca	15		
15	-	Sing It With Joe	Joe 'Mr. Piano' Henderson	Polygon	4		F
16	-	You My Love	Frank Sinatra	Capitol	7		
17	7	Softly Softly	Ruby Murray	Columbia	23		
18	-	Cool Water	Frankie Laine	Philips	22		
19	-	Crazy Otto Rag	Stargazers	Decca	3		
20	-	Stowaway	Barbara Lyon	Columbia	8		F

◆ Latin American dance craze the mambo had its finest moment thanks to Perez Prado's transatlantic smash 'Cherry Pink And Apple Blossom White'.

◆ Sixteen months after they had simultaneously climbed the American Top 20, versions of 'Stranger In Paradise' by Tony Bennett, Tony Martin and The Four Aces also battled it out on the British chart. The song which was adapted from classical composer Borodin's 'Polovtsian Dances' came from the musical *Kismet*.

1955

July 1955

This Mnth	Prev Mnth	Title	Artist	Label	Wks	(US 20 Pos)	
1	7	Dreamboat	Alma Cogan	HMV	16		
2	3	Unchained Melody	Jimmy Young	Decca	19		
3	2	Unchained Melody	Al Hibbler	Brunswick	17	(5)	F L
4	1	Cherry Pink And Apple Blossom White	Eddie Calvert	Columbia	21		
5	14	I Wonder	Dickie Valentine	Decca	15		
6	-	Evermore	Ruby Murray	Columbia	17		
7	18	Cool Water	Frankie Laine	Philips	22		
8	5	Earth Angel	Crew-Cuts	Mercury	20	(8)	L
9	9	Where Will The Baby's Dimple Be	Rosemary Clooney	Philips	13		
10	-	Rose Marie	Slim Whitman	London	19		F
11	4	Stranger In Paradise	Tony Bennett	Philips	16	(2)	F
12	-	Every Day Of My Life	Malcolm Vaughan	HMV	16		F
13	-	Ev'rywhere	David Whitfield	Decca	20		
14	20	Stowaway	Barbara Lyon	Columbia	8		F L
15	6	Cherry Pink And Apple Blossom White	Perez Prado	HMV	17	(1)	F
16	8	Stranger In Paradise	Tony Martin	HMV	13	(10)	F
17	-	Strange Lady In Town	Frankie Laine	Philips	13		
18	-	Sincerely	McGuire Sisters	Vogue Coral	4	(1)	
19	10	If You Believe	Johnnie Ray	Philips	11		
20	13	Unchained Melody	Les Baxter	Capitol	9	(2)	F L

August 1955

This Mnth	Prev Mnth	Title	Artist	Label	Wks	(US 20 Pos)	
1	10	Rose Marie	Slim Whitman	London	19		F
2	7	Cool Water	Frankie Laine	Philips	22		
3	6	Evermore	Ruby Murray	Columbia	17		
4	1	Dreamboat	Alma Cogan	HMV	16		
5	13	Ev'rywhere	David Whitfield	Decca	20		
6	12	Every Day Of My Life	Malcolm Vaughan	HMV	16		F
7	-	Learnin' The Blues	Frank Sinatra	Capitol	13	(2)	
8	17	Strange Lady In Town	Frankie Laine	Philips	13		
9	2	Unchained Melody	Jimmy Young	Decca	19		
10	5	I Wonder	Dickie Valentine	Decca	15		
11	4	Cherry Pink And Apple Blossom White	Eddie Calvert	Columbia	21		
12	3	Unchained Melody	Al Hibbler	Brunswick	17	(5)	F L
13	-	Mama	David Whitfield	Decca	11		
14	-	Indian Love Call	Slim Whitman	London American	12	(10)	
15	-	John And Julie	Eddie Calvert	Columbia	11		
16	-	The Breeze And I	Caterina Valente	Polydor	14	(13)	F L
17	8	Earth Angel	Crew-Cuts	Mercury	20	(8)	L
18	9	Where Will The Baby's Dimple Be	Rosemary Clooney	Philips	13		
19	14	Stowaway	Barbara Lyon	Columbia	8		F L
20	-	You My Love	Frank Sinatra	Capitol	7		

◆ Despite its failure in the US, 'Rose Marie' (from the 1925 musical of the same name) by Florida C&W artist Slim Whitman, held the top spot in Britain for 11 successive weeks – a record he held until 1991 when it was broken by Bryan Adams.

◆ Among the earliest R&B songs to chart in Britain were 'Earth Angel' and 'Sincerely', albeit the sanitized American pop versions by the Crew-Cuts and the McGuire Sisters respectively.

1955

This Mnth	Prev Mnth	Title	Artist	Label	Wks	(US 20 Pos)	
1	1	**Rose Marie**	Slim Whitman	London	19		F
2	7	**Learnin' The Blues**	Frank Sinatra	Capitol	13	(2)	
3	2	**Cool Water**	Frankie Laine	Philips	22		
4	5	**Ev'rywhere**	David Whitfield	Decca	20		
5	16	**The Breeze And I**	Caterina Valente	Polydor	14	(13)	F L
6	3	**Evermore**	Ruby Murray	Columbia	17		
7	8	**Strange Lady In Town**	Frankie Laine	Philips	13		
8	15	**John And Julie**	Eddie Calvert	Columbia	11		
9	6	**Every Day Of My Life**	Malcolm Vaughan	HMV	16		F
10	14	**Indian Love Call**	Slim Whitman	London American	12	(10)	
11	-	**Close The Door**	Stargazers	Decca	9		
12	-	**The Man From Laramie**	Jimmy Young	Decca	12		
13	-	**Love Me Or Leave Me**	Sammy Davis Jr.	Brunswick	6	(10)	
14	-	**Stars Shine In Your Eyes**	Ronnie Hilton	HMV	7		
15	-	**Something's Gotta Give**	Sammy Davis Jr.	Brunswick	7	(9)	F
16	-	**That's How A Love Song Was Born**	Ray Burns	Columbia	6		L
17	-	**Blue Star**	Cyril Stapleton	Decca	12		
18	13	**Mama**	David Whitfield	Decca	11		
19	4	**Dreamboat**	Alma Cogan	HMV	16		
20	-	**China Doll**	Slim Whitman	London American	2		

This Mnth	Prev Mnth	Title	Artist	Label	Wks	(US 20 Pos)	
1	12	**The Man From Laramie**	Jimmy Young	Decca	12		
2	17	**Blue Star**	Cyril Stapleton	Decca	12		
3	1	**Rose Marie**	Slim Whitman	London	19		F
4	3	**Cool Water**	Frankie Laine	Philips	22		
5	-	**Yellow Rose Of Texas**	Mitch Miller	Philips	13	(1)	F L
6	4	**Ev'rywhere**	David Whitfield	Decca	20		
7	5	**The Breeze And I**	Caterina Valente	Polydor	14	(13)	F L
8	-	**Hernando's Hideaway**	Johnston Brothers	Decca	13		
9	2	**Learnin' The Blues**	Frank Sinatra	Capitol	13	(2)	
10	11	**Close The Door**	Stargazers	Decca	9		
11	-	**Hey There**	Rosemary Clooney	Philips	11	(1)	
12	-	**Rock Around The Clock**	Bill Haley & His Comets	Brunswick	17	(1)	G
13	-	**Hernando's Hideaway**	Johnnie Ray	Philips	5	(24)	
14	-	**Hey There**	Johnnie Ray	Philips	9		
15	10	**Indian Love Call**	Slim Whitman	London American	12	(10)	
16	-	**I'll Come When You Call**	Ruby Murray	Columbia	7		
17	9	**Every Day Of My Life**	Malcolm Vaughan	HMV	16		F
18	6	**Evermore**	Ruby Murray	Columbia	17		
19	13	**Love Me Or Leave Me**	Sammy Davis Jr.	Brunswick	6	(10)	
20	-	**Go On By**	Alma Cogan	HMV	4		

◆ Slim Whitman was not the only American artist hitting with a recording that had either failed in their homeland or had not merited release there. Other acts with Anglo-aimed singles included Rosemary Clooney, Johnnie Ray, Frank Sinatra and Frankie Laine. The latter was enjoying two UK-only successes 'Strange Lady In Town' and 'Cool Water'.

◆ American composer Jerry Ross died aged 29, as his compositions, 'Hernando's Hideaway' and 'Hey There', held three places in the UK Top 5.

1955

November 1955

This Mnth	Prev Mnth	Title	Artist	Label	Wks	(US 20 Pos)	
1	8	Hernando's Hideaway	Johnston Brothers	Decca	13		
2	12	Rock Around The Clock	Bill Haley & His Comets	Brunswick	17	(1)	G
3	1	The Man From Laramie	Jimmy Young	Decca	12		
4	14	Hey There	Johnnie Ray	Philips	9		
5	11	Hey There	Rosemary Clooney	Philips	11	(1)	
6	2	Blue Star	Cyril Stapleton	Decca	12		
7	5	Yellow Rose Of Texas	Mitch Miller	Philips	13	(1)	F L
8	16	I'll Come When You Call	Ruby Murray	Columbia	7		
9	-	Let's Have A Ding Dong	Winifred Atwell	Decca	10		
10	6	Ev'rywhere	David Whitfield	Decca	20		
11	-	Song Of The Dreamer	Johnnie Ray	Philips	5		
12	-	Love Is A Many Splendoured Thing	Four Aces	Brunswick	13	(1)	
13	4	Cool Water	Frankie Laine	Philips	22		
14	-	Twenty Tiny Fingers	Stargazers	Decca	11		L
15	3	Rose Marie	Slim Whitman	London	19		F
16	-	Yellow Rose Of Texas	Gary Miller	Nixa	5		F
17	7	The Breeze And I	Caterina Valente	Polydor	14	(13)	F L
18	-	Ain't That A Shame	Pat Boone	London American	9	(2)	F
19	-	Meet Me On The Corner	Max Bygraves	HMV	11		
20	-	Yellow Rose Of Texas	Ronnie Hilton	HMV	2		

December 1955

This Mnth	Prev Mnth	Title	Artist	Label	Wks	(US 20 Pos)	
1	2	Rock Around The Clock	Bill Haley & His Comets	Brunswick	17	(1)	G
2	-	Christmas Alphabet	Dickie Valentine	Decca	7		
3	12	Love Is A Many Splendoured Thing	Four Aces	Brunswick	13	(1)	
4	9	Let's Have A Ding Dong	Winifred Atwell	Decca	10		
5	19	Meet Me On The Corner	Max Bygraves	HMV	11		
6	14	Twenty Tiny Fingers	Stargazers	Decca	11		L
7	7	Yellow Rose Of Texas	Mitch Miller	Philips	13	(1)	F L
8	1	Hernando's Hideaway	Johnston Brothers	Decca	13		
9	-	Suddenly There's A Valley	Petula Clark	Nixa	10		
10	18	Ain't That A Shame	Pat Boone	London American	9	(2)	F
11	-	Hawkeye	Frankie Laine	Philips	8		
12	-	When You Lose The One You Love	David Whitfield	Decca	11	(62)	
13	-	Suddenly There's A Valley	Jo Stafford	Philips	6	(21)	L
14	-	The Singing Dogs (Medley)	Singing Dogs	Nixa	4		F L
15	-	Never Do A Tango With An Eskimo	Alma Cogan	HMV	5		
16	4	Hey There	Johnnie Ray	Philips	9		
17	5	Hey There	Rosemary Clooney	Philips	11	(1)	
18	-	Suddenly There's A Valley	Lee Lawrence	Columbia	3		L
19	6	Blue Star	Cyril Stapleton	Decca	12		
20	-	On With The Motley	Harry Secombe	Philips	3		F

◆ Thanks to its exposure in the hit film *The Blackboard Jungle*, 'Rock Around The Clock' by Bill Haley & The Comets became the first rock'n'roll record to top the UK chart.

◆ Balladeer Jimmy Young became the first British artist to clock up two successive UK No. 1s. The record that completed the double was his version of the American film theme 'The Man From Laramie', a song which failed to chart Stateside.

1956

This Mnth	Prev Mnth	Title	Artist	Label	Wks	(US 20 Pos)	
1	1	**Rock Around The Clock**	Bill Haley & His Comets	Brunswick	17	(1)	G
2	3	**Love Is A Many Splendoured Thing**	Four Aces	Brunswick	13	(1)	
3	-	**Rock-A-Beatin' Boogie**	Bill Haley & His Comets	Brunswick	8	(23)	
4	-	**Sixteen Tons**	Tennessee Ernie Ford	Capitol	11	(1)	
5	-	**The Ballad Of Davy Crockett**	Bill Hayes	London American	9	(1)	F L
6	5	**Meet Me On The Corner**	Max Bygraves	HMV	11		
7	-	**Love And Marriage**	Frank Sinatra	Capitol	8	(6)	
8	-	**The Ballad Of Davy Crockett**	Tennessee Ernie Ford	Capitol	7	(6)	L
9	15	**Never Do A Tango With An Eskimo**	Alma Cogan	HMV	5		
10	12	**When You Lose The One You Love**	David Whitfield	Decca	11	(62)	
11	6	**Twenty Tiny Fingers**	Stargazers	Decca	11		L
12	9	**Suddenly There's A Valley**	Petula Clark	Nixa	10		
13	-	**Rock Island Line**	Lonnie Donegan	Decca	14	(8)	F
14	-	**The Tender Trap**	Frank Sinatra	Capitol	9	(24)	
15	-	**Pickin' A Chicken**	Eve Boswell	Parlophone	10		F L
16	-	**Sixteen Tons**	Frankie Laine	Philips	3		
17	11	**Hawkeye**	Frankie Laine	Philips	8		
18	-	**Someone On Your Mind**	Jimmy Young	Decca	5		
19	10	**Ain't That A Shame**	Pat Boone	London American	9	(2)	F
20	2	**Christmas Alphabet**	Dickie Valentine	Decca	7		

1	4	**Sixteen Tons**	Tennessee Ernie Ford	Capitol	11	(1)	
2	14	**The Tender Trap**	Frank Sinatra	Capitol	9	(24)	
3	5	**The Ballad Of Davy Crockett**	Bill Hayes	London American	9	(1)	F L
4	-	**Memories Are Made Of This**	Dean Martin	Capitol	14	(1)	
5	-	**Zambesi**	Lou Busch	Capitol	15	(75)	F L
6	7	**Love And Marriage**	Frank Sinatra	Capitol	8	(6)	
7	-	**Only You**	Hilltoppers	London American	21	(15)	F
8	13	**Rock Island Line**	Lonnie Donegan	Decca	14	(8)	F
9	8	**The Ballad Of Davy Crockett**	Tennessee Ernie Ford	Capitol	7	(6)	L
10	-	**Dreams Can Tell A Lie**	Nat 'King' Cole	Capitol	9		
11	-	**It's Almost Tomorrow**	Dream Weavers	Brunswick	16	(8)	F L
12	3	**Rock-A-Beatin' Boogie**	Bill Haley & His Comets	Brunswick	8	(23)	
13	-	**Rock And Roll Waltz**	Kay Starr	HMV	18	(1)	L
14	-	**Band Of Gold**	Don Cherry	Philips	11	(5)	F L
15	-	**Robin Hood**	Gary Miller	Nixa	6		
16	2	**Love Is A Many Splendoured Thing**	Four Aces	Brunswick	13	(1)	
17	-	**Robin Hood**	Dick James	Parlophone	8		F
18	15	**Pickin' A Chicken**	Eve Boswell	Parlophone	10		F L
19	-	**Memories Are Made Of This**	Dave King	Decca	13		F
20	-	**Young And Foolish**	Edmund Hockridge	Nixa	7		F

◆ As Mercury Records had no UK outlet, the Platters' US smashes, 'Only You' and 'The Great Pretender', were not released in the UK until Autumn 1956. This left the way clear for The Hilltoppers and Jimmy Parkinson.

◆ Lonnie Donegan's 'Rock Island Line' introduced the transatlantic public to skiffle – a do-it-yourself folk/blues based music that launched a thousand British groups.

1956

March 1956

This Mnth	Prev Mnth	Title	Artist	Label	Wks (US 20 Pos)	
1	11	**It's Almost Tomorrow**	Dream Weavers	Brunswick	16 (8)	F L
2	4	**Memories Are Made Of This**	Dean Martin	Capitol	14 (1)	
3	13	**Rock And Roll Waltz**	Kay Starr	HMV	18 (1)	L
4	5	**Zambesi**	Lou Busch	Capitol	15 (75)	F L
5	7	**Only You**	Hilltoppers	London American	21 (15)	F
6	19	**Memories Are Made Of This**	Dave King	Decca	13	F
7	14	**Band Of Gold**	Don Cherry	Philips	11 (5)	F L
8	-	**See You Later Alligator**	Bill Haley & His Comets	Brunswick	11 (6)	
9	20	**Young And Foolish**	Edmund Hockridge	Nixa	7	F
10	8	**Rock Island Line**	Lonnie Donegan	Decca	14 (8)	F
11	-	**The Great Pretender**	Jimmy Parkinson	Columbia	10	F
12	-	**Poor People Of Paris**	Winifred Atwell	Decca	15	
13	2	**The Tender Trap**	Frank Sinatra	Capitol	9 (24)	
14	1	**Sixteen Tons**	Tennessee Ernie Ford	Capitol	11 (1)	
15	-	**Chain Gang**	Jimmy Young	Decca	5	
16	-	**Theme From 'The Three Penny Opera'**	Dick Hyman Trio	MGM	9 (10)	F L
17	10	**Dreams Can Tell A Lie**	Nat 'King' Cole	Capitol	9	
18	-	**Zambesi**	Eddie Calvert	Columbia	5	
19	-	**In Old Lisbon**	Frank Chacksfield	Decca	4	L
20	18	**Pickin' A Chicken**	Eve Boswell	Parlophone	10	F L

April 1956

This Mnth	Prev Mnth	Title	Artist	Label	Wks (US 20 Pos)	
1	12	**Poor People Of Paris**	Winifred Atwell	Decca	15	
2	1	**It's Almost Tomorrow**	Dream Weavers	Brunswick	16 (8)	F L
3	3	**Rock And Roll Waltz**	Kay Starr	HMV	18 (1)	L
4	5	**Only You**	Hilltoppers	London American	21 (15)	F
5	6	**Memories Are Made Of This**	Dave King	Decca	13	F
6	4	**Zambesi**	Lou Busch	Capitol	15 (75)	F L
7	2	**Memories Are Made Of This**	Dean Martin	Capitol	14 (1)	
8	8	**See You Later Alligator**	Bill Haley & His Comets	Brunswick	11 (6)	
9	16	**Theme From 'The Three Penny Opera'**	Dick Hyman Trio	MGM	9 (10)	F L
10	-	**My September Love**	David Whitfield	Decca	21	
11	11	**The Great Pretender**	Jimmy Parkinson	Columbia	10	F
12	-	**A Tear Fell**	Teresa Brewer	Vogue/Coral	15 (9)	
13	-	**Willie Can**	Alma Cogan	HMV	7	
14	-	**No Other Love**	Ronnie Hilton	HMV	13	
15	-	**Theme From 'The Threepenny Opera'**	Billy Vaughn	London American	5 (37)	L
16	15	**Chain Gang**	Jimmy Young	Decca	5	
17	18	**Zambesi**	Eddie Calvert	Columbia	5	
18	-	**Theme From The Threepenny Opera**	Louis Armstrong	Philips	7	
19	7	**Band Of Gold**	Don Cherry	Philips	11 (5)	F L
20	-	**You Can't Be True To Two**	Dave King	Decca	7	

◆ George Martin had three productions simultaneously in the UK Top 20. The records being by TV personality Eamonn Andrews, Eve Boswell and (later Beatles' publisher) Dick James.

◆ For the first time in Britain an album sold enough copies to enter the best selling records chart. The LP **Songs For Swinging Lovers** contained such standards as 'Pennies From Heaven', 'Makin' Whoopee' and 'I've Got You Under My Skin'.

1956

This Mnth	Prev Mnth	Title	Artist	Label	Wks (US 20 Pos)	
1	14	**No Other Love**	Ronnie Hilton	HMV	13	
2	1	**Poor People Of Paris**	Winifred Atwell	Decca	15	
3	12	**A Tear Fell**	Teresa Brewer	Vogue/Coral	15 (9)	
4	3	**Rock And Roll Waltz**	Kay Starr	HMV	18 (1)	L
5	10	**My September Love**	David Whitfield	Decca	21	
6	2	**It's Almost Tomorrow**	Dream Weavers	Brunswick	16 (8)	F L
7	4	**Only You**	Hilltoppers	London American	21 (15)	F
8	-	**I'll Be Home**	Pat Boone	London American	23 (6)	
9	-	**Lost John/Stewball**	Lonnie Donegan	Pye Nixa	14 (58)	
10	-	**Main Title Theme From The Man With The Golden Arm**	Billy May	Capitol	6 (49)	F L
11	18	**Theme From The Threepenny Opera**	Louis Armstrong	Philips	7	
12	20	**You Can't Be True To Two**	Dave King	Decca	7	
13	-	**Heartbreak Hotel**	Elvis Presley	HMV	19 (1)	F
14	-	**The Happy Whistler**	Don Robertson	Capitol	7 (9)	F L
15	8	**See You Later Alligator**	Bill Haley & His Comets	Brunswick	11 (6)	
16	5	**Memories Are Made Of This**	Dave King	Decca	13	F
17	7	**Memories Are Made Of This**	Dean Martin	Capitol	14 (1)	
18	-	**Blue Suede Shoes**	Carl Perkins	London American	7 (3)	F L
19	-	**Mountain Greenery**	Mel Torme	Vogue/Coral	17	F
20	9	**Theme From 'The Three Penny Opera'**	Dick Hyman Trio	MGM	9 (10)	F L

This Mnth	Prev Mnth	Title	Artist	Label	Wks (US 20 Pos)	
1	8	**I'll Be Home**	Pat Boone	London American	23 (6)	
2	9	**Lost John/Stewball**	Lonnie Donegan	Pye Nixa	14 (58)	
3	1	**No Other Love**	Ronnie Hilton	HMV	13	
4	13	**Heartbreak Hotel**	Elvis Presley	HMV	19 (1)	F
5	3	**A Tear Fell**	Teresa Brewer	Vogue/Coral	15 (9)	
6	-	**Hot Diggity**	Perry Como	HMV	12 (2)	
7	-	**The Saints Rock 'n Roll**	Bill Haley & His Comets	Brunswick	22 (18)	
8	5	**My September Love**	David Whitfield	Decca	21	
9	-	**Blue Suede Shoes**	Elvis Presley	HMV	8 (20)	
10	-	**Too Young To Go Steady**	Nat 'King' Cole	Capitol	10	
11	14	**The Happy Whistler**	Don Robertson	Capitol	7 (9)	F L
12	-	**Moonglow/Theme From 'Picnic'**	Morris Stoloff	Brunswick	8 (2)	F L
13	2	**Poor People Of Paris**	Winifred Atwell	Decca	15	
14	4	**Rock And Roll Waltz**	Kay Starr	HMV	18 (1)	L
15	18	**Blue Suede Shoes**	Carl Perkins	London American	7 (3)	F L
16	7	**Only You**	Hilltoppers	London American	21 (15)	F
17	10	**Main Title Theme From The Man With The Golden Arm**	Billy May	Capitol	6 (49)	F L
18	-	**Songs For Swinging Lovers (L.P.)**	Frank Sinatra	Capitol	5	
19	-	**Hot Diggity**	Michael Holliday	Columbia	4	
20	-	**Gal With The Yaller Shoes**	Michael Holliday	Columbia	3	

◆ In the month that Elvis and Carl Perkins debuted on the British chart and Alan Freed was first heard in Europe, the first Eurovision Song Contest was held: it was won by Lys Assia from Switzerland with a song called 'Refrains'.

◆ The British singles chart was extended to a Top 30.

◆ As Elvis Presley was first seen on the front cover of *NME*, Britain's Lonnie Donegan appeared on the cover of the noted US music magazine *Cash Box*.

July 1956

This Mnth	Prev Mnth	Title	Artist	Label	Wks	(US 20 Pos)	
1	1	I'll Be Home	Pat Boone	London American	23	(6)	
2	4	Heartbreak Hotel	Elvis Presley	HMV	19	(1)	F
3	-	All Star Hit Parade	Various Artists	Decca	8		F L
4	-	Why Do Fools Fall In Love	Frankie Lymon/The Teenagers	Columbia	15	(6)	F
5	-	I'm Walking Backwards For Christmas/Bluebottle Blues	Goons	Decca	8		F
6	6	Hot Diggity	Perry Como	HMV	12	(2)	
7	2	Lost John/Stewball	Lonnie Donegan	Pye Nixa	14	(58)	
8	-	Experiments With Mice	Johnny Dankworth	Parlophone	8	(61)	F
9	-	The Wayward Wind	Gogi Grant	London American	9	(1)	F L
10	7	The Saints Rock 'n Roll	Bill Haley & His Comets	Brunswick	22	(18)	
11	-	Wayward Wind	Tex Ritter	Capitol	11	(28)	F L
12	8	My September Love	David Whitfield	Decca	21		
13	-	Who Are We	Ronnie Hilton	HMV	8		
14	-	Walk Hand In Hand	Tony Martin	HMV	13	(21)	L
15	-	Whatever Will Be Will Be	Doris Day	Philips	20	(3)	
16	12	Moonglow/Theme From 'Picnic'	Morris Stoloff	Brunswick	8	(2)	F L
17	3	No Other Love	Ronnie Hilton	HMV	13		
18	18	Songs For Swinging Lovers (L.P.)	Frank Sinatra	Capitol	5		
19	5	A Tear Fell	Teresa Brewer	Vogue/Coral	15	(9)	
20	10	Too Young To Go Steady	Nat 'King' Cole	Capitol	10		

August 1956

This Mnth	Prev Mnth	Title	Artist	Label	Wks	(US 20 Pos)	
1	15	Whatever Will Be Will Be	Doris Day	Philips	20	(3)	
2	4	Why Do Fools Fall In Love	Frankie Lymon/The Teenagers	Columbia	15	(6)	F
3	14	Walk Hand In Hand	Tony Martin	HMV	13	(21)	L
4	-	Sweet Old-Fashioned Girl	Teresa Brewer	Vogue/Coral	13	(12)	L
5	-	Mountain Greenery	Mel Torme	Vogue/Coral	17		F
6	2	Heartbreak Hotel	Elvis Presley	HMV	19	(1)	F
7	1	I'll Be Home	Pat Boone	London American	23	(6)	
8	11	Wayward Wind	Tex Ritter	Capitol	11	(28)	F L
9	10	The Saints Rock 'n Roll	Bill Haley & His Comets	Brunswick	22	(18)	
10	13	Who Are We	Ronnie Hilton	HMV	8		
11	-	Rockin' Through The Rye	Bill Haley & His Comets	Brunswick	19	(78)	
12	3	All Star Hit Parade	Various Artists	Decca	8		F L
13	-	Serenade	Slim Whitman	London American	8		
14	5	I'm Walking Backwards For Christmas/Bluebottle Blues	Goons	Decca	8		F
15	-	Walk Hand In Hand	Ronnie Carroll	Philips	7		F
16	9	The Wayward Wind	Gogi Grant	London American	9	(1)	F L
17	8	Experiments With Mice	Johnny Dankworth	Parlophone	8	(61)	F
18	6	Hot Diggity	Perry Como	HMV	12	(2)	
19	-	I Almost Lost My Mind	Pat Boone	London American	6	(2)	
20	-	Left Bank	Winifred Atwell	Decca	5		

◆ Britain's first rock'n' roll riots were reported, as the film *Rock Around The Clock* went on general release. The film had teenagers jiving in the aisles and, sometimes, slashing cinema seats.

◆ At a time when American artists ruled the UK charts, Frankie Lymon & The Teenagers became the first black American act to top the British hit parade.

1956

This Mnth	Prev Mnth	Title	Artist	Label	Wks	(US 20 Pos)	
1	1	Whatever Will Be Will Be	Doris Day	Philips	20	(3)	
2	-	Lay Down Your Arms	Anne Shelton	Philips	13	(59)	
3	11	Rockin' Through The Rye	Bill Haley & His Comets	Brunswick	19	(78)	
4	2	Why Do Fools Fall In Love	Frankie Lymon/The Teenagers	Columbia	15	(6)	F
5	4	Sweet Old-Fashioned Girl	Teresa Brewer	Vogue/Coral	13	(12)	L
6	3	Walk Hand In Hand	Tony Martin	HMV	13	(21)	L
7	-	The Great Pretender/Only You	Platters	Mercury	10	(2)	F
8	-	Bloodnok's Rock 'n' Roll Call/ Ying Tong Song	Goons	Decca	8		
9	5	Mountain Greenery	Mel Torme	Vogue/Coral	17		F
10	9	The Saints Rock 'n Roll	Bill Haley & His Comets	Brunswick	22	(18)	
11	-	Bring A Little Water Sylvie/ Dead Or Alive	Lonnie Donegan	Pye Nixa	8		
12	-	A Woman In Love	Frankie Laine	Philips	19	(19)	
13	-	Born To Be With You	Chordettes	London American	8	(8)	
14	13	Serenade	Slim Whitman	London American	8		
15	-	Hound Dog	Elvis Presley	HMV	22	(1)	
16	-	I Want You I Need You I Love You	Elvis Presley	HMV	6	(1)	
17	6	Heartbreak Hotel	Elvis Presley	HMV	19	(1)	F
18	19	I Almost Lost My Mind	Pat Boone	London American	6	(2)	
19	-	Rock Around The Clock	Bill Haley & His Comets	Brunswick	11		
20	-	I'm In Love Again	Fats Domino	London American	5	(4)	F

1	12	A Woman In Love	Frankie Laine	Philips	19	(19)	
2	2	Lay Down Your Arms	Anne Shelton	Philips	13	(59)	
3	15	Hound Dog	Elvis Presley	HMV	22	(1)	
4	1	Whatever Will Be Will Be	Doris Day	Philips	20	(3)	
5	-	Giddy-Up-A-Ding-Dong	Freddie Bell & The Bellboys	Mercury	8		F L
6	3	Rockin' Through The Rye	Bill Haley & His Comets	Brunswick	19	(78)	
7	7	The Great Pretender/Only You	Platters	Mercury	10	(2)	F
8	8	Bloodnok's Rock 'n' Roll Call/ Ying Tong Song	Goons	Decca	8		
9	11	Bring A Little Water Sylvie/ Dead Or Alive	Lonnie Donegan	Pye Nixa	8		
10	19	Rock Around The Clock	Bill Haley & His Comets	Brunswick	11		
11	-	Just Walkin' In The Rain	Johnnie Ray	Philips	18	(3)	
12	-	When Mexico Gave Up The Rumba	Mitchell Torok	Brunswick	15		F L
13	10	The Saints Rock 'n Roll	Bill Haley & His Comets	Brunswick	22	(18)	
14	-	More	Perry Como	HMV	8	(4)	
15	13	Born To Be With You	Chordettes	London American	8	(8)	
16	-	Razzle Dazzle	Bill Haley & His Comets	Brunswick	4	(15)	
17	-	See You Later Alligator	Bill Haley & His Comets	Brunswick	6	(6)	
18	4	Why Do Fools Fall In Love	Frankie Lymon/The Teenagers	Columbia	15	(6)	F
19	-	More	Jimmy Young	Decca	14		
20	5	Sweet Old-Fashioned Girl	Teresa Brewer	Vogue/Coral	13	(12)	L

◆ The first British hit with "rock" in the title came from the very popular radio comedy team The Goons (Peter Sellers, Harry Secombe and Spike Milligan). The B-side, 'Ying Tong Song', returned to the Top 10 in 1973.

◆ In the *NME* poll, Elvis was runner-up to Bill Haley as World's Most Outstanding Vocal Personality, and to Frank Sinatra as World's Outstanding Singer. In the *Billboard* DJ poll he was voted Most Played Male Pop and C&W Artist.

November 1956

This Mnth	Prev Mnth	Title	Artist	Label	Wks	(US 20 Pos)	
1	11	**Just Walkin' In The Rain**	Johnnie Ray	Philips	18	(3)	
2	1	**A Woman In Love**	Frankie Laine	Philips	19	(19)	
3	3	**Hound Dog**	Elvis Presley	HMV	22	(1)	
4	-	**My Prayer**	Platters	Mercury	10	(1)	
5	19	**More**	Jimmy Young	Decca	14		
6	6	**Rockin' Through The Rye**	Bill Haley & His Comets	Brunswick	19	(78)	
7	10	**Rock Around The Clock**	Bill Haley & His Comets	Brunswick	11		
8	12	**When Mexico Gave Up The Rumba**	Mitchell Torok	Brunswick	15		F L
9	-	**Green Door**	Frankie Vaughan	Philips	15		
10	2	**Lay Down Your Arms**	Anne Shelton	Philips	13	(59)	
11	-	**Rip It Up**	Bill Haley & His Comets	Brunswick	14	(25)	
12	-	**Make It A Party**	Winifred Atwell	Decca	10		
13	4	**Whatever Will Be Will Be**	Doris Day	Philips	20	(3)	
14	5	**Giddy-Up-A-Ding-Dong**	Freddie Bell & The Bellboys	Mercury	8		F L
15	-	**St. Therese Of The Roses**	Malcolm Vaughan	HMV	18		
16	-	**The Green Door**	Jim Lowe	London American	5	(2)	F L
17	-	**Love Me As If There Were No Tomorrow**	Nat 'King' Cole	Capitol	7		
18	-	**Blue Moon**	Elvis Presley	HMV	8	(55)	
19	14	**More**	Perry Como	HMV	8	(4)	
20	-	**Cindy, Oh Cindy**	Eddie Fisher	HMV	13	(10)	L

December 1956

This Mnth	Prev Mnth	Title	Artist	Label	Wks	(US 20 Pos)	
1	1	**Just Walkin' In The Rain**	Johnnie Ray	Philips	18	(3)	
2	9	**Green Door**	Frankie Vaughan	Philips	15		
3	15	**St. Therese Of The Roses**	Malcolm Vaughan	HMV	18		
4	11	**Rip It Up**	Bill Haley & His Comets	Brunswick	14	(25)	
5	20	**Cindy, Oh Cindy**	Eddie Fisher	HMV	13	(10)	L
6	4	**My Prayer**	Platters	Mercury	10	(1)	
7	-	**True Love**	Bing Crosby & Grace Kelly	Capitol	23	(5)	
8	2	**A Woman In Love**	Frankie Laine	Philips	19	(19)	
9	12	**Make It A Party**	Winifred Atwell	Decca	10		
10	3	**Hound Dog**	Elvis Presley	HMV	22	(1)	
11	5	**More**	Jimmy Young	Decca	14		
12	18	**Blue Moon**	Elvis Presley	HMV	8	(55)	
13	8	**When Mexico Gave Up The Rumba**	Mitchell Torok	Brunswick	15		F L
14	-	**Christmas Island**	Dickie Valentine	Decca	3		
15	-	**Love Me Tender**	Elvis Presley	HMV	9	(1)	
16	-	**Two Different Worlds**	Ronnie Hilton	HMV	7		
17	-	**A House With Love In It**	Vera Lynn	Decca	6		
18	-	**Cindy Oh Cindy**	Tony Brent	Columbia	3		
19	-	**Moonlight Gambler**	Frankie Laine	Philips	9	(5)	
20	-	**Singing The Blues**	Guy Mitchell	Philips	20	(1)	

◆ Although they failed to enter the Top 100 in their homeland, American rock'n'roll records by Freddie Bell and The Bellboys ('Giddy-Up-A-Ding-Dong') and Mitchell Torok ('When Mexico Gave Up The Rhumba') were big British hits.

◆ For several weeks Bill Haley & The Comets had five singles in the Top 20.

1957

This Mnth	Prev Mnth	Title	Artist	Label	Wks	(US 20 Pos)	
1	20	Singing The Blues	Guy Mitchell	Philips	20	(1)	
2	-	Singing The Blues	Tommy Steele	Decca	10		
3	3	St. Therese Of The Roses	Malcolm Vaughan	HMV	18		
4	1	Just Walkin' In The Rain	Johnnie Ray	Philips	18	(3)	
5	2	Green Door	Frankie Vaughan	Philips	15		
6	7	True Love	Bing Crosby & Grace Kelly	Capitol	23	(5)	
7	5	Cindy, Oh Cindy	Eddie Fisher	HMV	13	(10)	L
8	-	Friendly Persuasion	Pat Boone	London American	17	(9)	
9	-	Garden Of Eden	Frankie Vaughan	Philips	12		
10	10	Hound Dog	Elvis Presley	HMV	22	(1)	
11	4	Rip It Up	Bill Haley & His Comets	Brunswick	14	(25)	
12	15	Love Me Tender	Elvis Presley	HMV	9	(1)	
13	-	Blueberry Hill	Fats Domino	London American	10	(3)	
14	19	Moonlight Gambler	Frankie Laine	Philips	9	(5)	
15	8	A Woman In Love	Frankie Laine	Philips	19	(19)	
16	-	Don't You Rock Me Daddy-O	Lonnie Donegan	Pye Nixa	16		
17	-	Garden Of Eden	Gary Miller	Pye Nixa	2		
18	13	When Mexico Gave Up The Rumba	Mitchell Torok	Brunswick	15		F L
19	11	More	Jimmy Young	Decca	14		
20	9	Make It A Party	Winifred Atwell	Decca	10		

This Mnth	Prev Mnth	Title	Artist	Label	Wks	(US 20 Pos)	
1	9	Garden Of Eden	Frankie Vaughan	Philips	12		
2	1	Singing The Blues	Guy Mitchell	Philips	20	(1)	
3	8	Friendly Persuasion	Pat Boone	London American	17	(9)	
4	6	True Love	Bing Crosby & Grace Kelly	Capitol	23	(5)	
5	16	Don't You Rock Me Daddy-O	Lonnie Donegan	Pye Nixa	16		
6	3	St. Therese Of The Roses	Malcolm Vaughan	HMV	18		
7	13	Blueberry Hill	Fats Domino	London American	10	(3)	
8	-	Young Love	Tab Hunter	London American	17	(1)	F
9	2	Singing The Blues	Tommy Steele	Decca	10		
10	-	Don't Forbid Me	Pat Boone	London American	14	(3)	
11	7	Cindy, Oh Cindy	Eddie Fisher	HMV	13	(10)	L
12	-	Don't Knock The Rock	Bill Haley & His Comets	Brunswick	7	(45)	
13	-	Don't You Rock Me Daddy-O	Vipers Skiffle Group	Parlophone	6		F
14	10	Hound Dog	Elvis Presley	HMV	22	(1)	
15	5	Green Door	Frankie Vaughan	Philips	15		
16	-	Rock-A-Bye Your Baby (With A Dixie Melody)	Jerry Lewis	Brunswick	5	(10)	F L
17	4	Just Walkin' In The Rain	Johnnie Ray	Philips	18	(3)	
18	11	Rip It Up	Bill Haley & His Comets	Brunswick	14	(25)	
19	-	Adoration Waltz	David Whitfield	Decca	8		
20	-	You Don't Owe Me A Thing	Johnnie Ray	Philips	10	(10)	

◆ Less than three months after his chart debut, Tommy Steele (who was already filming his life story!) became the first British rock'n'roll artist to top the charts. His version of 'Singing The Blues' replaced Guy Mitchell's at No. 1.

◆ Britain launched its first pop TV shows: *Cool For Cats*, where professional dancers performed choreographed routines to current records, and the very influential *6-5 Special* which featured live artists.

March 1957

This Mnth	Prev Mnth	Title	Artist	Label	Wks	(US 20 Pos)	
1	8	Young Love	Tab Hunter	London American	17	(1)	F
2	10	Don't Forbid Me	Pat Boone	London American	14	(3)	
3	-	Knee Deep In The Blues	Guy Mitchell	Philips	11	(21)	
4	5	Don't You Rock Me Daddy-O	Lonnie Donegan	Pye Nixa	16		
5	2	Singing The Blues	Guy Mitchell	Philips	20	(1)	
6	-	Long Tall Sally	Little Richard	London American	14	(6)	F
7	1	Garden Of Eden	Frankie Vaughan	Philips	12		
8	4	True Love	Bing Crosby & Grace Kelly	Capitol	23	(5)	
9	-	Banana Boat Song	Harry Belafonte	HMV	14	(5)	F
10	3	Friendly Persuasion	Pat Boone	London American	17	(9)	
11	-	Banana Boat Song	Shirley Bassey	Philips	6		.F
12	19	Adoration Waltz	David Whitfield	Decca	8		
13	-	Young Love	Sonny James	Capitol	7	(2)	F L
14	12	Don't Knock The Rock	Bill Haley & His Comets	Brunswick	7	(45)	
15	7	Blueberry Hill	Fats Domino	London American	10	(3)	
16	-	The Girl Can't Help It	Little Richard	London American	10	(49)	
17	-	Wisdom Of A Fool	Norman Wisdom	Columbia	4		L
18	6	St. Therese Of The Roses	Malcolm Vaughan	HMV	18		
19	20	You Don't Owe Me A Thing	Johnnie Ray	Philips	10	(10)	
20	16	Rock-A-Bye Your Baby (With A Dixie Melody)	Jerry Lewis	Brunswick	5	(10)	F L

April 1957

This Mnth	Prev Mnth	Title	Artist	Label	Wks	(US 20 Pos)	
1	1	Young Love	Tab Hunter	London American	17	(1)	F
2	-	Cumberland Gap	Lonnie Donegan	Pye Nixa	11		
3	9	Banana Boat Song	Harry Belafonte	HMV	14	(5)	F
4	2	Don't Forbid Me	Pat Boone	London American	14	(3)	
5	6	Long Tall Sally	Little Richard	London American	14	(6)	F
6	3	Knee Deep In The Blues	Guy Mitchell	Philips	11	(21)	
7	-	Look Homeward Angel	Johnnie Ray	Philips	10	(36)	
8	4	Don't You Rock Me Daddy-O	Lonnie Donegan	Pye Nixa	16		
9	8	True Love	Bing Crosby & Grace Kelly	Capitol	23	(5)	
10	16	The Girl Can't Help It	Little Richard	London American	10	(49)	
11	-	Baby Baby	Frankie Lymon/The Teenagers	Columbia	8		L
12	-	Ninety-Nine Ways	Tab Hunter	London American	10	(12)	L
13	-	Heart	Max Bygraves	Decca	7		
14	5	Singing The Blues	Guy Mitchell	Philips	20	(1)	
15	-	Cumberland Gap	Vipers Skiffle Group	Parlophone	4		L
16	-	I'm Not A Juvenile Delinquent	Frankie Lymon/The Teenagers	Columbia	4		
17	19	You Don't Owe Me A Thing	Johnnie Ray	Philips	10	(10)	
18	-	I'll Take You Home Again Kathleen	Slim Whitman	London American	11	(93)	
19	-	When I Fall In Love	Nat 'King' Cole	Capitol	19		
20	-	Freight Train	Chas McDevitt Skiffle Group	Oriole	14	(40)	F L

◆ Bill Haley & The Comets received an amazing media welcome to Britain, where *Rock Around The Clock* had became the first million seller. However, UK interest in them quickly faded and they left with minimal press coverage, and no future recordings made it into the Top 20.

◆ In April, Little Richard had three singles in the UK Top 20 and 14-year-old Frankie Lymon & The Teenagers had two. The youthful group, who successfully toured Britain and topped the bill at the London Palladium, were not to chart again.

1957

This Mnth	Prev Mnth	Title	Artist	Label	Wks	(US 20 Pos)
1	-	**Rock-A-Billy**	Guy Mitchell	Philips	11	(10)
2	-	**Butterfly**	Andy Williams	London American	12	(4) F
3	2	**Cumberland Gap**	Lonnie Donegan	Pye Nixa	11	
4	19	**When I Fall In Love**	Nat 'King' Cole	Capitol	19	
5	12	**Ninety-Nine Ways**	Tab Hunter	London American	10	(12) L
6	11	**Baby Baby**	Frankie Lymon/The Teenagers	Columbia	8	L
7	-	**Yes Tonight Josephine**	Johnnie Ray	Philips	15	
8	3	**Banana Boat Song**	Harry Belafonte	HMV	14	(5) F
9	20	**Freight Train**	Chas McDevitt Skiffle Group	Oriole	14	(40) F L
10	18	**I'll Take You Home Again Kathleen**	Slim Whitman	London American	11	(93)
11	-	**Too Much**	Elvis Presley	HMV	8	(1)
12	1	**Young Love**	Tab Hunter	London American	17	(1) F
13	7	**Look Homeward Angel**	Johnnie Ray	Philips	10	(36)
14	5	**Long Tall Sally**	Little Richard	London American	14	(6) F
15	-	**Chapel Of The Roses**	Malcolm Vaughan	HMV	7	
16	10	**The Girl Can't Help It**	Little Richard	London American	10	(49)
17	-	**Mr. Wonderful**	Peggy Lee	Brunswick	13	(25) F
18	-	**Butterfly**	Charlie Gracie	Parlophone	3	(3) F
19	-	**Butterfingers**	Tommy Steele	Decca	15	
20	4	**Don't Forbid Me**	Pat Boone	London American	14	(3)

1	7	**Yes Tonight Josephine**	Johnnie Ray	Philips	15	
2	4	**When I Fall In Love**	Nat 'King' Cole	Capitol	19	
3	2	**Butterfly**	Andy Williams	London American	12	(4) F
4	-	**Gamblin' Man/Putting On The Style**	Lonnie Donegan	Pye Nixa	18	
5	-	**Around The World**	Ronnie Hilton	HMV	15	
6	-	**Around The World**	Bing Crosby	Brunswick	14	(25)
7	1	**Rock-A-Billy**	Guy Mitchell	Philips	11	(10)
8	-	**Little Darlin'**	Diamonds	Mercury	15	(2) F L
9	9	**Freight Train**	Chas McDevitt Skiffle Group	Oriole	14	(40) F L
10	17	**Mr. Wonderful**	Peggy Lee	Brunswick	13	(25) F
11	-	**Around The World**	Gracie Fields	Columbia	7	F L
12	-	**A White Sport Coat**	King Brothers	Parlophone	11	F
13	-	**We Will Make Love**	Russ Hamilton	Oriole	16	F
14	11	**Too Much**	Elvis Presley	HMV	8	(1)
15	10	**I'll Take You Home Again Kathleen**	Slim Whitman	London American	11	(93)
16	15	**Chapel Of The Roses**	Malcolm Vaughan	HMV	7	
17	-	**All Shook Up**	Elvis Presley	HMV	18	(1)
18	-	**Fabulous**	Charlie Gracie	Parlophone	13	(16)
19	-	**Island In The Sun**	Harry Belafonte	RCA	22	(30)
20	3	**Cumberland Gap**	Lonnie Donegan	Pye Nixa	11	

◆ Skiffle, now reaching its peak of popularity, had its first chart topper with Lonnie Donegan's adaptation of the traditional American folk song 'Cumberland Gap'.

◆ Amazingly, Nat 'King' Cole's version of the 1952 film theme 'When I Fall In Love' (which did not chart in America) returned to the UK Top 5 in 1987.

July 1957

This Mnth	Prev Mnth	Title	Artist	Label	Wks	(US 20 Pos)	
1	17	**All Shook Up**	Elvis Presley	HMV	18	(1)	
2	4	**Gamblin' Man/Putting On The Style**	Lonnie Donegan	Pye Nixa	18		
3	8	**Little Darlin'**	Diamonds	Mercury	15	(2)	F L
4	13	**We Will Make Love**	Russ Hamilton	Oriole	16		F
5	5	**Around The World**	Ronnie Hilton	HMV	15		
6	1	**Yes Tonight Josephine**	Johnnie Ray	Philips	15		
7	12	**A White Sport Coat**	King Brothers	Parlophone	11		F
8	2	**When I Fall In Love**	Nat 'King' Cole	Capitol	19		
9	6	**Around The World**	Bing Crosby	Brunswick	14	(25)	
10	-	**Butterfingers**	Tommy Steele	Decca	15		
11	10	**Mr. Wonderful**	Peggy Lee	Brunswick	13	(25)	
12	-	**Teddy Bear**	Elvis Presley	HMV	18	(1)	
13	-	**Love Letters In The Sand**	Pat Boone	London American	21	(1)	
14	18	**Fabulous**	Charlie Gracie	Parlophone	13	(16)	
15	9	**Freight Train**	Chas McDevitt Skiffle Group	Oriole	14	(40)	F L
16	-	**Lucille**	Little Richard	London American	7	(21)	
17	19	**Island In The Sun**	Harry Belafonte	RCA	22	(30)	
18	-	**Bye Bye Love**	Everly Brothers	London American	13	(2)	F
19	3	**Butterfly**	Andy Williams	London American	12	(4)	F
20	-	**I Like Your Kind Of Love**	Andy Williams	London American	2	(10)	

August 1957

1	13	**Love Letters In The Sand**	Pat Boone	London American	21	(1)	
2	1	**All Shook Up**	Elvis Presley	HMV	18	(1)	
3	12	**Teddy Bear**	Elvis Presley	HMV	18	(1)	
4	17	**Island In The Sun**	Harry Belafonte	RCA	22	(30)	
5	2	**Gamblin' Man/Putting On The Style**	Lonnie Donegan	Pye Nixa	18		
6	4	**We Will Make Love**	Russ Hamilton	Oriole	16		F
7	3	**Little Darlin'**	Diamonds	Mercury	15	(2)	F L
8	18	**Bye Bye Love**	Everly Brothers	London American	13	(2)	F
9	-	**Last Train To San Fernando**	Johnny Duncan & The Blue Grass Boys	Columbia	16		F L
10	-	**Diana**	Paul Anka	Columbia	23	(1)	F G
11	5	**Around The World**	Ronnie Hilton	HMV	15		
12	-	**With All My Heart**	Petula Clark	Pye Nixa	16		
13	10	**Butterfingers**	Tommy Steele	Decca	15		
14	9	**Around The World**	Bing Crosby	Brunswick	14	(25)	
15	16	**Lucille**	Little Richard	London American	7	(21)	
16	14	**Fabulous**	Charlie Gracie	Parlophone	13	(16)	
17	6	**Yes Tonight Josephine**	Johnnie Ray	Philips	15		
18	8	**When I Fall In Love**	Nat 'King' Cole	Capitol	19		
19	7	**A White Sport Coat**	King Brothers	Parlophone	11		F
20	-	**Start Movin'**	Sal Mineo	Philips	6	(9)	F L

◆ The first successful British rock-related group were The King Brothers. This youthful trio scored the first of their hits with a cover of Marty Robbins' 'A White Sport Coat'.

◆ John Lennon and Paul McCartney met for the first time at a Church Garden Fete as fellow Merseyside singer/songwriter Russ Hamilton earned a pot of gold for his double sided transatlantic smash, 'We Will Make Love'/'Rainbow'.

1957

This Mnth	Prev Mnth	Title	Artist	Label	Wks	(US 20 Pos)	
1	10	**Diana**	Paul Anka	Columbia	23	(1)	F G
2	1	**Love Letters In The Sand**	Pat Boone	London American	21	(1)	
3	9	**Last Train To San Fernando**	Johnny Duncan & The Blue Grass Boys	Columbia	16		F L
4	4	**Island In The Sun**	Harry Belafonte	RCA	22	(30)	
5	12	**With All My Heart**	Petula Clark	Pye Nixa	16		
6	-	**Water Water/Handful Of Songs**	Tommy Steele	Decca	13		
7	2	**All Shook Up**	Elvis Presley	HMV	18	(1)	
8	-	**Wanderin' Eyes/I Love You So Much It Hurts**	Charlie Gracie	London American	12	(71)	L
9	-	**Paralysed**	Elvis Presley	HMV	9	(59)	
10	8	**Bye Bye Love**	Everly Brothers	London American	13	(2)	F
11	-	**Tammy**	Debbie Reynolds	Vogue Coral	15	(1)	F L
12	3	**Teddy Bear**	Elvis Presley	HMV	18	(1)	
13	5	**Gamblin' Man/Putting On The Style**	Lonnie Donegan	Pye Nixa	18		
14	16	**Fabulous**	Charlie Gracie	Parlophone	13	(16)	
15	-	**Jenny Jenny**	Little Richard	London American	5	(10)	
16	6	**We Will Make Love**	Russ Hamilton	Oriole	16		F
17	-	**Stardust**	Billy Ward & His Dominoes	London American	6	(14)	F L
18	-	**Shiralee**	Tommy Steele	Decca	3		
19	7	**Little Darlin'**	Diamonds	Mercury	15	(2)	F L
20	-	**Build Your Love**	Johnnie Ray	Philips	3	(58)	L

This Mnth	Prev Mnth	Title	Artist	Label	Wks	(US 20 Pos)	
1	1	**Diana**	Paul Anka	Columbia	23	(1)	F G
2	2	**Love Letters In The Sand**	Pat Boone	London American	21	(1)	
3	11	**Tammy**	Debbie Reynolds	Vogue Coral	15	(1)	F L
4	4	**Island In The Sun**	Harry Belafonte	RCA	22	(30)	
5	-	**That'll Be The Day**	Crickets	Vogue Coral	12	(1)	F
6	3	**Last Train To San Fernando**	Johnny Duncan & The Blue Grass Boys	Columbia	16		F L
7	8	**Wanderin' Eyes/I Love You So Much It Hurts**	Charlie Gracie	London American	12	(71)	L
8	5	**With All My Heart**	Petula Clark	Pye Nixa	16		
9	-	**Party**	Elvis Presley	RCA	14		
10	6	**Water Water/Handful Of Songs**	Tommy Steele	Decca	13		
11	12	**Teddy Bear**	Elvis Presley	HMV	18	(1)	
12	-	**Remember You're Mine/There's A Goldmine In The Sky**	Pat Boone	London American	13	(10)	
13	7	**All Shook Up**	Elvis Presley	HMV	18	(1)	
14	-	**Man On Fire/Wanderin' Eyes**	Frankie Vaughan	Philips	11		
15	-	**Whole Lotta Shakin' Goin' On**	Jerry Lee Lewis	London American	7	(3)	F
16	9	**Paralysed**	Elvis Presley	HMV	9	(59)	
17	-	**My Dixie Darling**	Lonnie Donegan	Pye Nixa	8		
18	17	**Stardust**	Billy Ward & His Dominoes	London American	6	(14)	F L
19	15	**Jenny Jenny**	Little Richard	London American	5	(10)	
20	-	**Call Rosie On The Phone**	Guy Mitchell	Philips	3		

◆ Fifteen-year-old Paul Anka topped the transatlantic chart with his composition 'Diana' (written about his childhood babysitter), which went on to sell over a million in Britain.

◆ *NME* readers voted Pat Boone World's Outstanding Male Singer, Elvis World's Outstanding Musical Personality, Doris Day World's Top Female Singer and The Platters World's Top Group.

1957

November 1957

This Mnth	Prev Mnth	Title	Artist	Label	Wks (US 20 Pos)
1	5	That'll Be The Day	Crickets	Vogue Coral	12 (1) F
2	9	Party	Elvis Presley	RCA	14
3	3	Tammy	Debbie Reynolds	Vogue Coral	15 (1) F L
4	12	Remember You're Mine/There's A Goldmine In The Sky	Pat Boone	London American	13 (10)
5	-	Be My Girl	Jim Dale	Parlophone	12 (1) F L
6	1	Diana	Paul Anka	Columbia	23 (1) F G
7	14	Man On Fire/Wanderin' Eyes	Frankie Vaughan	Philips	11
8	-	Mary's Boy Child	Harry Belafonte	RCA	9 (12) G
9	-	I Love You Baby	Paul Anka	Columbia	13 (97)
10	-	Gotta Have Something In The Bank Frank	Frankie Vaughan & The Kaye Sisters	Philips	7
11	-	Wake Up Little Susie	Everly Brothers	London American	11 (1)
12	17	My Dixie Darling	Lonnie Donegan	Pye Nixa	8
13	15	Whole Lotta Shakin' Goin' On	Jerry Lee Lewis	London American	7 (3) F
14	10	Water Water/Handful Of Songs	Tommy Steele	Decca	13
15	2	Love Letters In The Sand	Pat Boone	London American	21 (1)
16	7	Wanderin' Eyes/I Love You So Much It Hurts	Charlie Gracie	London American	12 (71) L
17	-	Santa Bring My Baby Back To Me	Elvis Presley	RCA	7
18	8	With All My Heart	Petula Clark	Pye Nixa	16
19	-	Alone	Petula Clark	Pye Nixa	9
20	-	Ma He's Making Eyes At Me	Johnny Otis Show	Capitol	15 F

December 1957

This Mnth	Prev Mnth	Title	Artist	Label	Wks (US 20 Pos)
1	8	Mary's Boy Child	Harry Belafonte	RCA	9 (12) G
2	20	Ma He's Making Eyes At Me	Johnny Otis Show	Capitol	15 F
3	11	Wake Up Little Susie	Everly Brothers	London American	11 (1)
4	9	I Love You Baby	Paul Anka	Columbia	13 (97)
5	-	My Special Angel	Malcolm Vaughan	HMV	14
6	5	Be My Girl	Jim Dale	Parlophone	12 F L
7	-	Let's Have A Ball	Winifred Atwell	Decca	5
8	19	Alone	Petula Clark	Pye Nixa	9
9	-	Reet Petite	Jackie Wilson	Coral	11 (62) F
10	2	Party	Elvis Presley	RCA	14
11	-	All The Way	Frank Sinatra	Capitol	16 (15)
12	4	Remember You're Mine/There's A Goldmine In The Sky	Pat Boone	London American	13 (10)
13	17	Santa Bring My Baby Back To Me	Elvis Presley	RCA	7
14	6	Diana	Paul Anka	Columbia	23 (1) F G
15	-	Great Balls Of Fire	Jerry Lee Lewis	London American	11 (2)
16	-	He's Got The Whole World In His Hands	Laurie London	Parlophone	7 (2) F L
17	1	That'll Be The Day	Crickets	Vogue Coral	12 (1) F
18	10	Gotta Have Something In The Bank Frank	Frankie Vaughan/Kaye Sisters	Philips	7
19	-	April Love	Pat Boone	London American	17 (1)
20	7	Man On Fire/Wanderin' Eyes	Frankie Vaughan	Philips	11

◆ Elvis Presley had a record seven singles in the UK Top 30. In America Elvis' **Christmas Album**, with unprecedented American advance orders, replaced his **Lovin' You** at the top.

◆ Johnny Otis, who had been America's top R&B act of 1950, had a surprise British hit with a revival of 'Ma He's Making Eyes At Me', a flop in the USA.

1958

January 1958

This Mnth	Prev Mnth	Title	Artist	Label	Wks	(US 20 Pos)	
1	2	Ma He's Making Eyes At Me	Johnny Otis Show	Capitol	15		F
2	15	Great Balls Of Fire	Jerry Lee Lewis	London American	11	(2)	
3	11	All The Way	Frank Sinatra	Capitol	16	(15)	
4	5	My Special Angel	Malcolm Vaughan	HMV	14		
5	9	Reet Petite	Jackie Wilson	Coral	11	(62)	F
6	-	Peggy Sue	Buddy Holly	Coral	12	(3)	F
7	-	Oh, Boy!	Crickets	Coral	12	(11)	
8	3	Wake Up Little Susie	Everly Brothers	London American	11	(1)	
9	4	I Love You Baby	Paul Anka	Columbia	13	(97)	
10	-	Kisses Sweeter Than Wine	Jimmie Rodgers	Columbia	10	(8)	F
11	-	Kisses Sweeter Than Wine	Frankie Vaughan	Philips	8		
12	19	April Love	Pat Boone	London American	17	(1)	
13	-	Jailhouse Rock	Elvis Presley	RCA	13	(1)	
14	-	The Story Of My Life	Michael Holliday	Columbia	14		
15	1	Mary's Boy Child	Harry Belafonte	RCA	9	(12)	G
16	8	Alone	Petula Clark	Pye Nixa	9		
17	-	Jack O' Diamonds	Lonnie Donegan	Pye Nixa	6		
18	14	Diana	Paul Anka	Columbia	23	(1)	F G
19	-	At The Hop	Danny & The Juniors	HMV	13	(1)	F L
20	-	Story Of My Life	Gary Miller	Pye Nixa	5		L

February 1958

This Mnth	Prev Mnth	Title	Artist	Label	Wks	(US 20 Pos)	
1	14	The Story Of My Life	Michael Holliday	Columbia	14		
2	13	Jailhouse Rock	Elvis Presley	RCA	13	(1)	
3	19	At The Hop	Danny & The Juniors	HMV	13	(1)	F L
4	7	Oh, Boy!	Crickets	Coral	12	(11)	
5	-	Magic Moments	Perry Como	RCA	15	(3)	
6	3	All The Way	Frank Sinatra	Capitol	16	(15)	
7	-	Love Me Forever	Marion Ryan	Pye Nixa	10		F L
8	6	Peggy Sue	Buddy Holly	Coral	12	(3)	F
9	12	April Love	Pat Boone	London American	17	(1)	
10	-	You Are My Destiny	Paul Anka	Columbia	10	(9)	
11	2	Great Balls Of Fire	Jerry Lee Lewis	London American	11	(2)	
12	-	Bony Moronie	Larry Williams	London American	7	(14)	F L
13	1	Ma He's Making Eyes At Me	Johnny Otis Show	Capitol	15		F
14	4	My Special Angel	Malcolm Vaughan	HMV	14		
15	-	Raunchy	Bill Justis	London American	4	(2)	F L
16	10	Kisses Sweeter Than Wine	Jimmie Rodgers	Columbia	10	(8)	F
17	-	Witchcraft	Frank Sinatra	Capitol	6	(20)	
18	11	Kisses Sweeter Than Wine	Frankie Vaughan	Philips	8		
19	-	Sugartime	McGuire Sisters	Coral	3	(7)	
20	-	Mandy	Eddie Calvert	Columbia	11		L

◆ Petula Clark had a hat-trick of hits with covers of US pop songs, 'With All My Heart', 'Alone' and 'Baby Lover'. When she recorded original material in the mid-1960s she became one of the top acts in America.

◆ Elvis Presley's 'Jailhouse Rock', with record advance orders of 250,000, became the first record to enter the chart at No. 1. Meanwhile, in America, 'Don't', became Presley's tenth chart topper in less than two years.

March 1958

This Mnth	Prev Mnth	Title	Artist	Label	Wks	(US 20 Pos)	
1	5	**Magic Moments**	Perry Como	RCA	15	(3)	
2	1	**The Story Of My Life**	Michael Holliday	Columbia	14		
3	2	**Jailhouse Rock**	Elvis Presley	RCA	13	(1)	
4	-	**Don't**	Elvis Presley	RCA	10	(1)	
5	3	**At The Hop**	Danny & The Juniors	HMV	13	(1)	F L
6	10	**You Are My Destiny**	Paul Anka	Columbia	10	(9)	
7	-	**Nairobi**	Tommy Steele	Decca	10		
8	7	**Love Me Forever**	Marion Ryan	Pye Nixa	10		F L
9	-	**Good Golly Miss Molly**	Little Richard	London American	7	(13)	
10	9	**April Love**	Pat Boone	London American	17	(1)	
11	4	**Oh, Boy!**	Crickets	Coral	12	(11)	
12	6	**All The Way**	Frank Sinatra	Capitol	16	(15)	
13	-	**Whole Lotta Woman**	Marvin Rainwater	MGM	14	(60)	F
14	-	**Catch A Falling Star**	Perry Como	RCA	7	(3)	
15	-	**Can't Get Along Without You/ We're Not Alone**	Frankie Vaughan	Philips	3		
16	-	**Baby Lover**	Petula Clark	Pye Nixa	4		
17	20	**Mandy**	Eddie Calvert	Columbia	11		L
18	-	**Maybe Baby**	Crickets	Coral	8	(18)	
19	-	**La Dee Dah**	Jackie Dennis	Decca	7		F L
20	8	**Peggy Sue**	Buddy Holly	Coral	12	(3)	F

April 1958

This Mnth	Prev Mnth	Title	Artist	Label	Wks	(US 20 Pos)	
1	1	**Magic Moments**	Perry Como	RCA	15	(3)	
2	13	**Whole Lotta Woman**	Marvin Rainwater	MGM	14	(60)	F
3	7	**Nairobi**	Tommy Steele	Decca	10		
4	-	**Swingin' Shepherd Blues**	Ted Heath	Decca	10		L
5	18	**Maybe Baby**	Crickets	Coral	8	(18)	
6	19	**La Dee Dah**	Jackie Dennis	Decca	7		F L
7	-	**Tequila**	Champs	London American	7	(1)	F L
8	4	**Don't**	Elvis Presley	RCA	10	(1)	
9	-	**A Wonderful Time Up There**	Pat Boone	London American	14	(4)	
10	-	**Who's Sorry Now**	Connie Francis	MGM	20	(5)	F
11	2	**The Story Of My Life**	Michael Holliday	Columbia	14		
12	-	**It's Too Soon To Know**	Pat Boone	London American	8	(4)	
13	17	**Mandy**	Eddie Calvert	Columbia	11		L
14	14	**Catch A Falling Star**	Perry Como	RCA	7	(3)	
15	-	**Breathless**	Jerry Lee Lewis	London American	6	(9)	
16	9	**Good Golly Miss Molly**	Little Richard	London American	7	(13)	
17	-	**To Be Loved**	Malcolm Vaughan	HMV	8		
18	5	**At The Hop**	Danny & The Juniors	HMV	13	(1)	F L
19	3	**Jailhouse Rock**	Elvis Presley	RCA	13	(1)	
20	-	**Lollipop**	Chordettes	London American	5	(2)	L

◆ Successful songwriter Hal David's collaboration with newcomer Burt Bacharach produced two successive UK No. 1s: 'The Story Of My Life' and 'Magic Moments'.

◆ Buddy Holly & The Crickets had a very successful tour of Britain, at a time when they were charting with four hits: 'Oh, Boy!', 'Peggy Sue', 'Maybe Baby' and 'Listen To Me'.

◆ Jerry Lee Lewis's British tour was cut short when the media discovered that his bigamously married third wife was his 14-year-old second cousin.

1955

This Mnth	Prev Mnth	Title	Artist	Label	Wks	(US 20 Pos)	
1	10	**Who's Sorry Now**	Connie Francis	MGM	20	(5)	F
2	2	**Whole Lotta Woman**	Marvin Rainwater	MGM	14	(60)	F
3	9	**A Wonderful Time Up There**	Pat Boone	London American	14	(4)	
4	-	**Tom Hark**	Elias & His Zigzag Jive Flutes	Columbia	12		F L
5	-	**Wear My Ring Around Your Neck**	Elvis Presley	RCA	7	(2)	
6	-	**Lollipop**	Mudlarks	Columbia	9		F
7	-	**Grand Coolie Dam**	Lonnie Donegan	Pye Nixa	9		
8	4	**Swingin' Shepherd Blues**	Ted Heath	Decca	10		L
9	20	**Lollipop**	Chordettes	London American	5	(2)	L
10	15	**Breathless**	Jerry Lee Lewis	London American	6	(9)	
11	7	**Tequila**	Champs	London American	7	(1)	F L
12	1	**Magic Moments**	Perry Como	RCA	15	(3)	
13	12	**It's Too Soon To Know**	Pat Boone	London American	8	(4)	
14	-	**You Need Hands/ Tulips From Amsterdam**	Max Bygraves	Decca	21		
15	-	**On The Street Where You Live**	Vic Damone	Philips	15	(8)	F L
16	-	**I May Never Pass This Way Again**	Robert Earl	Philips	9		F
17	-	**Kewpie Doll**	Perry Como	RCA	5	(12)	
18	17	**To Be Loved**	Malcolm Vaughan	HMV	8		
19	-	**Kewpie Doll**	Frankie Vaughan	Philips	9		
20	5	**Maybe Baby**	Crickets	Coral	8	(18)	

This Mnth	Prev Mnth	Title	Artist	Label	Wks	(US 20 Pos)	
1	1	**Who's Sorry Now**	Connie Francis	MGM	20	(5)	F
2	15	**On The Street Where You Live**	Vic Damone	Philips	15	(8)	F L
3	4	**Tom Hark**	Elias & His Zigzag Jive Flutes	Columbia	12		F L
4	-	**Stairway Of Love**	Michael Holliday	Columbia	11		
5	14	**You Need Hands/ Tulips From Amsterdam**	Max Bygraves	Decca	21		
6	-	**All I Have To Do Is Dream/ Claudette**	Everly Brothers	London American	19	(1)	
7	-	**Witch Doctor**	Don Lang	HMV	10		L
8	3	**A Wonderful Time Up There**	Pat Boone	London American	14	(4)	
9	-	**Army Game**	TV Cast	HMV	6		F L
10	6	**Lollipop**	Mudlarks	Columbia	9		F
11	19	**Kewpie Doll**	Frankie Vaughan	Philips	9		
12	7	**Grand Coolie Dam**	Lonnie Donegan	Pye Nixa	9		
13	-	**Twilight Time**	Platters	Mercury	12	(1)	
14	-	**Book Of Love**	Mudlarks	Columbia	7		L
15	5	**Wear My Ring Around Your Neck**	Elvis Presley	RCA	7	(2)	
16	-	**I May Never Pass This Way Again**	Perry Como	RCA	4		
17	-	**Big Man**	Four Preps	Capitol	12	(6)	F L
18	17	**Kewpie Doll**	Perry Como	RCA	5	(12)	
19	-	**Witch Doctor**	David Seville	London	5	(1)	F
20	16	**I May Never Pass This Way Again**	Robert Earl	Philips	9		F

◆ Jack Good, producer of *6-5 Special*, launched *Oh Boy!*, a TV show which first introduced the public to such acts as Cliff Richard and Billy Fury.

◆ A track recorded on the streets of South Africa by a tin-whistle band in 1956, 'Tom Hark' by Elias & His Zigzag Jive Flutes, was the year's most unexpected UK hit.

1958

This Mnth	Prev Mnth	Title	Artist	Label	Wks (US 20 Pos)		
1	6	**All I Have To Do Is Dream/ Claudette**	Everly Brothers	London American	19	(1)	
2	2	**On The Street Where You Live**	Vic Damone	Philips	15	(8)	F L
3	5	**You Need Hands/ Tulips From Amsterdam**	Max Bygraves	Decca	21		
4	17	**Big Man**	Four Preps	Capitol	12	(6)	F L
5	13	**Twilight Time**	Platters	Mercury	12	(1)	
6	1	**Who's Sorry Now**	Connie Francis	MGM	20	(5)	F
7	-	**Sugar Moon**	Pat Boone	London American	10	(10)	
8	14	**Book Of Love**	Mudlarks	Columbia	7		L
9	-	**Rave On**	Buddy Holly	Coral	12	(41)	
10	7	**Witch Doctor**	Don Lang	HMV	10		L
11	4	**Stairway Of Love**	Michael Holliday	Columbia	11		
12	-	**Sally Don't You Grieve/ Betty, Betty, Betty**	Lonnie Donegan	Pye Nixa	6		
13	-	**The Purple People Eater**	Sheb Wooley	MGM	6	(1)	F L
14	3	**Tom Hark**	Elias & His Zigzag Jive Flutes	Columbia	12		F L
15	-	**Endless Sleep**	Marty Wilde	Philips	12		F
16	-	**I'm Sorry I Made You Cry**	Connie Francis	MGM	7	(36)	
17	9	**Army Game**	TV Cast	HMV	6		F L
18	-	**On The Street Where You Live**	David Whitfield	Decca	8		L
19	-	**Hard Headed Woman**	Elvis Presley	RCA	8	(1)	
20	11	**Kewpie Doll**	Frankie Vaughan	Philips	9		

This Mnth	Prev Mnth	Title	Artist	Label	Wks (US 20 Pos)		
1	1	**All I Have To Do Is Dream/ Claudette**	Everly Brothers	London American	19	(1)	
2	-	**When**	Kalin Twins	Brunswick	16	(5)	F L
3	19	**Hard Headed Woman**	Elvis Presley	RCA	8	(1)	
4	-	**Return To Me**	Dean Martin	Capitol	16	(4)	
5	3	**You Need Hands/ Tulips From Amsterdam**	Max Bygraves	Decca	21		
6	15	**Endless Sleep**	Marty Wilde	Philips	12		F
7	4	**Big Man**	Four Preps	Capitol	12	(6)	F L
8	9	**Rave On**	Buddy Holly	Coral	12	(41)	
9	5	**Twilight Time**	Platters	Mercury	12	(1)	
10	-	**Patricia**	Perez Prado	RCA	11	(2)	L
11	7	**Sugar Moon**	Pat Boone	London American	10	(10)	
12	6	**Who's Sorry Now**	Connie Francis	MGM	20	(5)	F
13	-	**Think It Over**	Crickets	Coral	5	(27)	
14	2	**On The Street Where You Live**	Vic Damone	Philips	15	(8)	F L
15	16	**I'm Sorry I Made You Cry**	Connie Francis	MGM	7	(36)	
16	-	**Splish Splash**	Charlie Drake	Parlophone	9		F
17	12	**Sally Don't You Grieve/ Betty, Betty, Betty**	Lonnie Donegan	Pye Nixa	6		
18	-	**Fever**	Peggy Lee	Capitol	8	(8)	L
19	-	**Carolina Moon/Stupid Cupid**	Connie Francis	MGM	17	(14)	
20	-	**Poor Little Fool**	Ricky Nelson	London American	13	(1)	F

◆ One of the most recorded songs of the year, 'On The Street Where You Live', took noted US balladeer Vic Damone to the top. His version had also outpaced all the competition in the USA two years earlier.

◆ Cliff Richard's debut single, 'Move It' (composed by Ian Samwell from his backing group, The Drifters), only narrowly missed topping the chart.

1958

◆ Johnny Otis's biggest American hit, 'Willie & The Hand Jive', was inspired by a digital dance started in British coffee bars and popularized on *6-5 Special*.

◆ In August, the month that both Michael Jackson and Madonna were born, George Harrison joined John Lennon and Paul McCartney's group, The Quarry Men.

November 1958

This Mnth	Prev Mnth	Title	Artist	Label	Wks	(US 20 Pos)	
1	12	**It's All In The Game**	Tommy Edwards	MGM	15	(1)	F L
2	18	**Hoots Mon**	Lord Rockingham's XI	Decca	16		F
3	2	**Bird Dog**	Everly Brothers	London American	16	(2)	
4	11	**Come Prima**	Marino Marini	Durium	13		L
5	7	**A Certain Smile**	Johnny Mathis	Fontana	14	(21)	F
6	14	**More Than Ever (Come Prima)**	Malcolm Vaughan	HMV	13		
7	1	**Carolina Moon/Stupid Cupid**	Connie Francis	MGM	17	(14)	
8	5	**Move It**	Cliff Richard	Columbia	11		F
9	-	**Tea For Two Cha Cha**	Tommy Dorsey Orchestra	Brunswick	16	(7)	F L
10	-	**It's Only Make Believe**	Conway Twitty	MGM	14	(1)	F
11	4	**King Creole**	Elvis Presley	RCA	9		
12	-	**My True Love**	Jack Scott	London American	8	(3)	F
13	-	**Love Makes The World Go Round**	Perry Como	RCA	13	(33)	
14	-	**Tom Dooley**	Lonnie Donegan	Pye Nixa	12		
15	6	**Born Too Late**	Poni-Tails	HMV	10	(7)	F L
16	-	**Someday**	Jodie Sands	HMV	8	(95)	F L
17	-	**Someday**	Ricky Nelson	London American	8		
18	3	**Volare**	Dean Martin	Capitol	12	(15)	
19	17	**Western Movies**	Olympics	HMV	7	(8)	F L
20	-	**Come On Let's Go**	Tommy Steele	Decca	11		

December 1958

This Mnth	Prev Mnth	Title	Artist	Label	Wks	(US 20 Pos)	
1	10	**It's Only Make Believe**	Conway Twitty	MGM	14	(1)	F
2	2	**Hoots Mon**	Lord Rockingham's XI	Decca	16		F
3	14	**Tom Dooley**	Lonnie Donegan	Pye Nixa	12		
4	1	**It's All In The Game**	Tommy Edwards	MGM	15	(1)	F L
5	9	**Tea For Two Cha Cha**	Tommy Dorsey Orchestra	Brunswick	16	(7)	F L
6	-	**Tom Dooley**	Kingston Trio	Capitol	12	(1)	F L
7	13	**Love Makes The World Go Round**	Perry Como	RCA	13	(33)	
8	-	**High Class Baby**	Cliff Richard	Columbia	9		
9	6	**More Than Ever (Come Prima)**	Malcolm Vaughan	HMV	13		
10	5	**A Certain Smile**	Johnny Mathis	Fontana	14	(21)	F
11	17	**Someday**	Ricky Nelson	London American	8		
12	20	**Come On Let's Go**	Tommy Steele	Decca	11		
13	4	**Come Prima**	Marino Marini	Durium	13		L
14	-	**The Day The Rains Came**	Jane Morgan	London American	13	(21)	F L
15	-	**Mary's Boy Child**	Harry Belafonte	RCA	5		G
16	3	**Bird Dog**	Everly Brothers	London American	16	(2)	
17	-	**Mandolins In The Moonlight**	Perry Como	RCA	8	(47)	
18	-	**More Party Pops**	Russ Conway	Columbia	3		F
19	-	**Real Love**	Ruby Murray	Columbia	3		
20	8	**Move It**	Cliff Richard	Columbia	11		F

◆ *NME* poll winners included Elvis (World's Outstanding Male), Connie Francis (World's Outstanding Female), the Everly Brothers (World's Outstanding Group) and Cliff Richard, whose act had been labelled "crude" and "vulgar" was Favourite New Singer.

◆ Italian songs were enjoying an unprecedented amount of success in the UK. Three versions of Domenico Modugno's US chart topper, 'Volare', charted alongside two recordings of 'Come Prima' and Dean Martin's multi-lingual 'Return To Me'.

1959

This Mnth	Prev Mnth	Title	Artist	Label	Wks	(US 20 Pos)	
1	1	It's Only Make Believe	Conway Twitty	MGM	14	(1)	F
2	14	The Day The Rains Came	Jane Morgan	London American	13	(21)	F L
3	2	Hoots Mon	Lord Rockingham's XI	Decca	16		F
4	5	Tea For Two Cha Cha	Tommy Dorsey Orchestra	Brunswick	16	(7)	F L
5	3	Tom Dooley	Lonnie Donegan	Pye Nixa	12		
6	-	Baby Face	Little Richard	London American	10	(41)	
7	-	To Know Him, Is To Love Him	Teddy Bears	London American	11	(1)	F L
8	6	Tom Dooley	Kingston Trio	Capitol	12	(1)	F L
9	-	Kiss Me Honey Honey Kiss Me	Shirley Bassey	Philips	13		
10	7	Love Makes The World Go Round	Perry Como	RCA	13	(33)	
11	12	Come On Let's Go	Tommy Steele	Decca	11		
12	8	High Class Baby	Cliff Richard	Columbia	9		
13	-	One Night/I Got Stung	Elvis Presley	RCA	10	(4)	
14	-	As I Love You	Shirley Bassey	Philips	16		
15	17	Mandolins In The Moonlight	Perry Como	RCA	8	(47)	
16	4	It's All In The Game	Tommy Edwards	MGM	15	(1)	F L
17	-	You Always Hurt The One You Love	Connie Francis	MGM	5		
18	-	Smoke Gets In Your Eyes	Platters	Mercury	19	(1)	
19	-	Chantilly Lace	Big Bopper	Mercury	4	(6)	F L
20	-	Problems	Everly Brothers	London American	9	(2)	

This Mnth	Prev Mnth	Title	Artist	Label	Wks	(US 20 Pos)	
1	14	As I Love You	Shirley Bassey	Philips	16		
2	13	One Night/I Got Stung	Elvis Presley	RCA	10	(4)	
3	9	Kiss Me Honey Honey Kiss Me	Shirley Bassey	Philips	13		
4	18	Smoke Gets In Your Eyes	Platters	Mercury	19	(1)	
5	7	To Know Him is To Love Him	Teddy Bears	London American	11	(1)	F L
6	-	Does Your Chewing Gum Lose It's Flavour	Lonnie Donegan	Pye Nixa	11	(5)	
7	6	Baby Face	Little Richard	London American	10	(41)	
8	20	Problems	Everly Brothers	London American	9	(2)	
9	2	The Day The Rains Came	Jane Morgan	London American	13	(21)	F L
10	-	(All Of A Sudden) My Heart Sings	Paul Anka	Columbia	12	(15)	
11	-	A Pub With No Beer	Slim Dusty	Columbia	13		F L
12	-	Petite Fleur	Chris Barber's Jazz Band	Pye Nixa	18	(5)	F L
13	-	The Little Drummer Boy	Beverley Sisters	Decca	11		
14	-	High School Confidential	Jerry Lee Lewis	London American	4	(22)	
15	1	It's Only Make Believe	Conway Twitty	MGM	14	(1)	F
16	4	Tea For Two Cha Cha	Tommy Dorsey Orchestra	Brunswick	16	(7)	F L
17	-	My Happiness	Connie Francis	MGM	13	(2)	
18	-	Little Drummer Boy	Harry Simeone Chorale	Top Rank	4	(13)	F L
19	-	Apple Blossom Time	Rosemary June	Pye-Int	3		F L
20	-	Gigi	Billy Eckstine	Mercury	12		

◆ Among the acts charting with revivals of standard songs were US acts Little Richard, Paul Anka, the late Tommy Dorsey's Orchestra, Tommy Edwards, The Platters, Connie Francis and chart debutante Rosemary June.

◆ Lonnie Donegan, whose UK hit 'Does Your Chewing Gum Lose Its Flavour' reached the American Top 3 in 1961, signed a record £10,000 recording deal.

1959

March 1959

This Mnth	Prev Mnth	Title	Artist	Label	Wks (US 20 Pos)	
1	4	**Smoke Gets In Your Eyes**	Platters	Mercury	19 (1)	
2	1	**As I Love You**	Shirley Bassey	Philips	16	
3	-	**Side Saddle**	Russ Conway	Columbia	25	
4	11	**A Pub With No Beer**	Slim Dusty	Columbia	13	F L
5	12	**Petite Fleur**	Chris Barber's Jazz Band	Pye Nixa	18 (5)	F L
6	17	**My Happiness**	Connie Francis	MGM	13 (2)	
7	13	**The Little Drummer Boy**	Beverley Sisters	Decca	11	
8	6	**Does Your Chewing Gum Lose It's Flavour**	Lonnie Donegan	Pye Nixa	11 (5)	
9	-	**Stagger Lee**	Lloyd Price	HMV	11 (1)	F
10	10	**(All Of A Sudden) My Heart Sings**	Paul Anka	Columbia	12 (15)	
11	-	**It Doesn't Matter Anymore**	Buddy Holly	Coral	21 (13)	
12	2	**One Night/I Got Stung**	Elvis Presley	RCA	10 (4)	
13	20	**Gigi**	Billy Eckstine	Mercury	12	
14	3	**Kiss Me Honey Honey Kiss Me**	Shirley Bassey	Philips	13	
15	-	**Tomboy**	Perry Como	RCA	10 (29)	
16	8	**Problems**	Everly Brothers	London American	9 (2)	
17	-	**C'mon Everybody**	Eddie Cochran	London American	10 (35)	
18	5	**To Know Him is To Love Him**	Teddy Bears	London American	11 (1)	F L
19	-	**Wonderful Secret Of Love**	Robert Earl	Philips	4	L
20	18	**Little Drummer Boy**	Harry Simeone Chorale	Top Rank	4 (13)	F L

April 1959

This Mnth	Prev Mnth	Title	Artist	Label	Wks (US 20 Pos)	
1	3	**Side Saddle**	Russ Conway	Columbia	25	
2	11	**It Doesn't Matter Anymore**	Buddy Holly	Coral	21 (13)	
3	1	**Smoke Gets In Your Eyes**	Platters	Mercury	19 (1)	
4	5	**Petite Fleur**	Chris Barber's Jazz Band	Pye Nixa	18 (5)	F L
5	6	**My Happiness**	Connie Francis	MGM	13 (2)	
6	9	**Stagger Lee**	Lloyd Price	HMV	11 (1)	F
7	-	**Donna**	Marty Wilde	Philips	11	
8	2	**As I Love You**	Shirley Bassey	Philips	16	
9	13	**Gigi**	Billy Eckstine	Mercury	12	
10	-	**Charlie Brown**	Coasters	London American	11 (2)	
11	4	**A Pub With No Beer**	Slim Dusty	Columbia	13	F L
12	17	**C'mon Everybody**	Eddie Cochran	London American	10 (35)	
13	15	**Tomboy**	Perry Como	RCA	10 (29)	
14	7	**The Little Drummer Boy**	Beverley Sisters	Decca	11	
15	-	**Wait For Me**	Malcolm Vaughan	HMV	8	L
16	-	**Sing Little Birdie**	Pearl Carr & Teddy Johnson	Columbia	5	F
17	-	**A Fool Such As I/ I Need Your Love Tonight**	Elvis Presley	RCA	14 (2)	
18	8	**Does Your Chewing Gum Lose It's Flavour**	Lonnie Donegan	Pye Nixa	11 (5)	
19	-	**By The Light Of The Silvery Moon**	Little Richard	London American	3	
20	10	**(All Of A Sudden) My Heart Sings**	Paul Anka	Columbia	12 (15)	

◆ For the first time three British records simultaneously made the US Top 20: 'Petite Fleur' by Chris Barber, 'The Children's Marching Song' by Cyril Stapleton and 'Manhattan Spiritual' by Reg Owen - all instrumentals.

◆ Both the Beverly Sisters and The Harry Simone Chorale clicked with the Christmas song 'The Little Drummer Boy'.

1959

This Mnth	Prev Mnth	Title	Artist	Label	Wks	(US 20 Pos)	
1	17	A Fool Such As I/ I Need Your Love Tonight	Elvis Presley	RCA	14	(2)	
2	2	It Doesn't Matter Anymore	Buddy Holly	Coral	21	(13)	
3	1	Side Saddle	Russ Conway	Columbia	25		
4	7	Donna	Marty Wilde	Philips	11		
5	-	It's Late	Ricky Nelson	London American	18	(9)	
6	4	Petite Fleur	Chris Barber's Jazz Band	Pye Nixa	18	(5)	F L
7	-	I've Waited So Long	Anthony Newley	Decca	13		
8	-	Come Softly To Me	Fleetwoods	London American	8	(1)	F L
9	10	Charlie Brown	Coasters	London American	11	(2)	
10	-	Come Softly To Me	Frankie Vaughan/Kaye Sisters	Philips	8		
11	-	I Go Ape	Neil Sedaka	RCA	10	(42)	F
12	-	Mean Streak	Cliff Richard	Columbia	8		
13	3	Smoke Gets In Your Eyes	Platters	Mercury	19	(1)	
14	12	C'mon Everybody	Eddie Cochran	London American	10	(35)	
15	-	Fort Worth Jail	Lonnie Donegan	Pye Nixa	4		
16	-	Roulette	Russ Conway	Columbia	18		
17	-	Guitar Boogie Shuffle	Bert Weedon	Top Rank	8		F L
18	-	May You Always	McGuire Sisters	Coral	5	(11)	L
19	-	Idle On Parade (EP)	Anthony Newley	Decca	2		F
20	6	Stagger Lee	Lloyd Price	HMV	11	(1)	F

This Mnth	Prev Mnth	Title	Artist	Label	Wks	(US 20 Pos)	
1	1	A Fool Such As I/ I Need Your Love Tonight	Elvis Presley	RCA	14	(2)	
2	16	Roulette	Russ Conway	Columbia	18		
3	2	It Doesn't Matter Anymore	Buddy Holly	Coral	21	(13)	
4	7	I've Waited So Long	Anthony Newley	Decca	13		
5	5	It's Late	Ricky Nelson	London American	18	(9)	
6	-	Dream Lover	Bobby Darin	London American	17	(2)	
7	3	Side Saddle	Russ Conway	Columbia	25		
8	-	A Teenager In Love	Marty Wilde	Philips	13		
9	17	Guitar Boogie Shuffle	Bert Weedon	Top Rank	8		F L
10	12	Mean Streak	Cliff Richard	Columbia	8		
11	11	I Go Ape	Neil Sedaka	RCA	10	(42)	F
12	-	May You Always	Joan Regan	HMV	10		L
13	6	Petite Fleur	Chris Barber's Jazz Band	Pye Nixa	18	(5)	F L
14	4	Donna	Marty Wilde	Philips	11		
15	10	Come Softly To Me	Frankie Vaughan/Kaye Sisters	Philips	8		
16	-	Peter Gunn Theme	Duane Eddy	London American	10	(27)	
17	8	Come Softly To Me	Fleetwoods	London American	8	(1)	F L
18	-	Battle Of New Orleans	Lonnie Donegan	Pye	14		
19	9	Charlie Brown	Coasters	London American	11	(2)	
20	-	A Teenager In Love	Craig Douglas	Top Rank	8		F

◆ American rockers faring better in Britain included Little Richard, Eddie Cochran (whose 'C'mon Everybody' revisited the UK Top 20 in 1988) and the late Buddy Holly, whose 'It Doesn't Matter Anymore' topped the chart.

◆ The year's most successful singles artist in the UK was not a rock performer but easy-on-the-ear honky tonk pianist Russ Conway, whose self composed singles 'Side Saddle' and 'Roulette' both headed the chart.

1959

This Mnth	Prev Mnth	Title	Artist	Label	Wks	(US 20 Pos)	
1	6	**Dream Lover**	Bobby Darin	London American	17	(2)	
2	18	**Battle Of New Orleans**	Lonnie Donegan	Pye	14		
3	8	**A Teenager In Love**	Marty Wilde	Philips	13		
4	2	**Roulette**	Russ Conway	Columbia	18		
5	16	**Peter Gunn Theme**	Duane Eddy	London American	10	(27)	
6	-	**Personality**	Anthony Newley	Decca	9		
7	-	**Living Doll**	Cliff Richard	Columbia	19	(30)	
8	1	**A Fool Such As I/ I Need Your Love Tonight**	Elvis Presley	RCA	14	(2)	
9	-	**Goodbye Jimmy, Goodbye**	Ruby Murray	Columbia	11		L
10	5	**It's Late**	Ricky Nelson	London American	18	(9)	
11	-	**Lipstick On Your Collar**	Connie Francis	MGM	15	(5)	
12	4	**I've Waited So Long**	Anthony Newley	Decca	13		
13	7	**Side Saddle**	Russ Conway	Columbia	25		
14	-	**Personality**	Lloyd Price	HMV	7	(2)	L
15	12	**May You Always**	Joan Regan	HMV	10		L
16	-	**Big Hunk O' Love**	Elvis Presley	RCA	8	(1)	
17	3	**It Doesn't Matter Anymore**	Buddy Holly	Coral	21	(13)	
18	20	**A Teenager In Love**	Craig Douglas	Top Rank	8		F
19	-	**Poor Jenny**	Everly Brothers	London American	7	(22)	
20	-	**I Know**	Perry Como	RCA	12	(47)	

This Mnth	Prev Mnth	Title	Artist	Label	Wks	(US 20 Pos)	
1	7	**Living Doll**	Cliff Richard	Columbia	19	(30)	
2	1	**Dream Lover**	Bobby Darin	London American	17	(2)	
3	2	**Battle Of New Orleans**	Lonnie Donegan	Pye	14		
4	11	**Lipstick On Your Collar**	Connie Francis	MGM	15	(5)	
5	-	**Lonely Boy**	Paul Anka	Columbia	13	(1)	
6	16	**Big Hunk O' Love**	Elvis Presley	RCA	8	(1)	
7	3	**A Teenager In Love**	Marty Wilde	Philips	13		
8	4	**Roulette**	Russ Conway	Columbia	18		
9	-	**The Heart Of A Man**	Frankie Vaughan	Philips	12		
10	-	**Only Sixteen**	Craig Douglas	Top Rank	14		
11	-	**Someone**	Johnny Mathis	Fontana	13	(35)	
12	6	**Personality**	Anthony Newley	Decca	9		
13	-	**Ragtime Cowboy Joe**	Chipmunks	London American	5	(16)	L
14	20	**I Know**	Perry Como	RCA	12	(47)	
15	5	**Peter Gunn Theme**	Duane Eddy	London American	10	(27)	
16	10	**It's Late**	Ricky Nelson	London American	18	(9)	
17	9	**Goodbye Jimmy, Goodbye**	Ruby Murray	Columbia	11		L
18	-	**China Tea**	Russ Conway	Columbia	10		
19	-	**Tallahassee Lassie**	Tommy Steele	Decca	3		
20	-	**Mona Lisa**	Conway Twitty	MGM	12	(29)	L

◆ As Cliff Richard scored his first No. 1 with 'Living Doll', Duane Eddy hit with his version of 'Peter Gunn Theme' – in 1986 both artists returned to the Top 10 with re-recordings of the compositions.

◆ Mantovani, who had five albums on the US Top 30 stereo album chart, became the first British-based act to top the American LP chart when **Film Encores** moved into the top slot.

◆ Marty Wilde, Frankie Vaughan, Craig Douglas and Tommy Steele were just some of the artists in the 1950s whose UK hit tally was bolstered by cover versions of songs from the US chart.

1959

This Mnth	Prev Mnth	Title	Artist	Label	Wks	(US 20 Pos)
1	10	Only Sixteen	Craig Douglas	Top Rank	14	
2	1	Living Doll	Cliff Richard	Columbia	19	(30)
3	5	Lonely Boy	Paul Anka	Columbia	13	(1)
4	-	Here Comes Summer	Jerry Keller	London American	12	(14) F L
5	18	China Tea	Russ Conway	Columbia	10	
6	4	Lipstick On Your Collar	Connie Francis	MGM	15	(5)
7	11	Someone	Johnny Mathis	Fontana	13	(35)
8	20	Mona Lisa	Conway Twitty	MGM	12	(29) L
9	9	The Heart Of A Man	Frankie Vaughan	Philips	12	
10	3	Battle Of New Orleans	Lonnie Donegan	Pye	14	
11	2	Dream Lover	Bobby Darin	London American	17	(2)
12	-	40 Miles Of Bad Road	Duane Eddy	London American	9	(9)
13	-	('Til) I Kissed You	Everly Brothers	London American	14	(4)
14	-	Just A Little Too Much	Ricky Nelson	London American	8	(9)
15	-	Sal's Got A Sugar Lip	Lonnie Donegan	Pye	3	
16	14	I Know	Perry Como	RCA	12	(47)
17	6	Big Hunk O' Love	Elvis Presley	RCA	8	(1)
18	-	The Three Bells	Browns	RCA	11	(1) F L
19	-	High Hopes	Frank Sinatra	Capitol	12	(30)
20	8	Roulette	Russ Conway	Columbia	18	

1	-	Mack The Knife	Bobby Darin	London American	14	(1)
2	4	Here Comes Summer	Jerry Keller	London American	12	(14) F L
3	13	('Til) I Kissed You	Everly Brothers	London American	14	(4)
4	1	Only Sixteen	Craig Douglas	Top Rank	14	
5	2	Living Doll	Cliff Richard	Columbia	19	(30)
6	18	The Three Bells	Browns	RCA	11	(1) F L
7	-	Sea Of Love	Marty Wilde	Philips	11	
8	-	Travellin' Light	Cliff Richard	Columbia	16	
9	19	High Hopes	Frank Sinatra	Capitol	12	(30)
10	-	Broken Hearted Melody	Sarah Vaughan	Mercury	12	(7) F
11	8	Mona Lisa	Conway Twitty	MGM	12	(29) L
12	7	Someone	Johnny Mathis	Fontana	13	(35)
13	3	Lonely Boy	Paul Anka	Columbia	13	(1)
14	5	China Tea	Russ Conway	Columbia	10	
15	14	Just A Little Too Much	Ricky Nelson	London American	8	(9)
16	-	Red River Rock	Johnny & The Hurricanes	London American	13	(5) F
17	12	40 Miles Of Bad Road	Duane Eddy	London American	9	(9)
18	-	Peggy Sue Got Married	Buddy Holly	Coral	5	
19	-	Makin' Love	Floyd Robinson	RCA	7	(20) F L
20	9	The Heart Of A Man	Frankie Vaughan	Philips	12	

◆ To avoid confusion with US hit makers The Drifters, Cliff Richard's group changed their name to The Shadows.

◆ Emile Ford became the first British-based black male performer to top the charts. His Johnny Otis-styled revival of 'What Do You Want To Make Those Eyes At Me For' sold over a million in the UK alone.

November 1959

This Mnth	Prev Mnth	Title	Artist	Label	Wks	(US 20 Pos)	
1	8	**Travellin' Light**	Cliff Richard	Columbia	16		
2	1	**Mack The Knife**	Bobby Darin	London American	14	(1)	
3	16	**Red River Rock**	Johnny & The Hurricanes	London American	13	(5)	F
4	-	**What Do You Want To Make Those Eyes At Me For**	Emile Ford & The Checkmates	Pye	18		F
5	3	**('Til) I Kissed You**	Everly Brothers	London American	14	(4)	
6	7	**Sea Of Love**	Marty Wilde	Philips	11		
7	-	**Put Your Head On My Shoulder**	Paul Anka	Columbia	10	(2)	
8	10	**Broken Hearted Melody**	Sarah Vaughan	Mercury	12	(7)	F
9	9	**High Hopes**	Frank Sinatra	Capitol	12	(30)	
10	6	**The Three Bells**	Browns	RCA	11	(1)	F L
11	19	**Makin' Love**	Floyd Robinson	RCA	7	(20)	F L
12	-	**Oh! Carol**	Neil Sedaka	RCA	14	(9)	
13	-	**One More Sunrise (Morgen)**	Dickie Valentine	Pye	7		L
14	-	**Teen Beat**	Sandy Nelson	Top Rank	8	(4)	F
15	-	**What Do You Want**	Adam Faith	Parlophone	15		F
16	2	**Here Comes Summer**	Jerry Keller	London American	12	(14)	F L
17	-	**Mr. Blue**	Mike Preston	Decca	5		F
18	-	**Snow Coach**	Russ Conway	Columbia	8		
19	11	**Mona Lisa**	Conway Twitty	MGM	12	(29)	L
20	4	**Only Sixteen**	Craig Douglas	Top Rank	14		

December 1959

This Mnth	Prev Mnth	Title	Artist	Label	Wks	(US 20 Pos)	
1	15	**What Do You Want**	Adam Faith	Parlophone	15		F
2	4	**What Do You Want To Make Those Eyes At Me For**	Emile Ford & The Checkmates	Pye	18		F
3	12	**Oh! Carol**	Neil Sedaka	RCA	14	(9)	
4	1	**Travellin' Light**	Cliff Richard	Columbia	16		
5	-	**Seven Little Girls Sitting In The Back Seat**	Avons	Columbia	10		F L
6	3	**Red River Rock**	Johnny & The Hurricanes	London American	13	(5)	F
7	7	**Put Your Head On My Shoulder**	Paul Anka	Columbia	10	(2)	
8	18	**Snow Coach**	Russ Conway	Columbia	8		
9	-	**Rawhide**	Frankie Laine	Philips	13		L
10	-	**More And More Party Pops**	Russ Conway	Columbia	5		
11	2	**Mack The Knife**	Bobby Darin	London American	14	(1)	
12	-	**Little White Bull**	Tommy Steele	Decca	12		
13	-	**Piano Party**	Winifred Atwell	Decca	5		L
14	14	**Teen Beat**	Sandy Nelson	Top Rank	8	(4)	F
15	-	**Among My Souvenirs**	Connie Francis	MGM	6	(7)	
16	-	**Staccato's Theme**	Elmer Bernstein	Capitol	10		F L
17	-	**Jingle Bell Rock**	Max Bygraves	Decca	3		
18	5	**('Til) I Kissed You**	Everly Brothers	London American	14	(4)	
19	-	**Little Donkey**	Beverley Sisters	Decca	4		L
20	6	**Sea Of Love**	Marty Wilde	Philips	11		

◆ Among the many other new groups in Britain were Johnny & The Moondogs (members included three Beatles) who reached the final in a TV *Star Search*.

◆ Transatlantic star Guy Mitchell, who had made his chart debut in 1950, ended the decade with the No. 1 single in America, 'Heartaches By The Number'.

1960

This Mnth	Prev Mnth	Title	Artist	Label	Wks	(US 20 Pos)	
1	2	**What Do You Want To Make Those Eyes At Me For**	Emile Ford & The Checkmates	Pye	18		F
2	1	**What Do You Want**	Adam Faith	Parlophone	15		F
3	3	**Oh! Carol**	Neil Sedaka	RCA	14	(9)	
4	16	**Staccato's Theme**	Elmer Bernstein	Capitol	10		F L
5	5	**Seven Little Girls Sitting In The Back Seat**	Avons	Columbia	10		F L
6	12	**Little White Bull**	Tommy Steele	Decca	12		
7	-	**Starry Eyed**	Michael Holliday	Columbia	9		L
8	9	**Rawhide**	Frankie Laine	Philips	13		L
9	-	**Why**	Anthony Newley	Decca	12		
10	-	**Way Down Yonder In New Orleans**	Freddy Cannon	Top Rank	11	(3)	
11	-	**Heartaches By The Number**	Guy Mitchell	Philips	9	(1)	L
12	-	**Bad Boy**	Marty Wilde	Philips	7	(45)	
13	6	**Travellin' Light**	Cliff Richard	Columbia	16		
14	-	**Be My Guest**	Fats Domino	London American	7	(8)	
15	-	**Voice In The Wilderness**	Cliff Richard	Columbia	10		
16	-	**In The Mood**	Ernie Fields	London American	5	(4)	F L
17	-	**Some Kind-A Earthquake**	Duane Eddy	London American	5	(37)	
18	15	**Among My Souvenirs**	Connie Francis	MGM	6	(7)	
19	-	**Reveille Rock**	Johnny & The Hurricanes	London American	4	(25)	
20	10	**More And More Party Pops**	Russ Conway	Columbia	5		

This Mnth	Prev Mnth	Title	Artist	Label	Wks	(US 20 Pos)	
1	9	**Why**	Anthony Newley	Decca	12		
2	15	**Voice In The Wilderness**	Cliff Richard	Columbia	10		
3	10	**Way Down Yonder In New Orleans**	Freddy Cannon	Top Rank	11	(3)	
4	-	**Poor Me**	Adam Faith	Parlophone	11		
5	7	**Starry Eyed**	Michael Holliday	Columbia	9		L
6	-	**Pretty Blue Eyes**	Craig Douglas	Top Rank	8		
7	-	**On A Slow Boat To China**	Emile Ford	Pye	9		
8	1	**What Do You Want To Make Those Eyes At Me For**	Emile Ford & The Checkmates	Pye	18		F
9	-	**Beyond The Sea (La Mer)**	Bobby Darin	London American	6	(6)	
10	11	**Heartaches By The Number**	Guy Mitchell	Philips	9	(1)	L
11	-	**Running Bear**	Johnny Preston	Mercury	12	(1)	F
12	-	**Summer Set**	Acker Bilk	Columbia	10		F
13	-	**Misty**	Johnny Mathis	Fontana	6	(12)	
14	2	**What Do You Want**	Adam Faith	Parlophone	15		F
15	-	**Harbour Lights**	Platters	Mercury	7	(8)	L
16	4	**Staccato's Theme**	Elmer Bernstein	Capitol	10		F L
17	6	**Little White Bull**	Tommy Steele	Decca	12		
18	-	**You Got What It Takes**	Marv Johnson	London American	10	(10)	F
19	8	**Rawhide**	Frankie Laine	Philips	13		L
20	3	**Oh! Carol**	Neil Sedaka	RCA	14	(9)	

◆ Cliff Richard & The Shadows set a new record when 19.5 million people watched them on *Sunday Night At The London Palladium*. The following day they flew to the USA to tour with American chart stars Frankie Avalon, Freddy Cannon and Bobby Rydell.

◆ Elvis Presley set foot in Britain for the only time when changing planes in Scotland on his way back to the US from Germany to be demobbed.

1960

March 1960

This Mnth	Prev Mnth	Title	Artist	Label	Wks	(US 20 Pos)
1	4	**Poor Me**	Adam Faith	Parlophone	11	
2	11	**Running Bear**	Johnny Preston	Mercury	12	(1) F
3	-	**Delaware**	Perry Como	RCA	8	(22)
4	1	**Why**	Anthony Newley	Decca	12	
5	7	**On A Slow Boat To China**	Emile Ford & The Checkmates	Pye	9	
6	18	**You Got What It Takes**	Marv Johnson	London American	10	(10) F
7	-	**Theme From 'A Summer Place'**	Percy Faith	Philips	12	(1) F L
8	12	**Summer Set**	Acker Bilk	Columbia	10	F
9	2	**Voice In The Wilderness**	Cliff Richard	Columbia	10	
10	-	**What In The World's Come Over You**	Jack Scott	Top Rank	7	(5) L
11	3	**Way Down Yonder In New Orleans**	Freddy Cannon	Top Rank	11	(3)
12	6	**Pretty Blue Eyes**	Craig Douglas	Top Rank	8	
13	-	**Be Mine**	Lance Fortune	Pye	7	F L
14	-	**Fings Ain't What They Used T'be**	Max Bygraves	Decca	10	
15	-	**My Old Man's A Dustman**	Lonnie Donegan	Pye	9	
16	-	**Who Could Be Bluer**	Jerry Lordan	Parlophone	5	F L
17	9	**Beyond The Sea (La Mer)**	Bobby Darin	London American	6	(6)
18	-	**Beatnik Fly**	Johnny & The Hurricanes	London American	9	(15)
19	-	**Bonnie Came Back**	Duane Eddy	London American	4	(26)
20	-	**Royal Event**	Russ Conway	Columbia	3	

April 1960

This Mnth	Prev Mnth	Title	Artist	Label	Wks	(US 20 Pos)
1	15	**My Old Man's A Dustman**	Lonnie Donegan	Pye	9	
2	-	**Fall In Love With You**	Cliff Richard	Columbia	11	
3	-	**Handy Man**	Jimmy Jones	MGM	17	(2) F
4	-	**Do You Mind**	Anthony Newley	Decca	12	(91)
5	14	**Fings Ain't What They Used T'Be**	Max Bygraves	Decca	10	
6	-	**Stuck On You**	Elvis Presley	RCA	8	(1)
7	7	**Theme From 'A Summer Place'**	Percy Faith	Philips	12	(1) F L
8	2	**Running Bear**	Johnny Preston	Mercury	12	(1) F
9	18	**Beatnik Fly**	Johnny & The Hurricanes	London American	9	(15)
10	-	**Someone Else's Baby**	Adam Faith	Parlophone	10	
11	-	**Cathy's Clown**	Everly Brothers	Warner	14	(1)
12	3	**Delaware**	Perry Como	RCA	8	(22)
13	-	**Wild One**	Bobby Rydell	Columbia	8	(2) F
14	6	**You Got What It Takes**	Marv Johnson	London American	10	(10) F
15	-	**Sweet Nothin's**	Brenda Lee	Brunswick	13	(4) F
16	10	**What In The World's Come Over You**	Jack Scott	Top Rank	7	(5) L
17	-	**Clementine**	Bobby Darin	London American	6	(21)
18	-	**Standing On The Corner**	King Brothers	Parlophone	6	
19	1	**Poor Me**	Adam Faith	Parlophone	11	
20	-	**Footsteps**	Steve Lawrence	HMV	10	(7) F

◆ British teen idol Adam Faith scored his second successive No. 1 single.

◆ *Record Retailer* introduced Britain's first Top 50 single and Top 20 album charts.

◆ The Everly Brothers' initial release on Warner Brothers, their own composition 'Cathy's Clown', topped the chart on both sides of the Atlantic.

1960

This Mnth	Prev Mnth	Title	Artist	Label	Wks	(US 20 Pos)	
1	11	Cathy's Clown	Everly Brothers	Warner	14	(1)	
2	10	Someone Else's Baby	Adam Faith	Parlophone	10		
3	3	Handy Man	Jimmy Jones	MGM	17	(2)	F
4	4	Do You Mind	Anthony Newley	Decca	12	(91)	
5	15	Sweet Nothin's	Brenda Lee	Brunswick	13	(4)	F
6	-	Cradle Of Love	Johnny Preston	Mercury	11	(7)	
7	-	Shazam	Duane Eddy	London American	9	(45)	
8	2	Fall In Love With You	Cliff Richard	Columbia	11		
9	18	Standing On The Corner	King Brothers	Parlophone	6		
10	20	Footsteps	Steve Lawrence	HMV	10	(7)	F
11	6	Stuck On You	Elvis Presley	RCA	8	(1)	
12	-	Three Steps To Heaven	Eddie Cochran	London American	12		
13	-	Heart Of A Teenage Girl	Craig Douglas	Top Rank	5		
14	7	Theme From 'A Summer Place'	Percy Faith	Philips	12	(1)	F L
15	1	My Old Man's A Dustman	Lonnie Donegan	Pye	9		
16	-	Stairway To Heaven	Neil Sedaka	RCA	7	(9)	
17	5	Fings Ain't What They Used T'be	Max Bygraves	Decca	10		
18	-	Mama	Connie Francis	MGM	11	(8)	
19	9	Beatnik Fly	Johnny & The Hurricanes	London American	9	(15)	
20	-	Let The Little Girl Dance	Billy Bland	London American	3	(7)	F L

This Mnth	Prev Mnth	Title	Artist	Label	Wks	(US 20 Pos)	
1	1	Cathy's Clown	Everly Brothers	Warner	14	(1)	
2	6	Cradle Of Love	Johnny Preston	Mercury	11	(7)	
3	3	Handy Man	Jimmy Jones	MGM	17	(2)	F
4	12	Three Steps To Heaven	Eddie Cochran	London American	12		
5	5	Sweet Nothin's	Brenda Lee	Brunswick	13	(4)	F
6	-	Robot Man	Connie Francis	MGM	11		
7	-	I Wanna Go Home	Lonnie Donegan	Pye	9		
8	7	Shazam	Duane Eddy	London American	9	(45)	
9	18	Mama	Connie Francis	MGM	11	(8)	
10	2	Someone Else's Baby	Adam Faith	Parlophone	10		
11	-	Ain't Misbehavin'	Tommy Bruce & The Bruisers	Columbia	11		F L
12	-	Sixteen Reasons	Connie Stevens	Warner	7	(3)	F L
13	-	He'll Have To Go	Jim Reeves	RCA	6	(2)	F
14	16	Stairway To Heaven	Neil Sedaka	RCA	7	(9)	
15	10	Footsteps	Steve Lawrence	HMV	10	(7)	F
16	-	Good Timin'	Jimmy Jones	MGM	13	(3)	L
17	-	Down Yonder	Johnny & The Hurricanes	London American	5	(48)	
18	-	Lucky Five	Russ Conway	Columbia	4		
19	4	Do You Mind	Anthony Newley	Decca	12	(91)	
20	20	Let The Little Girl Dance	Billy Bland	London American	3	(7)	F L

◆ Gene Vincent was injured and Eddie Cochran killed in a car crash in England. Cochran's first posthumous release, 'Three Steps To Heaven' topped the UK chart.

◆ The Silver Beetles (Beatles) toured Scotland as backing band to little heralded rocker Johnny Gentle, and appeared alongside Gerry & The Pacemakers at a gig on Merseyside.

July 1960

This Mnth	Prev Mnth	Title	Artist	Label	Wks	(US 20 Pos)	
1	16	Good Timin'	Jimmy Jones	MGM	13	(3)	L
2	-	Please Don't Tease	Cliff Richard	Columbia	13		
3	11	Ain't Misbehavin'	Tommy Bruce & The Bruisers	Columbia	11		F L
4	-	Shakin' All Over	Johnny Kidd & The Pirates	HMV	12		F
5	-	What A Mouth	Tommy Steele	Decca	7		L
6	6	Robot Man	Connie Francis	MGM	11		
7	-	Made You	Adam Faith	Parlophone	7		
8	4	Three Steps To Heaven	Eddie Cochran	London American	12		
9	-	Angela Jones	Michael Cox	Triumph	7		F L
10	-	Look For A Star	Garry Mills	Top Rank	7	(26)	F L
11	1	Cathy's Clown	Everly Brothers	Warner	14	(1)	
12	-	When Will I Be Loved	Everly Brothers	London American	12	(8)	
13	9	Mama	Connie Francis	MGM	11	(8)	
14	-	When Johnny Comes Marching Home	Adam Faith	Parlophone	7		
15	7	I Wanna Go Home	Lonnie Donegan	Pye	9		
16	17	Down Yonder	Johnny & The Hurricanes	London American	5	(48)	
17	-	If She Should Come To You	Anthony Newley	Decca	9	(67)	
18	-	Itsy Bitsy Teenie Weenie Yellow Polka Dot Bikini	Brian Hyland	London American	9	(1)	F
19	2	Cradle Of Love	Johnny Preston	Mercury	11	(7)	
20	3	Handy Man	Jimmy Jones	MGM	17	(2)	F

August 1960

This Mnth	Prev Mnth	Title	Artist	Label	Wks	(US 20 Pos)	
1	2	Please Don't Tease	Cliff Richard	Columbia	13		
2	-	Apache	Shadows	Columbia	15		F
3	-	A Mess Of Blues	Elvis Presley	RCA	14	(32)	
4	4	Shakin' All Over	Johnny Kidd & The Pirates	HMV	12		F
5	-	Because They're Young	Duane Eddy	London American	14	(4)	
6	12	When Will I Be Loved	Everly Brothers	London American	12	(8)	
7	1	Good Timin'	Jimmy Jones	MGM	13	(3)	L
8	17	If She Should Come To You	Anthony Newley	Decca	9	(67)	
9	-	Tie Me Kangaroo Down Sport	Rolf Harris	Columbia	8	(3)	F
10	18	Itsy Bitsy Teenie Weenie Yellow Polka Dot Bikini	Brian Hyland	London American	9	(1)	F
11	10	Look For A Star	Garry Mills	Top Rank	7	(26)	F L
12	-	I'm Sorry	Brenda Lee	Brunswick	8	(1)	
13	-	Paper Roses	Kaye Sisters	Philips	10		L
14	-	Girl Of My Best Friend	Elvis Presley	RCA	12		
15	3	Ain't Misbehavin'	Tommy Bruce & The Bruisers	Columbia	11		F L
16	-	As Long As He Needs Me	Shirley Bassey	Columbia	22		
17	-	Everybody's Somebody's Fool	Connie Francis	MGM	10	(1)	
18	6	Robot Man	Connie Francis	MGM	11		
19	-	Mais Oui	King Brothers	Parlophone	3		
20	14	When Johnny Comes Marching Home	Adam Faith	Parlophone	7		

◆ After several unsuccessful singles, Cliff Richard's backing group, The Shadows, had a No. 1 hit with 'Apache'. They also recorded one of the earliest video discs, which was seen on European video juke boxes.

◆ The Beatles, with Pete Best on drums, played outside of Liverpool for the first time when they started a three month stand at the Indra club in Hamburg, Germany.

1960

This Mnth	Prev Mnth	Title	Artist	Label	Wks	(US 20 Pos)	
1	2	Apache	Shadows	Columbia	15		F
2	5	Because They're Young	Duane Eddy	London American	14	(4)	
3	-	Tell Laura I Love Her	Ricky Valance	Columbia	12		F L
4	3	A Mess Of Blues	Elvis Presley	RCA	14	(32)	
5	14	Girl Of My Best Friend	Elvis Presley	RCA	12		
6	-	Only The Lonely	Roy Orbison	London American	15	(2)	F
7	16	As Long As He Needs Me	Shirley Bassey	Columbia	22		
8	1	Please Don't Tease	Cliff Richard	Columbia	13		
9	17	Everybody's Somebody's Fool	Connie Francis	MGM	10	(1)	
10	6	When Will I Be Loved	Everly Brothers	London American	12	(8)	
11	-	How About That	Adam Faith	Parlophone	10		
12	13	Paper Roses	Kaye Sisters	Philips	10		L
13	-	Nine Times Out Of Ten	Cliff Richard	Columbia	8		
14	-	Love Is Like A Violin	Ken Dodd	Decca	7		F
15	8	If She Should Come To You	Anthony Newley	Decca	9	(67)	
16	-	Walk-Don't Run	Ventures	Top Rank	8	(2)	F
17	4	Shakin' All Over	Johnny Kidd & The Pirates	HMV	12		F
18	-	Walk Don't Run	John Barry Seven	Columbia	9		
19	12	I'm Sorry	Brenda Lee	Brunswick	8	(1)	
20	9	Tie Me Kangaroo Down Sport	Rolf Harris	Columbia	8	(3)	F

This Mnth	Prev Mnth	Title	Artist	Label	Wks	(US 20 Pos)	
1	6	Only The Lonely	Roy Orbison	London American	15	(2)	F
2	3	Tell Laura I Love Her	Ricky Valance	Columbia	12		F L
3	7	As Long As He Needs Me	Shirley Bassey	Columbia	22		
4	11	How About That	Adam Faith	Parlophone	10		
5	13	Nine Times Out Of Ten	Cliff Richard	Columbia	8		
6	-	So Sad (To Watch Good Love Go Bad)	Everly Brothers	Warner	8	(7)	
7	18	Walk Don't Run	John Barry Seven	Columbia	9		
8	1	Apache	Shadows	Columbia	15		F
9	-	Chain Gang	Sam Cooke	RCA	8	(2)	F
10	-	Let's Think About Living	Bob Luman	Warner	9	(7)	F L
11	16	Walk-Don't Run	Ventures	Top Rank	8	(2)	F
12	5	Girl Of My Best Friend	Elvis Presley	RCA	12		
13	-	Dreamin'	Johnny Burnette	London American	12	(11)	F
14	-	Please Help Me, I'm Falling	Hank Locklin	RCA	7	(8)	F L
15	-	Rocking Goose	Johnny & The Hurricanes	London American	15	(60)	
16	4	A Mess Of Blues	Elvis Presley	RCA	14	(32)	
17	2	Because They're Young	Duane Eddy	London American	14	(4)	
18	-	MacDonald's Cave	Piltdown Men	Capitol	6		F
19	9	Everybody's Somebody's Fool	Connie Francis	MGM	10	(1)	
20	-	My Love For You	Johnny Mathis	Fontana	11	(47)	

◆ Sam Cooke's current US hit, 'Wonderful World' (which he had written with Herb Alpert), was a transatlantic Top 10 hit for Herman's Hermits in 1965, and became a major British hit by Cooke in 1986 (21 years after his death!)

◆ Elvis Presley's 'It's Now Or Never', which had record UK advance orders, sold over 750,000 copies in its first week and passed the million mark 40 days later. Meanwhile, in America, his revival of 'Are You Lonesome Tonight' became his 15th chart topping single.

November 1960

This Mnth	Prev Mnth	Title	Artist	Label	Wks	(US 20 Pos)	
1	-	**It's Now Or Never**	Elvis Presley	RCA	14	(1)	G
2	3	**As Long As He Needs Me**	Shirley Bassey	Columbia	22		
3	13	**Dreamin'**	Johnny Burnette	London American	12	(11)	F
4	1	**Only The Lonely**	Roy Orbison	London American	15	(2)	F
5	15	**Rocking Goose**	Johnny & The Hurricanes	London American	15	(60)	
6	-	**My Heart Has A Mind Of Its Own**	Connie Francis	MGM	8	(1)	
7	-	**Save The Last Dance For Me**	Drifters	London American	14	(1)	
8	10	**Let's Think About Living**	Bob Luman	Warner	9	(7)	F L
9	-	**Goodness Gracious Me**	Peter Sellers & Sophia Loren	Parlophone	12		
10	20	**My Love For You**	Johnny Mathis	Fontana	11	(47)	
11	18	**MacDonald's Cave**	Piltdown Men	Capitol	6		F
12	-	**Man Of Mystery**	Shadows	Columbia	10		
13	9	**Chain Gang**	Sam Cooke	RCA	8	(2)	F
14	4	**How About That**	Adam Faith	Parlophone	10		
15	-	**Mr. Custer**	Charlie Drake	Parlophone	4		
16	7	**Walk Don't Run**	John Barry Seven	Columbia	9		
17	-	**The Stranger**	Shadows	Columbia	4		
18	-	**Kommotion**	Duane Eddy	London American	3	(78)	
19	6	**So Sad (To Watch Good Love Go Bad)**	Everly Brothers	Warner	8	(7)	
20	5	**Nine Times Out Of Ten**	Cliff Richard	Columbia	8		

December 1960

This Mnth	Prev Mnth	Title	Artist	Label	Wks	(US 20 Pos)	
1	1	**It's Now Or Never**	Elvis Presley	RCA	14	(1)	G
2	7	**Save The Last Dance For Me**	Drifters	London American	14	(1)	
3	-	**I Love You**	Cliff Richard	Columbia	12		
4	-	**Strawberry Fair**	Anthony Newley	Decca	8		
5	9	**Goodness Gracious Me**	Peter Sellers & Sophia Loren	Parlophone	12		
6	-	**Little Donkey**	Nina & Frederick	Columbia	7		F
7	5	**Rocking Goose**	Johnny & The Hurricanes	London American	15	(60)	
8	12	**Man Of Mystery**	Shadows	Columbia	10		
9	-	**Poetry In Motion**	Johnny Tillotson	London American	13	(2)	F L
10	-	**Lonely Pup (In A Christmas Shop)**	Adam Faith	Parlophone	7		
11	-	**Gurney Slade**	Max Harris	Fontana	6		F L
12	6	**My Heart Has A Mind Of Its Own**	Connie Francis	MGM	8	(1)	
13	2	**As Long As He Needs Me**	Shirley Bassey	Columbia	22		
14	-	**Perfidia**	Ventures	London American	9	(15)	L
15	3	**Dreamin'**	Johnny Burnette	London American	12	(11)	F
16	10	**My Love For You**	Johnny Mathis	Fontana	11	(47)	
17	-	**Blue Angel**	Roy Orbison	London American	8	(9)	
18	-	**Lively**	Lonnie Donegan	Pye	6		
19	-	**Ol' Macdonald**	Frank Sinatra	Capitol	4	(25)	
20	-	**Counting Teardrops**	Emile Ford & The Checkmates	Pye	9		L

◆ Instrumentals were big business in Britain – at times accounting for 30% of the chart. The hottest instrumental acts were The Shadows, Johnny & The Hurricanes, Duane Eddy and American session-group The Piltdown Men.

◆ Frankie Vaughan, one of the top UK singers of the 1950s, became the first UK pop performer to be the subject of the US TV show *This Is Your Life* – an estimated 40 million viewers saw the show.

1961

January 1961

This Mnth	Prev Mnth	Title	Artist	Label	Wks	(US 20 Pos)	
1	9	Poetry In Motion	Johnny Tillotson	London American	13	(2)	F L
2	3	I Love You	Cliff Richard	Columbia	12		
3	2	Save The Last Dance For Me	Drifters	London American	14	(1)	
4	-	Portrait Of My Love	Matt Monro	Parlophone	10		F
5	1	It's Now Or Never	Elvis Presley	RCA	14	(1)	G
6	14	Perfidia	Ventures	London American	9	(15)	L
7	20	Counting Teardrops	Emile Ford & The Checkmates	Pye	9		L
8	-	Are You Lonesome Tonight?	Elvis Presley	RCA	10	(1)	
9	5	Goodness Gracious Me	Peter Sellers & Sophia Loren	Parlophone	12		
10	-	Buona Sera	Acker Bilk	Columbia	8		
11	-	Pepe	Duane Eddy	London American	8	(18)	
12	10	Lonely Pup (In A Christmas Shop)	Adam Faith	Parlophone	7		
13	-	Stay	Maurice Williams & The Zodiacs	Top Rank	6	(1)	F L
14	7	Rocking Goose	Johnny & The Hurricanes	London American	15	(60)	
15	-	Sway	Bobby Rydell	Columbia	5	(14)	
16	17	Blue Angel	Roy Orbison	London American	8	(9)	
17	4	Strawberry Fair	Anthony Newley	Decca	8		
18	8	Man Of Mystery	Shadows	Columbia	10		
19	-	You're Sixteen	Johnny Burnette	London American	8	(8)	
20	-	Sailor	Petula Clark	Pye	9		

February 1961

		Title	Artist	Label	Wks	(US 20 Pos)	
1	8	Are You Lonesome Tonight?	Elvis Presley	RCA	10	(1)	
2	20	Sailor	Petula Clark	Pye	9		
3	-	Rubber Ball	Bobby Vee	London American	7	(6)	F
4	19	You're Sixteen	Johnny Burnette	London American	8	(8)	
5	11	Pepe	Duane Eddy	London American	8	(18)	
6	4	Portrait Of My Love	Matt Monro	Parlophone	10		F
7	-	F.B.I.	Shadows	Columbia	11		
8	1	Poetry In Motion	Johnny Tillotson	London American	13	(2)	F L
9	-	Walk Right Back	Everly Brothers	Warner	11	(7)	
10	-	Sailor	Anne Shelton	Philips	5		L
11	-	Rubber Ball	Marty Wilde	Philips	4		L
12	-	Who Am I/This Is It	Adam Faith	Parlophone	9		
13	10	Buona Sera	Acker Bilk	Columbia	8		
14	-	Will You Love Me Tomorrow	Shirelles	Top Rank	9	(1)	F L
15	-	Calendar Girl	Neil Sedaka	RCA	8	(4)	
16	2	I Love You	Cliff Richard	Columbia	12		
17	-	Many Tears Ago	Connie Francis	MGM	5	(7)	
18	7	Counting Teardrops	Emile Ford & The Checkmates	Pye	9		L
19	13	Stay	Maurice Williams & The Zodiacs	Top Rank	6	(1)	F L
20	-	Riders In The Sky	Ramrods	London American	7	(30)	F L

◆ Trad (based on old-time New Orleans- styled traditional jazz) was the latest UK music craze, with Acker Bilk, Kenny Ball and Chris Barber at the forefront of it.

◆ New transatlantic stars included the Buddy Holly-influenced 17-year-old Bobby Vee and singer/songwriter Johnny Tillotson whose 'Poetry In Motion' topped the chart on both sides of the Atlantic

March 1961

This Mnth	Prev Mnth	Title	Artist	Label	Wks	(US 20 Pos)	
1	9	**Walk Right Back**	Everly Brothers	Warner	11	(7)	
2	-	**Are You Sure**	Allisons	Fontana	12		F L
3	-	**Theme For A Dream**	Cliff Richard	Columbia	9		
4	14	**Will You Love Me Tomorrow**	Shirelles	Top Rank	9	(1)	F L
5	-	**Wooden Heart**	Elvis Presley	RCA	14		
6	7	**F.B.I.**	Shadows	Columbia	11		
7	20	**Riders In The Sky**	Ramrods	London American	7	(30)	F L
8	-	**My Kind Of Girl**	Matt Monro	Parlophone	7	(18)	
9	2	**Sailor**	Petula Clark	Pye	9		
10	15	**Calendar Girl**	Neil Sedaka	RCA	8	(4)	
11	-	**Exodus**	Ferrante & Teicher	London American	10	(2)	F L
12	12	**Who Am I/This Is It**	Adam Faith	Parlophone	9		
13	1	**Are You Lonesome Tonight?**	Elvis Presley	RCA	10	(1)	
14	-	**Wheels**	String-A-Longs	London American	6	(3)	F L
15	-	**Samantha**	Kenny Ball	Pye Jazz	10		F
16	-	**And The Heavens Cried**	Anthony Newley	Decca	7		
17	-	**Lazy River**	Bobby Darin	London American	8	(14)	
18	-	**Let's Jump The Broomstick**	Brenda Lee	Brunswick	4		
19	-	**Ja-Da**	Johnny & The Hurricanes	London American	3	(86)	L
20	3	**Rubber Ball**	Bobby Vee	London American	7	(6)	F

April 1961

This Mnth	Prev Mnth	Title	Artist	Label	Wks	(US 20 Pos)	
1	5	**Wooden Heart**	Elvis Presley	RCA	14		
2	2	**Are You Sure**	Allisons	Fontana	12		F L
3	17	**Lazy River**	Bobby Darin	London American	8	(14)	
4	-	**You're Driving Me Crazy**	Temperance Seven	Parlophone	12		F
5	11	**Exodus**	Ferrante & Teicher	London American	10	(2)	F L
6	3	**Theme For A Dream**	Cliff Richard	Columbia	9		
7	-	**Where The Boys Are**	Connie Francis	MGM	6	(4)	
8	-	**Blue Moon**	Marcels	Pye International	9	(1)	F L
9	1	**Walk Right Back**	Everly Brothers	Warner	11	(7)	
10	16	**And The Heavens Cried**	Anthony Newley	Decca	7		
11	-	**Gee Whiz It's You**	Cliff Richard	Columbia	8		
12	8	**My Kind Of Girl**	Matt Monro	Parlophone	7	(18)	
13	6	**F.B.I.**	Shadows	Columbia	11		
14	15	**Samantha**	Kenny Ball	Pye Jazz	10		F
15	-	**Warpaint**	Brook Brothers	Pye	9		F
16	-	**African Waltz**	Johnny Dankworth	Columbia	8		L
17	4	**Will You Love Me Tomorrow**	Shirelles	Top Rank	9	(1)	F L
18	-	**A Hundred Pounds Of Clay**	Craig Douglas	Top Rank	6		
19	-	**Don't Treat Me Like A Child**	Helen Shapiro	Columbia	11		F
20	-	**Baby Sittin' Boogie**	Buzz Clifford	Fontana	3	(6)	F L

◆ The Allisons were the most talked about new act. The duo's self-composed 'Are You Sure' dethroned Elvis at the top and came runner-up in the most publicized Eurovision Song Contest to date.

◆ Ex-Drifter Ben E. King released 'Stand By Me' a song he had originally written for the group. It was a US Top 10 hit in both 1961 and 1986, and even topped the UK chart in 1987!

1961

May 1961

This Mnth	Prev Mnth	Title	Artist	Label	Wks	(US 20 Pos)	
1	8	Blue Moon	Marcels	Pye International	9	(1)	F L
2	4	You're Driving Me Crazy	Temperance Seven	Parlophone	12		F
3	-	On The Rebound	Floyd Cramer	RCA	9	(4)	F L
4	-	Runaway	Del Shannon	London American	16	(1)	F
5	-	More Than I Can Say	Bobby Vee	London American	9	(61)	
6	19	Don't Treat Me Like A Child	Helen Shapiro	Columbia	11		F
7	1	Wooden Heart	Elvis Presley	RCA	14		
8	-	Theme From Dixie	Duane Eddy	London American	6	(39)	
9	-	Frightened City	Shadows	Columbia	11		
10	-	Easy Going Me	Adam Faith	Parlophone	5		
11	18	A Hundred Pounds Of Clay	Craig Douglas	Top Rank	6		
12	-	What'd I Say	Jerry Lee Lewis	London American	6	(30)	L
13	16	African Waltz	Johnny Dankworth	Columbia	8		L
14	-	You'll Never Know	Shirley Bassey	Columbia	8		
15	11	Gee Whiz It's You	Cliff Richard	Columbia	8		
16	15	Warpaint	Brook Brothers	Pye	9		F
17	3	Lazy River	Bobby Darin	London American	8	(14)	
18	-	Surrender	Elvis Presley	RCA	10	(1)	
19	-	But I Do	Clarence 'Frogman' Henry	Pye International	13	(4)	F
20	5	Exodus	Ferrante & Teicher	London American	10	(2)	F L

June 1961

1	4	Runaway	Del Shannon	London American	16	(1)	F
2	18	Surrender	Elvis Presley	RCA	10	(1)	
3	19	But I Do	Clarence 'Frogman' Henry	Pye International	13	(4)	F
4	9	Frightened City	Shadows	Columbia	11		
5	14	You'll Never Know	Shirley Bassey	Columbia	8		
6	-	Hello Mary Lou/Travellin' Man	Ricky Nelson	London American	15	(9)	
7	-	Halfway To Paradise	Billy Fury	Decca	18		
8	-	Have A Drink On Me	Lonnie Donegan	Pye	8		
9	-	Pasadena	Temperance Seven	Parlophone	12		
10	5	More Than I Can Say	Bobby Vee	London American	9	(61)	
11	-	Temptation	Everly Brothers	Warner	12	(27)	
12	-	Little Devil	Neil Sedaka	RCA	6	(11)	
13	3	On The Rebound	Floyd Cramer	RCA	9	(4)	F L
14	-	I've Told Every Little Star	Linda Scott	Columbia	6	(3)	F L
15	-	Running Scared	Roy Orbison	London American	9	(1)	
16	12	What'd I Say	Jerry Lee Lewis	London American	6	(30)	L
17	-	A Girl Like You	Cliff Richard	Columbia	12		
18	-	Pop Goes The Weasel	Anthony Newley	Decca	6	(85)	
19	-	Well I Ask You	Eden Kane	Decca	16		F
20	1	Blue Moon	Marcels	Pye International	9	(1)	F L

◆ Elvis Presley's 'Surrender', which like its predecessor, 'It's Now Or Never', was based on an old Italian ballad, had a record 460,000 advance orders.

◆ The first American artist to appear on new pop TV show *Thank Your Lucky Stars* was Gene Vincent. This show, more than any other, would spread the Merseybeat sound.

◆ British teen idol Billy Fury clocked up his biggest hit to date with a cover of Tony Orlando's 'Halfway To Paradise'.

July 1961

This Mnth	Prev Mnth	Title	Artist	Label	Wks	(US 20 Pos)	
1	11	Temptation	Everly Brothers	Warner	12	(27)	
2	1	Runaway	Del Shannon	London American	16	(1)	F
3	19	Well I Ask You	Eden Kane	Decca	16		F
4	6	Hello Mary Lou/Travellin' Man	Ricky Nelson	London American	15	(9)	
5	17	A Girl Like You	Cliff Richard	Columbia	12		
6	9	Pasadena	Temperance Seven	Parlophone	12		
7	7	Halfway To Paradise	Billy Fury	Decca	18		
8	3	But I Do	Clarence 'Frogman' Henry	Pye International	13	(4)	F
9	15	Running Scared	Roy Orbison	London American	9	(1)	
10	-	You Don't Know	Helen Shapiro	Columbia	14		
11	-	You Always Hurt The One You Love	Clarence 'Frogman' Henry	Pye International	9	(12)	L
12	2	Surrender	Elvis Presley	RCA	10	(1)	
13	-	Time	Craig Douglas	Top Rank	10		
14	18	Pop Goes The Weasel	Anthony Newley	Decca	6	(85)	
15	-	Romeo	Petula Clark	Pye	11		
16	-	Moody River	Pat Boone	London American	6	(1)	
17	4	Frightened City	Shadows	Columbia	11		
18	-	Weekend	Eddie Cochran	London American	3		L
19	-	Don't You Know It	Adam Faith	Parlophone	6		
20	-	Breakin' In A Brand New Broken Heart	Connie Francis	MGM	2	(7)	

August 1961

This Mnth	Prev Mnth	Title	Artist	Label	Wks	(US 20 Pos)	
1	10	You Don't Know	Helen Shapiro	Columbia	14		
2	3	Well I Ask You	Eden Kane	Decca	16		F
3	-	Johnny Remember Me	John Leyton	Top Rank	11		F
4	7	Halfway To Paradise	Billy Fury	Decca	18		
5	15	Romeo	Petula Clark	Pye	11		
6	11	You Always Hurt The One You Love	Clarence 'Frogman' Henry	Pye International	9	(12)	L
7	6	Pasadena	Temperance Seven	Parlophone	12		
8	1	Temptation	Everly Brothers	Warner	12	(27)	
9	19	Don't You Know It	Adam Faith	Parlophone	6		
10	13	Time	Craig Douglas	Top Rank	10		
11	5	A Girl Like You	Cliff Richard	Columbia	12		
12	4	Hello Mary Lou/Travellin' Man	Ricky Nelson	London American	15	(9)	
13	-	Quarter To Three	Gary U.S. Bonds	Top Rank	9	(1)	L
14	-	Reach For The Stars/ Climb Ev'ry Mountain	Shirley Bassey	Columbia	11		
15	2	Runaway	Del Shannon	London American	16	(1)	F
16	-	Climb Ev'ry Mountain	Shirley Bassey	Columbia	6		
17	-	Baby I Don't Care	Buddy Holly	Coral	6		
18	-	Marcheta	Karl Denver	Decca	7		F
19	-	That's My Home	Acker Bilk	Columbia	9		
20	-	Cupid	Sam Cooke	RCA	7	(17)	

◆ 'Michael', a 19th century slave song, gave American folk quintet The Highwaymen an unexpected transatlantic No. 1, despite heavy British competition from Lonnie Donegan. Incidentally, Donegan's 1959 UK hit 'Chewing Gum' was now huge in the USA.

◆ The Shadows became the first British rock act to top the UK album chart. Their boss, Cliff Richard, would be the second with his **21 Today** LP.

1961

September 1961

This Mnth	Prev Mnth	Title	Artist	Label	Wks	(US 20 Pos)
1	3	Johnny Remember Me	John Leyton	Top Rank	11	F
2	1	You Don't Know	Helen Shapiro	Columbia	14	
3	14	Reach For The Stars/ Climb Ev'ry Mountain	Shirley Bassey	Columbia	11	
4	-	Wild In The Country	Elvis Presley	RCA	8	(26)
5	-	Kon-Tiki	Shadows	Columbia	8	
6	20	Cupid	Sam Cooke	RCA	7	(17)
7	2	Well I Ask You	Eden Kane	Decca	16	F
8	-	Michael	Highwaymen	HMV	10	(1) F L
9	19	That's My Home	Acker Bilk	Columbia	9	
10	5	Romeo	Petula Clark	Pye	11	
11	-	Michael Row The Boat	Lonnie Donegan	Pye	6	
12	-	Jealousy	Billy Fury	Decca	8	
13	4	Halfway To Paradise	Billy Fury	Decca	18	
14	-	Get Lost	Eden Kane	Decca	8	
15	13	Quarter To Three	Gary U.S. Bonds	Top Rank	9	(1) L
16	-	How Many Tears	Bobby Vee	London American	5	(63)
17	-	Together	Connie Francis	MGM	6	(6)
18	-	Hats Off To Larry	Del Shannon	London American	8	(5)
19	11	A Girl Like You	Cliff Richard	Columbia	12	
20	-	You'll Answer To Me	Cleo Laine	Fontana	9	F L

October 1961

This Mnth	Prev Mnth	Title	Artist	Label	Wks	(US 20 Pos)
1	-	Walkin' Back To Happiness	Helen Shapiro	Columbia	15	(100)
2	8	Michael	Highwaymen	HMV	10	(1) F L
3	-	Wild Wind	John Leyton	Top Rank	6	
4	20	You'll Answer To Me	Cleo Laine	Fontana	9	F L
5	12	Jealousy	Billy Fury	Decca	8	
6	-	Sucu-Sucu	Laurie Johnson	Pye	10	F L
7	5	Kon-Tiki	Shadows	Columbia	8	
8	18	Hats Off To Larry	Del Shannon	London American	8	(5)
9	4	Wild In The Country	Elvis Presley	RCA	8	(26)
10	-	When The Girl In Your Arms Is The Girl In Your Heart	Cliff Richard	Columbia	7	
11	-	Bless You	Tony Orlando	Fontana	7	(15) F L
12	14	Get Lost	Eden Kane	Decca	8	
13	-	Mexicali Rose	Karl Denver	Decca	9	
14	1	Johnny Remember Me	John Leyton	Top Rank	11	F
15	-	You Must Have Been A Beautiful Baby	Bobby Darin	London American	8	(5)
16	-	Granada	Frank Sinatra	Reprise	4	(64)
17	-	Hit The Road Jack	Ray Charles	HMV	8	(1)
18	17	Together	Connie Francis	MGM	6	(6)
19	-	My Boomerang Won't Come Back	Charlie Drake	Parlophone	6	(21) L
20	2	You Don't Know	Helen Shapiro	Columbia	14	

◆ 15-year-old London schoolgirl Helen Shapiro had two successive chart toppers with the British songs 'You Don't Know' and 'Walkin' Back To Happiness'. Both records sold over a million copies worldwide.

◆ Unusually. three hitsby British acts also reached the US Top 10: 'Midnight In Moscow' by Kenny Ball, 'Stranger On The Shore' by Acker Bilk and 'Let's Get Together' by 14-year-old Hayley Mills.

November 1961

This Mnth	Prev Mnth	Title	Artist	Label	Wks	(US 20 Pos)	
1	-	His Latest Flame	Elvis Presley	RCA	8	(4)	
2	1	Walkin' Back To Happiness	Helen Shapiro	Columbia	15	(100)	
3	-	Take Good Care Of My Baby	Bobby Vee	London American	11	(1)	
4	-	Big Bad John	Jimmy Dean	Philips	11	(1)	F L
5	10	When The Girl In Your Arms Is The Girl In Your Heart	Cliff Richard	Columbia	7		
6	-	Take Five	Dave Brubeck Quartet	Fontana	10	(25)	F
7	17	Hit The Road Jack	Ray Charles	HMV	8	(1)	
8	-	The Time Has Come	Adam Faith	Parlophone	8		
9	6	Sucu-Sucu	Laurie Johnson	Pye	10		F L
10	13	Mexicali Rose	Karl Denver	Decca	9		
11	-	Tower Of Strength	Frankie Vaughan	Philips	10		
12	-	Moon River	Danny Williams	HMV	12		F
13	11	Bless You	Tony Orlando	Fontana	7	(15)	F L
14	15	You Must Have Been A Beautiful Baby	Bobby Darin	London American	8	(5)	
15	3	Wild Wind	John Leyton	Top Rank	6		
16	-	Runaround Sue	Dion	Top Rank	5	(1)	F
17	-	The Savage	Shadows	Columbia	5		
18	-	Let's Get Together	Hayley Mills	Decca	5	(8)	F L
19	-	Midnight In Moscow	Kenny Ball	Pye Jazz	11	(2)	
20	4	You'll Answer To Me	Cleo Laine	Fontana	9		F L

December 1961

This Mnth	Prev Mnth	Title	Artist	Label	Wks	(US 20 Pos)	
1	11	Tower Of Strength	Frankie Vaughan	Philips	10		
2	12	Moon River	Danny Williams	HMV	12		F
3	3	Take Good Care Of My Baby	Bobby Vee	London American	11	(1)	
4	19	Midnight In Moscow	Kenny Ball	Pye Jazz	11	(2)	
5	-	Stranger On The Shore	Mr. Acker Bilk	Columbia	33	(1)	G
6	-	I'll Get By	Shirley Bassey	Columbia	6		
7	2	Walkin' Back To Happiness	Helen Shapiro	Columbia	15	(100)	
8	1	His Latest Flame	Elvis Presley	RCA	8	(4)	
9	-	Johnny Will	Pat Boone	London American	8	(35)	
10	6	Take Five	Dave Brubeck Quartet	Fontana	10	(25)	F
11	-	Let There Be Drums	Sandy Nelson	London American	9	(7)	L
12	4	Big Bad John	Jimmy Dean	Philips	11	(1)	F L
13	8	The Time Has Come	Adam Faith	Parlophone	8		
14	-	My Friend The Sea	Petula Clark	Pye	4		
15	-	So Long Baby	Del Shannon	London American	6	(28)	
16	-	Don't Bring Lulu	Dorothy Provine	Warner	6		F L
17	-	Happy Birthday, Sweet Sixteen	Neil Sedaka	RCA	11	(6)	
18	-	I Cried For You	Ricky Stevens	Columbia	4		F L
19	17	The Savage	Shadows	Columbia	5		
20	-	I'd Never Find Another You	Billy Fury	Decca	11		

◆ Mantovani received five American gold albums while fellow Briton Matt Monro was voted Most Promising Artist in the *Billboard* DJ Poll.

◆ American hits from C&W stars Leroy Van Dyke, Jimmy Dean and Patsy Cline also scored in Britain, although, in the case of Cline's 'Crazy' it was 30 years later!

◆ EMI Records proudly announced that **The Black And White Minstrel Show** by The George Mitchell Minstrels (which was based on the act's very popular TV series) was the company's first album to sell over 100,000 copies in the UK.

1962

This Mnth	Prev Mnth	Title	Artist	Label	Wks	(US 20 Pos)	
1	5	**Stranger On The Shore**	Mr. Acker Bilk	Columbia	33	(1)	G
2	20	**I'd Never Find Another You**	Billy Fury	Decca	11		
3	11	**Let There Be Drums**	Sandy Nelson	London American	9	(7)	L
4	-	**The Young Ones**	Cliff Richard	Columbia	13		G
5	17	**Happy Birthday, Sweet Sixteen**	Neil Sedaka	RCA	11	(6)	
6	-	**Multiplication**	Bobby Darin	London American	8	(30)	
7	-	**Let's Twist Again**	Chubby Checker	Columbia	18	(8)	
8	2	**Moon River**	Danny Williams	HMV	12		F
9	4	**Midnight In Moscow**	Kenny Ball	Pye Jazz	11	(2)	
10	9	**Johnny Will**	Pat Boone	London American	8	(35)	
11	-	**Run To Him**	Bobby Vee	Liberty	9	(2)	
12	-	**The Twist**	Chubby Checker	Columbia	5	(1)	F
13	1	**Tower Of Strength**	Frankie Vaughan	Philips	10		
14	-	**The Lion Sleeps Tonight**	Tokens	RCA	4	(1)	F L
15	-	**Walk On By**	Leroy Van Dyke	Mercury	9	(5)	F L
16	15	**So Long Baby**	Del Shannon	London American	6	(28)	
17	-	**Forget Me Not**	Eden Kane	Decca	9		
18	-	**Language Of Love**	John D. Loudermilk	RCA	4	(32)	F L
19	-	**Toy Balloons**	Russ Conway	Columbia	5		L
20	-	**Cryin' In The Rain**	Everly Brothers	Warner	9	(6)	

This Mnth	Prev Mnth	Title	Artist	Label	Wks	(US 20 Pos)	
1	4	**The Young Ones**	Cliff Richard	Columbia	13		G
2	7	**Let's Twist Again**	Chubby Checker	Columbia	18	(8)	
3	-	**Rock-A-Hula-Baby**	Elvis Presley	RCA	9	(23)	
4	17	**Forget Me Not**	Eden Kane	Decca	9		
5	15	**Walk On By**	Leroy Van Dyke	Mercury	9	(5)	F L
6	5	**Happy Birthday, Sweet Sixteen**	Neil Sedaka	RCA	11	(6)	
7	20	**Cryin' In The Rain**	Everly Brothers	Warner	9	(6)	
8	2	**I'd Never Find Another You**	Billy Fury	Decca	11		
9	1	**Stranger On The Shore**	Mr. Acker Bilk	Columbia	33	(1)	G
10	11	**Run To Him**	Bobby Vee	Liberty	9	(2)	
11	6	**Multiplication**	Bobby Darin	London American	8	(30)	
12	-	**A Little Bitty Tear**	Burl Ives	Brunswick	6	(9)	F L
13	-	**Peppermint Twist**	Joey Dee & The Starliters	Columbia	5	(1)	F L
14	-	**Wimoweh**	Karl Denver	Decca	10		
15	-	**Lonesome**	Adam Faith	Parlophone	4		
16	-	**Can't Help Falling In Love**	Elvis Presley	RCA	13	(2)	
17	-	**The Comancheros**	Lonnie Donegan	Pye	4		
18	-	**March Of The Siamese Children**	Kenny Ball	Pye Jazz	8	(88)	
19	3	**Let There Be Drums**	Sandy Nelson	London American	9	(7)	L
20	12	**The Twist**	Chubby Checker	Columbia	5	(1)	F

◆ The theme from Cliff Richard's film *The Young Ones* racked up 500.000 advance orders and entered the UK chart at No. 1. It went on to sell over a million in Britain. The soundtrack album also topped the chart.

◆ Elvis Presley earned his 29th gold single with the double-sided 'Rock-A-Hula Baby' and 'Can't Help Falling In Love'. The single came from the soundtrack album to the film *Blue Hawaii*, which topped the chart for four months on both sides of the Atlantic. 'Can't Help Falling In Love' charted again later for Andy Williams, The Stylistics and UB40.

March 1962

This Mnth	Prev Mnth	Title	Artist	Label	Wks	(US 20 Pos)	
1	18	**March Of The Siamese Children**	Kenny Ball	Pye Jazz	8	(88)	
2	-	**Tell Me What He Said**	Helen Shapiro	Columbia	10		
3	2	**Let's Twist Again**	Chubby Checker	Columbia	18	(8)	
4	-	**Wonderful Land**	Shadows	Columbia	16		
5	16	**Can't Help Falling In Love**	Elvis Presley	RCA	13	(2)	
6	14	**Wimoweh**	Karl Denver	Decca	10		
7	1	**The Young Ones**	Cliff Richard	Columbia	13		G
8	3	**Rock-A-Hula-Baby**	Elvis Presley	RCA	9	(23)	
9	9	**Stranger On The Shore**	Mr. Acker Bilk	Columbia	33	(1)	G
10	-	**Hole In The Ground**	Bernard Cribbins	Parlophone	7		F
11	-	**Twistin' The Night Away**	Sam Cooke	RCA	12	(9)	
12	-	**Dream Baby**	Roy Orbison	London American	11	(4)	
13	-	**Softly As I Leave You**	Matt Monro	Parlophone	8		
14	-	**Hey! Baby**	Bruce Channel	Mercury	9	(1)	F
15	7	**Cryin' In The Rain**	Everly Brothers	Warner	9	(6)	
16	-	**The Wanderer**	Dion	HMV	6	(2)	
17	4	**Forget Me Not**	Eden Kane	Decca	9		
18	12	**A Little Bitty Tear**	Burl Ives	Brunswick	6	(9)	F L
19	5	**Walk On By**	Leroy Van Dyke	Mercury	9	(5)	F L
20	-	**Hey Little Girl**	Del Shannon	London American	12	(38)	

April 1962

This Mnth	Prev Mnth	Title	Artist	Label	Wks	(US 20 Pos)	
1	4	**Wonderful Land**	Shadows	Columbia	16		
2	14	**Hey! Baby**	Bruce Channel	Mercury	9	(1)	F
3	12	**Dream Baby**	Roy Orbison	London American	11	(4)	
4	-	**When My Little Girl Is Smiling**	Jimmy Justice	Pye	9		F
5	11	**Twistin' The Night Away**	Sam Cooke	RCA	12	(9)	
6	2	**Tell Me What He Said**	Helen Shapiro	Columbia	10		
7	20	**Hey Little Girl**	Del Shannon	London American	12	(38)	
8	5	**Can't Help Falling In Love**	Elvis Presley	RCA	13	(2)	
9	-	**Never Goodbye**	Karl Denver	Decca	7		
10	-	**Speak To Me Pretty**	Brenda Lee	Brunswick	9		
11	3	**Let's Twist Again**	Chubby Checker	Columbia	18	(8)	
12	6	**Wimoweh**	Karl Denver	Decca	10		
13	-	**When My Little Girl Is Smiling**	Craig Douglas	Top Rank	6		
14	-	**Dr. Kildare Theme**	Johnny Spence	Parlophone	5		F L
15	9	**Stranger On The Shore**	Mr. Acker Bilk	Columbia	33	(1)	G
16	1	**March Of The Siamese Children**	Kenny Ball	Pye Jazz	8	(88)	
17	-	**Love Letters**	Ketty Lester	London American	9	(5)	F L
18	-	**Nut Rocker**	B. Bumble & The Stingers	Top Rank	11	(23)	F L
19	-	**Wonderful World Of The Young**	Danny Williams	HMV	7		L
20	-	**Ev'rybody's Twistin'**	Frank Sinatra	Reprise	5	(75)	

◆ Alexis Korner's group, Blues Incorporated (which at times included Charlie Watts, Jack Bruce, Ginger Baker, Mick Jagger and Brian Jones), played their debut gig at a club in Ealing.

◆ British trad star Acker Bilk topped the US chart with 'Stranger On The Shore'. In the 1962 *Billboard* DJ poll he won awards for Top Instrumentalist and Top Instrumental Single.

1962

This Mnth	Prev Mnth	Title	Artist	Label	Wks	(US 20 Pos)	
1	18	**Nut Rocker**	B. Bumble & The Stingers	Top Rank	11	(23)	F L
2	1	**Wonderful Land**	Shadows	Columbia	16		
3	17	**Love Letters**	Ketty Lester	London American	9	(5)	F L
4	-	**Good Luck Charm**	Elvis Presley	RCA	14	(1)	
5	10	**Speak To Me Pretty**	Brenda Lee	Brunswick	9		
6	-	**I'm Looking Out The Window**	Cliff Richard	Columbia	11		
7	7	**Hey Little Girl**	Del Shannon	London American	12	(38)	
8	4	**When My Little Girl Is Smiling**	Jimmy Justice	Pye	9		F
9	-	**As You Like It**	Adam Faith	Parlophone	10		
10	2	**Hey! Baby**	Bruce Channel	Mercury	9	(1)	F
11	19	**Wonderful World Of The Young**	Danny Williams	HMV	7		L
12	3	**Dream Baby**	Roy Orbison	London American	11	(4)	
13	5	**Twistin' The Night Away**	Sam Cooke	RCA	12	(9)	
14	-	**Come Outside**	Mike Sarne & Wendy Richard	Parlophone	14		F
15	-	**Last Night Was Made For Love**	Billy Fury	Decca	11		
16	-	**The Party's Over**	Lonnie Donegan	Pye	5		
17	15	**Stranger On The Shore**	Mr. Acker Bilk	Columbia	33	(1)	G
18	20	**Ev'rybody's Twistin'**	Frank Sinatra	Reprise	5	(75)	
19	-	**Let's Talk About Love**	Helen Shapiro	Columbia	3		
20	-	**I Don't Know Why**	Eden Kane	Decca	7		

This Mnth	Prev Mnth	Title	Artist	Label	Wks	(US 20 Pos)	
1	4	**Good Luck Charm**	Elvis Presley	RCA	14	(1)	
2	14	**Come Outside**	Mike Sarne & Wendy Richard	Parlophone	14		F
3	6	**I'm Looking Out The Window**	Cliff Richard	Columbia	11		
4	-	**A Picture Of You**	Joe Brown & The Bruvvers	Piccadilly	14		F
5	-	**Ginny Come Lately**	Brian Hyland	HMV	10	(21)	
6	15	**Last Night Was Made For Love**	Billy Fury	Decca	11		
7	20	**I Don't Know Why**	Eden Kane	Decca	7		
8	9	**As You Like It**	Adam Faith	Parlophone	10		
9	1	**Nut Rocker**	B. Bumble & The Stingers	Top Rank	11	(23)	F L
10	-	**The Green Leaves Of Summer**	Kenny Ball	Pye Jazz	9	(87)	
11	-	**Do You Wanna Dance**	Cliff Richard	Columbia	6		
12	17	**Stranger On The Shore**	Mr. Acker Bilk	Columbia	33	(1)	G
13	-	**I Can't Stop Loving You**	Ray Charles	HMV	12	(1)	
14	3	**Love Letters**	Ketty Lester	London American	9	(5)	F L
15	-	**Theme From Dr. Kildare (Three Stars Will Shine Tonight)**	Richard Chamberlain	MGM	4	(10)	F
16	-	**Ain't That Funny**	Jimmy Justice	Pye	8		L
17	-	**A Little Love, A Little Kiss**	Karl Denver	Decca	3		
18	2	**Wonderful Land**	Shadows	Columbia	16		
19	-	**Here Comes That Feeling**	Brenda Lee	Brunswick	8	(89)	
20	-	**Follow That Dream E.P.**	Elvis Presley	RCA	6	(15)	

◆ Three years after his first tour was scrapped (following the discovery that he had married his 14-year-old second cousin), Jerry Lee Lewis made a triumphant return to the UK. The piano-pounding performer helped re-awaken interest in wild rock'n'roll and breathed more life into the burgeoning British beat boom.

◆ The Beatles, attrac-ted a record 900 crowd to the Cavern Club after their successful EMI audition. Meanwhile, the Dave Clark Five released their debut single 'That's What I Said'.

◆ Mick Jagger met Brian Jones for the first time at the Ealing Jazz Club and decided to form a group.

July 1962

This Mnth	Prev Mnth	Title	Artist	Label	Wks 20	(US Pos)	
1	12	I Can't Stop Loving You	Ray Charles	HMV	12	(1)	
2	4	A Picture Of You	Joe Brown & The Bruvvers	Piccadilly	14		F
3	2	Come Outside	Mike Sarne & Wendy Richard	Parlophone	14		F
4	-	I Remember You	Frank Ifield	Columbia	19	(5)	F G
5	1	Good Luck Charm	Elvis Presley	RCA	14	(1)	
6	18	Here Comes That Feeling	Brenda Lee	Brunswick	8	(89)	
7	-	English Country Garden	Jimmie Rodgers	Columbia	9		L
8	5	Ginny Come Lately	Brian Hyland	HMV	10	(21)	
9	-	Don't Ever Change	Crickets	Liberty	9		L
10	-	Speedy Gonzales	Pat Boone	London American	12	(6)	
11	-	Our Favourite Melodies	Craig Douglas	Columbia	6		
12	10	The Green Leaves Of Summer	Kenny Ball	Pye Jazz	9	(87)	
13	3	I'm Looking Out The Window	Cliff Richard	Columbia	11		
14	15	Ain't That Funny	Jimmy Justice	Pye	8		L
15	6	Last Night Was Made For Love	Billy Fury	Decca	11		
16	-	Yes My Darling Daughter	Eydie Gorme	CBS	5		F
17	12	Stranger On The Shore	Mr. Acker Bilk	Columbia	33	(1)	G
18	-	Right Said Fred	Bernard Cribbins	Parlophone	6		L
19	19	Follow That Dream E.P.	Elvis Presley	RCA	6	(15)	
20	-	Ya Ya Twist	Petula Clark	Pye	5		

August 1962

This Mnth	Prev Mnth	Title	Artist	Label	Wks 20	(US Pos)	
1	4	I Remember You	Frank Ifield	Columbia	19	(5)	F G
2	10	Speedy Gonzales	Pat Boone	London American	12	(6)	
3	-	Guitar Tango	Shadows	Columbia	10		
4	-	Things	Bobby Darin	London American	12	(3)	
5	1	I Can't Stop Loving You	Ray Charles	HMV	12	(1)	
6	-	Roses Are Red	Ronnie Carroll	Philips	11		
7	2	A Picture Of You	Joe Brown & The Bruvvers	Piccadilly	14		F
8	9	Don't Ever Change	Crickets	Liberty	9		L
9	-	Once Upon A Dream	Billy Fury	Decca	8		
10	-	Little Miss Lonely	Helen Shapiro	Columbia	7		L
11	-	Let There Be Love	Nat 'King' Cole	Capitol	7		
12	-	Breaking Up Is Hard To Do	Neil Sedaka	RCA	11	(1)	
13	-	Sealed With A Kiss	Brian Hyland	HMV	8	(3)	
14	6	Here Comes That Feeling	Brenda Lee	Brunswick	8	(89)	
15	3	Come Outside	Mike Sarne & Wendy Richard	Parlophone	14		F
16	17	Right Said Fred	Bernard Cribbins	Parlophone	6		L
17	-	Roses Are Red (My Love)	Bobby Vinton	Columbia	4	(1)	F
18	-	Vacation	Connie Francis	MGM	4	(9)	L
19	7	English Country Garden	Jimmie Rodgers	Columbia	9		L
20	-	So Do I	Kenny Ball	Pye Jazz	3		

◆ Ringo Starr replaced drummer Pete Best in The Beatles, who recorded their Parlophone debut, 'Love Me Do'. The record, which took 17 takes, was a US No. 1 in 1964 and finally made the UK Top 10 twenty years later! Another group who were to change 1960s music, The Rolling Stones, made their live debut at the Marquee club in London.

◆ Frank Ifield scored the first of three successive No. 1s with 'I Remember You', which spent seven weeks at No. 1 in Britain and sold over a million copies.

1962

This Mnth	Prev Mnth	Title	Artist	Label	Wks	(US 20 Pos)	
1	-	She's Not You	Elvis Presley	RCA	11	(5)	
2	1	I Remember You	Frank Ifield	Columbia	19	(5)	F G
3	6	Roses Are Red	Ronnie Carroll	Philips	11		
4	-	It'll Be Me	Cliff Richard	Columbia	8		
5	4	Things	Bobby Darin	London American	12	(3)	
6	13	Sealed With A Kiss	Brian Hyland	HMV	10	(3)	
7	12	Breaking Up Is Hard To Do	Neil Sedaka	RCA	11	(1)	
8	-	Telstar	Tornados	Decca	19	(1)	F
9	2	Speedy Gonzales	Pat Boone	London American	12	(6)	
10	3	Guitar Tango	Shadows	Columbia	10		
11	-	Don't That Beat All	Adam Faith	Parlophone	8		
12	-	Sheila	Tommy Roe	HMV	11	(1)	F
13	-	The Loco-Motion	Little Eva	London American	12	(1)	F
14	-	Ballad Of Paladin	Duane Eddy	RCA	7	(33)	
15	9	Once Upon A Dream	Billy Fury	Decca	8		
16	-	Pick A Bale Of Cotton	Lonnie Donegan	Pye	5		L
17	-	You Don't Know Me	Ray Charles	HMV	8	(2)	
18	-	Will I What	Mike Sarne	Parlophone	5		L
19	-	Main Title Theme From 'Man With The Golden Arm'	Jet Harris	Decca	6		F
20	5	I Can't Stop Loving You	Ray Charles	HMV	13	(1)	

This Mnth	Prev Mnth	Title	Artist	Label	Wks	(US 20 Pos)	
1	8	Telstar	Tornados	Decca	19	(1)	F
2	12	Sheila	Tommy Roe	HMV	11	(1)	F
3	13	The Loco-Motion	Little Eva	London American	12	(1)	F
4	-	It Might As Well Rain Until September	Carole King	London American	9	(22)	F
5	1	She's Not You	Elvis Presley	RCA	11	(5)	
6	-	Ramblin' Rose	Nat 'King' Cole	Capitol	10	(2)	
7	17	You Don't Know Me	Ray Charles	HMV	8	(2)	
8	4	It'll Be Me	Cliff Richard	Columbia	8		
9	-	What Now My Love	Shirley Bassey	Columbia	8		
10	-	Venus In Blue Jeans	Mark Wynter	Pye	9		F
11	2	I Remember You	Frank Ifield	Columbia	19	(5)	F G
12	11	Don't That Beat All	Adam Faith	Parlophone	8		
13	-	Let's Dance	Chris Montez	London American	13	(4)	F
14	6	Sealed With A Kiss	Brian Hyland	HMV	10	(3)	
15	-	Sherry	Four Seasons	Stateside	10	(1)	F
16	-	Lonely	Acker Bilk	Columbia	5		
17	3	Roses Are Red	Ronnie Carroll	Philips	11		
18	-	Swiss Maid	Del Shannon	London American	12	(64)	
19	-	Lovesick Blues	Frank Ifield	Columbia	14	(44)	
20	5	Things	Bobby Darin	London American	12	(3)	

◆ Despite the fact that their current UK singles failed to enter the US Top 100, American performers Jimmie Rodgers, The Crickets (with a vocal from Glen Campbell), Eydie Gormé and Nat 'King' Cole had major British hits. Also faring far better in Britain were new releases from Brenda Lee, Duane Eddy and Carole King.

◆ Rock'n'roll great Little Richard played his first shows on British shores. He was supported by The Beatles, whom he thought "sounded like a black American act".

November 1962

This Mnth	Prev Mnth	Title	Artist	Label	Wks (US 20 Pos)	
1	19	**Lovesick Blues**	Frank Ifield	Columbia	14 (44)	
2	13	**Let's Dance**	Chris Montez	London American	13 (4)	F
3	1	**Telstar**	Tornados	Decca	19 (1)	F
4	18	**Swiss Maid**	Del Shannon	London American	12 (64)	
5	10	**Venus In Blue Jeans**	Mark Wynter	Pye	9	F
6	3	**The Loco-Motion**	Little Eva	London American	12 (1)	F
7	-	**Bobby's Girl**	Susan Maughan	Philips	12	FL
8	15	**Sherry**	Four Seasons	Stateside	10 (1)	F
9	-	**Devil Woman**	Marty Robbins	CBS	10 (16)	L
10	6	**Ramblin' Rose**	Nat 'King' Cole	Capitol	10 (2)	
11	-	**No One Can Make My Sunshine Smile**	Everly Brothers	Warner	7	
12	4	**It Might As Well Rain Until September**	Carole King	London American	9 (22)	F
13	2	**Sheila**	Tommy Roe	HMV	11 (1)	F
14	-	**Dance With The Guitar Man**	Duane Eddy	RCA	11 (12)	
15	-	**Sun Arise**	Rolf Harris	Columbia	11 (61)	
16	-	**Oh Lonesome Me**	Craig Douglas	Decca	4	L
17	9	**What Now My Love**	Shirley Bassey	Columbia	8	
18	-	**Return To Sender**	Elvis Presley	RCA	11 (2)	
19	-	**A Forever Kind Of Love**	Bobby Vee	Liberty	5	
20	-	**Kid Galahad E.P.**	Elvis Presley	RCA	3	

December 1962

This Mnth	Prev Mnth	Title	Artist	Label	Wks (US 20 Pos)	
1	18	**Return To Sender**	Elvis Presley	RCA	11 (2)	
2	1	**Lovesick Blues**	Frank Ifield	Columbia	14 (44)	
3	15	**Sun Arise**	Rolf Harris	Columbia	11 (61)	
4	-	**The Next Time**	Cliff Richard	Columbia	12	
5	14	**Dance With The Guitar Man**	Duane Eddy	RCA	11 (12)	
6	2	**Let's Dance**	Chris Montez	London American	13 (4)	F
7	7	**Bobby's Girl**	Susan Maughan	Philips	12	F L
8	4	**Swiss Maid**	Del Shannon	London American	12 (64)	
9	-	**Rockin' Around The Christmas Tree**	Brenda Lee	Brunswick	4 (14)	
10	3	**Telstar**	Tornados	Decca	19 (1)	F
11	-	**Dance On**	Shadows	Columbia	10	
12	-	**Bachelor Boy**	Cliff Richard	Columbia	12 (99)	
13	-	**It Only Took A Minute**	Joe Brown & The Bruvvers	Piccadilly	8	
14	9	**Devil Woman**	Marty Robbins	CBS	10 (16)	L
15	-	**The Main Attraction**	Pat Boone	London American	5	L
16	8	**Sherry**	Four Seasons	Stateside	10 (1)	F
17	-	**Your Cheatin' Heart**	Ray Charles	HMV	4 (29)	
18	-	**Up On The Roof**	Kenny Lynch	HMV	7	F
19	5	**Venus In Blue Jeans**	Mark Wynter	Pye	9	F
20	19	**A Forever Kind Of Love**	Bobby Vee	Liberty	5	

◆ Big winners at the *NME* poll were Elvis, Brenda Lee and The Everly Brothers, with The Beatles being voted 8th most popular British group.

◆ The first British group to top the American charts were instrumental combo The Tornados with 'Telstar'. The record's producer/composer, Joe Meek, earlier turned down a chance to work with The Beatles.

1963

This Mnth	Prev Mnth	Title	Artist	Label	Wks	(US 20 Pos)	
1	11	Dance On	Shadows	Columbia	10		
2	1	Return To Sender	Elvis Presley	RCA	11	(2)	
3	4	The Next Time	Cliff Richard	Columbia	12		
4	12	Bachelor Boy	Cliff Richard	Columbia	12	(99)	
5	5	Dance With The Guitar Man	Duane Eddy	RCA	11	(12)	
6	-	Like I Do	Maureen Evans	Oriole	9		F L
7	3	Sun Arise	Rolf Harris	Columbia	11	(61)	
8	2	Lovesick Blues	Frank Ifield	Columbia	14	(44)	
9	-	Globetrotter	Tornados	Decca	8		
10	-	Diamonds	Jet Harris & Tony Meehan	Decca	10		F
11	-	Go Away Little Girl	Mark Wynter	Pye	7		
12	18	Up On The Roof	Kenny Lynch	HMV	7		F
13	10	Telstar	Tornados	Decca	19	(1)	F
14	-	Coming Home Baby	Mel Tormé	London American	4	(36)	L
15	13	It Only Took A Minute	Joe Brown & The Bruvvers	Piccadilly	8		
16	7	Bobby's Girl	Susan Maughan	Philips	12		F L
17	-	Don't You Think It's Time	Mike Berry	HMV	7		F
18	6	Let's Dance	Chris Montez	London American	13	(4)	F
19	-	Little Town Flirt	Del Shannon	London American	8	(12)	
20	-	Desafinado	Stan Getz & Charlie Byrd	HMV	5	(15)	F L

This Mnth	Prev Mnth	Title	Artist	Label	Wks	(US 20 Pos)	
1	10	Diamonds	Jet Harris & Tony Meehan	Decca	10		F
2	-	Wayward Wind	Frank Ifield	Columbia	10		
3	19	Little Town Flirt	Del Shannon	London American	8	(12)	
4	-	Please Please Me	Beatles	Parlophone	10	(3)	F
5	9	Globetrotter	Tornados	Decca	8		
6	4	Bachelor Boy	Cliff Richard	Columbia	12	(99)	
7	-	Loop De Loop	Frankie Vaughan	Philips	8		
8	17	Don't You Think It's Time	Mike Berry	HMV	7		F
9	-	The Night Has A Thousand Eyes	Bobby Vee	Liberty	8	(3)	L
10	-	All Alone Am I	Brenda Lee	Brunswick	7	(3)	
11	-	Island Of Dreams	Springfields	Philips	12		F
12	6	Like I Do	Maureen Evans	Oriole	9		F L
13	1	Dance On	Shadows	Columbia	10		
14	3	The Next Time	Cliff Richard	Columbia	12		
15	-	Sukiyaki	Kenny Ball	Pye Jazz	5		
16	-	Walk Right In	Rooftop Singers	Fontana	5	(1)	F L
17	-	That's What Love Will Do	Joe Brown & The Bruvvers	Piccadilly	9		L
18	-	Big Girls Don't Cry	Four Seasons	Stateside	5	(1)	
19	2	Return To Sender	Elvis Presley	RCA	11	(2)	
20	-	Summer Holiday	Cliff Richard	Columbia	11		

◆ The Beatles' second single 'Please Please Me' topped the chart. It put Merseybeat on the musical map and launched the Beat Boom. In America it was rush released but failed to click.

◆ Rock instrumentals reached new heights in February when records by (ex-Shadows) Jet Harris & Tony Meehan, The Tornados and The Shadows took the top three spots.

March 1963

This Mnth	Prev Mnth	Title	Artist	Label	Wks	(US 20 Pos)	
1	20	**Summer Holiday**	Cliff Richard	Columbia	11		
2	4	**Please Please Me**	Beatles	Parlophone	10	(3)	F
3	-	**Like I've Never Been Gone**	Billy Fury	Decca	10		
4	17	**That's What Love Will Do**	Joe Brown & The Bruvvers	Piccadilly	9		L
5	9	**The Night Has A Thousand Eyes**	Bobby Vee	Liberty	8	(3)	L
6	-	**Foot Tapper**	Shadows	Columbia	9		
7	11	**Island Of Dreams**	Springfields	Philips	12		F
8	2	**Wayward Wind**	Frank Ifield	Columbia	10		
9	-	**Charmaine**	Bachelors	Decca	9		F
10	-	**One Broken Heart For Sale**	Elvis Presley	RCA	5	(11)	
11	7	**Loop De Loop**	Frankie Vaughan	Philips	8		
12	-	**Hey Paula**	Paul & Paula	Philips	7	(1)	F
13	-	**From A Jack To A King**	Ned Miller	London American	12	(6)	F L
14	-	**Tell Him**	Billie Davis	Decca	5		F L
15	1	**Diamonds**	Jet Harris & Tony Meehan	Decca	10		F
16	-	**Say Wonderful Things**	Ronnie Carroll	Philips	8	(91)	L
17	-	**Rhythm Of The Rain**	Cascades	Warner	10	(3)	F L
18	-	**How Do You Do It?**	Gerry & The Pacemakers	Columbia	11	(9)	F
19	-	**Brown Eyed Handsome Man**	Buddy Holly	Coral	10		
20	16	**Walk Right In**	Rooftop Singers	Fontana	5	(1)	F L

April 1963

This Mnth	Prev Mnth	Title	Artist	Label	Wks	(US 20 Pos)	
1	18	**How Do You Do It?**	Gerry & The Pacemakers	Columbia	11	(9)	F
2	13	**From A Jack To A King**	Ned Miller	London American	12	(6)	F L
3	6	**Foot Tapper**	Shadows	Columbia	9		
4	19	**Brown Eyed Handsome Man**	Buddy Holly	Coral	10		
5	17	**Rhythm Of The Rain**	Cascades	Warner	10	(3)	F L
6	-	**Say I Won't Be There**	Springfields	Philips	8		L
7	16	**Say Wonderful Things**	Ronnie Carroll	Philips	8	(91)	L
8	1	**Summer Holiday**	Cliff Richard	Columbia	11		
9	-	**The Folk Singer**	Tommy Roe	HMV	7	(84)	
10	-	**Nobody's Darlin' But Mine**	Frank Ifield	Columbia	8		
11	-	**From Me To You**	Beatles	Parlophone	15	(41)	
12	3	**Like I've Never Been Gone**	Billy Fury	Decca	10		
13	-	**In Dreams**	Roy Orbison	London American	13	(7)	
14	9	**Charmaine**	Bachelors	Decca	9		F
15	-	**Walk Like A Man**	Four Seasons	Stateside	6	(1)	
16	-	**Can't Get Used To Losing You**	Andy Williams	CBS	10	(2)	
17	7	**Island Of Dreams**	Springfields	Philips	12		F
18	-	**Robot**	Tornados	Decca	5		
19	4	**That's What Love Will Do**	Joe Brown & The Bruvvers	Piccadilly	9		L
20	-	**Let's Turkey Trot**	Little Eva	London American	6	(20)	

◆ The Scopitone video juke box was launched – it cost 5p a play to see acts like Craig Douglas and The Mudlarks – it proved to be a five minute wonder.

◆ Word came from Australia that The Bee Gees, an Everly Brothers influenced act, who originally hailed from Manchester, had signed with Festival Records. After making a name for themselves down under they became superstars later in the decade.

◆ The Beatles' manager Brian Epstein also looked after Billy J. Kramer & The Dakotas who had two successive No. 1s and Gerry & The Pacemakers who achieved three.

1963

This Mnth	Prev Mnth	Title	Artist	Label	Wks	(US 20 Pos)	
1	11	From Me To You	Beatles	Parlophone	15	(41)	
2	-	Scarlett O'Hara	Jet Harris & Tony Meehan	Decca	11		
3	16	Can't Get Used To Losing You	Andy Williams	CBS	10	(2)	
4	1	How Do You Do It?	Gerry & The Pacemakers	Columbia	11	(9)	F
5	13	In Dreams	Roy Orbison	London American	13	(7)	
6	10	Nobody's Darlin' But Mine	Frank Ifield	Columbia	8		
7	-	Do You Want To Know A Secret	Billy J. Kramer & The Dakotas	Parlophone	10		F
8	-	Two Kinds Of Teardrops	Del Shannon	London American	8	(50)	
9	-	Lucky Lips	Cliff Richard	Columbia	9	(62)	
10	2	From A Jack To A King	Ned Miller	London American	12	(6)	F L
11	-	Losing You	Brenda Lee	Brunswick	9	(6)	
12	6	Say I Won't Be There	Springfields	Philips	8		L
13	-	He's So Fine	Chiffons	Stateside	5	(1)	F
14	-	Deck Of Cards	Wink Martindale	London American	15		L
15	-	When Will You Say I Love You	Billy Fury	Decca	7		
16	-	Young Lovers	Paul & Paula	Philips	6	(6)	L
17	5	Rhythm Of The Rain	Cascades	Warner	10	(3)	F L
18	-	Take These Chains From My Heart	Ray Charles	HMV	13	(8)	
19	4	Brown Eyed Handsome Man	Buddy Holly	Coral	10		
20	9	The Folk Singer	Tommy Roe	HMV	7	(84)	

This Mnth	Prev Mnth	Title	Artist	Label	Wks	(US 20 Pos)	
1	-	I Like It	Gerry & The Pacemakers	Columbia	12	(17)	
2	7	Do You Want To Know A Secret	Billy J. Kramer & The Dakotas	Parlophone	10		F
3	1	From Me To You	Beatles	Parlophone	15	(41)	
4	18	Take These Chains From My Heart	Ray Charles	HMV	13	(8)	
5	-	If You Gotta Make A Fool Of Somebody	Freddie & The Dreamers	Columbia	9		F
6	-	Atlantis	Shadows	Columbia	11		
7	15	When Will You Say I Love You	Billy Fury	Decca	7		
8	14	Deck Of Cards	Wink Martindale	London American	15		L
9	2	Scarlett O'Hara	Jet Harris & Tony Meehan	Decca	11		
10	9	Lucky Lips	Cliff Richard	Columbia	9	(62)	
11	-	Falling	Roy Orbison	London American	8	(22)	
12	5	In Dreams	Roy Orbison	London American	13	(7)	
13	-	Bo Diddley	Buddy Holly	Coral	8		
14	8	Two Kinds Of Teardrops	Del Shannon	London American	8	(50)	
15	16	Young Lovers	Paul & Paula	Philips	6	(6)	L
16	-	Da Doo Ron Ron	Crystals	London American	10	(3)	
17	-	The Ice Cream Man	Tornados	Decca	4		L
18	-	It's My Party	Lesley Gore	Mercury	8	(1)	F
19	-	Forget Him	Bobby Rydell	Cameo Parkway	9	(4)	L
20	-	Confessin'	Frank Ifield	Columbia	11	(58)	

◆ Early examples of R&B covers in the "Beat Boom" included Freddie & The Dreamers' 'If You Gotta Make a Fool Of Somebody' and The Rolling Stones' version of Chuck Berry's 'Come On'. The late Buddy Holly hit the Top 5 with revivals of Chuck's 'Brown Eyed Handsome Man' and Bo Diddley's eponymous song, while in America The Beach Boys turned Berry's 'Sweet Little 16' into 'Surfin' USA' and Lonnie Mack charted with Chuck's 'Memphis'.

July 1963

This Mnth	Prev Mnth	Title	Artist	Label	Wks	(US 20 Pos)	
1	20	Confessin'	Frank Ifield	Columbia	11	(58)	
2	1	I Like It	Gerry & The Pacemakers	Columbia	12	(17)	
3	6	Atlantis	Shadows	Columbia	11		
4	-	Devil In Disguise	Elvis Presley	RCA	8	(3)	
5	16	Da Doo Ron Ron	Crystals	London American	10	(3)	
6	4	Take These Chains From My Heart	Ray Charles	HMV	13	(8)	
7	-	Sweets For My Sweet	Searchers	Pye	10		F
8	8	Deck Of Cards	Wink Martindale	London American	15		L
9	-	Welcome To My World	Jim Reeves	RCA	9		
10	18	It's My Party	Lesley Gore	Mercury	8	(1)	F
11	-	Twist And Shout	Brian Poole & The Tremeloes	Decca	9		F
12	13	Bo Diddley	Buddy Holly	Coral	8		
13	5	If You Gotta Make A Fool Of Somebody	Freddie & The Dreamers	Columbia	9		F
14	3	From Me To You	Beatles	Parlophone	15	(41)	
15	11	Falling	Roy Orbison	London American	8	(22)	
16	-	Twist And Shout E.P.	Beatles	Parlophone	15	(2)	
17	-	Sukiyaki	Kyu Sakamoto	HMV	9	(1)	F L
18	2	Do You Want To Know A Secret	Billy J. Kramer & The Dakotas	Parlophone	10		F
19	19	Forget Him	Bobby Rydell	Cameo Parkway	9	(4)	L
20	-	You Can Never Stop Me Loving You	Kenny Lynch	HMV	6		L

August 1963

This Mnth	Prev Mnth	Title	Artist	Label	Wks	(US 20 Pos)	
1	7	Sweets For My Sweet	Searchers	Pye	10		F
2	1	Confessin'	Frank Ifield	Columbia	11	(58)	
3	16	Twist And Shout E.P.	Beatles	Parlophone	15	(2)	
4	-	Bad To Me	Billy J. Kramer & The Dakotas	Parlophone	10	(9)	
5	11	Twist And Shout	Brian Poole & The Tremeloes	Decca	9		F
6	-	In Summer	Billy Fury	Decca	8		
7	4	Devil In Disguise	Elvis Presley	RCA	8	(3)	
8	-	Wipe Out	Surfaris	London American	8	(2)	F L
9	-	I'm Telling You Now	Freddie & The Dreamers	Columbia	7	(1)	
10	-	Theme From 'The Legion's Last Patrol'	Ken Thorne & His Orchestra	HMV	10		F L
11	5	Da Doo Ron Ron	Crystals	London American	10	(3)	
12	17	Sukiyaki	Kyu Sakamoto	HMV	9	(1)	F L
13	-	I'll Never Get Over You	Johnny Kidd & The Pirates	HMV	10		L
14	-	It's All In The Game	Cliff Richard	Columbia	9	(25)	
15	3	Atlantis	Shadows	Columbia	11		
16	-	You Don't Have To Be A Baby To Cry	Caravelles	Decca	7	(3)	F L
17	2	I Like It	Gerry & The Pacemakers	Columbia	12	(17)	
18	-	She Loves You	Beatles	Parlophone	24	(1)	G
19	6	Take These Chains From My Heart	Ray Charles	HMV	13	(8)	
20	20	You Can Never Stop Me Loving You	Kenny Lynch	HMV	6		L

◆ The Beatles' debut LP **Please Please Me** topped the chart for 30 weeks and the single 'She Loves You', which had record advance orders and sold over a million in the UK, cemented their position as Britain's top group.

◆ *Ready Steady Go* was launched – it was the British pop TV show which best reflected the times. Early guests included the Rolling Stones.

1963

This Mnth	Prev Mnth	Title	Artist	Label	Wks	(US 20 Pos)	
1	18	She Loves You	Beatles	Parlophone	24	(1)	G
2	14	It's All In The Game	Cliff Richard	Columbia	9	(25)	
3	4	Bad To Me	Billy J. Kramer & The Dakotas	Parlophone	10	(9)	
4	-	I Want To Stay Here	Steve Lawrence & Eydie Gormé	CBS	8	(28)	L
5	13	I'll Never Get Over You	Johnny Kidd & The Pirates	HMV	10		L
6	9	I'm Telling You Now	Freddie & The Dreamers	Columbia	7	(1)	
7	-	Just Like Eddie	Heinz	Decca	10		F
8	16	You Don't Have To Be A Baby To Cry	Caravelles	Decca	7	(3)	F L
9	-	Applejack	Jet Harris & Tony Meehan	Decca	8		L
10	-	Do You Love Me	Brian Poole & The Tremeloes	Decca	11		
11	10	Theme From 'The Legion's Last Patrol'	Ken Thorne & His Orchestra	HMV	10		F L
12	8	Wipe Out	Surfaris	London American	8	(2)	F L
13	-	Then He Kissed Me	Crystals	London American	10	(6)	
14	-	If I Had A Hammer	Trini Lopez	Reprise	10	(3)	F L
15	1	Sweets For My Sweet	Searchers	Pye	10		F
16	-	Still	Karl Denver	Decca	6		L
17	3	Twist And Shout E.P.	Beatles	Parlophone	15	(2)	
18	-	Dance On	Kathy Kirby	Decca	5		F
19	-	Shindig	Shadows	Columbia	7		
20	-	Wishing	Buddy Holly	Coral	5		L

1	10	Do You Love Me	Brian Poole & The Tremeloes	Decca	11		
2	13	Then He Kissed Me	Crystals	London American	10	(6)	
3	1	She Loves You	Beatles	Parlophone	24	(1)	G
4	14	If I Had A Hammer	Trini Lopez	Reprise	10	(3)	F L
5	-	Blue Bayou	Roy Orbison	London American	10	(29)	
6	-	The First Time	Adam Faith	Parlophone	8		
7	-	You'll Never Walk Alone	Gerry & The Pacemakers	Columbia	15	(48)	
8	19	Shindig	Shadows	Columbia	7		
9	-	I (Who Have Nothing)	Shirley Bassey	Columbia	9		
10	9	Applejack	Jet Harris & Tony Meehan	Decca	8		L
11	17	Twist And Shout E.P.	Beatles	Parlophone	15	(2)	
12	2	It's All In The Game	Cliff Richard	Columbia	9	(25)	
13	7	Just Like Eddie	Heinz	Decca	10		F
14	-	Hello Little Girl	Fourmost	Parlophone	6		F
15	4	I Want To Stay Here	Steve Lawrence & Eydie Gormé	CBS	8	(28)	L
16	-	Ain't Gonna Kiss Ya (E.P.)	Searchers	Pye	4		
17	-	Searchin'	Hollies	Parlophone	4		F
18	-	Everybody	Tommy Roe	HMV	4	(3)	
19	-	Memphis Tennessee	Chuck Berry	Pye International	7		
20	-	Be My Baby	Ronettes	London American	7	(2)	F

◆ Eric Clapton and Tom McGuinness (later of Manfred Mann) joined Casey Jones & The Engineers, and John Mayall launched The Bluesbreakers which included John McVie (later a founder of Fleetwood Mac.)

◆ As the year ended, The Beatles had five records in the Top 20 singles (including 2 EPs and an album) and the top two albums. The LP **With The Beatles** entered at No. 1 as did 'I Want To Hold Your Hand', which smashed all UK sales records, selling a million copies in three days. A big US launch was planned for early 1964.

November 1963

This Mnth	Prev Mnth	Title	Artist	Label	Wks	(US 20 Pos)	
1	3	**She Loves You**	Beatles	Parlophone	24	(1)	G
2	7	**You'll Never Walk Alone**	Gerry & The Pacemakers	Columbia	15	(48)	
3	-	**Sugar And Spice**	Searchers	Pye	7	(44)	
4	20	**Be My Baby**	Ronettes	London American	7	(2)	F
5	9	**I (Who Have Nothing)**	Shirley Bassey	Columbia	9		
6	5	**Blue Bayou**	Roy Orbison	London American	10	(29)	
7	-	**Don't Talk To Him**	Cliff Richard	Columbia	10		
8	-	**Secret Love**	Kathy Kirby	Decca	12		
9	19	**Memphis Tennessee**	Chuck Berry	Pye International	7		
10	1	**Do You Love Me**	Brian Poole & The Tremeloes	Decca	11		
11	-	**I'll Keep You Satisfied**	Billy J. Kramer & The Dakotas	Parlophone	6	(30)	
12	-	**You Were Made For Me**	Freddie & The Dreamers	Columbia	11	(21)	
13	2	**Then He Kissed Me**	Crystals	London American	10	(6)	
14	-	**Maria Elena**	Los Indios Tabajaras	RCA	12	(6)	F L
15	-	**Fools Rush In**	Rick Nelson	London American	5	(12)	
16	6	**The First Time**	Adam Faith	Parlophone	8		
17	4	**If I Had A Hammer**	Trini Lopez	Reprise	10	(3)	F L
18	-	**Blowin' In The Wind**	Peter, Paul & Mary	Warner	5	(2)	F
19	-	**It's Almost Tomorrow**	Mark Wynter	Pye	6		L
20	-	**I Only Want To Be With You**	Dusty Springfield	Philips	14	(12)	F

December 1963

This Mnth	Prev Mnth	Title	Artist	Label	Wks	(US 20 Pos)	
1	-	**I Want To Hold Your Hand**	Beatles	Parlophone	13	(1)	G
2	1	**She Loves You**	Beatles	Parlophone	24	(1)	G
3	8	**Secret Love**	Kathy Kirby	Decca	12		
4	-	**Glad All Over**	Dave Clark Five	Columbia	14	(6)	F
5	12	**You Were Made For Me**	Freddie & The Dreamers	Columbia	11	(21)	
6	7	**Don't Talk To Him**	Cliff Richard	Columbia	10		
7	20	**I Only Want To Be With You**	Dusty Springfield	Philips	14	(12)	F
8	-	**Dominique**	Singing Nun	Philips	8	(1)	FL
9	14	**Maria Elena**	Los Indios Tabajaras	RCA	12	(6)	FL
10	-	**Twenty Four Hours From Tulsa**	Gene Pitney	UA	13	(17F)	
11	11	**I'll Keep You Satisfied**	Billy J. Kramer & The Dakotas	Parlophone	6	(30)	
12	-	**Twist And Shout (E.P.)**	Beatles	Parlophone	15	(2)	
13	2	**You'll Never Walk Alone**	Gerry & The Pacemakers	Columbia	15	(48)	
14	-	**Geronimo**	Shadows	Columbia	6		
15	-	**With The Beatles L.P.**	Beatles	Parlophone	5		
16	-	**Swinging On A Star**	Big Dee Irwin	Colpix	10	(38)	FL
17	-	**I Wanna Be Your Man**	Rolling Stones	Decca	8		
18	19	**It's Almost Tomorrow**	Mark Wynter	Pye	6		L
19	-	**All I Want For Christmas Is A Beatle**	Dora Bryan	Fontana	3		FL
20	4	**Be My Baby**	Ronettes	London American	7	(2)	F

◆ For the first time, British acts, The Beatles and Cliff Richard (who had been voted Most Promising Male Singer in the top US teen magazine, *16*), won awards in the World section of the *NME* readers poll.

◆ UK acts scoring with US songs included Brian Poole & The Tremeloes, Gerry & The Pacemakers, Cliff Richard, Shirley Bassey, Kathy Kirby, Mark Wynter, The Hollies, The Searchers ('Ain't Gonna Kiss Ya') and The Beatles ('Twist And Shout').

1964

This Mnth	Prev Mnth	Title	Artist	Label	Wks (US 20 Pos)	
1	4	**Glad All Over**	Dave Clark Five	Columbia	14 (6)	F
2	1	**I Want To Hold Your Hand**	Beatles	Parlophone	13 (1)	G
3	7	**I Only Want To Be With You**	Dusty Springfield	Philips	14 (12)	F
4	-	**Hippy Hippy Shake**	Swinging Blue Jeans	HMV	10 (24)	F
5	2	**She Loves You**	Beatles	Parlophone	24 (1)	G
6	10	**Twenty Four Hours From Tulsa**	Gene Pitney	UA	13 (17)	F
7	16	**Swinging On A Star**	Big Dee Irwin	Colpix	10 (38)	F
8	5	**You Were Made For Me**	Freddie & The Dreamers	Columbia	11 (21)	
9	8	**Dominique**	Singing Nun	Philips	8 (1)	F
10	-	**Stay**	Hollies	Parlophone	7	
11	3	**Secret Love**	Kathy Kirby	Decca	12	
12	9	**Maria Elena**	Los Indios Tabajaras	RCA	12 (6)	F
13	17	**I Wanna Be Your Man**	Rolling Stones	Decca	8	
14	-	**Kiss Me Quick**	Elvis Presley	RCA	6 (34)	
15	-	**We Are In Love**	Adam Faith	Parlophone	6	
16	6	**Don't Talk To Him**	Cliff Richard	Columbia	10	
17	-	**As Usual**	Brenda Lee	Brunswick	10 (12)	
18	-	**Needles And Pins**	Searchers	Pye	9 (13)	
19	14	**Geronimo**	Shadows	Columbia	6	
20	-	**I'm The One**	Gerry & The Pacemakers	Columbia	9 (82)	

1	18	**Needles And Pins**	Searchers	Pye	9 (13)	
2	20	**I'm The One**	Gerry & The Pacemakers	Columbia	9 (82)	
3	4	**Hippy Hippy Shake**	Swinging Blue Jeans	HMV	10 (24)	F
4	-	**Diane**	Bachelors	Decca	11 (10)	
5	1	**Glad All Over**	Dave Clark Five	Columbia	14 (6)	F
6	17	**As Usual**	Brenda Lee	Brunswick	10 (12)	
7	-	**5-4-3-2-1**	Manfred Mann	HMV	7	F
8	-	**Don't Blame Me**	Frank Ifield	Columbia	7	L
9	-	**Anyone Who Had A Heart**	Cilla Black	Parlophone	11	F
10	-	**I Think Of You**	Merseybeats	Fontana	11	F
11	6	**Twenty Four Hours From Tulsa**	Gene Pitney	UA	13 (17)	F
12	2	**I Want To Hold Your Hand**	Beatles	Parlophone	13 (1)	G
13	-	**Baby I Love You**	Ronettes	London American	7 (24)	L
14	3	**I Only Want To Be With You**	Dusty Springfield	Philips	14 (12)	F
15	-	**I'm The Lonely One**	Cliff Richard	Columbia	4 (92)	
16	10	**Stay**	Hollies	Parlophone	7	
17	-	**Bits And Pieces**	Dave Clark Five	Columbia	9 (4)	
18	-	**Candy Man**	Brian Poole & The Tremeloes	Decca	6	
19	-	**For You**	Rick Nelson	Brunswick	4 (6)	L
20	7	**Swinging On A Star**	Big Dee Irwin	Colpix	10 (38)	F L

◆ *Top Of The Pops* was launched. The TV show based on the Top 20 chart is still running thirty years later. Soon afterwards the first pirate radio station Radio Caroline started broadcasting from a ship in the North Sea.

◆ The Dave Clark Five's 'Bits And Pieces' had 250,000 advance orders and The Beatles 'Can't Buy Me Love' piled up record UK advance orders of over a million.

March 1964

This Mnth	Prev Mnth	Title	Artist	Label	Wks	(US 20 Pos)	
1	9	Anyone Who Had A Heart	Cilla Black	Parlophone	11		F
2	17	Bits And Pieces	Dave Clark Five	Columbia	9	(4)	
3	-	Little Children	Billy J. Kramer & The Dakotas	Parlophone	9	(7)	
4	-	Not Fade Away	Rolling Stones	Decca	9	(48)	
5	4	Diane	Bachelors	Decca	11	(10)	
6	-	Just One Look	Hollies	Parlophone	9	(44)	
7	10	I Think Of You	Merseybeats	Fontana	11		F
8	-	Boys Cry	Eden Kane	Fontana	7		L
9	1	Needles And Pins	Searchers	Pye	9	(13)	
10	-	I Love You Because	Jim Reeves	RCA	26		
11	18	Candy Man	Brian Poole & The Tremeloes	Decca	6		
12	-	Let Me Go, Lover	Kathy Kirby	Decca	6		
13	-	That Girl Belongs To Yesterday	Gene Pitney	UA	7	(49)	
14	2	I'm The One	Gerry & The Pacemakers	Columbia	9	(82)	
15	-	Stay Awhile	Dusty Springfield	Philips	6	(38)	
16	-	Over You	Freddie & The Dreamers	Columbia	5		
17	6	As Usual	Brenda Lee	Brunswick	10	(12)	
18	-	Can't Buy Me Love	Beatles	Parlophone	9	(1)	G
19	7	5-4-3-2-1	Manfred Mann	HMV	7		F
20	-	Theme For Young Lovers	Shadows	Columbia	6		

April 1964

This Mnth	Prev Mnth	Title	Artist	Label	Wks	(US 20 Pos)	
1	18	Can't Buy Me Love	Beatles	Parlophone	9	(1)	G
2	-	I Believe	Bachelors	Decca	11	(33)	
3	3	Little Children	Billy J. Kramer & The Dakotas	Parlophone	9	(7)	
4	-	A World Without Love	Peter & Gordon	Columbia	9	(1)	F
5	10	I Love You Because	Jim Reeves	RCA	26		
6	6	Just One Look	Hollies	Parlophone	9	(44)	
7	4	Not Fade Away	Rolling Stones	Decca	9	(48)	
8	-	Tell Me When	Applejacks	Decca	8		F
9	13	That Girl Belongs To Yesterday	Gene Pitney	UA	7	(49)	
10	-	My Boy Lollipop	Millie	Fontana	10	(2)	F L
11	2	Bits And Pieces	Dave Clark Five	Columbia	9	(4)	
12	1	Anyone Who Had A Heart	Cilla Black	Parlophone	11		F
13	5	Diane	Bachelors	Decca	11	(10)	
14	-	Good Golly Miss Molly	Swinging Blue Jeans	HMV	5	(43)	
15	-	Move Over Darling	Doris Day	CBS	8		L
16	-	Everything's Alright	Mojos	Decca	6		F L
17	20	Theme For Young Lovers	Shadows	Columbia	6		
18	-	Don't Throw Your Love Away	Searchers	Pye	8	(16)	
19	-	Mockingbird Hill	Migil Five	Pye	6		F L
20	-	Viva Las Vegas	Elvis Presley	RCA	4	(29)	

◆ Blue beat was in with 'Madness' (Prince Buster) and 'Oh Carolina' (Folkes Brothers) selling well. A top 1980s band named themselves after the first track and the latter was a No. 1 in 1993 for Shaggy.

◆ Mods and Rockers clashed on British beaches, teenagers and drugs were linked for the first time in the press and the first drug-related British records, Mickey Finn's 'Pills' and 'Purple Pill Eater' by The Wild Ones, were released.

1961

This Mnth	Prev Mnth	Title	Artist	Label	Wks	(US 20 Pos)	
1	18	Don't Throw Your Love Away	Searchers	Pye	8	(16)	
2	10	My Boy Lollipop	Millie	Fontana	10	(2)	F L
3	-	Juliet	Four Pennies	Philips	10		F
4	2	I Believe	Bachelors	Decca	11	(33)	
5	4	A World Without Love	Peter & Gordon	Columbia	9	(1)	F
6	-	Don't Let The Sun Catch You Crying	Gerry & The Pacemakers	Columbia	6	(4)	
7	5	I Love You Because	Jim Reeves	RCA	26		
8	-	It's Over	Roy Orbison	London American	14	(9)	
9	-	A Little Loving	Fourmost	Parlophone	8		L
10	-	Walk On By	Dionne Warwick	Pye International	9	(6)	F
11	-	Constantly	Cliff Richard	Columbia	8		
12	-	You're My World	Cilla Black	Parlophone	10	(26)	
13	1	Can't Buy Me Love	Beatles	Parlophone	9	(1)	G
14	15	Move Over Darling	Doris Day	CBS	8		L
15	19	Mockingbird Hill	Migil Five	Pye	6		F L
16	-	Don't Turn Around	Merseybeats	Fontana	5		
17	-	The Rise & Fall Of Flingel Bunt	Shadows	Columbia	8		
18	16	Everything's Alright	Mojos	Decca	6		F L
19	-	I Will	Billy Fury	Decca	6		
20	-	Hubble Bubble Toil And Trouble	Manfred Mann	HMV	4		

1	12	You're My World	Cilla Black	Parlophone	10	(26)	
2	8	It's Over	Roy Orbison	London American	14	(9)	
3	-	Someone Someone	Brian Poole & The Tremeloes	Decca	11	(97)	
4	-	No Particular Place To Go	Chuck Berry	Pye International	7	(10)	
5	-	Here I Go Again	Hollies	Parlophone	7		
6	-	My Guy	Mary Wells	Stateside	8	(1)	F
7	17	The Rise & Fall Of Flingel Bunt	Shadows	Columbia	8		
8	11	Constantly	Cliff Richard	Columbia	8		
9	3	Juliet	Four Pennies	Philips	10		F
10	-	Shout	Lulu	Decca	7	(94)	F
11	-	Hello, Dolly!	Louis Armstrong	London American	8	(1)	
12	-	Can't You See That She's Mine	Dave Clark Five	Columbia	6	(4)	
13	7	I Love You Because	Jim Reeves	RCA	26		
14	-	Ramona	Bachelors	Decca	8		
15	10	Walk On By	Dionne Warwick	Pye International	9	(6)	F
16	9	A Little Loving	Fourmost	Parlophone	8		L
17	2	My Boy Lollipop	Millie	Fontana	10	(2)	F L
18	-	You're No Good	Swinging Blue Jeans	HMV	8	(97)	L
19	-	Nobody I Know	Peter & Gordon	Columbia	5	(12)	
20	-	Non Ho L'Eta Per Amarti	Gigliola Cinquetti	Decca	4		F

◆ The Rolling Stones' eponymous debut album knocked The Beatles off the top after 51 consecutive weeks at the top.
◆ Peter & Gordon's 'World Without Love' was the eighth Lennon & McCartney song to top the UK chart in 14 months, and their fifth in the USA in less than five months.

◆ Mary Wells's last recording for Motown, 'My Guy', gave the label their first major transatlantic hit.
◆ Irish trio The Bachelors had two singles in the UK Top 10 while The Beatles had nine in the equivalent Canadian chart!

1964

July 1964

This Mnth	Prev Mnth	Title	Artist	Label	Wks	(US 20 Pos)	
1	-	**House Of The Rising Sun**	Animals	Columbia	7	(1)	F
2	-	**Hold Me**	P.J. Proby	Decca	8	(70)	F
3	2	**It's Over**	Roy Orbison	London American	14	(9)	
4	-	**It's All Over Now**	Rolling Stones	Decca	11	(26)	
5	-	**I Won't Forget You**	Jim Reeves	RCA	19	(93)	
6	3	**Someone Someone**	Brian Poole & The Tremeloes	Decca	11	(97)	
7	18	**You're No Good**	Swinging Blue Jeans	HMV	8	(97)	L
8	14	**Ramona**	Bachelors	Decca	8		
9	-	**A Hard Day's Night**	Beatles	Parlophone	11	(1)	
10	11	**Hello, Dolly!**	Louis Armstrong	London American	8	(1)	
11	-	**I Just Don't Know What To Do With Myself**	Dusty Springfield	Philips	9		
12	-	**On The Beach**	Cliff Richard	Columbia	8		
13	-	**Kissin' Cousins**	Elvis Presley	RCA	6	(12)	
14	6	**My Guy**	Mary Wells	Stateside	8	(1)	F
15	19	**Nobody I Know**	Peter & Gordon	Columbia	5	(12)	
16	12	**Can't You See That She's Mine**	Dave Clark Five	Columbia	6	(4)	
17	1	**You're My World**	Cilla Black	Parlophone	10	(26)	
18	-	**Call Up The Groups**	Barron Knights	Columbia	9		F
19	10	**Shout**	Lulu	Decca	7	(94)	F
20	-	**Do Wah Diddy Diddy**	Manfred Mann	HMV	10	(1)	

August 1964

This Mnth	Prev Mnth	Title	Artist	Label	Wks	(US 20 Pos)	
1	9	**A Hard Day's Night**	Beatles	Parlophone	11	(1)	
2	20	**Do Wah Diddy Diddy**	Manfred Mann	HMV	10	(1)	
3	18	**Call Up The Groups**	Barron Knights	Columbia	9		F
4	4	**It's All Over Now**	Rolling Stones	Decca	11	(26)	
5	5	**I Won't Forget You**	Jim Reeves	RCA	19	(93)	
6	-	**Tobacco Road**	Nashville Teens	Decca	8	(14)	F
7	11	**I Just Don't Know What To Do With Myself**	Dusty Springfield	Philips	9		
8	-	**I Get Around**	Beach Boys	Capitol	8	(1)	F
9	12	**On The Beach**	Cliff Richard	Columbia	8		
10	-	**Have I The Right?**	Honeycombs	Pye	11	(5)	F
11	-	**It's Only Make Believe**	Billy Fury	Decca	5		
12	1	**House Of The Rising Sun**	Animals	Columbia	7	(1)	F
13	-	**From A Window**	Billy J. Kramer & The Dakotas	Parlophone	4	(23)	
14	-	**Someday We're Gonna Love Again**	Searchers	Pye	5	(34)	
15	2	**Hold Me**	P.J. Proby	Decca	8	(70)	F
16	-	**It's For You**	Cilla Black	Parlophone	6	(79)	
17	-	**Wishin' And Hopin'**	Merseybeats	Fontana	6		
18	-	**You Really Got Me**	Kinks	Pye	9	(7)	F
19	-	**I Found Out The Hard Way**	Four Pennies	Philips	3		
20	3	**It's Over**	Roy Orbison	London American	14	(9)	

◆ The Rolling Stones caused their first fan riots on tour in Britain. The quintet also clocked up their first UK chart topper, 'It's All Over Now', which was recorded in Chicago during their relatively disappointing debut US tour.

◆ The death of US country singer Jim Reeves (the top selling solo artist in Britain in 1964) resulted in a record eight of his albums simultaneously making the Top 20.

71

1964

This Mnth	Prev Mnth	Title	Artist	Label	Wks (US 20 Pos)	
1	10	**Have I The Right?**	Honeycombs	Pye	11 (5)	F
2	18	**You Really Got Me**	Kinks	Pye	9 (7)	F
3	5	**I Won't Forget You**	Jim Reeves	RCA	19 (93)	
4	-	**I Wouldn't Trade You For The World**	Bachelors	Decca	11 (69)	
5	-	**The Crying Game**	Dave Berry	Decca	7	
6	-	**I'm Into Something Good**	Herman's Hermits	Columbia	10 (13)	F
7	-	**Rag Doll**	Four Seasons	Philips	9 (1)	
8	2	**Do Wah Diddy Diddy**	Manfred Mann	HMV	10 (1)	
9	-	**As Tears Go By**	Marianne Faithfull	Decca	10 (22)	F
10	1	**A Hard Day's Night**	Beatles	Parlophone	11 (1)	
12	-	**Where Did Our Love Go**	Supremes	Stateside	10 (1)	F
13	-	**She's Not There**	Zombies	Decca	6 (2)	F L
14	16	**It's For You**	Cilla Black	Parlophone	6 (79)	
15	-	**Such A Night**	Elvis Presley	RCA	5 (16)	
16	-	**The Wedding**	Julie Rogers	Mercury	13 (10)	F L
17	8	**I Get Around**	Beach Boys	Capitol	8 (1)	F
18	-	**Oh Pretty Woman**	Roy Orbison	London American	12 (1)	
19	4	**It's All Over Now**	Rolling Stones	Decca	11 (26)	
20	-	**Everybody Loves Somebody**	Dean Martin	Reprise	7 (1)	

This Mnth	Prev Mnth	Title	Artist	Label	Wks (US 20 Pos)	
1	17	**Oh Pretty Woman**	Roy Orbison	London American	12 (1)	
2	11	**Where Did Our Love Go**	Supremes	Stateside	10 (1)	F
3	6	**I'm Into Something Good**	Herman's Hermits	Columbia	10 (13)	F
4	15	**The Wedding**	Julie Rogers	Mercury	13 (10)	F L
5	7	**Rag Doll**	Four Seasons	Philips	9 (1)	
6	-	**When You Walk In The Room**	Searchers	Pye	8 (35)	
7	4	**I Wouldn't Trade You For The World**	Bachelors	Decca	11 (69)	
8	3	**I Won't Forget You**	Jim Reeves	RCA	19 (93)	
9	-	**(There's) Always Something There To Remind Me**	Sandie Shaw	Pye	5 (52)	F
10	-	**I'm Crying**	Animals	Columbia	6 (19)	
11	-	**We're Through**	Hollies	Parlophone	7	
12	-	**Walk Away**	Matt Monro	Parlophone	11 (23)	
13	-	**Together**	P.J. Proby	Decca	6	
14	19	**Everybody Loves Somebody**	Dean Martin	Reprise	7 (1)	
15	9	**As Tears Go By**	Marianne Faithfull	Decca	10 (22)	F
16	-	**The Twelfth Of Never**	Cliff Richard	Columbia	6	
17	1	**Have I The Right?**	Honeycombs	Pye	11 (5)	F
18	-	**How Soon**	Henry Mancini & His Orchestra	RCA	4	L
19	-	**One Way Love**	Cliff Bennett & The Rebel Rousers	Parlophone	4	F
20	2	**You Really Got Me**	Kinks	Pye	9 (7)	F

◆ 60s superstars The Kinks and Herman's Hermits debuted on the UK chart, while the High Numbers (Who), Joe Cocker and Rod Stewart released unsuccessful singles.

◆ There was an upsurge of interest in "death discs" with Twinkle's self-penned 'Terry' and the US hit 'Leader Of The Pack' by the Shangri-La's (a hit in 1965, 1972 and 1976) both motoring up the chart. However, J. Frank Wilson's ghoulish American smash 'Last Kiss' was a stiff on this side of the Atlantic.

November 1964

This Mnth	Prev Mnth	Title	Artist	Label	Wks	(US 20 Pos)	
1	-	Baby Love	Supremes	Stateside	10	(1)	
2	1	Oh Pretty Woman	Roy Orbison	London American	12	(1)	
3	-	Sha La La	Manfred Mann	HMV	7	(12)	
4	-	He's In Town	Rockin' Berries	Piccadilly	7		F
5	-	All Day And All Of The Night	Kinks	Pye	9	(7)	
6	12	Walk Away	Matt Monro	Parlophone	11	(23)	
7	-	Um Um Um Um Um Um	Wayne Fontana & The Mindbenders	Fontana	7		F
8	4	The Wedding	Julie Rogers	Mercury	13	(10)	F L
9	6	When You Walk In The Room	Searchers	Pye	8	(35)	
10	-	Tokyo Melody	Helmut Zacharias Orchestra	Polydor	6		F L
11	-	There's A Heartache Following Me	Jim Reeves	RCA	10		
12	16	The Twelfth Of Never	Cliff Richard	Columbia	6		
13	-	Google Eye	Nashville Teens	Decca	3		L
14	-	Don't Bring Me Down	Pretty Things	Fontana	5		F
15	-	I'm Gonna Be Strong	Gene Pitney	Stateside	10	(9)	
16	9	(There's) Always Something There To Remind Me	Sandie Shaw	Pye	5	(52)	F
17	-	Little Red Rooster	Rolling Stones	Decca	8		
18	2	Where Did Our Love Go	Supremes	Stateside	10	(1)	F
19	19	One Way Love	Cliff Bennett/Rebel Rousers	Parlophone	4		F
20	-	Remember (Walkin' In The Sand)	Shangri-Las	Red Bird	3	(5)	F

December 1964

This Mnth	Prev Mnth	Title	Artist	Label	Wks	(US 20 Pos)	
1	-	I Feel Fine	Beatles	Parlophone	10	(1)	G
2	15	I'm Gonna Be Strong	Gene Pitney	Stateside	10	(9)	
3	-	Downtown	Petula Clark	Pye	12	(1)	
4	17	Little Red Rooster	Rolling Stones	Decca	8		
5	-	Walk Tall	Val Doonican	Decca	10		F
6	-	Pretty Paper	Roy Orbison	London American	6	(15)	
7	1	Baby Love	Supremes	Stateside	10	(1)	
8	-	I Understand	Freddie & The Dreamers	Columbia	8	(36)	L
9	11	There's A Heartache Following Me	Jim Reeves	RCA	10		
10	5	All Day And All Of The Night	Kinks	Pye	9	(7)	
11	-	No Arms Could Ever Hold You	Bachelors	Decca	7	(27)	
12	10	Tokyo Melody	Helmut Zacharias Orchestra	Polydor	6		F L
13	-	Losing You	Dusty Springfield	Philips	5	(91)	
14	7	Um Um Um Um Um Um	Wayne Fontana/Mindbenders	Fontana	7		F
15	-	I Could Easily Fall	Cliff Richard	Columbia	8		
16	-	Message To Martha (Kentucky Bluebird)	Adam Faith	Parlophone	6		L
17	4	He's In Town	Rockin' Berries	Piccadilly	7		F
18	-	Somewhere	P.J. Proby	Liberty	8	(91)	
19	-	Blue Christmas	Elvis Presley	RCA	3		
20	-	Terry	Twinkle	Decca	9		F L

◆ The Beach Boys, who had a successful UK visit, ended the year topping the US album listings with Beach Boys Concert.

◆ 'Oh Pretty Woman' by Roy Orbison, was the only American record to top the transatlantic charts since 'I Can't Stop Loving You' by Ray Charles in 1962.

1965

This Mnth	Prev Mnth	Title	Artist	Label	Wks	(US 20 Pos)	
1	-	Yeh Yeh	Georgie Fame	Columbia	8	(21)	F
2	1	I Feel Fine	Beatles	Parlophone	10	(1)	G
3	20	Terry	Twinkle	Decca	9		F L
4	-	Girl Don't Come	Sandie Shaw	Pye	9	(42)	
5	-	Go Now!	Moody Blues	Decca	9	(10)	F
6	3	Downtown	Petula Clark	Pye	12	(1)	
7	5	Walk Tall	Val Doonican	Decca	10		F
8	18	Somewhere	P.J. Proby	Liberty	8	(91)	
9	15	I Could Easily Fall	Cliff Richard	Columbia	8		
10	2	I'm Gonna Be Strong	Gene Pitney	Stateside	10	(9)	
11	-	Cast Your Fate To The Wind	Sounds Orchestral	Piccadilly	10	(10)	F L
12	-	Ferry Across The Mersey	Gerry & The Pacemakers	Columbia	7	(6)	
13	11	No Arms Could Ever Hold You	Bachelors	Decca	7	(27)	
14	8	I Understand	Freddie & The Dreamers	Columbia	8	(36)	L
15	-	You've Lost That Lovin' Feelin'	Cilla Black	Parlophone	5		
16	-	Come Tomorrow	Manfred Mann	HMV	7	(50)	
17	-	What Have They Done To The Rain	Searchers	Pye	6	(29)	
18	-	Baby Please Don't Go	Them	Decca	6		F
19	16	Message To Martha (Kentucky Bluebird)	Adam Faith	Parlophone	6		L
20	-	You've Lost That Lovin' Feelin'	Righteous Brothers	London American	7	(1)	F

This Mnth	Prev Mnth	Title	Artist	Label	Wks	(US 20 Pos)	
1	20	You've Lost That Lovin' Feelin'	Righteous Brothers	London American	7	(1)	F
2	-	Tired Of Waiting For You	Kinks	Pye	7	(6)	
3	-	Keep Searchin' (We'll Follow The Sun)	Del Shannon	Stateside	8	(9)	L
4	-	I'll Never Find Another You	Seekers	Columbia	11	(4)	F
5	16	Come Tomorrow	Manfred Mann	HMV	7	(50)	
6	-	The Special Years	Val Doonican	Decca	8		
7	5	Go Now!	Moody Blues	Decca	9	(10)	F
8	-	Game Of Love	Wayne Fontana & The Mindbenders	Fontana	7	(1)	
9	-	Don't Let Me Be Misunderstood	Animals	Columbia	7	(15)	
10	11	Cast Your Fate To The Wind	Sounds Orchestral	Piccadilly	10	(10)	F L
11	15	You've Lost That Lovin' Feelin'	Cilla Black	Parlophone	5		
12	-	Funny How Love Can Be	Ivy League	Piccadilly	6		F
13	18	Baby Please Don't Go	Them	Decca	6		F
14	-	It Hurts So Much	Jim Reeves	RCA	6		
15	12	Ferry Across The Mersey	Gerry & The Pacemakers	Columbia	7	(6)	
16	-	Leader Of The Pack	Shangri-Las	Red Bird	4	(1)	
17	1	Yeh Yeh	Georgie Fame	Columbia	8	(21)	F
18	4	Girl Don't Come	Sandie Shaw	Pye	9	(42)	
19	3	Terry	Twinkle	Decca	9		F L
20	-	Yes I Will	Hollies	Parlophone	7		

◆ Folk rivals Bob Dylan and Donovan debuted on the UK singles chart in the same week.

◆ An all-star Motown package tour played to half empty houses. The Temptations' US chart topper, 'My Girl', finally hit in the UK in 1992. Fellow American, P.J. Proby, who was faring far better, was banned by the BBC, a major theatre chain and American show *Shindig*, after splitting his trousers on stage.

1965

March 1965

This Mnth	Prev Mnth	Title	Artist	Label	Wks	(US 20 Pos)	
1	-	It's Not Unusual	Tom Jones	Decca	9	(10)	F
2	4	I'll Never Find Another You	Seekers	Columbia	11	(4)	F
3	-	Silhouettes	Herman's Hermits	Columbia	9	(5)	
4	-	Come And Stay With Me	Marianne Faithfull	Decca	7	(26)	
5	-	The Last Time	Rolling Stones	Decca	9	(9)	
6	-	I'll Stop At Nothing	Sandie Shaw	Pye	7	(97)	
7	-	I Must Be Seeing Things	Gene Pitney	Stateside	6	(31)	
8	8	Game Of Love	Wayne Fontana & The Mindbenders	Fontana	7	(1)	
9	9	Don't Let Me Be Misunderstood	Animals	Columbia	7	(15)	
10	20	Yes I Will	Hollies	Parlophone	7		
11	-	Goodbye My Love	Searchers	Pye	5	(52)	
12	6	The Special Years	Val Doonican	Decca	8		
13	12	Funny How Love Can Be	Ivy League	Piccadilly	6		F
14	-	I Apologise	P.J. Proby	Liberty	5		
15	-	Goodnight	Roy Orbison	London American	5	(21)	
16	14	It Hurts So Much	Jim Reeves	RCA	6		
17	2	Tired Of Waiting For You	Kinks	Pye	7	(6)	
18	-	Concrete And Clay	Unit 4 Plus 2	Decca	9	(28)	F
19	-	Honey I Need	Pretty Things	Fontana	3		L
20	-	The Minute You're Gone	Cliff Richard	Columbia	9		

April 1965

This Mnth	Prev Mnth	Title	Artist	Label	Wks	(US 20 Pos)	
1	20	The Minute You're Gone	Cliff Richard	Columbia	9		
2	-	For Your Love	Yardbirds	Columbia	7	(6)	F
3	18	Concrete And Clay	Unit 4 Plus 2	Decca	9	(28)	F
4	-	Catch The Wind	Donovan	Pye	8	(23)	F
5	5	The Last Time	Rolling Stones	Decca	9	(9)	
6	-	Here Comes The Night	Them	Decca	8	(24)	L
7	-	Times They Are A-Changin'	Bob Dylan	CBS	7		F
8	-	I Can't Explain	Who	Brunswick	7	(93)	F
9	-	Stop! In The Name Of Love	Supremes	Tamla Motown	6	(1)	
10	1	It's Not Unusual	Tom Jones	Decca	9	(10)	F
11	3	Silhouettes	Herman's Hermits	Columbia	9	(5)	
12	-	Ticket To Ride	Beatles	Parlophone	9	(1)	
13	11	Goodbye My Love	Searchers	Pye	5	(52)	
14	-	Little Things	Dave Berry	Decca	6		
15	4	Come And Stay With Me	Marianne Faithfull	Decca	7	(26)	
16	-	I'll Be There	Gerry & The Pacemakers	Columbia	4	(14)	L
17	-	You're Breakin' My Heart	Keely Smith	Reprise	5		F L
18	-	Everybody's Gonna Be Happy	Kinks	Pye	3		
19	2	I'll Never Find Another You	Seekers	Columbia	11	(4)	F
20	-	Pop Go The Workers	Barron Knights	Columbia	8		

◆ David Bowie's group, The Mannish Boys (named, as were the Rolling Stones, after a Muddy Waters' song), signed to Parlophone and released their debut single, 'I Pity The Fool' (a cover of Bobby Bland's R&B success).

◆ Bob Dylan concluded a very successful tour of Britain (the subject of the film *Don't Look Back*) where his album Bringing It All Back Home followed Freewheelin' at No. 1.

1965

This Mnth	Prev Mnth	Title	Artist	Label	Wks	(US 20 Pos)	
1	12	Ticket To Ride	Beatles	Parlophone	9	(1)	
2	-	King Of The Road	Roger Miller	Philips	9	(4)	F
3	-	True Love Ways	Peter & Gordon	Columbia	10	(14)	
4	-	A World Of Our Own	Seekers	Columbia	11	(19)	
5	-	Where Are You Now (My Love)	Jackie Trent	Pye	7		F L
6	20	Pop Go The Workers	Barron Knights	Columbia	8		
7	-	Bring It On Home To Me	Animals	Columbia	8	(32)	
8	6	Here Comes The Night	Them	Decca	8	(24)	L
9	1	The Minute You're Gone	Cliff Richard	Columbia	9		
10	-	Wonderful World	Herman's Hermits	Columbia	7	(4)	
11	-	Oh No Not My Baby	Manfred Mann	HMV	5		
12	-	Subterranean Homesick Blues	Bob Dylan	CBS	6	(39)	
13	-	This Little Bird	Marianne Faithfull	Decca	7	(32)	
14	4	Catch The Wind	Donovan	Pye	8	(23)	F
15	-	Long Live Love	Sandie Shaw	Pye	9		
16	14	Little Things	Dave Berry	Decca	6		
17	9	Stop! In The Name Of Love	Supremes	Tamla Motown	6	(1)	
18	3	Concrete And Clay	Unit 4 Plus 2	Decca	9	(28)	F
19	-	Poor Man's Son	Rockin' Berries	Piccadilly	7		L
20	-	The Clapping Song	Shirley Ellis	London American	8	(8)	F L

This Mnth	Prev Mnth	Title	Artist	Label	Wks	(US 20 Pos)	
1	15	Long Live Love	Sandie Shaw	Pye	9		
2	-	Crying In The Chapel	Elvis Presley	RCA	11	(3)	
3	-	The Price Of Love	Everly Brothers	Warner	10		
4	-	Trains And Boats And Planes	Burt Bacharach	London American	7		F L
5	19	Poor Man's Son	Rockin' Berries	Piccadilly	7		L
6	4	A World Of Our Own	Seekers	Columbia	11	(19)	
7	20	The Clapping Song	Shirley Ellis	London American	8	(8)	F L
8	-	I'm Alive	Hollies	Parlophone	10		
9	13	This Little Bird	Marianne Faithfull	Decca	7	(32)	
10	-	Marie	Bachelors	Decca	6	(15)	
11	5	Where Are You Now (My Love)	Jackie Trent	Pye	7		F L
12	3	True Love Ways	Peter & Gordon	Columbia	10	(14)	
13	-	Colours	Donovan	Pye	6	(61)	
14	-	Set Me Free	Kinks	Pye	6	(23)	
15	-	You've Never Been In Love Like This Before	Unit 4 Plus 2	Decca	5	(95)	L
16	1	Ticket To Ride	Beatles	Parlophone	9	(1)	
17	-	Anyway Anyhow Anywhere	Who	Brunswick	6		
18	-	Trains And Boats And Planes	Billy J. Kramer & The Dakotas	Parlophone	4	(47)	L
19	2	King Of The Road	Roger Miller	Philips	9	(4)	F
20	-	Looking Through The Eyes Of Love	Gene Pitney	Stateside	8	(28)	

◆ Cliff Richard clocked up his first No. 1 since the start of the beat boom with his Nashville-recorded version of Sonny James's country hit 'The Minute You're Gone'.

◆ Merseybeat pioneers Gerry & The Pacemakers and Billy J. Kramer & The Dakotas enjoyed their last Top 20 entries. From now on The Beatles were Epstein's only hitmaking group.

July 1965

This Mnth	Prev Mnth	Title	Artist	Label	Wks	(US 20 Pos)	
1	8	I'm Alive	Hollies	Parlophone	10		
2	-	Heart Full Of Soul	Yardbirds	Columbia	9	(9)	
3	2	Crying In The Chapel	Elvis Presley	RCA	11	(3)	
4	-	Mr. Tambourine Man	Byrds	CBS	9	(1)	F
5	20	Looking Through The Eyes Of Love	Gene Pitney	Stateside	8	(28)	
6	-	To Know You Is To Love You	Peter & Gordon	Columbia	6	(24)	
7	-	Tossing And Turning	Ivy League	Piccadilly	8		L
8	3	The Price Of Love	Everly Brothers	Warner	10		
9	-	Leave A Little Love	Lulu	Decca	5		
10	13	Colours	Donovan	Pye	6	(61)	
11	-	In The Middle Of Nowhere	Dusty Springfield	Philips	6		
12	17	Anyway Anyhow Anywhere	Who	Brunswick	6		
13	-	You've Got Your Troubles	Fortunes	Decca	9	(7)	F
14	-	There But For Fortune	Joan Baez	Fontana	7	(50)	F
15	4	Trains And Boats And Planes	Burt Bacharach	London American	7		F L
16	1	Long Live Love	Sandie Shaw	Pye	9		
17	-	Wooly Bully	Sam The Sham & The Pharaohs	MGM	6	(2)	F L
18	-	On My Word	Cliff Richard	Columbia	5		
19	14	Set Me Free	Kinks	Pye	6	(23)	
20	-	We Gotta Get Out Of This Place	Animals	Columbia	8	(13)	

August 1965

This Mnth	Prev Mnth	Title	Artist	Label	Wks	(US 20 Pos)	
1	-	Help!	Beatles	Parlophone	10	(1)	
2	20	We Gotta Get Out Of This Place	Animals	Columbia	8	(13)	
3	13	You've Got Your Troubles	Fortunes	Decca	9	(7)	F
4	4	Mr. Tambourine Man	Byrds	CBS	9	(1)	F
5	-	Catch Us If You Can	Dave Clark Five	Columbia	6	(4)	
6	-	Everyone's Gone To The Moon	Jonathan King	Decca	7	(17)	F
7	-	A Walk In The Black Forest	Horst Jankowski	Mercury	12	(12)	F L
8	7	Tossing And Turning	Ivy League	Piccadilly	8		L
9	14	There But For Fortune	Joan Baez	Fontana	7	(50)	F
10	-	I Got You Babe	Sonny & Cher	Atlantic	9	(1)	F
11	-	Zorba's Dance	Marcello Minerbi	Durium	10		F L
12	-	Summer Nights	Marianne Faithfull	Decca	5	(24)	L
13	-	In Thoughts Of You	Billy Fury	Decca	5		L
14	2	Heart Full Of Soul	Yardbirds	Columbia	9	(9)	
15	-	All I Really Want To Do	Byrds	CBS	5	(40)	
16	-	With These Hands	Tom Jones	Decca	4	(27)	
17	17	Wooly Bully	Sam The Sham & The Pharaohs	MGM	6	(2)	F L
18	11	In The Middle Of Nowhere	Dusty Springfield	Philips	6		
19	-	Don't Make My Baby Blue	Shadows	Columbia	5		
20	-	He's Got No Love	Searchers	Pye	5	(79)	

◆ The Rolling Stones played the prestigious London Palladium. Supporting them were Steam Packet featuring Rod Stewart.

◆ The Righteous Brothers' revival of 'Unchained Melody' became a transatlantic success. It would repeat that feat in 1990.

◆ Appearing at the National Jazz & Blues Festival at Richmond were such artists as The Spencer Davis Group, Manfred Mann, Rod Stewart, The Who and The Yardbirds.

1965

This Mnth	Prev Mnth	Title	Artist	Label	Wks	(US 20 Pos)	
1	-	(I Can't Get No) Satisfaction	Rolling Stones	Decca	10	(1)	
2	-	Make It Easy On Yourself	Walker Brothers	Philips	10	(16)	
3	10	I Got You Babe	Sonny & Cher	Atlantic	9	(1)	F
4	7	A Walk In The Black Forest	Horst Jankowski	Mercury	12	(12)	F L
5	-	Like A Rolling Stone	Bob Dylan	CBS	8	(2)	
6	1	Help!	Beatles	Parlophone	10	(1)	
7	11	Zorba's Dance	Marcello Minerbi	Durium	10		F L
8	-	Look Through Any Window	Hollies	Parlophone	8	(32)	
9	15	All I Really Want To Do	Byrds	CBS	5	(40)	
10	-	Tears	Ken Dodd	Columbia	21		G
11	-	Laugh At Me	Sonny	Atlantic	6	(10)	F L
12	-	All I Really Want To Do	Cher	Liberty	5	(15)	F
13	-	That's The Way	Honeycombs	Pye	7		L
14	-	What's New Pussycat?	Tom Jones	Decca	5	(3)	
15	6	Everyone's Gone To The Moon	Jonathan King	Decca	7	(17)	F
16	-	Eve Of Destruction	Barry McGuire	RCA	10	(1)	F L
17	-	Unchained Melody	Righteous Brothers	London American	3	(4)	
18	-	See My Friend	Kinks	Pye	4		
19	-	Il Silenzio	Nini Rosso	Durium	7		F L
20	-	Just A Little Bit Better	Herman's Hermits	Columbia	5	(7)	

This Mnth	Prev Mnth	Title	Artist	Label	Wks	(US 20 Pos)	
1	10	Tears	Ken Dodd	Columbia	21		G
2	-	If You Gotta Go, Go Now	Manfred Mann	HMV	8		
3	16	Eve Of Destruction	Barry McGuire	RCA	10	(1)	F
4	-	Almost There	Andy Williams	CBS	10	(67)	
5	2	Make It Easy On Yourself	Walker Brothers	Philips	10	(16)	
6	-	Hang On Sloopy	McCoys	Immediate	9	(1)	F
7	8	Look Through Any Window	Hollies	Parlophone	8	(32)	
8	19	Il Silenzio	Nini Rosso	Durium	7		F L
9	1	(I Can't Get No) Satisfaction	Rolling Stones	Decca	10	(1)	
10	-	Message Understood	Sandie Shaw	Pye	5		
11	-	Baby Don't Go	Sonny & Cher	Reprise	5	(8)	
12	4	A Walk In The Black Forest	Horst Jankowski	Mercury	12	(12)	F L
13	-	Some Of Your Lovin'	Dusty Springfield	Philips	6		
14	-	Evil Hearted You/Still I'm Sad	Yardbirds	Columbia	6		
15	5	Like A Rolling Stone	Bob Dylan	CBS	8	(2)	
16	3	I Got You Babe	Sonny & Cher	Atlantic	10	(1)	F
17	-	It's Good News Week	Hedgehoppers Anonymous	Decca	6	(48)	F L
18	-	In The Midnight Hour	Wilson Pickett	Atlantic	4	(21)	F
19	-	What Cha Gonna Do About It	Small Faces	Decca	5		F
20	-	Yesterday Man	Chris Andrews	Decca	11	(94)	F

◆ After a long absence, US groups started to chart again in Britain, with newcomers The Byrds, Sam The Sham & The Pharaohs and The Walker Brothers leading the way.

◆ Two British records which sold over a million in the UK but failed to even chart Stateside were: 'Tears' by Ken Dodd and 'The Carnival Is Over' by The Seekers.

◆ In a year when rock giants The Beatles, The Rolling Stones and Bob Dylan were the only acts to top the UK album chart, the longest running No. 1 was the MOR soundtrack album **The Sound Of Music**.

1965

November 1965

This Mnth	Prev Mnth	Title	Artist	Label	Wks (US 20 Pos)	
1	-	Get Off Of My Cloud	Rolling Stones	Decca	8 (1)	
2	1	Tears	Ken Dodd	Columbia	21	G
3	20	Yesterday Man	Chris Andrews	Decca	11 (94)	F
4	-	The Carnival Is Over	Seekers	Columbia	14	G
5	-	Here It Comes Again	Fortunes	Decca	7 (27)	
6	14	Evil Hearted You/Still I'm Sad	Yardbirds	Columbia	6	
7	-	It's My Life	Animals	Columbia	6 (23)	
8	17	It's Good News Week	Hedgehoppers Anonymous	Decca	6 (48)	F L
9	-	Yesterday	Matt Monro	Parlophone	7	L
10	-	My Generation	Who	Brunswick	10 (74)	
11	4	Almost There	Andy Williams	CBS	10 (67)	
12	-	1-2-3	Len Barry	Brunswick	11 (2)	F
13	-	Positively 4th Street	Bob Dylan	CBS	9 (7)	
14	-	Love Is Strange	Everly Brothers	Warner	4	L
15	3	Eve Of Destruction	Barry McGuire	RCA	10 (1)	F L
16	-	Wind Me Up (Let Me Go)	Cliff Richard	Columbia	12	
17	-	A Lover's Concerto	Toys	Stateside	9 (2)	F L
18	6	Hang On Sloopy	McCoys	Immediate	9 (1)	F L
19	2	If You Gotta Go, Go Now	Manfred Mann	HMV	8	
20	-	Princess In Rags	Gene Pitney	Stateside	8 (37)	

December 1965

This Mnth	Prev Mnth	Title	Artist	Label	Wks (US 20 Pos)	
1	4	The Carnival Is Over	Seekers	Columbia	14	G
2	16	Wind Me Up (Let Me Go)	Cliff Richard	Columbia	12	
3	10	My Generation	Who	Brunswick	10 (74)	
4	12	1-2-3	Len Barry	Brunswick	11 (2)	F
5	-	Day Tripper/We Can Work it Out	Beatles	Parlophone	10 (5)	G
6	2	Tears	Ken Dodd	Columbia	21	G
7	-	The River	Ken Dodd	Columbia	11	
8	17	A Lovers Concerto	Toys	Stateside	9 (2)	F L
9	-	Maria	P.J. Proby	Liberty	6	L
10	20	Princess In Rags	Gene Pitney	Stateside	8 (37)	
11	1	Get Off Of My Cloud	Rolling Stones	Decca	8 (1)	
12	-	My Ship Is Coming In	Walker Brothers	Philips	10 (63)	
13	13	Positively 4th Street	Bob Dylan	CBS	9 (7)	
14	-	Let's Hang On!	Four Seasons	Philips	11 (3)	
15	-	Rescue Me	Fontella Bass	Chess	7 (4)	F L
16	3	Yesterday Man	Chris Andrews	Decca	11 (94)	F
17	-	Don't Bring Me Your Heartaches	Paul & Barry Ryan	Decca	4	F
18	7	It's My Life	Animals	Columbia	6 (23)	
19	-	To Whom It Concerns	Chris Andrews	Decca	5	L
20	-	Tell Me Why	Elvis Presley	RCA	4 (33)	

◆ As The Stones scored their fifth successive UK No. 1 with 'Get Off Of My Cloud', Motown (America's top label in 1965) act The Supremes notched up their sixth American topper, 'I Hear A Symphony'.

◆ Decca Records released Marc Bolan's debut disc, 'The Wizard'. The label also recorded the first solo tracks by Van Morrison, whose group, Them, had temporarily disbanded.

1966

January 1966

This Mnth	Prev Mnth	Title	Artist	Label	Wks	(US 20 Pos)	
1	5	Day Tripper/We Can Work it Out	Beatles	Parlophone	10	(1)	G
2	-	Keep On Runnin'	Spencer Davis Group	Fontana	10	(76)	F
3	12	My Ship Is Coming In	Walker Brothers	Philips	10	(63)	
4	2	Wind Me Up (Let Me Go)	Cliff Richard	Columbia	12		
5	7	The River	Ken Dodd	Columbia	11		
6	1	The Carnival Is Over	Seekers	Columbia	14		G
7	14	Let's Hang On!	Four Seasons	Philips	11	(3)	
8	-	Till The End Of The Day	Kinks	Pye	8	(50)	
9	6	Tears	Ken Dodd	Columbia	21		G
10	-	Spanish Flea	Herb Alpert	Pye International	12	(27)	F
11	-	A Must To Avoid	Herman's Hermits	Columbia	7	(8)	
12	4	1-2-3	Len Barry	Brunswick	11	(2)	F
13	-	Merrie Gentle Pops	Barron Knights	Columbia	5		
14	-	Michelle	Overlanders	Pye	6		F L
15	3	My Generation	Who	Brunswick	10	(74)	
16	15	Rescue Me	Fontella Bass	Chess	7	(4)	F L
17	-	My Girl	Otis Redding	Atlantic	7		F
18	-	A Hard Day's Night	Peter Sellers	Parlophone	4		L
19	8	A Lovers Concerto	Toys	Stateside	9	(2)	F L
20	19	To Whom It Concerns	Chris Andrews	Decca	5		L

February 1966

1	-	You Were On My Mind	Crispian St. Peters	Decca	8	(36)	F
2	10	Spanish Flea	Herb Alpert	Pye International	12	(27)	F
3	-	These Boots Are Made For Walkin'	Nancy Sinatra	Reprise	10	(1)	F
4	-	Love's Just A Broken Heart	Cilla Black	Parlophone	6		
5	-	A Groovy Kind Of Love	Mindbenders	Fontana	10	(2)	F
6	14	Michelle	Overlanders	Pye	6		F L
7	2	Keep On Runnin'	Spencer Davis Group	Fontana	10	(76)	F
8	-	19th Nervous Breakdown	Rolling Stones	Decca	7	(2)	
9	11	A Must To Avoid	Herman's Hermits	Columbia	7	(8)	
10	-	Mirror Mirror	Pinkerton's Assorted Colours	Decca	4		F L
11	-	Tomorrow	Sandie Shaw	Pye	5		
12	-	Like A Baby	Len Barry	Brunswick	4	(27)	L
13	-	Girl	St. Louis Union	Decca	5		F L
14	-	My Love	Petula Clark	Pye	6	(1)	
15	1	Day Tripper/We Can Work it Out	Beatles	Parlophone	10	(1)	G
16	17	My Girl	Otis Redding	Atlantic	7		F
17	7	Let's Hang On!	Four Seasons	Philips	11	(3)	
18	-	Sha La La La Lee	Small Faces	Decca	8		
19	3	My Ship Is Coming In	Walker Brothers	Philips	10	(63)	
20	-	Michelle	David & Jonathan	Columbia	4	(18)	F

◆ Cover versions were still rife with re-treads of recent songs from The Walker Brothers, Cliff Richard, Otis Redding, Crispian St. Peters, The Mindbend-ers and The Hollies.

◆ A casual remark by John Lennon, which compared the popularity of The Beatles to Jesus, went virtually unnoticed in the UK. However, it caused problems in some American states.

1966

March 1966

This Mnth	Prev Mnth	Title	Artist	Label	Wks	(US 20 Pos)	
1	5	A Groovy Kind Of Love	Mindbenders	Fontana	10	(2)	F
2	18	Sha La La La Lee	Small Faces	Decca	8		
3	-	Barbara Ann	Beach Boys	Capitol	8	(2)	
4	3	These Boots Are Made For Walkin'	Nancy Sinatra	Reprise	10	(1)	F
5	-	Backstage	Gene Pitney	Stateside	6	(25)	
6	-	I Can't Let Go	Hollies	Parlophone	6	(42)	
7	-	The Sun Ain't Gonna Shine Anymore	Walker Brothers	Philips	7	(13)	
8	8	19th Nervous Breakdown	Rolling Stones	Decca	7	(2)	
9	14	My Love	Petula Clark	Pye	6	(1)	
10	2	Spanish Flea	Herb Alpert	Pye International	12	(27)	F
11	-	Make The World Go Away	Eddy Arnold	RCA	10	(6)	F L
12	-	Shapes Of Things	Yardbirds	Columbia	7	(11)	
13	-	Lightnin' Strikes	Lou Christie	MGM	5	(1)	F
14	-	Dedicated Follower Of Fashion	Kinks	Pye	8	(36)	
15	-	Inside-Looking Out	Animals	Decca	4	(34)	
16	1	You Were On My Mind	Crispian St. Peters	Decca	8	(36)	F
17	11	Tomorrow	Sandie Shaw	Pye	5		
18	-	What Now My Love	Sonny & Cher	Atlantic	5	(14)	
19	-	Elusive Butterfly	Bob Lind	Fontana	5	(5)	F L
20	-	This Golden Ring	Fortunes	Decca	2	(82)	

April 1966

This Mnth	Prev Mnth	Title	Artist	Label	Wks	(US 20 Pos)	
1	-	Somebody Help Me	Spencer Davis Group	Fontana	7	(47)	
2	-	Hold Tight	Dave Dee, Dozy, Beaky, Mick & Tich	Fontana	10		F
3	-	The Sound Of Silence	Bachelors	Decca	9		
4	-	Elusive Butterfly	Val Doonican	Decca	8		
5	7	The Sun Ain't Gonna Shine Anymore	Walker Brothers	Philips	7	(13)	
6	-	Substitute	Who	Reaction	9		
7	19	Elusive Butterfly	Bob Lind	Fontana	5	(5)	F L
8	-	You Don't Have To Say You Love Me	Dusty Springfield	Philips	10	(4)	
9	14	Dedicated Follower Of Fashion	Kinks	Pye	8	(36)	
10	11	Make The World Go Away	Eddy Arnold	RCA	10	(6)	F L
11	-	Bang Bang (My Baby Shot Me Down)	Cher	Liberty	8	(2)	
12	12	Shapes Of Things	Yardbirds	Columbia	7	(11)	
13	6	I Can't Let Go	Hollies	Parlophone	6	(42)	
14	-	I Put A Spell On You	Alan Price Set	Decca	5	(80)	F
15	-	Alfie	Cilla Black	Parlophone	7	(95)	
16	-	Pied Piper	Crispian St. Peters	Decca	8	(4)	L
17	-	Someday One Day	Seekers	Columbia	6		
18	2	Sha La La La Lee	Small Faces	Decca	8		
19	3	Barbara Ann	Beach Boys	Capitol	8	(2)	
20	-	Pretty Flamingo	Manfred Mann	HMV	7	(29)	

◆ US soul music continued to thrive. Stevie Wonder had his first UK hit, 'Uptight'. James Brown had the whole of *Ready Steady Go* devoted to him, and Wilson Pickett and Mary Wells also had successful appearances on the show.

◆ The Beatles played their last UK date, alongside the Stones and The Who, at the *NME* poll winners' concert. They started their final World tour by returning to Hamburg.

1966

This Mnth	Prev Mnth	Title	Artist	Label	Wks	(US Pos)	
1	20	Pretty Flamingo	Manfred Mann	HMV	7	(29)	
2	-	Sloop John B	Beach Boys	Capitol	9	(3)	
3	-	Daydream	Lovin' Spoonful	Pye International	8	(2)	F
4	8	You Don't Have To Say You Love Me	Dusty Springfield	Philips	10	(4)	
5	16	Pied Piper	Crispian St. Peters	Decca	8	(4)	L
6	11	Bang Bang (My Baby Shot Me Down)	Cher	Liberty	8	(2)	
7	-	Wild Thing	Troggs	Fontana	8	(1)	F
8	-	Shotgun Wedding	Roy 'C'	Island	6		F
9	2	Hold Tight	Dave Dee, Dozy, Beaky, Mick & Tich	Fontana	10		F
10	-	Sorrow	Merseys	Fontana	8		L
11	-	Paint It, Black	Rolling Stones	Decca	7	(1)	
12	-	Homeward Bound	Simon & Garfunkel	CBS	7	(5)	F
13	3	The Sound Of Silence	Bachelors	Decca	9		
14	-	Strangers In The Night	Frank Sinatra	Reprise	13	(1)	
15	15	Alfie	Cilla Black	Parlophone	7	(95)	
16	-	Rainy Day Women Nos. 12 & 35	Bob Dylan	CBS	5	(2)	
17	-	Monday Monday	Mamas & The Papas	RCA	10	(1)	F
18	-	Hey Girl	Small Faces	Decca	5		
19	-	Promises	Ken Dodd	Columbia	8		
20	1	Somebody Help Me	Spencer Davis Group	Fontana	7	(47)	

This Mnth	Prev Mnth	Title	Artist	Label	Wks	(US Pos)	
1	14	Strangers In The Night	Frank Sinatra	Reprise	13	(1)	
2	17	Monday Monday	Mamas & The Papas	RCA	10	(1)	F
3	10	Sorrow	Merseys	Fontana	8		L
4	11	Paint It, Black	Rolling Stones	Decca	7	(1)	
5	-	When A Man Loves A Woman	Percy Sledge	Atlantic	9	(1)	F
6	7	Wild Thing	Troggs	Fontana	8	(1)	F
7	-	Don't Bring Me Down	Animals	Decca	6	(12)	
8	19	Promises	Ken Dodd	Columbia	8		
9	2	Sloop John B	Beach Boys	Capitol	9	(3)	
10	-	Paperback Writer	Beatles	Parlophone	7	(1)	
11	16	Rainy Day Women Nos. 12 & 35	Bob Dylan	CBS	5	(2)	
12	-	Over Under Sideways Down	Yardbirds	Columbia	5	(13)	L
13	18	Hey Girl	Small Faces	Decca	5		
14	-	Don't Answer Me	Cilla Black	Parlophone	6		
15	-	Sunny Afternoon	Kinks	Pye	9	(14)	
16	-	Nothing Comes Easy	Sandie Shaw	Pye	4		
17	-	River Deep Mountain High	Ike & Tina Turner	London American	9	(88)	F
18	8	Shotgun Wedding	Roy 'C'	Island	6		F
19	1	Pretty Flamingo	Manfred Mann	HMV	7	(29)	
20	-	Nobody Needs Your Love	Gene Pitney	Stateside	9		

◆ Like their earlier US No. 1s, 'Mrs. Brown You've Got A Lovely Daughter' and 'I'm Henry VIII I Am', Herman's Hermits latest American hit, a revival of George Formby's music hall favourite 'Leaning On The Lamp Post', was not deemed suitable for release in the group's homeland.

◆ American trio The Walker Brothers applied to become British Citizens, soon after British duo Chad & Jeremy had requested US citizenship.

◆ Frank Sinatra scored the only solo transatlantic chart topper of his career with Bert Kaempfert's composition 'Strangers In The Night'.

1966

July 1966

This Mnth	Prev Mnth	Title	Artist	Label	Wks	(US 20 Pos)	
1	15	Sunny Afternoon	Kinks	Pye	9	(14)	
2	17	River Deep Mountain High	Ike & Tina Turner	London American	9	(88)	F
3	20	Nobody Needs Your Love	Gene Pitney	Stateside	9		
4	-	Get Away	Georgie Fame	Columbia	7	(70)	
5	1	Strangers In The Night	Frank Sinatra	Reprise	13	(1)	
6	-	Bus Stop	Hollies	Parlophone	7	(5)	
7	10	Paperback Writer	Beatles	Parlophone	7	(1)	
8	-	Out Of Time	Chris Farlowe	Immediate	8		F L
9	-	Black Is Black	Los Bravos	Decca	9	(4)	F
10	-	Hideaway	Dave Dee, Dozy, Beaky, Mick & Tich	Fontana	6		
11	-	I Couldn't Live Without Your Love	Petula Clark	Pye	7	(9)	
12	14	Don't Answer Me	Cilla Black	Parlophone	6		
13	5	When A Man Loves A Woman	Percy Sledge	Atlantic	9	(1)	F
14	-	Love Letters	Elvis Presley	RCA	7	(19)	
15	2	Monday Monday	Mamas & The Papas	RCA	10	(1)	F
16	-	With A Girl Like You	Troggs	Fontana	8	(29)	
17	-	The More I See You	Chris Montez	Pye International	9	(16)	
18	-	Goin' Back	Dusty Springfield	Philips	6		
19	-	Lana	Roy Orbison	London American	5		
20	7	Don't Bring Me Down	Animals	Decca	6	(12)	

August 1966

This Mnth	Prev Mnth	Title	Artist	Label	Wks	(US 20 Pos)	
1	16	With A Girl Like You	Troggs	Fontana	8	(29)	
2	9	Black Is Black	Los Bravos	Decca	9	(4)	F
3	17	The More I See You	Chris Montez	Pye International	9	(16)	
4	-	Mama	Dave Berry	Decca	10		L
5	-	God Only Knows	Beach Boys	Capitol	9	(39)	
6	8	Out Of Time	Chris Farlowe	Immediate	8		F L
7	-	Yellow Submarine/Eleanor Rigby	Beatles	Parlophone	9	(2)	
8	-	Visions	Cliff Richard	Columbia	8		
9	-	Summer In The City	Lovin' Spoonful	Kama Sutra	7	(1)	L
10	14	Love Letters	Elvis Presley	RCA	7	(19)	
11	11	I Couldn't Live Without Your Love	Petula Clark	Pye	7	(9)	
12	-	Hi-Lili-Hi-Lo	Alan Price Set	Decca	7		
13	-	They're Coming To Take Me Away Ha-Haaa!	Napoleon XIV	Warner	6	(3)	F L
14	4	Get Away	Georgie Fame	Columbia	7	(70)	
15	1	Sunny Afternoon	Kinks	Pye	9	(14)	
16	18	Goin' Back	Dusty Springfield	Philips	6		
17	-	Lovers Of The World Unite	David & Jonathan	Columbia	7		L
18	-	I Saw Her Again	Mamas & The Papas	RCA	6	(5)	
19	-	I Want You	Bob Dylan	CBS	5	(20)	
20	-	All Or Nothing	Small Faces	Decca	8		

◆ 'They're Coming To Take Me Away Ha-Haaa!' was one of the strangest transatlantic hits of all time. This "madman's monologue" was released by recording engineer-cum-successful MOR songsmith Jerry Samuels under the apt name Napoleon XIV. It cost him $15 to record and sold half a million copies in its first week.

1966

This Mnth	Prev Mnth	Title	Artist	Label	Wks	(US 20 Pos)	
1	20	All Or Nothing	Small Faces	Decca	8		
2	7	Yellow Submarine/Eleanor Rigby	Beatles	Parlophone	9	(2)	
3	5	God Only Knows	Beach Boys	Capitol	9	(39)	
4	-	Too Soon To Know	Roy Orbison	London American	10	(68)	
5	-	Distant Drums	Jim Reeves	RCA	19	(45)	
6	13	They're Coming To Take Me Away Ha-Haaa!	Napoleon XIV	Warner	6	(3)	F L
7	17	Lovers Of The World Unite	David & Jonathan	Columbia	7		L
8	4	Mama	Dave Berry	Decca	10		L
9	-	Working In The Coal Mine	Lee Dorsey	Stateside	6	(8)	F
10	-	Got To Get You Into My Life	Cliff Bennett & The Rebel Rousers	Parlophone	5		L
11	-	Just Like A Woman	Manfred Mann	Fontana	6		
12	1	With A Girl Like You	Troggs	Fontana	8	(29)	
13	-	I'm A Boy	Who	Reaction	10		
14	8	Visions	Cliff Richard	Columbia	8		
15	-	Little Man	Sonny & Cher	Atlantic	6	(21)	
16	-	You Can't Hurry Love	Supremes	Tamla Motown	8	(1)	
17	18	I Saw Her Again	Mamas & The Papas	RCA	6	(5)	
18	12	Hi-Lili-Hi-Lo	Alan Price Set	Decca	7		
19	9	Summer In The City	Lovin' Spoonful	Kama Sutra	7	(1)	L
20	-	When I Come Home	Spencer Davis Group	Fontana	4		

This Mnth	Prev Mnth	Title	Artist	Label	Wks	(US 20 Pos)	
1	5	Distant Drums	Jim Reeves	RCA	19	(45)	
2	-	Bend It	Dave Dee, Dozy, Beaky, Mick & Tich	Fontana	9		
3	13	I'm A Boy	Who	Reaction	10		
4	-	Winchester Cathedral	New Vaudeville Band	Fontana	9	(1)	F
5	16	You Can't Hurry Love	Supremes	Tamla Motown	8	(1)	
6	-	Have You Seen Your Mother, Baby, Standing In The Shadow	Rolling Stones	Decca	6	(9)	
7	-	Guantanamera	Sandpipers	Pye International	9	(9)	F L
8	15	Little Man	Sonny & Cher	Atlantic	6	(21)	
9	-	All I See Is You	Dusty Springfield	Philips	7	(20)	
10	-	I Can't Control Myself	Troggs	Page One	9	(43)	
11	-	Walk With Me	Seekers	Columbia	6		
12	4	Too Soon To Know	Roy Orbison	London American	10	(68)	
13	-	Reach Out I'll Be There	Four Tops	Tamla Motown	10	(1)	F
14	-	Stop Stop Stop	Hollies	Parlophone	8	(7)	
15	-	Sunny	Georgie Fame	Columbia	4		
16	-	Sunny	Bobby Hebb	Philips	3	(2)	F L
17	1	All Or Nothing	Small Faces	Decca	8		
18	-	Another Tear Falls	Walker Brothers	Philips	3		
19	-	No Milk Today	Herman's Hermits	Columbia	7	(35)	
20	2	Yellow Submarine/Eleanor Rigby	Beatles	Parlophone	9	(2)	

◆ The *NME* announced "The British Beat Boom is over". They pointed out there were now more American records on the US chart than British, and that sales of UK records in America were dropping. *NME* concluded, "Whatever happens, Britain has made her mark upon the world of pop, America now accepts us as a force to be reckoned with – the dark days when British hits in America were regarded as flukes are over."

November 1966

This Mnth	Prev Mnth	Title	Artist	Label	Wks 20	(US Pos)	
1	13	Reach Out I'll Be There	Four Tops	Tamla Motown	10	(1)	F
2	14	Stop Stop Stop	Hollies	Parlophone	8	(7)	
3	-	Semi-Detached Surburban Mr.James	Manfred Mann	Fontana	8		
4	-	High Time	Paul Jones	HMV	8		F
5	-	Good Vibrations	Beach Boys	Capitol	11	(1)	
6	10	I Can't Control Myself	Troggs	Page One	9	(43)	
7	1	Distant Drums	Jim Reeves	RCA	19	(45)	
8	-	Gimme Some Loving	Spencer Davis Group	Fontana	7	(7)	
9	-	If I Were A Carpenter	Bobby Darin	Atlantic	7	(8)	L
10	19	No Milk Today	Herman's Hermits	Columbia	7	(35)	
11	4	Winchester Cathedral	New Vaudeville Band	Fontana	9	(1)	F
12	-	Holy Cow	Lee Dorsey	Stateside	8	(23)	L
13	7	Guantanamera	Sandpipers	Pye International	9	(9)	F L
14	-	Green Green Grass Of Home	Tom Jones	Decca	15	(11)	G
15	-	Time Drags By	Cliff Richard	Columbia	4		
16	-	A Fool Am I	Cilla Black	Parlophone	4		
17	2	Bend It	Dave Dee, Dozy, Beaky etc.	Fontana	9		
18	-	What Would I Be	Val Doonican	Decca	11		
19	-	I've Got You Under My Skin	Four Seasons	Philips	5	(9)	
20	-	Help Me Girl	Eric Burdon & The Animals	Decca	4	(29)	

December 1966

1	14	Green Green Grass Of Home	Tom Jones	Decca	15	(11)	G
2	18	What Would I Be	Val Doonican	Decca	11		
3	5	Good Vibrations	Beach Boys	Capitol	11	(1)	
4	-	Morningtown Ride	Seekers	Columbia	10	(44)	
5	-	Friday On My Mind	Easybeats	UA	9	(16)	F
6	-	My Mind's Eye	Small Faces	Decca	6		
7	-	Dead End Street	Kinks	Pye	9	(73)	
8	8	Gimme Some Loving	Spencer Davis Group	Fontana	7	(7)	
9	-	What Becomes Of The Brokenhearted	Jimmy Ruffin	Tamla Motown	7	(7)	F
10	3	Semi-Detached Surburban Mr.James	Manfred Mann	Fontana	8		
11	-	Sunshine Superman	Donovan	Pye	7	(1)	
12	12	Holy Cow	Lee Dorsey	Stateside	8	(23)	L
13	-	Just One Smile	Gene Pitney	Stateside	6	(64)	
14	-	You Keep Me Hangin' On	Supremes	Tamla Motown	7	(1)	
15	-	Save Me	Dave Dee, Dozy, Beaky, Mick & Tich	Fontana	7		
16	7	Distant Drums	Jim Reeves	RCA	19	(45)	
17	-	If Every Day Was Like Christmas	Elvis Presley	RCA	4		
18	1	Reach Out I'll Be There	Four Tops	Tamla Motown	10	(1)	F
19	4	High Time	Paul Jones	HMV	8		F
20	-	There Won't Be Many Coming Home	Roy Orbison	London American	3		L

◆ The Beach Boys were mobbed when they arrived for a British tour. They ousted The Beatles as World's Top Group in the *NME* poll, and their transatlantic No. 1, 'Good Vibrations', showed how good pop records could be.

◆ A chart survey showed that the oddly named Dave Dee, Dozy, Beaky, Mick & Tich were the most successful singles act in the UK during 1966. The group went almost unnoticed across the Atlantic.

1967

January 1967

This Mnth	Prev Mnth	Title	Artist	Label	Wks	(US 20 Pos)	
1	1	Green Green Grass Of Home	Tom Jones	Decca	15	(11)	G
2	4	Morningtown Ride	Seekers	Columbia	10	(44)	
3	-	Happy Jack	Who	Reaction	7	(24)	
4	11	Sunshine Superman	Donovan	Pye	7	(1)	
5	-	I'm A Believer	Monkees	RCA	10	(1)	F
6	-	In The Country	Cliff Richard	Columbia	6		
7	15	Save Me	Dave Dee, Dozy, Beaky, Mick & Tich	Fontana	7		
8	-	Matthew And Son	Cat Stevens	Deram	7		F
9	-	Any Way That You Want Me	Troggs	Page One	5		
10	-	Night Of Fear	Move	Deram	7		F
11	7	Dead End Street	Kinks	Pye	9	(73)	
12	2	What Would I Be	Val Doonican	Decca	11		
13	-	Sittin' In The Park	Georgie Fame	Columbia	7		
14	14	You Keep Me Hangin' On	Supremes	Tamla Motown	7	(1)	
15	-	Pamela Pamela	Wayne Fontana	Fontana	6		L
16	-	Standing In The Shadows Of Love	Four Tops	Tamla Motown	4	(6)	
17	-	I Feel Free	Cream	Reaction	4		F
18	-	Hey Joe	Jimi Hendrix Experience	Polydor	5		F
19	3	Good Vibrations	Beach Boys	Capitol	11	(1)	
20	5	Friday On My Mind	Easybeats	UA	9	(16)	F

February 1967

This Mnth	Prev Mnth	Title	Artist	Label	Wks	(US 20 Pos)	
1	5	I'm A Believer	Monkees	RCA	10	(1)	F
2	-	Let's Spend The Night Together/Ruby Tuesday	Rolling Stones	Decca	7	(1)	
3	-	I've Been A Bad Bad Boy	Paul Jones	HMV	6		L
4	-	This Is My Song	Petula Clark	Pye	10	(3)	
5	8	Matthew And Son	Cat Stevens	Deram	7		F
6	10	Night Of Fear	Move	Deram	7		F
7	-	Release Me	Engelbert Humperdinck	Decca	15	(4)	F G
8	1	Green Green Grass Of Home	Tom Jones	Decca	15	(11)	G
9	-	Sugar Town	Nancy Sinatra	Reprise	5	(5)	
10	18	Hey Joe	Jimi Hendrix Experience	Polydor	5		F
11	-	Snoopy Vs The Red Baron	Royal Guardsmen	Stateside	8	(2)	F L
12	-	Peek-A-Boo	New Vaudeville Band	Fontana	7	(72)	
13	-	I Won't Come In While He's There	Jim Reeves	RCA	5		
14	-	Here Comes My Baby	Tremeloes	CBS	7	(13)	F
15	16	Standing In The Shadows Of Love	Four Tops	Tamla Motown	4	(6)	
16	-	I'm A Man	Spencer Davis Group	Fontana	3	(10)	L
17	-	Let Me Cry On Your Shoulder	Ken Dodd	Columbia	3		
18	-	Penny Lane/Strawberry Fields Forever	Beatles	Parlophone	8	(1)	
19	-	Mellow Yellow	Donovan	Pye	5	(2)	
20	17	I Feel Free	Cream	Reaction	4		F

◆ Tom Jones had his biggest UK hit with 'Green Green Grass Of Home'. Engelbert Humperdinck – who shared Jones's manager – also struck UK gold with a revi-val of another US country hit, 'Release Me'.

◆ Pink Floyd, The Jimi Hendrix Experience, Cream and The Monkees debuted on the UK chart. The Monkees' TV show was successful in Britain, catapulting them to the top of the charts.

1967

March 1967

This Mnth	Prev Mnth	Title	Artist	Label	Wks	(US 20 Pos)	
1	7	Release Me	Engelbert Humperdinck	Decca	15	(4)	F G
2	18	Penny Lane/Strawberry Fields..	Beatles	Parlophone	8	(1)	
3	4	This Is My Song	Petula Clark	Pye	10	(3)	
4	-	Edelweiss	Vince Hill	Columbia	11		
5	14	Here Comes My Baby	Tremeloes	CBS	7	(13)	F
6	-	On A Carousel	Hollies	Parlophone	7	(11)	
7	-	There's A Kind Of Hush	Herman's Hermits	Columbia	7	(4)	
8	-	Georgy Girl	Seekers	Columbia	7	(2)	
9	-	Detroit City	Tom Jones	Decca	6	(27)	
10	11	Snoopy Vs The Red Baron	Royal Guardsmen	Stateside	8	(2)	F L
11	19	Mellow Yellow	Donovan	Pye	5	(2)	
12	12	Peek-A-Boo	New Vaudeville Band	Fontana	7	(72)	
13	-	This Is My Song	Harry Secombe	Philips	9		L
14	1	I'm A Believer	Monkees	RCA	10	(1)	F
15	-	Give It To Me	Troggs	Page One	4		
16	-	Simon Smith & His Amazing Dancing Bear	Alan Price Set	Decca	7		
17	-	I Was Kaiser Bill's Batman	Whistling Jack Smith	Deram	7	(20)	F L
18	-	Memories Are Made Of This	Val Doonican	Decca	5		
19	13	I Won't Come In While He's There	Jim Reeves	RCA	5		
20	2	Let's Spend The Night Together/Ruby Tuesday	Rolling Stones	Decca	7	(1)	

April 1967

This Mnth	Prev Mnth	Title	Artist	Label	Wks	(US 20 Pos)	
1	-	Somethin' Stupid	Nancy & Frank Sinatra	Reprise	11	(1)	
2	-	Puppet On A String	Sandie Shaw	Pye	13		
3	1	Release Me	Engelbert Humperdinck	Decca	15	(4)	F G
4	13	This Is My Song	Harry Secombe	Philips	9		L
5	-	A Little Bit Me, A Little Bit You	Monkees	RCA	8	(2)	
6	16	Simon Smith & His Amazing Dancing Bear	Alan Price Set	Decca	7		
7	17	I Was Kaiser Bill's Batman	Whistling Jack Smith	Deram	7	(20)	F L
8	-	Ha Ha Said The Clown	Manfred Mann	Fontana	7		
9	4	Edelweiss	Vince Hill	Columbia	11		
10	-	It's All Over	Cliff Richard	Columbia	6		
11	-	Purple Haze	Jimi Hendrix Experience	Track	8	(65)	
12	2	Penny Lane/Strawberry Fields Forever	Beatles	Parlophone	8	(1)	
13	8	Georgy Girl	Seekers	Columbia	7	(2)	
14	-	Bernadette	Four Tops	Tamla Motown	5	(4)	
15	3	This Is My Song	Petula Clark	Pye	10	(3)	
16	-	I'm Gonna Get Me A Gun	Cat Stevens	Deram	5		
17	18	Memories Are Made Of This	Val Doonican	Decca	5		
18	-	Happy Together	Turtles	London American	6	(1)	F
19	-	I Can Hear The Grass Grow	Move	Deram	6		
20	-	Touch Me Touch Me	Dave Dee, Dozy, Beaky, Mick & Tich	Fontana	3		

◆ Acts making their UK stage debuts included Otis Redding and Sam & Dave (on a Stax Records package show) and The Jeff Beck Group with vocalist Rod Stewart.

◆ The Beatles' album **Sergeant Pepper's Lonely Hearts Club Band** was released to much critical acclaim – it helped shape the future of pop and rock music.

1967

This Mnth	Prev Mnth	Title	Artist	Label	Wks	(US 20 Pos)	
1	2	**Puppet On A String**	Sandie Shaw	Pye	13		
2	-	**Dedicated To The One I Love**	Mamas & The Papas	RCA	10	(2)	
3	1	**Somethin' Stupid**	Nancy & Frank Sinatra	Reprise	11	(1)	
4	-	**Silence Is Golden**	Tremeloes	CBS	10	(11)	
5	-	**The Boat That I Row**	Lulu	Columbia	6		
6	-	**Pictures Of Lily**	Who	Track	6	(51)	
7	-	**Funny Familiar Forgotten Feeling**	Tom Jones	Decca	7	(49)	
8	11	**Purple Haze**	Jimi Hendrix Experience	Track	8	(65)	
9	-	**Seven Drunken Nights**	Dubliners	Major Minor	9		F
10	5	**A Little Bit Me, A Little Bit You**	Monkees	RCA	8	(2)	
11	19	**I Can Hear The Grass Grow**	Move	Deram	6		
12	-	**Waterloo Sunset**	Kinks	Pye	7		
13	-	**Then I Kissed Her**	Beach Boys	Capitol	8		
14	8	**Ha Ha Said The Clown**	Manfred Mann	Fontana	7		
15	-	**Hi-Ho Silver Lining**	Jeff Beck	Columbia	5		F
16	16	**I'm Gonna Get Me A Gun**	Cat Stevens	Deram	5		
17	-	**The Wind Cries Mary**	Jimi Hendrix Experience	Track	5		
18	3	**Release Me**	Engelbert Humperdinck	Decca	15	(4)	F G
19	-	**New York Mining Disaster 1941**	Bee Gees	Polydor	5	(14)	F
20	18	**Happy Together**	Turtles	London American	6	(1)	F

This Mnth	Prev Mnth	Title	Artist	Label	Wks	(US 20 Pos)	
1	-	**A Whiter Shade Of Pale**	Procol Harum	Deram	11	(5)	F
2	4	**Silence Is Golden**	Tremeloes	CBS	10	(11)	
3	12	**Waterloo Sunset**	Kinks	Pye	7		
4	-	**There Goes My Everything**	Engelbert Humperdinck	Decca	13	(20)	
5	-	**The Happening**	Supremes	Tamla Motown	8	(1)	
6	13	**Then I Kissed Her**	Beach Boys	Capitol	8		
7	2	**Dedicated To The One I Love**	Mamas & The Papas	RCA	10	(2)	
8	-	**Sweet Soul Music**	Arthur Conley	Atlantic	9	(2)	F L
9	-	**Carrie-Anne**	Hollies	Parlophone	8	(9)	
10	17	**The Wind Cries Mary**	Jimi Hendrix Experience	Track	5		
11	-	**Okay!**	Dave Dee, Dozy, Beaky, Mick & Tich	Fontana	6		
12	-	**Finchley Central**	New Vaudeville Band	Fontana	6		L
13	9	**Seven Drunken Nights**	Dubliners	Major Minor	9		F
14	6	**Pictures Of Lily**	Who	Track	6	(51)	
15	-	**Paper Sun**	Traffic	Island	5	(94)	F
16	1	**Puppet On A String**	Sandie Shaw	Pye	13		
17	-	**Roses Of Picardy**	Vince Hill	Columbia	4		
18	-	**Groovin'**	Young Rascals	Atlantic	7	(1)	F L
19	3	**Somethin' Stupid**	Nancy & Frank Sinatra	Reprise	11	(1)	
20	19	**New York Mining Disaster 1941**	Bee Gees	Polydor	5	(14)	F

◆ After coming second on five occasions the UK finally won the Eurovision Song Contest thanks to barefoot Sandie Shaw's bouncy 'Puppet On A String'.

◆ The Monkees, who continued adding to their transatlantic toppers, had a very successful British live debut at Wembley.

1967

July 1967

This Mnth	Prev Mnth	Title	Artist	Label	Wks	(US 20 Pos)	
1	1	**A Whiter Shade Of Pale**	Procol Harum	Deram	11	(5)	F
2	-	**Alternate Title**	Monkees	RCA	8		
3	4	**There Goes My Everything**	Engelbert Humperdinck	Decca	13	(20)	
4	-	**She'd Rather Be With Me**	Turtles	London American	10	(3)	
5	-	**It Must Be Him (Seul Sur Son Etoile)**	Vikki Carr	Liberty	10	(3)	F L
6	-	**All You Need Is Love**	Beatles	Parlophone	10	(1)	
7	9	**Carrie-Anne**	Hollies	Parlophone	8	(9)	
8	-	**See Emily Play**	Pink Floyd	Columbia	7		
9	-	**If I Were A Rich Man**	Topol	CBS	6		F L
10	-	**San Francisco (Be Sure To Wear Some Flowers In Your Hair)**	Scott McKenzie	CBS	14	(4)	F L
11	18	**Groovin'**	Young Rascals	Atlantic	7	(1)	F L
12	15	**Paper Sun**	Traffic	Island	5	(94)	F
13	-	**Respect**	Aretha Franklin	Atlantic	5	(1)	F
14	11	**Okay!**	Dave Dee, Dozy, Beaky, Mick & Tich	Fontana	6		
15	-	**Here Come The Nice**	Small Faces	Immediate	6		
16	8	**Sweet Soul Music**	Arthur Conley	Atlantic	9	(2)	F L
17	-	**Seven Rooms Of Gloom**	Four Tops	Tamla Motown	5	(14)	
18	5	**The Happening**	Supremes	Tamla Motown	8	(1)	
19	-	**Don't Sleep In The Subway**	Petula Clark	Pye	4	(5)	
20	-	**You Only Live Twice/Jackson**	Nancy Sinatra	Reprise	5	(44)	

August 1967

This Mnth	Prev Mnth	Title	Artist	Label	Wks	(US 20 Pos)	
1	10	**San Francisco (Be Sure To Wear Some Flowers In Your Hair)**	Scott McKenzie	CBS	14	(4)	F L
2	6	**All You Need Is Love**	Beatles	Parlophone	10	(1)	
3	-	**I'll Never Fall In Love Again**	Tom Jones	Decca	10	(6)	
4	-	**Death Of A Clown**	Dave Davies	Pye	7		F
5	-	**I Was Made To Love Her**	Stevie Wonder	Tamla Motown	9	(2)	
6	5	**It Must Be Him (Seul Sur Son Etoile)**	Vikki Carr	Liberty	10	(3)	F L
7	-	**Up Up And Away**	Johnny Mann Singers	Liberty	7		F L
8	-	**Just Loving You**	Anita Harris	CBS	15		F L
9	4	**She'd Rather Be With Me**	Turtles	London American	10	(3)	
10	-	**Even The Bad Times Are Good**	Tremeloes	CBS	9	(36)	
11	2	**Alternate Title**	Monkees	RCA	8		
12	-	**Creeque Alley**	Mamas & The Papas	RCA	6	(5)	L
13	8	**See Emily Play**	Pink Floyd	Columbia	7		
14	-	**The House That Jack Built**	Alan Price Set	Decca	7		
15	3	**There Goes My Everything**	Engelbert Humperdinck	Decca	13	(20)	
16	-	**Let's Pretend**	Lulu	Columbia	4		
17	-	**Gin House Blues**	Amen Corner	Deram	5		F
18	1	**A Whiter Shade Of Pale**	Procol Harum	Deram	11	(5)	F
19	20	**You Only Live Twice/Jackson**	Nancy Sinatra	Reprise	5	(44)	
20	-	**Pleasant Valley Sunday**	Monkees	RCA	4	(3)	

◆ The UK government banned pirate radio stations and then launched Radio 1 – their own Top 40 station.

◆ Engelbert Humperdinck, one of the few acts not experimenting with psychedelic sounds, earned his second UK million seller of 1967 with 'The Last Waltz'.

◆ Beatles manager Brian Epstein and Bob Dylan's inspiration, folk singer/songwriter Woody Guthrie, died.

1967

This Mnth	Prev Mnth	Title	Artist	Label	Wks (US 20 Pos)	
1	-	The Last Waltz	Engelbert Humperdinck	Decca	20 (25)	G
2	3	I'll Never Fall In Love Again	Tom Jones	Decca	10 (6)	
3	1	San Francisco (Be Sure To Wear Some Flowers In Your Hair)	Scott McKenzie	CBS	14 (4)	F L
4	-	Excerpt From A Teenage Opera	Keith West	Parlophone	11	F L
5	-	Itchycoo Park	Small Faces	Immediate	11 (16)	
6	10	Even The Bad Times Are Good	Tremeloes	CBS	9 (36)	
7	-	Let's Go To San Francisco	Flowerpot Men	Deram	7	F L
8	-	We Love You/Dandelion	Rolling Stones	Decca	6 (14)	
9	8	Just Loving You	Anita Harris	CBS	15	F L
10	-	Heroes And Villains	Beach Boys	Capitol	5 (12)	
11	14	The House That Jack Built	Alan Price Set	Decca	7	
12	5	I Was Made To Love Her	Stevie Wonder	Tamla Motown	9 (2)	
13	-	Reflections	Diana Ross & The Supremes	Tamla Motown	8 (2)	
14	-	Flowers In The Rain	Move	Regal Zonophone	10	
15	-	The Day I Met Marie	Cliff Richard	Columbia	8	
16	2	All You Need Is Love	Beatles	Parlophone	10 (1)	
17	-	Hole In My Shoe	Traffic	Island	10	
18	20	Pleasant Valley Sunday	Monkees	RCA	4 (3)	
19	-	There Must Be A Way	Frankie Vaughan	Columbia	14	L
20	4	Death Of A Clown	Dave Davies	Pye	7	F

1	-	Massachusetts	Bee Gees	Polydor	10 (11)	
2	1	The Last Waltz	Engelbert Humperdinck	Decca	20 (25)	G
3	17	Hole In My Shoe	Traffic	Island	10	
4	14	Flowers In The Rain	Move	Regal Zonophone	10	
5	-	The Letter	Box Tops	Stateside	8 (1)	F
6	4	Excerpt From A Teenage Opera	Keith West	Parlophone	11	F L
7	13	Reflections	Diana Ross & The Supremes	Tamla Motown	8 (2)	
8	19	There Must Be A Way	Frankie Vaughan	Columbia	14	L
9	-	Homburg	Procol Harum	Regal Zonophone	7 (34)	
10	5	Itchycoo Park	Small Faces	Immediate	11 (16)	
11	-	From The Underworld	Herd	Fontana	8	F
12	-	When Will The Good Apples Fall	Seekers	Columbia	6	L
13	15	The Day I Met Marie	Cliff Richard	Columbia	8	
14	7	Let's Go To San Francisco	Flowerpot Men	Deram	7	F L
15	-	Baby, Now That I Found You	Foundations	Pye	9 (11)	F
16	-	Zabadak	Dave Dee, Dozy, Beaky, Mick & Tich	Fontana	8 (52)	
17	-	Ode To Billie Joe	Bobbie Gentry	Capitol	6 (1)	F
18	9	Just Loving You	Anita Harris	CBS	15	F L
19	-	Black Velvet Band	Dubliners	Major Minor	5	
20	2	I'll Never Fall In Love Again	Tom Jones	Decca	10 (6)	

◆ Innovative US act The Mothers Of Invention, whose **Freak Out** album was a milestone in rock, made a successful UK debut.

◆ The Beatles closed the year with 'Hello Goodbye' topping the transatlantic charts. However, in 1967, they were replaced as the world's most successful act by The Monkees, who, among other achievements, chalked up a (still unbeaten) record of four American chart topping albums in one calendar year.

1967

November 1967

This Mnth	Prev Mnth	Title	Artist	Label	Wks (US 20 Pos)	
1	15	**Baby, Now That I Found You**	Foundations	Pye	9 (11)	F
2	1	**Massachusetts**	Bee Gees	Polydor	10 (11)	
3	16	**Zabadak**	Dave Dee, Dozy, Beaky, Mick & Tich	Fontana	8 (52)	
4	-	**Autumn Almanac**	Kinks	Pye	7	
5	2	**The Last Waltz**	Engelbert Humperdinck	Decca	20 (25)	G
6	-	**Love Is All Around**	Troggs	Page One	7 (7)	L
7	11	**From The Underworld**	Herd	Fontana	8	F
8	-	**San Franciscan Nights**	Eric Burdon & The Animals	MGM	5 (9)	
9	9	**Homburg**	Procol Harum	Regal Zonophone	7 (34)	
10	-	**There Is A Mountain**	Donovan	Pye	5 (11)	
11	8	**There Must Be A Way**	Frankie Vaughan	Columbia	14	L
12	-	**Let The Heartaches Begin**	Long John Baldry	Pye	9 (88)	F
13	3	**Hole In My Shoe**	Traffic	Island	10	
14	-	**If The Whole World Stopped Loving**	Val Doonican	Pye	13	
15	-	**I Can See For Miles**	Who	Track	4 (9)	
16	-	**Everybody Knows**	Dave Clark Five	Columbia	8 (43)	
17	4	**Flowers In The Rain**	Move	Regal Zonophone	10	
18	5	**The Letter**	Box Tops	Stateside	8 (1)	F
19	-	**I Feel Love Comin' On**	Felice Taylor	President	6	F L
20	12	**When Will The Good Apples Fall**	Seekers	Columbia	6	L

December 1967

This Mnth	Prev Mnth	Title	Artist	Label	Wks (US 20 Pos)	
1	-	**Hello Goodbye**	Beatles	Parlophone	10 (1)	
2	14	**If The Whole World Stopped Loving**	Val Doonican	Pye	13	
3	12	**Let The Heartaches Begin**	Long John Baldry	Pye	9 (88)	F
4	-	**Something's Gotten Hold Of My Heart**	Gene Pitney	Stateside	9	
5	-	**I'm Comin' Home**	Tom Jones	Decca	12 (57)	
6	16	**Everybody Knows**	Dave Clark Five	Columbia	8 (43)	
7	-	**All My Love**	Cliff Richard	Columbia	8	
8	-	**Careless Hands**	Des O'Connor	Columbia	9	F
9	-	**Daydream Believer**	Monkees	RCA	12 (1)	
10	-	**World**	Bee Gees	Polydor	10	
11	-	**Thank U Very Much**	Scaffold	Parlophone	8 (69)	F
12	-	**Magical Mystery Tour (Double E.P.)**	Beatles	Parlophone	9	
13	6	**Love Is All Around**	Troggs	Page One	7 (7)	L
14	-	**Here We Go Round The Mulberry Bush**	Traffic	Island	7	L
15	5	**The Last Waltz**	Engelbert Humperdinck	Decca	20 (25)	G
16	1	**Baby, Now That I Found You**	Foundations	Pye	9 (11)	F
17	19	**I Feel Love Comin' On**	Felice Taylor	President	6	F L
18	-	**Kites**	Simon Dupree & The Big Sound	Parlophone	8	F L
19	-	**Walk Away Renee**	Four Tops	Tamla Motown	8 (14)	
20	3	**Zabadak**	Dave Dee, Dozy, Beaky etc.	Fontana	8 (52)	

◆ In the year that US record sales first topped the $1 billion mark and, for the first time, albums outsold singles, the gap between the American and British markets widened, with only 25% of Top 20 hits scoring in both countries.

◆ 'To Sir With Love' by Lulu topped the US chart but was only a B-side in the UK.
◆ Critically acclaimed UK underground band Pink Floyd joined burgeoning teen idols Amen Corner and The Move to support headliner Jimi Hendrix on tour.

1968

This Mnth	Prev Mnth	Title	Artist	Label	Wks	(US 20 Pos)	
1	1	Hello Goodbye	Beatles	Parlophone	10	(1)	
2	12	Magical Mystery Tour (Double E.P.)	Beatles	Parlophone	9		
3	-	Ballad Of Bonnie & Clyde	Georgie Fame	CBS	8	(7)	
4	19	Walk Away Renee	Four Tops	Tamla Motown	8	(14)	
5	9	Daydream Believer	Monkees	RCA	12	(1)	
6	5	I'm Comin' Home	Tom Jones	Decca	12	(57)	
7	11	Thank U Very Much	Scaffold	Parlophone	8	(69)	F
8	-	Everlasting Love	Love Affair	CBS	10		F
9	2	If The Whole World Stopped Loving	Val Doonican	Pye	13		
10	10	World	Bee Gees	Polydor	10		
11	18	Kites	Simon Dupree & The Big Sound	Parlophone	8		F L
12	-	Am I That Easy To Forget	Engelbert Humperdinck	Decca	9	(18)	
13	4	Something's Gotten Hold Of My Heart	Gene Pitney	Stateside	9		
14	-	Tin Soldier	Small Faces	Immediate	8	(73)	
15	14	Here We Go Round The Mulberry Bush	Traffic	Island	7		L
16	-	Judy In Disguise (With Glasses)	John Fred & His Playboy Band	Pye International	7	(1)	F L
17	8	Careless Hands	Des O'Connor	Columbia	9		F
18	-	In And Out Of Love	Diana Ross & The Supremes	Tamla Motown	7	(9)	
19	-	Everything I Am	Plastic Penny	Page One	5		F L
20	-	She Wears My Ring	Solomon King	Columbia	11		F L

1	8	Everlasting Love	Love Affair	CBS	10		F
2	-	Mighty Quinn	Manfred Mann	Fontana	8	(10)	
3	12	Am I That Easy To Forget	Engelbert Humperdinck	Decca	9	(18)	
4	-	Bend Me Shape Me	Amen Corner	Deram	9		
5	16	Judy In Disguise (With Glasses)	John Fred & His Playboy Band	Pye International	7	(1)	F L
6	20	She Wears My Ring	Solomon King	Columbia	11		F L
7	-	Suddenly You Love Me	Tremeloes	CBS	8	(44)	
8	-	Gimme Little Sign	Brenton Wood	Liberty	7	(9)	F L
9	3	Ballad Of Bonnie & Clyde	Georgie Fame	CBS	8	(7)	
10	-	Pictures Of Matchstick Men	Status Quo	Pye	7	(12)	F
11	19	Everything I Am	Plastic Penny	Page One	5		F L
12	-	I Can Take Or Leave Your Lovin'	Herman's Hermits	Columbia	6	(22)	
13	-	Darlin'	Beach Boys	Capitol	9	(19)	
14	-	Fire Brigade	Move	Regal Zonophone	8		
15	-	Words	Bee Gees	Polydor	7	(15)	
16	-	Cinderella Rockafella	Esther & Abi Ofarim	Philips	9	(68)	F
17	5	Daydream Believer	Monkees	RCA	12	(1)	
18	-	Don't Stop The Carnival	Alan Price Set	Decca	4		
19	14	Tin Soldier	Small Faces	Immediate	8	(73)	
20	2	Magical Mystery Tour (Double E.P.)	Beatles	Parlophone	9		

◆ Music from *Magical Mystery Tour* kept the Beatles at the top, although the film itself was their first commercial and critical flop. Meanwhile, their previous project, **Sergeant Pepper**, grabbed four Grammies.

◆ Newcomers Love Affair were splashed over the front pages of the tabloids when they admitted that only lead singer Steve Ellis was actually on their chart topping cover of 'Everlasting Love'. This revelation did not stop them being elevated to teen idol status.

March 1968

This Mnth	Prev Mnth	Title	Artist	Label	Wks	(US 20 Pos)	
1	16	**Cinderella Rockafella**	Esther & Abi Ofarim	Philips	9	(68)	F
2	-	**Legend Of Xanadu**	Dave Dee, Dozy, Beaky, Mick & Tich	Fontana	8		
3	14	**Fire Brigade**	Move	Regal Zonophone	8		
4	-	**Rosie**	Don Partridge	Columbia	9		F
5	-	**Jennifer Juniper**	Donovan	Pye	6	(26)	
6	-	**Delilah**	Tom Jones	Decca	11	(15)	
7	2	**Mighty Quinn**	Manfred Mann	Fontana	8	(10)	
8	-	**(Sittin' On) The Dock Of The Bay**	Otis Redding	Stax	8	(1)	
9	-	**Green Tambourine**	Lemon Pipers	Pye International	6	(1)	F L
10	6	**She Wears My Ring**	Solomon King	Columbia	11		F L
11	4	**Bend Me Shape Me**	Amen Corner	Deram	9		
12	10	**Pictures Of Matchstick Men**	Status Quo	Pye	7	(12)	F
13	15	**Words**	Bee Gees	Polydor	7	(15)	
14	-	**Me The Peaceful Heart**	Lulu	Columbia	5	(53)	
15	13	**Darlin'**	Beach Boys	Capitol	9	(19)	
16	-	**Lady Madonna**	Beatles	Parlophone	6	(4)	
17	-	**What A Wonderful World**	Louis Armstrong	HMV	16	(32)	L
18	7	**Suddenly You Love Me**	Tremeloes	CBS	8	(44)	
19	-	**If I Were A Carpenter**	Four Tops	Tamla Motown	6	(20)	
20	8	**Gimme Little Sign**	Brenton Wood	Liberty	7	(9)	F L

April 1968

This Mnth	Prev Mnth	Title	Artist	Label	Wks	(US 20 Pos)	
1	-	**Congratulations**	Cliff Richard	Columbia	9	(99)	
2	17	**What A Wonderful World**	Louis Armstrong	HMV	16	(32)	L
3	6	**Delilah**	Tom Jones	Decca	11	(15)	
4	-	**If I Only Had Time**	John Rowles	MCA	11		F
5	8	**(Sittin' On) The Dock Of The Bay**	Otis Redding	Stax	8	(1)	
6	16	**Lady Madonna**	Beatles	Parlophone	6	(4)	
7	-	**Simon Says**	1910 Fruitgum Co.	Pye International	12	(4)	F L
8	-	**Step Inside Love**	Cilla Black	Parlophone	5		
9	19	**If I Were A Carpenter**	Four Tops	Tamla Motown	6	(20)	
10	-	**Jennifer Eccles**	Hollies	Parlophone	6	(40)	
11	-	**Can't Take My Eyes Off You**	Andy Williams	CBS	9		
12	1	**Cinderella Rockafella**	Esther & Abi Ofarim	Philips	9	(68)	F
13	-	**I Can't Let Maggie Go**	Honeybus	Deram	6		F L
14	-	**Captain Of Your Ship**	Reperata & The Delrons	Bell	5		F L
15	-	**Ain't Nothin' But A Housparty**	Showstoppers	Beacon	9		F L
16	-	**Valleri**	Monkees	RCA	5	(3)	
17	4	**Rosie**	Don Partridge	Columbia	9		F
18	2	**Legend Of Xanadu**	Dave Dee, Dozy, Beaky, Mick & Tich	Fontana	8		
19	-	**Love Is Blue (L'Amour Est Bleu)**	Paul Mauriat	Philips	5	(1)	F L
20	-	**Something Here In My Heart (Keeps A-Tellin' Me No)**	Paper Dolls	Pye	5		F L

◆ Status Quo (who subsequently had more UK chart singles than The Beatles or Stones) debuted on the Top 20. Fellow superstars Genesis released their first single, as did Elton John, described by his label as "1968's greatest new talent".

◆ Pink Floyd, Jethro Tull and Tyrannosaurus Rex appeared at the first free concert in London's Hyde Park.

1968

This Mnth	Prev Mnth	Title	Artist	Label	Wks	(US 20 Pos)	
1	2	What A Wonderful World	Louis Armstrong	HMV	16	(32)	L
2	-	Lazy Sunday	Small Faces	Immediate	7		
3	-	A Man Without Love	Engelbert Humperdinck	Decca	9	(19)	
4	7	Simon Says	1910 Fruitgum Co.	Pye International	12	(4)	F L
5	-	Young Girl	Gary Puckett & The Union Gap	CBS	12	(2)	F
6	11	Can't Take My Eyes Off You	Andy Williams	CBS	9		
7	-	I Don't Want Our Loving To Die	Herd	Fontana	8		L
8	4	If I Only Had Time	John Rowles	MCA	11		F
9	-	Honey	Bobby Goldsboro	UA	11	(1)	F
10	1	Congratulations	Cliff Richard	Columbia	9	(99)	
11	-	White Horses	Jacky	Philips	9		F L
12	10	Jennifer Eccles	Hollies	Parlophone	6	(40)	
13	-	Rainbow Valley	Love Affair	CBS	8		
14	15	Ain't Nothin' But A Houseparty	Showstoppers	Beacon	9		F L
15	13	I Can't Let Maggie Go	Honeybus	Deram	6		F L
16	20	Something Here In My Heart (Keeps A-Tellin' Me No)	Paper Dolls	Pye	5		F L
17	3	Delilah	Tom Jones	Decca	11	(15)	
18	-	Sleepy Joe	Herman's Hermits	Columbia	6	(61)	
19	-	Joanna	Scott Walker	Philips	7		F
20	-	Cry Like A Baby	Box Tops	Bell	5	(2)	L

This Mnth	Prev Mnth	Title	Artist	Label	Wks	(US 20 Pos)	
1	5	Young Girl	Gary Puckett & The Union Gap	CBS	12	(2)	F
2	9	Honey	Bobby Goldsboro	UA	11	(1)	F
3	-	Jumping Jack Flash	Rolling Stones	Decca	9	(3)	
4	3	A Man Without Love	Engelbert Humperdinck	Decca	9	(19)	
5	-	This Wheel's On Fire	Julie Driscoll, Brian Auger & The Trinity	Marmalade	8		F L
6	13	Rainbow Valley	Love Affair	CBS	8		
7	-	Do You Know The Way To San José	Dionne Warwick	Pye International	8	(10)	
8	-	Blue Eyes	Don Partridge	Columbia	8		L
9	-	Hurdy Gurdy Man	Donovan	Pye	7	(5)	
10	7	I Don't Want Our Loving To Die	Herd	Fontana	8		L
11	19	Joanna	Scott Walker	Philips	7		F
12	-	Baby Come Back	Equals	President	12	(32)	F
13	1	What A Wonderful World	Louis Armstrong	HMV	16	(32)	L
14	-	I Pretend	Des O'Connor	Columbia	15		
15	2	Lazy Sunday	Small Faces	Immediate	7		
16	4	Simon Says	1910 Fruitgum Co.	Pye International	12	(4)	F L
17	18	Sleepy Joe	Herman's Hermits	Columbia	6	(61)	
18	-	Lovin' Things	Marmalade	CBS	6		F
19	-	Son Of Hickory Hollers Tramp	O.C. Smith	CBS	9	(40)	F L
20	-	Helule Helule	Tremeloes	CBS	5		

◆ American hits in Britain included: transatlantic No. 1 'Young Girl' by Gary Puckett & The Union Gap, 'Honey ' by Bobby Goldsboro, 'What A Wonderful World' by 66-year-old Louis Armstrong and rock's biggest seller, 'Rock Around The Clock' by Bill Haley.

◆ For a while street busker Don Partridge stopped playing outside theatres and headlined inside, thanks to two successive Top 5 singles, 'Rosie' and 'Blue Eyes'.

July 1968

This Mnth	Prev Mnth	Title	Artist	Label	Wks	(US 20 Pos)	
1	12	**Baby Come Back**	Equals	President	12	(32)	F
2	14	**I Pretend**	Des O'Connor	Columbia	15		
3	19	**Son Of Hickory Hollers Tramp**	O.C. Smith	CBS	9	(40)	F L
4	-	**Yesterday Has Gone**	Cupid's Inspiration	Nems	7		F L
5	-	**Yummy Yummy Yummy**	Ohio Express	Pye International	9	(4)	F L
6	-	**Mony Mony**	Tommy James & The Shondells	Major Minor	11	(3)	F L
7	3	**Jumping Jack Flash**	Rolling Stones	Decca	9	(3)	
8	-	**My Name Is Jack**	Manfred Mann	Fontana	5		
9	-	**MacArthur Park**	Richard Harris	RCA	7	(2)	F L
10	8	**Blue Eyes**	Don Partridge	Columbia	8		L
11	18	**Lovin' Things**	Marmalade	CBS	6		F
12	9	**Hurdy Gurdy Man**	Donovan	Pye	7	(5)	
13	-	**Hush Not A Word To Mary**	John Rowles	MCA	5		L
14	-	**Fire**	Crazy World Of Arthur Brown	Track	10	(2)	F L
15	-	**One More Dance**	Esther & Abi Ofarim	Philips	4		L
16	1	**Young Girl**	Gary Puckett & The Union Gap	CBS	12	(2)	F
17	-	**This Guy's In Love With You**	Herb Alpert	A&M	11	(1)	
18	-	**Mrs. Robinson**	Simon & Garfunkel	CBS	7	(1)	
19	5	**This Wheel's On Fire**	Julie Driscoll, Brian Auger & The Trinity	Marmalade	8		F L
20	-	**I Close My Eyes And Count To Ten**	Dusty Springfield	Philips	6		

August 1968

This Mnth	Prev Mnth	Title	Artist	Label	Wks	(US 20 Pos)	
1	6	**Mony Mony**	Tommy James & The Shondells	Major Minor	11	(3)	F L
2	14	**Fire**	Crazy World Of Arthur Brown	Track	10	(2)	F L
3	17	**This Guy's In Love With You**	Herb Alpert	A&M	11	(1)	
4	2	**I Pretend**	Des O'Connor	Columbia	15		
5	20	**I Close My Eyes And Count To Ten**	Dusty Springfield	Philips	6		
6	-	**Help Yourself**	Tom Jones	Decca	10	(35)	
7	18	**Mrs. Robinson**	Simon & Garfunkel	CBS	7	(1)	
8	-	**Sunshine Girl**	Herman's Hermits	Columbia	8		
9	-	**Dance To The Music**	Sly & The Family Stone	Direction	7	(8)	F
10	-	**Do It Again**	Beach Boys	Capitol	10	(20)	
11	-	**Last Night In Soho**	Dave Dee, Dozy, Beaky, Mick & Tich	Fontana	6		
12	-	**I've Gotta Get A Message To You**	Bee Gees	Polydor	11	(8)	
13	9	**MacArthur Park**	Richard Harris	RCA	7	(2)	F L
14	-	**Keep On**	Bruce Channel	Bell	6		L
15	1	**Baby Come Back**	Equals	President	12	(32)	F
16	-	**High In The Sky**	Amen Corner	Deram	9		
17	-	**Days**	Kinks	Pye	6		
18	5	**Yummy Yummy Yummy**	Ohio Express	Pye International	9	(4)	F L
19	-	**I Say A Little Prayer**	Aretha Franklin	Atlantic	8	(10)	
20	3	**Son Of Hickory Hollers Tramp**	O.C. Smith	CBS	9	(40)	F L

◆ The Beatles launched their own label, Apple, and released their animated film *Yellow Submarine*. Incidentally, the group's No. 1 rivals of 1967, the Monkees, had their last US Top 20 entry with a Leiber & Stoller song, 'D.W. Washburn'.

◆ Cream announced they were splitting up, as did The Yardbirds. The Hollies started to make solo records, Janis Joplin quit Big Brother & The Holding Company, and Dennis Edwards replaced singer David Ruffin in The Temptations.

1968

This Mnth	Prev Mnth	Title	Artist	Label	Wks (US 20 Pos)	
1	12	**I've Gotta Get A Message To You**	Bee Gees	Polydor	11 (8)	
2	10	**Do It Again**	Beach Boys	Capitol	10 (20)	
3	19	**I Say A Little Prayer**	Aretha Franklin	Atlantic	8 (10)	
4	-	**Hold Me Tight**	Johnny Nash	Regal Zonophone	10 (5)	F
5	-	**Hey Jude**	Beatles	Apple	10 (1)	
6	-	**Those Were The Days**	Mary Hopkin	Apple	14 (2)	F
7	3	**This Guy's In Love With You**	Herb Alpert	A&M	11 (1)	
8	16	**High In The Sky**	Amen Corner	Deram	9	
9	6	**Help Yourself**	Tom Jones	Decca	10 (35)	
10	-	**Jesamine**	Casuals	Decca	11	F L
11	-	**On The Road Again**	Canned Heat	Liberty	7 (16)	F
12	-	**Lady Willpower**	Gary Puckett & The Union Gap	CBS	10 (2)	
13	-	**Dream A Little Dream Of Me**	Mama Cass	RCA	7 (12)	F
14	-	**Little Arrows**	Leapy Lee	MCA	13 (16)	F
15	1	**Mony Mony**	Tommy James & The Shondells	Major Minor	11 (3)	F L
16	2	**Fire**	Crazy World Of Arthur Brown	Track	10 (2)	F L
17	-	**Hard To Handle**	Otis Redding	Atlantic	6 (51)	L
18	9	**Dance To The Music**	Sly & The Family Stone	Direction	7 (8)	F
19	-	**Classical Gas**	Mason Williams	Warner	8 (2)	F L
20	8	**Sunshine Girl**	Herman's Hermits	Columbia	8	

This Mnth	Prev Mnth	Title	Artist	Label	Wks (US 20 Pos)	
1	6	**Those Were The Days**	Mary Hopkin	Apple	14 (2)	F
2	5	**Hey Jude**	Beatles	Apple	10 (1)	
3	10	**Jesamine**	Casuals	Decca	11	F L
4	14	**Little Arrows**	Leapy Lee	MCA	13 (16)	F L
5	12	**Lady Willpower**	Gary Puckett & The Union Gap	CBS	10 (2)	
6	-	**My Little Lady**	Tremeloes	CBS	7	
7	-	**Red Balloon**	Dave Clark Five	Columbia	6	
8	-	**A Day Without Love**	Love Affair	CBS	7	
9	4	**Hold Me Tight**	Johnny Nash	Regal Zonophone	10 (5)	F
10	-	**Les Bicyclettes De Belsize**	Engelbert Humperdinck	Decca	7 (31)	
11	19	**Classical Gas**	Mason Williams	Warner	8 (2)	F L
12	-	**Ice In The Sun**	Status Quo	Pye	6 (70)	
13	1	**I've Gotta Get A Message To You**	Bee Gees	Polydor	11 (8)	
14	-	**Light My Fire**	José Feliciano	RCA	8 (3)	F L
15	-	**The Good, The Bad And The Ugly**	Hugo Montenegro & Orchestra	RCA	15 (2)	F L
16	3	**I Say A Little Prayer**	Aretha Franklin	Atlantic	8 (10)	
17	-	**Listen To Me**	Hollies	Parlophone	6	
18	-	**Hello, I Love You**	Doors	Elektra	6 (1)	F
19	8	**High In The Sky**	Amen Corner	Deram	9	
20	-	**Only One Woman**	Marbles	Polydor	8	F L

◆ The Album **Beat of the Brass** ended a fantastic run of eight consecutive Top 10 LPs for Herb Alpert & The Tijuana Brass

◆ John Sebastian left The Lovin' Spoonful, Eric Burdon disbanded The Animals and Graham Nash left The Hollies (to form Crosby, Stills & Nash). Also Mama Cass left The Mamas & The Papas, Peter Tork quit The Monkees and Cream's farewell American tour grossed over $700,000.

November 1968

This Mnth	Prev Mnth	Title	Artist	Label	Wks (US 20 Pos)	
1	15	The Good, The Bad And The Ugly	Hugo Montenegro & Orchestra	RCA	15 (2)	F L
2	-	With A Little Help From My Friends	Joe Cocker	Regal Zonophone	8 (68)	F
3	-	Eloise	Barry Ryan	MGM	9 (86)	F L
4	1	Those Were The Days	Mary Hopkin	Apple	14 (2)	F
5	-	This Old Heart Of Mine	Isley Brothers	Tamla Motown	10 (12)	F
6	20	Only One Woman	Marbles	Polydor	8	F L
7	-	All Along The Watchtower	Jimi Hendrix Experience	Track	6 (20)	
8	14	Light My Fire	Jose Feliciano	RCA	8 (3)	F L
9	-	Breakin' Down The Walls Of Heartache	Johnny Johnson & The Bandwagon	Direction	11	F
10	4	Little Arrows	Leapy Lee	MCA	13 (16)	F L
11	3	Jesamine	Casuals	Decca	11	F L
12	2	Hey Jude	Beatles	Apple	10 (1)	
13	-	Elenore	Turtles	London American	5 (6)	L
14	10	Les Bicyclettes De Belsize	Engelbert Humperdinck	Decca	7 (31)	
15	-	Ain't Got No - I Got Life/ Do What You Gotta Do	Nina Simone	RCA	12 (94)	F
16	-	Lily The Pink	Scaffold	Parlophone	12	
17	17	Listen To Me	Hollies	Parlophone	6	
18	6	My Little Lady	Tremeloes	CBS	7	
19	8	A Day Without Love	Love Affair	CBS	7	
20	-	Mexico	Long John Baldry	Pye	4	L

December 1968

This Mnth	Prev Mnth	Title	Artist	Label	Wks (US 20 Pos)	
1	16	Lily The Pink	Scaffold	Parlophone	12	
2	15	Ain't Got No - I Got Life/ Do What You Gotta Do	Nina Simone	RCA	12 (94)	F
3	1	The Good, The Bad And The Ugly	Hugo Montenegro & Orchestra	RCA	15 (2)	F L
4	-	One Two Three O'Leary	Des O'Connor	Columbia	9	
5	-	Build Me Up Buttercup	Foundations	Pye	9 (3)	
6	-	I'm The Urban Spaceman	Bonzo Dog Doo-Dah Band	Liberty	10	F L
7	5	This Old Heart Of Mine	Isley Brothers	Tamla Motown	10 (12)	F
8	9	Breakin' Down The Walls Of Heartache	Johnny Johnson & The Bandwagon	Direction	11	F
9	-	Race With The Devil	Gun	CBS	7	F L
10	-	I'm A Tiger	Lulu	Columbia	10	
11	-	Sabre Dance	Love Sculpture	Parlophone	8	F L
12	3	Eloise	Barry Ryan	MGM	9 (86)	F L
13	-	May I Have The Next Dream With You	Malcolm Roberts	Major Minor	8	F
14	-	Ob-La-Di Ob-La-Da	Marmalade	CBS	10	
15	-	Harper Valley P.T.A.	Jeannie C. Riley	Polydor	5 (1)	F L
16	13	Elenore	Turtles	London American	5 (6)	L
17	-	Albatross	Fleetwood Mac	Blue Horizon	13	F
18	-	Private Number	Judy Clay & William Bell	Stax	9 (75)	F L
19	-	A Minute Of Your Time	Tom Jones	Decca	7 (48)	
20	7	All Along The Watchtower	Jimi Hendrix Experience	Track	6 (20)	

◆ Double album, **The Beatles**, topped the charts, and the group's seven minute single, 'Hey Jude', amassed world sales of five million. The first solo Beatle LPs were released by George and John, and a single on their Apple imprint, 'Those Were The Days' by Mary Hopkin, became an international hit.

1969

This Mnth	Prev Mnth	Title	Artist	Label	Wks	(US 20 Pos)	
1	14	**Ob-La-Di Ob-La-Da**	Marmalade	CBS	10		
2	1	**Lily The Pink**	Scaffold	Parlophone	12		
3	17	**Albatross**	Fleetwood Mac	Blue Horizon	13		F
4	5	**Build Me Up Buttercup**	Foundations	Pye	9	(3)	
5	6	**I'm The Urban Spaceman**	Bonzo Dog Doo-Dah Band	Liberty	10		F L
6	-	**For Once In My Life**	Stevie Wonder	Tamla Motown	10	(2)	
7	11	**Sabre Dance**	Love Sculpture	Parlophone	8		F L
8	-	**Something's Happening**	Herman's Hermits	Columbia	8		
9	2	**Ain't Got No - I Got Life/ Do What You Gotta Do**	Nina Simone	RCA	12	(94)	F
10	-	**Son-Of-A Preacher Man**	Dusty Springfield	Philips	6	(10)	
11	18	**Private Number**	Judy Clay & William Bell	Stax	9	(75)	F L
12	4	**One Two Three O'Leary**	Des O'Connor	Columbia	9		
13	-	**Blackberry Way**	Move	Regal Zonophone	8		
14	10	**I'm A Tiger**	Lulu	Columbia	10		
15	-	**Fox On The Run**	Manfred Mann	Fontana	6	(97)	
16	9	**Race With The Devil**	Gun	CBS	7		F L
17	3	**The Good, The Bad And The Ugly**	Hugo Montenegro & Orchestra	RCA	15	(2)	F L
18	-	**Love Child**	Diana Ross & The Supremes	Tamla Motown	9	(1)	
19	-	**Stop Her On Sight (SOS)/ Headline News**	Edwin Starr	Polydor	5	(48)	F
20	19	**A Minute Of Your Time**	Tom Jones	Decca	7	(48)	

This Mnth	Prev Mnth	Title	Artist	Label	Wks	(US 20 Pos)	
1	3	**Albatross**	Fleetwood Mac	Blue Horizon	13		F
2	13	**Blackberry Way**	Move	Regal Zonophone	8		
3	6	**For Once In My Life**	Stevie Wonder	Tamla Motown	10	(2)	
4	-	**Dancing In The Street**	Martha & The Vandellas	Tamla Motown	7		F
5	-	**You Got Soul**	Johnny Nash	Major Minor	6	(58)	
6	-	**Please Don't Go**	Donald Peers	Columbia	9		F L
7	1	**Ob-La-Di Ob-La-Da**	Marmalade	CBS	10		
8	-	**I'm Gonna Make You Love Me**	Diana Ross & The Supremes & The Temptations	Tamla Motown	7	(2)	
9	-	**To Love Somebody**	Nina Simone	RCA	5		
10	-	**(If Paradise Is) Half As Nice**	Amen Corner	Immediate	7		
11	15	**Fox On The Run**	Manfred Mann	Fontana	6	(97)	
12	-	**Where Do You Go To My Lovely**	Peter Sarstedt	UA	10	(70)	F
13	8	**Something's Happening**	Herman's Hermits	Columbia	8		
14	-	**I Guess I'll Always Love You**	Isley Brothers	Tamla Motown	5	(61)	
15	11	**Private Number**	Judy Clay & William Bell	Stax	9	(75)	F L
16	19	**Stop Her On Sight (SOS)/ Headline News**	Edwin Starr	Polydor	5	(48)	F
17	-	**The Way It Used To Be**	Engelbert Humperdinck	Decca	8	(42)	
18	-	**I'll Pick A Rose For My Rose**	Marv Johnson	Tamla Motown	6		L
19	2	**Lily The Pink**	Scaffold	Parlophone	12		
20	-	**Mrs. Robinson (E.P.)**	Simon & Garfunkel	CBS	1		

◆ Martha & The Vandellas' 1964 American hit 'Dancing In The Streets' finally reached the UK Top 20 as did label-mates The Isley Brothers' 1966 recording of 'I Guess I'll Always Love You'.

◆ Led Zeppelin debuted in the US (supported by fellow newcomers Jethro Tull). They would become one of the biggest selling and most influential acts of all time.

1969

March 1969

This Mnth	Prev Mnth	Title	Artist	Label	Wks	(US 20 Pos)	
1	12	**Where Do You Go To My Lovely**	Peter Sarstedt	UA	10	(70)	F
2	-	**Surround Yourself With Sorrow**	Cilla Black	Parlophone	9		
3	-	**I Heard It Through The Grapevine**	Marvin Gaye	Tamla Motown	10	(1)	
4	17	**The Way It Used To Be**	Engelbert Humperdinck	Decca	8	(42)	
5	6	**Please Don't Go**	Donald Peers	Columbia	9		F L
6	-	**Gentle On My Mind**	Dean Martin	Reprise	12		L
7	-	**Wichita Lineman**	Glen Campbell	Ember	6	(3)	F
8	-	**Monsieur Dupont**	Sandie Shaw	Pye	8		L
9	10	**(If Paradise Is) Half As Nice**	Amen Corner	Immediate	7		
10	-	**First Of May**	Bee Gees	Polydor	6	(37)	
11	8	**I'm Gonna Make You Love Me**	Diana Ross & The Supremes & The Temptations	Tamla Motown	7	(2)	
12	-	**You've Lost That Lovin' Feelin'**	Righteous Brothers	London American	6		
13	-	**Sorry Suzanne**	Hollies	Parlophone	7	(56)	
14	-	**If I Can Dream**	Elvis Presley	RCA	6	(12)	
15	-	**Good Times (Better Times)**	Cliff Richard	Columbia	7		
16	4	**Dancing In The Street**	Martha & The Vandellas	Tamla Motown	7		F
17	18	**I'll Pick A Rose For My Rose**	Marv Johnson	Tamla Motown	6		L
18	-	**Games People Play**	Joe South	Capitol	8	(12)	F L
19	2	**Blackberry Way**	Move	Regal Zonophone	8		
20	1	**Albatross**	Fleetwood Mac	Blue Horizon	13		F

April 1969

This	Prev	Title	Artist	Label	Wks	(US)	
1	3	**I Heard It Through The Grapevine**	Marvin Gaye	Tamla Motown	10	(1)	
2	-	**Israelites**	Desmond Dekker & The Aces	Pyramid	8	(9)	
3	6	**Gentle On My Mind**	Dean Martin	Reprise	12		L
4	-	**Boom Bang-A-Bang**	Lulu	Columbia	7		
5	-	**Goodbye**	Mary Hopkin	Apple	9	(13)	
6	13	**Sorry Suzanne**	Hollies	Parlophone	7	(56)	
7	-	**In The Bad Bad Old Days**	Foundations	Pye	7	(51)	L
8	-	**Pinball Wizard**	Who	Track	8	(19)	
9	18	**Games People Play**	Joe South	Capitol	8	(12)	F L
10	-	**Windmills Of Your Mind**	Noel Harrison	Reprise	9		F L
11	8	**Monsieur Dupont**	Sandie Shaw	Pye	8		L
12	-	**I Can Hear Music**	Beach Boys	Capitol	7	(24)	
13	2	**Surround Yourself With Sorrow**	Cilla Black	Parlophone	9		
14	1	**Where Do You Go To My Lovely**	Peter Sarstedt	UA	10	(70)	F
15	-	**Get Back**	Beatles with Billy Preston	Apple	10	(1)	
16	-	**Come Back And Shake Me**	Clodagh Rodgers	RCA	8		F
17	-	**Harlem Shuffle**	Bob & Earl	Island	7	(44)	F L
18	-	**Cupid**	Johnny Nash	Major Minor	6	(39)	
19	-	**Get Ready**	Temptations	Tamla Motown	5	(29)	
20	10	**First Of May**	Bee Gees	Polydor	6	(37)	

◆ Cream's **Goodbye Cream** album was a Top 3 entry - although the film of the same name was panned. Ex-Cream members Eric Clapton and Ginger Baker were planning a new group (Blind Faith) with Stevie Winwood.

◆ Headliners at the first Country Music Festival in Britain included George Jones, Tammy Wynette, Conway Twitty and Loretta Lynn. Fellow Nashville superstar Johnny Cash appeared on a TV special with Bob Dylan.

1969

This Mnth	Prev Mnth	Title	Artist	Label	Wks	(US 20 Pos)	
1	15	**Get Back**	Beatles with Billy Preston	Apple	10	(1)	
2	-	**Man Of The World**	Fleetwood Mac	Immediate	9		
3	-	**My Sentimental Friend**	Herman's Hermits	Columbia	7		
4	5	**Goodbye**	Mary Hopkin	Apple	9	(13)	
5	16	**Come Back And Shake Me**	Clodagh Rodgers	RCA	8		F
6	-	**My Way**	Frank Sinatra	Reprise	9	(27)	
7	-	**Behind A Painted Smile**	Isley Brothers	Tamla Motown	7		
8	8	**Pinball Wizard**	Who	Track	8	(19)	
9	2	**Israelites**	Desmond Dekker & The Aces	Pyramid	8	(9)	
10	-	**Dizzy**	Tommy Roe	Stateside	10	(1)	L
11	-	**The Boxer**	Simon & Garfunkel	CBS	7	(7)	
12	-	**(I'm A) Road Runner**	Jr. Walker & The All Stars	Tamla Motown	6	(20)	F
13	17	**Harlem Shuffle**	Bob & Earl	Island	7	(44)	F L
14	18	**Cupid**	Johnny Nash	Major Minor	6	(39)	
15	-	**Ragamuffin Man**	Manfred Mann	Fontana	6		
16	3	**Gentle On My Mind**	Dean Martin	Reprise	12		L
17	-	**Love Me Tonight**	Tom Jones	Decca	6	(13)	
18	10	**Windmills Of Your Mind**	Noel Harrison	Reprise	9		F L
19	-	**Aquarius/Let The Sunshine In (Medley)**	Fifth Dimension	Liberty	4	(1)	F
20	-	**I'm Living In Shame**	Diana Ross & The Supremes	Tamla Motown	3	(10)	

This Mnth	Prev Mnth	Title	Artist	Label	Wks	(US 20 Pos)	
1	-	**Ballad Of John And Yoko**	Beatles	Apple	8	(8)	
2	10	**Dizzy**	Tommy Roe	Stateside	10	(1)	L
3	-	**Oh Happy Day**	Edwin Hawkins Singers	Buddah	8	(4)	F L
4	-	**Time Is Tight**	Booker T. & The M.G.'s	Stax	10	(6)	F
5	1	**Get Back**	Beatles with Nilly Preston	Apple	10	(1)	
6	6	**My Way**	Frank Sinatra	Reprise	9	(27)	
7	-	**Living In The Past**	Jethro Tull	Island	6	(11)	F
8	-	**The Tracks Of My Tears**	Smokey Robinson & The Miracles	Tamla Motown	6		F
9	2	**Man Of The World**	Fleetwood Mac	Immediate	9		
10	11	**The Boxer**	Simon & Garfunkel	CBS	7	(7)	
11	-	**(Your Love Keeps Lifting Me) Higher And Higher**	Jackie Wilson	MCA	6	(6)	
12	-	**Big Ship**	Cliff Richard	Columbia	5		
13	-	**In The Ghetto**	Elvis Presley	RCA	11	(3)	
14	15	**Ragamuffin Man**	Manfred Mann	Fontana	6		
15	17	**Love Me Tonight**	Tom Jones	Decca	6	(13)	
16	-	**Something In The Air**	Thunderclap Newman	Track	8	(37)	F L
17	3	**My Sentimental Friend**	Herman's Hermits	Columbia	7		
18	-	**I'd Rather Go Blind**	Chicken Shack	Blue Horizon	5		F L
19	-	**Galveston**	Glen Campbell	Ember	5	(4)	
20	7	**Behind A Painted Smile**	Isley Brothers	Tamla Motown	7		

◆ Shortly after marrying Bee Gee Maurice Gibb, Lulu won the Eurovision Song Contest (in an unprecedented four-way tie!) with 'Boom Bang-A-Bang'. The victory did not help her career, as this archetypal entry was her last major UK hit for five years.

◆ Blind Faith's debut show in London's Hyde Park was watched by a crowd of 150,000.

◆ Meanwhile, the first successful rock opera *Tommy* by The Who simultaneously entered the UK and US album charts.

July 1969

This Mnth	Prev Mnth	Title	Artist	Label	Wks	(US 20 Pos)	
1	16	**Something In The Air**	Thunderclap Newman	Track	8	(37)	F L
2	13	**In The Ghetto**	Elvis Presley	RCA	11	(3)	
3	-	**Hello Susie**	Amen Corner	Immediate	6		L
4	-	**Way Of Life**	Family Dogg	Bell	8		F L
5	1	**Ballad Of John And Yoko**	Beatles	Apple	8	(8)	
6	-	**Break Away**	Beach Boys	Capitol	6	(63)	
7	-	**Honky Tonk Women**	Rolling Stones	Decca	12	(1)	
8	-	**Proud Mary**	Creedence Clearwater Revival	Liberty	6	(2)	F
9	7	**Living In The Past**	Jethro Tull	Island	6	(11)	F
10	-	**Give Peace A Chance**	Plastic Ono Band	Apple	7	(14)	F
11	-	**It Mek**	Desmond Dekker & The Aces	Pyramid	5		
12	4	**Time Is Tight**	Booker T. & The M.G.'s	Stax	10	(6)	F
13	-	**Lights Of Cincinatti**	Scott Walker	Philips	5		L
14	-	**Baby Make It Soon**	Marmalade	CBS	7		
15	3	**Oh Happy Day**	Edwin Hawkins Singers	Buddah	8	(4)	F L
16	-	**Frozen Orange Juice**	Peter Sarstedt	UA	4		L
17	-	**Gimme Gimme Good Lovin'**	Crazy Elephant	Major Minor	5	(12)	F L
18	-	**Saved By The Bell**	Robin Gibb	Polydor	10		F L
19	12	**Big Ship**	Cliff Richard	Columbia	5		
20	-	**That's The Way God Planned It**	Billy Preston	Apple	6	(62)	F

August 1969

This Mnth	Prev Mnth	Title	Artist	Label	Wks	(US 20 Pos)	
1	7	**Honky Tonk Women**	Rolling Stones	Decca	12	(1)	
2	18	**Saved By The Bell**	Robin Gibb	Polydor	10		F L
3	-	**Make Me An Island**	Joe Dolan	Pye	10		F
4	10	**Give Peace A Chance**	Plastic Ono Band	Apple	7	(14)	F
5	-	**My Cherie Amour**	Stevie Wonder	Tamla Motown	9	(4)	
6	-	**Goodnight Midnight**	Clodagh Rodgers	RCA	8		
7	-	**Conversations**	Cilla Black	Parlophone	7		
8	2	**In The Ghetto**	Elvis Presley	RCA	11	(3)	
9	-	**In The Year 2525 (Exordium & Terminus)**	Zager & Evans	RCA	9	(1)	F L
10	-	**Bringing On Back The Good Times**	Love Affair	CBS	6		L
11	-	**Early In The Morning**	Vanity Fare	Page One	6	(12)	
12	-	**Too Busy Thinking About My Baby**	Marvin Gaye	Tamla Motown	8	(4)	
13	-	**Wet Dream**	Max Romeo	Unity	6		F L
14	14	**Baby Make It Soon**	Marmalade	CBS	7		
15	1	**Something In The Air**	Thunderclap Newman	Track	8	(37)	F L
16	20	**That's The Way God Planned It**	Billy Preston	Apple	6	(62)	F
17	11	**It Mek**	Desmond Dekker & The Aces	Pyramid	5		
18	-	**Viva Bobbie Joe**	Equals	President	8		
19	-	**Goo Goo Barabajagal (Love Is Hot)**	Donovan & Jeff Beck Group	Pye	4	(36)	L
20	-	**Curly**	Move	Regal Zonophone	7		

◆ The Rolling Stones attracted 250,000 fans to Hyde Park – during the show they paid tribute to ex-member Brian Jones who had drowned just days before. Other British shows included the Isle of Wight Festival headlined by Bob Dylan, and The National Jazz & Blues Festival featuring The Who, Yes and King Crimson.

1969

This Mnth	Prev Mnth	Title	Artist	Label	Wks	(US 20 Pos)	
1	-	Bad Moon Rising	Creedence Clearwater Revival	Liberty	11	(2)	
2	9	In The Year 2525 (Exordium & Terminus)	Zager & Evans	RCA	9	(1)	F L
3	-	Don't Forget To Remember	Bee Gees	Polydor	11	(73)	
4	-	Je T'Aime...Moi Non Plus	Jane Birkin & Serge Gainsbourg	Fontana/ Major Minor	13	(58)	F L
5	-	Natural Born Bugie	Humble Pie	Immediate	7		F L
6	12	Too Busy Thinking About My Baby	Marvin Gaye	Tamla Motown	8	(4)	
7	18	Viva Bobbie Joe	Equals	President	8		
8	5	My Cherie Amour	Stevie Wonder	Tamla Motown	9	(4)	
9	1	Honky Tonk Women	Rolling Stones	Decca	12	(1)	
10	-	Good Morning Starshine	Oliver	CBS	10	(3)	F L
11	-	I'll Never Fall In Love Again	Bobbie Gentry	Capitol	9		
12	2	Saved By The Bell	Robin Gibb	Polydor	10		F L
13	3	Make Me An Island	Joe Dolan	Pye	10		F
14	-	A Boy Named Sue	Johnny Cash	CBS	9	(2)	F
15	20	Curly	Move	Regal Zonophone	7		
16	11	Early In The Morning	Vanity Fare	Page One	6	(12)	
17	-	It's Getting Better	Mama Cass	Stateside	6	(30)	L
18	-	Throw Down A Line	Cliff Richard	Columbia	6		
19	-	I'm A Better Man	Engelbert Humperdinck	Decca	4	(38)	
20	-	Cloud Nine	Temptations	Tamla Motown	3	(6)	

This Mnth	Prev Mnth	Title	Artist	Label	Wks	(US 20 Pos)	
1	4	Je T'Aime...Moi Non Plus	Jane Birkin & Serge Gainsbourg	Fontana/ Major Minor	13	(58)	F L
2	11	I'll Never Fall In Love Again	Bobbie Gentry	Capitol	9		
3	14	A Boy Named Sue	Johnny Cash	CBS	9	(2)	F
4	-	Lay Lady Lay	Bob Dylan	CBS	7	(7)	
5	1	Bad Moon Rising	Creedence Clearwater Revival	Liberty	11	(2)	
6	-	I'm Gonna Make You Mine	Lou Christie	Buddah	8	(10)	L
7	10	Good Morning Starshine	Oliver	CBS	10	(3)	F L
8	-	Nobody's Child	Karen Young	Major Minor	12		F L
9	3	Don't Forget To Remember	Bee Gees	Polydor	11	(73)	
10	18	Throw Down A Line	Cliff Richard	Columbia	6		
11	17	It's Getting Better	Mama Cass	Stateside	6	(30)	L
12	-	He Ain't Heavy, He's My Brother	Hollies	Parlophone	8	(7)	
13	-	Space Oddity	David Bowie	Philips	8	(15)	F
14	-	Oh Well	Fleetwood Mac	Reprise	10	(55)	
15	-	Sugar Sugar	Archies	RCA	17	(1)	F L
16	-	Hare Krishna	Radha Krishna Temple	Apple	5		F L
17	2	In The Year 2525 (Exordium & Terminus)	Zager & Evans	RCA	9	(1)	F L
18	5	Natural Born Bugie	Humble Pie	Immediate	7		F L
19	-	Do What You Gotta Do	Four Tops	Tamla Motown	1		
20	7	Viva Bobbie Joe	Equals	President	8		

◆ nitially Zager & Evans only pressed 1000 copies of their pessimistic peek into the future, 'In The Year 2525'. As in the best fairy tales it sold five million copies and topped the charts.

◆ As the year closed, Elton John first collaborated with songwriter Bernie Taupin, Rod Stewart joined The Faces and Jimi Hendrix unveiled his Band Of Gypsies.

November 1969

This Mnth	Prev Mnth	Title	Artist	Label	Wks	(US 20 Pos)	
1	15	**Sugar Sugar**	Archies	RCA	17	(1)	F L
2	14	**Oh Well**	Fleetwood Mac	Reprise	10	(55)	
3	-	**The Return Of Django**	Upsetters	Upsetter	8		F L
4	-	**(Call Me) Number One**	Tremeloes	CBS	11		
5	12	**He Ain't Heavy, He's My Brother**	Hollies	Parlophone	**8**	(7)	
6	8	**Nobody's Child**	Karen Young	Major Minor	13		F L
7	-	**Wonderful World Beautiful People**	Jimmy Cliff	Trojan	9	(25)	F
8	6	**I'm Gonna Make You Mine**	Lou Christie	Buddah	8	(10)	L
9	-	**Something/Come Together**	Beatles	Apple	9	(1)	
10	-	**Love's Been Good To Me**	Frank Sinatra	Reprise	7	(75)	
11	13	**Space Oddity**	David Bowie	Philips	8	(15)	F
12	-	**Delta Lady**	Joe Cocker	Regal Zonophone	5	(69)	
13	-	**Sweet Dream**	Jethro Tull	Chrysalis	6		
14	2	**I'll Never Fall In Love Again**	Bobbie Gentry	Capitol	10		
15	-	**Ruby, Don't Take Your Love To Town**	Kenny Rogers & The First Edition	Reprise	16	(6)	F
16	-	**Yester-Me, Yester-You, Yesterday**	Stevie Wonder	Tamla Motown	9	(7)	
17	-	**What Does It Take To Win Your Love**	Jr. Walker & The All Stars	Tamla Motown	5	(4)	
18	3	**A Boy Named Sue**	Johnny Cash	CBS	9	(2)	F
19	-	**Cold Turkey**	Plastic Ono Band	Apple	5	(30)	
20	1	**Je T'Aime...Moi Non Plus**	Jane Birkin & Serge Gainsbourg	Fontana/MajorMinor	13	(58)	F L

December 1969

1	1	**Sugar Sugar**	Archies	RCA	17	(1)	F L
2	15	**Ruby, Don't Take Your Love To Town**	Kenny Rogers & The First Edition	Reprise	16	(6)	F
3	-	**Two Little Boys**	Rolf Harris	Columbia	16		
4	16	**Yester-Me, Yester-You, Yesterday**	Stevie Wonder	Tamla Motown	**9**	(7)	
5	-	**Melting Pot**	Blue Mink	Philips	10		F
6	4	**(Call Me) Number One**	Tremeloes	CBS	11		
7	-	**Suspicious Minds**	Elvis Presley	RCA	11	(1)	
8	-	**Winter World Of Love**	Engelbert Humperdinck	Decca	9	(16)	
9	-	**Liquidator**	Harry J. & The All Stars	Trojan	13		F L
10	-	**All I Have To Do Is Dream**	Bobbie Gentry & GlenCampbell	Capitol	10	(27)	L
11	-	**Onion Song**	Marvin Gaye & Tammi Terrell	Tamla Motown	8	(50)	L
12	9	**Something/Come Together**	Beatles	Apple	9	(1)	
13	7	**Wonderful World Beautiful People**	Jimmy Cliff	Trojan	9	(25)	F
14	-	**Tracy**	Cuff Links	MCA	9	(9)	F
15	-	**Love Is All**	Malcolm Roberts	Major Minor	6		L
16	-	**Durham Town (The Leavin')**	Roger Whittaker	Columbia	9		F
17	2	**Oh Well**	Fleetwood Mac	Reprise	10	(55)	
18	-	**Without Love**	Tom Jones	Decca	6	(5)	
19	13	**Sweet Dream**	Jethro Tull	Chrysalis	6		
20	6	**Nobody's Child**	Karen Young	Major Minor	13		F L

◆ The Rolling Stones toured the US for the first time in three years. Their record breaking tour was marred by the death of a fan during their set at Altamont. The festival attracted 300,000 people.

◆ Jane Birkin and Serge Gainsbourg, survived both a BBC ban and being dropped by its original label. Their orgasmic ode became the first foreign language record to top the UK chart.

1970

This Mnth	Prev Mnth	Title	Artist	Label	Wks	(US 20 Pos)	
1	3	Two Little Boys	Rolf Harris	Columbia	16		
2	2	Ruby, Don't Take Your Love To Town	Kenny Rogers & First Edition	Reprise	16	(6)	F
3	10	All I Have To Do Is Dream	Bobbie Gentry & Glen Campbell	Capitol	10	(27)	L
4	7	Suspicious Minds	Elvis Presley	RCA	11	(1)	
5	14	Tracy	Cuff Links	MCA	9	(9)	F
6	1	Sugar Sugar	Archies	RCA	17	(1)	F L
7	5	Melting Pot	Blue Mink	Philips	10		F
8	-	Good Old Rock 'n' Roll	Dave Clark Five	Columbia	8		
9	-	Reflections Of My Life	Marmalade	Decca	7	(10)	
10	-	Come And Get It	Badfinger	Apple	7	(7)	F
11	4	Yester-Me, Yester-You, Yesterday	Stevie Wonder	Tamla Motown	9	(7)	
12	18	Without Love	Tom Jones	Decca	6	(5)	
13	16	Durham Town (The Leavin')	Roger Whittaker	Columbia	9		F
14	9	Liquidator	Harry J. & The All Stars	Trojan	13		F L
15	-	Love Grows (Where My Rosemary Goes)	Edison Lighthouse	Bell	10	(5)	F L
16	-	Friends	Arrival	Decca	5		F
17	8	Winter World Of Love	Engelbert Humperdinck	Decca	9	(16)	
18	11	Onion Song	Marvin Gaye & Tammi Terrell	Tamla Motown	8	(50)	
19	-	Someday We'll Be Together	Diana Ross & The Supremes	Tamla Motown	5	(1)	
20	-	Leavin' On A Jet Plane	Peter, Paul & Mary	Warner	9	(1)	L

This Mnth	Prev Mnth	Title	Artist	Label	Wks	(US 20 Pos)	
1	15	Love Grows (Where My Rosemary Goes)	Edison Lighthouse	Bell	10	(5)	F L
2	20	Leavin' On A Jet Plane	Peter, Paul & Mary	Warner	9	(1)	L
3	-	Let's Work Together	Canned Heat	Liberty	9	(26)	L
4	-	The Witch's Promise/Teacher	Jethro Tull	Chrysalis	5		
5	-	Temma Harbour	Mary Hopkin	Apple	6	(39)	
6	1	Two Little Boys	Rolf Harris	Columbia	16		
7	-	I Want You Back	Jackson Five	Tamla Motown	9	(1)	F
8	10	Come And Get It	Badfinger	Apple	7	(7)	F
9	9	Reflections Of My Life	Marmalade	Decca	7	(10)	
10	-	Wand'rin' Star	Lee Marvin	Paramount	11		F L
11	-	Venus	Shocking Blue	Penny Farthing	5	(1)	F L
12	-	I'm A Man	Chicago	CBS	6	(49)	F
13	-	Instant Karma	Lennon, Ono & The Plastic Ono Band	Apple	6	(3)	
14	2	Ruby, Don't Take Your Love To Town	Kenny Rogers & First Edition	Reprise	16	(6)	F
15	-	I Can't Get Next To You	Temptations	Tamla Motown	5	(1)	
16	16	Friends	Arrival	Decca	5		F
17	-	My Baby Loves Lovin'	White Plains	Deram	5	(13)	F
18	-	Years May Come, Years May Go	Herman's Hermits	Columbia	7		
19	3	All I Have To Do Is Dream	Bobbie Gentry & Glen Campbell	Capitol	10	(27)	L
20	-	United We Stand	Brotherhood Of Man	Deram	6	(13)	F

◆ American Ron Dante was the lead vocalist of transatlantic hit makers The Archies and The Cuff Links, while Englishman Tony Burrows sang in three transatlantic hit acts, Edison Lighthouse, White Plains and Brotherhood Of Man.

◆ Davy Jones quit The Monkees, British teen idol Steve Ellis left Love Affair and Joe Cocker split from the Grease Band before joining the *Mad Dogs And Englishmen* tour.

March 1970

This Mnth	Prev Mnth	Title	Artist	Label	Wks	(US 20 Pos)	
1	10	Wand'rin' Star	Lee Marvin	Paramount	11		F L
2	-	Bridge Over Troubled Water	Simon & Garfunkel	CBS	13	(1)	L
3	7	I Want You Back	Jackson Five	Tamla Motown	9	(1)	F
4	-	Let It Be	Beatles	Apple	6	(1)	
5	3	Let's Work Together	Canned Heat	Liberty	9	(26)	L
6	13	Instant Karma	Lennon/Ono/Plastic Ono Band	Apple	6	(3)	
7	-	That Same Old Feeling	Pickettywitch	Pye	8	(67)	F
8	18	Years May Come, Years May Go	Herman's Hermits	Columbia	7		
9	1	Love Grows (Where My Rosemary Goes)	Edison Lighthouse	Bell	10	(5)	F L
10	-	Na Na Hey Hey Kiss Him Goodbye	Steam	Fontana	6	(1)	F L
11	-	Don't Cry Daddy	Elvis Presley	RCA	7	(6)	
12	-	Can't Help Falling In Love	Andy Williams	CBS	11	(88)	
13	-	Raindrops Keep Fallin' On My Head	Sacha Distel	Warner	5		F L
14	20	United We Stand	Brotherhood Of Man	Deram	6	(13)	F
15	-	Something's Burning	Kenny Rogers & First Edition	Reprise	8	(11)	
16	-	Everybody Get Together	Dave Clark Five	Columbia	5		L
17	2	Leavin' On A Jet Plane	Peter, Paul & Mary	Warner	9	(1)	L
18	17	My Baby Loves Lovin'	White Plains	Deram	5	(13)	F
19	-	Young Gifted And Black	Bob & Marcia	Harry J.	8		F
20	-	Knock Knock Who's There	Mary Hopkin	Apple	7	(92)	

April 1970

This Mnth	Prev Mnth	Title	Artist	Label	Wks	(US 20 Pos)	
1	2	Bridge Over Troubled Water	Simon & Garfunkel	CBS	13	(1)	L
2	12	Can't Help Falling In Love	Andy Williams	CBS	11	(88)	
3	20	Knock Knock Who's There	Mary Hopkin	Apple	7	(92)	
4	-	All Kinds Of Everything	Dana	Rex	8		F
5	19	Young Gifted And Black	Bob & Marcia	Harry J.	8		F
6	-	Spirit In The Sky	Norman Greenbaum	Reprise	11	(3)	F L
7	1	Wand'rin' Star	Lee Marvin	Paramount	11		F L
8	7	That Same Old Feeling	Pickettywitch	Pye	8	(67)	F
9	-	Gimme Dat Ding	Pipkins	Columbia	6	(9)	F L
10	-	Farewell Is A Lonely Sound	Jimmy Ruffin	Tamla Motown	7		
11	15	Something's Burning	Kenny Rogers & The First Edition	Reprise	8	(11)	
12	-	I Can't Help Myself	Four Tops	Tamla Motown	5	(1)	
13	4	Let It Be	Beatles	Apple	6	(1)	
14	-	Never Had A Dream Come True	Stevie Wonder	Tamla Motown	7	(26)	
15	-	When Julie Comes Around	Cuff Links	MCA	6	(41)	L
16	11	Don't Cry Daddy	Elvis Presley	RCA	7	(6)	
17	16	Everybody Get Together	Dave Clark Five	Columbia	5		L
18	-	Good Morning Freedom	Blue Mink	Philips	4		
19	10	Na Na Hey Hey Kiss Him Goodbye	Steam	Fontana	6	(1)	F L
20	-	You're Such A Good Looking Woman	Joe Dolan	Pye	4		L

◆ Simon & Garfunkel topped the single and album charts with the multi Grammy winning Bridge Over Troubled Water. The album headed the UK charts for a record 41 weeks and remained in the Top 10 for 126 weeks!

◆ The new year heralded the introduction of the Minimoog. This instrument, an early synthesizer, was to greatly influence the recording scene over the next decades.

1970

This Mnth	Prev Mnth	Title	Artist	Label	Wks	(US 20 Pos)	
1	-	Back Home	England World Cup Squad	Pye	9		F
2	6	Spirit In The Sky	Norman Greenbaum	Reprise	11	(3)	F L
3	-	House Of The Rising Sun	Frijid Pink	Deram	8	(7)	F L
4	4	All Kinds Of Everything	Dana	Rex	8		F
5	-	Daughter Of Darkness	Tom Jones	Decca	9	(13)	
6	-	Question	Moody Blues	Threshold	9	(21)	
7	-	Yellow River	Christie	CBS	11	(23)	F
8	1	Bridge Over Troubled Water	Simon & Garfunkel	CBS	13	(1)	L
9	-	Travellin' Band	Creedence Clearwater Revival	Liberty	7	(2)	
10	2	Can't Help Falling In Love	Andy Williams	CBS	11	(88)	
11	-	I Can't Tell The Bottom From The Top	Hollies	Parlophone	5	(82)	
12	-	Brontosaurus	Move	Regal Zonophone	6		
13	14	Never Had A Dream Come True	Stevie Wonder	Tamla Motown	7	(26)	
14	-	I Don't Believe In If Anymore	Roger Whittaker	Columbia	8		
15	15	When Julie Comes Around	Cuff Links	MCA	6	(41)	L
16	9	Gimme Dat Ding	Pipkins	Columbia	6	(9)	F L
17	10	Farewell Is A Lonely Sound	Jimmy Ruffin	Tamla Motown	7		
18	-	Honey Come Back	Glen Campbell	Capitol	10	(19)	
19	18	Good Morning Freedom	Blue Mink	Philips	4		
20	-	Up The Ladder To The Roof	Supremes	Tamla Motown	6	(10)	

This Mnth	Prev Mnth	Title	Artist	Label	Wks	(US 20 Pos)	
1	7	Yellow River	Christie	CBS	11	(23)	F
2	-	In The Summertime	Mungo Jerry	Dawn	13	(3)	F
3	-	Groovin' With Mr. Bloe	Mr. Bloe	DJM	10		F L
4	18	Honey Come Back	Glen Campbell	Capitol	10	(19)	
5	1	Back Home	England World Cup Squad	Pye	9		F
6	-	Cottonfields	Beach Boys	Capitol	12		
7	-	Everything Is Beautiful	Ray Stevens	CBS	8	(1)	F
8	6	Question	Moody Blues	Threshold	9	(21)	
9	20	Up The Ladder To The Roof	Supremes	Tamla Motown	6	(10)	
10	-	Sally	Gerry Monroe	Chapter One	9		F
11	-	Abraham Martin & John	Marvin Gaye	Tamla Motown	7		
12	-	All Right Now	Free	Island	11	(4)	F
13	-	The Green Manalishi (With The Two Prong Crown)	Fleetwood Mac	Reprise	9		
14	-	ABC	Jackson Five	Tamla Motown	5	(1)	
15	14	I Don't Believe In If Anymore	Roger Whittaker	Columbia	8		
16	5	Daughter Of Darkness	Tom Jones	Decca	9	(13)	
17	-	Goodbye Sam Hello Samantha	Cliff Richard	Columbia	10		
18	2	Spirit In The Sky	Norman Greenbaum	Reprise	11	(3)	F L
19	-	It's All In The Game	Four Tops	Tamla Motown	9	(24)	
20	-	Down The Dustpipe	Status Quo	Pye	6		

◆ Grateful Dead made their UK debut at the Hollywood Rock Music Festival, where newcomers Mungo Jerry (whose 'In The Summertime' would sell seven million worldwide) were the surprise hit. One of several other UK festivals was the Bath Festival Of Blues And Progressive Music, whose headliners included Led Zeppelin, The Byrds, Donovan, Santana, Steppenwolf, Pink Floyd, John Mayall and Frank Zappa.

July 1970

This Mnth	Prev Mnth	Title	Artist	Label	Wks	(US Pos)	
1	2	In The Summertime	Mungo Jerry	Dawn	13	(3)	F
2	12	All Right Now	Free	Island	11	(4)	F
3	-	Up Around The Bend	Creedence Clearwater Revival	Liberty	8	(4)	
4	19	It's All In The Game	Four Tops	Tamla Motown	9	(24)	
5	3	Groovin' With Mr. Bloe	Mr. Bloe	DJM	10		F L
6	6	Cottonfields	Beach Boys	Capitol	12		
7	10	Sally	Gerry Monroe	Chapter One	9		F
8	17	Goodbye Sam Hello Samantha	Cliff Richard	Columbia	10		
9	-	Love Of The Common People	Nicky Thomas	Trojan	7		F L
10	-	Lola	Kinks	Pye	10	(9)	
11	-	Something	Shirley Bassey	UA	12	(55)	
12	13	The Green Manalishi (With The Two Prong Crown)	Fleetwood Mac	Reprise	9		
13	20	Down The Dustpipe	Status Quo	Pye	6		
14	-	The Wonder Of You	Elvis Presley	RCA	16	(9)	
15	1	Yellow River	Christie	CBS	11	(23)	F
16	4	Honey Come Back	Glen Campbell	Capitol	10	(19)	
17	-	Lady D'Arbanville	Cat Stevens	Island	8		
18	11	Abraham Martin & John	Marvin Gaye	Tamla Motown	7		
19	-	Neanderthal Man	Hotlegs	Fontana	9	(22)	F L
20	-	Love Like A Man	Ten Years After	Deram	6	(98)	F L

August 1970

This Mnth	Prev Mnth	Title	Artist	Label	Wks	(US Pos)	
1	14	The Wonder Of You	Elvis Presley	RCA	16	(9)	
2	19	Neanderthal Man	Hotlegs	Fontana	9	(22)	F L
3	10	Lola	Kinks	Pye	10	(9)	
4	11	Something	Shirley Bassey	UA	12	(55)	
5	2	All Right Now	Free	Island	11	(4)	F
6	1	In The Summertime	Mungo Jerry	Dawn	13	(3)	F
7	-	Rainbow	Marmalade	Decca	8	(51)	
8	-	I'll Say Forever My Love	Jimmy Ruffin	Tamla Motown	8	(77)	
9	-	Natural Sinner	Fair Weather	RCA	6		F L
10	-	The Tears Of A Clown	Smokey Robinson & The Miracles	Tamla Motown	10	(1)	
11	3	Up Around The Bend	Creedence Clearwater Revival	Liberty	8	(4)	
12	17	Lady D'Arbanville	Cat Stevens	Island	8		
13	4	It's All In The Game	Four Tops	Tamla Motown	9	(24)	
14	20	Love Like A Man	Ten Years After	Deram	6	(98)	F L
15	-	Big Yellow Taxi	Joni Mitchell	Reprise	5	(67)	F L
16	-	The Love You Save	Jackson Five	Tamla Motown	4	(1)	
17	-	25 Or 6 To 4	Chicago	CBS	7	(4)	
18	-	Signed, Sealed, Delivered I'm Yours	Stevie Wonder	Tamla Motown	5	(3)	
19	9	Love Of The Common People	Nicky Thomas	Trojan	7		F L
20	-	Sweet Inspiration	Johnny Johnson & The Bandwagon	Bell	5		

◆ The first of numerous hits by British football teams quickly shot to the top; it was by England's World Cup Squad (the winners of the previous World Cup) with the stirring 'Back Home'.

◆ Just weeks before his untimely death, Jimi Hendrix appeared at the Isle Of Wight Festival which also showcased The Who, The Doors, Chicago, Emerson, Lake & Palmer, The Moody Blues and Free, whose debut hit, 'All Right Now', returned to the UK Top 20 in 1973 and again in 1991.

1970

September 1970

This Mnth	Prev Mnth	Title	Artist	Label	Wks	(US 20 Pos)	
1	10	The Tears Of A Clown	Smokey Robinson/The Miracles	Tamla Motown	10	(1)	
2	1	The Wonder Of You	Elvis Presley	RCA	16	(9)	
3	-	Give Me Just A Little More Time	Chairmen Of The Board	Invictus	8	(3)	F
4	-	Mama Told Me Not To Come	Three Dog Night	Stateside	8	(1)	F L
5	-	Band Of Gold	Freda Payne	Invictus	11	(3)	F L
6	-	Make It With You	Bread	Elektra	7	(1)	F
7	-	Love Is Life	Hot Chocolate	RAK	8		F
8	-	Wild World	Jimmy Cliff	Island	5		L
9	17	25 Or 6 To 4	Chicago	CBS	7	(4)	
10	7	Rainbow	Marmalade	Decca	8	(51)	
11	-	You Can Get It If You Really Want	Desmond Dekker	Trojan	10		
12	-	Which Way You Goin' Billy	Poppy Family	Decca	7	(2)	F L
13	2	Neanderthal Man	Hotlegs	Fontana	9	(22)	F L
14	4	Something	Shirley Bassey	UA	12	(55)	
15	20	Sweet Inspiration	Johnny Johnson & The Bandwagon	Bell	5		
16	-	Montego Bay	Bobby Bloom	Polydor	8	(8)	F L
17	-	It's So Easy	Andy Williams	CBS	4		
18	9	Natural Sinner	Fair Weather	RCA	6		F L
19	-	Don't Play That Song	Aretha Franklin	Atlantic	5	(11)	
20	-	Black Night	Deep Purple	Harvest	10	(66)	F

October 1970

This Mnth	Prev Mnth	Title	Artist	Label	Wks	(US 20 Pos)	
1	5	Band Of Gold	Freda Payne	Invictus	11	(3)	F L
2	20	Black Night	Deep Purple	Harvest	10	(66)	F
3	11	You Can Get It If You Really Want	Desmond Dekker	Trojan	10		
4	-	Paranoid	Black Sabbath	Vertigo	8	(61)	F
5	16	Montego Bay	Bobby Bloom	Polydor	8	(8)	F L
6	-	Me And My Life	Tremeloes	CBS	9		L
7	-	Ain't No Mountain High Enough	Diana Ross	Tamla Motown	7	(1)	F
8	-	(They Long To Be) Close To You	Carpenters	A&M	8	(1)	F
9	12	Which Way You Goin' Billy	Poppy Family	Decca	7	(2)	F L
10	-	Patches	Clarence Carter	Atlantic	8	(4)	F L
11	-	Ball Of Confusion	Temptations	Tamla Motown	7	(3)	
12	-	Woodstock	Matthews Southern Comfort	Uni	8	(23)	F L
13	1	The Tears Of A Clown	Smokey Robinson & The Miracles	Tamla Motown	10	(1)	
14	3	Give Me Just A Little More Time	Chairmen Of The Board	Invictus	8	(3)	F
15	2	The Wonder Of You	Elvis Presley	RCA	16	(9)	
16	-	Strange Band	Family	Reprise	5		F
17	-	Black Pearl	Horace Faith	Trojan	4		F L
18	-	Still Water (Love)	Four Tops	Tamla Motown	6	(11)	
19	7	Love Is Life	Hot Chocolate	RAK	8		F
20	-	Gasoline Alley Bred	Hollies	Parlophone	4		

◆ The *Melody Maker* poll showed Janis Joplin as Top Female Singer and, after eight years, The Beatles were replaced as Top Group by Led Zeppelin. Incidentally, Zeppelin billed their sixth US tour as "The Greatest Live Event Since The Beatles".

◆ Matthews' Southern Comfort's version of 'Woodstock' topped the chart despite the "Summer of Love" being no more than a distant memory.

108

November 1970

This Mnth	Prev Mnth	Title	Artist	Label	Wks (US 20 Pos)	
1	12	Woodstock	Matthews Southern Comfort	Uni	8 (23)	F L
2	10	Patches	Clarence Carter	Atlantic	8 (4)	F L
3	-	War	Edwin Starr	Tamla Motown	8 (1)	
4	-	Indian Reservation	Don Fardon	Young Blood	11 (20)	F L
5	-	Voodoo Chile	Jimi Hendrix Experience	Track	10	L
6	-	The Witch	Rattles	Decca	5 (79)	F L
7	-	Ruby Tuesday	Melanie	Buddah	7 (52)	F
8	-	San Bernadino	Christie	CBS	6 (100)	L
9	6	Me And My Life	Tremeloes	CBS	9	L
10	2	Black Night	Deep Purple	Harvest	10 (66)	F
11	-	It's Wonderful	Jimmy Ruffin	Tamla Motown	8	
12	1	Band Of Gold	Freda Payne	Invictus	11 (3)	F L
13	11	Ball Of Confusion	Temptations	Tamla Motown	7 (3)	
14	-	Cracklin' Rosie	Neil Diamond	Uni	13 (1)	F
15	-	I Hear You Knocking	Dave Edmunds	MAM	12 (4)	F
16	-	Julie, Do Ya Love Me	White Plains	Deram	9	
17	-	Ride A White Swan	T. Rex	Fly	14 (76)	F
18	4	Paranoid	Black Sabbath	Vertigo	8 (61)	F
19	18	Still Water (Love)	Four Tops	Tamla Motown	6 (11)	
20	-	I've Lost You	Elvis Presley	RCA	8 (32)	

December 1970

This Mnth	Prev Mnth	Title	Artist	Label	Wks (US 20 Pos)	
1	15	I Hear You Knocking	Dave Edmunds	MAM	12 (4)	F
2	-	When I'm Dead And Gone	McGuinness Flint	Capitol	10 (47)	F
3	14	Cracklin' Rosie	Neil Diamond	Uni	13 (1)	F
4	-	It's Only Make Believe	Glen Campbell	Capitol	10 (10)	
5	-	You've Got Me Dangling On A String	Chairmen Of The Board	Invictus	10 (38)	
6	17	Ride A White Swan	T. Rex	Fly	14 (76)	F
7	5	Voodoo Chile	Jimi Hendrix Experience	Track	10	L
8	-	I'll Be There	Jackson Five	Tamla Motown	11 (1)	
9	-	Home Lovin' Man	Andy Williams	CBS	9	
10	4	Indian Reservation	Don Fardon	Young Blood	11 (20)	F L
11	-	My Prayer	Gerry Monroe	Chapter One	7	
12	-	Grandad	Clive Dunn	Columbia	14	F L
13	-	Nothing Rhymed	Gilbert O'Sullivan	MAM	7	F
14	20	I've Lost You	Elvis Presley	RCA	8 (32)	
15	16	Julie, Do Ya Love Me	White Plains	Deram	9	
16	-	Lady Barbara	Herman's Hermits	RAK	6	L
17	-	Blame It On The Pony Express	Johnny Johnson & The Bandwagon	Bell	8	L
18	11	It's Wonderful	Jimmy Ruffin	Tamla Motown	8	
19	8	San Bernadino	Christie	CBS	6 (100)	L
20	1	Woodstock	Matthews Southern Comfort	Uni	8 (23)	F L

◆ Double Grammy winners, The Carpenters, had their first transatlantic hit , '(They Long To Be) Close To You'. Also debuting on the UK chart were Neil Diamond, Gilbert O' Sullivan and T-Rex, while the US chart welcomed Dawn, James Taylor, and the stars of the latest pop-oriented TV series, The Partridge Family, featuring teen idol David Cassidy.
◆ The price of all record papers in Britain rose to 5p (12c).

1971

January 1971

January 1971

This Mnth	Prev Mnth	Title	Artist	Label	Wks	(US 20 Pos)	
1	12	Grandad	Clive Dunn	Columbia	14		F L
2	1	I Hear You Knocking	Dave Edmunds	MAM	12	(4)	F
3	6	Ride A White Swan	T. Rex	Fly	14	(76)	F
4	8	I'll Be There	Jackson Five	Tamla Motown	11	(1)	
5	2	When I'm Dead And Gone	McGuinness Flint	Capitol	10	(47)	F
6	3	Cracklin' Rosie	Neil Diamond	Uni	13	(1)	F
7	17	Blame It On The Pony Express	Johnny Johnson & The Bandwagon	Bell	8		L
8	4	It's Only Make Believe	Glen Campbell	Capitol	10	(10)	
9	-	Ape Man	Kinks	Pye	9	(45)	
10	9	Home Lovin' Man	Andy Williams	CBS	9		
11	13	Nothing Rhymed	Gilbert O'Sullivan	MAM	7		F
12	-	My Sweet Lord	George Harrison	Apple	12	(1)	F
13	-	Black Skin Blue Eyed Boys	Equals	President	6		L
14	5	You've Got Me Dangling On A String	Chairmen Of The Board	Invictus	10	(38)	
15	-	Amazing Grace	Judy Collins	Elektra	13	(15)	
16	-	The Pushbike Song	Mixtures	Polydor	13	(44)	F L
17	-	You Don't Have To Say You Love Me	Elvis Presley	RCA	6	(11)	
18	16	Lady Barbara	Herman's Hermits	RAK	6		L
19	11	My Prayer	Gerry Monroe	Chapter One	7		
20	-	You're Ready Now	Frankie Valli	Philips	6		F

February 1971

This Mnth	Prev Mnth	Title	Artist	Label	Wks	(US 20 Pos)	
1	12	My Sweet Lord	George Harrison	Apple	12	(1)	F
2	16	The Pushbike Song	Mixtures	Polydor	13	(44)	F L
3	-	Stoned Love	Supremes	Tamla Motown	8	(7)	
4	-	Resurrection Shuffle	Ashton Gardner & Dyke	Capitol	9	(40)	F L
5	15	Amazing Grace	Judy Collins	Elektra	13	(15)	
6	-	No Matter What	Badfinger	Apple	8	(8)	
7	1	Grandad	Clive Dunn	Columbia	14		F L
8	-	Your Song	Elton John	DJM	6	(8)	F
9	-	Candida	Dawn	Bell	6	(3)	F
10	9	Ape Man	Kinks	Pye	9	(45)	
11	-	It's Impossible	Perry Como	RCA	11	(10)	
12	3	Ride A White Swan	T. Rex	Fly	14	(76)	F
13	20	You're Ready Now	Frankie Valli	Philips	6		F
14	-	She's A Lady	Tom Jones	Decca	5	(2)	
15	-	Baby Jump	Mungo Jerry	Dawn	9		
16	4	I'll Be There	Jackson Five	Tamla Motown	11	(1)	
17	-	Rupert	Jackie Lee	Pye	5		F L
18	17	You Don't Have To Say You Love Me	Elvis Presley	RCA	6	(11)	
19	-	(Come 'Round Here) I'm The One You Need	Smokey Robinson & The Miracles	Tamla Motown	4		
20	-	Sweet Caroline	Neil Diamond	Uni	7	(4)	

◆ George Harrison's triple LP, **All Things Must Pass**, topped the American charts, and his single 'My Sweet Lord' was a transatlantic No. 1. Soon afterwards, a court ruled that he had "unconsciously plagiarised" The Chiffons' (with whom The Beatles had toured in 1964) 'He's So Fine' when writing this hit.

March 1971

This Mnth	Prev Mnth	Title	Artist	Label	Wks (US 20 Pos)	
1	15	**Baby Jump**	Mungo Jerry	Dawn	9	
2	-	**Another Day**	Paul McCartney	Apple	9 (5)	F
3	1	**My Sweet Lord**	George Harrison	Apple	12 (1)	F
4	11	**It's Impossible**	Perry Como	RCA	11 (10)	
5	-	**Rose Garden**	Lynn Anderson	CBS	10 (3)	F L
6	-	**Hot Love**	T. Rex	Fly	12 (72)	
7	2	**The Pushbike Song**	Mixtures	Polydor	13 (44)	F L
8	20	**Sweet Caroline**	Neil Diamond	Uni	7 (4)	
9	5	**Amazing Grace**	Judy Collins	Elektra	13 (15)	
10	4	**Resurrection Shuffle**	Ashton Gardner & Dyke	Capitol	9 (40)	F L
11	-	**Tomorrow Night**	Atomic Rooster	B&C	5	F
12	3	**Stoned Love**	Supremes	Tamla Motown	8 (7)	
13	-	**Everything's Tuesday**	Chairmen Of The Board	Invictus	5 (38)	
14	-	**Bridget The Midget (The Queen Of The Blues)**	Ray Stevens	CBS	9 (50)	
15	-	**Power To The People**	John Lennon & The Plastic Ono Band	Apple	6 (11)	
16	-	**Strange Kind Of Woman**	Deep Purple	Harvest	5	
17	-	**Forget Me Not**	Martha & The Vandellas	Tamla Motown	3 (93)	L
18	-	**Who Put The Lights Out**	Dana	Rex	3	
19	-	**Rose Garden**	New World	RAK	5	F
20	-	**Jack In The Box**	Clodagh Rodgers	RCA	6	L

April 1971

This Mnth	Prev Mnth	Title	Artist	Label	Wks (US 20 Pos)	
1	6	**Hot Love**	T. Rex	Fly	12 (72)	
2	14	**Bridget The Midget (The Queen Of The Blues)**	Ray Stevens	CBS	9 (50)	
3	5	**Rose Garden**	Lynn Anderson	CBS	10 (3)	F L
4	20	**Jack In The Box**	Clodagh Rodgers	RCA	6	L
5	-	**There Goes My Everything**	Elvis Presley	RCA	6 (21)	
6	-	**Walkin'**	C.C.S.	RAK	7	
7	2	**Another Day**	Paul McCartney	Apple	9 (5)	F
8	-	**If Not For You**	Olivia Newton-John	Pye International	6 (25)	F
9	15	**Power To The People**	John Lennon	Apple	6 (11)	
10	-	**(Where Do I Begin) Love Story**	Andy Williams	CBS	8 (9)	
11	-	**Double Barrel**	Dave & Ansil Collins	Technique	9 (22)	F
12	1	**Baby Jump**	Mungo Jerry	Dawn	9	
13	4	**It's Impossible**	Perry Como	RCA	11 (10)	
14	-	**Mozart Symphony No. 40 In G Minor**	Waldo De Los Rios	A&M	10 (67)	F L
15	16	**Strange Kind Of Woman**	Deep Purple	Harvest	5	
16	8	**Sweet Caroline**	Neil Diamond	Uni	7 (4)	
17	-	**Funny Funny**	Sweet	RCA	6	F
18	3	**My Sweet Lord**	George Harrison	Apple	12 (1)	F
19	7	**The Pushbike Song**	Mixtures	Polydor	13 (44)	F L
20	-	**Something Old, Something New**	Fantastics	Bell	3	F L

◆ Judy Collins's live recording of the ancient hymn 'Amazing Grace' spent an amazing 67 weeks on the chart. Only Frank Sinatra's 'My Way' can claim a longer residence.

◆ Swedish quartet, The Engaged Couples, made their debut at a Gothenburg nightclub. They later changed their name to Abba.

1971

This Mnth	Prev Mnth	Title	Artist	Label	Wks	(US 20 Pos)	
1	-	Knock Three Times	Dawn	Bell	13	(1)	
2	-	Brown Sugar/Bitch/Let It Rock	Rolling Stones	Rolling Stone	9	(1)	
3	11	Double Barrel	Dave & Ansil Collins	Technique	9	(22)	F
4	-	It Don't Come Easy	Ringo Starr	Apple	8	(4)	F
5	14	Mozart Symphony No. 40 In G Minor	Waldo De Los Rios	A&M	10	(67)	F L
6	-	Indiana Wants Me	R. Dean Taylor	Tamla Motown	9	(5)	
7	-	Remember Me	Diana Ross	Tamla Motown	7	(16)	
8	1	Hot Love	T. Rex	Fly	12	(72)	
9	-	Jig A Jig	East Of Eden	Deram	6		F L
10	10	(Where Do I Begin) Love Story	Andy Williams	CBS	8	(9)	
11	-	Heaven Must Have Sent You	Elgins	Tamla Motown	9	(50)	F L
12	-	Malt And Barley Blues	McGuinness Flint	Capitol	7		L
13	-	Un Banc, Un Arbre, Une Rue	Severine	Philips	4		F L
14	2	Bridget The Midget (The Queen Of The Blues)	Ray Stevens	CBS	9	(50)	
15	-	My Brother Jake	Free	Island	7		
16	-	Sugar Sugar	Sakkarin	RCA	5		F L
17	17	Funny Funny	Sweet	RCA	6		F
18	-	It's A Sin To Tell A Lie	Gerry Monroe	Chapter One	5		L
19	-	Rosetta	Fame And Price Together	CBS	5		L
20	20	Something Old, Something New	Fantastics	Bell	3		F L

This Mnth	Prev Mnth	Title	Artist	Label	Wks	(US 20 Pos)	
1	1	Knock Three Times	Dawn	Bell	13	(1)	
2	-	I Did What I Did For Maria	Tony Christie	MCA	9		F
3	11	Heaven Must Have Sent You	Elgins	Tamla Motown	9	(50)	F L
4	-	I'm Gonna Run Away From You	Tami Lynn	Mojo	8		F L
5	-	I Am ...I Said	Neil Diamond	Uni	8	(4)	
6	6	Indiana Wants Me	R. Dean Taylor	Tamla Motown	9	(5)	
7	-	Lady Rose	Mungo Jerry	Dawn	7		
8	-	Banner Man	Blue Mink	Regal Zonophone	9		
9	15	My Brother Jake	Free	Island	7		
10	-	Chirpy Chirpy Cheep Cheep	Middle Of The Road	RCA	12		F
11	-	Rags To Riches	Elvis Presley	RCA	6	(33)	
12	2	Brown Sugar/Bitch/Let It Rock	Rolling Stones	Rolling Stone	9	(1)	
13	-	He's Gonna Step On You Again	John Kongos	Fly	8	(70)	F
14	12	Malt And Barley Blues	McGuinness Flint	Capitol	7		L
15	-	Oh You Pretty Thing	Peter Noone	Rak	6		F L
16	9	Jig A Jig	East Of Eden	Deram	6		F L
17	-	I Think Of You	Perry Como	RCA	5	(53)	
18	-	Don't Let It Die	Hurricane Smith	Columbia	8		F
19	-	Co-Co	Sweet	RCA	10	(99)	
20	5	Mozart Symphony No. 40 In G Minor	Waldo De Los Rios	A&M	10	(67)	F L

◆ Photogenic Irish vocalist Clodagh Rodgers had her last hit with the UK's entry to the Eurovision Song Contest, 'Jack In A Box'. The winner 'Un Banc, Un Arbre, Une Rue' by Severine from Monaco also charted.

◆ Eric Clapton won a poll in *NME* for Greatest All-Time Guitarist, with Jimi Hendrix and B.B. King in runner-up positions.

July 1971

This Mnth	Prev Mnth	Title	Artist	Label	Wks	(US 20 Pos)	
1	10	Chirpy Chirpy Cheep Cheep	Middle Of The Road	RCA	12		F
2	19	Co-Co	Sweet	RCA	10	(99)	
3	18	Don't Let It Die	Hurricane Smith	Columbia	8		F
4	8	Banner Man	Blue Mink	Regal Zonophone	9		
5	-	Me And You And A Dog Named Boo	Lobo	Philips	9	(5)	F
6	-	Get It On	T. Rex	Fly	9	(10)	
7	-	Black And White	Greyhound	Trojan	8		F
8	13	He's Gonna Step On You Again	John Kongos	Fly	8	(70)	F
9	-	Just My Imagination (Runnin' Away With Me)	Temptations	Tamla Motown	8	(1)	
10	-	Monkey Spanner	Dave & Ansil Collins	Technique	8		L
11	4	I'm Gonna Run Away From You	Tami Lynn	Mojo	8		F L
12	-	Tom-Tom Turnaround	New World	RAK	10		
13	2	I Did What I Did For Maria	Tony Christie	MCA	9		F
14	-	Pied Piper	Bob & Marcia	Trojan	5		L
15	7	Lady Rose	Mungo Jerry	Dawn	7		
16	-	River Deep-Mountain High	Supremes & Four Tops	Tamla	6	(14)	
17	-	I Don't Blame You At All	Smokey Robinson & The Miracles	Tamla Motown	5	(18)	
18	-	When You Are A King	White Plains	Deram	5		L
19	-	Never Ending Song Of Love	New Seekers	Philips	12		F
20	-	Tonight	Move	Harvest	5		

August 1971

This Mnth	Prev Mnth	Title	Artist	Label	Wks	(US 20 Pos)	
1	19	Never Ending Song Of Love	New Seekers	Philips	12		F
2	6	Get It On	T. Rex	Fly	9	(10)	
3	-	I'm Still Waiting	Diana Ross	Tamla Motown	11	(63)	
4	-	Devil's Answer	Atomic Rooster	B&C	7		L
5	-	In My Own Time	Family	Reprise	8		
6	1	Chirpy Chirpy Cheep Cheep	Middle Of The Road	RCA	12		F
7	12	Tom-Tom Turnaround	New World	RAK	10		
8	-	Won't Get Fooled Again	Who	Track	6	(15)	
9	-	What Are You Doing Sunday	Dawn	Bell	7	(39)	
10	5	Me And You And A Dog Named Boo	Lobo	Philips	9	(5)	F
11	2	Co-Co	Sweet	RCA	10	(99)	
12	-	Heartbreak Hotel/Hound Dog	Elvis Presley	RCA	5		
13	-	Leap Up And Down (Wave Your Knickers In The Air)	St. Cecilia	Polydor	7		F L
14	-	Soldier Blue	Buffy Sainte-Marie	RCA	8		F L
15	10	Monkey Spanner	Dave & Ansil Collins	Technique	8		L
16	-	Let Your Yeah Be Yeah	Pioneers	Trojan	6		F L
17	-	Bangla Desh	George Harrison	Apple	4	(23)	
18	7	Black And White	Greyhound	Trojan	8		F
19	-	Get Down And Get With It	Slade	Polydor	4		F
20	-	Hey Girl Don't Bother Me	Tams	Probe	11	(41)	F L

◆ Glitter-Rock (aka Glam Rock) was off and running in Britain, thanks to hits from Sweet, T-Rex and chart newcomers Slade.

◆ The Tams' seven-year-old 'Hey Girl Don't Bother Me' was one of several re-issues on the British chart – others came from Tami Lynn, The Elgins and even Elvis, with a coupling of 'Heartbreak Hotel' and 'Hound Dog'.

1971

This Mnth	Prev Mnth	Title	Artist	Label	Wks	(US 20 Pos)	
1	20	Hey Girl Don't Bother Me	Tams	Probe	11	(41)	F L
2	3	I'm Still Waiting	Diana Ross	Tamla Motown	11	(63)	
3	1	Never Ending Song Of Love	New Seekers	Philips	12		F
4	-	Did You Ever	Nancy Sinatra & Lee Hazlewood	Reprise	9		L
5	9	What Are You Doing Sunday	Dawn	Bell	7	(39)	
6	14	Soldier Blue	Buffy Sainte-Marie	RCA	8		F L
7	-	Back Street Luv	Curved Air	Warner	6		F L
8	-	Nathan Jones	Supremes	Tamla Motown	7	(16)	
9	-	It's Too Late	Carole King	A&M	6	(1)	L
10	16	Let Your Yeah Be Yeah	Pioneers	Trojan	6		F L
11	5	In My Own Time	Family	Reprise	8		
12	-	I Believe (In Love)	Hot Chocolate	RAK	6		
13	-	Maggie May	Rod Stewart	Mercury	14	(1)	F
14	-	You've Got A Friend	James Taylor	Warner	9	(1)	F L
15	-	Tweedle Dee Tweedle Dum	Middle Of The Road	RCA	9		
16	-	Cousin Norman	Marmalade	Decca	7		
17	2	Get It On	T. Rex	Fly	9	(10)	
18	17	Bangla Desh	George Harrison	Apple	4	(23)	
19	-	Tap Turns On The Water	C.C.S.	RAK	7		L
20	-	For All We Know	Shirley Bassey	UA	10		

1	13	Maggie May	Rod Stewart	Mercury	14	(1)	F
2	15	Tweedle Dee Tweedle Dum	Middle Of The Road	RCA	9		
3	14	You've Got A Friend	James Taylor	Warner	9	(1)	F L
4	1	Hey Girl Don't Bother Me	Tams	Probe	11	(41)	F L
5	4	Did You Ever	Nancy Sinatra & Lee Hazlewood	Reprise	9		L
6	20	For All We Know	Shirley Bassey	UA	10		
7	19	Tap Turns On The Water	C.C.S.	RAK	7		L
8	-	Witch Queen Of New Orleans	Redbone	Epic	8	(21)	F L
9	-	Freedom Come Freedom Go	Fortunes	Capitol	7	(72)	
10	16	Cousin Norman	Marmalade	Decca	7		
11	-	Simple Game	Four Tops	Tamla Motown	8	(90)	
12	-	Sultana	Titanic	CBS	7		F L
13	-	Life Is A Long Song/Up The Pool	Jethro Tull	Chrysalis	5		L
14	8	Nathan Jones	Supremes	Tamla Motown	7	(16)	
15	-	Butterfly	Danyel Gerard	CBS	5	(78)	F L
16	12	I Believe (In Love)	Hot Chocolate	RAK	6		
17	-	Another Time Another Place	Engelbert Humperdinck	Decca	4	(43)	
18	-	You Don't Have To Be In The Army To Fight In The War	Mungo Jerry	Dawn	3		
19	7	Back Street Luv	Curved Air	Warner	6		F L
20	-	Keep On Dancing	Bay City Rollers	Bell	5		F

◆ Cliff Richard, who received an Ivor Novello award for his outstanding services to British music, was heavily promoting newcomer Olivia Newton-John on his weekly TV series.

◆ English comedian Benny Hill topped the chart with the novelty 'Ernie (The Fastest Milkman In The West)', which was loosely based on an earlier record by American humorist Frank Gallup.

1971

November 1971

This Mnth	Prev Mnth	Title	Artist	Label	Wks	(US 20 Pos)	
1	-	Coz I Luv You	Slade	Polydor	10		
2	1	Maggie May	Rod Stewart	Mercury	14	(1)	F
3	-	Till	Tom Jones	Decca	10	(41)	
4	-	Tired Of Being Alone	Al Green	London American	6	(11)	F
5	8	Witch Queen Of New Orleans	Redbone	Epic	8	(21)	F L
6	-	Johnny Reggae	Piglets	Bell	7		F L
7	-	I Will Return	Springwater	Polydor	6		F L
8	11	Simple Game	Four Tops	Tamla Motown	8	(90)	
9	-	The Night They Drove Old Dixie Down	Joan Baez	Vanguard	7	(3)	L
10	-	Banks Of The Ohio	Olivia Newton-John	Pye International	8	(94)	
11	-	Gypsys Tramps & Thieves	Cher	MCA	9	(1)	
12	-	Look Around	Vince Hill	Columbia	6		L
13	-	Jeepster	T. Rex	Fly	10		
14	12	Sultana	Titanic	CBS	7		F L
15	-	Brandy	Scott English	Horse	5	(91)	F L
16	-	Ernie (The Fastest Milkman In The West)	Benny Hill	Columbia	10		L
17	6	For All We Know	Shirley Bassey	UA	10		
18	2	Tweedle Dee Tweedle Dum	Middle Of The Road	RCA	9		
19	-	Run, Baby Run (Back Into My Arms)	Newbeats	London American	6		L
20	-	Surrender	Diana Ross	Tamla Motown	5	(38)	

December 1971

This Mnth	Prev Mnth	Title	Artist	Label	Wks	(US 20 Pos)	
1	16	Ernie (The Fastest Milkman In The.West)	Benny Hill	Columbia	10		L
2	13	Jeepster	T. Rex	Fly	10		
3	1	Coz I Luv You	Slade	Polydor	10		
4	-	Tokoloshe Man	John Kongos	Fly	7		L
5	11	Gypsys Tramps & Thieves	Cher	MCA	9	(1)	
6	-	Theme From 'Shaft'	Isaac Hayes	Stax	8	(1)	F
7	-	Something Tells Me (Something Is Gonna Happen Tonight)	Cilla Black	Parlophone	8		L
8	10	Banks Of The Ohio	Olivia Newton-John	Pye International	8	(94)	
9	-	No Matter How I Try	Gilbert O'Sullivan	MAM	9		
10	3	Till	Tom Jones	Decca	10	(41)	
11	6	Johnny Reggae	Piglets	Bell	7		F L
12	19	Run, Baby Run (Back Into My Arms)	Newbeats	London American	6		L
13	-	Softly Whispering I Love You	Congregation	Columbia	8	(29)	F L
14	-	Sing A Song Of Freedom	Cliff Richard	Columbia	4		
15	7	I Will Return	Springwater	Polydor	6		F L
16	20	Surrender	Diana Ross	Tamla Motown	5	(38)	
17	-	I'd Like To Teach The World To Sing	New Seekers	Polydor	12	(7)	
18	-	Soley Soley	Middle Of The Road	RCA	8		L
19	-	It Must Be Love	Labi Siffre	Pye International	6		F
20	-	Fireball	Deep Purple	Harvest	6		L

◆ Led Zeppelin's un-titled fourth album, which contained the FM classic 'Stairway To Heaven', was released. It spent five years on the American chart and sold eleven million in the US alone.

◆ Slade followed their first No. 1, 'Coz I Luv You', with another four phonetically spelled chart toppers. They were the first act to regularly misspell titles.

1972

This Mnth	Prev Mnth	Title	Artist	Label	Wks	(US 20 Pos)	
1	17	I'd Like To Teach The World To Sing	New Seekers	Polydor	12	(7)	
2	13	Softly Whispering I Love You	Congregation	Columbia	8	(29)	F L
3	-	Mother Of Mine	Neil Reid	Decca	14		F L
4	18	Soley Soley	Middle Of The Road	RCA	8		L
5	1	Ernie (The Fastest Milkman In The West)	Benny Hill	Columbia	10		L
6	-	I Just Can't Help Believing	Elvis Presley	RCA	8		
7	7	Something Tells Me (Something Is Gonna Happen Tonight)	Cilla Black	Parlophone	8		L
8	-	Sleepy Shores	Johnny Pearson Orchestra	Penny Farthing	7		F L
9	2	Jeepster	T. Rex	Fly	10		
10	9	No Matter How I Try	Gilbert O'Sullivan	MAM	9		
11	-	Brand New Key	Melanie	Buddah	7	(1)	L
12	-	Horse With No Name	America	Warner	7	(1)	F L
13	6	Theme From 'Shaft'	Isaac Hayes	Stax	8	(1)	F
14	-	Stay With Me	Faces	Warner	5	(17)	F
15	-	Morning Has Broken	Cat Stevens	Island	4	(6)	
16	-	Morning	Val Doonican	Philips	6		L
17	4	Tokoloshe Man	John Kongos	Fly	7		L
18	-	Telegram Sam	T. Rex	T. Rex	7	(67)	
19	-	Where Did Our Love Go	Donnie Elbert	London American	5	(15)	F
20	-	Let's Stay Together	Al Green	London American	7	(1)	

This	Prev	Title	Artist	Label	Wks	(US Pos)	
1	18	Telegram Sam	T. Rex	T. Rex	7	(67)	
2	-	Son Of My Father	Chicory Tip	CBS	9		F
3	3	Mother Of Mine	Neil Reid	Decca	14		F L
4	-	Have You Seen Her	Chi-Lites	MCA	7	(3)	F
5	1	I'd Like To Teach The World To Sing	New Seekers	Polydor	12	(7)	
6	12	Horse With No Name	America	Warner	7	(1)	F L
7	-	Look Wot You Dun	Slade	Polydor	7		
8	20	Let's Stay Together	Al Green	London American	7	(1)	
9	-	American Pie	Don McLean	UA	11	(1)	F
10	11	Brand New Key	Melanie	Buddah	7	(1)	L
11	-	All I Ever Need Is You	Sonny & Cher	MCA	6	(7)	L
12	-	Storm In A Teacup	Fortunes	Capitol	6		L
13	14	Stay With Me	Faces	Warner	5	(17)	F
14	-	Moon River	Greyhound	Trojan	4		
15	19	Where Did Our Love Go	Donnie Elbert	London American	5	(15)	F
16	-	Day After Day	Badfinger	Apple	6	(4)	L
17	-	Without You	Nilsson	RCA	13	(1)	F L
18	6	I Just Can't Help Believing	Elvis Presley	RCA	8		
19	-	Baby I'm A Want You	Bread	Elektra	4	(3)	
20	-	Got To Be There	Michael Jackson	Tamla Motown	6	(4)	F

◆ Pink Floyd pre-viewed their **Dark Side Of The Moon** album at London's new home of rock music, The Rainbow Theatre. The LP, which was released a year later, smashed all longevity records.
◆ As Paul McCartney (& Wings) played his first dates since leaving The Beatles, John Lennon was having problems renewing his US visa. Ringo Starr, meanwhile, was making a film about Britain's latest pop sensations, T-Rex, whose live shows were "creating hysteria not seen since the early days of The Beatles".

March 1972

This Mnth	Prev Mnth	Title	Artist	Label	Wks	(US 20 Pos)	
1	17	**Without You**	Nilsson	RCA	13	(1)	F L
2	9	**American Pie**	Don McLean	UA	11	(1)	F
3	2	**Son Of My Father**	Chicory Tip	CBS	9		F
4	-	**Beg Steal Or Borrow**	New Seekers	Polydor	9	(81)	
5	-	**Mother & Child Reunion**	Paul Simon	CBS	7	(4)	F
6	20	**Got To Be There**	Michael Jackson	Tamla Motown	6	(4)	F
7	-	**Blue Is The Colour**	Chelsea F.C.	Penny Farthing	7		F L
8	-	**Alone Again (Naturally)**	Gilbert O'Sullivan	MAM	7	(1)	
9	7	**Look Wot You Dun**	Slade	Polydor	7		
10	-	**Meet Me On The Corner**	Lindisfarne	Charisma	6		F
11	-	**Poppa Joe**	Sweet	RCA	5		
12	3	**Mother Of Mine**	Neil Reid	Decca	14		F L
13	12	**Storm In A Teacup**	Fortunes	Capitol	6		L
14	-	**I Can't Help Myself**	Donnie Elbert	Avco	5	(22)	L
15	16	**Day After Day**	Badfinger	Apple	6	(4)	L
16	4	**Have You Seen Her**	Chi-Lites	MCA	7	(3)	F
17	-	**Hold Your Head Up**	Argent	Epic	7	(5)	F
18	-	**Floy Joy**	Supremes	Tamla Motown	6	(16)	
19	-	**Say You Don't Mind**	Colin Blunstone	Epic	3		F L
20	-	**Desiderata**	Les Crane	Warner	7	(8)	F L

April 1972

This Mnth	Prev Mnth	Title	Artist	Label	Wks	(US 20 Pos)	
1	1	**Without You**	Nilsson	RCA	13	(1)	F L
2	4	**Beg Steal Or Borrow**	New Seekers	Polydor	9	(81)	
3	-	**Amazing Grace**	Royal Scots Dragoon Guards	RCA	11	(11)	F
4	-	**Sweet Talkin' Guy**	Chiffons	London American	8		L
5	17	**Hold Your Head Up**	Argent	Epic	7	(5)	F
6	-	**Back Off Boogaloo**	Ringo Starr	Apple	8	(9)	
7	8	**Alone Again (Naturally)**	Gilbert O'Sullivan	MAM	7	(1)	
8	-	**The Young New Mexican Puppeteer**	Tom Jones	Decca	7	(80)	
9	20	**Desiderata**	Les Crane	Warner	7	(8)	F L
10	-	**Heart Of Gold**	Neil Young	Reprise	5	(1)	F L
11	10	**Meet Me On The Corner**	Lindisfarne	Charisma	6		F
12	2	**American Pie**	Don McLean	UA	11	(1)	F
13	18	**Floy Joy**	Supremes	Tamla Motown	6	(16)	
14	-	**Until It's Time For You To Go**	Elvis Presley	RCA	6	(40)	
15	-	**Debora/One Inch Rock**	Tyrannosaurus Rex	Magni Fly	6		
16	-	**Run Run Run**	Jo Jo Gunne	Asylum	7	(27)	F L
17	-	**Crying Laughing Loving Lying**	Labi Siffre	Pye International	5		
18	-	**It's One Of Those Nights (Yes Love)**	Partridge Family	Bell	5	(20)	
19	-	**Come What May**	Vicky Leandros	Philips	8		F L
20	5	**Mother & Child Reunion**	Paul Simon	CBS	7	(4)	F

◆ 'I'd Like To Teach The World To Sing' by The New Seekers was not the first recording from a TV advertisement, but this Coca Cola commercial was the one which proved that major UK hits can come via this route. Since then many more have charted in Britain.

◆ Among the record nine re-issued singles in the UK Top 50 were Procol Harum's 'A Whiter Shade of Pale' and tracks by The Chiffons and The Drifters.

1972

This Mnth	Prev Mnth	Title	Artist	Label	Wks	(US 20 Pos)	
1	3	Amazing Grace	Royal Scots Dragoon Guards	RCA	11	(11)	F
2	-	Could It Be Forever/Cherish	David Cassidy	Bell	9	(37)	F
3	19	Come What May	Vicky Leandros	Philips	8		F L
4	-	A Thing Called Love	Johnny Cash	CBS	7		L
5	-	Rocket Man	Elton John	DJM	8	(6)	
6	-	Metal Guru	T. Rex	EMI	8		
7	-	Tumbling Dice	Rolling Stones	Rolling Stone	6	(7)	
8	-	Radancer	Marmalade	Decca	6		
9	16	Run Run Run	Jo Jo Gunne	Asylum	7	(27)	F L
10	6	Back Off Boogaloo	Ringo Starr	Apple	8	(9)	
11	4	Sweet Talkin' Guy	Chiffons	London American	8		L
12	-	At The Club/Saturday Night At The Movies	Drifters	Atlantic	9	(43)	
13	15	Debora/One Inch Rock	Tyrannosaurus Rex	Magni Fly	6		
14	-	Oh Babe What Would You Say?	Hurricane Smith	Columbia	7	(3)	L
15	-	Take A Look Around	Temptations	Tamla Motown	5	(30)	
16	-	Leeds United	Leeds United F.C.	Chapter One	5		F L
17	8	The Young New Mexican Puppeteer	Tom Jones	Decca	7	(80)	
18	1	Without You	Nilsson	RCA	13	(1)	F L
19	-	Stir It Up	Johnny Nash	CBS	5	(12)	
20	14	Until It's Time For You To Go	Elvis Presley	RCA	6	(40)	

This Mnth	Prev Mnth	Title	Artist	Label	Wks	(US 20 Pos)	
1	6	Metal Guru	T. Rex	EMI	8		
2	-	Vincent	Don McLean	UA	9	(12)	
3	12	At The Club/Saturday Night At The Movies	Drifters	Atlantic	9	(43)	
4	-	Lady Eleanor	Lindisfarne	Charisma	6	(82)	
5	14	Oh Babe What Would You Say?	Hurricane Smith	Columbia	7	(3)	L
6	-	California Man	Move	Harvest	8		L
7	5	Rocket Man	Elton John	DJM	8	(6)	
8	-	Rockin' Robin	Michael Jackson	Tamla Motown	7	(2)	
9	-	Take Me Bak 'Ome	Slade	Polydor	9	(97)	
10	-	Sister Jane	New World	RAK	6		L
11	2	Could It Be Forever/Cherish	David Cassidy	Bell	9	(37)	F
12	-	Mary Had A Little Lamb	Wings	Apple	7	(28)	
13	1	Amazing Grace	Royal Scots Dragoon Guards	RCA	11	(11)	F
14	-	Isn't Life Strange	Moody Blues	Threshold	4	(29)	
15	-	Rock & Roll Part 2	Gary Glitter	Bell	10	(7)	F
16	3	Come What May	Vicky Leandros	Philips	8		F L
17	-	Doobedood'ndoobe Doobedood'ndoobe	Diana Ross	Tamla Motown	3		
18	-	A Whiter Shade Of Pale	Procol Harum	Magnifly	4		
19	4	A Thing Called Love	Johnny Cash	CBS	7		L
20	16	Leeds United	Leeds United F.C.	Chapter One	5		F L

♦ Clyde McPhatter, founder of The Drifters and one of the most imitated R&B singers in the 1950s, died of drink related causes.

♦ The Electric Light Orchestra and Roxy Music made their UK debuts, as Slade embarked on their first UK tour (supported by Status Quo). Other firsts included David Bowie's chart album, **The Rise And Fall Of Ziggy Stardust And The Spiders From Mars**, and Bob Marley's first hit as composer of American reggae star Johnny Nash's 'Stir It Up'.

1972

July 1972

This Mnth	Prev Mnth	Title	Artist	Label	Wks	(US 20 Pos)	
1	-	**Puppy Love**	Donny Osmond	MGM	12	(3)	F
2	15	**Rock & Roll Part 2**	Gary Glitter	Bell	10	(7)	F
3	9	**Take Me Bak 'Ome**	Slade	Polydor	9	(97)	
4	-	**Little Willie**	Sweet	RCA	8	(3)	
5	-	**Circles**	New Seekers	Polydor	8	(87)	
6	-	**Sylvia's Mother**	Dr. Hook	CBS	8	(5)	F
7	-	**I Can See Clearly Now**	Johnny Nash	CBS	9	(1)	
8	-	**An American Trilogy**	Elvis Presley	RCA	5	(66)	
9	2	**Vincent**	Don McLean	UA	9	(12)	
10	8	**Rockin' Robin**	Michael Jackson	Tamla Motown	7	(2)	
11	-	**Ooh-Wakka-Doo-Wakka-Day**	Gilbert O'Sullivan	MAM	6		
12	-	**Breaking Up Is Hard To Do**	Partridge Family	Bell	9	(28)	
13	-	**Join Together**	Who	Track	6	(17)	
14	6	**California Man**	Move	Harvest	8		L
15	12	**Mary Had A Little Lamb**	Paul McCartney	Apple	7	(28)	
16	-	**Seaside Shuffle**	Terry Dactyl & The Dinosaurs	UK	8		F L
17	-	**School's Out**	Alice Cooper	Warner	9	(7)	F
18	-	**Mad About You**	Bruce Ruffin	Rhino	5		L
19	-	**Walkin' In The Rain With The One I Love**	Love Unlimited	Uni	4	(14)	F
20	-	**Little Bit Of Love**	Free	Island	5		

August 1972

This Mnth	Prev Mnth	Title	Artist	Label	Wks	(US 20 Pos)	
1	17	**School's Out**	Alice Cooper	Warner	9	(7)	F
2	16	**Seaside Shuffle**	Terry Dactyl & The Dinosaurs	UK	8		F L
3	1	**Puppy Love**	Donny Osmond	MGM	12	(3)	F
4	-	**Silver Machine**	Hawkwind	UA	10		F L
5	12	**Breaking Up Is Hard To Do**	Partridge Family	Bell	9	(28)	
6	-	**Popcorn**	Hot Butter	Pye International	8	(9)	F L
7	6	**Sylvia's Mother**	Dr. Hook	CBS	8	(5)	F
8	2	**Rock & Roll Part 2**	Gary Glitter	Bell	10	(7)	F
9	7	**I Can See Clearly Now**	Johnny Nash	CBS	9	(1)	
10	-	**You Wear It Well**	Rod Stewart	Mercury	7	(13)	
11	-	**All The Young Dudes**	Mott The Hoople	CBS	6	(37)	F
12	5	**Circles**	New Seekers	Polydor	8	(87)	
13	-	**It's Four In The Morning**	Faron Young	Mercury	10	(92)	F L
14	-	**10538 Overture**	Electric Light Orchestra	Harvest	6		F
15	-	**Run To Me**	Bee Gees	Polydor	5	(16)	
16	-	**Automatically Sunshine**	Supremes	Tamla Motown	4	(37)	L
17	-	**Layla**	Derek & The Dominoes	Polydor	5	(10)	F L
18	-	**Starman**	David Bowie	RCA	6	(65)	
19	18	**Mad About You**	Bruce Ruffin	Rhino	5		L
20	-	**The Loco-Motion**	Little Eva	London American	5		L

◆ Wembley Stadium hosted its first pop concert and 45,000 50s fans turned out to watch Bill Haley, Chuck Berry, Little Richard, Jerry Lee Lewis and Bo Diddley (filmed as *The London Rock And Roll Show*).

◆ The successful album-oriented TV show, *The Old Grey Whistle Test,* kicked off - it helped launch many less commercial acts in the 1970s.

1972

This Mnth	Prev Mnth	Title	Artist	Label	Wks	(US 20 Pos)	
1	-	Mama Weer All Crazee Now	Slade	Polydor	7	(76)	
2	10	You Wear It Well	Rod Stewart	Mercury	7	(13)	
3	13	It's Four In The Morning	Faron Young	Mercury	10	(92)	F L
4	-	Sugar Me	Lynsey De Paul	MAM	6		F
5	-	Virginia Plain	Roxy Music	Island	6		F
6	-	Standing In The Road	Blackfoot Sue	Jam	6		F L
7	11	All The Young Dudes	Mott The Hoople	CBS	6	(37)	F
8	-	How Can I Be Sure	David Cassidy	Bell	8	(25)	
9	-	I Get The Sweetest Feeling	Jackie Wilson	MCA	6	(34)	
10	-	Children Of The Revolution	T. Rex	EMI	7		
11	-	Ain't No Sunshine	Michael Jackson	Tamla Motown	6		
12	4	Silver Machine	Hawkwind	UA	10		F L
13	17	Layla	Derek & The Dominoes	Polydor	5	(10)	F L
14	1	School's Out	Alice Cooper	Warner	9	(7)	F
15	-	Too Young	Donny Osmond	MGM	5	(13)	
16	-	Living In Harmony	Cliff Richard	Columbia	4		
17	20	The Loco-Motion	Little Eva	London American	5		L
18	6	Popcorn	Hot Butter	Pye International	8	(9)	F L
19	-	Come On Over To My Place	Drifters	Atlantic	6	(60)	
20	-	Wig Wam Bam	Sweet	RCA	7		

This Mnth	Prev Mnth	Title	Artist	Label	Wks	(US 20 Pos)	
1	-	Mouldy Old Dough	Lieutenant Pigeon	Decca	11		F
2	8	How Can I Be Sure	David Cassidy	Bell	8	(25)	
3	-	You're A Lady	Peter Skellern	Decca	7	(50)	F
4	-	I Didn't Know I Loved You (Till I Saw You Rock 'n' Roll)	Gary Glitter	Bell	7	(35)	
5	20	Wig Wam Bam	Sweet	RCA	7		
6	-	Donna	10cc	UK	9		F
7	10	Children Of The Revolution	T. Rex	EMI	7		
8	-	Burning Love	Elvis Presley	RCA	6	(2)	
9	-	In A Broken Dream	Python Lee Jackson	Youngblood	7	(56)	F L
10	15	Too Young	Donny Osmond	MGM	5	(13)	
11	-	Big Six	Judge Dread	Big Shot	8		F
12	-	Elected	Alice Cooper	Warner	7	(26)	
13	-	John I'm Only Dancing	David Bowie	RCA	5		
14	-	There Are More Questions Than Answers	Johnny Nash	CBS	6		
15	-	Clair	Gilbert O'Sullivan	MAM	8	(2)	
16	19	Come On Over To My Place	Drifters	Atlantic	6	(60)	
17	3	It's Four In The Morning	Faron Young	Mercury	10	(92)	F L
18	1	Mama Weer All Crazee Now	Slade	Polydor	7	(76)	
19	-	Suzanne Beware Of The Devil	Dandy Livingstone	Horse	5		F L
20	-	Goodbye To Love/I Won't Last A Day Without You	Carpenters	A&M	6	(7)	

◆ Making their debuts were Wizzard, formed by ex-Move and Electric Light Orchestra front man Roy Wood, and 10cc, a collection of Manchester's finest, who had evolved from The Mindbenders and Hot Legs.

◆ Compilation albums of 1950s hits held the top spot for 14 consecutive weeks, and re-issues of earlier hits continued to clog the charts, the latest coming from Americans Neil Sedaka, The Shangri-Las, Chris Montez and Roy C.

November 1972

This Mnth	Prev Mnth	Title	Artist	Label	Wks	(US Pos)	
1	15	Clair	Gilbert O'Sullivan	MAM	8	(2)	
2	1	Mouldy Old Dough	Lieutenant Pigeon	Decca	11		F
3	-	Leader Of The Pack	Shangri-Las	Kama Sutra	6		
4	-	Loop Di Love	Shag	UK	7		F L
5	-	My Ding-A-Ling	Chuck Berry	Chess	10	(1)	
6	6	Donna	10cc	UK	9		F
7	12	Elected	Alice Cooper	Warner	7	(26)	
8	9	In A Broken Dream	Python Lee Jackson	Youngblood	7	(56)	F L
9	20	Goodbye To Love/I Won't Last A Day Without You	Carpenters	A&M	6	(7)	
10	-	Crazy Horses	Osmonds	MGM	12	(14)	F
11	-	Why	Donny Osmond	MGM	9	(13)	
12	-	Crocodile Rock	Elton John	DJM	10	(1)	
13	-	Let's Dance	Chris Montez	London American	5		L
14	-	Hallelujah Freedom	Junior Campbell	Deram	5		F
15	-	I'm Stone In Love With You	Stylistics	Avco	5	(10)	
16	-	Here I Go Again	Archie Bell & The Drells	Atlantic	3		F
17	14	There Are More Questions Than Answers	Johnny Nash	CBS	6		
18	-	Burlesque	Family	Reprise	5		L
19	8	Burning Love	Elvis Presley	RCA	6	(2)	
20	3	You're A Lady	Peter Skellern	Decca	7	(50)	F

December 1972

This Mnth	Prev Mnth	Title	Artist	Label	Wks	(US Pos)	
1	5	My Ding-A-Ling	Chuck Berry	Chess	10	(1)	
2	10	Crazy Horses	Osmonds	MGM	12	(14)	F
3	-	Gudbuy T'Jane	Slade	Polydor	9	(68)	
4	11	Why	Donny Osmond	MGM	9	(13)	
5	-	Long Haired Lover From Liverpool	Little Jimmy Osmond	MGM	14	(38)	F
6	-	Solid Gold Easy Action	T. Rex	EMI	8		
7	12	Crocodile Rock	Elton John	DJM	10	(1)	
8	-	Ben	Michael Jackson	Tamla Motown	8	(1)	
9	-	Angel/What Made Milwaukee Famous	Rod Stewart	Mercury	5	(40)	
10	-	Happy Xmas (War Is Over)	John & Yoko/Plastic Ono Band	Apple	5		
11	-	Stay With Me	Blue Mink	Regal Zonophone	5		
12	-	Shotgun Wedding	Roy 'C'	UK	7		L
13	-	Lookin' Through The Windows	Jackson Five	Tamla Motown	6	(16)	
14	-	Rock Me Baby	David Cassidy	Bell	5	(38)	
15	-	Nights In White Satin	Moody Blues	Deram	6	(2)	
16	-	Lay Down	Strawbs	A&M	4		F
17	1	Clair	Gilbert O'Sullivan	MAM	8	(2)	
18	-	Help Me Make It Through The Night	Gladys Knight & The Pips	Tamla Motown	7	(33)	
19	15	I'm Stone In Love With You	Stylistics	Avco	5	(10)	
20	-	Little Drummer Boy	Royal Scots Dragoon Guards	RCA	4		L

◆ With Osmond-mania at its height in the UK, nine-year-old Little Jimmy's minor US hit, 'Long Haired Lover From Liverpool', became the biggest British seller by any of the family.

◆ The Moody Blues' US tour was a resounding success. The group, who had a transatlantic hit with the five-year-old, 'Nights in White Satin', topped the album chart with Seventh Sojourn.

◆ American band The New York Dolls made an impressive if not highly publicized UK debut.

1973

This Mnth	Prev Mnth	Title	Artist	Label	Wks	(US 20 Pos)	
1	5	Long Haired Lover From Liverpool	Little Jimmy Osmond	MGM	14	(38)	F
2	-	The Jean Genie	David Bowie	RCA	8	(71)	
3	-	Hi Hi Hi/C Moon	Wings	Apple	6	(10)	
4	6	Solid Gold Easy Action	T. Rex	EMI	8		
5	2	Crazy Horses	Osmonds	MGM	12	(14)	F
6	-	Ball Park Incident	Wizzard	Harvest	6		F
7	-	You're So Vain	Carly Simon	Elektra	8	(1)	F
8	-	Blockbuster	Sweet	RCA	10	(73)	
9	-	Big Seven	Judge Dread	Big Shot	7		
10	-	Always On My Mind	Elvis Presley	RCA	5		
11	3	Gudbuy T'Jane	Slade	Polydor	9	(68)	
12	12	Shotgun Wedding	Roy 'C'	UK	7		L
13	15	Nights In White Satin	Moody Blues	Deram	6	(2)	
14	10	Happy Xmas (War Is Over)	John & Yoko & The Plastic Ono Band	Apple	5		
15	1	My Ding-A-Ling	Chuck Berry	Chess	10	(1)	
16	18	Help Me Make It Through The Night	Gladys Knight & The Pips	Tamla Motown	7	(33)	
17	8	Ben	Michael Jackson	Tamla Motown	8	(1)	
18	-	Do You Wanna Touch Me (Oh Yeah)	Gary Glitter	Bell	7		
19	-	Wishing Well	Free	Island	5		
20	-	Can't Keep It In	Cat Stevens	Island	4		

This Mnth	Prev Mnth	Title	Artist	Label	Wks	(US 20 Pos)	
1	8	Blockbuster	Sweet	RCA	10	(73)	
2	18	Do You Wanna Touch Me (Oh Yeah)	Gary Glitter	Bell	7		
3	-	Part Of The Union	Strawbs	A&M	9		L
4	-	Daniel	Elton John	DJM	6	(2)	
5	7	You're So Vain	Carly Simon	Elektra	8	(1)	F
6	1	Long Haired Lover From Liverpool	Little Jimmy Osmond	MGM	14	(38)	F
7	-	Sylvia	Focus	Polydor	6	(89)	L
8	-	Roll Over Beethoven	Electric Light Orchestra	Harvest	5	(42)	
9	-	Paper Plane	Status Quo	Vertigo	5		
10	19	Wishing Well	Free	Island	5		
11	-	Whiskey In The Jar	Thin Lizzy	Decca	6		F
12	-	If You Don't Know Me By Now	Harold Melvin & The Blue Notes	CBS	4	(3)	F
13	2	The Jean Genie	David Bowie	RCA	8	(71)	
14	-	Superstition	Stevie Wonder	Tamla Motown	5	(1)	
15	-	Me And Mrs. Jones	Billy Paul	Epic	4	(1)	F L
16	-	Cindy Incidentally	Faces	Warner	7	(48)	
17	-	Baby I Love You	Dave Edmunds	Rockfield	6		
18	-	Lookin' Through The Eyes Of Love	Partridge Family	Bell	5	(39)	
19	6	Ball Park Incident	Wizzard	Harvest	6		F
20	20	Can't Keep It In	Cat Stevens	Island	4		

◆ Local glam rock greats, Sweet, Gary Glitter, T-Rex, David Bowie and Slade vied for the affection of British teeny boppers with American superstars The Osmonds and David Cassidy.

◆ Pink Floyd's album **Dark Side Of The Moon** entered the US chart, where it has remained for a record smashing 17 years (selling over 12 million copies)!

March 1973

This Mnth	Prev Mnth	Title	Artist	Label	Wks (US 20 Pos)	
1	-	**Cum On Feel The Noize**	Slade	Polydor	7 (98)	
2	-	**Feel The Need In Me**	Detroit Emeralds	Janus	7 (90)	F
3	-	**20th Century Boy**	T. Rex	EMI	6	
4	16	**Cindy Incidentally**	Faces	Warner	7 (48)	
5	-	**The Twelfth Of Never**	Donny Osmond	MGM	9 (8)	
6	-	**Killing Me Softly With His Song**	Roberta Flack	Atlantic	8 (1)	
7	-	**Hello Hurray**	Alice Cooper	Warner	8 (35)	
8	3	**Part Of The Union**	Strawbs	A&M	9	L
9	-	**Power To All Our Friends**	Cliff Richard	EMI	7	
10	1	**Blockbuster**	Sweet	RCA	10 (73)	
11	-	**Gonna Make You An Offer You Can't Refuse**	Jimmy Helms	Cube	5	F L
12	7	**Sylvia**	Focus	Polydor	6 (89)	L
13	-	**Doctor My Eyes**	Jackson Five	Tamla Motown	5	
14	17	**Baby I Love You**	Dave Edmunds	Rockfield	6	
15	-	**Get Down**	Gilbert O'Sullivan	MAM	8 (7)	
16	11	**Whiskey In The Jar**	Thin Lizzy	Decca	6	F
17	2	**Do You Wanna Touch Me (Oh Yeah)**	Gary Glitter	Bell	7	
18	18	**Lookin' Through The Eyes Of Love**	Partridge Family	Bell	5 (39)	
19	-	**Never Never Never**	Shirley Bassey	UA	8 (48)	L
20	-	**Heart Of Stone**	Kenny	RAK	6	F L

April 1973

This Mnth	Prev Mnth	Title	Artist	Label	Wks (US 20 Pos)	
1	-	**Tie A Yellow Ribbon Round The Old Oak Tree**	Dawn	Bell	17 (1)	
2	15	**Get Down**	Gilbert O'Sullivan	MAM	8 (7)	
3	-	**I'm A Clown/Some Kind Of A Summer**	David Cassidy	Bell	8	
4	5	**The Twelfth Of Never**	Donny Osmond	MGM	9 (8)	
5	-	**Tweedle Dee**	Little Jimmy Osmond	MGM	7 (59)	
6	-	**Hello Hello I'm Back Again**	Gary Glitter	Bell	10	
7	9	**Power To All Our Friends**	Cliff Richard	EMI	7	
8	19	**Never Never Never**	Shirley Bassey	UA	8 (48)	L
9	-	**Love Train**	O'Jays	CBS	6 (1)	
10	-	**Pyjamarama**	Roxy Music	Island	6	
11	-	**All Because Of You**	Geordie	EMI	6	F
12	-	**Drive-In Saturday**	David Bowie	RCA	7	
13	-	**Crazy**	Mud	RAK	5	F
14	20	**Heart Of Stone**	Kenny	RAK	6	F L
15	-	**My Love**	Paul McCartney & Wings	Apple	6 (1)	
16	-	**Amanda**	Stuart Gillies	Philips	5	F L
17	6	**Killing Me Softly With His Song**	Roberta Flack	Atlantic	8 (1)	
18	2	**Feel The Need In Me**	Detroit Emeralds	Janus	7 (90)	F
19	-	**Why Can't We Live Together**	Timmy Thomas	Mojo	4 (3)	F L
20	1	**Cum On Feel The Noize**	Slade	Polydor	7 (98)	

◆ Reluctant guitar hero Eric Clapton made his live comeback after two years with a performance at London's Rainbow Theatre. Pete Townshend organized the show which also featured Steve Winwood, Ron Wood and Jim Capaldi.

◆ As John Lennon denied that The Beatles would re-unite, the group's compilation album 1967-1970 was replaced at the top of the US chart by Red Rose Speedway from Paul McCartney & Wings.

1973

May 1973

This Mnth	Prev Mnth	Title	Artist	Label	Wks	(US 20 Pos)
1	1	Tie A Yellow Ribbon Round The Old Oak Tree	Dawn	Bell	17	(1)
2	-	Hell Raiser	Sweet	RCA	6	
3	-	See My Baby Jive	Wizzard	Harvest	10	
4	6	Hello Hello I'm Back Again	Gary Glitter	Bell	10	
5	12	Drive-In Saturday	David Bowie	RCA	7	
6	-	Giving It All Away	Roger Daltrey	Track	6	(83) F
7	-	Brother Louie	Hot Chocolate	RAK	6	
8	-	And I Love You So	Perry Como	RCA	12	(29)
9	15	My Love	Paul McCartney & Wings	Apple	6	(1)
10	-	No More Mr. Nice Guy	Alice Cooper	Warner	4	(25)
11	11	All Because Of You	Geordie	EMI	6	F
12	-	Also Sprach Zarathustra (2001)	Deodata	CTI	5	(2) F L
13	-	Wonderful Dream	Ann-Marie David	Epic	4	F L
14	5	Tweedle Dee	Little Jimmy Osmond	MGM	7	(59)
15	-	One And One Is One	Medicine Head	Polydor	7	F
16	2	Get Down	Gilbert O'Sullivan	MAM	8	(7)
17	3	I'm A Clown/Some Kind Of A Summer	David Cassidy	Bell	8	
18	-	Big Eight	Judge Dread	Big Shot	5	
19	-	Can The Can	Suzi Quatro	RAK	7	(56) F
20	-	Broken Down Angel	Nazareth	Mooncrest	5	F

June 1973

This Mnth	Prev Mnth	Title	Artist	Label	Wks	(US 20 Pos)
1	19	Can The Can	Suzi Quatro	RAK	7	(56) F
2	-	Rubber Bullets	10cc	UK	9	(73)
3	3	See My Baby Jive	Wizzard	Harvest	10	
4	15	One And One Is One	Medicine Head	Polydor	7	F
5	-	Albatross	Fleetwood Mac	CBS	8	
6	8	And I Love You So	Perry Como	RCA	12	(29)
7	-	The Groover	T. Rex	EMI	5	
8	-	Stuck In The Middle With You	Stealer's Wheel	A&M	6	(6) F L
9	1	Tie A Yellow Ribbon Round The Old Oak Tree	Dawn	Bell	17	(1)
10	-	Walking In The Rain	Partridge Family	Bell	5	L
11	-	You Are The Sunshine Of My Life	Stevie Wonder	Tamla Motown	5	(1)
12	-	Welcome Home	Peters & Lee	Philips	15	F
13	-	Snoopy Vs. The Red Baron	Hotshots	Mooncrest	8	F L
14	-	Give Me Love (Give Me Peace On Earth)	George Harrison	Apple	6	(1)
15	2	Hell Raiser	Sweet	RCA	6	
16	-	Walk On The Wild Side	Lou Reed	RCA	4	(16) F L
17	-	Live And Let Die	Wings	Apple	7	(2)
18	20	Broken Down Angel	Nazareth	Mooncrest	5	F
19	-	Skweeze Me Pleeze Me	Slade	Polydor	6	
20	12	Also Sprach Zarathustra (2001)	Deodata	CTI	5	(2) F L

◆ Fleetwood Mac's re-issued instrumental 'Albatross' peaked at No. 2, narrowly failing to become the first record to top the UK chart on two separate occasions.

◆ 'Monster Mash' by Bobby 'Boris' Pickett & The Crypt Kickers, which had topped the US chart in 1962, not only returned to the Top 10 but also hit in re-issue-mad Britain for the first time.

1973

This Mnth	Prev Mnth	Title	Artist	Label	Wks	(US 20 Pos)	
1	12	**Welcome Home**	Peters & Lee	Philips	15		F
2	19	**Skweeze Me Pleeze Me**	Slade	Polydor	6		
3	-	**Life On Mars**	David Bowie	RCA	8		
4	-	**Born To Be With You**	Dave Edmunds	Rockfield	7		
5	13	**Snoopy Vs. The Red Baron**	Hotshots	Mooncrest	8		F L
6	-	**Take Me To The Mardi Gras**	Paul Simon	CBS	5		
7	2	**Rubber Bullets**	10cc	UK	9	(73)	
8	-	**Saturday Night's Alright For Fighting**	Elton John	DJM	5	(12)	
9	-	**I'm The Leader Of The Gang (I Am)**	Gary Glitter	Bell	8		
10	5	**Albatross**	Fleetwood Mac	CBS	8		
11	-	**Going Home**	Osmonds	MGM	6	(36)	
12	-	**Alright Alright Alright**	Mungo Jerry	Dawn	6		
13	-	**Randy**	Blue Mink	EMI	5		L
14	17	**Live And Let Die**	Wings	Apple	7	(2)	
15	-	**Gaye**	Clifford T. Ward	Charisma	5		F L
16	14	**Give Me Love (Give Me Peace On Earth)**	George Harrison	Apple	6	(1)	
17	-	**Honaloochie Boogie**	Mott The Hoople	CBS	3		
18	7	**The Groover**	T. Rex	EMI	5		
19	-	**Can You Do It**	Geordie	EMI	4		L
20	-	**Step By Step**	Joe Simon	Mojo	3	(37)	F L

This	Prev	Title	Artist	Label	Wks	(US Pos)	
1	9	**I'm The Leader Of The Gang (I Am)**	Gary Glitter	Bell	8		
2	1	**Welcome Home**	Peters & Lee	Philips	15		F
3	-	**Yesterday Once More**	Carpenters	A&M	8	(2)	
4	-	**48 Crash**	Suzi Quatro	RAK	5		
5	12	**Alright Alright Alright**	Mungo Jerry	Dawn	6		
6	-	**Spanish Eyes**	Al Martino	Capitol	13		L
7	11	**Going Home**	Osmonds	MGM	6	(36)	
8	-	**You Can Do Magic**	Limmie & The Family Cookin'	Avco	7	(84)	F
9	3	**Life On Mars**	David Bowie	RCA	8		
10	-	**Touch Me In The Morning**	Diana Ross	Tamla Motown	6	(1)	
11	-	**Ying Tong Song**	Goons	Decca	4		L
12	-	**Bad Bad Boy**	Nazareth	Mooncrest	5		
13	-	**(Dancing) On A Saturday Night**	Barry Blue	Bell	9		F
14	-	**Young Love**	Donny Osmond	MGM	7	(25)	
15	-	**Smarty Pants**	First Choice	Bell	5	(56)	L
16	13	**Randy**	Blue Mink	EMI	5		L
17	15	**Gaye**	Clifford T. Ward	Charisma	5		F L
18	-	**All Right Now**	Free	Island	3		
19	-	**Rising Sun**	Medicine Head	Polydor	5		L
20	-	**Summer (The First Time)**	Bobby Goldsboro	UA	5	(21)	

◆ David Bowie and Jethro Tull (who topped the US LP chart with A Passion Play) announced that their touring days were over. The Everly Brothers split up and Ray Davis quit The Kinks. More permanent, however, were the dissolution of The Doors and Eno's departure from Roxy Music.

◆ Soon after Freddie Mercury's debut single 'I Can Hear Music' (as Larry Lurex) failed to click, his group Queen's first 45, 'Keep Yourself Alive' also fell by the wayside. Despite this disappointing chart start, they went on to become one of the biggest selling and most influential British acts of all time.

1973

This Mnth	Prev Mnth	Title	Artist	Label	Wks	(US 20 Pos)	
1	-	**Angel Fingers**	Wizzard	Harvest	8		
2	14	**Young Love**	Donny Osmond	MGM	7	(25)	
3	-	**Rock On**	David Essex	CBS	7	(5)	F
4	13	**(Dancing) On A Saturday Night**	Barry Blue	Bell	9		F
5	6	**Spanish Eyes**	Al Martino	Capitol	13		L
6	-	**Angie**	Rolling Stones	Rolling Stone	5	(1)	
7	8	**You Can Do Magic**	Limmie & The Family Cookin'	Avco	7	(84)	F
8	-	**Oh No Not My Baby**	Rod Stewart	Mercury	5	(59)	
9	-	**Say, Has Anybody Seen My Sweet Gypsy Rose**	Dawn	Bell	5	(3)	L
10	-	**Like Sister And Brother**	Drifters	Bell	6		
11	3	**Yesterday Once More**	Carpenters	A&M	8	(2)	
12	-	**Ballroom Blitz**	Sweet	RCA	6	(5)	
13	-	**Pick Up The Pieces**	Hudson-Ford	A&M	4		F
14	-	**Monster Mash**	Bobby 'Boris' Pickett & The Crypt Kickers	London American	6	(10)	F L
15	-	**The Dean And I**	10cc	UK	4		
16	20	**Summer (The First Time)**	Bobby Goldsboro	UA	5	(21)	
17	-	**Eye Level**	Simon Park Orchestra	Columbia	10		F G L
18	2	**Welcome Home**	Peters & Lee	Philips	15		F
19	-	**For The Good Times**	Perry Como	RCA	10		L
20	1	**I'm The Leader Of The Gang (I Am)**	Gary Glitter	Bell	8		

This Mnth	Prev Mnth	Title	Artist	Label	Wks	(US 20 Pos)	
1	17	**Eye Level**	Simon Park Orchestra	Columbia	10		F G L
2	-	**My Friend Stan**	Slade	Polydor	6		
3	-	**Nutbush City Limits**	Ike & Tina Turner	UA	7	(22)	L
4	12	**Ballroom Blitz**	Sweet	RCA	6	(5)	
5	14	**Monster Mash**	Bobby 'Boris' Pickett & The Crypt Kickers	London American	6	(10)	F L
6	-	**The Laughing Gnome**	David Bowie	Deram	6		
7	19	**For The Good Times**	Perry Como	RCA	10		L
8	-	**Daydreamer/The Puppy Song**	David Cassidy	Bell	8		
9	-	**Caroline**	Status Quo	Vertigo	8		
10	-	**Goodbye Yellow Brick Road**	Elton John	DJM	7	(2)	
11	1	**Angel Fingers**	Wizzard	Harvest	8		
12	-	**Joybringer**	Manfred Mann's Earth Band	Vertigo	5		L
13	-	**A Hard Rain's Gonna Fall**	Bryan Ferry	Island	5		F
14	-	**Sorrow**	David Bowie	RCA	8		
15	-	**Ghetto Child**	Detroit Spinners	Atlantic	6	(29)	
16	8	**Oh No Not My Baby**	Rod Stewart	Mercury	5	(59)	
17	5	**Spanish Eyes**	Al Martino	Capitol	13		L
18	-	**All The Way From Memphis**	Mott The Hoople	CBS	4		
19	-	**Showdown**	Electric Light Orchestra	Harvest	5	(53)	
20	-	**That Lady (Pt. 1)**	Isley Brothers	Epic	2	(6)	

◆ It was announced that David Bowie had sold over eight million units in Britain in two years, making him the biggest seller since The Beatles.

◆ Hottest producer/ songwriters in Britain in 1973 were Nicky Chinn & Mike Chapman, who were responsible for hits from Sweet, American rocker Suzi Quatro and new teen idols Mud.

November 1973

This Mnth	Prev Mnth	Title	Artist	Label	Wks	(US 20 Pos)	
1	-	**Let Me In**	Osmonds	MGM	9	(36)	
2	14	**Sorrow**	David Bowie	RCA	8		
3	8	**Daydreamer/The Puppy Song**	David Cassidy	Bell	8		
4	-	**Top Of The World**	Carpenters	A&M	8	(1)	
5	-	**Dyna-Mite**	Mud	RAK	7		
6	1	**Eye Level**	Simon Park Orchestra	Columbia	10		F G L
7	-	**I Love You Love Me Love**	Gary Glitter	Bell	12		G
8	15	**Ghetto Child**	Detroit Spinners	Atlantic	6	(29)	
9	7	**For The Good Times**	Perry Como	RCA	10		L
10	-	**Photograph**	Ringo Starr	Apple	5	(1)	
11	-	**This Flight Tonight**	Nazareth	Mooncrest	5		
12	9	**Caroline**	Status Quo	Vertigo	8		
13	-	**When I Fall In Love**	Donny Osmond	MGM	9	(14)	
14	10	**Goodbye Yellow Brick Road**	Elton John	DJM	7	(2)	
15	-	**Do You Wanna Dance**	Barry Blue	Bell	6		
16	19	**Showdown**	Electric Light Orchestra	Harvest	5	(53)	
17	-	**Deck Of Cards**	Max Bygraves	Pye	5		L
18	-	**Paper Roses**	Marie Osmond	MGM	11	(5)	F L
19	2	**My Friend Stan**	Slade	Polydor	6		
20	-	**Won't Somebody Dance With Me**	Lynsey De Paul	MAM	5		

December 1973

This Mnth	Prev Mnth	Title	Artist	Label	Wks	(US 20 Pos)	
1	7	**I Love You Love Me Love**	Gary Glitter	Bell	12		G
2	-	**My Coo-Ca-Choo**	Alvin Stardust	Magnet	12		F
3	-	**You Won't Find Another Fool Like Me**	New Seekers	Polydor	12		
4	18	**Paper Roses**	Marie Osmond	MGM	11	(5)	F L
5	-	**Lamplight**	David Essex	CBS	11	(71)	
6	-	**Merry Xmas Everybody**	Slade	Polydor	7		G
7	-	**Why Oh Why Oh Why**	Gilbert O'Sullivan	MAM	10		
8	-	**Roll Away The Stone**	Mott The Hoople	CBS	9		
9	-	**I Wish It Could Be Christmas Everyday**	Wizzard	Harvest	7		
10	-	**Street Life**	Roxy Music	Island	8		
11	13	**When I Fall In Love**	Donny Osmond	MGM	9	(14)	
12	5	**Dyna-Mite**	Mud	RAK	7		
13	1	**Let Me In**	Osmonds	MGM	9	(36)	
14	-	**Truck On (Tyke)**	T. Rex	EMI	7		
15	-	**The Show Must Go On**	Leo Sayer	Chrysalis	9		F
16	15	**Do You Wanna Dance**	Barry Blue	Bell	6		
17	-	**Helen Wheels**	Paul McCartney & Wings	Apple	4	(10)	
18	-	**Forever**	Roy Wood	Harvest	9		
19	-	**Loving And Free/Amoureuse**	Kiki Dee	Rocket	5		F
20	10	**Photograph**	Ringo Starr	Apple	5	(1)	

◆ John Rostill of The Shadows was electrocuted in his studio. His death came days after his song 'Let Me Be There' gave Olivia Newton-John her first American pop hit and days before her record became the first UK recording to crack the US country Top 10.

1974

This Mnth	Prev Mnth	Title	Artist	Label	Wks	(US 20 Pos)	
1	3	You Won't Find Another Fool Like Me	New Seekers	Polydor	12		
2	15	The Show Must Go On	Leo Sayer	Chrysalis	9		F
3	6	Merry Xmas Everybody	Slade	Polydor	7		G
4	2	My Coo-Ca-Choo	Alvin Stardust	Magnet	12		F
5	-	Dance With The Devil	Cozy Powell	RAK	10	(49)	F
6	1	I Love You Love Me Love	Gary Glitter	Bell	12		G
7	18	Forever	Roy Wood	Harvest	9		
8	4	Paper Roses	Marie Osmond	MGM	11	(5)	F L
9	-	Radar Love	Golden Earring	Track	6	(13)	F L
10	9	I Wish It Could Be Christmas Everyday	Wizzard	Harvest	7		
11	-	Pool Hall Richard/I Wish It Would Rain	Faces	Warner	7		
12	-	Love On A Mountain Top	Robert Knight	Monument	10		F
13	5	Lamplight	David Essex	CBS	11	(71)	
14	-	Teenage Rampage	Sweet	RCA	6		
15	-	Tiger Feet	Mud	RAK	8		
16	8	Roll Away The Stone	Mott The Hoople	CBS	9		
17	-	Solitaire	Andy Williams	CBS	8		L
18	10	Street Life	Roxy Music	Island	8		
19	7	Why Oh Why Oh Why	Gilbert O'Sullivan	MAM	10		
20	14	Truck On (Tyke)	T. Rex	EMI	7		

This Mnth	Prev Mnth	Title	Artist	Label	Wks	(US 20 Pos)	
1	15	Tiger Feet	Mud	RAK	8		
2	14	Teenage Rampage	Sweet	RCA	6		
3	17	Solitaire	Andy Williams	CBS	8		L
4	-	The Man Who Sold The World	Lulu	Polydor	6		
5	5	Dance With The Devil	Cozy Powell	RAK	10	(49)	F
6	-	Devil Gate Drive	Suzi Quatro	RAK	7		
7	-	Rockin' Roll Baby	Stylistics	Avco	6	(14)	
8	-	All Of My Life	Diana Ross	Tamla Motown	6		
9	2	The Show Must Go On	Leo Sayer	Chrysalis	9		F
10	-	The Wombling Song	Wombles	CBS	7		F
11	1	You Won't Find Another Fool Like Me	New Seekers	Polydor	12		
12	-	How Come	Ronnie Lane	GM	4		F L
13	9	Radar Love	Golden Earring	Track	6	(13)	F L
14	7	Forever	Roy Wood	Harvest	9		
15	12	Love On A Mountain Top	Robert Knight	Monument	10		F
16	-	Jealous Mind	Alvin Stardust	Magnet	6		
17	4	My Coo-Ca-Choo	Alvin Stardust	Magnet	12		F
18	-	Teenage Lament '74	Alice Cooper	Warner	3	(48)	L
19	-	Teenage Dream	Marc Bolan & T. Rex	EMI	3		
20	-	Rebel Rebel	David Bowie	RCA	5	(64)	

◆ Newcomers who were creating interest included: Queen, Leo Sayer, Alvin Stardust, Bad Company, The Wombles, and a new-look Bay City Rollers.

◆ The main winners in the *NME* poll were David Bowie (Top Male), Diana Ross (Top Female) and Yes (Top Group). Incidentally, Yes, who quickly sold out their Madison Square Garden shows, scored their first UK chart topper with the LP **Tales From Topographic Oceans**.

March 1974

This Mnth	Prev Mnth	Title	Artist	Label	Wks	(US 20 Pos)	
1	-	The Air That I Breathe	Hollies	Polydor	7	(6)	
2	-	Billy, Don't Be A Hero	Paper Lace	Bus Stop	9	(96)	F
3	16	Jealous Mind	Alvin Stardust	Magnet	6		
4	-	You're Sixteen	Ringo Starr	Apple	7	(1)	L
5	-	The Most Beautiful Girl	Charlie Rich	CBS	9	(1)	F
6	6	Devil Gate Drive	Suzi Quatro	RAK	7		
7	-	Remember (Sha-La-La)	Bay City Rollers	Bell	6		
8	-	Jet	Paul McCartney & Wings	Apple	6	(7)	
9	10	The Wombling Song	Wombles	CBS	7		F
10	-	It's You	Freddie Starr	Tiffany	6		F L
11	20	Rebel Rebel	David Bowie	RCA	5	(64)	
12	-	I Get A Little Sentimental Over You	New Seekers	Polydor	6		L
13	-	Candle In The Wind	Elton John	DJM	6		
14	-	Ma He's Making Eyes At Me	Lena Zavaroni	Philips	6	(91)	F L
15	-	Emma	Hot Chocolate	RAK	7	(8)	
16	-	School Love	Barry Blue	Bell	5		L
17	1	Tiger Feet	Mud	Rak	8		
18	-	Seasons In The Sun	Terry Jacks	Bell	9	(1)	F
19	-	Never, Never Gonna Give Ya Up	Barry White	Pye International	4	(7)	F
20	-	Love's Theme	Love Unlimited Orchestra	Pye	6	(1)	F L

April 1974

This Mnth	Prev Mnth	Title	Artist	Label	Wks	(US 20 Pos)	
1	18	Seasons In The Sun	Terry Jacks	Bell	9	(1)	F
2	-	Angel Face	Glitter Band	Bell	7		F
3	-	Everyday	Slade	Polydor	5		
4	-	Remember Me This Way	Gary Glitter	Bell	6		
5	-	You Are Everything	Diana Ross	Tamla Motown	7		
6	2	Billy, Don't Be A Hero	Paper Lace	Bus Stop	9	(96)	F
7	15	Emma	Hot Chocolate	RAK	7	(8)	
8	-	The Cat Crept In	Mud	RAK	6		
9	-	Doctor's Orders	Sunny	CBS	5		F L
10	-	Seven Seas Of Rhye	Queen	EMI	6		F
11	-	Remember You're A Womble	Wombles	CBS	9		
12	5	The Most Beautiful Girl	Charlie Rich	CBS	9	(1)	F
13	12	I Get A Little Sentimental Over You	New Seekers	Polydor	6		L
14	-	I'm Gonna Knock On Your Door	Little Jimmy Osmond	MGM	4		L
15	-	Waterloo	Abba	Epic	7	(6)	F
16	-	Homely Girl	Chi-Lites	Brunswick	6	(54)	
17	-	Rock Around The Clock	Bill Haley & His Comets	MCA	5		L
18	-	A Walkin' Miracle	Limmie & The Family Cookin'	Avco	5		L
19	-	Long Live Love	Olivia Newton-John	Pye International	4		
20	-	Jambalaya	Carpenters	A&M	5		

◆ Soon after Elvis and Priscilla ended their marriage, Cher filed for divorce from Sonny and John Lennon and Yoko Ono temporarily separated.

◆ Rick Wakeman quit Yes and his solo album **Journey To The Centre Of The Earth** reached the transatlantic Top 3. Also stretching their wings were Bill Wyman, who became the first Rolling Stone to release a solo album, and The Who's Roger Daltrey, who staged his first solo concert.

1974

This Mnth	Prev Mnth	Title	Artist	Label	Wks	(US 20 Pos)	
1	15	**Waterloo**	Abba	Epic	7	(6)	F
2	-	**Don't Stay Away Too Long**	Peters & Lee	Philips	8		
3	-	**Shang-A-Lang**	Bay City Rollers	Bell	6		
4	-	**Sugar Baby Love**	Rubettes	Polydor	7	(37)	F
5	11	**Remember You're A Womble**	Wombles	CBS	9		
6	-	**Rock 'n' Roll Winter**	Wizzard	Warner	4		
7	16	**Homely Girl**	Chi-Lites	Brunswick	6	(54)	
8	-	**The Night Chicago Died**	Paper Lace	Bus Stop	6	(1)	
9	18	**A Walkin' Miracle**	Limmie & The Family Cookin'	Avco	5		L
10	-	**Red Dress**	Alvin Stardust	Magnet	5		
11	8	**The Cat Crept In**	Mud	RAK	6		
12	1	**Seasons In The Sun**	Terry Jacks	Bell	9	(1)	F
13	-	**This Town Ain't Big Enough For Both Of Us**	Sparks	Island	6		F
14	-	**He's Misstra Know It All**	Stevie Wonder	Tamla Motown	5		
15	-	**I Can't Stop**	Osmonds	MCA	5	(96)	
16	5	**You Are Everything**	Diana Ross	Tamla Motown	7		
17	9	**Doctor's Orders**	Sunny	CBS	5		F L
18	-	**Long Legged Woman Dressed In Black**	Mungo Jerry	Dawn	5		L
19	-	**Spiders & Snakes**	Jim Stafford	MGM	4	(3)	F
20	-	**Break The Rules**	Status Quo	Vertigo	4		

1	-	**Hey Rock And Roll**	Showaddywaddy	Bell	8		F
2	-	**There's A Ghost In My House**	R. Dean Taylor	Tamla Motown	7		L
3	-	**The Streak**	Ray Stevens	Janus	7	(1)	
4	13	**This Town Ain't Big Enough For Both Of Us**	Sparks	Island	6		F
5	4	**Sugar Baby Love**	Rubettes	Polydor	7	(37)	F
6	-	**Judy Teen**	Cockney Rebel	EMI	6		F
7	-	**Always Yours**	Gary Glitter	Bell	6		
8	-	**Jarrow Song**	Alan Price	Warner	5		L
9	8	**The Night Chicago Died**	Paper Lace	Bus Stop	6	(1)	
10	-	**A Touch Too Much**	Arrows	RAK	5		F L
11	-	**I See A Star**	Mouth & McNeal	Decca	5		F L
12	-	**Go (Before You Break My Heart)**	Gigliola Cinquetti	CBS	4		L
13	-	**She**	Charles Aznavour	Barclay	8		F L
14	-	**If I Didn't Care**	David Cassidy	Bell	4		
15	2	**Don't Stay Away Too Long**	Peters & Lee	Philips	8		
16	-	**Liverpool Lou**	Scaffold	Warner	4		L
17	-	**I'd Love You To Want Me**	Lobo	UK	6	(2)	L
18	-	**One Man Band**	Leo Sayer	Chrysalis	5	(96)	
19	-	**The In Crowd**	Bryan Ferry	Island	4		
20	3	**Shang-A-Lang**	Bay City Rollers	Bell	6		

◆ NME writers selected **Sergeant Pepper** (The Beatles), **Blonde On Blonde** (Bob Dylan) and **Pet Sounds** (Beach Boys) as the three greatest albums ever recorded.

◆ Bill Haley & The Comets' original 1954 recording of 'Rock Around The Clock' returned to the chart; it was the fifth separate visit to the UK Top 20 for the single.

◆ As Blue Swede put Sweden on the US musical map, Abba gave Scandinavia its biggest British hit, with their Eurovision winner, 'Waterloo'.

1974

This Mnth	Prev Mnth	Title	Artist	Label	Wks	(US 20 Pos)	
1	13	She	Charles Aznavour	Barclay	8		F L
2	-	Kissin' In The Back Row Of The Movies	Drifters	Bell	8		
3	-	Bangin' Man	Slade	Polydor	5		
4	-	Rock Your Baby	George McCrae	Jayboy	9	(1)	F
5	17	I'd Love You To Want Me	Lobo	UK	6	(2)	L
6	-	Young Girl	Gary Puckett & The Union Gap	CBS	6		L
7	-	Band On The Run	Paul McCartney & Wings	Apple	6	(1)	
8	7	Always Yours	Gary Glitter	Bell	6		
9	-	Banana Rock	Wombles	CBS	5		
10	-	Wall Street Shuffle	10cc	UK	5		
11	1	Hey Rock And Roll	Showaddywaddy	Bell	8		F
12	18	One Man Band	Leo Sayer	Chrysalis	5	(96)	
13	-	Born With A Smile On My Face	Stephanie De Sykes	Bradley's	6		F
14	-	The Six Teens	Sweet	RCA	5		
15	-	If You Go Away	Terry Jacks	Bell	4	(68)	L
16	3	The Streak	Ray Stevens	Janus	7	(1)	
17	-	When Will I See You Again	Three Degrees	Philly International	10	(2)	
18	-	Guilty	Pearls	Bell	4		F L
19	-	Beach Baby	First Class	UK	4	(4)	F L
20	-	Going Down The Road	Roy Wood	Harvest	3		

This Mnth	Prev Mnth	Title	Artist	Label	Wks	(US 20 Pos)	
1	17	When Will I See You Again	Three Degrees	Philly International	10	(2)	
2	-	You Make Me Feel Brand New	Stylistics	Avco	9	(2)	
3	4	Rock Your Baby	George McCrae	Jayboy	9	(1)	F
4	-	Summerlove Sensation	Bay City Rollers	Bell	7		
5	13	Born With A Smile On My Face	Stephanie De Sykes	Bradley's	6		F
6	-	Rocket	Mud	RAK	5		
7	-	Rock The Boat	Hues Corporation	RCA	5	(1)	F L
8	-	What Becomes Of The Brokenhearted	Jimmy Ruffin	Tamla Motown	8		
9	-	Amateur Hour	Sparks	Island	5		
10	7	Band On The Run	Paul McCartney & Wings	Apple	6	(1)	
11	-	I'm Leaving It (All) Up To You	Donny & Marie Osmond	MGM	8	(4)	F
12	-	I Shot The Sheriff	Eric Clapton	RSO	4	(1)	F
13	-	It's Only Rock 'n Roll (But I Like It)	Rolling Stones	Rolling Stone	4	(16)	
14	-	Tonight	Rubettes	Polydor	5		
15	2	Kissin' In The Back Row Of The...	Drifters	Bell	8		
16	-	Love Me For A Reason	Osmonds	MGM	7	(10)	
17	-	Mr. Soft	Cockney Rebel	EMI	5		
18	6	Young Girl	Gary Puckett & The Union Gap	CBS	6		L
19	-	Honey Honey	Sweet Dreams	Bradley's	6	(68)	F L
20	-	Just For You	Glitter Band	Bell	4		

◆ American oldies on the UK chart included Gary Puckett's 'Young Girl', 'Baby Love' by The Supremes and Jimmy Ruffin's 'What Becomes Of The Broken Hearted'.

◆ The Moody Blues opened the world's first quadrophonic (a system with four separate soundtracks as compared to stereo's two) recording studio in West London. One of the first projects recorded there was Blue Jays, a transatlantic Top 20 album by Moody members Justin Hayward & John Lodge.

131

1974

September 1974

This Mnth	Prev Mnth	Title	Artist	Label	Wks	(US 20 Pos)		
1	-	Kung Fu Fighting	Carl Douglas	Pye	8	(1)	F	L
2	16	Love Me For A Reason	Osmonds	MGM	7	(10)		
3	-	Annie's Song	John Denver	RCA	9	(1)	F	L
4	-	Y Viva Espana	Sylvia	Sonet	8			L
5	11	I'm Leaving It (All) Up To You	Donny & Marie Osmond	MGM	8	(4)	F	
6	-	Hang On In There Baby	Johnny Bristol	MGM	7	(8)	F	L
7	-	You You You	Alvin Stardust	Magnet	6			
8	1	When Will I See You Again	Three Degrees	Philly International	10	(2)		
9	8	What Becomes Of The Brokenhearted	Jimmy Ruffin	Tamla Motown	8			
10	-	Queen Of Clubs	KC & The Sunshine Band	Jayboy	6	(66)	F	
11	-	Na Na Na	Cozy Powell	RAK	6			L
12	-	Can't Get Enough Of Your Love, Babe	Barry White	Pye International	6	(1)		
13	19	Honey Honey	Sweet Dreams	Bradley's	6	(68)	F	L
14	2	You Make Me Feel Brand New	Stylistics	Avco	9	(2)		
15	17	Mr. Soft	Cockney Rebel	EMI	5			
16	-	The Black Eyed Boys	Paper Lace	Bus Stop	4	(41)		
17	-	Baby Love	Diana Ross & The Supremes	Tamla Motown	3			L
18	-	Rock 'n' Roll Lady	Showaddywaddy	Bell	4			
19	-	Rock Me Gently	Andy Kim	Capitol	5	(1)	F	L
20	-	Long Tall Glasses	Leo Sayer	Chrysalis	5	(9)		

October 1974

This Mnth	Prev Mnth	Title	Artist	Label	Wks	(US 20 Pos)		
1	-	Sad Sweet Dreamer	Sweet Sensation	Pye	7	(14)	F	
2	3	Annie's Song	John Denver	RCA	9	(1)	F	L
3	-	Gee Baby	Peter Shelley	Magnet	6	(81)	F	
4	19	Rock Me Gently	Andy Kim	Capitol	5	(1)	F	L
5	-	Everything I Own	Ken Boothe	Trojan	9		F	
6	20	Long Tall Glasses	Leo Sayer	Chrysalis	5	(9)		
7	1	Kung Fu Fighting	Carl Douglas	Pye	8	(1)	F	L
8	6	Hang On In There Baby	Johnny Bristol	MGM	7	(8)	F	L
9	-	Far Far Away	Slade	Polydor	5			
10	-	I Get A Kick Out Of You	Gary Shearston	Charisma	5		F	L
11	-	Farewell/Bring It On Home To Me	Rod Stewart	Mercury	4			
12	-	Reggae Tune	Andy Fairweather-Low	A&M	4		F	
13	-	(You're) Having My Baby	Paul Anka & Odia Coates	UA	6	(1)		L
14	-	All Of Me Loves All Of You	Bay City Rollers	Bell	6			
15	7	You You You	Alvin Stardust	Magnet	6			
16	12	Can't Get Enough Of Your Love Babe	Barry White	Pye International	6	(1)		
17	-	I Can't Leave You Alone	George McCrae	Jayboy	5	(50)		
18	-	Knock On Wood	David Bowie	RCA	4			
19	10	Queen Of Clubs	KC & The Sunshine Band	Jayboy	6	(66)	F	
20	-	Gonna Make You A Star	David Essex	CBS	9			

◆ Mama Cass, of The Mamas & The Papas, was found dead in Nilsson's London apartment. Four years later, The Who's extrovert drummer Keith Moon was to die in the same Park Street flat.

◆ Elton John re-signed with MCA Records. The five album deal netted him a record $8 million.

1974

November 1974

This Mnth	Prev Mnth	Title	Artist	Label	Wks (US 20 Pos)	
1	20	Gonna Make You A Star	David Essex	CBS	9	
2	-	Killer Queen	Queen	EMI	6 (12)	
3	5	Everything I Own	Ken Boothe	Trojan	9	F
4	-	(Hey There) Lonely Girl	Eddie Holman	ABC	7	F L
5	14	All Of Me Loves All Of You	Bay City Rollers	Bell	6	
6	-	You're The First, The Last, My Everything	Barry White	20th Century	9 (2)	
7	9	Far Far Away	Slade	Polydor	5	
8	-	Down On The Beach Tonight	Drifters	Bell	5	
9	-	Let's Put It All Together	Stylistics	Avco	5 (18)	
10	-	Let's Get Together Again	Glitter Band	Bell	5	
11	-	Pepper Box	Peppers	Spark	5	F L
12	13	(You're) Having My Baby	Paul Anka & Odia Coates	UA	6 (1)	L
13	-	Juke Box Jive	Rubettes	Polydor	9	
14	17	I Can't Leave You Alone	George McCrae	Jayboy	5 (50)	
15	-	The Wild One	Suzi Quatro	RAK	5	
16	-	All I Want Is You	Roxy Music	Island	6	
17	-	Oh Yes! You're Beautiful	Gary Glitter	Bell	7	
18	-	No Honestly	Lynsey De Paul	Jet	4	
19	-	Never Turn Your Back On Mother Earth	Sparks	Island	4	
20	-	Magic	Pilot	EMI	5 (5)	F

December 1974

This Mnth	Prev Mnth	Title	Artist	Label	Wks (US 20 Pos)	
1	6	You're The First, The Last, My Everything	Barry White	20th Century	9 (2)	
2	-	You Ain't Seen Nothin' Yet	Bachman-Turner Overdrive	Mercury	9 (1)	F L
3	13	Juke Box Jive	Rubettes	Polydor	9	
4	17	Oh Yes! You're Beautiful	Gary Glitter	Bell	7	
5	-	Lonely This Christmas	Mud	RAK	8	
6	-	My Boy	Elvis Presley	RCA	9 (20)	
7	-	Tell Him	Hello	Bell	6	F
8	-	Get Dancing	Disco Tex & The Sex-O-Lettes	Chelsea	8 (10)	F
9	-	Streets Of London	Ralph McTell	Reprise	9	F L
10	-	Ire Feelings (Skanga)	Rupie Edwards	Cactus	6	F L
11	-	Lucy In The Sky With Diamonds	Elton John	DJM	8 (1)	
12	1	Gonna Make You A Star	David Essex	CBS	9	
13	-	Wombling Merry Christmas	Wombles	CBS	5	
14	20	Magic	Pilot	EMI	5 (5)	F
15	-	You Can Make Me Dance Sing Or Anything	Rod Stewart & The Faces	Warner	4	L
16	-	The In Betweenies/Father Christmas Do Not Touch Me	Goodies	Bradley's	6	F
17	-	Too Good To Be Forgotten	Chi-Lites	Brunswick	4	
18	4	(Hey There) Lonely Girl	Eddie Holman	ABC	7	F L
19	-	Down Down	Status Quo	Vertigo	8	
20	2	Killer Queen	Queen	EMI	6 (12)	

◆ British soul singers were making their mark. In the UK teenage Manchester group Sweet Sensation topped the chart with their debut 'Sad Sweet Dreamer' and in the USA Carl Douglas repeated his UK success by reaching No. 1 with 'Kung Fu Fighting'.

◆ The Drifters, who started as a trend-setting R&B act in 1953, were now resident in Britain and scored their third successive UK-written Top 10 hit, 'Down On The Beach Tonight'. Another US R&B group who would soon follow in their footsteps were The Three Degrees.

1975

This Mnth	Prev Mnth	Title	Artist	Label	Wks	(US 20 Pos)	
1	9	**Streets Of London**	Ralph McTell	Reprise	9		F L
2	19	**Down Down**	Status Quo	Vertigo	8		
3	5	**Lonely This Christmas**	Mud	RAK	8		
4	-	**The Bump**	Kenny	RAK	6		F
5	-	**Never Can Say Goodbye**	Gloria Gaynor	MGM	5	(9)	F
6	-	**Ms Grace**	Tymes	RCA	5	(91)	L
7	8	**Get Dancing**	Disco Tex & The Sex-O-Lettes	Chelsea	8	(10)	F
8	-	**I Can Help**	Billy Swan	Monument	7	(1)	F L
9	13	**Wombling Merry Christmas**	Wombles	CBS	5		
10	6	**My Boy**	Elvis Presley	RCA	9	(20)	
11	16	**The In Betweenies/Father Christmas Do Not Touch Me**	Goodies	Bradley's	6		F
12	3	**Juke Box Jive**	Rubettes	Polydor	9		
13	-	**Stardust**	David Essex	CBS	4		
14	-	**Are You Ready To Rock**	Wizzard	Warner	5		L
15	2	**You Ain't Seen Nothin' Yet**	Bachman-Turner Overdrive	Mercury	9	(1)	F L
16	-	**Help Me Make It Through The Night**	John Holt	Trojan	6		F L
17	-	**Crying Over You**	Ken Boothe	Trojan	4		L
18	-	**Morning Side Of The Mountain**	Donny & Marie Osmond	MGM	5	(8)	
19	1	**You're The First, The Last, My...**	Barry White	20th Century	9	(2)	
20	11	**Lucy In The Sky With Diamonds**	Elton John	DJM	8	(1)	

This Mnth	Prev Mnth	Title	Artist	Label	Wks	(US 20 Pos)	
1	-	**January**	Pilot	EMI	6	(87)	L
2	-	**Goodbye My Love**	Glitter Band	Bell	6		
3	-	**Sugar Candy Kisses**	Mac & Katie Kissoon	Polydor	5		F
4	-	**Please Mr. Postman**	Carpenters	A&M	7	(1)	
5	4	**The Bump**	Kenny	RAK	6		F
6	18	**Morning Side Of The Mountain**	Donny & Marie Osmond	MGM	5	(8)	
7	-	**Angie Baby**	Helen Reddy	Capitol	6	(1)	F L
8	6	**Ms Grace**	Tymes	RCA	5	(91)	L
9	5	**Never Can Say Goodbye**	Gloria Gaynor	MGM	5	(9)	F
10	-	**Make Me Smile (Come Up And See Me)**	Steve Harley & Cockney Rebel	EMI	6	(96)	
11	-	**Black Superman (Muhammad Ali)**	Johnny Wakelin & The Kinshasa Band	Pye	4	(21)	F
12	-	**Promised Land**	Elvis Presley	RCA	5	(14)	
13	16	**Help Me Make It Through The Night**	John Holt	Trojan	6		F L
14	-	**Footsee**	Wigan's Chosen Few	Disco Demand	5		F L
15	-	**Now I'm Here**	Queen	EMI	5		
16	-	**Shame, Shame, Shame**	Shirley And Company	All Platinum	5	(12)	F L
17	-	**Purely By Coincidence**	Sweet Sensation	Pye	4		L
18	-	**Star On A TV Show**	Stylistics	Avco	4	(47)	
19	-	**Boogie On Reggae Woman**	Stevie Wonder	Tamla Motown	3	(3)	
20	-	**The Secrets That You Keep**	Mud	RAK	5		

◆ Status Quo, who have put more singles in the UK charts than any other group, went up to the top for the only time in their long career with 'Down Down'.

◆ American acts whose current records were faring far better in Britain included: *Kojak* actor Telly Savalas, The Tymes, The Moments & The Whatnauts, Johnny Mathis and Love Unlimited.

1975

March 1975

This Mnth	Prev Mnth	Title	Artist	Label	Wks	(US 20 Pos)	
1	-	If	Telly Savalas	MCA	7		F L
2	-	Only You Can	Fox	GTO	7	(53)	F
3	-	Bye Bye Baby	Bay City Rollers	Bell	11		
4	10	Make Me Smile (Come Up And See Me)	Steve Harley & Cockney Rebel	EMI	6	(96)	
5	20	The Secrets That You Keep	Mud	RAK	5		
6	-	My Eyes Adored You	Frankie Valli	Private Stock	5	(1)	
7	-	Pick Up The Pieces	Average White Band	Atlantic	5	(1)	F
8	-	There's A Whole Lot Of Loving	Guys & Dolls	Magnet	7		F
9	4	Please Mr. Postman	Carpenters	A&M	7	(1)	
10	-	What Am I Gonna Do With You	Barry White	20th Century	6	(8)	
11	16	Shame, Shame, Shame	Shirley And Company	All Platinum	5	(12)	F L
12	-	Girls	Moments And Whatnauts	All Platinum	6		F
13	-	Please Tell Him I Said Hello	Dana	GTO	6		
14	-	Fancy Pants	Kenny	RAK	6		
15	-	Mandy	Barry Manilow	Arista	4	(1)	F
16	-	I'm Stone In Love With You	Johnny Mathis	CBS	6		
17	-	I Can Do It	Rubettes	State	6		
18	-	Dreamer	Supertramp	A&M	4	(15)	F
19	14	Footsee	Wigan's Chosen Few	Disco Demand	5		F L
20	-	It May Be Winter Outside (But In My Heart It's Spring)	Love Unlimited	20th Century	4	(83)	L

April 1975

1	3	Bye Bye Baby	Bay City Rollers	Bell	11		
2	-	Fox On The Run	Sweet	RCA	6	(5)	
3	-	Swing Your Daddy	Jim Gilstrap	Chelsea	7	(55)	F L
4	-	Love Me Love My Dog	Peter Shelley	Magnet	6		L
5	-	Funky Gibbon/Sick Man Blues	Goodies	Bradley's	6	(79)	
6	8	There's A Whole Lot Of Loving	Guys & Dolls	Magnet	7		F
7	12	Girls	Moments And Whatnauts	All Platinum	6		F
8	14	Fancy Pants	Kenny	RAK	6		
9	17	I Can Do It	Rubettes	State	6		
10	-	Honey	Bobby Goldsboro	UA	6		L
11	-	Play Me Like You Play Your Guitar	Duane Eddy & Rebelettes	GTO	5		
12	-	The Ugly Duckling	Mike Reid	Pye	4		F L
13	10	What Am I Gonna Do With You	Barry White	20th Century	6	(8)	
14	-	Let Me Be The One	Shadows	EMI	3		
15	-	Philadelphia Freedom	Elton John	DJM	6	(1)	
16	-	Skiing In The Snow	Wigan's Ovation	Spark	4		F L
17	-	Life Is A Minestone	10cc	Mercury	5		
18	-	Oh Boy	Mud	RAK	6		
19	-	Reach Out I'll Be There	Gloria Gaynor	MGM	4	(60)	
20	-	Loving You	Minnie Riperton	Epic	6	(1)	F L

◆ Disco was taking over the chart, with hits by Gloria Gaynor, Disco Tex, Barry White, Shirley & Co., Labelle and B. T. Express. Another type of dance music selling well in the UK was northern soul – the biggest hit from obscure Canadian band Wigan's Chosen Few.

135

1975

This Mnth	Prev Mnth	Title	Artist	Label	Wks 20	(US Pos)	
1	18	**Oh Boy**	Mud	RAK	6		
2	20	**Loving You**	Minnie Riperton	Epic	6	(1)	F L
3	-	**Stand By Your Man**	Tammy Wynette	Epic	8		F
4	-	**Hurt So Good**	Susan Cadogan	Magnet	6		F L
5	-	**Let Me Try Again**	Tammy Jones	Epic	6		F L
6	10	**Honey**	Bobby Goldsboro	UA	6		L
7	-	**I Wanna Dance Wit Choo'**	Disco Tex & The Sex-O-Lettes	Chelsea	5	(23)	L
8	-	**The Way We Were/Try To Remember (Medley)**	Gladys Knight & The Pips	Buddah	7	(11)	
9	-	**Sing Baby Sing**	Stylistics	Avco	7		
10	-	**Only Yesterday**	Carpenters	A&M	5	(4)	
11	-	**The Night**	Frankie Valli & Four Seasons	Mowest	5		
12	-	**Whispering Grass**	Windsor Davies & Don Estelle	EMI	9		F L
13	1	**Bye Bye Baby**	Bay City Rollers	Bell	11		
14	-	**Thanks For The Memory (Wham Bam Thank You Mam)**	Slade	Polydor	5		
15	-	**Take Good Care Of Yourself**	Three Degrees	Philly Int.	4		
16	-	**A Little Love And Understanding**	Gilbert Becaud	Decca	5		F L
17	-	**The Tears I Cried**	Glitter Band	Bell	5		
18	-	**Don't Do It Baby**	Mac & Katie Kissoon	State	4		
19	-	**Three Steps To Heaven**	Showaddywaddy	Bell	8		
20	-	**Send In The Clowns**	Judy Collins	Elektra	5	(19)	L

This Mnth	Prev Mnth	Title	Artist	Label	Wks 20	(US Pos)	
1	12	**Whispering Grass**	Windsor Davies & Don Estelle	EMI	9		F L
2	19	**Three Steps To Heaven**	Showaddywaddy	Bell	8		
3	-	**I'm Not In Love**	10cc	Mercury	8	(2)	
4	-	**The Proud One**	Osmonds	MGM	6	(22)	L
5	3	**Stand By Your Man**	Tammy Wynette	Epic	8		F
6	9	**Sing Baby Sing**	Stylistics	Avco	7		
7	-	**The Hustle**	Van McCoy	Avco	8	(1)	F
8	8	**The Way We Were/Try To Remember (Medley)**	Gladys Knight & The Pips	Buddah	7	(11)	
9	-	**Listen To What The Man Said**	Wings	Capitol	5	(1)	
10	20	**Send In The Clowns**	Judy Collins	Elektra	5	(19)	L
11	-	**Disco Stomp**	Hamilton Bohannon	Brunswick	7		F L
12	-	**Disco Queen**	Hot Chocolate	RAK	4	(28)	
13	-	**Autobahn**	Kraftwerk	Vertigo	5	(25)	F
14	-	**Tears On My Pillow**	Johnny Nash	CBS	9		L
15	-	**Roll Over Lay Down**	Status Quo	Vertigo	5		
16	-	**The Israelites**	Desmond Dekker & The Aces	Cactus	5		
17	-	**Oh What A Shame**	Roy Wood	Jet	4		L
18	-	**Doing Alright With The Boys**	Gary Glitter	Bell	4		
19	-	**Baby I Love You, OK**	Kenny	RAK	4		
20	14	**Thanks For The Memory (Wham Bam Thank You Mam)**	Slade	Polydor	5		

◆ A 12 city American tour by The Beach Boys and Chicago (whose **Chicago VIII** was a chart topper) was seen by 700,000, who paid over $7 million. The Beach Boys then joined Elton John, Rufus and The Eagles, playing to 80,000 at London's Wembley Stadium.

◆ Groundbreaking German group Kraftwerk had a transatlantic Top 40 hit with 'Autobahn'. Their electro-pop sound was a blueprint for many later electronic-dance acts.

July 1975

This Mnth	Prev Mnth	Title	Artist	Label	Wks	(US 20 Pos)	
1	14	**Tears On My Pillow**	Johnny Nash	CBS	9		L
2	-	**Misty**	Ray Stevens	Janus	7	(14)	L
3	7	**The Hustle**	Van McCoy	Avco	8	(1)	F
4	-	**Have You Seen Her/Oh Girl**	Chi-Lites	Brunswick	5		
5	3	**I'm Not In Love**	10cc	Mercury	8	(2)	
6	-	**Give A Little Love**	Bay City Rollers	Bell	7		
7	11	**Disco Stomp**	Hamilton Bohannon	Brunswick	7		F L
8	-	**Eighteen With A Bullet**	Pete Wingfield	Island	5	(15)	F L
9	-	**Barbados**	Typically Tropical	Gull	9		F L
10	1	**Whispering Grass**	Windsor Davies & Don Estelle	EMI	9		F L
11	18	**Doing Alright With The Boys**	Gary Glitter	Bell	4		
12	-	**Moonshine Sally**	Mud	RAK	4		
13	-	**Rollin' Stone**	David Essex	CBS	4		
14	-	**Je T'Aime (Moi Non Plus)**	Judge Dread	Cactus	6		
15	2	**Three Steps To Heaven**	Showaddywaddy	Bell	8		
16	-	**Jive Talkin'**	Bee Gees	RSO	7	(1)	
17	-	**Sealed With A Kiss**	Brian Hyland	ABC	8		L
18	-	**D.I.V.O.R.C.E.**	Tammy Wynette	Epic	4	(63)	
19	-	**My White Bicycle**	Nazareth	Mooncrest	4		
20	19	**Baby I Love You, OK**	Kenny	RAK	4		

August 1975

		Title	Artist	Label	Wks	(US 20 Pos)	
1	9	**Barbados**	Typically Tropical	Gull	9		F L
2	-	**Can't Give You Anything (But My Love)**	Stylistics	Avco	8	(51)	
3	-	**If You Think You Know How To Love Me**	Smokey	RAK	7	(96)	F
4	6	**Give A Little Love**	Bay City Rollers	Bell	7		
5	16	**Jive Talkin'**	Bee Gees	RSO	7	(1)	
6	-	**The Last Farewell**	Roger Whittaker	EMI	9	(19)	
7	-	**It's Been So Long**	George McCrae	Jayboy	7		
8	17	**Sealed With A Kiss**	Brian Hyland	ABC	8		L
9	-	**It's In His Kiss**	Linda Lewis	Arista	5		L
10	-	**Blanket On The Ground**	Billie Jo Spears	UA	6	(78)	F
11	-	**Delilah**	Sensational Alex Harvey Band	Vertigo	5		F
12	-	**Sailing**	Rod Stewart	Warner	9	(58)	
13	1	**Tears On My Pillow**	Johnny Nash	CBS	9		L
14	-	**Sherry**	Adrian Baker	Magnet	4		F L
15	-	**Dolly My Love**	Moments	All Platinum	5		L
16	-	**That's The Way (I Like It)**	KC & The Sunshine Band	Jayboy	6	(1)	
17	14	**Je T'Aime (Moi Non Plus)**	Judge Dread	Cactus	6		
18	-	**The Best Thing That Ever Happened**	Gladys Knight & The Pips	Buddah	6	(3)	
19	2	**Misty**	Ray Stevens	Janus	7	(14)	L
20	-	**El Bimbo**	Bimbo Jet	EMI	4	(43)	F L

◆ Paul McCartney, who had yet to score a solo No. 1 single in his homeland, notched up his fourth American chart topping single, 'Listen To What The Man Said', and another transatlantic album topper, **Venus And Mars.**

◆ Soon after David Bowie announced "rock'n'roll is dead", he had his biggest American hit with 'Fame', co-written with John Lennon.

1975

This Mnth	Prev Mnth	Title	Artist	Label	Wks	(US Pos)	
1	12	Sailing	Rod Stewart	Warner	9	(58)	
2	6	The Last Farewell	Roger Whittaker	EMI	9	(19)	
3	-	Moonlighting	Leo Sayer	Chrysalis	6		
4	-	Summertime City	Mike Batt	Epic	5		F L
5	-	Funky Moped/Magic Roundabout	Jasper Carrott	DJM	10		F L
6	-	A Child's Prayer	Hot Chocolate	RAK	5		
7	2	Can't Give You Anything (But My Love)	Stylistics	Avco	8	(51)	
8	16	That's The Way (I Like It)	KC & The Sunshine Band	Jayboy	6	(1)	
9	-	I'm On Fire	5000 Volts	Philips	6	(26)	F
10	-	Heartbeat	Showaddywaddy	Bell	5		
11	-	Julie Ann	Kenny	RAK	5		L
12	7	It's Been So Long	George McCrae	Jayboy	7		
13	-	Hold Me Close	David Essex	CBS	8		
14	18	The Best Thing That Ever Happened	Gladys Knight & The Pips	Buddah	6	(3)	
15	10	Blanket On The Ground	Billie Jo Spears	UA	6	(78)	F
16	-	There Goes My First Love	Drifters	Bell	8		
17	-	Motor Biking	Chris Spedding	RAK	4		F L
18	-	Fattie Bum-Bum	Carl Malcolm	UK	5		F L
19	-	Love In The Sun	Glitter Band	Bell	4		
20	-	I Only Have Eyes For You	Art Garfunkel	CBS	8	(18)	F

This Mnth	Prev Mnth	Title	Artist	Label	Wks	(US Pos)	
1	13	Hold Me Close	David Essex	CBS	8		
2	20	I Only Have Eyes For You	Art Garfunkel	CBS	8	(18)	F
3	16	There Goes My First Love	Drifters	Bell	8		
4	-	It's Time For Love	Chi-Lites	Brunswick	5	(94)	
5	-	Una Paloma Blanca	Jonathan King	UK	6		L
6	-	Who Loves You	Four Seasons	Warner	5	(3)	
7	-	S.O.S.	Abba	Epic	6	(15)	
8	-	Scotch On The Rocks	Band Of The Black Watch	Spark	7		F L
9	-	Feelings	Morris Albert	Decca	6	(6)	F L
10	5	Funky Moped/Magic Roundabout	Jasper Carrott	DJM	10		F L
11	-	Paloma Blanca	George Baker Selection	Warner	4	(26)	F L
12	18	Fattie Bum-Bum	Carl Malcolm	UK	5		F L
13	9	I'm On Fire	5000 Volts	Philips	6	(26)	F
14	1	Sailing	Rod Stewart	Warner	9	(58)	
15	-	Space Oddity	David Bowie	RCA	8	(15)	
16	-	L-L-Lucy	Mud	Private Stock	4		
17	-	Don't Play Your Rock 'n' Roll To Me	Smokey	RAK	4		
18	3	Moonlighting	Leo Sayer	Chrysalis	6		
19	10	Heartbeat	Showaddywaddy	Bell	5		
20	-	Big Ten	Judge Dread	Cactus	4		

◆ Shortly before his group The Faces finally called it a day, lead singer Rod Stewart had the biggest British hit of his long and successful career with 'Sailing'. The single, which failed to make the American Top 40, returned to the Top 3 the following year, after its use as the theme to the BBC TV documentary *Sailor*, and was also a minor hit in 1987, with royalties being donated to the Zeebrugge Ferry Disaster Fund.

November 1975

This Mnth	Prev Mnth	Title	Artist	Label	Wks	(US 20 Pos)	
1	15	**Space Oddity**	David Bowie	RCA	8	(15)	
2	-	**Love Is The Drug**	Roxy Music	Island	6	(30)	
3	-	**D.I.V.O.R.C.E.**	Billy Connolly	Polydor	6		F L
4	-	**Rhinestone Cowboy**	Glen Campbell	Capitol	6	(1)	L
5	-	**Love Hurts**	Jim Capaldi	Island	6	(97)	F L
6	-	**You Sexy Thing**	Hot Chocolate	RAK	9	(3)	
7	2	**I Only Have Eyes For You**	Art Garfunkel	CBS	8	(18)	F
8	-	**Imagine**	John Lennon	Apple	5		G
9	-	**Hold Back The Night**	Trammps	Buddah	5	(35)	F
10	-	**Blue Guitar**	Justin Hayward & John Lodge	Threshold	5	(94)	F
11	-	**What A Diff'rence A Day Makes**	Esther Phillips	Kudu	5	(20)	F L
12	-	**Bohemian Rhapsody**	Queen	EMI	14	(9)	G
13	9	**Feelings**	Morris Albert	Decca	6	(6)	F L
14	-	**New York Groove**	Hello	Bell	4		L
15	-	**Sky High**	Jigsaw	Splash	5	(3)	F L
16	7	**S.O.S.**	Abba	Epic	6	(15)	
17	3	**There Goes My First Love**	Drifters	Bell	8		
18	-	**This Old Heart Of Mine**	Rod Stewart	Riva	5		
19	-	**Right Back Where We Started From**	Maxine Nightingale	UA	5	(2)	F
20	-	**Money Honey**	Bay City Rollers	Bell	8	(9)	

December 1975

This Mnth	Prev Mnth	Title	Artist	Label	Wks	(US 20 Pos)	
1	12	**Bohemian Rhapsody**	Queen	EMI	14	(9)	G
2	6	**You Sexy Thing**	Hot Chocolate	RAK	9	(3)	
3	-	**Trail Of The Lonesome Pine**	Laurel & Hardy	UA	7		F L
4	-	**Na Na Is The Saddest Word**	Stylistics	Avco	7		
5	20	**Money Honey**	Bay City Rollers	Bell	8	(9)	
6	-	**Let's Twist Again**	Chubby Checker	London American	8		
7	-	**All Around My Hat**	Steeleye Span	Chrysalis	7		L
8	-	**I Believe In Father Christmas**	Greg Lake	Manticore	6	(95)	F L
9	-	**Happy To Be On An Island In The Sun**	Demis Roussos	Philips	7		F
10	-	**Show Me You're A Woman**	Mud	Private Stock	6		
11	18	**This Old Heart Of Mine**	Rod Stewart	Riva	5		
12	-	**Golden Years**	David Bowie	RCA	7	(10)	
13	5	**Love Hurts**	Jim Capaldi	Island	6	(97)	F L
14	8	**Imagine**	John Lennon	Apple	5		G
15	-	**Renta Santa**	Chris Hill	Philips	3		F
16	-	**It's Gonna Be A Cold Cold Christmas**	Dana	GTO	5		
17	15	**Sky High**	Jigsaw	Splash	5	(3)	F L
18	3	**D.I.V.O.R.C.E.**	Billy Connolly	Polydor	6		F L
19	-	**Can I Take You Home Little Girl**	Drifters	Bell	6		
20	-	**In For A Penny**	Slade	Polydor	3		

◆ Queen's 'Bohemian Rhapsody' topped the chart and sold more than a million. In 1991, after Freddie Mercury's death, it returned and repeated the feat.

◆ The latest oldies to chart included Chubby Checker's 'Let's Twist Again' from 1961, David Bowie's 'Space Oddity' from 1969 and Laurel & Hardy's 1937 recording 'The Trail Of The Lonesome Pine'.

◆ Elton John's US tour closed with a spectacular show at the Dodger Stadium in L.A.

1976

This Mnth	Prev Mnth	Title	Artist	Label	Wks	(US 20 Pos)	
1	1	**Bohemian Rhapsody**	Queen	EMI	14	(9)	G
2	-	**Glass Of Champagne**	Sailor	Epic	8		F
3	-	**Mamma Mia**	Abba	Epic	8	(32)	
4	-	**Wide Eyed And Legless**	Andy Fairweather-Low	A&M	7		L
5	6	**Let's Twist Again**	Chubby Checker	London American	8		
6	3	**Trail Of The Lonesome Pine**	Laurel & Hardy	UA	7		F L
7	-	**In Dulce Jubilo/On Horseback**	Mike Oldfield	Virgin	4		F
8	-	**Art For Art's Sake**	10cc	UK			
9	-	**King Of The Cops**	Billy Howard	Penny Farthing	6		F L
10	8	**I Believe In Father Christmas**	Greg Lake	Manticore	6	(95)	F L
11	-	**Love Machine**	Miracles	Tamla Motown	7	( )	L
12	16	**It's Gonna Be A Cold Cold Christmas**	Dana	GTO	5		
13	12	**Golden Years**	David Bowie	RCA	7	(10)	
14	9	**Happy To Be On An Island In The Sun**	Demis Roussos	Philips	7		F
15	-	**We Do It**	R & J Stone	RCA	7		F L
16	-	**Forever & Ever**	Slik	Bell	7		F L
17	-	**Itchycoo Park**	Small Faces	Immediate	5		L
18	-	**Let The Music Play**	Barry White	20th Century	4	(32)	
19	19	**Can I Take You Home Little Girl**	Drifters	Bell	6		
20	2	**You Sexy Thing**	Hot Chocolate	RAK	9	(3)	

This Mnth	Prev Mnth	Title	Artist	Label	Wks	(US 20 Pos)	
1	16	**Forever & Ever**	Slik	Bell	7		L
2	-	**December '63 (Oh What A Night)**	Four Seasons	Warner	8	(1)	
3	3	**Mamma Mia**	Abba	Epic	8	(32)	
4	-	**Love To Love You Baby**	Donna Summer	GTO	6	(2)	F
5	11	**Love Machine**	Miracles	Tamla Motown	7	(1)	L
6	-	**Rodrigo's Guitar Concerto De Aranjuez**	Manuel & His Music Of TheMountains	EMI	6		L
7	15	**We Do It**	R & J Stone	RCA	7		F L
8	-	**No Regrets**	Walker Brothers	GTO	5		L
9	-	**I Love To Love (But My Baby Loves To Dance)**	Tina Charles	CBS	7		F
10	-	**Convoy**	C.W. McCall	MGM	7	(1)	F L
11	-	**Dat**	Pluto Shervington	Opal	5		F
12	-	**Moonlight Serenade/Little Brown Jug/In The Mood**	Glenn Miller	RCA	5		F L
13	-	**It Should Have Been Me**	Yvonne Fair	Tamla Motown	5	(85)	F L
14	-	**Low Rider**	War	UA	5	(7)	F
15	1	**Bohemian Rhapsody**	Queen	EMI	14	(9)	G
16	-	**Evil Woman**	Electric Light Orchestra	JET	4	(10)	
17	-	**Squeeze Box**	Who	Polydor	6	(16)	
18	-	**Walk Away From Love**	David Ruffin	Tamla	4	(9)	F L
19	-	**Midnight Rider**	Paul Davidson	Tropical	4		F L
20	-	**Rain**	Status Quo	Vertigo	5		

◆ Thirteen years after taking the US charts by storm, The Four Seasons had their only transatlantic No. 1, 'December '63 (Oh What A Night)'.

◆ In Britain, album chart toppers included 1950s star Slim Whitman and 1960s chart regular Roy Orbison, whilst 1940s favourite Glenn Miller returned to the singles chart!

March 1976

This Mnth	Prev Mnth	Title	Artist	Label	Wks	(US 20 Pos)	
1	9	I Love To Love (But My Baby...)	Tina Charles	CBS	7		F
2	10	Convoy	C.W. McCall	MGM	7	(1)	F L
3	-	Love Really Hurts Without You	Billy Ocean	GTO	8	(22)	F
4	2	December '63 (Oh What A Night)	Four Seasons	Warner	8	(1)	
5	-	You Don't Have To Say You Love Me	Guys & Dolls	Magnet	5		L
6	-	People Like You And People Like Me	Glitter Band	Bell	6		L
7	-	Save Your Kisses For Me	Brotherhood Of Man	Pye	13	(27)	G
8	13	It Should Have Been Me	Yvonne Fair	Tamla Motown	5	(85)	F L
9	6	Rodrigo's Guitar Concerto...	Manuel/Music Of The Moutains	EMI	6		F L
10	-	You See The Trouble With Me	Barry White	20th Century	7		
11	-	I Wanna Stay With You	Gallagher & Lyle	A&M	6	(49)	F
12	-	(Do The) Spanish Hustle	Fatback Band	Polydor	4		
13	20	Rain	Status Quo	Vertigo	5		
14	11	Dat	Pluto Shervington	Opal	5		F
15	-	Funky Weekend	Stylistics	Avco	4	(76)	
16	-	Falling Apart At The Seams	Marmalade	Target	6	(49)	L
17	-	Miss You Nights	Cliff Richard	EMI	4		
18	-	Yesterday	Beatles	Apple	6		
19	17	Squeeze Box	Who	Polydor	6	(16)	
20	-	I Love Music	O'Jays	Philly International	4	(5)	

April 1976

This Mnth	Prev Mnth	Title	Artist	Label	Wks	(US 20 Pos)	
1	7	Save Your Kisses For Me	Brotherhood Of Man	Pye	13	(27)	G
2	-	Music	John Miles	Decca	7	(88)	
3	10	You See The Trouble With Me	Barry White	20th Century	7		
4	-	Fernando	Abba	Epic	12	(13)	
5	-	I'm Mandy Fly Me	10cc	Mercury	6	(60)	
6	-	Jungle Rock	Hank Mizell	Charly	9		F L
7	-	Pinball Wizard	Elton John	DJM	4		
8	-	Theme From Mahogany (Do You Know Where You're Going To)	Diana Ross	Tamla Motown	5	(1)	
9	3	Love Really Hurts Without You	Billy Ocean	GTO	8	(22)	F
10	18	Yesterday	Beatles	Apple	6		
11	-	Girls Girls Girls	Sailor	Epic	5		L
12	11	I Wanna Stay With You	Gallagher & Lyle	A&M	6	(49)	F
13	16	Falling Apart At The Seams	Marmalade	Target	6	(49)	L
14	-	Hello Happiness	Drifters	Bell	5		
15	-	Love Me Like I Love You	Bay City Rollers	Bell	5		
16	-	Don't Stop It Now	Hot Chocolate	RAK	5	(42)	
17	-	Hey Jude	Beatles	Apple	4		
18	6	People Like You And People Like Me	Glitter Band	Bell	6		L
19	1	I Love To Love (But My Baby Loves To Dance)	Tina Charles	CBS	7		F
20	-	S-S-S-Single Bed	Fox	GTO	7		L

◆ Despite minimal British success Fleetwood Mac (with new members Stevie Nicks and Lindsey Buckingham) headed up the US LP chart with their eponymous album – it took 58 weeks to reach No. 1!

◆ The chart topper 'Save Your Kisses For Me' from mixed quartet Brotherhood Of Man went on to win the Eurovision Song Contest and sold over a million copies. Unlike all the earlier British entries this catchy single reached the US Top 40.

1976

This Mnth	Prev Mnth	Title	Artist	Label	Wks	(US 20 Pos)	
1	4	Fernando	Abba	Epic	12	(13)	
2	1	Save Your Kisses For Me	Brotherhood Of Man	Pye	13	(27)	G
3	6	Jungle Rock	Hank Mizell	Charly	9		F L
4	20	S-S-S-Single Bed	Fox	GTO	7		L
5	-	Silver Star	Four Seasons	Warner	5	(38)	L
6	-	More, More, More	Andrea True Connection	Buddah	7	(4)	F L
7	-	Arms Of Mary	Sutherland Brothers And Quiver	CBS	5	(81)	F L
8	-	Get Up And Boogie (That's Right)	Silver Convention	Magnet	6	(2)	F L
9	-	No Charge	J.J. Barrie	Power Exchange	7		F L
10	-	Convoy GB	Laurie Lingo & The Dipsticks	State	5		F L
11	-	Can't Help Falling In Love	Stylistics	Avco	6		
12	-	Fool To Cry	Rolling Stones	Rolling Stone	6	(10)	
13	-	Life Is Too Short Girl	Sheer Elegance	Pye International	6		L
14	8	Theme From Mahogany (Do You Where You're Going To)	Diana Ross	Tamla Motown	5	(1)	
15	-	My Resistance Is Low	Robin Sarstedt	Decca	5		F L
16	-	Combine Harvester (Brand New Key)	Wurzels	EMI	7		F
17	-	Love Hangover	Diana Ross	Tamla Motown	6	(1)	
18	-	Disco Connection	Isaac Hayes	ABC	5		L
19	11	Girls Girls Girls	Sailor	Epic	5		L
20	15	Love Me Like I Love You	Bay City Rollers	Bell	5		

This Mnth	Prev Mnth	Title	Artist	Label	Wks	(US 20 Pos)	
1	16	Combine Harvester (Brand New Key)	Wurzels	EMI	7		F
2	-	Silly Love Songs	Paul McCartney	Parlophone	8	(1)	
3	9	No Charge	J.J. Barrie	Power Exchange	7		F L
4	-	You To Me Are Everything	Real Thing	Pye International	8	(64)	F
5	15	My Resistance Is Low	Robin Sarstedt	Decca	7		F L
6	-	You Just Might See Me Cry	Our Kid	Polydor	7		F L
7	-	Let Your Love Flow	Bellamy Brothers	Warner	8	(1)	F
8	12	Fool To Cry	Rolling Stones	Rolling Stone	6	(10)	
9	1	Fernando	Abba	Epic	12	(13)	
10	-	Tonight's The Night (Gonna Be Alright)	Rod Stewart	Riva	7	(1)	
11	-	Jolene	Dolly Parton	RCA	6	(60)	F
12	-	Heart On My Sleeve	Gallagher & Lyle	A&M	7	(67)	L
13	-	Show Me The Way	Peter Frampton	A&M	5	(6)	F L
14	-	Devil Woman	Cliff Richard	EMI	4	(6)	
15	-	Midnight Train To Georgia	Gladys Knight & The Pips	Buddah	4	(1)	
16	7	Arms Of Mary	Sutherland Brothers & Quiver	CBS	7	(81)	F L
17	-	This Is It	Melba Moore	Buddah	4	(91)	F
18	-	Young Hearts Run Free	Candi Staton	Warner	9	(20)	F
19	17	Love Hangover	Diana Ross	Tamla Motown	6	(1)	
20	-	Shake It Down	Mud	Private Stock	2		

◆ The Rolling Stones, whose **Black And Blue** headed the American LP listings, played six nights at Earl's Court in London as part of their European tour. Other major UK events included The Who at Charlton Athletic Football Club and David Bowie at Wembley.

◆ A harbinger of the forthcoming British rockabilly revival was the success of 'Jungle Rock' by Hank Mizell. The old time rock'n'roll hit sold few copies in the USA when first released in 1957 but gave the 52-year-old sales manager a surprise European hit in 1976.

1976

July 1976

This Mnth	Prev Mnth	Title	Artist	Label	Wks	(US Pos)	
1	18	Young Hearts Run Free	Candi Staton	Warner	9	(20)	F
2	-	Roussos Phenomenon E.P.	Demis Roussos	Philips	9		
3	-	A Little Bit More	Dr. Hook	Capitol	11	(11)	
4	-	Kiss And Say Goodbye	Manhattans	CBS	8	(1)	F
5	4	You To Me Are Everything	Real Thing	Pye International	8	(64)	F
6	-	Don't Go Breaking My Heart	Elton John & Kiki Dee	Rocket	11	(1)	
7	-	Let's Stick Together	Bryan Ferry	Island	7		
8	6	You Just Might See Me Cry	Our Kid	Polydor	7		F L
9	-	Misty Blue	Dorothy Moore	Contempo	9	(3)	F
10	-	You're My Best Friend	Queen	EMI	5	(16)	
11	10	Tonight's The Night (Gonna Be Alright)	Rod Stewart	Riva	7	(1)	
12	-	Leader Of The Pack	Shangri-Las	Charly/Contempo	5		L
13	-	It Only Takes A Minute	One Hundred Ton & A Feather	UK	5		F L
14	-	The Boys Are Back In Town	Thin Lizzy	Vertigo	5	(12)	
15	-	You Are My Love	Liverpool Express	Warner	6		F
16	-	Heaven Must Be Missing An Angel	Tavares	Capitol	7	(15)	F
17	12	Heart On My Sleeve	Gallagher & Lyle	A&M	7	(67)	L
18	2	Silly Love Songs	Paul McCartney	Parlophone	8	(1)	
19	-	I Love To Boogie	T. Rex	EMI	5		
20	-	Man To Man	Hot Chocolate	RAK	4		

August 1976

This Mnth	Prev Mnth	Title	Artist	Label	Wks	(US Pos)	
1	6	Don't Go Breaking My Heart	Elton John & Kiki Dee	Rocket	11	(1)	
2	3	A Little Bit More	Dr. Hook	Capitol	11	(11)	
3	-	Jeans On	David Dundas	Air	6	(17)	F L
4	16	Heaven Must Be Missing An Angel	Tavares	Capitol	7	(15)	F
5	-	In Zaire	Johnny Wakelin	Pye	6		L
6	-	Now Is The Time	Jimmy James & The Vagabonds	Pye	6		F L
7	-	Dr Kiss Kiss	5000 Volts	Philips	6		L
8	-	Let 'Em In	Wings	Parlophone	8	(3)	
9	9	Misty Blue	Dorothy Moore	Contempo	9	(3)	F
10	-	You Should Be Dancing	Bee Gees	RSO	7	(1)	
11	2	Roussos Phenomenon E.P.	Demis Roussos	Philips	9		
12	-	Mystery Song	Status Quo	Vertigo	5		
13	-	Harvest For The World	Isley Brothers	Epic	4	(63)	
14	4	Kiss And Say Goodbye	Manhattans	CBS	8	(1)	F
15	-	Here Comes The Sun	Steve Harley	EMI	4		
16	-	You Don't Have To Go	Chi-Lites	Brunswick	7		L
17	-	Extended Play (E.P.)	Bryan Ferry	Island	6		
18	-	What I've Got In Mind	Billie Jo Spears	UA	5		L
19	1	Young Hearts Run Free	Candi Staton	Warner	9	(20)	F
20	-	You'll Never Find Another Love Like Mine	Lou Rawls	Philly International	4	(2)	F L

◆ A UK visit by The Ramones helped to heighten interest in punk. The Sex Pistols appeared on TV, and The Clash, The Buzzcocks and Siouxsie & The Banshees made their live debuts. Stiff Records was launched, and the first issue of fanzine *Sniffin' Glue* hit the streets.

◆ The Rolling Stones, Lynyrd Skynyrd, and 10cc attracted 200,000 to the Knebworth Festival, while 60,000 attended Queen's Hyde Park concert and Grateful Dead and Santana packed the crowds into Wembley.

1976

This Mnth	Prev Mnth	Title	Artist	Label	Wks	(US 20 Pos)	
1	-	**Dancing Queen**	Abba	Epic	12	(1)	
2	8	**Let 'Em In**	Wings	Parlophone	8	(3)	
3	-	**The Killing Of Georgie**	Rod Stewart	Riva	7	(30)	
4	16	**You Don't Have To Go**	Chi-Lites	Brunswick	7		L
5	-	**(Light Of Experience) Doina De Jale**	Georghe Zamfir	Epic	6		F L
6	-	**Can't Get By Without You**	Real Thing	Pye	8		
7	-	**16 Bars**	Stylistics	H & L	7		L
8	1	**Don't Go Breaking My Heart**	Elton John & Kiki Dee	Rocket	11	(1)	
9	18	**What I've Got In Mind**	Billie Jo Spears	UA	5		L
10	-	**Aria**	Acker Bilk	Pye	6		L
11	-	**Blinded By The Light**	Manfred Mann's Earth Band	Bronze	6	(1)	F
12	-	**I Am A Cider Drinker (Paloma Blanca)**	Wurzels	EMI	5		L
13	-	**I Only Wanna Be With You**	Bay City Rollers	Bell	6	(12)	
14	17	**Extended Play (E.P.)**	Bryan Ferry	Island	6		
15	10	**You Should Be Dancing**	Bee Gees	RSO	7	(1)	
16	-	**Mississippi**	Pussycat	Sonet	13		F L
17	2	**A Little Bit More**	Dr. Hook	Capitol	11	(11)	
18	-	**Dance Little Lady Dance**	Tina Charles	CBS	6		
19	20	**You'll Never Find Another Love Like Mine**	Lou Rawls	Philly International	4	(2)	F L
20	5	**In Zaire**	Johnny Wakelin	Pye	6		L

This Mnth	Prev Mnth	Title	Artist	Label	Wks	(US 20 Pos)	
1	16	**Mississippi**	Pussycat	Sonet	13		F L
2	1	**Dancing Queen**	Abba	Epic	12	(1)	
3	-	**Sailing**	Rod Stewart	Warner	8	(58)	
4	6	**Can't Get By Without You**	Real Thing	Pye	8		
5	-	**When Forever Has Gone**	Demis Roussos	Philips	7		L
6	-	**Disco Duck**	Rick Dees & His Cast Of Idiots	RSO	6	(1)	F L
7	-	**Howzat**	Sherbet	Epic	7	(61)	F L
8	-	**Girl Of My Best Friend**	Elvis Presley	RCA	6		
9	18	**Dance Little Lady Dance**	Tina Charles	CBS	6		
10	13	**I Only Wanna Be With You**	Bay City Rollers	Bell	6	(12)	
11	-	**Hurt**	Manhattans	CBS	8	(97)	L
12	-	**If You Leave Me Now**	Chicago	CBS	12	(1)	
13	-	**The Best Disco In Town**	Ritchie Family	Polydor	5	(17)	F L
14	12	**I Am A Cider Drinker (Paloma Blanca)**	Wurzels	EMI	5		L
15	-	**Summer Of My Life**	Simon May	Pye	6		F L
16	-	**Don't Take Away The Music**	Tavares	Capitol	7	(34)	
17	10	**Aria**	Acker Bilk	Pye	6		L
18	11	**Blinded By The Light**	Manfred Mann's Earth Band	Bronze	6	(1)	F
19	-	**I'll Meet You At Midnight**	Smokie	RAK	5		
20	-	**Loving And Free/Amoureuse**	Kiki Dee	Rocket	5		

◆ Britain's top solo artist, Cliff Richard, finally cracked the US Top 10 with 'Devil Woman'. His 20 date Russian tour was also a great success.

◆ Sid Bernstein, who had promoted The Beatles' famous Shea Stadium gig, reportedly offered the group $200 million to reform and tour for him.

1976

This Mnth	Prev Mnth	Title	Artist	Label	Wks	(US 20 Pos)	
1	12	If You Leave Me Now	Chicago	CBS	12	(1)	
2	1	Mississippi	Pussycat	Sonet	13		F L
3	-	You Make Me Feel Like Dancing	Leo Sayer	Chrysalis	7	(1)	
4	16	Don't Take Away The Music	Tavares	Capitol	7	(34)	
5	-	Play That Funky Music	Wild Cherry	Epic	7	(1)	F L
6	11	Hurt	Manhattans	CBS	8	(97)	L
7	5	When Forever Has Gone	Demis Roussos	Philips	7		L
8	-	If Not You	Dr. Hook	Capitol	6	(55)	
9	-	Under The Moon Of Love	Showaddywaddy	Bell	12		
10	-	Couldn't Get It Right	Climax Blues Band	BTM	6	(3)	F L
11	7	Howzat	Sherbet	Epic	7	(61)	F L
12	15	Summer Of My Life	Simon May	Pye	6		F L
13	-	Dancing With The Captain	Paul Nicholas	RSO	5		
14	-	Substitute	Who	Polydor	5		
15	-	Love And Affection	Joan Armatrading	A&M	5		F
16	-	Beautiful Noise	Neil Diamond	CBS	4		
17	-	Lost In France	Bonnie Tyler	RCA	5		F
18	-	Somebody To Love	Queen	EMI	8	(13)	
19	-	Jaws	Lalo Schifrin	CTI	4		F L
20	3	Sailing	Rod Stewart	Warner	8	(58)	

This Mnth	Prev Mnth	Title	Artist	Label	Wks	(US 20 Pos)	
1	9	Under The Moon Of Love	Showaddywaddy	Bell	12		
2	18	Somebody To Love	Queen	EMI	8	(13)	
3	-	Money Money Money	Abba	Epic	10	(56)	
4	-	Livin' Thing	Electric Light Orchestra	Jet	8	(13)	
5	-	When A Child Is Born (Soleado)	Johnny Mathis	CBS	8		
6	-	Love Me	Yvonne Elliman	RSO	8	(14)	F
7	1	If You Leave Me Now	Chicago	CBS	12	(1)	
8	3	You Make Me Feel Like Dancing	Leo Sayer	Chrysalis	7	(1)	
9	-	Lean On Me	Mud	Private Stock	7		L
10	-	Portsmouth	Mike Oldfield	Virgin	9		
11	-	Get Back	Rod Stewart	Riva	6		
12	17	Lost In France	Bonnie Tyler	RCA	5		F
13	8	If Not You	Dr. Hook	Capitol	6	(55)	
14	-	Sorry Seems To Be The Hardest Word	Elton John	Rocket	3	(6)	
15	-	Living Next Door To Alice	Smokie	RAK	7	(25)	
16	-	Bionic Santa	Chris Hill	Philips	5		L
17	-	Little Does She Know	Kursaal Flyers	CBS	6		F L
18	-	Dr. Love	Tina Charles	CBS	8		L
19	-	Stop Me (If You've Heard It All Before)	Billy Ocean	GTO	4		
20	-	Rock'n Me	Steve Miller Band	Mercury	4	(1)	F

♦ 'New Rose' by The Damned, widely accepted as the first British punk single, was released. The Sex Pistols' debut disc 'Anarchy In The UK' charted, but EMI, offended by their "disgraceful... aggressive behaviour", withdrew the record, paid them off with £40,000 ($100,000) and dropped them!

♦ One of the leading exponents of the current British craze Pub Rock, Dr. Feelgood (named after an earlier US R&B singer), took their R&B-styled live album **Stupidity** to the top without the benefit of a hit single.

1977

This Mnth	Prev Mnth	Title	Artist	Label	Wks	(US 20 Pos)	
1	-	Don't Give Up On Us	David Soul	Private Stock	12	(1)	F G
2	1	Under The Moon Of Love	Showaddywaddy	Bell	12		
3	3	Money Money Money	Abba	Epic	10	(56)	
4	5	When A Child Is Born (Soleado)	Johnny Mathis	CBS	8		
5	18	Dr. Love	Tina Charles	CBS	8		L
6	10	Portsmouth	Mike Oldfield	Virgin	9		
7	15	Living Next Door To Alice	Smokie	RAK	7	(25)	
8	-	Things We Do For Love	10cc	Mercury	8	(5)	
9	-	Side Show	Barry Biggs	Dynamic	9		F L
10	-	Don't Cry For Me Argentina	Julie Covington	MCA	10		F
11	-	Wild Side Of Life	Status Quo	Vertigo	9		
12	-	I Wish	Stevie Wonder	Tamla Motown	6	(1)	
13	2	Somebody To Love	Queen	EMI	8	(13)	
14	-	Grandma's Party	Paul Nicholas	RSO	8		L
15	-	You're More Than A Number In My Little Red Book	Drifters	Arista	6		L
16	9	Lean On Me	Mud	Private Stock	7		L
17	-	Isn't She Lovely	David Parton	Pye	7		F L
18	4	Livin' Thing	Electric Light Orchestra	Jet	8	(13)	
19	-	Fairytale	Dana	GTO	6		L
20	16	Bionic Santa	Chris Hill	Philips	5		L

1	10	Don't Cry For Me Argentina	Julie Covington	MCA	10		F
2	1	Don't Give Up On Us	David Soul	Private Stock	12	(1)	F G
3	-	When I Need You	Leo Sayer	Chrysalis	9	(1)	
4	9	Side Show	Barry Biggs	Dynamic	9		F L
5	17	Isn't She Lovely	David Parton	Pye	7		F L
6	-	Don't Leave Me This Way	Harold Melvin & The Blue Notes	Philly Int.	7		L
7	-	Daddy Cool	Boney M	Atlantic	6	(65)	F
8	-	Jack In The Box	Moments	All Platinum	6		L
9	-	Boogie Nights	Heatwave	GTO	10	(2)	F
10	-	Car Wash	Rose Royce	MCA	6	(1)	F
11	-	Suspicion	Elvis Presley	RCA	6		
12	15	You're More Than A Number In My Little Red Book	Drifters	Arista	6		L
13	-	Chanson D'Amour	Manhattan Transfer	Atlantic	11		F
14	-	Sing Me	Brothers	Bus Stop	6		F L
15	-	Don't Believe A Word	Thin Lizzy	Vertigo	4		
16	8	Things We Do For Love	10cc	Mercury	8	(5)	
17	11	Wild Side Of Life	Status Quo	Vertigo	9		
18	-	This Is Tomorrow	Bryan Ferry	Polydor	6		
19	-	Romeo	Mr. Big	EMI	7	(87)	F L
20	12	I Wish	Stevie Wonder	Tamla Motown	6	(1)	

◆ American actor David Soul's version of the British-written 'Don't Give Up On Us', topped the transatlantic charts and sold a million copies in the UK alone.
Interestingly, teen-heartthrob Soul had previously recorded unsuccessfully in 1966 as The Covered Man (advertisements showed him with a bag on his head)!
◆ Punk was making the headlines, and most major labels quickly clambered onto the fast moving bandwagon. United Artists signed The Stranglers, Polydor nabbed The Jam and A&M briefly inked The Sex Pistols.

March 1977

This Mnth	Prev Mnth	Title	Artist	Label	Wks	(US 20 Pos)	
1	13	**Chanson D'Amour**	Manhattan Transfer	Atlantic	11		F
2	9	**Boogie Nights**	Heatwave	GTO	10	(2)	F
3	3	**When I Need You**	Leo Sayer	Chrysalis	9	(1)	
4	19	**Romeo**	Mr. Big	EMI	7	(87)	F L
5	-	**Knowing Me Knowing You**	Abba	Epic	11	(14)	
6	-	**Sound And Vision**	David Bowie	RCA	9	(69)	
7	-	**Torn Between Two Lovers**	Mary MacGregor	Ariola America	8	(1)	F L
8	1	**Don't Cry For Me Argentina**	Julie Covington	MCA	10		F
9	-	**When**	Showaddywaddy	Arista	8		
10	18	**This Is Tomorrow**	Bryan Ferry	Polydor	6		
11	-	**Baby I Know**	Rubettes	State	7		L
12	-	**Rockaria**	Electric Light Orchestra	Jet	5		
13	-	**What Can I Say**	Boz Scaggs	CBS	5	(42)	F
14	6	**Don't Leave Me This Way**	Harold Melvin & The Blue Notes	Philly Int.	7		L
15	14	**Sing Me**	Brothers	Bus Stop	6		F L
16	2	**Don't Give Up On Us**	David Soul	Private Stock	12	(1)	F G
17	-	**Moody Blue**	Elvis Presley	RCA	5	(31)	
18	-	**Don't Leave Me This Way**	Thelma Houston	Motown	4	(1)	F L
19	8	**Jack In The Box**	Moments	All Platinum	6		L
20	-	**Going In With My Eyes Open**	David Soul	Private Stock	6	(54)	

April 1977

This Mnth	Prev Mnth	Title	Artist	Label	Wks	(US 20 Pos)	
1	5	**Knowing Me Knowing You**	Abba	Epic	11	(14)	
2	20	**Going In With My Eyes Open**	David Soul	Private Stock	6	(54)	
3	-	**I Don't Want To Put A Hold On You**	Berni Flint	EMI	8		F L
4	-	**Red Light Spells Danger**	Billy Ocean	GTO	9		
5	9	**When**	Showaddywaddy	Arista	8		
6	-	**Sunny**	Boney M	Atlantic	6		
7	6	**Sound And Vision**	David Bowie	RCA	9	(69)	
8	-	**Oh Boy**	Brotherhood Of Man	Pye	7		
9	1	**Chanson D'Amour**	Manhattan Transfer	Atlantic	11		F
10	-	**You Don't Have To Be A Star (To Be In My Show)**	Marilyn McCoo & Billy Davis Jr	ABC	5	(1)	F L
11	17	**Moody Blue**	Elvis Presley	RCA	5	(31)	
12	-	**Free**	Deniece Williams	CBS	9	(25)	F
13	-	**Have I The Right?**	Dead End Kids	CBS	7		F L
14	-	**Sir Duke**	Stevie Wonder	Motown	7	(1)	
15	-	**Lay Back In The Arms Of Someone**	Smokie	RAK	6		
16	-	**Love Hit Me**	Maxine Nightingale	UA	3		L
17	-	**Gimme Some**	Brendon	Magnet	5		F L
18	7	**Torn Between Two Lovers**	Mary MacGregor	Ariola America	8	(1)	F L
19	-	**Pearl's A Singer**	Elkie Brooks	A&M	6		F
20	2	**Boogie Nights**	Heatwave	GTO	10	(2)	F

◆ Two American acts faring better in Britain were Manhattan Transfer with the chart-topping single 'Chanson D'Amour', and 53-year-old country singer Slim Whitman, who had a No. 1 album, **Red River Valley** – neither record charted Stateside.

◆ The Sex Pistols topped some charts with 'God Save The Queen'. The Clash and The Stranglers had hit albums and newcomers The Boomtown Rats and Adam & The Ants attracted media acclaim.

1977

May 1977

This Mnth	Prev Mnth	Title	Artist	Label	Wks	(US 20 Pos)	
1	-	I Don't Want To Talk About It/ First Cut Is The Deepest	Rod Stewart	Riva	10	(46)	
2	12	Free	Deniece Williams	CBS	9	(25)	F
3	-	Ain't Gonna Bump No More (WithNo Big Fat Woman)	Joe Tex	Epic	8	(12)	F L
4	14	Sir Duke	Stevie Wonder	Motown	7	(1)	
5	-	The Shuffle	Van McCoy	H & L	8		L
6	-	Whodunit	Tavares	Capitol	7	(22)	
7	-	Evergreen ('A Star Is Born')	Barbra Streisand	CBS	12	(1)	
8	-	Hotel California	Eagles	Asylum	5	(1)	L
9	-	Good Morning Judge	10cc	Mercury	7	(69)	
10	-	Lucille	Kenny Rogers	UA	10	(5)	
11	13	Have I The Right?	Dead End Kids	CBS	7		F L
12	4	Red Light Spells Danger	Billy Ocean	GTO	9		
13	-	Mah Na Mah Na	Piero Umiliani	EMI International	5	(55)	F L
14	19	Pearl's A Singer	Elkie Brooks	A&M	6		F
15	-	Solsbury Hill	Peter Gabriel	Charisma	5	(68)	F
16	1	Knowing Me Knowing You	Abba	Epic	11	(14)	
17	-	Got To Give It Up	Marvin Gaye	Motown	6	(1)	
18	-	How Much Love	Leo Sayer	Chrysalis	5	(17)	
19	-	Lonely Boy	Andrew Gold	Asylum	5	(7)	F
20	3	I Don't Want To Put A Hold On You	Berni Flint	EMI	8		F L

June 1977

This Mnth	Prev Mnth	Title	Artist	Label	Wks	(US 20 Pos)	
1	10	Lucille	Kenny Rogers	UA	10	(5)	
2	1	I Don't Want To Talk About It/ First Cut Is The Deepest	Rod Stewart	Riva	10	(46)	
3	7	Evergreen ('A Star Is Born')	Barbra Streisand	CBS	12	(1)	
4	-	God Save The Queen	Sex Pistols	Virgin	6		F
5	3	Ain't Gonna Bump No More (With No Big Fat Woman)	Joe Tex	Epic	8	(12)	F L
6	-	Show You The Way To Go	Jacksons	Epic	7	(28)	
7	-	You're Moving Out Today	Carole Bayer Sager	Elektra	7	(69)	F L
8	-	Halfway Down The Stairs	Muppets	Pye	6		F
9	5	The Shuffle	Van McCoy	H & L	8		L
10	17	Got To Give It Up	Marvin Gaye	Motown	6	(1)	
11	9	Good Morning Judge	10cc	Mercury	7	(69)	
12	-	Telephone Line	Electric Light Orchestra	Jet	7	(7)	
13	-	Lido Shuffle	Boz Scaggs	CBS	7	(11)	L
14	-	O.K.	Rock Follies	Polydor	4		F L
15	-	Baby Don't Change Your Mind	Gladys Knight & The Pips	Buddah	7	(52)	
16	-	So You Win Again	Hot Chocolate	RAK	10	(31)	
17	-	Too Hot To Handle/Slip Your Disc To This	Heatwave	GTO	7		
18	-	Fanfare For The Common Man	Emerson, Lake & Palmer	Atlantic	10		F L
19	13	Mah Na Mah Na	Piero Umiliani	EMI International	5	(55)	F L
20	-	Spot The Pigeon (E.P.)	Genesis	Charisma	2		F

◆ US cult heroes Blondie, Television, Talking Heads and The Ramones toured the UK, and The Damned became the first UK punk act to perform at CBGB's in New York.

◆ Debuting in the UK Top 20 were Genesis with 'Spot The Pigeon' and their former lead singer, Peter Gabriel, with 'Solsbury Hill'.

July 1977

This Mnth	Prev Mnth	Title	Artist	Label	Wks	(US 20 Pos)	
1	16	**So You Win Again**	Hot Chocolate	RAK	10	(31)	
2	18	**Fanfare For The Common Man**	Emerson, Lake & Palmer	Atlantic	10		F L
3	15	**Baby Don't Change Your Mind**	Gladys Knight & The Pips	Buddah	7	(52)	
4	-	**Ma Baker**	Boney M	Atlantic	10	(96)	
5	-	**I Feel Love**	Donna Summer	GTO	9	(6)	
6	6	**Show You The Way To Go**	Jacksons	Epic	7	(28)	
7	-	**Sam**	Olivia Newton-John	EMI	7	(20)	
8	-	**Peaches/Go Buddy Go**	Stranglers	UA	7		F
9	-	**Angelo**	Brotherhood Of Man	Pye	11		
10	-	**Pretty Vacant**	Sex Pistols	Virgin	5		
11	-	**Oh Lori**	Alessi	A&M	8		F L
12	7	**You're Moving Out Today**	Carole Bayer Sager	Elektra	7	(69)	F L
13	1	**Lucille**	Kenny Rogers	UA	10	(5)	
14	3	**Evergreen (Love Theme From 'A Star Is Born')**	Barbra Streisand	CBS	12	(1)	
15	-	**Slow Down**	John Miles	Decca	6	(34)	L
16	-	**You're Gonna Get Next To Me**	Bo Kirkland & Ruth Davis	EMI International	5		F L
17	-	**Feel The Need In Me**	Detroit Emeralds	Atlantic	8	(90)	L
18	-	**Do What You Wanna Do**	T-Connection	TK	3	(46)	F
19	12	**Telephone Line**	Electric Light Orchestra	Jet	7	(7)	
20	8	**Halfway Down The Stairs**	Muppets	Pye	6		F

August 1977

This Mnth	Prev Mnth	Title	Artist	Label	Wks	(US 20 Pos)	
1	9	**Angelo**	Brotherhood Of Man	Pye	11		
2	5	**I Feel Love**	Donna Summer	GTO	9	(6)	
3	-	**You Got What It Takes**	Showaddywaddy	Arista	8		
4	-	**Float On**	Floaters	ABC	9	(2)	F L
5	4	**Ma Baker**	Boney M	Atlantic	10	(96)	
6	-	**We're All Alone**	Rita Coolidge	A&M	8	(7)	F L
7	-	**The Crunch**	Rah Band	Good Earth	8		F
8	-	**It's Your Life**	Smokie	RAK	6		
9	-	**Easy**	Commodores	Motown	6	(4)	
10	-	**Something Better Change/ Straighten Out**	Stranglers	UA	5		
11	2	**Fanfare For The Common Man**	Emerson, Lake & Palmer	Atlantic	10		F L
12	1	**So You Win Again**	Hot Chocolate	RAK	10	(31)	
13	-	**That's What Friends Are For**	Deniece Williams	CBS	7		
14	-	**Roadrunner**	Jonathan Richman & The Modern Lovers	Berserkley	3		F
15	10	**Pretty Vacant**	Sex Pistols	Virgin	5		
16	-	**Nights On Broadway**	Candi Staton	Warner	8		
17	11	**Oh Lori**	Alessi	A&M	8		F L
18	-	**Nobody Does It Better**	Carly Simon	Elektra	8	(2)	
19	-	**Way Down**	Elvis Presley	RCA	10	(18)	
20	17	**Feel The Need In Me**	Detroit Emeralds	Atlantic	8	(90)	L

◆ As one of the era's top female singers Debbie Harry, and her group Blondie, signed with Chrysalis, an earlier teen queen, Connie Francis, was the first woman to top the UK LP chart.

◆ The Bay City Rollers, whose star had already waned in the UK, scored their last American Top 20 entry, as new teen idols Shaun Cassidy (David's brother) and Andy Gibb (Brother of the Bee Gees) debuted on the chart.

1977

This Mnth	Prev Mnth	Title	Artist	Label	Wks	(US 20 Pos)	
1	19	**Way Down**	Elvis Presley	RCA	10	(18)	
2	-	**Magic Fly**	Space	Pye International	8		F L
3	-	**Silver Lady**	David Soul	Private Stock	11	(52)	
4	-	**Oxygene Part IV**	Jean-Michel Jarre	Polydor	7		F L
5	4	**Float On**	Floaters	ABC	9	(2)	F L
6	-	**Deep Down Inside**	Donna Summer	Casablanca	7		
7	16	**Nights On Broadway**	Candi Staton	Warner	8		
8	18	**Nobody Does It Better**	Carly Simon	Elektra	8	(2)	
9	1	**Angelo**	Brotherhood Of Man	Pye	11		
10	13	**That's What Friends Are For**	Deniece Williams	CBS	7		
11	3	**You Got What It Takes**	Showaddywaddy	Arista	8		
12	-	**Telephone Man**	Meri Wilson	Pye International	7	(18)	F L
13	7	**The Crunch**	Rah Band	Good Earth	8		F
14	-	**Do Anything You Wanna Do**	Rods	Island	7		F L
15	-	**Tulane**	Steve Gibbons Band	Polydor	4		F L
16	-	**Dancin' In The Moonlight (It's Caught Me In The Spotlight)**	Thin Lizzy	Vertigo	4		
17	-	**Looking After Number One**	Boomtown Rats	Ensign	5		F
18	-	**Best Of My Love**	Emotions	CBS	7	(1)	F
19	2	**I Feel Love**	Donna Summer	GTO	9	(6)	
20	-	**Wonderous Stories**	Yes	Atlantic	7		F L

This	Prev	Title	Artist	Label	Wks	(US Pos)	
1	3	**Silver Lady**	David Soul	Private Stock	11	(52)	
2	-	**Black Is Black**	La Belle Epoque	Harvest	9		F L
3	18	**Best Of My Love**	Emotions	CBS	7	(1)	F
4	-	**I Remember Elvis Presley (The King Is Dead)**	Danny Mirror	Sonet	6		F L
5	1	**Way Down**	Elvis Presley	RCA	10	(18)	
6	-	**Yes Sir I Can Boogie**	Baccara	RCA	9		F
7	-	**You're In My Heart**	Rod Stewart	Riva	8	(4)	
8	-	**From New York To L.A.**	Patsy Gallant	EMI	5		F L
9	2	**Magic Fly**	Space	Pye International	8		F L
10	-	**Black Betty**	Ram Jam	Epic	8	(18)	F
11	-	**No More Heroes**	Stranglers	UA	6		
12	12	**Telephone Man**	Meri Wilson	Pye International	7	(18)	F L
13	20	**Wonderous Stories**	Yes	Atlantic	7		F L
14	6	**Deep Down Inside**	Donna Summer	Casablanca	7		
15	-	**Star Wars Theme - Cantina Band**	Meco	RCA	5	(1)	F L
16	4	**Oxygene Part IV**	Jean-Michel Jarre	Polydor	7		F L
17	-	**Rockin' All Over The World**	Status Quo	Vertigo	10		
18	-	**Sunshine After The Rain**	Elkie Brooks	A&M	4		
19	-	**I Remember Yesterday**	Donna Summer	GTO	5		
20	-	**Holidays In The Sun**	Sex Pistols	Virgin	5		

◆ Marc Bolan, front man of the highly successful glam rock duo T-Rex, died in a car crash. He was a major figure in British rock music.

◆ Bing Crosby died. The well-loved singer, who had amassed 299 American Top 20 hits, found himself back in the British Top 10 with the evergreen 'White Christmas'.

1977

This Mnth	Prev Mnth	Title	Artist	Label	Wks	(US 20 Pos)	
1	-	**The Name Of The Game**	Abba	Epic	9	(12)	
2	17	**Rockin' All Over The World**	Status Quo	Vertigo	10		
3	-	**We Are The Champions**	Queen	EMI	8	(4)	
4	6	**Yes Sir I Can Boogie**	Baccara	RCA	9		F
5	7	**You're In My Heart**	Rod Stewart	Riva	8	(4)	
6	-	**2-4-6-8 Motorway**	Tom Robinson Band	EMI	6		F
7	2	**Black Is Black**	La Belle Epoque	Harvest	9		F L
8	-	**Calling Occupants Of Interplanetary Craft**	Carpenters	A&M	6	(32)	L
9	-	**How Deep Is Your Love**	Bee Gees	RSO	11	(1)	
10	-	**Needles And Pins**	Smokie	RAK	6	(68)	
11	-	**Dancin' Party**	Showaddywaddy	Arista	9		
12	-	**Live In Trouble**	Barron Knights	Epic	5		
13	-	**Virginia Plain**	Roxy Music	Polydor	5		
14	10	**Black Betty**	Ram Jam	Epic	8	(18)	F
15	20	**Holidays In The Sun**	Sex Pistols	Virgin	5		
16	-	**Daddy Cool/The Girl Can't Help It**	Darts	Magnet	10		F
17	1	**Silver Lady**	David Soul	Private Stock	11	(52)	
18	-	**She's Not There**	Santana	CBS	5	(27)	F L
19	-	**Mull Of Kintyre/Girls' School**	Wings	Capitol	13	(33)	P
20	-	**Hot Track E.P.**	Nazareth	Mountain	4		L

This Mnth	Prev Mnth	Title	Artist	Label	Wks	(US 20 Pos)	
1	19	**Mull Of Kintyre/Girls' School**	Wings	Capitol	13	(33)	P
2	-	**The Floral Dance**	Brighouse & Rastrick Brass Band	Transatlantic	10		F L
3	9	**How Deep Is Your Love**	Bee Gees	RSO	11	(1)	
4	-	**I Will**	Ruby Winters	Creole	9		F
5	16	**Daddy Cool/The Girl Can't Help It**	Darts	Magnet	10		F
6	11	**Dancin' Party**	Showaddywaddy	Arista	9		
7	-	**Egyptian Reggae**	Jonathan Richman & The Modern Lovers	Berserkley	6		L
8	-	**Belfast**	Boney M	Atlantic	7		
9	3	**We Are The Champions**	Queen	EMI	8	(4)	
10	-	**Love's Unkind**	Donna Summer	GTO	10		
11	2	**Rockin' All Over The World**	Status Quo	Vertigo	10		
12	-	**White Christmas**	Bing Crosby	MCA	4		G
13	-	**It's A Heartache**	Bonnie Tyler	RCA	9	(3)	
14	-	**Love Of My Life**	Dooleys	GTO	5		
15	-	**Put Your Love In Me**	Hot Chocolate	RAK	6		
16	1	**The Name Of The Game**	Abba	Epic	9	(12)	
17	-	**Mary Of The Fourth Form**	Boomtown Rats	Ensign	5		
18	-	**Watching The Detectives**	Elvis Costello	Stiff	5		F
19	-	**My Way**	Elvis Presley	RCA	6	(22)	
20	12	**Live In Trouble**	Barron Knights	Epic	5		

◆ The Vortex opened. Among the early headliners were Adam & The Ants, controversial girl group The Slits and Siouxsie & The Banshees.

◆ Understandably, British punk had few initial takers Stateside. However the Sex Pistols' chart topping UK debut LP **Never Mind the Bollocks** and Elvis Costello's **My Aim Is True** (which included musical contributions from Huey Lewis) were minor US successes.

1978

This Mnth	Prev Mnth	Title	Artist	Label	Wks	(US 20 Pos)	
1	1	**Mull Of Kintyre/Girls' School**	Wings	Capitol	13	(33)	P
2	10	**Love's Unkind**	Donna Summer	GTO	10		
3	13	**It's A Heartache**	Bonnie Tyler	RCA	9	(3)	
4	2	**The Floral Dance**	Brighouse/Rastrick Brass Band	Transatlantic	10		F L
5	-	**Don't It Make My Brown Eyes Blue**	Crystal Gayle	UA	8	(2)	F
6	-	**Dance Dance Dance (Yowsah Yowsah Yowsah)**	Chic	Atlantic	8	(6)	F
7	-	**Uptown Top Ranking**	Althia And Donna	Lightning	8		F L
8	3	**How Deep Is Your Love**	Bee Gees	RSO	11	(1)	
9	-	**Let's Have A Quiet Night In**	David Soul	Private Stock	7		
10	4	**I Will**	Ruby Winters	Creole	9		F
11	-	**Native New Yorker**	Odyssey	RCA	7	(21)	F
12	-	**Who Pays The Ferryman**	Yannis Markopoulos	BBC	4		F L
13	5	**Daddy Cool/The Girl Can't Help It**	Darts	Magnet	10		F
14	-	**Figaro**	Brotherhood Of Man	Pye	9		
15	-	**Jamming/Punky Reggae Party**	Bob Marley & The Wailers	Island	5		
16	-	**Only Women Bleed**	Julie Covington	Virgin	4		L
17	-	**I Love You**	Donna Summer	Casablanca	3	(37)	
18	19	**My Way**	Elvis Presley	RCA	6	(22)	
19	-	**Lovely Day**	Bill Withers	CBS	6	(30)	
20	-	**If I Had Words**	Scott Fitzgerald/Yvonne Keeley	Pepper	7		F L

1	14	**Figaro**	Brotherhood Of Man	Pye	9		
2	-	**Take A Chance On Me**	Abba	Epic	10	(3)	
3	20	**If I Had Words**	Scott Fitzgerald/Yvonne Keeley	Pepper	7		F L
4	7	**Uptown Top Ranking**	Althia And Donna	Lightning	8		F L
5	-	**Come Back My Love**	Darts	Magnet	10		
6	-	**Sorry I'm A Lady**	Baccara	RCA	5		L
7	1	**Mull Of Kintyre/Girls' School**	Wings	Capitol	13	(33)	P
8	11	**Native New Yorker**	Odyssey	RCA	7	(21)	F
9	19	**Lovely Day**	Bill Withers	CBS	6	(30)	
10	-	**Wishing On A Star**	Rose Royce	Warner	8		
11	-	**Hotlegs/I Was Only Joking**	Rod Stewart	Riva	6	(28)	
12	-	**Mr. Blue Sky**	Electric Light Orchestra	Jet	8	(35)	
13	2	**Love's Unkind**	Donna Summer	GTO	10		
14	-	**Love Is Like Oxygen**	Sweet	Polydor	5	(8)	L
15	-	**The Groove Line**	Heatwave	GTO	5	(7)	
16	15	**Jamming/Punky Reggae Party**	Bob Marley & The Wailers	Island	5		
17	-	**Drummer Man**	Tonight	Target	3		F L
18	-	**Just One More Night**	Yellow Dog	Virgin	5		F L
19	3	**It's A Heartache**	Bonnie Tyler	RCA	9	(3)	
20	6	**Dance Dance Dance (Yowsah Yowsah Yaowsah)**	Chic	Atlantic	8	(6)	F

◆ British acts working the USA included Genesis, David Bowie, The Stranglers, The Jam and The Sex Pistols, whose leader, Johnny Rotten, announced at the end of their short and controversial tour, that they were disbanding. .

◆ Pink Floyd's Dave Gilmour helped Kate Bush get a record deal with EMI. The multi-talented teenager's first single 'Wuthering Heights' shot her to instant stardom in Britain.

March 1978

This Mnth	Prev Mnth	Title	Artist	Label	Wks	(US Pos)	
1	-	Wuthering Heights	Kate Bush	EMI	9		F
2	2	Take A Chance On Me	Abba	Epic	10	(3)	
3	5	Come Back My Love	Darts	Magnet	10		
4	10	Wishing On A Star	Rose Royce	Warner	8		
5	.-	Denis	Blondie	Chrysalis	9		F
6	-	Stayin' Alive	Bee Gees	RSO	7	(1)	
7	-	Baker Street	Gerry Rafferty	UA	10	(2)	F
8	-	I Can't Stand The Rain	Eruption	Atlantic	8	(18)	F
9	12	Mr. Blue Sky	Electric Light Orchestra	Jet	8	(35)	
10	-	Matchstalk Men And Matchstalk Cats And Dogs	Brian & Michael	Pye	11		F L
11	-	Is This Love	Bob Marley & The Wailers	Island	6		
12	18	Just One More Night	Yellow Dog	Virgin	5		F L
13	-	Emotions	Samantha Sang	Private Stock	8	(3)	F L
14	1	Figaro	Brotherhood Of Man	Pye	9		
15	-	Free (E.P.)	Free	Island	4		L
16	-	Fantasy	Earth, Wind & Fire	CBS	4	(32)	
17	14	Love Is Like Oxygen	Sweet	Polydor	5	(8)	L
18	3	If I Had Words	Scott Fitzgerald/Yvonne Keeley	Pepper	7		F L
19	-	Ally's Tartan Army	Andy Cameron	Klub	5		F L
20	-	I Love The Sound Of Breaking Glass	Nick Lowe & His Cowboy Outfit	Radar	4		F

April 1978

This Mnth	Prev Mnth	Title	Artist	Label	Wks	(US Pos)	
1	10	Matchstalk Men And Matchstalk Cats And Dogs	Brian & Michael	Pye	11		F L
2	-	I Wonder Why	Showaddywaddy	Arista	7		
3	7	Baker Street	Gerry Rafferty	UA	10	(2)	F
4	-	If You Can't Give Me Love	Suzi Quatro	RAK	8	(45)	
5	5	Denis	Blondie	Chrysalis	9		F
6	1	Wuthering Heights	Kate Bush	EMI	9		F
7	-	Follow You Follow Me	Genesis	Charisma	7	(23)	
8	-	Never Let Her Slip Away	Andrew Gold	Asylum	8	(67)	
9	-	With A Little Luck	Wings	Parlophone	5	(1)	
10	-	Night Fever	Bee Gees	RSO	12	(1)	
11	8	I Can't Stand The Rain	Eruption	Atlantic	8	(18)	F
12	-	Too Much, Too Little, Too Late	Johnny Mathis & Deniece Williams	CBS	9	(1)	
13	20	I Love The Sound Of Breaking Glass	Nick Lowe & His Cowboy Outfit	Radar	4		F
14	19	Ally's Tartan Army	Andy Cameron	Klub	5		F L
15	-	Walk In Love	Manhattan Transfer	Atlantic	5		
16	-	Every 1's A Winner	Hot Chocolate	RAK	6	(6)	
17	-	Singin' In The Rain (Pt. 1)	Sheila B. Devotion	Carrere	4		F
18	-	Sometimes When We Touch	Dan Hill	20th Century	5	(3)	F L
19	11	Is This Love	Bob Marley & The Wailers	Island	6		
20	-	More Like The Movies	Dr. Hook	Capitol	5		

◆ For the third time in the 1970s, Free's recording of 'All Right Now' reached the UK Top 20. This time around it was on the 'Free EP'.

◆ As The Bee Gees scored their only transatlantic topper of the 1970s with the Grammy winning 'Night Fever', its parent album, **Saturday Night Fever**, started an 18 week run (a record for the decade) at the top in Britain.

1978

This Mnth	Prev Mnth	Title	Artist	Label	Wks	(US 20 Pos)	
1	-	Rivers Of Babylon/Brown Girl In The Ring	Boney M	Atlantic/Hansa	22	(30)	P
2	10	Night Fever	Bee Gees	RSO	12	(1)	
3	12	Too Much, Too Little, Too Late	Johnny Mathis/Deniece Williams	CBS	9	(1)	
4	-	Automatic Lover	Dee D. Jackson	Mercury	5		F L
5	8	Never Let Her Slip Away	Andrew Gold	Asylum	8	(67)	
6	-	Boy From New York City	Darts	Magnet	8		
7	-	Because The Night	Patti Smith Group	Arista	6	(13)	F L
8	-	Let's All Chant	Michael Zager Band	Private Stock	6	(36)	F L
9	1	Matchstalk Men And Matchstalk...	Brian & Michael	Pye	11		F L
10	-	Jack And Jill	Raydio	Arista	5	(8)	F
11	-	If I Can't Have You	Yvonne Elliman	RSO	7	(1)	L
12	-	Love Is In The Air	John Paul Young	Ariola	6	(7)	F L
13	-	She's So Modern	Boomtown Rats	Ensign	6		
14	-	Do It Again	Raffaella Carra	Epic	5		F L
15	4	If You Can't Give Me Love	Suzi Quatro	RAK	8	(45)	
16	-	More Than A Woman	Tavares	Capitol	6	(32)	
17	-	Everybody Dance	Chic	Atlantic	5	(38)	
18	2	I Wonder Why	Showaddywaddy	Arista	7		
19	-	Bad Old Days	Co-Co	Ariola/Hansa	3		F L
20	-	(I'm Always Touched By Your) Presence Dear	Blondie	Chrysalis	5		

1	1	Rivers Of Babylon/Brown Girl In...	Boney M	Atlantic/Hansa	22	(30)	P
2	-	You're The One That I Want	John Travolta/Olivia Newton-John	RSO	17	(1)	F P
3	6	Boy From New York City	Darts	Magnet	8		
4	11	If I Can't Have You	Yvonne Elliman	RSO	7	(1)	L
5	2	Night Fever	Bee Gees	RSO	12	(1)	
6	-	Ca Plane Pour Moi	Plastic Bertrand	Sire	7		F L
7	-	Oh Carol	Smokie	RAK	6		
8	12	Love Is In The Air	John Paul Young	Ariola	6	(7)	F L
9	-	Davy's On The Road Again	Manfred Mann's Earth Band	Bronze	5		L
10	-	Annie's Song	James Galway	RCA Red Seal	8		F L
11	16	More Than A Woman	Tavares	Capitol	6	(32)	
12	-	Miss You	Rolling Stones	Rolling Stone	6	(1)	
13	7	Because The Night	Patti Smith Group	Arista	6	(13)	F L
14	-	The Smurf Song	Father Abraham & The Smurfs	Decca	11		F
15	-	Ole Ola (Muhler Brasileira)	Rod Stewart	Riva	3		
16	-	What A Waste	Ian Dury & The Blockheads	Stiff	4		F
17	-	Making Up Again	Goldie	Bronze	5		F L
18	-	Hi Tension	Hi Tension	Island	3		F
19	-	It Sure Brings Out The Love In Your Eyes	David Soul	Private Stock	4		L
20	-	Come To Me	Ruby Winters	Creole	4		L

◆ Boney M's double-sided chart topper, 'Rivers Of Babylon'/ 'Brown Girl In The Ring', which sold over two million in Britain, was the only American Top 40 entry for these regular European hit makers.

◆ Dire Straits' debut single 'Sultans Of Swing' was released. It caused little interest until 1979 when it first charted in the USA.

1978

July 1978

This Mnth	Prev Mnth	Title	Artist	Label	Wks	(US 20 Pos)	
1	2	You're The One That I Want	John Travolta & Olivia Newton-John	RSO	17	(1)	F P
2	14	The Smurf Song	Father Abraham & The Smurfs	Decca	11		F
3	-	Dancing In The City	Marshall Hain	Harvest	9	(43)	F L
4	-	Airport	Motors	Virgin	7		F
5	10	Annie's Song	James Galway	RCA Red Seal	8		F L
6	-	Like Clockwork	Boomtown Rats	Ensign	7		
7	-	Man With The Child In His Eyes	Kate Bush	EMI	6	(85)	
8	-	A Little Bit Of Soap	Showaddywaddy	Arista	6		
9	12	Miss You	Rolling Stones	Rolling Stone	6	(1)	
10	-	Substitute	Clout	Carrere	9	(67)	F L
11	-	Boogie Oogie Oogie	Taste Of Honey	Capitol	8	(1)	F L
12	-	No One Is Innocent/My Way	Sex Pistols	Virgin	5		
13	1	Rivers Of Babylon/Brown Girl In The Ring	Boney M	Atlantic/Hansa	22	(30)	P
14	-	Mind Blowing Decisions	Heatwave	GTO	4		
15	-	Used Ta Be My Girl	O'Jays	Philly International	5	(4)	L
16	-	Wild West Hero	Electric Light Orchestra	Jet	6		
17	-	Run For Home	Lindisfarne	Mercury	5	(33)	
18	17	Making Up Again	Goldie	Bronze	5		F L
19	9	Davy's On The Road Again	Manfred Mann's Earth Band	Bronze	5		L
20	-	Argentine Melody (Cancion De Argentina)	San Jose	MCA	3		F L

August 1978

This Mnth	Prev Mnth	Title	Artist	Label	Wks	(US 20 Pos)	
1	1	You're The One That I Want	John Travolta & Olivia Newton-John	RSO	17	(1)	F P
2	10	Substitute	Clout	Carrere	9	(67)	F L
3	11	Boogie Oogie Oogie	Taste Of Honey	Capitol	8	(1)	F L
4	13	Rivers Of Babylon/Brown Girl	Boney M	Atlantic/Hansa	22	(30)	P
5	-	Three Times A Lady	Commodores	Motown	10	(1)	
6	-	Forever Autumn	Justin Hayward	CBS	6	(47)	L
7	2	The Smurf Song	Father Abraham & The Smurfs	Decca	11		F
8	-	5-7-0-5	City Boy	Vertigo	5	(27)	F L
9	-	If The Kids Are United	Sham 69	Polydor	5		
10	-	It's Raining	Darts	Magnet	8		
11	3	Dancing In The City	Marshall Hain	Harvest	9	(43)	F L
12	-	Northern Lights	Renaissance	Warner	5		F L
13	16	Wild West Hero	Electric Light Orchestra	Jet	6		
14	-	Supernature	Cerrone	Atlantic	5	(70)	F L
15	8	A Little Bit Of Soap	Showaddywaddy	Arista	6		
16	6	Like Clockwork	Boomtown Rats	Ensign	7		
17	-	Dreadlock Holiday	10cc	Mercury	9	(44)	L
18	-	Come Back And Finish What You Started	Gladys Knight & The Pips	Buddah	5		
19	-	Stay	Jackson Browne	Asylum	4	(20)	F L
20	-	Baby Stop Crying	Bob Dylan	CBS	5		L

◆ The soundtrack album to John Travolta's latest box office smash *Grease* topped the American album chart for three months and it repeated that feat in Britain. It contained the transatlantic smash duets, 'You're The One That I Want' and 'Summer Nights' by Travolta and Olivia Newton-John (both selling over a million in the UK alone), as well as the chart topping title song by Frankie Valli.

1978

This Mnth	Prev Mnth	Title	Artist	Label	Wks	(US 20 Pos)	
1	5	**Three Times A Lady**	Commodores	Motown	10	(1)	
2	17	**Dreadlock Holiday**	10cc	Mercury	9	(44)	L
3	4	**Rivers Of Babylon/Brown Girl In The Ring**	Boney M	Atlantic/Hansa	22	(30)	P
4	-	**Oh What A Circus**	David Essex	Mercury	8		
5	-	**Jilted John**	Jilted John	EMI International	7		F L
6	10	**It's Raining**	Darts	Magnet	8		
7	1	**You're The One That I Want**	John Travolta/O. Newton-John	RSO	17	(1)	F P
8	-	**Kiss You All Over**	Exile	RAK	6	(1)	F L
9	-	**British Hustle/Peace On Earth**	Hi Tension	Island	5		L
10	-	**Hong Kong Garden**	Siouxsie & The Banshees	Polydor	5		F
11	14	**Supernature**	Cerrone	Atlantic	5	(70)	F L
12	-	**Grease**	Frankie Valli	RSO	6	(1)	L
13	-	**Picture This**	Blondie	Chrysalis	6		
14	-	**Summer Nights**	John Travolta/O. Newton-John	RSO	11	(5)	G
15	-	**An Everlasting Love**	Andy Gibb	RSO	5	(5)	F L
16	-	**Summer Night City**	Abba	Epic	5		
17	-	**It's Only Make Believe**	Child	Ariola Hansa	5		F L
18	-	**Forget About You**	Motors	Virgin	4		L
19	-	**Again And Again**	Status Quo	Vertigo	4		
20	-	**Love Don't Live Here Anymore**	Rose Royce	Whitfield	7	(32)	

This Mnth	Prev Mnth	Title	Artist	Label	Wks	(US 20 Pos)	
1	14	**Summer Nights**	John Travolta & Olivia Newton-John	RSO	11	(5)	G
2	-	**Rasputin**	Boney M	Atlantic/Hansa	7		
3	20	**Love Don't Live Here Anymore**	Rose Royce	Whitfield	7	(32)	
4	-	**Lucky Stars**	Dean Friedman	Lifesong	6		F L
5	-	**I Can't Stop Lovin' You (Though I Try)**	Leo Sayer	Chrysalis	6		
6	-	**Sandy**	John Travolta	Polydor	7		
7	-	**Sweet Talkin' Woman**	Electric Light Orchestra	Jet	7	(17)	
8	12	**Grease**	Frankie Valli	RSO	6	(1)	L
9	-	**You Make Me Feel (Mighty Real)**	Sylvester	Fantasy	5	(36)	F L
10	-	**Now That We've Found Love**	Third World	Island	4	(47)	F
11	-	**Talking In Your Sleep**	Crystal Gayle	UA	5	(18)	L
12	-	**Blame It On The Boogie**	Jacksons	Epic	7	(54)	
13	16	**Summer Night City**	Abba	Epic	5		
14	-	**Rat Trap**	Boomtown Rats	Ensign	9		
15	-	**Macarthur Park**	Donna Summer	Casablanca	6	(1)	
16	2	**Dreadlock Holiday**	10cc	Mercury	9	(44)	L
17	-	**A Rose Has To Die**	Dooleys	GTO	4		
18	8	**Kiss You All Over**	Exile	RAK	6	(1)	F L
19	1	**Three Times A Lady**	Commodores	Motown	10	(1)	
20	4	**Oh What A Circus**	David Essex	Mercury	8		

◆ Soon after The Who's original manager Pete Meaden committed suicide, the group's colourful and extrovert drummer Keith Moon died from drug and drink-related causes.

◆ It was reported that The Rolling Stones' US tour had grossed a record-breaking $6 million.

November 1978

This Mnth	Prev Mnth	Title	Artist	Label	Wks	(US 20 Pos)	
1	14	**Rat Trap**	Boomtown Rats	Ensign	9		
2	1	**Summer Nights**	John Travolta & Olivia Newton-John	RSO	11	(5)	G
3	6	**Sandy**	John Travolta	Polydor	7		
4	-	**Hopelessly Devoted To You**	Olivia Newton-John	RSO	5	(3)	
5	-	**Darlin'**	Frankie Miller	Chrysalis	7		F L
6	15	**Macarthur Park**	Donna Summer	Casablanca	6	(1)	
7	-	**My Best Friend's Girl**	Cars	Elektra	5	(35)	F
8	12	**Blame It On The Boogie**	Jacksons	Epic	7	(54)	
9	2	**Rasputin**	Boney M	Atlantic/Hansa	7		
10	-	**Pretty Little Angel Eyes**	Showaddywaddy	Arista	6		
11	7	**Sweet Talkin' Woman**	Electric Light Orchestra	Jet	7	(17)	
12	-	**Instant Replay**	Dan Hartman	Sky	6	(29)	F
13	-	**Givin' Up Givin' In**	Three Degrees	Ariola	5		
14	-	**Public Image**	Public Image Ltd.	Virgin	4		F
15	-	**Bicycle Race/Fat Bottomed Girls**	Queen	EMI	4	(24)	
16	-	**Da Ya Think I'm Sexy**	Rod Stewart	Riva	9	(1)	
17	4	**Lucky Stars**	Dean Friedman	Lifesong	6		F L
18	-	**Dippety Day**	Father Abraham & The Smurfs	Decca	5		
19	-	**Hurry Up Harry**	Sham 69	Polydor	5		
20	-	**Hanging On The Telephone**	Blondie	Chrysalis	7		

December 1978

This Mnth	Prev Mnth	Title	Artist	Label	Wks	(US 20 Pos)	
1	-	**Mary's Boy Child-Oh My Lord**	Boney M	Atlantic/Hansa	7	(85)	G
2	16	**Da Ya Think I'm Sexy**	Rod Stewart	Riva	9	(1)	
3	-	**Too Much Heaven**	Bee Gees	RSO	9	(1)	
4	-	**A Taste Of Aggro**	Barron Knights	Epic	8		
5	-	**I Lost My Heart To A Starship Trooper**	Sarah Brightman & Hot Gossip	Ariola	8		F
6	-	**Y.M.C.A.**	Village People	Mercury	10	(2)	F G
7	-	**Le Freak**	Chic	Atlantic	10	(1)	
8	-	**Always And Forever/Mind Blowing Decisions**	Heatwave	GTO	9	(18)	
9	20	**Hanging On The Telephone**	Blondie	Chrysalis	7		
10	-	**You Don't Bring Me Flowers**	Barbra & Neil	Columbia	6	(1)	
11	1	**Rat Trap**	Boomtown Rats	Ensign	9		
12	-	**Lay Your Love On Me**	Racey	RAK	9		F
13	-	**Don't Cry Out Loud**	Elkie Brooks	A&M	5		
14	4	**Hopelessly Devoted To You**	Olivia Newton-John	RSO	5	(3)	
15	10	**Pretty Little Angel Eyes**	Showaddywaddy	Arista	6		
16	7	**My Best Friend's Girl**	Cars	Elektra	5	(35)	F
17	-	**Greased Lightning**	John Travolta	Polydor	5	(47)	
18	-	**Song For Guy**	Elton John	Rocket	6		
19	12	**Instant Replay**	Dan Hartman	Sky	6	(29)	F
20	-	**In The Bush**	Musique	CBS	5	(58)	F L

◆ The film *Grease* continued to spawn hits, with three songs, 'Summer Nights', 'Sandy' and 'Hopelessly Devoted To You', taking slots in the British Top 4 in November.

◆ The Cars , who were voted Best New Band in *Rolling Stone,* started a European tour. Their debut hit, 'My Best Friend's Girl', was the first picture disc to be successfully marketed in Britain.

◆ Sex Pistol Sid Vicious was charged in New York with the murder of his girlfriend Nancy Spungen.

1979

This Mnth	Prev Mnth	Title	Artist	Label	Wks 20	(US Pos)	
1	6	Y.M.C.A.	Village People	Mercury	10	(2)	F G
2	-	Hit Me With Your Rhythm Stick	Ian Dury & The Blockheads	Stiff	10		
3	12	Lay Your Love On Me	Racey	RAK	9		F
4	-	September	Earth, Wind & Fire	CBS	7	(8)	
5	18	Song For Guy	Elton John	Rocket	6		
6	7	Le Freak	Chic	Atlantic	10	(1)	
7	-	A Little More Love	Olivia Newton-John	EMI	6	(3)	
8	4	A Taste Of Aggro	Barron Knights	Epic	8		
9	-	Hello This Is Joannie (Telephone Answering Machine Song)	Paul Evans	Spring	5		F L
10	10	You Don't Bring Me Flowers	Barbra & Neil	Columbia	6	(1)	
11	1	Mary's Boy Child-Oh My Lord	Boney M	Atlantic/Hansa	7	(85)	G
12	3	Too Much Heaven	Bee Gees	RSO	9	(1)	
13	-	I'm Every Woman	Chaka Khan	Warner	7	(21)	F
14	5	I Lost My Heart To A Starship Trooper	Sarah Brightman & Hot Gossip	Ariola	8		F
15	-	One Nation Under A Groove (Pt. 1)	Funkadelic	Warner	4	(28)	F L
16	-	Car 67	Driver 67	Logo	5		F L
17	-	I'll Put You Together Again	Hot Chocolate	RAK	4		
18	-	Women In Love	Three Degrees	Ariola	8		
19	-	Heart Of Glass	Blondie	Chrysalis	8	(1)	G
20	8	Always And Forever/Mind Blowing Decisions	Heatwave	GTO	9	(18)	

This Mnth	Prev Mnth	Title	Artist	Label	Wks 20	(US Pos)	
1	19	Heart Of Glass	Blondie	Chrysalis	8	(1)	G
2	18	Women In Love	Three Degrees	Ariola	8		
3	-	Chiquitita	Abba	Epic	7	(29)	
4	-	Don't Cry For Me Argentina	Shadows	EMI	6		
5	2	Hit Me With Your Rhythm Stick	Ian Dury & The Blockheads	Stiff	10		
6	-	I Was Made For Dancin'	Leif Garrett	Scotti Bros	5	(10)	F L
7	-	Contact	Edwin Starr	20th Century	6	(65)	
8	16	Car 67	Driver 67	Logo	5		F L
9	4	September	Earth, Wind & Fire	CBS	7	(8)	
10	-	Milk And Alcohol	Dr. Feelgood	UA	5		F L
11	-	Tragedy	Bee Gees	RSO	7	(1)	
12	1	Y.M.C.A.	Village People	Mercury	10	(2)	F G
13	7	A Little More Love	Olivia Newton-John	EMI	6	(3)	
14	-	My Life	Billy Joel	CBS	4	(3)	
15	-	Oliver's Army	Elvis Costello	Radar	9		
16	-	King Rocker	Generation X	Chrysalis	4		F L
17	-	Just The Way You Are	Barry White	20th Century	5		
18	9	Hello This Is Joannie (Telephone...)	Paul Evans	Spring	5		F L
19	-	I Will Survive	Gloria Gaynor	Polydor	9	(1)	
20	3	Lay Your Love On Me	Racey	RAK	9		F

◆ British single sales continued to amaze, with hits from the Village People ('Y.M.C.A.') and Blondie ('Heart Of Glass') selling more than a million and Ian Dury's 'Hit Me With Your Rhythm Stick', only narrowly missing.

◆ British success for local groups Dire Straits and Police only came after their respective singles 'Sultans Of Swing' and 'Roxanne' charted in America.

1979

March 1979

This Mnth	Prev Mnth	Title	Artist	Label	Wks	(US 20 Pos)	
1	19	I Will Survive	Gloria Gaynor	Polydor	9	(1)	
2	15	Oliver's Army	Elvis Costello	Radar	9		
3	11	Tragedy	Bee Gees	RSO	7	(1)	
4	-	Lucky Number	Lene Lovich	Stiff	7		F
5	-	Can You Feel The Force	Real Thing	Pye	7		
6	-	Something Else/Friggin' In The Riggin'	Sex Pistols	Virgin	7		
7	-	I Want Your Love	Chic	Atlantic	7	(7)	
8	1	Heart Of Glass	Blondie	Chrysalis	8	(1)	G
9	-	Keep On Dancin'	Gary's Gang	CBS	5	(41)	F L
10	7	Contact	Edwin Starr	20th Century	6	(65)	
11	-	Get Down	Gene Chandler	20th Century	5	(53)	F L
12	-	Into The Valley	Skids	Virgin	6		F
13	3	Chiquitita	Abba	Epic	7	(29)	
14	-	Painter Man	Boney M	Atlantic/Hansa	3		
15	-	Get It	Darts	Magnet	4		
16	-	Waiting For An Alibi	Thin Lizzy	Vertigo	4		
17	-	In The Navy	Village People	Mercury	6	(3)	
18	-	Don't Stop Me Now	Queen	EMI	4	(86)	
19	-	Sound Of The Suburbs	Members	Virgin	4		F L
20	6	I Was Made For Dancin'	Leif Garrett	Scotti Bros	5	(10)	F L

April 1979

This	Prev	Title	Artist	Label	Wks	(US Pos)	
1	-	Bright Eyes	Art Garfunkel	CBS	11		G L
2	-	Cool For Cats	Squeeze	A&M	7		
3	-	Some Girls	Racey	RAK	7		
4	17	In The Navy	Village People	Mercury	6	(3)	
5	1	I Will Survive	Gloria Gaynor	Polydor	9	(1)	
6	-	Shake Your Body (Down To The Ground)	Jacksons	Epic	6	(7)	
7	-	Sultans Of Swing	Dire Straits	Vertigo	5	(4)	F
8	-	He's The Greatest Dancer	Sister Sledge	Atlantic/Cotillion	5	(9)	
9	-	Silly Thing/Who Killed Bambi	Sex Pistols	Virgin	4		
10	-	The Runner	Three Degrees	Ariola	4		
11	7	I Want Your Love	Chic	Atlantic	7	(7)	
12	-	Hallelujah	Milk & Honey	Polydor	4		F L
13	6	Something Else/Friggin' In The Riggin'	Sex Pistols	Virgin	7		
14	-	Pop Muzik	M	MCA	9	(1)	F
15	-	Wow	Kate Bush	EMI	4		
16	-	Turn The Music Up	Players Association	Vanguard	4		F L
17	-	I Don't Wanna Lose You	Kandidate	RAK	5		F L
18	4	Lucky Number	Lene Lovich	Stiff	7		F
19	2	Oliver's Army	Elvis Costello	Radar	9		
20	-	The Logical Song	Supertramp	A&M	5	(6)	

◆ The biggest transatlantic hits of the period were Gloria Gaynor's smash 'I Will Survive' and Rod Stewart's disco-oriented 'Da Ya Think I'm Sexy'.

◆ The film *Quadrophenia*, based on The Who album, and featuring Sting and Toyah, premiered in London, on the night of The Who's first gig with new drummer Kenny Jones (Keith Moon having died in September 1978). Soon afterwards, The Who's movie *The Kids Are Alright* premiered in New York.

1976

This Mnth	Prev Mnth	Title	Artist	Label	Wks	(US 20 Pos)	
1	1	Bright Eyes	Art Garfunkel	CBS	11		G L
2	14	Pop Muzik	M	MCA	9	(1)	F
3	-	Hooray Hooray It's A Holi-Holiday	Boney M	Atlantic/Hansa	6		
4	-	Does Your Mother Know	Abba	Epic	6	(19)	
5	-	Knock On Wood	Amii Stewart	Atlantic/Hansa	6	(1)	F
6	-	Reunited	Peaches & Herb	CBS	7	(1)	F L
7	3	Some Girls	Racey	RAK	7		
8	-	Goodnight Tonight	Wings	Parlophone	5	(5)	
9	20	The Logical Song	Supertramp	A&M	5	(6)	
10	-	Dance Away	Roxy Music	Polydor	10	(44)	
11	-	One Way Ticket	Eruption	Atlantic/Hansa	6		L
12	-	Sunday Girl	Blondie	Chrysalis	8		
13	-	Banana Splits (Tra La La Song)	Dickies	A&M	3		F L
14	6	Shake Your Body (Down To The Ground)	Jacksons	Epic	6	(7)	
15	-	Parisienne Walkways	Gary Moore	MCA	5		F
16	12	Hallelujah	Milk & Honey	Polydor	4		F L
17	-	Love You Inside Out	Bee Gees	RSO	3	(1)	
18	-	Boys Keep Swingin'	David Bowie	RCA	6		
19	-	Roxanne	Police	A&M	5	(32)	F
20	2	Cool For Cats	Squeeze	A&M	7		

June 1979

This Mnth	Prev Mnth	Title	Artist	Label	Wks	(US 20 Pos)	
1	10	Dance Away	Roxy Music	Polydor	10	(44)	
2	12	Sunday Girl	Blondie	Chrysalis	8		
3	-	Boogie Wonderland	Earth, Wind & Fire With The Emotions	CBS	7	(6)	
4	-	Ring My Bell	Anita Ward	TK	7	(1)	F L
5	-	Ain't No Stoppin' Us Now	McFadden & Whitehead	Philly Int.	6	(13)	F L
6	-	Theme From The Deer Hunter (Cavatina)	Shadows	EMI	6		
7	-	Are 'Friends' Electric	Tubeway Army	Beggars Banquet	10		F L
8	-	Shine A Little Love	Electric Light Orchestra	Jet	6	(8)	
9	6	Reunited	Peaches & Herb	CBS	7	(1)	F L
10	-	Up The Junction	Squeeze	A&M	6		
11	-	We Are Family	Sister Sledge	Atlantic	4	(2)	
12	2	Pop Muzik	M	MCA	9	(1)	F
13	-	The Lone Ranger	Quantum Jump	Electric	5		F L
14	-	Hot Stuff	Donna Summer	Casablanca	4	(1)	
15	18	Boys Keep Swingin'	David Bowie	RCA	6		
16	-	H.A.P.P.Y. Radio	Edwin Starr	RCA	5	(79)	L
17	4	Does Your Mother Know	Abba	Epic	6	(19)	
18	-	Masquerade	Skids	Virgin	4		
19	15	Parisienne Walkways	Gary Moore	MCA	5		F
20	-	Night Owl	Gerry Rafferty	UA	5		L

◆ As the Sex Pistols clicked with Eddie Cochran's 'Something Else', German-based Eruption charted with a revival of another lesser known late 1950s song, Neil Sedaka's 'One Way Ticket'.

◆ Art Garfunkel's 'Bright Eyes', from the animated film *Watership Down,* topped the UK chart, selling over a million copies. Surprisingly it failed to chart in his homeland.

◆ For the first time in 16 years The Shadows had two successive Top 10 hits, 'Don't Cry For Me Argentina' and 'Theme From The Deer Hunter'.

July 1979

This Mnth	Prev Mnth	Title	Artist	Label	Wks	(US 20 Pos)	
1	7	Are 'Friends' Electric	Tubeway Army	Beggars Banquet	10		F L
2	-	Silly Games	Janet Kay	Scope	6		F L
3	-	C'mon Everybody	Sex Pistols	Virgin	5		L
4	-	Light My Fire-137 Disco Heaven (Medley)	Amii Stewart	Atlantic	5	(69)	
5	10	Up The Junction	Squeeze	A&M	6		
6	20	Night Owl	Gerry Rafferty	UA	5		L
7	-	Lady Lynda	Beach Boys	Caribou	4		
8	-	Good Times	Chic	Atlantic	5	(1)	
9	-	Wanted	Dooleys	GTO	7		
10	-	Girls Talk	Dave Edmunds	Swansong	5	(65)	
11	4	Ring My Bell	Anita Ward	Tk	7	(1)	F L
12	-	Babylon's Burning	Ruts	Virgin	4		F L
13	-	I Don't Like Mondays	Boomtown Rats	Ensign	9	(73)	
14	13	The Lone Ranger	Quantum Jump	Electric	5		F L
15	-	Living On The Front Line	Eddy Grant	Ensign	4		F
16	-	Breakfast In America	Supertramp	A&M	4	(62)	L
17	-	Maybe	Thom Pace	RSO	4		F L
18	-	Born To Be Alive	Patrick Hernandez	GEM	5	(16)	F L
19	-	My Sharona	Knack	Capitol	3		F L
20	-	Do Anything You Want To	Thin Lizzy	Vertigo	3		

August 1979

This Mnth	Prev Mnth	Title	Artist	Label	Wks	(US 20 Pos)	
1	13	I Don't Like Mondays	Boomtown Rats	Ensign	9	(73)	
2	-	We Don't Talk Anymore	Cliff Richard	EMI	10	(7)	
3	-	Angel Eyes/Voulez Vous	Abba	Epic	6	(64)	
4	-	Can't Stand Losing You	Police	A&M	6		
5	9	Wanted	Dooleys	GTO	7		
6	-	Reasons To Be Cheerful (Part 3)	Ian Dury & The Blockheads	Stiff	5		L
7	-	Hersham Boys	Sham 69	Polydor	4		L
8	-	After The Love Has Gone	Earth, Wind & Fire	CBS	6	2)	
9	-	The Diary Of Horace Wimp	Electric Light Orchestra	Jet	5		
10	-	Beat The Clock	Sparks	Virgin	4		L
11	10	Girls Talk	Dave Edmunds	Swansong	5	(65)	
12	-	Duke Of Earl	Darts	Magnet	6		
13	-	Bang Bang	B.A. Robertson	Asylum	7		F
14	18	Born To Be Alive	Patrick Hernandez	GEM	5	(16)	F L
15	19	My Sharona	Knack	Capitol	3		F L
16	-	Gangsters	Specials	2 Tone	6		F
17	16	Breakfast In America	Supertramp	A&M	4	(62)	L
18	-	Angel Eyes	Roxy Music	Polydor	7		
19	2	Silly Games	Janet Kay	Scope	6		F L
20	1	Are 'Friends' Electric	Tubeway Army	Beggars Banquet	10		F L

◆ West Indian sounds continued to gain popularity thanks in part to ska-based 2-Tone music, whose foremost purveyors, The Specials and Madness, debuted on the British chart.

◆ *Rolling Stone* called videotapes "The newest selling tool in rock", citing David Bowie's 'Boys Keep Swinging' and Queen's 'Bohemian Rhapsody' as good examples.

1979

This Mnth	Prev Mnth	Title	Artist	Label	Wks 20	(US Pos)	
1	2	We Don't Talk Anymore	Cliff Richard	EMI	10	(7)	
2	-	Cars	Gary Numan	Beggars Banquet	8	(9)	F
3	13	Bang Bang	B.A. Robertson	Asylum	7		F
4	-	Street Life	Crusaders	MCA	6	(36)	F L
5	-	Don't Bring Me Down	Electric Light Orchestra	Jet	6	(4)	
6	18	Angel Eyes	Roxy Music	Polydor	7		
7	-	If I Said You Had A Beautiful Body, Would You Hold It Against Me	Bellamy Brothers	Warner	7	(39)	L
8	-	Just When I Needed You Most	Randy Vanwarmer	Bearsville	5	(4)	F L
9	-	Love's Gotta Hold On Me	Dollar	Carrere	6		
10	-	Money	Flying Lizards	Virgin	5	(50)	F L
11	16	Gangsters	Specials	2 Tone	6		F
12	1	I Don't Like Mondays	Boomtown Rats	Ensign	9	(73)	
13	-	Message In A Bottle	Police	A&M	7	(74)	
14	8	After The Love Has Gone	Earth, Wind & Fire	CBS	6	(2)	
15	-	Gotta Go Home/El Lute	Boney M	Atlantic/Hansa	4		L
16	-	Ooh! What A Life	Gibson Brothers	Island	5		F
17	-	Strut Your Funky Stuff	Frantique	Philly Int.	4		F L
18	-	Sail On	Commodores	Motown	4	(4)	
19	12	Duke Of Earl	Darts	Magnet	6		
20	-	Reggae For It Now	Bill Lovelady	Charisma	4		F L

This Mnth	Prev Mnth	Title	Artist	Label	Wks 20	(US Pos)	
1	-	Video Killed The Radio Star	Buggles	Island	6	(40)	F
2	13	Message In A Bottle	Police	A&M	7	(74)	
3	-	Don't Stop Till You Get Enough	Michael Jackson	Epic	7	(1)	
4	-	Dreaming	Blondie	Chrysalis	6	(27)	
5	-	Whatever You Want	Status Quo	Vertigo	6		
6	-	Since You've Been Gone	Rainbow	Polydor	6	(57)	F
7	-	One Day At A Time	Lena Martell	Pye	8		F L
8	-	Every Day Hurts	Sad Café	RCA	6		F
9	2	Cars	Gary Numan	Beggars Banquet	8	(9)	F
10	7	If I Said You Had A Beautiful Body, Would You Hold It Against Me	Bellamy Brothers	Warner	7	(39)	L
11	-	When You're In Love With A Beautiful Woman	Dr. Hook	Capitol	9	(6)	
12	-	The Chosen Few	Dooleys	GTO	5		L
13	-	Kate Bush On Stage E.P.	Kate Bush	EMI	3		
14	9	Love's Gotta Hold On Me	Dollar	Carrere	6		
15	-	Queen Of Hearts	Dave Edmunds	Swansong	5		L
16	-	O.K. Fred	Erroll Dunkley	Scope	5		F L
17	-	Cruel To Be Kind	Nick Lowe	Radar	5	(12)	L
18	18	Sail On	Commodores	Motown	4	(4)	
19	-	Gimme Gimme Gimme (A Man After Midnight)	Abba	Epic	6		
20	-	Tusk	Fleetwood Mac	Warner	5	(8)	

◆ Disco performer Patrick Hernandez had his sole Top 20 entry with 'Born To Be Alive'. Among the Frenchman's backing vocalists in the early 1980s was a certain Madonna Ciccone.

◆ Almost overnight The Police became teen idols. They had two consecutive chart toppers, 'Message in A Bottle' and 'Walking on The Moon', and the first of five No. 1 LPs, **Regatta De Blanc**.

November 1979

This Mnth	Prev Mnth	Title	Artist	Label	Wks 20	(US Pos)	
1	11	When You're In Love With A...	Dr. Hook	Capitol	9	(6)	
2	7	One Day At A Time	Lena Martell	Pye	8		F L
3	-	Crazy Little Thing Called Love	Queen	EMI	7	(1)	
4	19	Gimme Gimme Gimme (A Man After Midnight)	Abba	Epic	6		
5	-	The Eton Rifles	Jam	Polydor	5		
6	8	Every Day Hurts	Sad Café	RCA	6		F
7	-	Still	Commodores	Motown	6	(1)	
8	20	Tusk	Fleetwood Mac	Warner	5	(8)	
9	-	Gonna Get Along Without You Now	Viola Wills	Ariola/Hansa	5		F L
10	-	On My Radio	Selecter	2 Tone	3		F
11	-	She's In Love With You	Suzi Quatro	RAK	4	(41)	L
12	1	Video Killed The Radio Star	Buggles	Island	6	(40)	F
13	-	The Sparrow	Ramblers	Decca	5		F L
14	-	No More Tears (Enough Is Enough)	Barbra Streisand/Donna Summer	Casablanca/CBS	8	(1)	
15	-	A Message To You Rudy/Nite Klub	Specials	2 Tone	4		
16	12	The Chosen Few	Dooleys	GTO	5		L
17	3	Don't Stop Till You Get Enough	Michael Jackson	Epic	7	(1)	
18	16	O.K. Fred	Erroll Dunkley	Scope	5		F L
19	-	Knocked It Off	B.A. Robertson	Asylum	4		
20	-	Ladies Night	Kool & The Gang	Mercury	4	(8)	F

December 1979

This Mnth	Prev Mnth	Title	Artist	Label	Wks 20	(US Pos)	
1	-	Walking On The Moon	Police	A&M	7		
2	-	Another Brick In The Wall (Pt. 2)	Pink Floyd	Harvest	8	(1)	G L
3	14	No More Tears (Enough Is Enough)	Barbra Streisand & D. Summer	Casablanca/CBS	8	(1)	
4	-	Que Sera Mi Vida (If You Should Go)	Gibson Brothers	Island	8		
5	-	I Only Want To Be With You	Tourists	Logo	7	(83)	F
6	-	Rapper's Delight	Sugarhill Gang	Sugarhill	7	(36)	F L
7	1	When You're In Love With A...	Dr. Hook	Capitol	9	(6)	
8	-	Confusion/Last Train To London	Electric Light Orchestra	Jet	6	(37)	
9	3	Crazy Little Thing Called Love	Queen	EMI	7	(1)	
10	-	One Step Beyond	Madness	Stiff	6		
11	-	I Have A Dream	Abba	Epic	6		
12	-	My Simple Heart	Three Degrees	Ariola	6		L
13	-	Day Trip To Bangor (Didn't We Have A Lovely Time)	Fiddler's Dram	Dingles	5		F L
14	-	Complex	Gary Numan	Beggars Banquet	4		
15	-	Off The Wall	Michael Jackson	Epic	4	(10)	
16	7	Still	Commodores	Motown	6	(1)	
17	-	Wonderful Christmastime	Paul McCartney	Parlophone	5		
18	-	Union City Blue	Blondie	Chrysalis	5		
19	-	Brass In Pocket	Pretenders	Real	9	(14)	F
20	5	The Eton Rifles	Jam	Polydor	5		

◆ Among the year's top record deals were Paul McCartney signing to Columbia for $20 million, and Paul Simon's seven album deal with Warner, which was reportedly worth $14 million.

◆ Annie Lennox first charted with The Tourists, 16-year-olds George Michael and Andrew Ridgeley formed a group and The Buggles warned that 'Video Killed The Radio Star'.

1980

This Mnth	Prev Mnth	Title	Artist	Label	Wks (US 20 Pos)
1	19	**Brass In Pocket**	Pretenders	Real	9 (14) F
2	2	**Another Brick In The Wall (Pt. 2)**	Pink Floyd	Harvest	8 (1) G L
3	11	**I Have A Dream**	Abba	Epic	6
4	-	**Please Don't Go**	KC & The Sunshine Band	TK	6 (1)
5	-	**With You I'm Born Again**	Billy Preston & Syreeta	Motown	5 (4) L
6	13	**Day Trip To Bangor (Didn't We Have A Lovely Time)**	Fiddler's Dram	Dingles	5 F L
7	5	**I Only Want To Be With You**	Tourists	Logo	7 (83) F
8	-	**My Girl**	Madness	Stiff	6
9	-	**Tears Of A Clown/Ranking Full Stop**	Beat	2 Tone	7 F
10	-	**I'm In The Mood For Dancing**	Nolans	Epic	8 F
11	6	**Rapper's Delight**	Sugarhill Gang	Sugarhill	7 (36) F L
12	12	**My Simple Heart**	Three Degrees	Ariola	6 L
13	1	**Walking On The Moon**	Police	A&M	7
14	-	**Is It Love You're After**	Rose Royce	Whitfield	6
15	-	**Green Onions**	Booker T. & The M.G.'s	Atlantic	4 L
16	-	**London Calling**	Clash	CBS	3
17	-	**John I'm Only Danncing (Again)**	David Bowie	RCA	5
18	-	**Better Love Next Time**	Dr. Hook	Capitol	4 (12)
19	-	**Babe**	Styx	A&M	6 (1) F L
20	17	**Wonderful Christmastime**	Paul McCartney	Parlophone	5

This Mnth	Prev Mnth	Title	Artist	Label	Wks (US 20 Pos)
1	-	**Too Much Too Young E.P. (Special AKA Live!)**	Specials	2 Tone	6
2	-	**Coward Of The County**	Kenny Rogers	UA	8 (3)
3	10	**I'm In The Mood For Dancing**	Nolans	Epic	8 F
4	-	**Someone's Looking At You**	Boomtown Rats	Ensign	5
5	-	**It's Different For Girls**	Joe Jackson	A&M	5
6	8	**My Girl**	Madness	Stiff	6
7	19	**Babe**	Styx	A&M	6 (1) F L
8	-	**Captain Beaky/Wilfred The Weasel**	Keith Michel	Polydor	5 F L
9	-	**And The Beat Goes On**	Whispers	Solar	7 (19) F
10	-	**I Hear You Now**	Jon & Vangelis	Polydor	6 (58) F
11	1	**Brass In Pocket**	Pretenders	Real	9 (14) F
12	-	**7 Teen**	Regents	Rialto	4 F L
13	5	**With You I'm Born Again**	Billy Preston & Syreeta	Motown	5 (4) L
14	-	**Carrie**	Cliff Richard	EMI	6 (34)
15	15	**Green Onions**	Booker T. & The M.G.'s	Atlantic	4 L
16	4	**Please Don't Go**	KC & The Sunshine Band	TK	6 (1)
17	-	**Atomic**	Blondie	Chrysalis	6 (39)
18	-	**Rock With You**	Michael Jackson	Epic	5 (1)
19	-	**I Can't Stand Up For Falling Down**	Elvis Costello	F. Beat	5
20	-	**Living By Numbers**	New Muzik	GTO	3 F L

◆ In the week that he was awarded an OBE by the Queen, Cliff Richard had the second US Top 10 entry of his long career with 'We Don't Talk Anymore'.

◆ Among the past hit makers who died as the decade dawned were Mantovani, R&B legends Amos Milburn and Professor Longhair, early rocker Larry Williams and million selling 1950s British balladeer David Whitfield.

March 1980

This Mnth	Prev Mnth	Title	Artist	Label	Wks	(US 20 Pos)	
1	-	**Together We Are Beautiful**	Fern Kinney	WEA	7		F L
2	-	**Take That Look Off Your Face**	Marti Webb	Polydor	6		F
3	17	**Atomic**	Blondie	Chrysalis	6	(39)	
4	-	**Games Without Frontiers**	Peter Gabriel	Charisma	5	(48)	
5	-	**All Night Long**	Rainbow	Polydor	6		
6	-	**Turning Japanese**	Vapors	UA	7	(36)	F L
7	9	**And The Beat Goes On**	Whispers	Solar	7	(19)	F
8	2	**Coward Of The County**	Kenny Rogers	UA	8	(3)	
9	14	**Carrie**	Cliff Richard	EMI	6	(34)	
10	19	**I Can't Stand Up For Falling Down**	Elvis Costello	F. Beat	5		
11	-	**So Lonely**	Police	A&M	5		
12	-	**Going Underground/Dreams Of Children**	Jam	Polydor	6		
13	-	**Dance Yourself Dizzy**	Liquid Gold	Polo	8		F
14	-	**Do That To Me One More Time**	Captain & Tennille	Casablanca	4	(1)	F L
15	18	**Rock With You**	Michael Jackson	Epic	5	(1)	
16	-	**Hands Off-She's Mine**	Beat	Go Feet	4		
17	-	**Working My Way Back To You- Forgive Me, Girl (Medley)**	Detroit Spinners	Atlantic	9	(2)	
18	-	**So Good To Be Back Home Again**	Tourists	Logo	5		L
19	-	**Riders In The Sky**	Shadows	EMI	4		L
20	-	**Cuba/Better Do It Salsa**	Gibson Brothers	Island	3	(81)	

April 1980

This Mnth	Prev Mnth	Title	Artist	Label	Wks	(US 20 Pos)	
1	17	**Working My Way Back To You**	Detroit Spinners	Atlantic	9	(2)	
2	13	**Dance Yourself Dizzy**	Liquid Gold	Polo	8		F
3	-	**King/Food For Thought**	UB40	Graduate	7		F
4	-	**Sexy Eyes**	Dr. Hook	Capitol	6	(5)	L
5	12	**Going Underground/ Dreams Of Children**	Jam	Polydor	6		
6	-	**Work Rest & Play (E.P.)**	Madness	Stiff	5		
7	-	**Poison Ivy**	Lambrettas	Rocket	5		F
8	-	**Call Me**	Blondie	Chrysalis	5	(1)	
9	-	**Turn It On Again**	Genesis	Charisma	4	(58)	
10	-	**January February**	Barbara Dickson	Epic	6		
11	6	**Turning Japanese**	Vapors	UA	7	(36)	F L
12	-	**Stomp!**	Brothers Johnson	A&M	5	(7)	F L
13	-	**Talk Of The Town**	Pretenders	Real	4		
14	-	**Silver Dream Machine (Pt. 1)**	David Essex	Mercury	7		
15	-	**Geno**	Dexy's Midnight Runners	Late Night Feelings	8		F
16	1	**Together We Are Beautiful**	Fern Kinney	WEA	7		F L
17	-	**Living After Midnight**	Judas Priest	CBS	4		
18	-	**Don't Push It, Don't Force It**	Leon Haywood	20th Century	6	(49)	F L
19	-	**Echo Beach**	Martha & The Muffins	Dindisc	4		F L
20	-	**Coming Up**	Paul McCartney	Parlophone	5	(1)	

◆ The first indie LP chart in the UK showed **Dirk Wears White Sox** by Adam & The Ants at No. 1.

◆ Mirror In The Bathroom' by 2-Tone act The Beat, was the UK's first digitally recorded hit. Another first was The Police's 'Six Pack' – six separate singles sold as a package – which reached the Top 20.

1980

This Mnth	Prev Mnth	Title	Artist	Label	Wks	(US 20 Pos)	
1	15	Geno	Dexy's Midnight Runners	Late Night...	8		F
2	-	What's Another Year	Johnny Logan	Epic	6		F
3	-	No Doubt About It	Hot Chocolate	RAK	8		
4	20	Coming Up	Paul McCartney	Parlophone	5	(1)	
5	-	Mirror In The Bathroom	Beat	Go Feet	5		
6	-	She's Out Of My Life	Michael Jackson	Epic	5	(10)	
7	14	Silver Dream Machine (Pt. 1)	David Essex	Mercury	7		
8	-	Hold On To My Love	Jimmy Ruffin	RSO	5	(10)	L
9	8	Call Me	Blondie	Chrysalis	5	(1)	
10	-	I Shoulda Loved Ya	Narada Michael Walden	Atlantic	5	(66)	F
11	-	The Groove	Rodney Franklin	CBS	4		F L
12	-	Toccata	Sky	Ariola	4		F L
13	-	Theme From M*A*S*H (Suicide Is Painless)	Mash	CBS	7		F L
14	-	My Perfect Cousin	Undertones	Sire	3		
15	-	Over You	Roxy Music	Polydor	7	(80)	
16	-	Don't Make Waves	Nolans	Epic	4		
17	-	We Are Glass	Gary Numan	Beggars Banquet	5		
18	-	Check Out The Groove	Bobby Thurston	Epic	3		F L
19	3	King/Food For Thought	UB40	Graduate	7		F
20	-	The Golden Years (E.P.)	Motorhead	Bronze	3		F

This Mnth	Prev Mnth	Title	Artist	Label	Wks	(US 20 Pos)	
1	-	Crying	Don McLean	EMI	9	(5)	
2	13	Theme From M*A*S*H (Suicide...)	Mash	CBS	7		F L
3	-	Funkytown	Lipps Inc.	Casablanca	8	(1)	F L
4	3	No Doubt About It	Hot Chocolate	Rak	8		
5	-	Back Together Again	Roberta Flack & Donny Hathaway	Atlantic	7	(56)	
6	-	Rat Race/Rude Buoys Outa Jail	Specials	2 Tone	6		
7	-	Let's Get Serious	Jermaine Jackson	Motown	5	(9)	F
8	15	Over You	Roxy Music	Polydor	7	(80)	
9	-	You Gave Me Love	Crown Heights Affair	De-Lite	6		F L
10	-	Everybody's Got To Learn Sometime	Korgis	Rialto	6	(18)	L
11	-	Behind The Groove	Teena Marie	Motown	5		F L
12	17	We Are Glass	Gary Numan	Beggars Banquet	5		
13	6	She's Out Of My Life	Michael Jackson	Epic	5	(10)	
14	-	Messages	Orchestral Manoeuvres In The Dark	Dindisc	4		F
15	-	Midnite Dynamos	Matchbox	Magnet	5		
16	-	Substitute	Liquid Gold	Polo	4		L
17	-	Let's Go Round Again Pt. 1	Average White Band	RCA	5	(53)	L
18	-	Breaking The Law	Judas Priest	CBS	3		L
19	-	D-a-a-ance	Lambrettas	Rocket	3		L
20	-	Simon Templar/Two Pints Of Lager And A Packet Of Crisps Please	Splodgenessabounds	Deram	4		F L

◆ American records creating interest in Britain included dance tracks from Crown Heights Affair and Teena Marie, a duet by Robert Flack & the late Donny Hathaway, and the chart topping ten-year-old TV series theme *M*A*S*H*.

◆ Two of the 1980s' most successful acts made their Top 20 debuts. UB40 scored with 'King' (a tribute to Martin Luther King) and Orchestral Manoeuvres In The Dark charted with 'Messages'.

July 1980

This Mnth	Prev Mnth	Title	Artist	Label	Wks	(US 20 Pos)	
1	-	**Xanadu**	Olivia Newton-John/ Electric Light Orchestra	Jet	8	(8)	
2	-	**Jump To The Beat**	Stacy Lattisaw	Atlantic	7		F L
3	-	**Use It Up And Wear It Out**	Odyssey	RCA	8		
4	1	**Crying**	Don McLean	EMI	9	(5)	
5	-	**Cupid-I've Loved You For A Long Time (Medley)**	Detroit Spinners	Atlantic	6	(4)	L
6	-	**My Way Of Thinking/I Think It's Going To Rain**	UB40	Graduate	6		
7	-	**Could You Be Loved**	Bob Marley & The Wailers	Island	6		
8	3	**Funkytown**	Lipps Inc.	Casablanca	8	(1)	F L
9	-	**Waterfalls**	Paul McCartney	Parlophone	5		
10	10	**Everybody's Got To Learn Sometime**	Korgis	Rialto	6	(18)	L
11	-	**Babooshka**	Kate Bush	EMI	6		
12	20	**Simon Templar/Two Pints Of Lager...**	Splodgenessabounds	Deram	4		F L
13	-	**To Be Or Not To Be**	B.A. Robertson	Asylum	3		
14	-	**More Than I Can Say**	Leo Sayer	Chrysalis	6	(2)	
15	5	**Back Together Again**	Roberta Flack/Donny Hathaway	Atlantic	7	(56)	
16	-	**747 (Strangers In The Night)**	Saxon	Carrere	4		
17	11	**Behind The Groove**	Teena Marie	Motown	5		F L
18	-	**Emotional Rescue**	Rolling Stones	Rolling Stone	5	(3)	
19	-	**Let's Hang On**	Darts	Magnet	4		L
20	-	**Love Will Tear Us Apart**	Joy Division	Factory	4		F

August 1980

This Mnth	Prev Mnth	Title	Artist	Label	Wks	(US 20 Pos)	
1	-	**The Winner Takes It All**	Abba	Epic	7	(8)	
2	-	**Upside Down**	Diana Ross	Motown	7	(1)	
3	-	**9 to 5 (A.K.A. Morning Train)**	Sheena Easton	EMI	9	(1)	F
4	-	**Oops Upside Your Head**	Gap Band	Mercury	8		F
5	-	**Ashes To Ashes**	David Bowie	RCA	7		
6	14	**More Than I Can Say**	Leo Sayer	Chrysalis	6	(2)	
7	3	**Use It Up And Wear It Out**	Odyssey	RCA	8		
8	-	**Oh Yeah (On The Radio)**	Roxy Music	Polydor	5		
9	-	**Give Me The Night**	George Benson	Warner	5	(4)	F
10	11	**Babooshka**	Kate Bush	EMI	6		
11	-	**Start**	Jam	Polydor	6		
12	7	**Could You Be Loved**	Bob Marley & The Wailers	Island	6		
13	-	**Tom Hark**	Piranhas	Sire	6		F
14	-	**Feels Like I'm In Love**	Kelly Marie	Calibre	9		F L
15	-	**Funkin' For Jamaica (N.Y.)**	Tom Browne	Arista	4		F L
16	1	**Xanadu**	Olivia Newton-John/E.L.O.	Jet	8	(8)	
17	-	**There There My Dear**	Dexy's Midnight Runners	Late Night Feelings	5		
18	-	**Mariana**	Gibson Brothers	Island	3		L
19	-	**Lip Up Fatty**	Bad Manners	Magnet	4		F
20	-	**Sunshine Of Your Smile**	Mike Berry	Polydor	6		L

◆ Critically acclaimed Manchester group Joy Division's 'Love Will Tear Us Apart' reached the Top 20 shortly after the group's leader Ian Curtis had committed suicide.

◆ Scottish singer Sheena Easton found herself with two singles in the Top 10 after being the subject of the TV series *The Big Time*. She went on to win the Grammy for Best New Artist of 1981.

1980

This Mnth	Prev Mnth	Title	Artist	Label	Wks	(US 20 Pos)	
1	14	**Feels Like I'm In Love**	Kelly Marie	Calibre	9		F L
2	11	**Start**	Jam	Polydor	6		
3	-	**Eighth Day**	Hazel O'Connor	A&M	6		F
4	5	**Ashes To Ashes**	David Bowie	RCA	7		
5	-	**One Day I'll Fly Away**	Randy Crawford	Warner	6		F
6	-	**It's Only Love/Beyond The Reef**	Elvis Presley	RCA	6	(51)	L
7	3	**9 to 5**	Sheena Easton	EMI	9	(1)	F
8	-	**Dreaming**	Cliff Richard	EMI	6	(10)	
9	-	**Modern Girl**	Sheena Easton	EMI	6	(18)	
10	-	**Master Blaster (Jammin')**	Stevie Wonder	Motown	6	(5)	
11	20	**Sunshine Of Your Smile**	Mike Berry	Polydor	6		L
12	13	**Tom Hark**	Piranhas	Sire	6		F
13	-	**Another One Bites The Dust**	Queen	EMI	5	(1)	
14	-	**I Die: You Die**	Gary Numan	Beggars Banquet	4		
15	-	**Can't Stop The Music**	Village People	Mercury	4		L
16	-	**Bank Robber**	Clash	CBS	4		
17	-	**Don't Stand So Close To Me**	Police	A&M	7	(10)	
18	-	**It's Still Rock And Roll To Me**	Billy Joel	CBS	6	(1)	
19	1	**The Winner Takes It All**	Abba	Epic	7	(8)	
20	-	**Baggy Trousers**	Madness	Stiff	7		

This Mnth	Prev Mnth	Title	Artist	Label	Wks	(US 20 Pos)	
1	17	**Don't Stand So Close To Me**	Police	A&M	7	(10)	
2	-	**D.I.S.C.O.**	Ottawan	Carrere	7		F
3	20	**Baggy Trousers**	Madness	Stiff	7		
4	10	**Master Blaster (Jammin')**	Stevie Wonder	Motown	6	(5)	
5	-	**My Old Piano**	Diana Ross	Motown	5		
6	-	**If You're Lookin' For A Way Out**	Odyssey	RCA	8		
7	-	**Et Les Oiseaux Chantaient (And The Birds Were Singing)**	Sweet People	Polydor	4		F L
8	-	**Amigo**	Black Slate	Ensign	4		F L
9	-	**What You're Proposing**	Status Quo	Vertigo	4		
10	-	**Woman In Love**	Barbra Streisand	CBS	8	(1)	
11	-	**When You Ask About Love**	Matchbox	Magnet	7		
12	5	**One Day I'll Fly Away**	Randy Crawford	Warner	6		F
13	-	**Killer On The Loose**	Thin Lizzy	Vertigo	4		
14	1	**Feels Like I'm In Love**	Kelly Marie	Calibre	9		F L
15	-	**Searching**	Change	WEA	3		
16	-	**Gotta Pull Myself Together**	Nolans	Epic	5		
17	13	**Another One Bites The Dust**	Queen	EMI	5	(1)	
18	-	**Casanova**	Coffee	De-Lite	4		F L
19	-	**Stereotype/International Jet Set**	Specials	2 Tone	1		
20	6	**It's Only Love/Beyond The Reef**	Elvis Presley	RCA	6	(51)	L

◆ On the album charts **Emotional Rescue** gave The Rolling Stones their only transatlantic No. 1 of the decade and singer/songwriter Kate Bush's **Never For Ever** became the first LP by a female British singer to head the UK charts. The Police had the year's top UK single and album with the Grammy winning 'Don't Stand So Close To Me' and **Zenyatta Mondatta**, both of which entered at No. 1.

◆ Abba's 'Super Trooper' gave them their ninth and last chart topper, as the album of the same name chalked up over a million British advance orders.

1980

This Mnth	Prev Mnth	Title	Artist	Label	Wks	(US 20 Pos)	
1	10	Woman In Love	Barbra Streisand	CBS	8	(1)	
2	-	The Tide Is High	Blondie	Chrysalis	9	(1)	
3	-	Special Brew	Bad Manners	Magnet	6		
4	-	Fashion	David Bowie	RCA	6	(70)	
5	-	Enola Gay	OMD	Dindisc	7		
6	-	I Could Be So Good For You	Dennis Waterman	EMI	6		F L
7	-	Dog Eat Dog	Adam & The Ants	CBS	6		F
8	-	Super Trouper	Abba	Epic	9	(45)	
9	-	Never Knew Love Like This Before	Stephanie Mills	20th Century	7	(6)	F L
10	11	When You Ask About Love	Matchbox	Magnet	7		
11	6	If You're Lookin' For A Way Out	Odyssey	RCA	8		
12	9	What You're Proposing	Status Quo	Vertigo	4		
13	2	D.I.S.C.O.	Ottawan	Carrere	7		F
14	-	The Earth Dies Screaming/ Dream A Lie	UB40	Graduate	5		
15	16	Gotta Pull Myself Together	Nolans	Epic	5		
16	-	Celebration	Kool & The Gang	De-Lite	5	(1)	
17	3	Baggy Trousers	Madness	Stiff	7		
18	-	(Just Like) Starting Over	John Lennon	Geffen	10	(1)	
19	-	All Out Of Love	Air Supply	Arista	4	(2)	F L
20	-	The Same Old Scene	Roxy Music	Polydor	3		

This Mnth	Prev Mnth	Title	Artist	Label	Wks	(US 20 Pos)	
1	8	Super Trouper	Abba	Epic	9	(45)	
2	-	There's No One Quite Like Grandma	St. Winifred's School Choir	MFP	6		F L
3	-	Embarrassment	Madness	Stiff	8		
4	-	Stop The Cavalry	Jona Lewie	Stiff	8		L
5	-	Banana Republic	Boomtown Rats	Ensign	7		L
6	18	(Just Like) Starting Over	John Lennon	Geffen	10	(1)	
7	-	To Cut A Long Story Short	Spandau Ballet	Reformation	8		F
8	-	De Do Do Do, De Da Da Da	Police	A&M	6	(10)	
9	2	The Tide Is High	Blondie	Chrysalis	9	(1)	
10	-	Do You Feel My Love	Eddy Grant	Ensign	4		
11	-	Runaway Boys	Stray Cats	Arista	6		F
12	-	Antmusic	Adam & The Ants	CBS	12		
13	16	Celebration	Kool & The Gang	De-Lite	5	(1)	
14	-	Lady	Kenny Rogers	UA	5	(1)	
15	9	Never Knew Love Like This Before	Stephanie Mills	20th Century	7	(6)	F L
16	6	I Could Be So Good For You	Dennis Waterman	EMI	6		F L
17	-	Lies/Don't Drive My Car	Status Quo	Vertigo	6		
18	-	Happy Xmas (War Is Over)	John & Yoko & The Plastic Ono Band	Apple	5		
19	-	Flash	Queen	EMI	8	(42)	
20	-	Rock 'n' Roll Ain't Noise Pollution	AC/DC	Atlantic	3		F

◆ Fleetwood Mac followed the record breaking **Rumours** album with **Tusk,** which reportedly cost over $1 million to record

◆ Queen notched up their second US chart topper of the year when 'Another One Bites The Dust' followed in the footsteps of their retro-rockabilly track 'Crazy Little Thing Called Love'.

1981

This Mnth	Prev Mnth	Title	Artist	Label	Wks	(US 20 Pos)	
1	-	Imagine	John Lennon	Apple	9		
2	12	Antmusic	Adam & The Ants	CBS	12		
3	18	Happy Xmas (War Is Over)	John & Yoko & The Plastic Ono Band	Apple	5		
4	6	(Just Like) Starting Over	John Lennon	Geffen	10	(1)	
5	4	Stop The Cavalry	Jona Lewie	Stiff	8		L
6	-	Do Nothing/Maggie's Farm	Specials	2 Tone	5		
7	19	Flash	Queen	EMI	8	(42)	
8	8	De Do Do Do, De Da Da Da	Police	A&M	6	(10)	
9	-	Woman	John Lennon	Geffen	7	(2)	
10	-	Too Nice To Talk To	Beat	Go Feet	4		
11	2	There's No One Quite Like Grandma	St. Winifred's School Choir	MFP	6		F L
12	-	In The Air Tonight	Phil Collins	Virgin	6	(19)	F
13	-	I Am The Beat	Look	MCA	5		F L
14	-	Rabbit	Chas & Dave	Rockney	6		
15	3	Embarrassment	Madness	Stiff	8		
16	1	Super Trouper	Abba	Epic	9	(45)	
17	-	Don't Stop The Music	Yarbrough & Peoples	Mercury	6	(19)	F L
18	17	Lies/Don't Drive My Car	Status Quo	Vertigo	6		
19	11	Runaway Boys	Stray Cats	Arista	6		F
20	-	I Ain't Gonna Stand For It	Stevie Wonder	Motown	4	(11)	

This Mnth	Prev Mnth	Title	Artist	Label	Wks	(US 20 Pos)	
1	9	Woman	John Lennon	Geffen	7	(2)	
2	-	Vienna	Ultravox	Chrysalis	10		F
3	12	In The Air Tonight	Phil Collins	Virgin	6	(19)	F
4	-	I Surrender	Rainbow	Polydor	6		
5	-	Shaddup You Face	Joe Dolce Music Theatre	Epic	6	(53)	F L
6	-	Return Of The Los Palmas 7	Madness	Stiff	7		
7	-	Oldest Swinger In Town	Fred Wedlock	Rocket	5		F L
8	-	Romeo And Juliet	Dire Straits	Vertigo	6		
9	-	Rapture	Blondie	Chrysalis	5	(1)	
10	1	Imagine	John Lennon	Apple	9		
11	-	Fade To Grey	Visage	Polydor	5		F
12	2	Antmusic	Adam & The Ants	CBS	12		
13	-	Rock This Town	Stray Cats	Arista	5	(9)	
14	17	Don't Stop The Music	Yarbrough & Peoples	Mercury	6	(19)	F L
15	-	We'll Bring The House Down	Slade	Cheapskate	4		
16	-	St. Valentine's Day Massacre E.P.	Motorhead & Girlschool	Bronze	5		
17	-	(Do) The Hucklebuck	Coast To Coast	Polydor	8		F L
18	-	Young Parisians	Adam & The Ants	Decca	4		
19	-	Message Of Love	Pretenders	Real	3		
20	-	Jealous Guy	Roxy Music	EG	7		

◆ In January, the late John Lennon held three of the Top 4 places in the UK chart. His recordings of 'Woman' and the re-released 'Imagine' hit the top, as did Roxy Music's interpretation of his composition 'Jealous Guy'.

◆ The rockabilly revival continued with American trio The Stray Cats and Welsh rocker Shakin' Stevens leading the way. Interest was also growing in Brit-funk, thanks to Freeez and Beggar & Co.

1981

March 1981

This Mnth	Prev Mnth	Title	Artist	Label	Wks	(US 20 Pos)	
1	20	**Jealous Guy**	Roxy Music	EG	7		
2	-	**Kings Of The Wild Frontier**	Adam & The Ants	CBS	6		
3	17	**(Do) The Hucklebuck**	Coast To Coast	Polydor	8		F L
4	2	**Vienna**	Ultravox	Chrysalis	10		F
5	-	**Kids In America**	Kim Wilde	RAK	8	(25)	F
6	-	**This Ole House**	Shakin' Stevens	Epic	9		
7	5	**Shaddup You Face**	Joe Dolce Music Theatre	Epic	6	(53)	F L
8	-	**Four From Toyah E.P.**	Toyah	Safari	7		F
9	-	**Reward**	Teardrop Explodes	Vertigo	4		F
10	-	**Southern Freeez**	Freeez	Beggars Banquet	4		F
11	16	**St. Valentine's Day Massacre E.P.**	Motorhead & Girlschool	Bronze	5		
12	-	**Something 'Bout You Baby I Like**	Status Quo	Vertigo	4		
13	-	**You Better You Bet**	Who	Polydor	4	(18)	L
14	4	**I Surrender**	Rainbow	Polydor	6		
15	-	**Once In A Lifetime**	Talking Heads	Sire	3	(91)	F
16	-	**Lately**	Stevie Wonder	Motown	7	(64)	
17	-	**Star**	Kiki Dee	Ariola	4		L
18	6	**Return Of The Los Palmas 7**	Madness	Stiff	7		
19	-	**(Somebody) Help Me Out**	Beggar & Co	Ensign	3		F L
20	-	**I Missed Again**	Phil Collins	Virgin	3	(19)	

April 1981

This Mnth	Prev Mnth	Title	Artist	Label	Wks	(US 20 Pos)	
1	6	**This Ole House**	Shakin' Stevens	Epic	9		
2	-	**Making Your Mind Up**	Bucks Fizz	RCA	8		F
3	16	**Lately**	Stevie Wonder	Motown	7	(64)	
4	-	**Einstein A Go-Go**	Landscape	RCA	7		F L
5	5	**Kids In America**	Kim Wilde	RAK	8	(25)	F
6	-	**Intuition**	Linx	Chrysalis	6		
7	-	**It's A Love Thing**	Whispers	Solar	7	(28)	L
8	-	**Chi Mai Theme (From The TV Series The Life And Times Of David Lloyd George)**	Ennio Morricone	BBC	8		F L
9	-	**Good Thing Going (We've Got A Good Thing Going)**	Sugar Minott	RCA	6		F L
10	-	**Capstick Comes Home/ Sheffield Grinder**	Tony Capstick	Dingles	4		F L
11	-	**Night Games**	Graham Bonnett	Vertigo	5		F L
12	-	**Can You Feel It**	Jacksons	Epic	6	(77)	
13	-	**D-Days**	Hazel O'Connor	Albion	5		
14	8	**Four From Toyah E.P.**	Toyah	Safari	7		F
15	-	**Attention To Me**	Nolans	Epic	7		
16	-	**What Becomes Of The Broken Hearted**	Dave Stewart & Colin Blunstone	Stiff	5		F
17	1	**Jealous Guy**	Roxy Music	Eg	7		
18	3	**(Do) The Hucklebuck**	Coast To Coast	Polydor	8		F L
19	-	**Just A Feeling**	Bad Manners	Magnet	5		
20	-	**Mind Of A Toy**	Visage	Polydor	3		

◆ Major new artists on the UK charts included Phil Collins (whose first solo album Face Value entered at No. 1), 'new romantics' Spandau Ballet and Duran Duran, Kim Wilde and influential bands New Order and Ultravox.

◆ The first demonstration of the CD took place in Europe. The revolutionary digital playback system for music, which utilised laser beam technology, was to vinyl as the most popular system of carrying recorded sound.

1981

This Mnth	Prev Mnth	Title	Artist	Label	Wks	(US 20 Pos)	
1	-	**Stars On 45**	Starsound	CBS	8	(1)	F
2	-	**Stand And Deliver**	Adam & The Ants	CBS	8		
3	-	**You Drive Me Crazy**	Shakin' Stevens	Epic	8		
4	-	**Grey Day**	Madness	Stiff	6		
5	8	**Chi Mai Theme (From The TV Series The Life And Times Of David Lloyd George)**	Ennio Morricone	BBC	8		F L
6	2	**Making Your Mind Up**	Bucks Fizz	RCA	8		F
7	-	**Chequered Love**	Kim Wilde	RAK	5		
8	-	**Ossie's Dream (Spurs Are On Their Way To Wembley)**	Tottenham Hotspur F.A. Cup Final Squad	Rockney	4		F
9	-	**Swords Of A Thousand Men**	Ten Pole Tudor	Stiff	6		F
10	-	**Keep On Loving You**	REO Speedwagon	Epic	5	(1)	F
11	9	**Good Thing Going (We've Got A Good Thing Going)**	Sugar Minott	RCA	6		F L
12	12	**Can You Feel It**	Jacksons	Epic	6	(77)	
13	15	**Attention To Me**	Nolans	Epic	7		
14	-	**Musclebound/Glow**	Spandau Ballet	Reformation	5		
15	-	**Stray Cat Strut**	Stray Cats	Arista	4	(3)	L
16	-	**Only Crying**	Keith Marshall	Arrival	4		F L
17	11	**Night Games**	Graham Bonnett	Vertigo	5		F L
18	-	**Bette Davis Eyes**	Kim Carnes	Emi America	5	(1)	F L
19	-	**I Want To Be Free**	Toyah	Safari	6		
20	7	**It's A Love Thing**	Whispers	Solar	7	(28)	L

1	-	**Being With You**	Smokey Robinson	Motown	7	(2)	F L
2	-	**One Day In Your Life**	Michael Jackson	Motown	8	(55)	
3	-	**More Than In Love**	Kate Robbins & Beyond	RCA	6		F L
4	-	**How 'Bout Us**	Champaign	CBS	7	(12)	F L
5	2	**Stand And Deliver**	Adam & The Ants	CBS	8		
6	3	**You Drive Me Crazy**	Shakin' Stevens	Epic	8		
7	-	**Will You**	Hazel O'Connor	A&M	5		L
8	-	**Going Back To My Roots**	Odyssey	RCA	7		
9	-	**Funeral Pyre**	Jam	Polydor	3		
10	19	**I Want To Be Free**	Toyah	Safari	6		
11	-	**Teddy Bear**	Red Sovine	Starday	4	(40)	F L
12	-	**All Stood Still**	Ultravox	Chrysalis	5		
13	-	**Ain't No Stoppin'**	Enigma	Creole	5		F
14	1	**Stars On 45**	Starsound	CBS·	8	(1)	F
15	9	**Swords Of A Thousand Men**	Ten Pole Tudor	Stiff	6		F
16	7	**Chequered Love**	Kim Wilde	RAK	5		
17	-	**Memory**	Elaine Paige	Polydor	6		F
18	-	**Chariots Of Fire - Titles**	Vangelis	Polydor	3	(1)	F L
19	18	**Bette Davis Eyes**	Kim Carnes	EMI America	5	(1)	F L
20	-	**Ghost Town**	Specials	2 Tone	8		

◆ A re-issue of his 1975 recording 'One Day In Your Life', which had previously failed to take Michael Jackson into the US Top 40, gave him his first British chart topper.

◆ Toni Basil's Word of Mouth (which included the future No. 1 'Mickey') claimed to be the first album to be simultaneously released on record and video.

◆ The first US shows by Britain's hottest act Adam & The Ants were successful, but American sales were minimal. In the UK their seventh chart entry in nine months, 'Stand And Deliver', came in at No. 1.

1981

July 1981

This Mnth	Prev Mnth	Title	Artist	Label	Wks	(US 20 Pos)	
1	20	**Ghost Town**	Specials	2 Tone	8		
2	-	**Can Can**	Bad Manners	Magnet	8		
3	2	**One Day In Your Life**	Michael Jackson	Motown	8	(55)	
4	-	**Body Talk**	Imagination	R&B	9		F
5	-	**Stars On 45 (Vol 2)**	Starsound	CBS	6		
6	8	**Going Back To My Roots**	Odyssey	RCA	7		
7	-	**Wordy Rappinghood**	Tom Tom Club	Island	5		F L
8	-	**No Woman No Cry**	Bob Marley & The Wailers	Island	6		
9	17	**Memory**	Elaine Paige	Polydor	6		F
10	-	**Motorhead Live**	Motorhead	Bronze	4		L
11	-	**You Might Need Somebody**	Randy Crawford	Warner	5		
12	1	**Being With You**	Smokey Robinson	Motown	7	(2)	F L
13	-	**Dancing On The Floor (Hooked On Love)**	Third World	CBS	6		L
14	-	**Razzamatazz**	Quincy Jones	A&M	3		L
15	-	**Chant No. 1 (I Don't Need This Pressure On)**	Spandau Ballet	Reformation	7		
16	-	**Piece Of The Action**	Bucks Fizz	RCA	5		
17	-	**Lay All Your Love On Me**	Abba	Epic	4		
18	3	**More Than In Love**	Kate Robbins & Beyond	RCA	6		F L
19	-	**Sat In Your Lap**	Kate Bush	EMI	4		
20	11	**Teddy Bear**	Red Sovine	Starday	4	(40)	F L

August 1981

This Mnth	Prev Mnth	Title	Artist	Label	Wks	(US 20 Pos)	
1	-	**Green Door**	Shakin' Stevens	Epic	6		
2	-	**Hooked On Classics**	Royal Philharmonic Orchestra	RCA	7	(10)	F L
3	-	**Happy Birthday**	Stevie Wonder	Motown	7		
4	15	**Chant No. 1 (I Don't Need This Pressure On)**	Spandau Ballet	Reformation	7		
5	-	**Back To The Sixties**	Tight Fit	Jive	6	(89)	F
6	-	**Girls On Film**	Duran Duran	EMI	6		
7	-	**Love Action (I Believe In Love)**	Human League	Virgin	7		
8	-	**Hold On Tight**	Electric Light Orchestra	Jet	9	(10)	
9	1	**Ghost Town**	Specials	2 Tone	8		
10	-	**For Your Eyes Only**	Sheena Easton	EMI	5	(4)	
11	-	**Japanese Boy**	Aneka	Hansa	7		F L
12	-	**Walk Right Now**	Jacksons	Epic	5	(73)	
13	2	**Can Can**	Bad Manners	Magnet	8		
14	-	**Tainted Love**	Soft Cell	Some Bizzare	9	(8)	F
15	-	**Caribbean Disco**	Lobo	Polydor	5		F L
16	-	**Water On Glass/Boys**	Kim Wilde	RAK	4		
17	5	**Stars On 45 (Vol 2)**	Starsound	CBS	6		
18	-	**New Life**	Depeche Mode	Mute	6		F
19	-	**Beach Boy Gold**	Gidea Park	Sonet	4		F L
20	13	**Dancing On The Floor (Hooked On Love)**	Third World	CBS	6		L

◆ When Soft Cell's revival of the northern soul favourite 'Tainted Love' was re-issued it became Britain's Top Single of 1981. It also went on to spend a record 43 weeks in the US Hot 100.

◆ Meat Loaf's long-awaited album, **Dead Ringer**, was the first LP by an American artist to enter the British chart at No. 1.

◆ The most successful purveyors of 2-Tone music, The Specials, topped the chart with their last single, 'Ghost Town'. It was their seventh Top 10 entry in two years.

1981

This Mnth	Prev Mnth	Title	Artist	Label	Wks	(US 20 Pos)	
1	14	**Tainted Love**	Soft Cell	Some Bizzare	9	(8)	F
2	11	**Japanese Boy**	Aneka	Hansa	7		F L
3	-	**Prince Charming**	Adam & The Ants	CBS	7		
4	-	**Wired For Sound**	Cliff Richard	EMI	6	(71)	
5	8	**Hold On Tight**	Electric Light Orchestra	Jet	9	(10)	
6	7	**Love Action (I Believe In Love)**	Human League	Virgin	7		
7	-	**Souvenir**	Orchestral Manoeuvres In The Dark	Dindisc	6		
8	-	**Hands Up (Give Me Your Heart)**	Ottawan	Carrere	8		L
9	-	**Start Me Up**	Rolling Stones	Rolling Stone	4	(2)	
10	-	**One In Ten**	UB40	Dep International	5		
11	-	**She's Got Claws**	Gary Numan	Beggars Banquet	4		
12	-	**Pretend**	Alvin Stardust	Stiff	6		
13	-	**Slow Hand**	Pointer Sisters	Planet	5	(2)	F
14	-	**Abacab**	Genesis	Charisma	4	(26)	
15	2	**Hooked On Classics**	Royal Philharmonic Orchestra	RCA	7	(10)	F L
16	-	**Endless Love**	Diana Ross & Lionel Richie	Motown	6	(1)	
17	-	**Everybody Salsa**	Modern Romance	WEA	3		F
18	-	**The Thin Wall**	Ultravox	Chrysalis	4		
19	15	**Caribbean Disco**	Lobo	Polydor	5		F L
20	1	**Green Door**	Shakin' Stevens	Epic	6		

1	-	**The Birdie Song (Birdie Dance)**	Tweets	PRT	8		F L
2	-	**It's My Party**	Dave Stewart & Barbara Gaskin	Broken	8	(72)	L
3	-	**Under Your Thumb**	Godley & Creme	Polydor	6		F
4	3	**Prince Charming**	Adam & The Ants	CBS	7		
5	8	**Hands Up (Give Me Your Heart)**	Ottawan	Carrere	8		L
6	-	**Thunder In Mountains**	Toyah	Safari	5		
7	-	**Invisible Sun**	Police	A&M	4		
8	-	**Just Can't Get Enough**	Depeche Mode	Mute	5		
9	-	**Shut Up**	Madness	Stiff	5		
10	-	**Happy Birthday**	Altered Images	Epic	7		F
11	-	**O Superman**	Laurie Anderson	Warner	4		F L
12	-	**Open Your Heart**	Human League	Virgin	5		
13	12	**Pretend**	Alvin Stardust	Stiff	6		
14	16	**Endless Love**	Diana Ross & Lionel Richie	Motown	6	(1)	
15	-	**A Good Year For The Roses**	Elvis Costello	F. Beat	6		L
16	-	**It's Raining**	Shakin' Stevens	Epic	5		
17	-	**Absolute Beginners**	Jam	Polydor	4		
18	7	**Souvenir**	Orchestral Manoeuvres In The Dark	Dindisc	6		
19	-	**Walkin' In The Sunshine**	Bad Manners	Magnet	5		
20	1	**Tainted Love**	Soft Cell	Some Bizzare	9	(8)	F

◆ The medley craze was at its height; artists scoring in this vein were Tight Fit, Gidea Park, Royal Philharmonic Orchestra and genre pioneers Starsound, who scored a second successive hit. Meanwhile in the USA, a segue single of past hits by The Beach Boys was riding high.

◆ The Rolling Stones' American tour grossed a record $35 million, with each Stone supposedly pocketing $4 million.

1981

November 1981

This Mnth	Prev Mnth	Title	Artist	Label	Wks	(US 20 Pos)	
1	-	Every Little Thing She Does Is Magic	Police	A&M	6	(3)	
2	-	Joan Of Arc	OMD	Dindisc	5		
3	-	When She Was My Girl	Four Tops	Casablanca	5	(11)	
4	-	Under Pressure	Queen & David Bowie	EMI	6	(29)	
5	10	Happy Birthday	Altered Images	Epic	7		F
6	-	Begin The Beguine (Volver A Empezar)	Julio Iglesias	CBS	8		F
7	-	Labelled With Love	Squeeze	A&M	6		
8	-	Favourite Shirts (Boy Meets Girl)	Haircut 100	Arista	5		F
9	-	Tonight I'm Yours (Don't Hurt Me)	Rod Stewart	Riva	6	(20)	
10	2	It's My Party	Dave Stewart & Barbara Gaskin	Broken	8	(72)	L
11	-	Physical	Olivia Newton-John	EMI	6	(1)	
12	-	Let's Groove	Earth, Wind & Fire	CBS	6	(3)	L
13	15	A Good Year For The Roses	Elvis Costello	F. Beat	6		L
14	-	Bed Sitter	Soft Cell	Some Bizzare	7		
15	-	I Go To Sleep	Pretenders	Real	5		
16	-	Hold Me	B.A. Robertson & Maggie Bell	Swansong	5		L
17	-	When You Were Sweet Sixteen	Fureys & Davey Arthur	Ritz	4		F L
18	1	The Birdie Song (Birdie Dance)	Tweets	PRT	8		F L
19	12	Open Your Heart	Human League	Virgin	5		
20	-	Why Do Fools Fall In Love	Diana Ross	Capitol	8	(7)	

December 1981

This	Prev	Title	Artist	Label	Wks	(US Pos)	
1	-	Don't You Want Me	Human League	Virgin	9	(1)	G
2	-	Daddy's Home	Cliff Richard	EMI	8	(23)	
3	6	Begin The Beguine (Volver A...)	Julio Iglesias	CBS	8		F
4	20	Why Do Fools Fall In Love	Diana Ross	Capitol	8	(7)	
5	14	Bed Sitter	Soft Cell	Some Bizzare	7		
6	-	One Of Us	Abba	Epic	7		L
7	-	Ant Rap	Adam & The Ants	CBS	7		
8	-	It Must Be Love	Madness	Stiff	7	(33)	
9	12	Let's Groove	Earth, Wind & Fire	CBS	6	(3)	L
10	-	Wedding Bells	Godley & Creme	Polydor	6		
11	4	Under Pressure	Queen & David Bowie	EMI	6	(29)	
12	-	Land Of Make Believe	Bucks Fizz	RCA	10		
13	15	I Go To Sleep	Pretenders	Real	5		
14	-	Rock 'n' Roll	Status Quo	Vertigo	6		
15	-	Cambodia	Kim Wilde	RAK	6		
16	-	Ay Ay Ay Ay Moosey	Modern Romance	WEA	4		
17	-	Spirits In The Material World	Police	A&M	5	(11)	
18	-	Mirror Mirror (Mon Amour)	Dollar	WEA	8		
19	-	Four More From Toyah E.P.	Toyah	Safari	2		L
20	8	Favourite Shirts (Boy Meets Girl)	Haircut 100	Arista	5		F

◆ The Human League's 'Don't You Want Me' sold almost 1.5 million in the UK alone. Six months later it topped the US chart and opened the doors to other British synth bands. The group's **Dare** album also reached No. 1 in Britain.

◆ Early rock songs enjoying a return to favour included 'Why Do Fools Fall In Love' by Diana Ross, 'It's My Party' by Dave Stewart & Barbara Gaskin and Cliff Richard's revival of 'Daddy's Home'.

1982

This Mnth	Prev Mnth	Title	Artist	Label	Wks	(US 20 Pos)	
1	12	Land Of Make Believe	Bucks Fizz	RCA	10		
2	1	Don't You Want Me	Human League	Virgin	9	(1)	G
3	-	Get Down On It	Kool & The Gang	De-Lite	7	(10)	
4	18	Mirror Mirror (Mon Amour)	Dollar	WEA	8		
5	-	I'll Find My Way Home	Jon & Vangelis	Polydor	8	(51)	L
6	7	Ant Rap	Adam & The Ants	CBS	7		
7	6	One Of Us	Abba	Epic	7		L
8	8	It Must Be Love	Madness	Stiff	7	(33)	
9	-	The Model/Computer Love	Kraftwerk	EMI	7		
10	-	Oh Julie	Shakin' Stevens	Epic	7		
11	-	I Could Be Happy	Altered Images	Epic	7		
12	-	Waiting For A Girl Like You	Foreigner	Atlantic	8	(2)	F
13	2	Daddy's Home	Cliff Richard	EMI	8	(23)	
14	-	Being Boiled	Human League	Virgin	5		
15	10	Wedding Bells	Godley & Creme	Polydor	6		
16	14	Rock 'n' Roll	Status Quo	Vertigo	6		
17	-	Dead Ringer For Love	Meat Loaf	Epic	6		
18	-	Young Turks	Rod Stewart	Riva	4	(5)	
19	-	Golden Brown	Stranglers	Liberty	7		
20	17	Spirits In The Material World	Police	A&M	5	(11)	

This	Prev	Title	Artist	Label	Wks	(US Pos)	
1	19	Golden Brown	Stranglers	Liberty	7		
2	9	The Model/Computer Love	Kraftwerk	EMI	7		
3	-	Maid Of Orleans (The Waltz Joan Of Arc)	Orchestral Manoeuvres In The Dark	Dindisc	7		
4	-	Town Called Malice/Precious	Jam	Polydor	6		
5	10	Oh Julie	Shakin' Stevens	Epic	7		
6	17	Dead Ringer For Love	Meat Loaf	Epic	6		
7	-	Arthur's Theme (Best That You Can Do)	Christopher Cross	Warner	6	(1)	F L
8	-	The Lion Sleeps Tonight	Tight Fit	Jive	9		
9	-	Say Hello Wave Goodbye	Soft Cell	Some Bizzare	6		
10	-	Love Plus One	Haircut 100	Arista	7	(37)	
11	-	I Can't Go For That (No Can Do)	Daryl Hall & John Oates	RCA	5	(1)	F
12	1	Land Of Make Believe	Bucks Fizz	RCA	10		
13	-	Drowning In Berlin	Mobiles	Rialto	5		F L
14	-	Senses Working Overtime	XTC	Virgin	5		L
15	-	Easier Said Than Done	Shakatak	Polydor	4		F
16	-	Centrefold	J. Geils Band	EMI America	6	(1)	F L
17	3	Get Down On It	Kool & The Gang	De-Lite	7	(10)	
18	14	Bein' Boiled	Human League	Virgin	5		
19	-	Let's Get It Up	AC/DC	Atlantic	2	(44)	
20	12	Waiting For A Girl Like You	Foreigner	Atlantic	8	(2)	F

◆ Retro rock'n'roller Shakin' Stevens scored his third No. 1 with 'Oh Julie' (covered in America by Barry Manilow). The Jam had their third chart topping single with 'Town Called Malice' and their only No. 1 LP, The Gift.

◆ UB40's new record deal with Dep International was described as "The best since Paul McCartney signed with Columbia".

March 1982

This Mnth	Prev Mnth	Title	Artist	Label	Wks	(US Pos)	
1	8	The Lion Sleeps Tonight	Tight Fit	Jive	9		
2	-	Mickey	Toni Basil	Radialchoice	6	(1)	F L
3	10	Love Plus One	Haircut 100	Arista	7	(37)	
4	-	It Ain't What You Do It's The Way That You Do It	Fun Boy Three & Bananarama	Chrysalis	5		
5	-	Seven Tears	Goombay Dance Band	Epic	7		F L
6	16	Centrefold	J. Geils Band	EMI America	6	(1)	F L
7	-	Poison Arrow	ABC	Neutron	6	(25)	
8	-	See You	Depeche Mode	Mute	5		
9	-	Go Wild In The Country	Bow Wow Wow	RCA	5		F
10	-	Run To The Hills	Iron Maiden	EMI	5		F
11	-	Classic	Adrian Gurvitz	RAK	5		F L
12	-	Just An Illusion	Imagination	R&B	7		
13	4	Town Called Malice/Precious	Jam	Polydor	6		
14	-	Quiereme Mucho (Yours)	Julio Iglesias	CBS	4		
15	-	Cardiac Arrest	Madness	Stiff	4		
16	-	Layla	Derek & The Dominoes	RSO	5		F L
17	9	Say Hello Wave Goodbye	Soft Cell	Some Bizzare	6		
18	-	Party Fears Two	Associates	Associates	3		F
19	-	Deutscher Girls	Adam & The Ants	Ego	4		
20	3	Maid Of Orleans (The Waltz Joan Of Arc)	Orchestral Manoeuvres In The Dark	Dindisc	7		

April 1982

This Mnth	Prev Mnth	Title	Artist	Label	Wks	(US Pos)	
1	-	My Camera Never Lies	Bucks Fizz	RCA	5		
2	-	Ain't No Pleasing You	Chas & Dave	Rockney	6		
3	5	Seven Tears	Goombay Dance Band	Epic	7		F L
4	12	Just An Illusion	Imagination	R&B	7		
5	-	Give Me Back My Heart	Dollar	WEA	6		
6	-	Ghosts	Japan	Virgin	5		
7	-	More Than This	Roxy Music	EG	5		
8	-	Ebony And Ivory	Paul McCartney & Stevie Wonder	Parlophone	7	(1)	
9	16	Layla	Derek & The Dominoes	RSO	5		F L
10	14	Quiereme Mucho (Yours)	Julio Iglesias	CBS	4		
11	-	Papa's Got A Brand New Pigbag	Pigbag	Y	5		F L
12	-	Have You Ever Been In Love	Leo Sayer	Chrysalis	3		
13	-	Dear John	Status Quo	Vertigo	4		
14	-	Is It A Dream	Classix Nouveaux	Liberty	3		F L
15	-	Night Birds	Shakatak	Polydor	4		
16	-	One Step Further	Bardo	Epic	4		F L
17	-	See Those Eyes	Altered Images	Epic	4		
18	7	Poison Arrow	ABC	Neutron	6	(25)	
19	-	Damned Don't Cry	Visage	Polydor	3		
20	-	Blue Eyes	Elton John	Rocket	4	(12)	

◆ Few pundits at the time would have prophesied that Bananarama, who made their chart debut alongside The Specials' off-shoot Fun Boy Three, would go on to amass more UK and US hits than any other female British group.

◆ In their homeland, British supergroup Asia's eponymous album, which headed the US chart for nine weeks, failed to make the Top 10.

1982

This Mnth	Prev Mnth	Title	Artist	Label	Wks	(US 20 Pos)
1	-	I Won't Let You Down	PhD	WEA	7	F L
2	8	Ebony And Ivory	Paul McCartney/Stevie Wonder	Parlophone	7	(1)
3	-	A Little Peace	Nicole	CBS	6	F L
4	-	I Love Rock 'n' Roll	Joan Jett & The Blackhearts	Epic	6	(1) F L
5	-	Only You	Yazoo	Mute	7	(67) F
6	-	Really Saying Something	Bananarama & Funboy Three	Deram	5	
7	-	This Time (We'll Get It Right)/ England We'll Fly The Flag	England World Cup Squad	England	5	
8	-	We Have A Dream	Scotland World Cup Squad	WEA	5	L
9	-	Girl Crazy	Hot Chocolate	RAK	6	
10	11	Papa's Got A Brand New Pigbag	Pigbag	Y	5	F L
11	-	Goody Two Shoes	Adam Ant	CBS	7	(12)
12	16	One Step Further	Bardo	Epic	4	F L
13	-	Forget Me Nots	Patrice Rushen	Elektra	5	(23) F L
14	-	House Of Fun	Madness	Stiff	6	
15	-	Fantasy Island	Tight Fit	Jive	7	L
16	-	I Can Make You Feel Good	Shalamar	Solar	5	
17	-	Fantastic Day	Haircut 100	Arista	5	
18	-	Shirley	Shakin' Stevens	Epic	2	
19	-	The Look Of Love (Part 1)	ABC	Neutron	7	(18)
20	-	Instinction	Spandau Ballet	Chrysalis	4	

This Mnth	Prev Mnth	Title	Artist	Label	Wks	(US 20 Pos)
1	11	Goody Two Shoes	Adam Ant	CBS	7	(12)
2	-	Torch	Soft Cell	Some Bizzare	6	
3	19	The Look Of Love (Part 1)	ABC	Neutron	7	(18)
4	14	House Of Fun	Madness	Stiff	6	
5	-	Hungry Like The Wolf	Duran Duran	EMI	8	(3)
6	-	I've Never Been To Me	Charlene	Motown	6	(3) F L
7	15	Fantasy Island	Tight Fit	Jive	7	L
8	-	Mama Used To Say	Junior	Mercury	7	(30) F
9	5	Only You	Yazoo	Mute	7	(67) F
10	-	I'm A Wonderful Thing (Baby)	Kid Creole & The Coconuts	Ze	5	F
11	-	I Want Candy	Bow Wow Wow	RCA	4	(62) L
12	-	Work That Body	Diana Ross	Capitol	5	(44)
13	-	3 X 3 (E.P.)	Genesis	Charisma	4	(32)
14	-	We Take Mystery (To Bed)	Gary Numan	Beggars Banquet	2	
15	-	Island Of Lost Souls	Blondie	Chrysalis	4	(37)
16	-	Club Country	Associates	Associates	4	L
17	13	Forget Me Nots	Patrice Rushen	Elektra	5	(23) F L
18	1	I Won't Let You Down	PhD	WEA	7	F L
19	-	Inside Out	Odyssey	RCA	7	L
20	-	Do I Do	Stevie Wonder	Motown	3	(13)

◆ Adam & The Ants split, and Adam's first solo effort, 'Goody Two Shoes', topped the UK listings and became his first US Top 20 entry.

◆ The Rolling Stones made their first UK appearance in six years. Their two Wembley shows attracted 140,000 fans.

◆ The UK's 500th chart topper was Eurovision Song Contest winner 'A Little Peace' by 17-year-old German Nicole (Hohloch). It entered at No. 8 – a record for a new artist.

July 1982

This Mnth	Prev Mnth	Title	Artist	Label	Wks	(US 20 Pos)	
1	-	Abracadabra	Steve Miller Band	Mercury	7	(1)	
2	-	Fame	Irene Cara	RSO	10	(4)	F
3	19	Inside Out	Odyssey	RCA	7		L
4	-	Happy Talk	Captain Sensible	A&M	4		F
5	-	A Night To Remember	Shalamar	Solar	6	(44)	
6	-	Music And Lights	Imagination	R&B	5		L
7	-	Da Da Da	Trio	Mobile Suit	5		F L
8	-	Shy Boy	Bananarama	London	7	(83)	
9	-	Now Those Days Are Gone	Bucks Fizz	RCA	5		
10	-	It Started With A Kiss	Hot Chocolate	RAK	8		
11	-	Don't Go	Yazoo	Mute	6		
12	-	No Regrets	Midge Ure	Chrysalis	5		F
13	6	I've Never Been To Me	Charlene	Motown	6	(3)	F L
14	-	Iko Iko	Natasha	Towerbell	5		F L
15	-	Driving In My Car	Madness	Stiff	6		
16	-	Come On Eileen	Dexy's Midnight Runners	Mercury	11	(1)	G
17	12	Work That Body	Diana Ross	Capitol	5	(44)	
18	-	Just Who Is The Five O'Clock Hero	Jam	Polydor	3		
19	-	Beatles Movie Medley	Beatles	Parlophone	4	(12)	
20	-	Night Train	Visage	Polydor	4		L

August 1982

This	Prev	Title	Artist	Label	Wks	(US Pos)	
1	16	Come On Eileen	Dexy's Midnight Runners	Mercury	11	(1)	G
2	2	Fame	Irene Cara	RSO	10	(4)	F
3	11	Don't Go	Yazoo	Mute	6		
4	10	It Started With A Kiss	Hot Chocolate	RAK	8		
5	-	Eye Of The Tiger	Survivor	Scotti Brothers	10	(1)	F
6	15	Driving My Car	Madness	Stiff	6		
7	-	Strange Little Girl	Stranglers	Liberty	5		
8	-	Stool Pigeon	Kid Creole & The Coconuts	Ze	5		
9	-	Can't Take My Eyes Off You	Boystown Gang	ERC	6		F L
10	-	My Girl Lollipop (My Boy Lollipop)	Bad Manners	Magnet	3		L
11	8	Shy Boy	Bananarama	London	7	(83)	
12	-	What	Soft Cell	Some Bizzare	5		
13	-	The Clapping Song	Belle Stars	Stiff	4		F
14	7	Da Da Da	Trio	Mobile Suit	5		F L
15	-	I Second That Emotion	Japan	Hansa	6		L
16	-	I Eat Cannibals Pt. 1	Toto Coelo	Radialchoice	5	(66)	F L
17	-	The Only Way Out	Cliff Richard	EMI	4	(64)	
18	-	Save A Prayer	Duran Duran	EMI	6	(16)	
19	-	Arthur Daley ('E's Alright)	Firm	Bark	3		F
20	-	John Wayne Is Big Leggy	Haysi Fantayzee	Regard	4		F

◆ Come On Eileen', by Dexy's Midnight Runners, which sold over a million in the UK, was Britain's top single of 1982 and went on to top the American charts too.

◆ Thanks to the TV series *Fame* (based on the 1980 film), Irene Cara's 'Fame' headed the British listings, two years after reaching the US Top 5. The film's soundtrack album also hit No. 1, being replaced by the million selling Kids From Fame from the TV series. This American series spawned five UK hit albums and four singles – none of which were successful in the act's homeland.

1982

This Mnth	Prev Mnth	Title	Artist	Label	Wks	(US 20 Pos)	
1	5	Eye Of The Tiger	Survivor	Scotti Brothers	10	(1)	F
2	18	Save A Prayer	Duran Duran	EMI	6	(16)	
3	-	Walking On Sunshine	Rocker's Revenge	London	8		F L
4	-	Private Investigations	Dire Straits	Vertigo	6		
5	1	Come On Eileen	Dexy's Midnight Runners	Mercury	11	(1)	G
6	-	Hi-Fidelity	Kids From 'Fame' (Featuring Valerie Landsberg)	RCA	6		F
7	-	All Of My Heart	ABC	Neutron	5		
8	-	Give Me Your Heart Tonight	Shakin' Stevens	Epic	4		
9	12	What	Soft Cell	Some Bizzare	5		
10	-	The Message	Grandmaster Flash, Melle Mel & The Furious Five	Sugar Hill	4	(62)	F
11	-	The Bitterest Pill (I Ever Had To Swallow)	Jam	Polydor	5		
12	16	I Eat Cannibals Pt. 1	Toto Coelo	Radialchoice	5	(66)	F L
13	-	There It Is	Shalamar	Solar	7		
14	9	Can't Take My Eyes Off You	Boystown Gang	ERC	6		F L
15	-	Nobody's Fool	Haircut 100	Arista	4		L
16	-	Today	Talk Talk	EMI	4		F
17	-	Saddle Up	David Christie	KR	5		F L
18	20	John Wayne Is Big Leggy	Haysi Fantayzee	Regard	4		F
19	-	Why	Carly Simon	WEA	5	(74)	
20	2	Fame	Irene Cara	RSO	10	(4)	F

This Mnth	Prev Mnth	Title	Artist	Label	Wks	(US 20 Pos)	
1	-	Pass The Dutchie	Musical Youth	MCA	6	(10)	F
2	-	Zoom	Fat Larry's Band	Virgin	7		F L
3	-	Do You Really Want To Hurt Me	Culture Club	Virgin	9	(2)	F
4	-	Hard To Say I'm Sorry	Chicago	Full Moon	6	(1)	
5	-	Starmaker	Kids From 'Fame'	RCA	7		
6	-	Love Come Down	Evelyn King	EMI	7	(17)	F L
7	-	Jackie Wilson Said	Dexy's Midnight Runners	Mercury	4		
8	13	There It Is	Shalamar	Solar	4		
9	-	Love Me Do	Beatles	Parlophone	5		
10	-	Just What I Always Wanted	Mari Wilson	Compact	5		F L
11	-	Lifeline	Spandau Ballet	Chrysalis	5		
12	-	Annie I'm Not Your Daddy	Kid Creole & The Coconuts	Ze	5		L
13	11	The Bitterest Pill (I Ever Had To Swallow)	Jam	Polydor	5		
14	-	Friend Or Foe	Adam Ant	CBS	4		
15	1	Eye Of The Tiger	Survivor	Scotti Brothers	10	(1)	F
16	3	Walking On Sunshine	Rocker's Revenge	London	8		F L
17	19	Why	Carly Simon	WEA	5	(74)	
18	-	House Of The Rising Sun	Animals	RAK	4		L
19	-	Danger Games	Pinkees	Creole	2		F L
20	-	Mad World	Tears For Fears	Mercury	7		F

◆ Survivor become the first US rock group to top the British charts in six years with their American No. 1, 'Eye of The Tiger'. The Steve Miller Band had nearly accomplished this feat just weeks earlier with 'Abracadabra'.

◆ Big American hits from the first British invasion, 'Love Me Do' by The Beatles and 'House Of The Rising Sun' by The Animals returned to the UK chart. Debuting on that chart were Culture Club, Wham! and Tears for Fears – artists who would help lead the second UK invasion.

November 1982

This Mnth	Prev Mnth	Title	Artist	Label	Wks 20	(US Pos)	
1	-	I Don't Wanna Dance	Eddy Grant	Ice	7	(53)	
2	-	Heartbreaker	Dionne Warwick	Arista	6	(10)	
3	20	Mad World	Tears For Fears	Mercury	7		F
4	3	Do You Really Want To Hurt Me	Culture Club	Virgin	9	(2)	F
5	-	(Sexual) Healing	Marvin Gaye	CBS	6	(3)	
6	-	Theme From Harry's Game	Clannad	RCA	4		F
7	-	Maneater	Daryl Hall & John Oates	RCA	4	(1)	
8	-	Ooh La La La (Let's Go Dancing)	Kool & The Gang	De-Lite	4	(30)	
9	-	The Girl Is Mine	Michael Jackson & Paul McCartney	Epic	3	(2)	
10	5	Starmaker	Kids From 'Fame'	RCA	7		
11	-	Mirror Man	Human League	Virgin	8	(30)	
12	-	I Wanna Do It With You	Barry Manilow	Arista	5		
13	-	Young Guns (Go For It)	Wham!	Innervision	9		F
14	-	Living On The Ceiling	Blancmange	London	6		F
15	12	Annie I'm Not Your Daddy	Kid Creole & The Coconuts	Ze	5		L
16	9	Love Me Do	Beatles	Parlophone	5		
17	-	I'll Be Satisfied	Shakin' Stevens	Epic	4		
18	-	Caroline (Live At The N.E.C.)	Status Quo	Vertigo	3		
19	-	Rio	Duran Duran	EMI	5	(14)	
20	11	Lifeline	Spandau Ballet	Chrysalis	5		

December 1982

This Mnth	Prev Mnth	Title	Artist	Label	Wks 20	(US Pos)	
1	-	Save Your Love	Renee And Renato	Hollywood	10		F L
2	-	Beat Surrender	Jam	Polydor	6		L
3	-	Time (Clock Of The Heart)	Culture Club	Virgin	8	(2)	
4	11	Mirror Man	Human League	Virgin	8	(30)	
5	-	Truly	Lionel Richie	Motown	7	(1)	
6	13	Young Guns (Go For It)	Wham!	Innervision	9		F
7	-	Our House	Madness	Stiff	8	(7)	
8	14	Living On The Ceiling	Blancmange	London	6		F
9	-	Best Years Of Our Lives	Modern Romance	WEA	8		
10	-	The Shakin' Stevens E.P.	Shakin' Stevens	Epic	4		
11	1	I Don't Wanna Dance	Eddy Grant	Ice	7	(53)	
12	19	Rio	Duran Duran	EMI	5	(14)	
13	-	Peace On Earth/Little DrummerBoy	David Bowie & Bing Crosby	RCA	4		
14	-	Wishing (If I Had A Photograph Of You)	Flock Of Seagulls	Jive	4	(26)	F L
15	-	Hymn	Ultravox	Chrysalis	8		
16	-	The Other Side Of Love	Yazoo	Mute	4		
17	-	You Can't Hurry Love	Phil Collins	Virgin	10	(10)	
18	2	Heartbreaker	Dionne Warwick	Arista	6	(10)	
19	-	Friends	Shalamar	Solar	6		
20	-	A Winter's Tale	David Essex	Mercury	6		

◆ Shortly after Musical Youth (featuring 11-year-old Kelvin Grant) became the youngest group to top the chart, David Bowie & the late Bing Crosby became the oldest duo to reach the Top 5.

◆ The 1980s' most influential British pop TV show, *The Tube,* was launched.

1983

This Mnth	Prev Mnth	Title	Artist	Label	Wks	(US 20 Pos)	
1	17	You Can't Hurry Love	Phil Collins	Virgin	10	(10)	
2	20	A Winter's Tale	David Essex	Mercury	6		
3	1	Save Your Love	Renee And Renato	Hollywood	10		F L
4	-	Orville's Song	Keith Harris & Orville	BBC	5		F L
5	-	Down Under	Men At Work	Epic	7	(1)	F L
6	9	Best Years Of Our Lives	Modern Romance	WEA	8		
7	7	Our House	Madness	Stiff	8	(7)	
8	-	The Story Of The Blues	Wah!	Eternal	6		F
9	3	Time (Clock Of The Heart)	Culture Club	Virgin	8	(2)	
10	-	Buffalo Gals	Malcolm McLaren & The World's Famous Supreme Team	Charisma	7		F
11	15	Hymn	Ultravox	Chrysalis	8		
12	-	Electric Avenue	Eddy Grant	Ice	5	(2)	
13	-	Heartache Avenue	Maisonettes	Ready Steady Go!	4		F L
14	10	The Shakin' Stevens E.P.	Shakin' Stevens	Epic	4		
15	-	All The Love In The World	Dionne Warwick	Arista	5		
16	13	Peace On Earth/Little Drummer Boy	David Bowie & Bing Crosby	RCA	4		
17	-	Steppin' Out	Joe Jackson	A&M	5	(6)	L
18	-	Cacharpaya (Andes Pumpsa Daesi)	Incantation	Beggars Banquet	4		F L
19	-	European Female	Stranglers	Epic	3		
20	-	If You Can't Stand The Heat	Bucks Fizz	RCA	6		

This Mnth	Prev Mnth	Title	Artist	Label	Wks	(US 20 Pos)	
1	-	Too Shy	Kajagoogoo	EMI	8	(5)	F
2	5	Down Under	Men At Work	Epic	7	(1)	F L
3	-	Sign Of The Times	Belle Stars	Stiff	7	(75)	L
4	-	Change	Tears For Fears	Mercury	6	(73)	
5	-	Up Where We Belong	Joe Cocker & Jennifer Warnes	Island	6	(1)	
6	12	Electric Avenue	Eddy Grant	Ice	5	(2)	
7	-	Wham Rap	Wham!	Innervision	5		
8	-	Gloria	Laura Branigan	Atlantic	6	(2)	F
9	-	Billie Jean	Michael Jackson	Epic	10	(1)	
10	-	Oh Diane	Fleetwood Mac	Warner	5		
11	1	You Can't Hurry Love	Phil Collins	Virgin	10	(10)	
12	-	Africa	Toto	CBS	6	(1)	
13	-	The Cutter	Echo & The Bunnymen	Korova	4		
14	8	The Story Of The Blues	Wah!	Eternal	6		F
15	-	Last Night A D.J. Saved My Life	Indeep	Sound Of New York	4		F L
16	-	New Year's Day	U2	Island	3	(53)	F
17	-	Never Gonna Give You Up	Musical Youth	MCA	5		L
18	-	Christian	China Crisis	Virgin	3		F
19	17	Steppin' Out	Joe Jackson	A&M	5	(6)	L
20	-	The Tunnel Of Love	Fun Boy Three	Chrysalis	5		

◆ Noteworthy newcomers on the UK chart included future transatlantic stars U2 (whose album War entered at No. 1), The Eurythmics and the Thompson Twins.

◆ Shortly after disbanding, The Jam had a record 15 singles in the UK Top 100, and lead singer Paul Weller signed a £250,000 deal for his new act Style Council.

March 1983

This Mnth	Prev Mnth	Title	Artist	Label	Wks	(US 20 Pos)	
1	-	Total Eclipse Of The Heart	Bonnie Tyler	CBS	8	(1)	
2	-	Sweet Dreams (Are Made Of This)	Eurythmics	RCA	7	(1)	F
3	9	Billie Jean	Michael Jackson	Epic	10	(1)	
4	-	Rock The Boat	Forrest	CBS	6		F
5	12	Africa	Toto	CBS	6	(1)	
6	-	Na Na Hey Hey Kiss Him Goodbye	Bananarama	London	5		
7	1	Too Shy	Kajagoogoo	EMI	8	(5)	F
8	-	Love On Your Side	Thompson Twins	Arista	5	(45)	F
9	-	Speak Like A Child	Style Council	Polydor	5		F
10	-	Tomorrow's (Just Another Day)/ Madness (Is All In The Mind)	Madness	Stiff	4		
11	17	Never Gonna Give You Up	Musical Youth	MCA	5		L
12	-	High Life	Modern Romance	WEA	3		
13	-	She Means Nothing To Me	Phil Everly & Cliff Richard	Capitol	4		F
14	-	Baby, Come To Me	Patti Austin & James Ingram	Qwest	5	(1)	F L
15	-	Communication	Spandau Ballet	Reformation	4	(59)	
16	-	Rip It Up	Orange Juice	Polydor	5		F L
17	20	The Tunnel Of Love	Fun Boy Three	Chrysalis	5		
18	-	Is There Something I Should Know	Duran Duran	EMI	5	(4)	
19	4	Change	Tears For Fears	Mercury	6	(73)	
20	-	Let's Dance	David Bowie	EMI America	8	(1)	

April 1983

This Mnth	Prev Mnth	Title	Artist	Label	Wks	(US 20 Pos)	
1	20	Let's Dance	David Bowie	EMI America	8	(1)	
2	18	Is There Something I Should Know	Duran Duran	EMI	5	(4)	
3	-	Church Of The Poison Mind	Culture Club	Virgin	6	(10)	
4	-	Boxer Beat	Joboxers	RCA	5		F
5	-	Breakaway	Tracey Ullman	Stiff	6	(70)	F
6	-	Beat It	Michael Jackson	Epic	6	(1)	
7	-	Words	F.R. David	Carrere	7	(62)	F L
8	-	Ooh To Be Ah	Kajagoogoo	EMI	5		
9	9	Speak Like A Child	Style Council	Polydor	5		F
10	2	Sweet Dreams (Are Made Of This)	Eurythmics	RCA	7	(1)	F
11	1	Total Eclipse Of The Heart	Bonnie Tyler	CBS	8	(1)	
12	-	Blue Monday	New Order	Factory	8		F
13	-	Fields Of Fire (400 Miles)	Big Country	Mercury	4	(52)	F
14	-	True	Spandau Ballet	Reformation	8	(4)	
15	-	Snot Rap	Kenny Everett	RCA	3		F L
16	-	Love Is A Stranger	Eurythmics	RCA	4	(23)	
17	-	Don't Talk To Me About Love	Altered Images	Epic	4		L
18	-	The House That Jack Built	Tracie	Respond	3		F L
19	16	Rip It Up	Orange Juice	Polydor	5		F L
20	-	Whistle Down The Wind	Nick Heyward	Arista	4		F

◆ CDs (which stored sounds digitally, thus eliminating most distortion) went on sale for the first time.

◆ Billy Fury, one of Britain's first home grown rock stars, died from heart problems, aged 41.

◆ Police scored the last of their five UK No. 1 singles and albums with 'Every Breath You Take' and **Synchronicity**. Both records also topped the US chart, with the latter holding sway for 17 weeks.

1983

This Mnth	Prev Mnth	Title	Artist	Label	Wks	(US 20 Pos)	
1	14	**True**	Spandau Ballet	Reformation	8	(4)	
2	-	**Temptation**	Heaven 17	Virgin	7		F
3	-	**Dancing Tight**	Galaxy Featuring Phil Fearon	Ensign	6		F
4	-	**(Keep Feeling) Fascination**	Human League	Virgin	6	(8)	
5	-	**Candy Girl**	New Edition	London	6	(46)	F
6	7	**Words**	F.R. David	Carrere	7	(62)	F L
7	-	**Pale Shelter**	Tears For Fears	Mercury	4		
8	-	**Can't Get Used To Losing You**	Beat	Go Feet	5		L
9	-	**Our Lips Are Sealed**	Fun Boy Three	Chrysalis	5		L
10	-	**We Are Detective**	Thompson Twins	Arista	4		
11	6	**Beat It**	Michael Jackson	Epic	6	(1)	
12	-	**Blind Vision**	Blancmange	London	4		
13	-	**Bad Boys**	Wham!	Innervision	8	(60)	
14	1	**Let's Dance**	David Bowie	EMI America	8	(1)	
15	-	**What Kinda Boy You Looking For (Girl)**	Hot Chocolate	RAK	4		
16	-	**True Love Ways**	Cliff Richard	EMI	4		
17	-	**Friday Night (Live Version)**	Kids From 'Fame'	RCA	4		L
18	3	**Church Of The Poison Mind**	Culture Club	Virgin	6	(10)	
19	-	**Every Breath You Take**	Police	A&M	8	(1)	
20	-	**Nobody's Diary**	Yazoo	Mute	7		

1	19	**Every Breath You Take**	Police	A&M	8	(1)	
2	13	**Bad Boys**	Wham!	Innervision	8	(60)	
3	20	**Nobody's Diary**	Yazoo	Mute	7		
4	-	**Buffalo Soldier**	Bob Marley & The Wailers	Island	6		
5	-	**China Girl**	David Bowie	EMI America	5	(10)	
6	-	**Love Town**	Booker Newberry III	Polydor	5		F L
7	-	**Flashdance....What A Feeling**	Irene Cara	Casablanca	9	(1)	L
8	5	**Candy Girl**	New Edition	London	6	(46)	F
9	-	**Just Got Lucky**	Joboxers	RCA	4	(36)	L
10	-	**Baby Jane**	Rod Stewart	Warner	9	(14)	
11	-	**Lady Love Me (One More Time)**	George Benson	Warner	5	(30)	
12	-	**Waiting For A Train**	Flash And The Pan	Ensign	5		F L
13	-	**I Guess That's Why They Call It The Blues**	Elton John	Rocket	6	(4)	
14	8	**Can't Get Used To Losing You**	Beat	Go Feet	5		L
15	-	**Wanna Be Startin' Something**	Michael Jackson	Epic	3	(5)	
16	2	**Temptation**	Heaven 17	Virgin	7		F
17	-	**Money Go Round (Pt.1)**	Style Council	Polydor	3		
18	-	**Hang On Now**	Kajagoogoo	EMI	3	(78)	
19	1	**True**	Spandau Ballet	Reformation	8	(4)	
20	-	**Dark Is The Night**	Shakatak	Polydor	2		

◆ David Bowie signed a $10 million deal with EMI, and the first release 'Let's Dance' (co-produced with Nile Rodgers) became his biggest transatlantic hit. He also launched his *Serious Moonlight* tour, which would be seen by over 2.5 million people.

◆ Blue Monday', the 12-inch only release from New Order, was released. It became the UK's biggest selling single on that particular format and spent nearly a year on the chart.

1983

This Mnth	Prev Mnth	Title	Artist	Label	Wks	(US 20 Pos)	
1	10	Baby Jane	Rod Stewart	Warner	9	(14)	
2	-	Wherever I Lay My Hat (That's My Home)	Paul Young	CBS	9	(70)	F
3	-	I.O.U.	Freeez	Beggars Banquet	9		L
4	-	Moonlight Shadow	Mike Oldfield	Virgin	9		
5	7	Flashdance....What A Feeling	Irene Cara	Casablanca	9	(1)	L
6	-	Come Live With Me	Heaven 17	Virgin	7		
7	-	War Baby	Tom Robinson	Panic	5		L
8	-	Who's That Girl	Eurythmics	RCA	6	(21)	
9	-	Double Dutch	Malcolm McLaren	Charisma	9		
10	-	It's Over	Funk Masters	Master Funk	4		F L
11	-	Dead Giveaway	Shalamar	Solar	5	(22)	
12	13	I Guess That's Why They Call It The Blues	Elton John	Rocket	6	(4)	
13	1	Every Breath You Take	Police	A&M	8	(1)	
14	-	Rock 'n' Roll Is King	Electric Light Orchestra	Jet	4	(19)	L
15	-	Take That Situation	Nick Heyward	Arista	3		
16	-	Cruel Summer	Bananarama	London	5	(9)	
17	-	Wrapped Around Your Finger	Police	A&M	4	(8)	
18	-	The Trooper	Iron Maiden	EMI	3		
19	5	China Girl	David Bowie	EMI America	5	(10)	
20	-	When We Were Young	Bucks Fizz	RCA	3		

1	-	Give It Up	KC & The Sunshine Band	Epic	9	(18)	L
2	-	Club Tropicana	Wham!	Innervision	7		
3	9	Double Dutch	Malcolm McLaren	Charisma	9		
4	3	I.O.U.	Freeez	Beggars Banquet	9		L
5	2	Wherever I Lay My Hat (That's My Home)	Paul Young	CBS	9	(70)	F
6	-	Long Hot Summer	Style Council	Polydor	5		
7	-	Gold	Spandau Ballet	Reformation	6	(29)	
8	-	I'm Still Standing	Elton John	Rocket	6	(12)	
9	-	Everything Counts	Depeche Mode	Mute	5		
10	-	The Crown	Gary Byrd & The GB Experience	Motown	5		F L
11	8	Who's That Girl	Eurythmics	RCA	6	(21)	
12	-	Rockit	Herbie Hancock	CBS	5	(71)	L
13	-	Big Log	Robert Plant	WEA	4	(20)	F L
14	16	Cruel Summer	Bananarama	London	5	(9)	
15	-	Wings Of A Dove	Madness	Stiff	6		
16	17	Wrapped Around Your Finger	Police	A&M	4	(8)	
17	-	It's Late	Shakin' Stevens	Epic	3		
18	4	Moonlight Shadow	Mike Oldfield	Virgin	9		
19	-	Watching You Watching Me	David Grant	Chrysalis	5		
20	6	Come Live With Me	Heaven 17	Virgin	7		

◆ David Bowie had ten albums in the British Top 100 (a feat bettered only by Elvis Presley), including the transatlantic Top 5 hit, **Let's Dance**.

◆ Stars of the Castle Donnington Rock Festival included ZZ Top, Meat Loaf, Twisted Sister and Whitesnake. Other successful live shows included Barry Manilow at Blenheim Palace, and The Prince's Trust Gala which included Duran Duran and Dire Straits.

1983

This Mnth	Prev Mnth	Title	Artist	Label	Wks	(US 20 Pos)	
1	-	Red Red Wine	UB40	Dep International	10	(34)	
2	15	Wings Of A Dove	Madness	Stiff	6		
3	-	Tonight I Celebrate My Love	Peabo Bryson & Roberta Flack	Capitol	7	(16)	F
4	-	What Am I Gonna Do	Rod Stewart	Warner	5	(35)	
5	-	Mama	Genesis	Virgin/Charisma	7	(73)	
6	-	Walking In The Rain	Modern Romance	WEA	6		L
7	1	Give It Up	KC & The Sunshine Band	Epic	9	(18)	L
8	-	The Sun Goes Down (Living It Up)	Level 42	Polydor	5		F
9	-	Karma Chameleon	Culture Club	Virgin	11	(1)	G
10	7	Gold	Spandau Ballet	Reformation	6	(29)	
11	8	I'm Still Standing	Elton John	Rocket	6	(12)	
12	-	Come Back And Stay	Paul Young	CBS	5	(22)	
13	-	Dolce Vita	Ryan Paris	Carrere	5		F L
14	2	Club Tropicana	Wham!	Innervision	7		
15	-	Chance	Big Country	Mercury	5		
16	6	Long Hot Summer	Style Council	Polydor	5		
17	-	Ol' Rag Blues	Status Quo	Vertigo	4		
18	19	Watching You Watching Me	David Grant	Chrysalis	5		
19	-	Confusion	New Order	Factory	3		
20	-	Modern Love	David Bowie	EMI America	6	(14)	

This Mnth	Prev Mnth	Title	Artist	Label	Wks	(US 20 Pos)	
1	9	Karma Chameleon	Culture Club	Virgin	11	(1)	G
2	20	Modern Love	David Bowie	EMI America	6	(14)	
3	-	They Don't Know	Tracey Ullman	Stiff	6	(8)	
4	-	Dear Prudence	Siouxsie & The Banshees	Wonderland	6		
5	-	New Song	Howard Jones	WEA	6	(27)	F
6	1	Red Red Wine	UB40	Dep International	10	(34)	
7	-	This Is Not A Love Song	Public Image Ltd.	Virgin	5		
8	-	Blue Monday	New Order	Factory	7		
9	-	In Your Eyes	George Benson	Warner	6		
10	-	All Night Long (All Night)	Lionel Richie	Motown	8	(1)	
11	-	(Hey You) The Rocksteady Crew	Rocksteady Crew	Virgin	6		F L
12	12	Come Back And Stay	Paul Young	CBS	5	(22)	
13	3	Tonight I Celebrate My Love	Peabo Bryson & Roberta Flack	Capitol	7	(16)	F
14	-	Superman (Gioca Jouer)	Black Lace	Flair	5		F
15	-	Tahiti (From Mutiny On The Bounty)	David Essex	Mercury	5		L
16	5	Mama	Genesis	Virgin	7	(73)	
17	-	Big Apple	Kajagoogoo	EMI	4		L
18	-	The Safety Dance	Men Without Hats	Statik	6	(3)	F L
19	13	Dolce Vita	Ryan Paris	Carrere	5		F L
20	15	Chance	Big Country	Mercury	5		

◆ As 'Wings Of A Dove' gave Madness their 16th successive Top 20 hit, 'Our House' became their only US Top 20 entry.

◆ Culture Club's only transatlantic chart topper, 'Karma Chameleon', was Britain's top single in 1983, selling nearly 1.5 million.

November 1983

This Mnth	Prev Mnth	Title	Artist	Label	Wks	(US 20 Pos)	
1	-	**Uptown Girl**	Billy Joel	CBS	12	(3)	
2	10	**All Night Long (All Night)**	Lionel Richie	Motown	8	(1)	
3	-	**Say Say Say**	Paul McCartney & Michael Jackson	Parlophone	9	(1)	
4	-	**Cry Just A Little Bit**	Shakin' Stevens	Epic	7	(67)	
5	-	**Puss 'n Boots**	Adam Ant	CBS	4		
6	-	**The Love Cats**	Cure	Fiction	5		
7	1	**Karma Chameleon**	Culture Club	Virgin	11	(1)	G
8	18	**The Safety Dance**	Men Without Hats	Statik	6	(3)	F L
9	-	**The Sun And The Rain**	Madness	Stiff	4	(72)	
10	-	**Union Of The Snake**	Duran Duran	EMI	4	(3)	
11	-	**Never Never**	Assembly	Mute	4		F L
12	-	**Please Don't Make Me Cry**	UB40	Dep International	5		
13	11	**(Hey You) The Rocksteady Crew**	Rocksteady Crew	Virgin	6		F L
14	3	**They Don't Know**	Tracey Ullman	Stiff	6	(8)	
15	5	**New Song**	Howard Jones	WEA	6	(27)	F
16	-	**Love Of The Common People**	Paul Young	CBS	10	(45)	
17	-	**Solid Bond In Your Heart**	Style Council	Polydor	3		
18	-	**Undercover Of The Night**	Rolling Stones	Rolling Stone	3	(9)	
19	-	**Calling Your Name**	Marilyn	Mercury	4		F L
20	-	**Unconditional Love**	Donna Summer	Mercury	2	(43)	

December 1983

This Mnth	Prev Mnth	Title	Artist	Label	Wks	(US 20 Pos)	
1	-	**Only You**	Flying Pickets	10	7		F
2	16	**Love Of The Common People**	Paul Young	CBS	10	(45)	
3	-	**Hold Me Now**	Thompson Twins	Arista	9	(3)	
4	-	**My Oh My**	Slade	RCA	7	(37)	
5	-	**Let's Stay Together**	Tina Turner	Capitol	8	(26)	F
6	1	**Uptown Girl**	Billy Joel	CBS	12	(3)	
7	-	**Victims**	Culture Club	Virgin	6		
8	-	**Please Don't Fall In Love**	Cliff Richard	EMI	6		
9	-	**Move Over Darling**	Tracey Ullman	Stiff	5		
10	-	**Islands In The Stream**	Kenny Rogers & Dolly Parton	RCA	7	(1)	L
11	-	**Tell Her About It**	Billy Joel	CBS	7	(1)	
12	-	**Thriller**	Michael Jackson	Epic	9	(4)	
13	19	**Calling Your Name**	Marilyn	Mercury	4		F L
14	-	**Marguerita Time**	Status Quo	Vertigo	6		
15	3	**Say Say Say**	Paul McCartney & Michael Jackson	Parlophone	9	(1)	
16	-	**What Is Love**	Howard Jones	WEA	8	(33)	
17	11	**Never Never**	Assembly	Mute	4		F L
18	4	**Cry Just A Little Bit**	Shakin' Stevens	Epic	7	(67)	
19	-	**Right By Your Side**	Eurythmics	RCA	4	(29)	
20	-	**That's All!**	Genesis	Charisma/virgin	4	(6)	

◆ In 1983, Michael Jackson not only had the biggest album, **Thriller**, he also earned the first platinum music video for *The Making Of Thriller*, and amassed seven US Top 10 singles –. the best yearly performance since The Beatles in 1964!

◆ Britain's most successful chart year in the US since 1964 ended with legendary hitmakers The Who splitting and chart regulars ELO starting a long sabbatical.

1984

This Mnth	Prev Mnth	Title	Artist	Label	Wks	(US 20 Pos)	
1	-	**Pipes Of Peace**	Paul McCartney	Parlophone	6		
2	16	**What Is Love**	Howard Jones	WEA	8	(33)	
3	-	**Relax**	Frankie Goes To Hollywood	ZTT	25	(10)	F G
4	14	**Marguerita Time**	Status Quo	Vertigo	6		
5	11	**Tell Her About It**	Billy Joel	CBS	7	(1)	
6	2	**Love Of The Common People**	Paul Young	CBS	10	(45)	
7	-	**A Rockin' Good Way**	Shaky & Bonnie	CBS	5		
8	-	**That's Living (Alright)**	Joe Fagin	Towerbell	7		F L
9	10	**Islands In The Stream**	Kenny Rogers & Dolly Parton	RCA	7	(1)	L
10	3	**Hold Me Now**	Thompson Twins	Arista	9	(3)	
11	1	**Only You**	Flying Pickets	10	7		F
12	7	**Victims**	Culture Club	Virgin	6		
13	-	**Bird Of Paradise**	Snowy White	Towerbell	4		F L
14	4	**My Oh My**	Slade	RCA	7	(37)	
15	-	**Nobody Told Me**	John Lennon	Ono/Polydor	3	(5)	L
16	12	**Thriller**	Michael Jackson	Epic	9	(4)	
17	-	**Wonderland**	Big Country	Mercury	4	(86)	
18	-	**Running With The Night**	Lionel Richie	Motown	2	(7)	
19	-	**Wishful Thinking**	China Crisis	Virgin	4		
20	5	**Let's Stay Together**	Tina Turner	Capitol	8	(26)	F

1	3	**Relax**	Frankie Goes To Hollywood	ZTT	25	(10)	F G
2	-	**Radio Ga Ga**	Queen	EMI	6	(16)	
3	-	**Girls Just Want To Have Fun**	Cyndi Lauper	Portrait	7	(2)	F
4	-	**Break My Stride**	Matthew Wilder	Epic	7	(5)	F L
5	-	**Doctor Doctor**	Thompson Twins	Arista	7	(11)	
6	8	**That's Living (Alright)**	Joe Fagin	Towerbell	7		F L
7	-	**Holiday**	Madonna	Sire	5	(16)	F
8	-	**New Moon On Monday**	Duran Duran	EMI	4	(10)	
9	-	**(Feels Like) Heaven**	Fiction Factory	CBS	4		F L
10	-	**99 Red Balloons**	Nena	Epic	8	(2)	F L
11	-	**My Ever Changing Moods**	Style Council	Polydor	4		
12	-	**Here Comes The Rain Again**	Eurythmics	RCA	5	(4)	
13	-	**The Killing Moon**	Echo & The Bunnymen	Korova	3		
14	-	**What Difference Does It Make**	Smiths	Rough Trade	4		F
15	-	**Somebody's Watching Me**	Rockwell	Motown	6	(2)	F L
16	-	**Love Theme From 'The Thorn Birds'**	Juan Martin	WEA	2		F L
17	-	**Wouldn't It Be Good**	Nik Kershaw	MCA	7	(46)	F
18	17	**Wonderland**	Big Country	Mercury	4	(86)	
19	-	**Michael Caine**	Madness	Stiff	3		
20	1	**Pipes Of Peace**	Paul McCartney	Parlophone	6		

◆ As 'Nobody Told Me' gave John Lennon his last transatlantic Top 20 hit, Paul McCartney scored his only British No. 1 of the 1980s, 'Pipes Of Peace', which, oddly, failed to chart Stateside.

◆ Despite being banned by the BBC, 'Relax' by Frankie Goes To Hollywood became one of Britain's biggest ever sellers.

March 1984

This Mnth	Prev Mnth	Title	Artist	Label	Wks 20	(US Pos)	
1	10	**99 Red Balloons**	Nena	Epic	8	(2)	F L
2	-	**Joanna/Tonight**	Kool & The Gang	De-Lite	7	(2)	
3	-	**Street Dance**	Break Machine	Record Shack	8		F
4	17	**Wouldn't It Be Good**	Nik Kershaw	MCA	7	(46)	F
5	1	**Relax**	Frankie Goes To Hollywood	ZTT	25	(10)	F G
6	-	**Hello**	Lionel Richie	Motown	10	(1)	
7	-	**An Innocent Man**	Billy Joel	CBS	7	(10)	
8	15	**Somebody's Watching Me**	Rockwell	Motown	6	(2)	F L
9	-	**It's Raining Men**	Weather Girls	CBS	6	(46)	F L
10	-	**Jump**	Van Halen	Warner	5	(1)	F
11	-	**What Do I Do**	Phil Fearon & Galaxy	Ensign	5		
12	-	**The Music Of Torvill & Dean EP**	Richard Hartley/ Michael Reed Orchestra	Safari	5		F L
13	-	**Run Runaway**	Slade	RCA	5	(20)	
14	-	**Robert De Niro's Waiting**	Bananarama	London	5	(95)	
15	5	**Doctor Doctor**	Thompson Twins	Arista	7	(11)	
16	-	**Your Love Is King**	Sade	Epic	5	(54)	F
17	-	**Hide And Seek**	Howard Jones	WEA	5		
18	-	**It's A Miracle**	Culture Club	Virgin	5	(13)	
19	2	**Radio Ga Ga**	Queen	EMI	6	(16)	
20	11	**My Ever Changing Moods**	Style Council	Polydor	4		

April 1984

This Mnth	Prev Mnth	Title	Artist	Label	Wks 20	(US Pos)	
1	6	**Hello**	Lionel Richie	Motown	10	(1)	
2	-	**You Take Me Up**	Thompson Twins	Arista	6	(44)	
3	-	**A Love Worth Waiting For**	Shakin' Stevens	Epic	6		
4	-	**People Are People**	Depeche Mode	Mute	6	(13)	
5	-	**Glad It's All Over/Damned On 45**	Captain Sensible	A&M	5		L
6	-	**Against All Odds (Take A Look At Me Now)**	Phil Collins	Virgin	8	(1)	
7	14	**Robert De Niro's Waiting**	Bananarama	London	5	(95)	
8	-	**I Want To Break Free**	Queen	EMI	9	(45)	
9	-	**Nelson Mandela**	Special AKA	2 Tone	4		L
10	18	**It's A Miracle**	Culture Club	Virgin	5	(13)	
11	-	**Ain't Nobody**	Rufus & Chaka Khan	Warner	6	(22)	F
12	9	**It's Raining Men**	Weather Girls	CBS	6	(46)	F L
13	-	**(When You Say You Love Somebody) In The Heart**	Kool & The Gang	De-Lite	4		
14	11	**What Do I Do**	Phil Fearon & Galaxy	Ensign	5		
15	-	**Wood Beez (Pray Like Aretha Franklin)**	Scritti Politti	Virgin	3	(91)	F
16	-	**P.Y.T. (Pretty Young Thing)**	Michael Jackson	Epic	3	(10)	
17	16	**Your Love Is King**	Sade	Epic	5	(54)	F
18	-	**The Reflex**	Duran Duran	EMI	8	(1)	
19	-	**Don't Tell Me**	Blancmange	London	6		L
20	-	**Cherry Oh Baby**	UB40	Dep International	3		

◆ The *NME* Poll showed New Order as Best Group, their 'Blue Monday' as Top Record, and fellow Mancunians The Smiths as Best New Group. In January, The Smiths' first three releases held the top three rungs on the Indie chart.

◆ The Beatles Exhibition Centre opened in Liverpool, Yoko Ono presented a cheque for £250,000 to Liverpool's Strawberry Fields old people's home (immortalized in The Beatles song 'Strawberry Fields Forever').

1984

This Mnth	Prev Mnth	Title	Artist	Label	Wks	(US 20 Pos)
1	18	**The Reflex**	Duran Duran	EMI	8	(1)
2	-	**Automatic**	Pointer Sisters	Planet	7	(5)
3	6	**Against All Odds (Take A Look At...)**	Phil Collins	Virgin	8	(1)
4	8	**I Want To Break Free**	Queen	EMI	9	(45)
5	-	**One Love/People Get Ready**	Bob Marley & The Wailers	Island	5	L
6	-	**Locomotion**	O.M.D.	Virgin	7	
7	-	**When You're Young And In Love**	Flying Pickets	10	5	L
8	19	**Don't Tell Me**	Blancmange	London	6	L
9	-	**Footloose**	Kenny Loggins	CBS	4	(1) F L
10	-	**Let's Hear It For The Boy**	Deniece Williams	CBS	7	(1) L
11	1	**Hello**	Lionel Richie	Motown	10	(1)
12	-	**Dancing Girls**	Nik Kershaw	MCA	3	
13	-	**The Lebanon**	Human League	Virgin	3	(64)
14	-	**I'm Falling**	Bluebells	London	4	F
15	-	**Love Games**	Belle & The Devotions	CBS	2	F L
16	-	**Wake Me Up Before You Go Go**	Wham!	Epic	8	(1)
17	-	**Break Dance Party**	Break Machine	Record Shack	4	L
18	13	**(When You Say You...) In The Heart**	Kool & The Gang	De-Lite	4	
19	-	**Somebody Else's Guy**	Jocelyn Brown	4th & Broadway	3	(75) F
20	2	**You Take Me Up**	Thompson Twins	Arista	6	(44)

This Mnth	Prev Mnth	Title	Artist	Label	Wks	(US 20 Pos)
1	16	**Wake Me Up Before You Go Go**	Wham!	Epic	8	(1)
2	-	**Two Tribes**	Frankie Goes To Hollywood	ZTT	14	(43) G
3	-	**Smalltown Boy**	Bronski Beat	Forbidden Fruit	7	(48) F
4	-	**High Energy**	Evelyn Thomas	Record Shack	5	(85) F L
5	10	**Let's Hear It For The Boy**	Deniece Williams	CBS	7	(1) L
6	-	**Dancing With Tears In My Eyes**	Ultravox	Chrysalis	5	
7	-	**Only When You Leave**	Spandau Ballet	Reformation	4	(34)
8	-	**Relax**	Frankie Goes To Hollywood	ZTT	25	(10) F G
9	-	**Sad Songs (Say So Much)**	Elton John	Rocket	5	(5)
10	-	**Pearl In The Shell**	Howard Jones	WEA	4	
11	-	**Searchin' (I Gotta Find A Man)**	Hazell Dean	Proto	5	F
12	-	**Groovin' (You're The Best Thing)/ Big Boss Groove)**	Style Council	Polydor	5	
13	-	**I Won't Let The Sun Go Down On Me**	Nik Kershaw	MCA	8	
14	1	**The Reflex**	Duran Duran	EMI	8	(1)
15	-	**Farewell My Summer Love**	Michael Jackson	Motown	6	(38)
16	-	**Heaven Knows I'm Miserable Now**	Smiths	Rough Trade	5	
17	-	**I Feel Like Buddy Holly**	Alvin Stardust	Stiff	5	
18	-	**Thinking Of You**	Sister Sledge	Cotillion/Atlantic	6	
19	2	**Automatic**	Pointer Sisters	Planet	7	(5)
20	4	**I Want To Break Free**	Queen	EMI	9	(45)

◆ The Beatles, who had recently had streets named after them in Liverpool, were made Freemen of that city – its highest honour.

◆ The late Bob Marley's **Legend** entered the LP chart at No. 1 and held that spot for three months.

◆ Frankie Goes To Hollywood's second single, 'Two Tribes', entered at No. 1 and spent nine weeks at the summit. Soon afterwards 'Relax' moved back up to No. 2. Both sold over a million.

July 1984

This Mnth	Prev Mnth	Title	Artist	Label	Wks	(US 20 Pos)	
1	2	**Two Tribes**	Frankie Goes To Hollywood	ZTT	14	(43)	G
2	-	**Relax**	Frankie Goes To Hollywood	ZTT	25	(10)	F G
3	-	**Time After Time**	Cyndi Lauper	Portrait	7	(1)	
4	13	**I Won't Let The Sun Go Down On Me**	Nik Kershaw	MCA	8		
5	-	**Hole In My Shoe**	neil	WEA	6		F L
6	-	**Jump (For My Love)**	Pointer Sisters	Planet	5	(3)	
7	-	**White Lines (Don't Don't Do It)**	Grandmaster Flash, Melle Mel & The Furious Five	Sugar Hill	12		L
8	-	**When Doves Cry**	Prince	Warner	8	(1)	F
9	-	**Breakin'...There's No Stopping Us**	Ollie & Jerry	Polydor	5	(9)	F L
10	-	**What's Love Got To Do With It**	Tina Turner	Capitol	10	(1)	
11	-	**Love Resurrection**	Alison Moyet	CBS	5	(82)	F
12	-	**Young At Heart**	Bluebells	London	6		
13	-	**Sister Of Mercy**	Thompson Twins	Arista	3		
14	3	**Smalltown Boy**	Bronski Beat	Forbidden	7	(48)	F
15	-	**Talking Loud And Clear**	Orchestral Manoeuvres In The Dark	Virgin	4		
16	15	**Farewell My Summer Love**	Michael Jackson	Motown	6	(38)	
17	-	**Stuck On You**	Lionel Richie	Motown	4	(3)	
18	1	**Wake Me Up Before You Go Go**	Wham!	Epic	8	(1)	
19	-	**Everybody's Laughing**	Phil Fearon & Galaxy	Ensign	5		
20	18	**Thinking Of You**	Sister Sledge	Cotillion/Atlantic	6		

August 1984

This Mnth	Prev Mnth	Title	Artist	Label	Wks	(US 20 Pos)	
1	1	**Two Tribes**	Frankie Goes To Hollywood	ZTT	14	(43)	G
2	-	**Careless Whisper**	George Michael	Epic	12	(1)	F G
3	10	**What's Love Got To Do With It**	Tina Turner	Capitol	10	(1)	
4	-	**Agadoo**	Black Lace	Flair	10		
5	-	**Relax**	Frankie Goes To Hollywood	ZTT	25	(10)	F G
6	8	**When Doves Cry**	Prince	Warner	8	(1)	F
7	-	**Whatever I Do (Wherever I Go)**	Hazell Dean	Proto	7		
8	5	**Hole In My Shoe**	neil	WEA	6		F L
9	-	**It's A Hard Life**	Queen	EMI	4	(72)	
10	-	**Self Control**	Laura Branigan	Atlantic	7	(4)	L
11	7	**White Lines (Don't Don't Do It)**	Grandmaster Flash, Melle Mel & The Furious Five	Sugar Hill	12		L
12	-	**Like To Get To Know You Well**	Howard Jones	WEA	7	(49)	
13	19	**Everybody's Laughing**	Phil Fearon & Galaxy	Ensign	5		
14	-	**On The Wings Of Love**	Jeffrey Osborne	A&M	5	(29)	L
15	-	**Down On The Street**	Shakatak	Polydor	4		L
16	-	**Closest Thing To Heaven**	Kane Gang	Kitchenware	5		F L
17	-	**I Just Called To Say I Love You**	Stevie Wonder	Motown	13	(1)	G
18	3	**Time After Time**	Cyndi Lauper	Portrait	7	(1)	
19	-	**Stuck On You**	Trevor Walters	Sanity	4		F L
20	12	**Young At Heart**	Bluebells	London	6		

◆ Elton John, Kool & The Gang and Brits winner Paul Young (whose **No Parlez** album sold over a million) performed in front of 72,000 at Wembley Stadium.

◆ Stevie Wonder's 36th British hit 'I Just Called To Say I Love You' was not only his first solo No. 1, but also Motown's first UK million seller. It was the third British million seller in a row to head the chart (following 'Two Tribes' and 'Careless Whisper').

1984

This Mnth	Prev Mnth	Title	Artist	Label	Wks	(US 20 Pos)	
1	16	I Just Called To Say I Love You	Stevie Wonder	Motown	13	(1)	G
2	2	Careless Whisper	George Michael	Epic	12	(1)	F G
3	4	Agadoo	Black Lace	Flair	10		
4	-	Ghostbusters	Ray Parker Jr.	Arista	17	(1)	
5	-	Dr. Beat	Miami Sound Machine	Epic	7		F
6	11	Like To Get To Know You Well	Howard Jones	WEA	7	(49)	
7	-	Passengers	Elton John	Rocket	5		
8	-	Pride (In The Name Of Love)	U2	Island	7	(33)	
9	9	Self Control	Laura Branigan	Atlantic	7	(4)	L
10	-	Big In Japan	Alphaville	WEA International	5	(66)	F L
11	-	Lost In Music	Sister Sledge	Cotillion/Atlantic	6		
12	-	Master And Servant	Depeche Mode	Mute	4	(87)	
13	-	I'll Fly For You	Spandau Ballet	Reformation	4		
14	6	Whatever I Do (Wherever I Go)	Hazell Dean	Proto	7		
15	-	Madame Butterfly	Malcolm McLaren	Charisma	4		L
16	1	Two Tribes	Frankie Goes To Hollywood	ZTT	14	(43)	G
17	10	White Lines (Don't Don't Do It)	Grandmaster Flash, Melle Mel & The Furious Five	Sugar Hill	12		L
18	-	A Letter To You	Shakin' Stevens	Epic	4		
19	-	Blue Jean	David Bowie	EMI America	4	(8)	
20	18	Stuck On You	Trevor Walters	Sanity	4		F L

This Mnth	Prev Mnth	Title	Artist	Label	Wks	(US 20 Pos)	
1	1	I Just Called To Say I Love You	Stevie Wonder	Motown	13	(1)	G
2	-	The War Song	Culture Club	Virgin	5	(17)	
3	-	Freedom	Wham!	Epic	8	(3)	
4	4	Ghostbusters	Ray Parker Jr.	Arista	17	(1)	
5	-	No More Lonely Nights (Ballad)	Paul McCartney	Parlophone	6	(6)	
6	-	Drive	Cars	Elektra	6	(3)	
7	-	Together In Electric Dreams	Giorgio Moroder & Phil Oakey	Virgin	6		L
8	-	Why?	Bronski Beat	Forbidden Fruit	5		
9	8	Pride (In The Name Of Love)	U2	Island	7	(33)	
10	-	Shout To The Top	Style Council	Polydor	4		
11	-	Purple Rain	Prince & The Revolution	Warner	4	(2)	
12	11	Lost In Music	Sister Sledge	Cotillion/Atlantic	6		
13	-	Missing You	John Waite	EMI	6	(1)	F L
14	-	If It Happens Again	UB40	Dep International	4		
15	-	I'm Gonna Tear Your Playhouse Down	Paul Young	CBS	3	(13)	
16	-	All Cried Out	Alison Moyet	CBS	6		
17	-	Love Kills	Freddie Mercury	CBS	4	(69)	F
18	19	Blue Jean	David Bowie	Emi America	4	(8)	
19	-	I Feel For You	Chaka Khan	Warner	8	(3)	
20	2	Careless Whisper	George Michael	Epic	12	(1)	F G

◆ Soon after releasing a duet with Cliff Richard, 'Two To The Power', Michael Jackson's 18-year-old sister Janet eloped with El Debarge, from the group Debarge.

◆ Bob Geldof and Midge Ure organized an all-star group, Band Aid, whose 'Do They Know It's Christmas' not only raised a fortune for the starving in Ethiopia but also became Britain's biggest ever seller (over 3.5 million).

November 1984

This Mnth	Prev Mnth	Title	Artist	Label	Wks	(US 20 Pos)	
1	19	I Feel For You	Chaka Khan	Warner	8	(3)	
2	-	The Wild Boys	Duran Duran	Parlophone	6	(2)	
3	3	Freedom	Wham!	Epic	8	(3)	
4	-	The Wanderer	Status Quo	Vertigo	5		
5	-	Caribbean Queen (No More Love On The Run)	Billy Ocean	Jive	6	(1)	
6	16	All Cried Out	Alison Moyet	CBS	6		
7	-	I Should Have Known Better	Jim Diamond	A&M	8		F
8	-	Never Ending Story	Limahl	EMI	7	(17)	L
9	-	Too Late For Goodbyes	Julian Lennon	Charisma	5	(5)	F
10	5	No More Lonely Nights (Ballad)	Paul McCartney	Parlophone	6	(6)	
11	7	Together In Electric Dreams	Giorgio Moroder & Phil Oakey	Virgin	6		L
12	-	Gimme All Your Lovin'	ZZ Top	Warner	4	(37)	F
13	-	Love's Great Adventure	Ultravox	Chrysalis	5		
14	-	Hard Habit To Break	Chicago	Full Moon	4	(3)	
15	-	I'm So Excited	Pointer Sisters	Planet	4	(9)	
16	1	I Just Called To Say I Love You	Stevie Wonder	Motown	13	(1)	G
17	-	The Riddle	Nik Kershaw	MCA	9		
18	13	Missing You	John Waite	EMI	6	(1)	F L
19	-	Sexcrime (Nineteen Eighty Four)	Eurythmics	Virgin	7	(81)	
20	6	Drive	Cars	Elektra	6	(3)	

December 1984

This Mnth	Prev Mnth	Title	Artist	Label	Wks	(US 20 Pos)	
1	-	The Power Of Love	Frankie Goes To Hollywood	ZTT	8		
2	18	The Riddle	Nik Kershaw	MCA	9		
3	-	We All Stand Together	Paul McCartney	Parlophone	7		
4	-	Like A Virgin	Madonna	Sire	10	(1)	
5	-	Do They Know It's Christmas	Band Aid	Mercury	8	(13)	F P
6	-	Teardrops	Shakin' Stevens	Epic	6		
7	7	I Should Have Known Better	Jim Diamond	A&M	8		F
8	-	Last Christmas/Everything She Wants	Wham!	Epic	8	(1)	G
9	20	Sexcrime (Nineteen Eighty Four)	Eurythmics	Virgin	7	(81)	
10	-	I Won't Run Away	Alvin Stardust	Chrysalis	6		L
11	1	I Feel For You	Chaka Khan	Warner	8	(3)	
12	-	Fresh	Kool & The Gang	De-Lite	7	(9)	
13	-	Nellie The Elephant	Toy Dolls	Volume	6		F L
14	-	Do The Conga	Black Lace	Flair	6		L
15	-	One Night In Bangkok	Murray Head	RCA	7	(3)	F L
16	8	Never Ending Story	Limahl	EMI	7	(17)	L
17	-	Everything Must Change	Paul Young	CBS	7	(56)	
18	-	Another Rock And Roll Christmas	Gary Glitter	Arista	3		L
19	15	Hard Habit To Break	Chicago	Full Moon	4	(3)	
20	-	Shout	Tears For Fears	Mercury	9	(1)	

◆ 'The Power Of Love' gave the year's most successful UK act, Frankie Goes To Hollywood, their third consecutive No. 1 with their first three hits, equalling a record set by fellow Liverpudlians Gerry & The Pacemakers.

◆ U2's first Top 5 entry 'Pride (In The Name Of Love)' was dedicated to Martin Luther King.

1985

This Mnth	Prev Mnth	Title	Artist	Label	Wks	(US 20 Pos)	
1	5	**Do They Know It's Christmas**	Band Aid	Mercury	8	(13)	F P
2	8	**Last Christmas/Everything She Wants**	Wham!	Epic	8	(1)	G
3	-	**I Want To Know What Love Is**	Foreigner	Atlantic	9	(1)	L
4	4	**Like A Virgin**	Madonna	Sire	10	(1)	
5	4	**Ghostbusters**	Ray Parker Jr.	Arista	17	(1)	
6	20	**Shout**	Tears For Fears	Mercury	9	(1)	
7	3	**We All Stand Together**	Paul McCartney	Parlophone	7		
8	18	**Everything Must Change**	Paul Young	CBS	7	(56)	
9	13	**Nellie The Elephant**	Toy Dolls	Volume	6		F L
10	-	**I Know Him So Well**	Elaine Paige & Barbara Dickson	RCA	10		L
11	-	**Step Off (Pt. 1)**	Grandmaster Melle Mel & The Furious Five	Sugar Hill	4		F L
12	-	**1999/Little Red Corvette**	Prince & The Revolution	Warner	7	(12)	
13	-	**Since Yesterday**	Strawberry Switchblade	Korova	5		F L
14	1	**The Power Of Love**	Frankie Goes To Hollywood	ZTT	8		
15	-	**Police Officer**	Smiley Culture	Fashion	3		F L
16	2	**The Riddle**	Nik Kershaw	MCA	9		
17	12	**Fresh**	Kool & The Gang	De-Lite	7	(9)	
18	-	**Love & Pride**	King	CBS	8	(55)	F
19	-	**Atmosphere**	Russ Abbot	Spirit	7		F
20	-	**Friends**	Amii Stewart	RCA	4		

This Mnth	Prev Mnth	Title	Artist	Label	Wks	(US 20 Pos)	
1	9	**I Know Him So Well**	Elaine Paige & Barbara Dickson	RCA	10		L
2	17	**Love & Pride**	King	CBS	8	(55)	F
3	-	**Solid**	Ashford & Simpson	Capitol	8	(12)	F L
4	3	**I Want To Know What Love Is**	Foreigner	Atlantic	9	(1)	L
5	11	**1999/Little Red Corvette**	Prince & The Revolution	Warner	7	(12)	
6	-	**Dancing In The Dark**	Bruce Springsteen	CBS	9	(2)	F
7	18	**Atmosphere**	Russ Abbot	Spirit	7		F
8	-	**Close (To The Edit)**	Art Of Noise	ZTT	4		F
9	5	**Shout**	Tears For Fears	Mercury	9	(1)	
10	-	**A New England**	Kirsty MacColl	Stiff	5		
11	-	**Run To You**	Bryan Adams	A&M	6	(6)	F
12	-	**Things Can Only Get Better**	Howard Jones	WEA	6	(5)	
13	12	**Since Yesterday**	Strawberry Switchblade	Korova	5		F L
14	-	**Sussudio**	Phil Collins	Virgin	4	(1)	
15	-	**Loverboy**	Billy Ocean	Jive	5	(2)	
16	-	**Thinking Of You**	Colour Field	Chrysalis	4		F L
17	-	**You Spin Me Round (Like A Record)**	Dead Or Alive	Epic	8	(11)	F
18	-	**Nightshift**	Commodores	Motown	8	(3)	
19	4	**Like A Virgin**	Madonna	Sire	10	(1)	
20	-	**Yah Mo B There**	James Ingram & Michael McDonald	A&M	2	(19)	

◆ Bruce Springsteen's 12 million selling **Born In The USA** topped the transatlantic charts as 'Dancing In The Dark' gave him his first major British hit.
◆ Wham! were voted British Group of the Year at the Brits, and George Michael became the youngest person to win the Songwriter of the Year trophy at the Ivor Novello Awards, where the transatlantic chart topper 'Careless Whisper' was named Most Performed Song of the Year.

1985

This Mnth	Prev Mnth	Title	Artist	Label	Wks	(US 20 Pos)
1	17	**You Spin Me Round (Like A Record)**	Dead Or Alive	Epic	8	(11) F
2	-	**Material Girl**	Madonna	Sire	6	(2)
3	1	**I Know Him So Well**	Elaine Paige & Barbara Dickson	RCA	10	L
4	18	**Nightshift**	Commodores	Motown	8	(3)
5	-	**Kiss Me**	Stephen 'Tin Tin' Duffy	10	6	F
6	-	**Easy Lover**	Philip Bailey & Phil Collins	CBS	9	(2) F L
7	-	**That Ole Devil Called Love**	Alison Moyet	CBS	6	
8	-	**The Last Kiss**	David Cassidy	Arista	5	L
9	-	**Everytime You Go Away**	Paul Young	CBS	6	(1)
10	-	**Do What You Do**	Jermaine Jackson	Arista	6	(13) L
11	6	**Dancing In The Dark**	Bruce Springsteen	CBS	9	(2) F
12	-	**Let's Go Crazy/Take Me With You**	Prince & The Revolution	Warner	4	(1)
13	3	**Solid**	Ashford & Simpson	Capitol	8	(12) F L
14	2	**Love & Pride**	King	CBS	4	(55) F
15	-	**We Close Our Eyes**	Go West	Chrysalis	8	(41) F
16	12	**Things Can Only Get Better**	Howard Jones	WEA	6	(5)
17	-	**Wide Boy**	Nik Kershaw	MCA	6	
18	-	**Pie Jesu**	Sarah Brightman & Paul Miles-Kingston	HMV	5	
19	10	**A New England**	Kirsty MacColl	Stiff	5	
20	-	**The Boys Of Summer**	Don Henley	Geffen	3	(5) F L

This Mnth	Prev Mnth	Title	Artist	Label	Wks	(US 20 Pos)
1	-	**Everybody Wants To Rule The World**	Tears For Fears	Mercury	9	(1)
2	6	**Easy Lover**	Philip Bailey & Phil Collins	CBS	9	(2) F L
3	-	**Welcome To The Pleasure Dome**	Frankie Goes To Hollywood	ZTT	5	(48)
4	15	**We Close Our Eyes**	Go West	Chrysalis	8	(41) F
5	-	**Move Closer**	Phyllis Nelson	Carrere	11	F L
6	-	**We Are The World**	USA For Africa	CBS	6	(1) F L
7	-	**Could It Be I'm Falling In Love**	David Grant & Jaki Graham	Chrysalis	6	
8	18	**Pie Jesu**	Sarah Brightman & Paul Miles-Kingston	HMV	5	
9	7	**That Ole Devil Called Love**	Alison Moyet	CBS	6	
10	9	**Everytime You Go Away**	Paul Young	CBS	6	(1)
11	-	**One More Night**	Phil Collins	Virgin	5	(1)
12	-	**Clouds Across The Moon**	Rah Band	RCA	5	L
13	-	**Spend The Night**	Coolnotes	Abstract Dance	4	F
14	17	**Wide Boy**	Nik Kershaw	MCA	6	
15	-	**The Heat Is On**	Glenn Frey	MCA	4	(2) F L
16	10	**Do What You Do**	Jermaine Jackson	Arista	6	(13) L
17	5	**Kiss Me**	Stephen 'Tin Tin' Duffy	10	6	F
18	2	**Material Girl**	Madonna	Sire	6	(2)
19	-	**I Feel Love**	Bronski Beat & Marc Almond	Forbidden Fruit	7	
20	-	**Don't You (Forget About Me)**	Simple Minds	Virgin	5	(1)

◆ Queen, Rod Stewart, Yes, Iron Maiden, AC/DC, Whitesnake, The Scorpions and Ozzy Osbourne were among the headliners at the massive *Rock In Rio* festival.

◆ Few Chinese noticed as Wham! became the first western pop group to play in China and to have records released there. In contrast, few Britons could have been unaware of Bruce Springsteen's UK tour.

1985

This Mnth	Prev Mnth	Title	Artist	Label	Wks	(US 20 Pos)	
1	-	**19**	Paul Hardcastle	Chrysalis	9	(15)	F
2	5	**Move Closer**	Phyllis Nelson	Carrere	11		F L
3	19	**I Feel Love**	Bronski Beat & Marc Almond	Forbidden Fruit	7		
4	1	**Everybody Wants To Rule The World**	Tears For Fears	Mercury	9	(1)	
5	-	**Feel So Real**	Steve Arrington	Atlantic	7		F L
6	-	**Rhythm Of The Night**	DeBarge	Gordy	6	(3)	F L
7	20	**Don't You (Forget About Me)**	Simple Minds	Virgin	5	(1)	
8	6	**We Are The World**	USA For Africa	CBS	6	(1)	F L
9	-	**The Unforgettable Fire**	U2	Island	3		
10	-	**I Was Born To Love You**	Freddie Mercury	CBS	5	(76)	
11	-	**Walls Come Tumbling Down!**	Style Council	Polydor	4		
12	-	**A View To Kill**	Duran Duran	Parlophone	7	(1)	
13	-	**Love Don't Live Here Anymore**	Jimmy Nail	Virgin	6		F
14	11	**One More Night**	Phil Collins	Virgin	5	(1)	
15	12	**Clouds Across The Moon**	Rah Band	RCA	5		L
16	-	**Kayleigh**	Marillion	EMI	9		
17	7	**Could It Be I'm Falling In Love**	David Grant & Jaki Graham	Chrysalis	6		
18	-	**Slave To Love**	Bryan Ferry	EG	4		
19	-	**Lover Come Back To Me**	Dead Or Alive	Epic	3	(75)	
20	-	**I Want Your Lovin' (Just A Little Bit)**	Curtis Hairston	London	2		F L

This Mnth	Prev Mnth	Title	Artist	Label	Wks	(US 20 Pos)	
1	16	**Kayleigh**	Marillion	EMI	9		
2	-	**You'll Never Walk Alone**	The Crowd	Spartan	6		F L
3	1	**19**	Paul Hardcastle	Chrysalis	9	(15)	F
4	12	**A View To Kill**	Duran Duran	Parlophone	7	(1)	
5	-	**Suddenly**	Billy Ocean	Jive	8	(4)	
6	-	**Obsession**	Animotion	Mercury	6	(6)	F L
7	-	**The Word Girl**	Scritti Politti Feat. Ranking Ann	Virgin	6		
8	-	**Frankie**	Sister Sledge	Atlantic	10	(75)	
9	-	**Crazy For You**	Madonna	Geffen	10	(1)	
10	-	**Out In The Fields**	Gary Moore & Phil Lynott	10	6		
11	-	**History**	Mai Tai	Virgin	7		F
12	-	**Cherish**	Kool & The Gang	De-Lite	12	(2)	L
13	-	**Walking On Sunshine**	Katrina & The Waves	Capitol	5	(9)	F
14	13	**Love Don't Live Here Anymore**	Jimmy Nail	Virgin	6		F
15	-	**Axel F**	Harold Faltermeyer	MCA	9	(3)	F L
16	6	**Rhythm Of The Night**	DeBarge	Gordy	6	(3)	F L
17	-	**Ben**	Marti Webb	Starblend	6		
18	-	**Call Me**	Go West	Chrysalis	3	(54)	
19	3	**I Feel Love**	Bronski Beat & Marc Almond	Forbidden Fruit	7		
20	-	**Johnny Come Home**	Fine Young Cannibals	London	7	(76)	F

◆ Paul Hardcastle, ex- keyboard player with Brit-funk band Direct Drive, took sampling to new heights with his groundbreaking transatlantic hit '19'. Its success helped make him the most in-demand remixer of the time.

◆ Dancing In The Street' by David Bowie & Mick Jagger, entered at No. 1. Proceeds from the hit helped the starving in Ethiopia.

July 1985

This Mnth	Prev Mnth	Title	Artist	Label	Wks	(US 20 Pos)	
1	8	**Frankie**	Sister Sledge	Atlantic	10	(75)	
2	15	**Axel F**	Harold Faltermeyer	MCA	9	(3)	F L
3	9	**Crazy For You**	Madonna	Geffen	10	(1)	
4	12	**Cherish**	Kool & The Gang	De-Lite	12	(2)	L
5	-	**I'm On Fire/Born In The U.S.A.**	Bruce Springsteen	CBS	7	(6)	
6	-	**There Must Be An Angel (Playing With My Heart)**	Eurythmics	RCA	8	(22)	
7	-	**My Toot Toot**	Denise La Salle	Epic	6		F L
8	17	**Ben**	Marti Webb	Starblend	6		
9	20	**Johnny Come Home**	Fine Young Cannibals	London	7	(76)	F
10	-	**Live Is Life**	Opus	Polydor	7	(32)	F L
11	11	**History**	Mai Tai	Virgin	7		F
12	5	**Suddenly**	Billy Ocean	Jive	8	(4)	
13	-	**Head Over Heels**	Tears For Fears	Mercury	4	(3)	
14	-	**Round And Round**	Jaki Graham	EMI	4		
15	1	**Kayleigh**	Marillion	EMI	9		
16	-	**Into The Groove**	Madonna	Sire	10		
17	2	**You'll Never Walk Alone**	The Crowd	Spartan	6		F L
18	-	**Turn It Up**	Conway Brothers	10	3		F L
19	-	**Money's Too Tight (To Mention)**	Simply Red	Elektra	3	(28)	F
20	-	**Living On Video**	Trans-X	Boiling Point	5	(61)	F L

August 1985

This Mnth	Prev Mnth	Title	Artist	Label	Wks	(US 20 Pos)	
1	16	**Into The Groove**	Madonna	Sire	10		
2	-	**We Don't Need Another Hero (Thunderdome)**	Tina Turner	Capitol	7	(2)	
3	-	**Money For Nothing**	Dire Straits	Vertigo	8	(1)	
4	6	**There Must Be An Angel (Playing With My Heart)**	Eurythmics	RCA	8	(22)	
5	-	**I Got You Babe**	UB40 Feat Chrissie Hynde	Dep International	8	(28)	
6	-	**Holiday**	Madonna	Sire	5		
7	-	**White Wedding**	Billy Idol	Chrysalis	8	(36)	
8	-	**Running Up That Hill**	Kate Bush	EMI	6	(30)	
9	-	**Drive**	Cars	Elektra	7		L
10	10	**Live Is Life**	Opus	Polydor	7	(32)	F L
11	4	**Cherish**	Kool & The Gang	De-Lite	12	(2)	L
12	-	**Say I'm Your No. 1**	Princess	Supreme	6		F
13	1	**Frankie**	Sister Sledge	Atlantic	10	(75)	
14	2	**Axel F**	Harold Faltermeyer	MCA	9	(3)	F L
15	-	**Don Quixote**	Nik Kershaw	MCA	3		L
16	-	**Tarzan Boy**	Baltimora	Columbia	7	(13)	F L
17	-	**Excitable**	Amazulu	Island	3		F
18	20	**Living On Video**	Trans-X	Boiling Point	5	(61)	F L
19	-	**Alone Without You**	King	CBS	5		
20	14	**Round And Round**	Jaki Graham	EMI	4		

◆ n September, a record nine re-issued singles were simultaneously in the UK Top 40, including re-mixes of Amii Stewart's 1979 'Knock On Wood' and 'Light My Fire' – the earliest of dozens of dance re-mixes to chart in Britain.

◆ Dire Straits scored simultaneous US chart-toppers with **Brothers In Arms** (which eventually sold six million in America, nearly four million in the UK and topped the chart in 22 countries!), and the Grammy winning 'Money For Nothing' on which co-writer Sting apeared.

1985

This Mnth	Prev Mnth	Title	Artist	Label	Wks	(US 20 Pos)	
1	-	**Dancing In The Street**	David Bowie & Mick Jagger	EMI America	7	(7)	
2	-	**Holding Out For A Hero**	Bonnie Tyler	CBS	8	(34)	L
3	16	**Tarzan Boy**	Baltimora	Columbia	7	(13)	F L
4	5	**I Got You Babe**	UB40 Feat. Chrissie Hynde	Dep International	8	(28)	
5	-	**Part Time Lover**	Stevie Wonder	Motown	5	(1)	
6	-	**Body And Soul**	Mai Tai	Virgin	6		L
7	1	**Into The Groove**	Madonna	Sire	10		
8	-	**Knock On Wood/Light My Fire**	Amii Stewart	Sedition	5		L
9	9	**Drive**	Cars	Elektra	7		L
10	-	**Lavender**	Marillion	EMI	5		
11	8	**Running Up That Hill**	Kate Bush	EMI	6	(30)	
12	12	**Say I'm Your No. 1**	Princess	Supreme	6		F
13	-	**If I Was**	Midge Ure	Chrysalis	7		
14	-	**Angel**	Madonna	Sire	5	(5)	
15	19	**Alone Without You**	King	CBS	5		
16	-	**The Power Of Love**	Huey Lewis & The News	Chrysalis	5	(1)	F
17	3	**Money For Nothing**	Dire Straits	Vertigo	8	(1)	
18	-	**Lean On Me (Ah-Li-Ayo)**	Red Box	Sire	8		F
19	-	**Body Rock**	Maria Vidal	EMI America	5	(48)	F L
20	-	**I Can Dream About You**	Dan Hartman	MCA	3	(6)	L

This Mnth	Prev Mnth	Title	Artist	Label	Wks	(US 20 Pos)	
1	-	**The Power Of Love**	Jennifer Rush	CBS	11	(57)	F G
2	13	**If I Was**	Midge Ure	Chrysalis	7		
3	-	**Trapped**	Colonel Abrams	MCA	10		F L
4	18	**Lean On Me (Ah-Li-Ayo)**	Red Box	Sire	7		
5	-	**Rebel Yell**	Billy Idol	Chrysalis	6	(46)	
6	5	**Part Time Lover**	Stevie Wonder	Motown	8	(1)	
7	-	**Take On Me**	A-Ha	Warner	9	(1)	F
8	-	**St. Elmo's Fire (Man In Motion)**	John Parr	London	6	(1)	F L
9	1	**Dancing In The Street**	David Bowie & Mick Jagger	EMI America	7	(7)	
10	2	**Holding Out For A Hero**	Bonnie Tyler	CBS	8	(34)	L
11	-	**Alive And Kicking**	Simple Minds	Virgin	6	(3)	
12	14	**Angel**	Madonna	Sire	5	(5)	
13	-	**Gambler**	Madonna	Geffen	6		
14	-	**Miami Vice Theme**	Jan Hammer	MCA	4	(1)	F
15	10	**Lavender**	Marillion	EMI	5		
16	19	**Body Rock**	Maria Vidal	EMI America	5	(48)	F L
17	16	**The Power Of Love**	Huey Lewis & The News	Chrysalis	5	(1)	F
18	-	**Slave To The Rhythm**	Grace Jones	ZTT	4		
19	-	**Nikita**	Elton John	Rocket	9	(7)	
20	-	**Single Life**	Cameo	Club	3		F

◆ Madonna became the first female to simultaneously hold the top 2 places, thanks to 'Into The Groove' (which only appeared on the 12" version of 'Angel' in the US) and a re-issue of 'Holiday'.

◆ It was claimed that Dire Straits' 'Brothers In Arms' was the first commercially succsseful CD single.

November 1985

This Mnth	Prev Mnth	Title	Artist	Label	Wks	(US 20 Pos)	
1	1	**The Power Of Love**	Jennifer Rush	CBS	11	(57)	F G
2	-	**A Good Heart**	Feargal Sharkey	Virgin	10	(67)	F
3	7	**Take On Me**	A-Ha	Warner	9	(1)	F
4	19	**Nikita**	Elton John	Rocket	9	(7)	
5	-	**Don't Break My Heart**	UB40	Dep International	8		
6	-	**Something About You**	Level 42	Polydor	6	(7)	
7	3	**Trapped**	Colonel Abrams	MCA	10		F L
8	-	**I'm Your Man**	Wham!	Epic	8	(3)	
9	-	**Road To Nowhere**	Talking Heads	EMI	6		
10	-	**One Vision**	Queen	EMI	4	(61)	
11	13	**Gambler**	Madonna	Geffen	6		
12	-	**Sisters Are Doin' It For Themselves**	Eurythmics & Aretha Franklin	RCA	5	(18)	
13	-	**Stairway To Heaven**	Far Corporation	Arista	4	(89)	F L
14	8	**St. Elmo's Fire (Man In Motion)**	John Parr	London	6	(1)	F L
15	-	**The Show**	Doug E. Fresh & The Get Fresh Crew	Cooltempo	6		F L
16	-	**The Taste Of Your Tears**	King	CBS	5		L
17	-	**Election Day**	Arcadia	Odeon	4	(6)	F L
18	11	**Alive And Kicking**	Simple Minds	Virgin	6	(3)	
19	-	**See The Day**	Dee C. Lee	CBS	8		F L
20	14	**Miami Vice Theme**	Jan Hammer	MCA	4	(1)	F

December 1985

This Mnth	Prev Mnth	Title	Artist	Label	Wks	(US 20 Pos)	
1	-	**Saving All My Love For You**	Whitney Houston	Arista	9	(1)	F
2	8	**I'm Your Man**	Wham!	Epic	8	(3)	
3	19	**See The Day**	Dee C. Lee	CBS	8		F L
4	-	**Separate Lives**	Phil Collins & Marilyn Martin	Virgin	8	(1)	
5	-	**Do They Know It's Christmas**	Band Aid	Mercury	5		L
6	-	**Merry Christmas Everyone**	Shakin' Stevens	Epic	6		
7	-	**Dress You Up**	Madonna	Sire	6	(5)	
8	-	**West End Girls**	Pet Shop Boys	Parlophone	8	(1)	
9	2	**A Good Heart**	Feargal Sharkey	Virgin	10	(67)	F
10	-	**Say You, Say Me**	Lionel Richie	Motown	7	( )	
11	15	**The Show**	Doug E. Fresh & The Get Fresh Crew	Cooltempo	6		F L
12	-	**We Built This City**	Starship	RCA	6	(1)	F
13	-	**Last Christmas**	Wham!	Epic	4		G
14	-	**Santa Claus Is Comin' To Town/My Hometown**	Bruce Springsteen	Epic	4		
15	5	**Don't Break My Heart**	UB40	Dep International	8		
16	-	**Don't Look Down-The Sequel**	Go West	Chrysalis	6	(39)	
17	-	**Walking In The Air**	Aled Jones	HMV	5		F L
18	9	**Road To Nowhere**	Talking Heads	EMI	6		
19	-	**Spies Like Us**	Paul McCartney	Parlophone	6	(7)	
20	4	**Nikita**	Elton John	Rocket	9	(7)	

◆ American Jennifer Rush topped the chart with 'The Power Of Love'. It became the first UK million seller by a female artist. In her homeland it failed to reach the Top 40. The song, however, became an American No. 1 by French-Canadian Celine Dion in 1994.

◆ NME writers chose The Jesus & Mary Chain's 'Never Understood' and **Psychocandy** as the Top Single and Album of the Year respectively.

1986

January 1986

This Mnth	Prev Mnth	Title	Artist	Label	Wks (US 20 Pos)	
1	8	**West End Girls**	Pet Shop Boys	Parlophone	8 (1)	F
2	-	**Hit That Perfect Beat**	Bronski Beat	Forbidden	7	
3	-	**The Sun Always Shines On T.V.**	A-Ha	Warner	7 (20)	
4	1	**Saving All My Love For You**	Whitney Houston	Arista	9 (1)	F
5	-	**Saturday Love**	Cherrelle & Alexander O'Neal	Tabu	5 (26)	F L
6	-	**Girlie Girlie**	Sophia George	Winner	5	F L
7	6	**Merry Christmas Everyone**	Shakin' Stevens	Epic	6	
8	-	**Walk Of Life**	Dire Straits	Vertigo	6 (7)	L
9	17	**Walking In The Air**	Aled Jones	HMV	5	F L
10	-	**You Little Thief**	Feargal Sharkey	Virgin	4	
11	-	**Broken Wings**	Mr Mister	RCA	4 (1)	F
12	7	**Dress You Up**	Madonna	Sire	6 (5)	
13	5	**Do They Know It's Christmas**	Band Aid	Mercury	5	L
14	2	**I'm Your Man**	Wham!	Epic	8 (3)	
15	4	**Separate Lives**	Phil Collins & Marilyn Martin	Virgin	8 (1)	
16	-	**Alice I Want You Just For Me**	Full Force	CBS	3	F L
17	13	**Last Christmas**	Wham!	Epic	4	G
18	-	**Who's Zoomin' Who**	Aretha Franklin	Arista	3 (7)	
19	-	**Russians**	Sting	A&M	3 (16)	
20	-	**It's Alright (Baby's Coming Back)**	Eurythmics	RCA	4 (78)	

February 1986

1	-	**When The Going Gets Tough, The Tough Get Going**	Billy Ocean	Jive	8 (2)	
2	-	**Borderline**	Madonna	Sire	6 (10)	
3	3	**The Sun Always Shines On T.V.**	A-Ha	Warner	7 (20)	
4	-	**Only Love**	Nana Mouskouri	Philips	6	F L
5	-	**System Addict**	Five Star	Tent	6	
6	8	**Walk Of Life**	Dire Straits	Vertigo	6 (7)	L
7	-	**Living In America**	James Brown	Scotti Bros	6 (4)	
8	-	**Eloise**	Damned	MCA	6	L
9	-	**The Phantom Of The Opera**	Sarah Brightman/Steve Harley	Polydor	4	
10	-	**Starting Together**	Su Pollard	Rainbow	5	F L
11	-	**The Captain Of Her Heart**	Double	Polydor	4 (16)	F L
12	-	**How Will I Know**	Whitney Houston	Arista	6 (1)	
13	-	**Suspicious Minds**	Fine Young Cannibals	London	5	
14	11	**Broken Wings**	Mr Mister	RCA	4 (1)	F
15	-	**Chain Reaction**	Diana Ross	Capitol	10 (66)	
16	5	**Saturday Love**	Cherrelle & Alexander O'Neal	Tabu	5 (26)	F L
17	-	**Rise**	Public Image Ltd.	Virgin	5	L
18	-	**Pull Up To The Bumper/La Vie En Rose**	Grace Jones	Island	4	L
19	-	**Burning Heart**	Survivor	Scotti Brothers	5 (2)	L
20	-	**Sanctify Yourself**	Simple Minds	Virgin	3 (14)	

◆ An *NME* survey showed that Madonna was the UK's Top Singles Artist in 1985 and that Bruce Springsteen was Top Album Artist.

◆ Annie Lennox again collected the Best Female Artist trophy at the Brit Awards. Other winners included Phil Collins (Best Male), Dire Straits (Best Group), Go West (Best Newcomer), Bruce Springsteen (Best International Artist) and Huey Lewis & The News (Best International Group).

1986

March 1986

This Mnth	Prev Mnth	Title	Artist	Label	Wks	(US 20 Pos)	
1	15	**Chain Reaction**	Diana Ross	Capitol	10	(66)	
2	-	**Manic Monday**	Bangles	CBS	6	(2)	F
3	1	**When The Going Gets Tough, The Tough Get Going**	Billy Ocean	Jive	8	(2)	
4	-	**Love Missile F1-11**	Sigue Sigue Sputnik	Parlophone	4		F
5	-	**Absolute Beginners**	David Bowie	Virgin	5	(53)	
6	-	**Hi Ho Silver**	Jim Diamond	A&M	7		L
7	10	**Starting Together**	Su Pollard	Rainbow	5		F L
8	19	**Burning Heart**	Survivor	Scotti Brothers	5	(2)	L
9	-	**Theme From New York New York**	Frank Sinatra	Reprise	3	(32)	L
10	-	**(Nothin' Serious) Just Buggin'**	Whistle	Champion	4		F L
11	12	**How Will I Know**	Whitney Houston	Arista	6	(1)	
12	-	**Living Doll**	Cliff Richard & The Young Ones	WEA	7		
13	-	**Kiss**	Prince & The Revolution	Paisley Park	4	(1)	
14	-	**The Power Of Love/Do You Believe In Love**	Huey Lewis & The News	Chrysalis	4		
15	8	**Eloise**	Damned	MCA	6		L
16	-	**Don't Waste My Time**	Paul Hardcastle	Chrysalis	4		
17	-	**Move Away**	Culture Club	Virgin	4	(12)	L
18	-	**Kyrie**	Mr. Mister	RCA	5	(1)	L
19	-	**Digging Your Scene**	Blow Monkeys	RCA	4	(14)	F
20	-	**Touch Me (I Want Your Body)**	Samantha Fox	Jive	6	(4)	F

April 1986

This Mnth	Prev Mnth	Title	Artist	Label	Wks	(US 20 Pos)	
1	12	**Living Doll**	Cliff Richard & The Young Ones	WEA	7		
2	-	**A Different Corner**	George Michael	Epic	7	(7)	
3	-	**Rock Me Amadeus**	Falco	A&M	9	(1)	F
4	20	**Touch Me (I Want Your Body)**	Samantha Fox	Jive	6	(4)	F
5	-	**A Kind Of Magic**	Queen	EMI	8	(42)	
6	-	**Wonderful World**	Sam Cooke	RCA	6		L
7	-	**You To Me Are Everything**	Real Thing	PRT	7		
8	-	**Peter Gunn**	Art Of Noise & Duane Eddy	China	4	(50)	
9	-	**Secret Lovers**	Atlantic Starr	A&M	6	(3)	F
10	-	**Train Of Thought**	A-Ha	Warner	3		
11	-	**Look Away**	Big Country	Mercury	5		
12	-	**All The Things She Said**	Simple Minds	Virgin	5	(28)	
13	1	**Chain Reaction**	Diana Ross	Capitol	10	(66)	
14	5	**Absolute Beginners**	David Bowie	Virgin	5	(53)	
15	-	**E=MC^2**	Big Audio Dynamite	CBS	4		F L
16	-	**What Have You Done For Me Lately**	Janet Jackson	A&M	6	(4)	F
17	-	**Can't Wait Another Minute**	Five Star	Tent	7	(41)	
18	-	**Just Say No**	Grange Hill Cast	BBC	3		F L
19	6	**Hi Ho Silver**	Jim Diamond	A&M	7		L
20	18	**Kyrie**	Mr. Mister	RCA	5	(1)	L

◆ Among the American re-releases hitting the heights were 'Borderline' by Madonna, 'The Power of Love' by Huey Lewis & The News and, perhaps most surprisingly, 'Theme From New York New York' by Frank Sinatra.

◆ Bob Geldof received an honorary knighthood for his charity work. Among the current charity hits were 'Everybody Wants To Run the World' (for Sports Aid) by Tears For Fears and an update of 'Living Doll' by Cliff Richard & The Young Ones (for Comic Relief).

1986

This Mnth	Prev Mnth	Title	Artist	Label	Wks	(US 20 Pos)	
1	-	Lessons In Love	Level 42	Polydor	7	(12)	
2	3	Rock Me Amadeus	Falco	A&M	9	(1)	F
3	-	On My Own	Patti Labelle/Michael McDonald	MCA	8	(1)	F L
4	-	The Chicken Song	Spitting Image	Virgin	6		F L
5	-	Live To Tell	Madonna	Sire	6	(1)	
6	16	What Have You Done For Me Lately	Janet Jackson	A&M	6	(4)	F
7	-	Sledgehammer	Peter Gabriel	Virgin	8	(1)	
8	17	Can't Wait Another Minute	Five Star	Tent	7	(41)	
9	-	Greatest Love Of All	Whitney Houston	Arista	5	(1)	
10	2	A Different Corner	George Michael	Epic	7	(7)	
11	-	Snooker Loopy	Matchroom Mob With Chas & Dave	Rockney	4		F L
12	-	Spirit In The Sky	Doctor & The Medics	IRS	9	(69)	F L
13	-	I Heard It Through The Grapevine	Marvin Gaye	Tamla Motown	4		L
14	-	Why Can't This Be Love	Van Halen	Warner	4	(3)	L
15	5	A Kind Of Magic	Queen	EMI	8	(42)	
16	18	Just Say No	Grange Hill Cast	BBC	3		F L
17	-	There'll Be Sad Songs (To Make You Cry)	Billy Ocean	Jive	4	(1)	
18	-	Rolling Home	Status Quo	Vertigo	3		
19	11	Look Away	Big Country	Mercury	5		
20	-	You And Me Tonight	Aurra	10	4		F L

This Mnth	Prev Mnth	Title	Artist	Label	Wks	(US 20 Pos)	
1	12	Spirit In The Sky	Doctor & The Medics	IRS	9	(69)	F L
2	-	Holding Back The Years	Simply Red	WEA	8	(1)	
3	-	I Can't Wait	Nu Shooz	Atlantic	7	(3)	F L
4	-	Addicted To Love	Robert Palmer	Island	7	(1)	
5	7	Sledgehammer	Peter Gabriel	Virgin	8	(1)	
6	-	Can't Get By Without You	Real Thing	PRT	6		L
7	-	The Edge Of Heaven/ Where Did Your Heart Go	Wham!	Epic	6	(10)	L
8	-	Hunting High And Low	A-Ha	Warner	5		
9	-	Set Me Free	Jaki Graham	EMI	5		
10	-	Everybody Wants To Run The World	Tears For Fears	Mercury	3		
11	-	Too Good To Be Forgotten	Amazulu	Island	6		
12	-	Vienna Calling	Falco	A&M	4	(18)	L
13	4	The Chicken Song	Spitting Image	Virgin	6		F L
14	-	Happy Hour	Housemartins	Go! Discs	7		F
15	3	On My Own	Patti Labelle/Michael McDonald	MCA	8	(1)	F L
16	-	New Beginning (Mamba Seyra)	Bucks Fizz	Polydor	5		L
17	1	Lessons In Love	Level 42	Polydor	7	(12)	
18	-	My Favourite Waste Of Time	Owen Paul	Epic	7		F L
19	-	Opportunities (Let's Make Lots Of Money)	Pet Shop Boys	Parlophone	4	(10)	
20	-	Amityville (The House On...)	Lovebug Starski	Epic	4		F L

◆ Sam Cooke's 'Wonderful World' (from 1960) and Marvin Gaye's 'I Heard it Through The Grapevine' (from 1968), were the first of many oldies that hit after being heard in Levis' jeans advertisements.

◆ Shortly before his last gig with Wham!, George Michael's 'A Different Corner' became the first British No. 1 sung, written, produced, arranged and played (all instruments!) by the same person.

July 1986

This Mnth	Prev Mnth	Title	Artist	Label	Wks	(US 20 Pos)	
1	-	**Papa Don't Preach**	Madonna	Sire	9	(1)	
2	18	**My Favourite Waste Of Time**	Owen Paul	Epic	7		F L
3	7	**The Edge Of Heaven/Where Did Your Heart Go**	Wham!	Epic	6	(10)	L
4	14	**Happy Hour**	Housemartins	Go! Discs	7		F
5	-	**Let's Go All The Way**	Sly Fox	Capitol	6	(7)	F L
6	-	**Venus**	Bananarama	London	5	(1)	
7	11	**Too Good To Be Forgotten**	Amazulu	Island	6		
8	-	**Every Beat Of My Heart**	Rod Stewart	Warner	6	(83)	
9	3	**I Can't Wait**	Nu Shooz	Atlantic	7	(3)	F L
10	-	**Sing Our Own Song**	UB40	Dep International	4		
11	-	**The Lady In Red**	Chris De Burgh	A&M	9	(3)	F
12	16	**New Beginning (Mamba Seyra)**	Bucks Fizz	Polydor	5		L
13	-	**Bang Zoom (Let's Go Go)**	Real Roxanne With Hitman Howie Tee	Cooltempo	4		F L
14	-	**Do Ya Do Ya (Wanna Please Me)**	Samantha Fox	Jive	3	(87)	
15	8	**Hunting High And Low**	A-Ha	Warner	5		
16	-	**Paranoimia**	Art Of Noise	China	3	(34)	
17	-	**Camouflage**	Stan Ridgway	IRS	6		F L
18	1	**Spirit In The Sky**	Doctor & The Medics	IRS	9	(69)	F L
19	-	**It's 'Orrible Being In Love (When You're 8½)**	Claire & Friends	BBC	3		F L
20	-	**Higher Love**	Steve Winwood	Island	3	(1)	F

August 1986

This Mnth	Prev Mnth	Title	Artist	Label	Wks	(US 20 Pos)	
1	11	**The Lady In Red**	Chris De Burgh	A&M	9	(3)	F
2	-	**So Macho/Cruising**	Sinitta	Fanfare	9		F
3	-	**I Want To Wake Up With You**	Boris Gardiner	Revue	9		
4	17	**Camouflage**	Stan Ridgway	IRS	6		F L
5	-	**Ain't Nothing Goin' On But The Rent**	Gwen Guthrie	Boiling Point	7	(42)	F L
6	1	**Papa Don't Preach**	Madonna	Sire	9	(1)	
7	-	**Anyone Can Fall In Love**	Anita Dobson	BBC	4		F L
8	5	**Let's Go All The Way**	Sly Fox	Capitol	6	(7)	F L
9	-	**Find The Time**	Five Star	Tent	4		
10	-	**Calling All The Heroes**	It Bites	Virgin	5		F L
11	8	**Every Beat Of My Heart**	Rod Stewart	Warner	6	(83)	
12	-	**What's The Colour Of Money?**	Hollywood Beyond	WEA	5		F L
13	-	**Shout**	Lulu	Jive/Decca	4		
14	-	**Panic**	Smiths	Rough Trade	4		
15	-	**I Didn't Mean To Turn You On**	Robert Palmer	Island	4	(2)	
16	-	**Dancing On The Ceiling**	Lionel Richie	Motown	4	(2)	
17	-	**Brother Louie**	Modern Talking	RCA	6		F L
18	-	**I Can Prove It**	Phil Fearon	Ensign	4		L
19	-	**We Don't Have To ...**	Jermaine Stewart	10	9	(5)	F
20	10	**Sing Our Own Song**	UB40	Dep International	4		

◆ Madonna's self-penned and produced 'Papa Don't Preach' was a transatlantic topper, as was her album **True Blue,** the first LP by an American female to enter the UK chart at the summit.

◆ Chicago club DJ Farley 'Jackmaster' Funk's 'Love Can't Turn You Around' is generally regarded as the earliest "house music" hit.

◆ Frankie Goes To Hollywood announced they were to disband, septet Madness shrunk to a quartet and Stiff Records closed – it was the end of another era in British pop.

1986

This Mnth	Prev Mnth	Title	Artist	Label	Wks	(US 20 Pos)	
1	-	**Don't Leave Me This Way**	Communards	London	9	(40)	F
2	19	**We Don't Have To ...**	Jermaine Stewart	10	9	(5)	F
3	3	**I Want To Wake Up With You**	Boris Gardiner	Revue	9		
4	-	**Glory Of Love**	Peter Cetera	Full Moon	7	(1)	F L
5	-	**(I Just) Died In Your Arms**	Cutting Crew	Siren	6	(1)	F L
6	-	**Rage Hard**	Frankie Goes To Hollywood	ZTT	4		
7	17	**Brother Louie**	Modern Talking	RCA	6		F L
8	-	**Word Up**	Cameo	Club	7	(6)	
9	-	**Holiday Rap**	M.C. Miker 'G' & Deejay Sven	Debut	3		F L
10	-	**Love Can't Turn Around**	Farley 'Jackmaster' Funk	D.J. International	6		F L
11	2	**So Macho/Cruising**	Sinitta	Fanfare	9		F
12	-	**Walk This Way**	Run D.M.C.	London	6	(4)	F
13	-	**Thorn In My Side**	Eurythmics	RCA	7	(68)	
14	-	**Human**	Human League	Virgin	5	(1)	
15	-	**Rain Or Shine**	Five Star	Tent	7		
16	-	**When I Think Of You**	Janet Jackson	A&M	4	(1)	
17	1	**The Lady In Red**	Chris De Burgh	A&M	9	(3)	F
18	-	**You Give Love A Bad Name**	Bon Jovi	Vertigo	3	(1)	F
19	-	**Sweet Freedom**	Michael McDonald	MCA	3	(7)	L
20	5	**Ain't Nothing Goin' On But The Rent**	Gwen Guthrie	Boiling Point	7	(42)	F L

This Mnth	Prev Mnth	Title	Artist	Label	Wks	(US 20 Pos)	
1	-	**True Blue**	Madonna	Sire	7	(3)	
2	15	**Rain Or Shine**	Five Star	Tent	7		
3	1	**Don't Leave Me This Way**	Communards	London	9	(40)	F
4	-	**You Can Call Me Al**	Paul Simon	Warner	6	(23)	
5	-	**Every Loser Wins**	Nick Berry	BBC	6		F
6	-	**In The Army Now**	Status Quo	Vertigo	7		
7	8	**Word Up**	Cameo	Club	7	(6)	
8	13	**Thorn In My Side**	Eurythmics	RCA	7	(68)	
9	-	**Suburbia**	Pet Shop Boys	Parlophone	5	(70)	
10	-	**I've Been Losing You**	A-Ha	Warner	4		
11	-	**All I Ask Of You**	Cliff Richard & Sarah Brightman	Polydor	8		
12	-	**Walk Like An Egyptian**	Bangles	CBS	8	(1)	
13	2	**We Don't Have To ...**	Jermaine Stewart	10	9	(5)	F
14	-	**(Forever) Live And Die**	Orchestral Manoeuvres In The Dark	Virgin	5	(19)	
15	-	**Always There**	Marti Webb	BBC	5		L
16	12	**Walk This Way**	Run D.M.C.	London	6	(4)	F
17	5	**(I Just) Died In Your Arms**	Cutting Crew	Siren	6	(1)	F L
18	-	**True Colors**	Cyndi Lauper	Portrait	5	(1)	
19	-	**Stuck With You**	Huey Lewis & The News	Chrysalis	4	(1)	L
20	-	**Montego Bay**	Amazulu	Island	3	(90)	

◆ Irish singer/songwriter Chris De Burgh, who had sold 10 million albums globally, gained his first UK Top 40 single with his 24th release, the chart topping 'The Lady In Red'. It was also his only US Top 20 entry.

◆ Status Quo scored their 20th Top 10 hit, 'In The Army Now'. The Beatles and The Rolling Stones were the only other groups to achieve this feat.

November 1986

This Mnth	Prev Mnth	Title	Artist	Label	Wks	(US 20 Pos)	
1	-	Take My Breath Away	Berlin	CBS	11	(1)	F
2	-	You Keep Me Hangin' On	Kim Wilde	MCA	7	(1)	
3	12	Walk Like An Egyptian	Bangles	CBS	8	(1)	
4	-	Showing Out (Get Fresh At The Weekend)	Mel & Kim	Supreme	6	(78)	F
5	6	In The Army Now	Status Quo	Vertigo	7		
6	5	Every Loser Wins	Nick Berry	BBC	6		F
7	-	Breakout	Swing Out Sister	Mercury	7	(6)	F
8	11	All I Ask Of You	Cliff Richard & Sarah Brightman	Polydor	8		
9	-	Livin' On A Prayer	Bon Jovi	Vertigo	10	(1)	
10	-	The Final Countdown	Europe	Epic	10	(8)	F
11	-	Through The Barricades	Spandau Ballet	Reformation	5		L
12	-	Don't Give Up	Peter Gabriel & Kate Bush	Virgin	4	(72)	
13	-	Notorious	Duran Duran	EMI	4	(2)	
14	-	For America	Red Box	Sire	5		L
15	-	Midas Touch	Midnight Star	Solar	4	(42)	L
16	1	True Blue	Madonna	Sire	7	(3)	
17	-	Don't Get Me Wrong	Pretenders	Real	4	(10)	
18	4	You Can Call Me Al	Paul Simon	Warner	6	(23)	
19	-	Each Time You Break My Heart	Nick Kamen	WEA	5		F
20	-	French Kissin' In The USA	Debbie Harry	Chrysalis	7	(57)	F

December 1986

This Mnth	Prev Mnth	Title	Artist	Label	Wks	(US 20 Pos)	
1	10	The Final Countdown	Europe	Epic	10	(8)	F
2	-	Sometimes	Erasure	Mute	10		F
3	-	Caravan Of Love	Housemartins	Go! Discs	6		
4	-	The Rain	Oran 'Juice' Jones	Def Jam	8	(9)	F L
5	9	Livin' On A Prayer	Bon Jovi	Vertigo	10	(1)	
6	1	Take My Breath Away	Berlin	CBS	11	(1)	F
7	-	Open Your Heart	Madonna	Sire	6	(1)	
8	-	Shake You Down	Gregory Abbott	CBS	7	(1)	F L
9	-	Reet Petite	Jackie Wilson	SMP	9		
10	-	So Cold The Night	Communards	London	6		
11	19	Each Time You Break My Heart	Nick Kamen	WEA	5		F
12	20	French Kissin' In The USA	Debbie Harry	Chrysalis	7	(57)	F
13	-	Cry Wolf	A-Ha	Warner	6	(50)	
14	7	Breakout	Swing Out Sister	Mercury	7	(6)	F
15	-	The Skye Boat Song	Roger Whittaker & Des O'Connor	Tembo	5		L
16	-	Is This Love	Alison Moyet	CBS	9		
17	2	You Keep Me Hangin' On	Kim Wilde	MCA	7	(1)	
18	4	Showing Out (Get Fesh At The Weekend)	Mel & Kim	Supreme	6	(78)	F
19	-	Big Fun	Gap Band	Total Experience	8		
20	-	Land Of Confusion	Genesis	Virgin	7	(4)	

◆ Take My Breath Away' (from the five million selling **Top Gun** soundtrack) gave Berlin a transatlantic chart-topper. It also returned to the British Top 3 in 1990.

◆ In October, for the first time, the top three US singles were by different solo female singers, Janet Jackson, Tina Turner and Cyndi Lauper. A month later female vocalists held a record Top 5 slots on the UK chart.

1987

This Mnth	Prev Mnth	Title	Artist	Label	Wks	(US 20 Pos)	
1	9	**Reet Petite**	Jackie Wilson	SMP	9		
2	16	**Is This Love**	Alison Moyet	CBS	9		
3	19	**Big Fun**	Gap Band	Total Experience	8		
4	-	**Jack Your Body**	Steve 'Silk' Hurley	DJ International	7		F L
5	-	**No More The Fool**	Elkie Brooks	Legend	8		L
6	3	**Caravan Of Love**	Housemartins	Go! Discs	6		
7	-	**C'est La Vie**	Robbie Nevil	Manhattan	5	(2)	F L
8	2	**Sometimes**	Erasure	Mute	10		F
9	1	**The Final Countdown**	Europe	Epic	10	(8)	F
10	7	**Open Your Heart**	Madonna	Sire	6	(1)	
11	4	**The Rain**	Oran 'Juice' Jones	Def Jam	8	(9)	F L
12	13	**Cry Wolf**	A-Ha	Warner	6	(50)	
13	-	**Surrender**	Swing Out Sister	Mercury	4		L
14	-	**Hymn To Her**	Pretenders	Real	5		
15	8	**Shake You Down**	Gregory Abbott	CBS	7	(1)	F L
16	-	**It Didn't Matter**	Style Council	Polydor	3		
17	-	**I Knew You Were Waiting (For Me)**	Aretha Franklin/George Michael	Epic	6	(1)	
18	-	**Down To Earth**	Curiosity Killed The Cat	Mercury	8		F
19	5	**Livin' On A Prayer**	Bon Jovi	Vertigo	10	(1)	
20	10	**So Cold The Night**	Communards	London	6		

This Mnth	Prev Mnth	Title	Artist	Label	Wks	(US 20 Pos)	
1	17	**I Knew You Were Waiting (For Me)**	Aretha Franklin/George Michael	Epic	6	(1)	
2	-	**Heartache**	Pepsi & Shirlie	Polydor	6	(78)	F
3	18	**Down To Earth**	Curiosity Killed The Cat	Mercury	8		F
4	-	**Almaz**	Randy Crawford	Warner	5		L
5	-	**It Doesn't Have To Be That Way**	Blow Monkeys	RCA	4		L
6	-	**Male Stripper**	Man 2 Man Meet Man Parrish	Bolts	7		F L
7	-	**Stand By Me**	Ben E. King	Atlantic	7	(9)	F L
8	-	**I Love My Radio**	Taffy	Transglobal	4		F L
9	-	**When A Man Loves A Woman**	Percy Sledge	Atlantic	6		L
10	4	**Jack Your Body**	Steve 'Silk' Hurley	DJ International	7		F L
11	-	**Stay Out Of My Life**	Five Star	Tent	4		
12	-	**The Music Of The Night/ Wishing You Were Somehow Here Again**	Michael Crawford/Sarah Brightman	Polydor	4		F L
13	-	**Running In The Family**	Level 42	Polydor	6	(83)	
14	-	**You Sexy Thing**	Hot Chocolate	EMI	4		
15	5	**No More The Fool**	Elkie Brooks	Legend	8		L
16	7	**C'est La Vie**	Robbie Nevil	Manhattan	5	(2)	F L
17	-	**Coming Around Again**	Carly Simon	Arista	5	(18)	L
18	-	**Shoplifters Of The World Unite**	Smiths	Rough Trade	2		
19	2	**Is This Love**	Alison Moyet	CBS	9		
20	-	**Once Bitten Twice Shy**	Vesta Williams	A&M	3		F L

◆ Ben E. King's 25-year-old 'Stand By Me' was a transatlantic Top 10 hit, while in Britain Percy Sledge's 1966 smash, 'When A Man Loves A Woman', scored again. Jackie Wilson's 29-year-old 'Reet Petite' hit the top and half the Top 10 in March were re-issues.

◆ *Record Mirror's* readers poll showed Prince as Top Male, Madonna as Top Female and The Smiths as Top Group.

March 1987

This Mnth	Prev Mnth	Title	Artist	Label	Wks	(US 20 Pos)	
1	-	**Everything I Own**	Boy George	Virgin	6		F
2	-	**I Get The Sweetest Feeling**	Jackie Wilson	SMP	6		
3	-	**Live It Up**	Mental As Anything	Epic	7		F L
4	-	**The Great Pretender**	Freddie Mercury	Parlophone	6		
5	7	**Stand By Me**	Ben E. King	Atlantic	7	(9)	F L
6	-	**Respectable**	Mel & Kim	Supreme	9		
7	9	**When A Man Loves A Woman**	Percy Sledge	Atlantic	6		L
8	-	**Crush On You**	Jets	MCA	6	(3)	F L
9	6	**Male Stripper**	Man 2 Man Meet Man Parrish	Bolts	7		F L
10	13	**Running In The Family**	Level 42	Polydor	6	(83)	
11	-	**Weak In The Presence Of Beauty**	Alison Moyet	CBS	6		
12	-	**Moonlighting ('Theme')**	Al Jarreau	WEA	4	(23)	F L
13	-	**Respect Yourself**	Bruce Willis	Motown	4	(5)	F
14	-	**The Right Thing**	Simply Red	WEA	4	(27)	
15	-	**It Doesn't Have To Be**	Erasure	Mute	5		
16	3	**Down To Earth**	Curiosity Killed The Cat	Mercury	8		F
17	17	**Coming Around Again**	Carly Simon	Arista	5	(18)	L
18	-	**With Or Without You**	U2	Island	6	(1)	
19	-	**Sign 'O' The Times**	Prince	Paisley Park	5	(3)	
20	-	**(You Gotta) Fight For Your Right (To Party)**	Beastie Boys	Def Jam	3	(7)	F

April 1987

This Mnth	Prev Mnth	Title	Artist	Label	Wks	(US 20 Pos)	
1	-	**Let It Be**	Ferry Aid	The Sun	5		F L
2	-	**La Isla Bonita**	Madonna	Sire	8	(4)	
3	6	**Respectable**	Mel & Kim	Supreme	9		
4	-	**Lean On Me**	Club Nouveau	King Jay	7	(1)	F L
5	-	**Let's Wait Awhile**	Janet Jackson	Breakout	6	(2)	
6	18	**With Or Without You**	U2	Island	6	(1)	
7	-	**If You Let Me Stay**	Terence Trent D'Arby	CBS	7	(68)	F
8	-	**Can't Be With You Tonight**	Judy Boucher	Orbitone	9		F
9	-	**Ever Fallen In Love**	Fine Young Cannibals	London	6		
10	11	**Weak In The Presence Of Beauty**	Alison Moyet	CBS	6		
11	-	**Living In A Box**	Living In A Box	Chrysalis	8	(17)	F
12	-	**The Irish Rover**	Pogues & The Dubliners	Stiff	3		
13	1	**Everything I Own**	Boy George	Virgin	6		F
14	2	**I Get The Sweetest Feeling**	Jackie Wilson	SMP	6		
15	-	**Ordinary Day**	Curiosity Killed The Cat	Mercury	3		
16	-	**The Slightest Touch**	Five Star	Tent	6		
17	-	**Wanted Dead Or Alive**	Bon Jovi	Vertigo	4	(7)	
18	19	**Sign 'O' The Times**	Prince	Paisley Park	5	(3)	
19	13	**Respect Yourself**	Bruce Willis	Motown	4	(5)	F
20	-	**Big Time**	Peter Gabriel	Charisma	3	(8)	

◆ Kate Bush, who was voted Best Female Artist at the Brit Awards, became the first British female to chalk up three No. 1 LPs when **The Whole Story** completed her hat-trick.

◆ This year's Prince's Trust Gala starred Eric Clapton, Bryan Adams, Ben E. King, Alison Moyet and new teeny bop idols Curiosity Killed The Cat. Acts enjoying sell out shows at Wembley included Americans Lionel Richie, Luther Vandross and Tina Turner and UK-based Duran Duran, David Bowie, U2 and The Pretenders.

1987

May 1987

This Mnth	Prev Mnth	Title	Artist	Label	Wks	(US 20 Pos)	
1	-	**Nothing's Gonna Stop Us Now**	Starship	RCA	11	(1)	L
2	8	**Can't Be With You Tonight**	Judy Boucher	Orbitone	9		F
3	-	**A Boy From Nowhere**	Tom Jones	Epic	8		
4	11	**Living In A Box**	Living In A Box	Chrysalis	8	(17)	F
5	-	**(Something Inside) So Strong**	Labi Siffre	China	7		L
6	2	**La Isla Bonita**	Madonna	Sire	8	(4)	
7	-	**Another Step (Closer To You)**	Kim Wilde & Junior	MCA	7		
8	16	**The Slightest Touch**	Five Star	Tent	6		
9	-	**Big Love**	Fleetwood Mac	Warner	5	(5)	
10	-	**Shattered Dreams**	Johnny Hates Jazz	Virgin	6	(2)	F
11	-	**Back And Forth**	Cameo	Club	5	(50)	L
12	-	**I Wanna Dance With Somebody (Who Loves Me)**	Whitney Houston	Arista	10	(1)	
13	4	**Lean On Me**	Club Nouveau	King Jay	7	(1)	F L
14	-	**Incommunicado**	Marillion	EMI	3		
15	-	**April Skies**	Jesus And Mary Chain	Blanco	3		
16	-	**To Be With You Again**	Level 42	Polydor	3		
17	7	**If You Let Me Stay**	Terence Trent D'Arby	CBS	7	(68)	
18	-	**Lil' Devil**	Cult	Beggars Banquet	4		
19	-	**Boops (Here To Go)**	Sly And Robbie	4th & Broadway	3		F L
20	-	**Hold Me Now**	Johnny Logan	Epic	7		L

June 1987

This Mnth	Prev Mnth	Title	Artist	Label	Wks	(US 20 Pos)	
1	12	**I Wanna Dance With Somebody (Who Loves Me)**	Whitney Houston	Arista	10	(1)	
2	20	**Hold Me Now**	Johnny Logan	Epic	7		L
3	1	**Nothing's Gonna Stop Us Now**	Starship	RCA	11	(1)	L
4	-	**I Want Your Sex**	George Michael	Epic	5	(2)	
5	-	**Star Trekkin'**	Firm	Bark	7		L
6	-	**I Still Haven't Found What I'm Looking For**	U2	Island	4	(1)	
7	-	**Jack Mix II**	Mirage	Debut	5		F
8	-	**Victim Of Love**	Erasure	Mute	4		
9	-	**Nothing's Gonna Stop Me Now**	Samantha Fox	Jive	5	(80)	
10	-	**Under The Boardwalk**	Bruce Willis	Motown	10	(59)	L
11	-	**Goodbye Stranger**	Pepsi & Shirlie	Polydor	4		L
12	10	**Shattered Dreams**	Johnny Hates Jazz	Virgin	6	(2)	F
13	-	**Wishing I Was Lucky**	Wet Wet Wet	Precious	5	(58)	F
14	-	**You're The Voice**	John Farnham	Wheatley	6	(82)	F L
15	-	**Serious**	Donna Allen	Portrait	3	(21)	F
16	-	**It's A Sin**	Pet Shop Boys	Parlophone	8	(9)	
17	-	**When Smokey Sings**	ABC	Neutron	4	(5)	L
18	-	**Looking For A New Love**	Jody Watley	MCA	3	(2)	F L
19	-	**Is This Love**	Whitesnake	EMI	5	(2)	
20	-	**No Sleep Till Brooklyn**	Beastie Boys	Def Jam	3		

◆ Headliners at Switzerland's Montreux Rock Festival included Whitney Houston, Cameo, Duran Duran, Spandau Ballet, Run DMC and The Beastie Boys. The latter two then toured Britain where The Beasties received a hammering from the British press for their alleged anti-social behaviour.

◆ The influx of old songs onto the chart continued and even classic old recordings such as Tom Jones's debut hit single 'It's Not Unusual' and The Beatles' **Sergeant Pepper** album returned to the Top 20.

July 1987

This Mnth	Prev Mnth	Title	Artist	Label	Wks (US 20 Pos)	
1	16	**It's A Sin**	Pet Shop Boys	Parlophone	8	(9)
2	10	**Under The Boardwalk**	Bruce Willis	Motown	10	(59) L
3	-	**Wishing Well**	Terence Trent D'Arby	CBS	6	(1)
4	5	**Star Trekkin'**	Firm	Bark	7	L
5	-	**Always**	Atlantic Starr	Warner	8	(1) L
6	-	**The Living Daylights**	A-Ha	Warner	5	
7	1	**I Wanna Dance With Somebody**			10	(1)
		(Who Loves Me)	WhitneyHouston	Arista		
8	-	**My Pretty One**	Cliff Richard	EMI	4	
9	-	**Who's That Girl**	Madonna	Sire	7	(1)
10	-	**Sweetest Smile**	Black	A&M	4	F
11	-	**Alone**	Heart	Capitol	7	(1) F
12	-	**F.L.M.**	Mel & Kim	Supreme	5	
13	14	**You're The Voice**	John Farnham	Wheatley	6	(82) F L
14	-	**Misfit**	Curiosity Killed The Cat	Mercury	4	(42)
15	19	**Is This Love**	Whitesnake	EMI	5	(2)
16	-	**Jive Talkin'**	Boogie Box High	Hardback	5	F L
17	-	**Let's Dance**	Chris Rea	Magnet	4	(81) L
18	17	**When Smokey Sings**	ABC	Neutron	4	(5) L
19	-	**La Bamba**	Los Lobos	Slash	6	(1) F
20	-	**A Little Boogie Woogie**			4	
		(In The Back Of My Mind)	Shakin' Stevens	Epic		

August 1987

1	19	**La Bamba**	Los Lobos	Slash	6	(1) F
2	-	**I Just Can't Stop Loving You**	Michael Jackson		6	(1)
			(duet with Seidah Garrett)	Epic		
3	-	**Call Me**	Spagna	CBS	6	F L
4	-	**True Faith**	New Order	Factory	6	
5	9	**Who's That Girl**	Madonna	Sire	7	(1)
6	11	**Alone**	Heart	Capitol	7	(1) F
7	5	**Always**	Atlantic Starr	Warner	8	(1) L
8	-	**Labour Of Love**	Hue & Cry	Circa	6	F
9	-	**Never Gonna Give You Up**	Rick Astley	RCA	10	(1) F
10	-	**Toy Boy**	Sinitta	Fanfare	8	
11	-	**Animal**	Def Leppard	Bludgeon Riffola	5	(19) F
12	-	**Sweet Little Mystery**	Wet Wet Wet	Precious	6	
13	-	**Somewhere Out There**	Linda Ronstadt	MCA	4	(2) F
14	-	**What Have I Done To**	Pet Shop Boys		6	(2)
		Deserve This	& Dusty Springfield	Parlophone		
15	16	**Jive Talkin'**	Boogie Box High	Hardback	5	F L
16	1	**It's A Sin**	Pet Shop Boys	Parlophone	8	(9)
17	-	**Just Don't Want To**			4	F L
		Be Lonely	Freddie McGregor	Germain		
18	-	**She's On It**	Beastie Boys	Def Jam	4	L
19	2	**Under The Boardwalk**	Bruce Willis	Motown	10	(59) L
20	-	**Funky Town**	Pseudo Echo	RCA	4	(6) F L

◆ The video for Peter Gabriel's 'Sledgehammer' won a record 10 MTV awards.

◆ Cliff Richard scored his 50th British Top 10 hit, 'My Pretty One', and Bananarama collected their 13th chart entry – a record for a British female group.

◆ Rick Astley had Britain's biggest selling single of 1987, 'Never Gonna Give You Up'.

1987

September 1987

This Mnth	Prev Mnth	Title	Artist	Label	Wks	(US 20 Pos)	
1	9	**Never Gonna Give You Up**	Rick Astley	RCA	10	(1)	F
2	-	**Wipeout**	Fat Boys & Beach Boys	Urban	7	(12)	F
3	-	**Heart And Soul**	T'Pau	Siren	6	(4)	F
4	14	**What Have I Done To Deserve This**	Pet Shop Boys/Dusty Springfield	Parlophone	6	(2)	
5	-	**Some People**	Cliff Richard	EMI	7		
6	10	**Toy Boy**	Sinitta	Fanfare	8		
7	-	**Pump Up The Volume**	M/A/R/R/S	4AD	8	(13)	F L
8	-	**Where The Streets Have No Name**	U2	Island	3	(13)	
9	-	**Wonderful Life**	Black	A&M	5		L
10	12	**Sweet Little Mystery**	Wet Wet Wet	Precious	6		
11	-	**Casanova**	Levert	Atlantic	5	(5)	F L
12	-	**Causing A Commotion**	Madonna	Sire	5	(2)	
13	-	**Bridge To Your Heart**	Wax	RCA	5		F L
14	3	**Call Me**	Spagna	CBS	6		F L
15	-	**House Nation**	House Master Boyz & The Rude Boy Of House	Magnetic Dance	4		F L
16	-	**It's Over**	Level 42	Polydor	4		
17	2	**I Just Can't Stop Loving You**	Michael Jackson	Epic	6	(1)	
18	-	**I Don't Want To Be A Hero**	Johnny Hates Jazz	Virgin	5	(31)	
19	-	**U Got The Look**	Prince	Paisley Park	4	(2)	
20	-	**Bad**	Michael Jackson	Epic	5	(1)	

October 1987

This Mnth	Prev Mnth	Title	Artist	Label	Wks	(US 20 Pos)	
1	-	**Crockett's Theme**	Jan Hammer	MCA	8		L
2	-	**Full Metal Jacket (I Wanna Be Your Drill Instructor)**	Abigail Mead & Nigel Goulding	Warner Bros.	6		F L
3	7	**Pump Up The Volume**	M/A/R/R/S	4AD	8	(13)	F L
4	-	**You Win Again**	Bee Gees	Warner Bros.	8	(75)	
5	-	**Crazy Crazy Nights**	Kiss	Vertigo	5	(65)	F
6	20	**Bad**	Michael Jackson	Epic	5	(1)	
7	1	**Never Gonna Give You Up**	Rick Astley	RCA	10	(1)	F
8	-	**I Need Love**	L.L. Cool J	CBS	5	(14)	F L
9	-	**The Circus**	Erasure	Mute	5		
10	5	**Some People**	Cliff Richard	EMI	7		
11	-	**I Found Lovin'**	Fatback Band	Master Mix	4		L
12	-	**Love In The First Degree/ Mr. Sleaze**	Bananarama/S.A.W.	London	6	(48)	
13	12	**Causing A Commotion**	Madonna	Sire	5	(2)	
14	-	**This Corrosion**	Sisters Of Mercy	Merciful Release	3		F
15	-	**Mony Mony**	Billy Idol	Chrysalis	6	(1)	
16	-	**Faith**	George Michael	Epic	5	(1)	
17	-	**Little Lies**	Fleetwood Mac	Warner Bros.	5	(4)	
18	-	**The Real Thing**	Jellybean Feat.\ Steven Dante	Chrysalis	4	(82)	F
19	15	**House Nation**	House Master Boyz/Rude Boy...	Magnetic Dance	4		F L
20	-	**Walk The Dinosaur**	Was (Not Was)	Fontana	5	(7)	F

◆ Introducing The Hardline According To Terence Trent D'Arby was the first debut album by an American act to enter the UK chart at No. 1. In his homeland it spent 26 weeks on the chart before reaching the Top 10.

◆ Half the songs on December's UK chart were oldies. Among them were re-issues of 'When I Fall In Love' by Nat 'King' Cole (1957) and 'My Baby Just Cares For Me' by Nina Simone (1959).

November 1987

This Mnth	Prev Mnth	Title	Artist	Label	Wks	(US 20 Pos)	
1	-	China In Your Hand	T'Pau	Siren	11		
2	-	Got My Mind Set On You	George Harrison	Dark Horse	9	(1)	L
3	-	Whenever You Need Somebody	Rick Astley	RCA	6		
4	4	You Win Again	Bee Gees	Warner	8	(75)	
5	-	Never Can Say Goodbye	Communards	London	7	(51)	
6	16	Faith	George Michael	Epic	5	(1)	
7	12	Love In The First Degree/ Mr. Sleaze	Bananarama/S.A.W.	London	6	(48)	
8	-	(I've Had) The Time Of My Life	Bill Medley & Jennifer Warnes	RCA	4	(1)	F
9	-	My Baby Just Cares For Me	Nina Simone	Charly	4		L
10	-	Barcelona	Freddie Mercury/M. Caballé	Polydor	4		
11	-	Here I Go Again	Whitesnake	EMI	5	(1)	
12	17	Little Lies	Fleetwood Mac	Warner	5	(4)	
13	-	Jack Mix IV	Mirage	Debut	4		L
14	-	So Emotional	Whitney Houston	Arista	6	(1)	
15	15	Mony Mony	Billy Idol	Chrysalis	6	(1)	
16	-	Criticize	Alexander O'Neal	Tabu	8	(70)	
17	1	Crockett's Theme	Jan Hammer	MCA	8		L
18	20	Walk The Dinosaur	Was (Not Was)	Fontana	5	(7)	F
19	-	I Don't Think That Man Should Sleep Alone	Ray Parker Jr.	Geffen	3	(68)	L
20	9	The Circus	Erasure	Mute	5		

December 1987

This Mnth	Prev Mnth	Title	Artist	Label	Wks	(US 20 Pos)	
1	1	China In Your Hand	T'Pau	Siren	11		
2	-	Always On My Mind	Pet Shop Boys	Parlophone	8	(4)	
3	-	The Way You Make Me Feel	Michael Jackson	Epic	7	(1)	
4	-	When I Fall In Love/My Arms Keep Missing You	Rick Astley	RCA	6		
5	-	What Do You Want To Make Those Eyes At Me For	Shakin' Stevens	Epic	5		
6	-	Letter From America	Proclaimers	Chrysalis	6		F
7	-	Love Letters	Alison Moyet	CBS	6		
8	2	Got My Mind Set On You	George Harrison	Dark Horse	9	(1)	L
9	16	Criticize	Alexander O'Neal	Tabu	8	(70)	
10	-	Rockin' Around The Christmas Tree	Mel & Kim (Smith & Wilde)	10	5		
11	-	Fairytale Of New York	Pogues Feat. Kirsty MacColl	Pogue Mahone	6		F
12	-	Who Found Who	Jellybean Feat. Elisa Fiorillo	Chrysalis	6	(16)	
13	14	So Emotional	Whitney Houston	Arista	6	(1)	
14	5	Never Can Say Goodbye	Communards	London	7	(51)	
15	-	The Look Of Love	Madonna	Sire	5		
16	-	Once Upon A Long Ago	Paul McCartney	Parlophone	3		
17	-	When I Fall In Love	Nat 'King' Cole	Capitol	4		L
18	-	Heaven Is A Place On Earth	Belinda Carlisle	Virgin	10	(1)	F
19	-	Ev'ry Time We Say Goodbye	Simply Red	Elektra	3		
20	-	Some Guys Have All The Luck	Maxi Priest	10	4		F

◆ 1987 was the year when "sampling" surfaced, three inch CDs were unsuccessfully launched, Japanese company Sony bought CBS Records and MTV debuted in Europe.

◆ The boundary breaking single 'Pump Up The Volume' by M/A/R/R/S was the first record to top the indie, dance and pop charts.

1988

This Mnth	Prev Mnth	Title	Artist	Label	Wks	(US 20 Pos)	
1	18	Heaven Is A Place On Earth	Belinda Carlisle	Virgin	10	(1)	F
2	2	Always On My Mind	Pet Shop Boys	Parlophone	8	(4)	
3	-	House Arrest	Krush	Club	7		F L
4	-	Stutter Rap (No Sleep 'Til Bedtime)	Morris Minor & The Majors	10/Virgin	5		F L
5	-	Angel Eyes (Home And Away)	Wet Wet Wet	Precious	6		
6	-	I Found Someone	Cher	Geffen	4	(10)	
7	-	Sign Your Name	Terence Trent D'Arby	CBS	6	(4)	
8	-	I Think We're Alone Now	Tiffany	MCA	9	(1)	F
9	-	Come Into My Life	Joyce Sims	London	5		L
10	11	Fairytale Of New York	Pogues Feat. Kirsty MacColl	Pogue Mahone	6		F
11	-	All Day And All Of The Night	Stranglers	Epic	4		
12	3	The Way You Make Me Feel	Michael Jackson	Epic	7	(1)	
13	7	Love Letters	Alison Moyet	CBS	6		
14	-	Rise To The Occasion	Climie Fisher	EMI	4		F
15	4	When I Fall In Love/My Arms Keep Missing You	Rick Astley	RCA	6		
16	10	Rockin' Around The Christmas Tree	Mel & Kim (Smith & Wilde)	10	5		
17	17	When I Fall In Love	Nat 'King' Cole	Capitol	4		
18	-	Heatseeker	AC/DC	Atlantic	3		
19	-	When Will I Be Famous	Bros	CBS	6	(83)	F
20	-	Rok Da House	Beatmasters Feat. Cookie Crew	Rhythm King	5		F

1	8	I Think We're Alone Now	Tiffany	MCA	9	(1)	F
2	-	Tell It To My Heart	Taylor Dayne	Arista	6	(7)	F
3	-	I Should Be So Lucky	Kylie Minogue	PWL	10	(28)	F
4	19	When Will I Be Famous	Bros	CBS	6	(83)	F
5	-	Get Outta My Dreams Get Into My Car	Billy Ocean	Jive	6	(1)	L
6	-	Candle In The Wind (Live)	Elton John	Rocket	5	(6)	
7	-	Shake Your Love	Debbie Gibson	Atlantic	5	(4)	F
8	-	Say It Again	Jermaine Stewart	10	5	(27)	
9	-	The Jack That House Built	Jack 'n' Chill	Oval	5		F L
10	-	Beat Dis	Bomb The Bass	Mister-Ron	5		F
11	20	Rok Da House	Beatmasters Feat. Cookie Crew	Rhythm King	5		F
12	7	Sign Your Name	Terence Trent D'Arby	CBS	6	(4)	
13	1	Heaven Is A Place On Earth	Belinda Carlisle	Virgin	10	(1)	F
14	-	O L'Amour	Dollar	London	5		L
15	-	Valentine	T'Pau	Siren	4		
16	-	Gimme Hope Jo'anna	Eddy Grant	Ice	5		L
17	3	House Arrest	Krush	Club	7		F L
18	-	Hot In The City	Billy Idol	Chrysalis	4	(23)	L
19	-	Tower Of Strength	Mission	Mercury	4		
20	-	Suedehead	Morrissey	HMV	3		F

◆ Female artists scored a record three successive No. 1s when Australian soap star Kylie Minogue followed transatlantic toppers Belinda Carlisle and Tiffany to the top spot.

◆ A survey showed that the richest people in the music business in Britain were Virgin Records' head Richard Branson followed by Paul McCartney and Elton John.

1988

March 1988

This Mnth	Prev Mnth	Title	Artist	Label	Wks	(US 20 Pos)	
1	3	I Should Be So Lucky	Kylie Minogue	PWL	10	(28)	F
2	-	Together Forever	Rick Astley	RCA	5	(1)	
3	-	Joe Le Taxi	Vanessa Paradis	FA Prods	6		F
4	10	Beat Dis	Bomb The Bass	Mister-Ron	5		F
5	-	Crash	Primitives	Lazy	5		F L
6	5	Get Outta My Dreams Get Into My Car	Billy Ocean	Jive	6	(1)	L
7	-	Doctorin' The House	Coldcut Featuring Yazz & The Plastic Population	Ahead Of Our Time	5		F
8	-	Don't Turn Around	Aswad	Mango	5		F
9	-	Ship Of Fools	Erasure	Mute	5		
10	16	Gimme Hope Jo'anna	Eddy Grant	Ice	5		L
11	-	I Get Weak	Belinda Carlisle	Virgin	5	(2)	
12	20	Suedehead	Morrissey	HMV	3		F
13	-	Love Is Contagious	Taja Sevelle	Paisley Park	3		F L
14	-	Drop The Boy	Bros	CBS	7		
15	-	Never/These Dreams	Heart	Capitol	5	(4)	
16	2	Tell It To My Heart	Taylor Dayne	Arista	6	(7)	F
17	-	That's The Way It Is	Mel & Kim	Supreme	3		L
18	-	Hazy Shade Of Winter	Bangles	Def Jam	3	(2)	
19	-	Can I Play With Madness	Iron Maiden	EMI	4		
20	-	Could've Been	Tiffany	MCA	5	(1)	

April 1988

This Mnth	Prev Mnth	Title	Artist	Label	Wks	(US 20 Pos)	
1	-	Heart	Pet Shop Boys	Parlophone	7		
2	-	Love Changes (Everything)	Climie Fisher	EMI	6	(23)	L
3	14	Drop The Boy	Bros	CBS	7		
4	20	Could've Been	Tiffany	MCA	5	(1)	
5	-	Everywhere	Fleetwood Mac	Warner Bros.	5	(14)	L
6	8	Don't Turn Around	Aswad	Mango	5		F
7	-	Cross My Broken Heart	Sinitta	Fanfare	5		
8	-	Who's Leaving Who	Hazell Dean	EMI	7		
9	-	Pink Cadillac	Natalie Cole	Manhattan	6	(5)	F
10	-	I'm Not Scared	Eighth Wonder	CBS	6		F
11	-	Theme From S'Express	S'Express	Rhythm King	7	(91)	F
12	19	Can I Play With Madness	Iron Maiden	EMI	4		
13	-	I Want You Back	Bananarama	London	6		
14	-	Stay On These Roads	A-Ha	Warner	4		
15	-	Prove Your Love	Taylor Dayne	Arista	4	(7)	L
16	-	Girlfriend	Pebbles	MCA	3	(5)	F L
17	-	Mary's Prayer	Danny Wilson	Virgin	6	(23)	F L
18	1	I Should Be So Lucky	Kylie Minogue	PWL	10	(28)	F
19	-	I Want You Back '88	Michael Jackson With The Jackson Five	Epic	5	(1)	
20	-	Only In My Dreams	Debbie Gibson	Atlantic	3	(4)	

◆ Expose became the first group to have four American Top 10 singles on their debut LP. Surprisingly, the female trio never had a major UK hit.

◆ Nelson Mandela's 70th birthday show was the most star-studded event since 'Live Aid'. Appearing were such notables as Bryan Adams, The Bee Gees, Natalie Cole, Phil Collins, Dire Straits, Eurythmics, Al Green, Whitney Houston, George Michael, Salt-N-Pepa, Sting and Stevie Wonder. The suprise hit of the show was Grammy winning American newcomer Tracy Chapman.

1988

This Mnth	Prev Mnth	Title	Artist	Label	Wks	(US 20 Pos)	
1	-	**Perfect**	Fairground Attraction	RCA	8	(80)	F
2	11	**Theme From S'express**	S'express	Rhythm King	7	(91)	F
3	-	**Blue Monday 1988**	New Order	Factory	6	(68)	
4	-	**With A Little Help From My Friends/She's Leaving Home**	Wet Wet Wet/ Billy Bragg & Cara Tivey	Childline	7		
5	-	**Loadsamoney (Doin' Up The House)**	Harry Enfield	Mercury	4		F L
6	17	**Mary's Prayer**	Danny Wilson	Virgin	6	(23)	F L
7	-	**Anfield Rap (Red Machine In Full Effect)**	Liverpool F.C.	Virgin	4		L
8	13	**I Want You Back**	Bananarama	London	6		
9	-	**Got To Be Certain**	Kylie Minogue	PWL	8		
10	8	**Who's Leaving Who**	Hazell Dean	EMI	7		
11	9	**Pink Cadillac**	Natalie Cole	Manhattan	6	(5)	F
12	-	**Divine Emotions**	Narada	Reprise	4		L
13	19	**I Want You Back '88**	Michael Jackson/Jackson Five	Epic	5	(1)	
14	-	**Alphabet Street**	Prince	Paisley Park	3	(8)	
15	-	**Circle In The Sand**	Belinda Carlisle	Virgin	5	(7)	
16	-	**The King Of Rock 'n' Roll**	Prefab Sprout	Kitchenware	4		F L
17	1	**Heart**	Pet Shop Boys	Parlophone	7		
18	-	**Somewhere In My Heart**	Aztec Camera	WEA	6		
19	-	**Let's All Chant**	Mick And Pat	PWL	4		F L
20	-	**Pump Up The Bitter**	Star Turn On 45 Pints	Pacific	2		F L

1	4	**With A Little Help From My Friends/She's Leaving...**	Wet Wet Wet/ Billy Bragg & Cara Tivey	Childline	7		
2	9	**Got To Be Certain**	Kylie Minogue	PWL	8		
3	-	**Doctorin' The Tardis**	Timelords	KLF Comms.	5	(66)	F L
4	18	**Somewhere In My Heart**	Aztec Camera	WEA	6		
5	-	**Voyage Voyage**	Desireless	CBS	6		F L
6	15	**Circle In The Sand**	Belinda Carlisle	Virgin	5	(7)	
7	-	**I Owe You Nothing**	Bros	CBS	7		
8	-	**My One Temptation**	Mica Paris	4th & Broadway	5	(97)	F
9	-	**Wild World**	Maxi Priest	10	6	(25)	
10	-	**Boys (Summertime Love)**	Sabrina	CBS	6		F L
11	1	**Perfect**	Fairground Attraction	RCA	8	(80)	F
12	-	**Check This Out**	L.A. Mix	Breakout	4		F L
13	-	**I Saw Him Standing There**	Tiffany	MCA	3	(7)	
14	-	**Everyday Is Like Sunday**	Morrissey	HMV	3		
15	16	**The King Of Rock 'n' Roll**	Prefab Sprout	Kitchenware	4		F L
16	-	**Chains Of Love**	Erasure	Mute	4	(12)	
17	-	**Tribute (Right On)**	Pasadenas	CBS	7	(52)	F
18	-	**Give A Little Love**	Aswad	Mango	6		
19	-	**The Twist (Yo, Twist)**	Fat Boys/Chubby Checker	Urban	7	(16)	L
20	-	**Love Will Save The Day**	Whitney Houston	Arista	2	(9)	

◆ Bros, whose UK tour incited mass hysteria among Britain's teenyboppers, topped the chart with a re-issue of their first single 'I Owe You Nothing'.

◆ Indie-dance act The Justified Ancients Of Mu Mu were convinced they knew the formula to get a UK No. 1 single. Their made-to-measure track 'Doctorin' The Tardis', released under the name The Timelords, not only reached the top, it also spent three months on the US chart.

July 1988

This Mnth	Prev Mnth	Title	Artist	Label	Wks	(US 20 Pos)	
1	-	Nothing's Gonna Change My Love For You	Glenn Medeiros	London	8	(12)	F
2	-	Push It/Tramp	Salt 'n' Pepa	Champion/ffrr	8	(19)	F
3	19	The Twist (Yo, Twist)	Fat Boys/Chubby Checker	Urban	7	(16)	L
4	7	I Owe You Nothing	Bros	CBS	7		
5	-	Fast Car	Tracy Chapman	Elektra	6	(6)	F L
6	-	Breakfast In Bed	UB40 Featuring Chrissie Hynde	Dep International	6		
7	10	Boys (Summertime Love)	Sabrina	CBS	6		F L
8	-	I Don't Want To Talk About It	Everything But The Girl	Blanco Y Negro	6		F
9	-	In The Air Tonight	Phil Collins	Virgin	5		
10	-	Roses Are Red	Mac Band Featuring The McCampbell Brothers	MCA	7		F L
11	17	Tribute (Right On)	Pasadenas	CBS	7	(52)	F
12	-	Dirty Diana	Michael Jackson	Epic	5	(1)	
13	-	I Want Your Love	Transvision Vamp	MCA	6		F
14	-	Don't Blame It On That Girl/ Wap Bam Boogie	Matt Bianco	WEA	6		L
15	9	Wild World	Maxi Priest	10	6	(25)	
16	-	Foolish Beat	Debbie Gibson	Atlantic	5	(1)	
17	3	Doctorin' The Tardis	Timelords	KLF	5	(66)	F L
18	-	You Came	Kim Wilde	MCA	7	(41)	
19	-	Love Bites	Def Leppard	Bludgeon Riffola	4	(1)	
20	-	Tougher Than The Rest	Bruce Springsteen	CBS	3		

August 1988

This Mnth	Prev Mnth	Title	Artist	Label	Wks	(US 20 Pos)	
1	-	The Only Way Is Up	Yazz & The Plastic Population	Big Life	9	(96)	
2	-	The Loco-Motion	Kylie Minogue	PWL	7	(3)	
3	18	You Came	Kim Wilde	MCA	7	(41)	
4	-	I Need You	B.V.S.M.P.	Debut	6		F L
5	-	Superfly Guy	S'Express	Rhythm King	6		
6	-	Find My Love	Fairground Attraction	RCA	6		L
7	-	The Evil That Men Do	Iron Maiden	EMI	3		
8	1	Nothing's Gonna Change My Love...	Glenn Medeiros	London	8	(12)	F
9	-	Reach Out I'll Be There	Four Tops	Motown	5		
10	-	Hands To Heaven	Breathe	Siren	6	(2)	F L
11	2	Push It/Tramp	Salt 'n' Pepa	Champion/ffrr	8	(19)	F
12	-	The Harder I Try	Brother Beyond	Parlophone	6		F
13	13	I Want Your Love	Transvision Vamp	MCA	6		F
14	-	Martha's Harbour	All About Eve	Mercury	3		F L
15	8	I Don't Want To Talk About It	Everything But The Girl	Blanco Y Negro	6		F
16	-	Hustle! (To The Music...)	Funky Worm	Fon	4		F L
17	10	Roses Are Red	Mac Band/McCampbell Brothers	MCA	7		F L
18	-	My Love	Julio Iglesias (featuring Stevie Wonder)	CBS	5	(80)	L
19	-	Good Tradition	Tanita Tikaram	WEA	4		F L
20	12	Dirty Diana	Michael Jackson	Epic	5	(1)	

◆ Two fans died at the *Monsters Of Rock* festival at Castle Donnington. Headlining were Iron Maiden, Kiss, Guns N' Roses, Megadeth and David Lee Roth.

◆ The Hollies' 19-year-old 'He Ain't Heavy, He's My Brother' hit the top. Other oldies returning included 'Lovely Day' by Bill Withers, 'Easy' by The Commodores and 'Reach Out I'll Be There' by The Four Tops.

1988

September 1988

This Mnth	Prev Mnth	Title	Artist	Label	Wks	(US 20 Pos)	
1	-	Groovy Kind Of Love	Phil Collins	Virgin	10	(1)	
2	-	Teardrops	Womack & Womack	4th & Broadway	11		
3	12	The Harder I Try	Brother Beyond	Parlophone	6		F
4	1	The Only Way Is Up	Yazz & The Plastic Population	Big Life	9	(96)	
5	-	He Ain't Heavy, He's My Brother	Hollies	EMI	7		L
6	-	Megablast/Don't Make Me Wait	Bomb The Bass	Mister-Ron	5		
7	-	The Race	Yello	Mercury	6		F L
8	18	My Love	Julio Iglesias/Stevie Wonder	CBS	5	(80)	L
9	2	The Loco-Motion	Kylie Minogue	PWL	7	(3)	
10	10	Hands To Heaven	Breathe	Siren	6	(2)	F L
11	-	Lovely Day	Bill Withers	CBS	5		L
12	-	I Quit	Bros	CBS	3		
13	-	Anything For You	Gloria Estefan/Miami Sound Machine	Epic	6	(1)	
14	-	Rush Hour	Jane Wiedlin	Manhattan	4	(9)	F L
15	-	Nothing Can Divide Us	Jason Donovan	PWL	7		F
16	-	Touchy!	A-Ha	Warner	3		
17	4	I Need You	B.V.S.M.P.	Debut	6		F L
18	-	I'm Gonna Be	Proclaimers	Chrysalis	5		
19	-	Big Fun	Inner City	10	7		F
20	6	Find My Love	Fairground Attraction	RCA	6		L

October 1988

This Mnth	Prev Mnth	Title	Artist	Label	Wks	(US 20 Pos)	
1	-	One Moment In Time	Whitney Houston	Arista	8	(5)	
2	2	Teardrops	Womack & Womack	4th & Broadway	11		
3	5	He Ain't Heavy, He's My Brother	Hollies	EMI	7		L
4	-	Don't Worry Be Happy	Bobby McFerrin	Manhattan	5	(1)	F L
5	-	Desire	U2	Island	4	(3)	
6	-	She Wants To Dance With Me	Rick Astley	RCA	7	(6)	
7	1	Groovy Kind Of Love	Phil Collins	Virgin	10	(1)	
8	-	A Little Respect	Erasure	Mute	8	(14)	
9	15	Nothing Can Divide Us	Jason Donovan	PWL	7		F
10	-	Wee Rule	Wee Papa Girl Rappers	Jive	6		F L
11	19	Big Fun	Inner City	10	7		F
12	-	Orinoco Flow	Enya	WEA	6	(24)	F
13	-	We Call It Acieed	D. Mob Feat. Gary Haisman	ffrr	6		F
14	11	Lovely Day	Bill Withers	CBS	5		L
15	-	Domino Dancing	Pet Shop Boys	Parlophone	4	(18)	
16	-	Never Trust A Stranger	Kim Wilde	MCA	6		
17	-	Je Ne Sais Pas Pourquoi	Kylie Minogue	PWL	6		
18	-	Riding On A Train	Pasadenas	CBS	5		
19	-	Harvest For The World	Christians	Island	4		
20	-	Burn It Up	Beatmasters With P.P. Arnold	Rhythm King	4		

◆ Even though it sold few copies in their homeland, 'Jackie' by Blue Zone charted in America. It featured vocalist Lisa Stansfield.

◆ The Proclaimers' current hit 'I'm Gonna Be', reached the US Top 20 five years later.

◆ U2's film *Rattle And Hum* premiered: the double album soundtrack sold a record one million copies in its first week in America and 300,000 in Britain.

November 1988

This Mnth	Prev Mnth	Title	Artist	Label	Wks	(US 20 Pos)	
1	-	Stand Up For Your Love Rights	Yazz	Big Life	6		
2	17	Je Ne Sais Pas Pourquoi	Kylie Minogue	PWL	6		
3	12	Orinoco Flow	Enya	WEA	6	(24)	F
4	-	The First Time	Robin Beck	Mercury	9		F L
5	-	Girl You Know It's True	Milli Vanilli	Cooltempo	6	(2)	F
6	-	She Makes My Day	Robert Palmer	EMI	5		
7	-	Real Gone Kid	Deacon Blue	CBS	5		F
8	-	He Ain't No Competition	Brother Beyond	Parlophone	4		
9	-	Need You Tonight	INXS	Mercury	5	(1)	F
10	-	Missing You	Chris De Burgh	A&M	6		L
11	-	Kiss	Art Of Noise & Tom Jones	China	4	(31)	L
12	-	1-2-3	Gloria Estefan & The Miami Sound Machine	Epic	3	(3)	
13	13	We Call It Acieed	D. Mob Feat. Gary Haisman	ffrr	6		F
14	-	Twist And Shout	Salt 'n' Pepa	ffrr	4		
15	1	One Moment In Time	Whitney Houston	Arista	8	(5)	
16	-	The Clairvoyant	Iron Maiden	EMI	3		
17	8	A Little Respect	Erasure	Mute	8	(14)	
18	-	Let's Stick Together	Bryan Ferry	EG	2		
19	19	Harvest For The World	Christians	Island	4		
20	-	Left To My Own Devices	Pet Shop Boys	Parlophone	4	(84)	

December 1988

This Mnth	Prev Mnth	Title	Artist	Label	Wks	(US 20 Pos)	
1	-	Mistletoe And Wine	Cliff Richard	EMI	7		
2	-	Cat Among The Pigeons/ Silent Night	Bros	CBS	6		
3	-	Especially For You	Kylie Minogue/Jason Donovan	PWL	10		
4	-	Suddenly	Angry Anderson	Food For Thought	8		F L
5	-	Two Hearts	Phil Collins	Virgin	8	(1)	
6	-	Crackers International (E.P.)	Erasure	Mute	10		
7	4	The First Time	Robin Beck	Mercury	9		F L
8	-	Smooth Criminal	Michael Jackson	Epic	8	(7)	
9	-	Take Me To Your Heart	Rick Astley	RCA	7		
10	-	Good Life	Inner City	10	8	(73)	
11	-	Burning Bridges (On And Off And On Again)	Status Quo	Vertigo	6		
12	10	Missing You	Chris De Burgh	A&M	6		L
13	-	Angel Of Harlem	U2	Island	4	(14)	
14	-	Say A Little Prayer	Bomb The Bass	Rhythm King	5		
15	20	Left To My Own Devices	Pet Shop Boys	Parlophone	4	(84)	
16	-	Downtown '88	Petula Clark	PRT	4		L
17	9	Need You Tonight	INXS	Mercury	5	(1)	F
18	-	Buffalo Stance	Neneh Cherry	Circa	7	(3)	F
19	-	Fine Time	New Order	Factory	4		
20	-	Loco In Acapulco	Four Tops	Arista	5		L

◆ Britain's fastest selling single of 1988 was 'Mistletoe And Wine', which gave Cliff Richard his 100th chart record and his 55th Top 10 hit (equalling Elvis Presley's record).

◆ Australian Kylie Minogue became the first female singer in the UK to have her first four singles sell over 250,000 copies each.

◆ Stock, Aitken & Waterman wrote and produced a record six singles in the Top 30 in October.

1989

This Mnth	Prev Mnth	Title	Artist	Label	Wks	(US 20 Pos)	
1	3	**Especially For You**	Kylie Minogue/Jason Donovan	PWL	10		
2	6	**Crackers International (E.P.)**	Erasure	Mute	10		
3	18	**Buffalo Stance**	Neneh Cherry	Circa	7	(3)	F
4	10	**Good Life**	Inner City	10	8	(73)	
5	-	**She Drives Me Crazy**	Fine Young Cannibals	London	6	(1)	
6	-	**The Living Years**	Mike + The Mechanics	WEA	7	(1)	F
7	4	**Suddenly**	Angry Anderson	Food For Thought	8		F L
8	-	**Four Letter Word**	Kim Wilde	MCA	6		
9	-	**Baby I Love Your Way/Freebird**	Will To Power	Epic	5	(1)	F L
10	20	**Loco In Acapulco**	Four Tops	Arista	5		L
11	-	**Something's Gotten Hold Of My Heart**	Marc Almond Featuring Gene Pitney	Parlophone	9		
12	-	**You Got It**	Roy Orbison	Virgin	6	(9)	
13	-	**Waiting For A Star To Fall**	Boy Meets Girl	RCA	4	(5)	F L
14	-	**Cuddly Toy**	Roachford	CBS	5		F L
15	11	**Burning Bridges (On And Off...)**	Status Quo	Vertigo	6		
16	-	**All She Wants Is**	Duran Duran	EMI	2	(22)	
17	1	**Mistletoe And Wine**	Cliff Richard	EMI	7		
18	-	**Keeping The Dream Alive**	Freiheit	CBS	4		F L
19	5	**Two Hearts**	Phil Collins	Virgin	8	(1)	
20	-	**You Are The One**	A-Ha	Warner	5		

This Mnth	Prev Mnth	Title	Artist	Label	Wks	(US 20 Pos)	
1	11	**Something's Gotten Hold Of My Heart**	Marc Almond Featuring Gene Pitney	Parlophone	9		
2	6	**The Living Years**	Mike + The Mechanics	WEA	7	(1)	F
3	-	**Love Train**	Holly Johnson	MCA	6	(65)	F
4	12	**You Got It**	Roy Orbison	Virgin	6	(9)	
5	-	**Love Changes Everything**	Michael Ball	Really Useful	8		F L
6	-	**My Prerogative**	Bobby Brown	MCA	6	(1)	F
7	14	**Cuddly Toy**	Roachford	CBS	5		F L
8	-	**Wait**	Robert Howard & Kym Mazelle	RCA	5		F L
9	-	**Belfast Child**	Simple Minds	Virgin	5		
10	-	**That's The Way Love Is**	Ten City	Atlantic	5		F L
11	-	**Fine Time**	Yazz	Big Life	4		
12	5	**She Drives Me Crazy**	Fine Young Cannibals	London	6	(1)	
13	-	**Last Of The Famous International Playboys**	Morrissey	HMV	2		
14	-	**Hold Me In Your Arms**	Rick Astley	RCA	4		
15	-	**Stop**	Sam Brown	A&M	7	(65)	F
16	1	**Especially For You**	Kylie Minogue/Jason Donovan	PWL	10		
17	-	**Leave Me Alone**	Michael Jackson	Epic	6		
18	2	**Crackers International (E.P.)**	Erasure	Mute	10		
19	-	**It's Only Love**	Simply Red	Elektra	2	(57)	
20	-	**Big Area**	Then Jerico	London	2		L

◆ A new album chart was introduced which contained only multi-artist albums, leaving the main chart for solo artist sets.
◆ American producers L.A. & Babyface had five singles simultaneously in the US Top 40. In Britain, Stock, Aitken & Waterman scored their 80th UK Top 75 hit in less than five years, and in March produced three of the Top 4 singles.
◆ The quasi-religious video for Madonna's transatlantic topper, 'Like A Prayer', caused a major controversy, resulting in Pepsi dropping an $8 million advertising campaign.

March 1989

This Mnth	Prev Mnth	Title	Artist	Label	Wks	(US 20 Pos)	
1	-	**Too Many Broken Hearts**	Jason Donovan	PWL	9		
2	-	**Help**	Bananarama/La Na Nee Nee Noo Noo	London	6		
3	15	**Stop**	Sam Brown	A&M	7	(65)	F
4	5	**Love Changes Everything**	Michael Ball	Really Useful	8		F L
5	-	**Can't Stay Away From You**	Gloria Estefan & The Miami Sound Machine	Epic	6	(6)	
6	17	**Leave Me Alone**	Michael Jackson	Epic	6		
7	-	**Hey Music Lover**	S'Express	Rhythm King	5		L
8	-	**This Time I Know It's For Real**	Donna Summer	Warner	8	(7)	
9	9	**Belfast Child**	Simple Minds	Virgin	5		
10	-	**Like A Prayer**	Madonna	Sire	7	(1)	
11	-	**Straight Up**	Paula Abdul	Siren	9	(1)	F
12	-	**I Don't Want A Lover**	Texas	Mercury	5	(77)	F
13	-	**Blow The House Down**	Living In A Box	Chrysalis	4		
14	-	**I'd Rather Jack**	Reynolds Girls	PWL	6		F L
15	-	**Keep On Movin'**	Soul II Soul Feat. Caron Wheeler	10	6	(11)	F
16	6	**My Prerogative**	Bobby Brown	MCA	6	(1)	F
17	-	**Turn Up The Bass**	Tyree Feat. Kool Rock Steady	ffrr	3		F L
18	-	**Every Rose Has Its Thorn**	Poison	Enigma	4	(1)	F
19	-	**Paradise City**	Guns N' Roses	Geffen	5	(5)	F
20	14	**Hold Me In Your Arms**	Rick Astley	RCA	4		

April 1989

This Mnth	Prev Mnth	Title	Artist	Label	Wks	(US 20 Pos)	
1	-	**Eternal Flame**	Bangles	CBS	9	(1)	L
2	10	**Like A Prayer**	Madonna	Sire	7	(1)	
3	11	**Straight Up**	Paula Abdul	Siren	9	(1)	F
4	-	**I Beg Your Pardon**	Kon Kan	Atlantic	7	(15)	F L
5	1	**Too Many Broken Hearts**	Jason Donovan	PWL	9		
6	8	**This Time I Know It's For Real**	Donna Summer	Warner	8	(7)	
7	-	**If You Don't Know Me By Now**	Simply Red	Elektra	7	(1)	
8	-	**Baby I Don't Care**	Transvision Vamp	MCA	8		
9	-	**Americanos**	Holly Johnson	MCA	7		
10	15	**Keep On Movin'**	Soul II Soul Feat. Caron Wheeler	10	6	(11)	F
11	19	**Paradise City**	Guns N' Roses	Geffen	5	(5)	F
12	-	**When Love Comes To Town**	U2 With B.B. King	Island	3	(68)	
13	-	**People Hold On**	Coldcut Feat. Lisa Stansfield	Ahead Of Our Time	4		L
14	-	**Good Thing**	Fine Young Cannibals	London	5	(1)	
15	14	**I'd Rather Jack**	Reynolds Girls	PWL	6		F L
16	-	**Lullaby**	Cure	Fiction	3	(74)	
17	-	**I Haven't Stopped Dancing Yet**	Pat & Mick	PWL	3		F L
18	-	**International Rescue**	Fuzzbox	WEA	4		F
19	-	**Don't Be Cruel**	Bobby Brown	MCA	3	(8)	
20	5	**Can't Stay Away From You**	Gloria Estefa/Miami Sound...	Epic	6	(6)	

◆ 1960s superstar Gene Pitney had his only No. 1 with a revival of his last Top 10 entry (from 1967), 'Something's Gotten Hold Of My Heart'. He shared billing on this re-recording with Marc Almond.

◆ TV's *Top Of The Pops* celebrated its 25th birthday.

◆ Wembley crowd-pullers included The Bee Gees, Bobby Brown, Bob Dylan, Elton John, R.E.M., Diana Ross and Stevie Wonder.

1989

This Mnth	Prev Mnth	Title	Artist	Label	Wks	(US 20 Pos)	
1	-	**Hand On Your Heart**	Kylie Minogue	PWL	7		
2	-	**Requiem**	London Boys	WEA	7		F
3	-	**Miss You Like Crazy**	Natalie Cole	EMI	8	(7)	
4	1	**Eternal Flame**	Bangles	CBS	9	(1)	L
5	-	**I Want It All**	Queen	Parlophone	4	(50)	
6	-	**Bring Me Edelweiss**	Edelweiss	WEA	5		F L
7	-	**Beds Are Burning**	Midnight Oil	CBS	5	(17)	F L
8	-	**Ferry 'Cross The Mersey**	Christians/Holly Johnson/Paul McCartney/Gerry Marsden & Stock Aitken Waterman	PWL	5		F L
9	8	**Baby I Don't Care**	Transvision Vamp	MCA	8		
10	-	**I'm Every Woman**	Chaka Khan	Warner	4		L
11	9	**Americanos**	Holly Johnson	MCA	7		
12	7	**If You Don't Know Me By Now**	Simply Red	Elektra	7	(1)	
13	-	**The Look**	Roxette	EMI	4	(1)	F
14	-	**Who's In The House**	Beatmasters	Rhythm King	4		
15	-	**Electric Youth**	Debbie Gibson	Atlantic	3	(11)	
16	-	**Every Little Step**	Bobby Brown	MCA	4	(3)	
17	-	**Your Mama Don't Dance**	Poison	Capitol	3	(10)	
18	14	**Good Thing**	Fine Young Cannibals	London	5	(1)	
19	-	**Manchild**	Neneh Cherry	Circa	5		
20	-	**Where Has All The Love Gone**	Yazz	Big Life	3		

1	-	**Sealed With A Kiss**	Jason Donovan	PWL	5		
2	3	**Miss You Like Crazy**	Natalie Cole	EMI	8	(7)	
3	-	**Express Yourself**	Madonna	Sire	5	(2)	
4	-	**The Best Of Me**	Cliff Richard	EMI	4		
5	-	**Right Back Where We Started From**	Sinitta	Fanfare	7	(84)	
6	-	**Back To Life (However Do You Want Me)**	Soul II Soul Featuring Caron Wheeler	10	10	(4)	
7	-	**Sweet Child O' Mine**	Guns N' Roses	Geffen	6	(1)	
8	8	**Ferry 'Cross The Mersey**	Christians, Holly Johnson etc.	PWL	5		F L
9	19	**Manchild**	Neneh Cherry	Circa	5		
10	-	**I Don't Wanna Get Hurt**	Donna Summer	Warner	5		
11	-	**On The Inside (Theme 'Prisoner- Cell Block H')**	Lynne Hamilton	A1	4		F L
12	-	**I Drove All Night**	Cyndi Lauper	Epic	6	(6)	
13	1	**Hand On Your Heart**	Kylie Minogue	PWL	7		
14	2	**Requiem**	London Boys	WEA	7		F
15	-	**Song For Whoever**	Beautiful South	Go! Discs	7		F
16	-	**It Is Time To Get Funky**	D. Mob Featuring LRS	London	5		
17	6	**Bring Me Edelweiss**	Edelweiss	WEA	5		F L
18	16	**Every Little Step**	Bobby Brown	MCA	4	(3)	
19	-	**Batdance**	Prince	Warner	5	(1)	
20	-	**Just Keep Rockin'**	Double Trouble & Rebel M.C.	Desire	7		F

◆ Stock, Aitken & Waterman scored a record three successive No. 1s with singles by Kylie Minogue, Jason Donovan and an all star group featuring Gerry (& The Pacemakers) Marsden, whose re-recording of 'Ferry Cross The Mersey' was the eighth charity chart topper in five years.

◆ Cliff Richard released his 100th single, 'The Best Of Me'. It coincided with the 100th anniversary of the first commercially released record.

This Mnth	Prev Mnth	Title	Artist	Label	Wks	(US 20 Pos)	
1	6	Back To Life (However Do You Want Me)	Soul II Soul Featuring Caron Wheeler	10	10	(4)	
2	-	London Nights	London Boys	Teldec/WEA	7		
3	15	Song For Whoever	Beautiful South	Go! Discs	7		F
4	-	You'll Never Stop Me From Loving You	Sonia	Chrysalis	8		F
5	-	Licence To Kill	Gladys Knight	MCA	7		L
6	-	It's Alright	Pet Shop Boys	Parlophone	4		
7	19	Batdance	Prince	Warner	5	(1)	
8	-	Ain't Nobody	Rufus & Chaka Khan	Warner	7	(22)	L
9	-	On Our Own	Bobby Brown	MCA	6	(2)	
10	-	Wind Beneath My Wings	Bette Midler	Atlantic	6	(1)	F L
11	12	I Drove All Night	Cyndi Lauper	Epic	6	(6)	
12	-	All I Want Is You	U2	Island	3	(83)	
13	-	Breakthru'	Queen	Parlophone	3		
14	-	Superwoman	Karyn White	Warner	4	(8)	F L
15	-	Don't Wanna Lose You	Gloria Estefan	Epic	6	(1)	
16	20	Just Keep Rockin'	Double Trouble & Rebel M.C.	Desire	7		F
17	5	Right Back Where We Started From	Sinitta	Fanfare	7	(84)	
18	-	Voodoo Ray (EP)	A Guy Called Gerald	Rham!	4		F L
19	1	Sealed With A Kiss	Jason Donovan	PWL	5		
20	-	Patience	Guns N' Roses	Geffen	3	(4)	

This	Prev	Title	Artist	Label	Wks	(US Pos)	
1	-	Swing The Mood	Jive Bunny & The Mastermixers	Music Factory	10	(11)	F
2	-	Wouldn't Change A Thing	Kylie Minogue	PWL	6		
3	-	French Kiss	Lil Louis	ffrr	7	(50)	F
4	-	Poison	Alice Cooper	Epic	7	(7)	L
5	4	You'll Never Stop Me From Loving...	Sonia	Chrysalis	8		F
6	15	Don't Wanna Lose You	Gloria Estefan	Epic	6	(1)	
7	-	Toy Soldiers	Martika	CBS	6	(1)	F
8	-	Too Much	Bros	CBS	4		
9	9	On Our Own	Bobby Brown	MCA	6	(2)	
10	-	You're History	Shakespear's Sister	ffrr	4		F
11	-	Losing My Mind	Liza Minnelli	Epic	3		F L
12	-	Ride On Time	Black Box	De Construction	14		F
13	-	Blame It On The Boogie	Big Fun	Jive	6		F
14	8	Ain't Nobody	Rufus & Chaka Khan	Warner	7	(22)	L
15	10	Wind Beneath My Wings	Bette Midler	Atlantic	6	(1)	F L
16	2	London Nights	London Boys	Teldec/WEA	7		
17	-	Hey D.J. I Can't Dance To That Music You're Playing/Ska Train	Beatmasters Featuring Betty Boo	Rhythm King	6		L
18	-	Days	Kirsty MacColl	Virgin	4		L
19	-	Do The Right Thing	Redhead Kingpin & The FBI	10	3		F L
20	1	Back To Life (However Do You ...)	Soul II Soul/Caron Wheeler	10	10	(4)	

◆ Madonna scored a record 16th successive Top 5 single in the USA with 'Cherish'. In the UK Kylie Minogue's 'Wouldn't Change A Thing' was the fourth of her six singles to enter in runner-up position (surprisingly she never had a record enter at No. 1).
◆ Paul McCartney started his first world tour for 13 years in Sweden, and The Pet Shop Boys, who chalked up their 12th Top 20 hit with 'It's Alright', toured the UK for the first time.

1989

This Mnth	Prev Mnth	Title	Artist	Label	Wks	(US 20 Pos)	
1	12	Ride On Time	Black Box	De Construction	14		F
2	1	Swing The Mood	Jive Bunny & Mastermixers	Music Factory	10	(11)	F
3	-	Sowing The Seeds Of Love	Tears For Fears	Fontana	5	(2)	
4	-	Right Here Waiting	Richard Marx	EMI	7	(1)	F
5	13	Blame It On The Boogie	Big Fun	Jive	6		F
6	-	Every Day (I Love You More)	Jason Donovan	PWL	4		
7	-	I Need Your Lovin'	Alyson Williams	Def Jam	7		L
8	-	The Time Warp	Damian	Jive	5		F L
9	-	The Best	Tina Turner	Capitol	7	(15)	
10	-	I Just Don't Have The Heart	Cliff Richard	EMI	5		
11	-	Numero Uno	Starlight	City Beat	6		F L
12	17	Hey D.J. I Can't Dance To That Music You're Playing/Ska Train	Beatmasters Featuring Betty Boo	Rhythm King	6		L
13	-	Pump Up The Jam	Technotronic Featuring Felly	Swanyard	9	(2)	F
14	-	Cherish	Madonna	Sire	5	(2)	
15	4	Poison	Alice Cooper	Epic	7	(7)	L
16	-	If Only I Could	Sydney Youngblood	Circa	9		F
17	7	Toy Soldiers	Martika	CBS	6	(1)	F
18	3	French Kiss	Lil Louis	ffrr	7	(50)	F
19	2	Wouldn't Change A Thing	Kylie Minogue	PWL	6		
20	-	Personal Jesus	Depeche Mode	Mute	3	(28)	

This Mnth	Prev Mnth	Title	Artist	Label	Wks	(US 20 Pos)	
1	1	Ride On Time	Black Box	De Construction	14		F
2	13	Pump Up The Jam	Technotronic Featuring Felly	Swanyard	9	(2)	F
3	16	If Only I Could	Sydney Youngblood	Circa	9		F
4	-	Street Tuff	Rebel MC/Double Trouble	Desire	8		L
5	-	That's What I Like	Jive Bunny & The Mastermixers	Music Factory	8	(69)	
6	-	We Didn't Start The Fire	Billy Joel	CBS	6	(1)	
7	-	Girl I'm Gonna Miss You	Milli Vanilli	Cooltempo	8	(1)	L
8	-	Sweet Surrender	Wet Wet Wet	Precious	5		
9	-	Drama!	Erasure	Mute	4		
10	-	If I Could Turn Back Time	Cher	Geffen	7	(3)	
11	-	Leave A Light On	Belinda Carlisle	Virgin	6	(11)	
12	-	You Keep It All In	Beautiful South	Go! Discs	5		
13	4	Right Here Waiting	Richard Marx	EMI	7	(1)	F
14	-	Room In Your Heart	Living In A Box	Chrysalis	7		L
15	9	The Best	Tina Turner	Capitol	7	(15)	
16	-	Wishing On A Star	Fresh 4 Featuring Lizz E	10	3		F L
17	-	Chocolate Box	Bros	CBS	2		
18	-	Name And Number	Curiosity Killed The Cat	Mercury	3		
19	-	The Road To Hell (Pt. 2)	Chris Rea	WEA	5		
20	14	Cherish	Madonna	Sire	5	(2)	

◆ In September, Italian records held the top three places in the UK dance chart with the chart topping 'Ride On Time' by Black Box outselling all other singles in 1989.

◆ Phonogram bought Island Records for $480 (£300) million with shareholders U2 making $48 (£30) million from the deal.

◆ Richard Marx's debut UK Top 20 entry, 'Right Here Waiting', had been his sixth successive US Top 3 entry.

November 1989

This Mnth	Prev Mnth	Title	Artist	Label	Wks	20 (US Pos)	
1	-	All Around The World	Lisa Stansfield	Arista	7	(3)	
2	7	Girl I'm Gonna Miss You	Milli Vanilli	Cooltempo	8	(1)	L
3	5	That's What I Like	Jive Bunny & The Mastermixers	Music Factory	8	(69)	L
4	-	Never Too Late	Kylie Minogue	PWL	5		
5	-	Another Day In Paradise	Phil Collins	Virgin	5	(1)	
6	4	Street Tuff	Rebel MC/Double Trouble	Desire	8		L
7	-	I Feel The Earth Move	Martika	CBS	6	(25)	
8	14	Room In Your Heart	Living In A Box	Chrysalis	7		L
9	-	You Got It (The Right Stuff)	New Kids On The Block	CBS	8	(3)	F
10	11	Leave A Light On	Belinda Carlisle	Virgin	6	(11)	
11	-	Don't Know Much	Linda Ronstadt (featuring Aaron Neville)	Elektra	7	(2)	L
12	-	Grand Piano	Mixmaster	BCM	4		F L
13	10	If I Could Turn Back Time	Cher	Geffen	7	(3)	
14	19	The Road To Hell (Pt. 2)	Chris Rea	WEA	5		
15	-	Infinite Dreams	Iron Maiden	EMI	2		
16	1	Ride On Time	Black Box	De Construction	14		F
17	-	I Want That Man	Deborah Harry	Chrysalis	4		L
18	-	Never Too Much (89 Remix)	Luther Vandross	Epic	3	(33)	
19	-	C'mon And Get My Love	D. Mob Featuring Cathy Dennis	Ffrr	4	(10)	
20	3	If Only I Could	Sydney Youngblood	Circa	9		F

December 1989

This Mnth	Prev Mnth	Title	Artist	Label	Wks	20 (US Pos)	
1	11	Don't Know Much	Linda Ronstadt (featuring Aaron Neville)	Elektra	7	(2)	L
2	9	You Got It (The Right Stuff)	New Kids On The Block	CBS	8	(3)	F
3	-	Lambada	Kaoma	CBS	9	(46)	F L
4	-	When You Come Back To Me	Jason Donovan	PWL	8		
5	-	Get A Life	Soul II Soul	10	8	(54)	
6	-	Eve Of The War	Jeff Wayne	CBS	6		F L
7	-	Let's Party	Jive Bunny & The Mastermixers	Music Factory	5		
8	-	I Don't Wanna Lose You	Tina Turner	Capitol	5	(9)	
9	-	Donald Where's Your Troosers	Andy Stewart	Stone	5	(77)	F L
10	-	Dear Jessie	Madonna	Sire	6		
11	-	Do They Know It's Christmas?	Band Aid II	PWL/Polydor	4		F L
12	-	Homely Girl	UB40	Dep International	4		
13	-	Can't Shake The Feeling	Big Fun	Jive	5		
14	-	Got To Get	Rob 'n' Raz Featuring Leila K	Arista	9		F L
15	1	All Around The World	Lisa Stansfield	Arista	7	(3)	
16	-	Fool's Gold/What The World Is Waiting For	Stone Roses	Silvertone	4		F
17	5	Another Day In Paradise	Phil Collins	Virgin	5	(1)	
18	-	In Private	Dusty Springfield	Parlophone	4		L
19	-	Sister	Bros	CBS	3		
20	-	Pacific	808 State	ZTT	4		F

◆ Jive Bunny & The Mastermixers scored a third successive No. 1 with their third release 'Let's Party', equalling the record set by Gerry & The Pacemakers and Frankie Goes To Hollywood.

◆ Stock, Aitken & Waterman produced a record breaking 11 of the year's Top 40 British singles.
◆ The decade ended with Band Aid II (a collection of current UK stars) topping the chart with an update of 'Do They Know It's Christmas'.

1990

January 1990

This Mnth	Prev Mnth	Title	Artist	Label	Wks	(US 20 Pos)	
1	-	Hangin' Tough	New Kids On The Block	CBS	6	(1)	
2	5	Get A Life	Soul II Soul	10	8	(54)	
3	4	When You Come Back To Me	Jason Donovan	PWL	8		
4	-	Touch Me	49ers	4th & Broadway	7		F
5	14	Got To Get	Rob 'n' Raz Featuring Leila K	Arista	9		F L
6	-	Got To Have Your Love	Mantronix Featuring Wondress	Capitol	7	(82)	F
7	-	Tears On My Pillow	Kylie Minogue	PWL	6		
8	-	The Magic Number/Buddy	De La Soul	Big Life	5		
9	11	Do They Know It's Christmas?	Band Aid II	PWL/Polydor	4		F L
10	10	Dear Jessie	Madonna	Sire	6		
11	3	Lambada	Kaoma	CBS	9	(46)	F L
12	-	Put Your Hands Together	D. Mob Featuring Nuff Juice	London	4		L
13	-	You Make Me Feel (Mighty Real)	Jimmy Somerville	London	4	(87)	
14	-	Going Back To My Roots/ Rich In Paradise	FPI Project	Rumour	4		F L
15	-	Deep Heat '89	Latino Rave	Deep Heat	6		F L
16	-	Could Have Told You So	Halo James	Epic	5		F L
17	7	Let's Party	Jive Bunny & The Mastermixers	Music Factory	5		
18	-	Listen To Your Heart	Sonia	Chrysalis	3		
19	-	Nothing Compares 2 U	Sinead O'Connor	Ensign	10	(1)	F L
20	9	Donald Where's Your Troosers	Andy Stewart	Stone	5	(77)	F L

February 1990

This Mnth	Prev Mnth	Title	Artist	Label	Wks	(US 20 Pos)	
1	19	Nothing Compares 2 U	Sinead O'Connor	Ensign	10	(1)	F L
2	-	Get Up (Before The Night Is Over)	Technotronic Feat. Ya Kid K	Swanyard	7	(7)	
3	-	Happenin' All Over Again	Lonnie Gordon	Supreme	6		F L
4	7	Tears On My Pillow	Kylie Minogue	PWL	6		
5	6	Got To Have Your Love	Mantronix Featuring Wondress	Capitol	7	(82)	F
6	-	I Wish It Would Rain Down	Phil Collins	Virgin	5	(3)	
7	-	Dub Be Good To Me	Beats International Featuring Lindy Layton	Go Beat	10	(76)	F
8	4	Touch Me	49ers	4th & Broadway	7		F
9	-	Walk On By	Sybil	PWL	5	(74)	
10	-	Instant Replay	Yell!	Fanfare	4		F L
11	-	I Don't Know Anybody Else	Black Box	Deconstruction	5	(23)	
12	16	Could Have Told You So	Halo James	Epic	5		F L
13	-	Live Together	Lisa Stansfield	Arista	3		
14	-	Nothing Ever Happens	Del Amitri	A&M	4		F
15	1	Hangin' Tough	New Kids On The Block	CBS	6	(1)	
16	-	Enjoy The Silence	Depeche Mode	Mute	6	(8)	
17	-	Just Like Jesse James	Cher	Geffen	4	(8)	
18	13	You Make Me Feel (Mighty Real)	Jimmy Somerville	London	4	(87)	
19	-	18 And Life	Skid Row	Atlantic	2	(4)	F
20	-	How Am I Supposed To Live Without You	Michael Bolton	CBS	6	(1)	F

◆ Ruby Turner became the first female British singer to top the US black music chart. A month later Lisa Stansfield followed in her footsteps.

◆ In February female-fronted singles held the top five places. Chart topper Sinead O'Connor also became the first Irish woman to top the LP chart.

March 1990

This Mnth	Prev Mnth	Title	Artist	Label	Wks	(US 20 Pos)	
1	7	Dub Be Good To Me	Beats International/Lindy Layton	Go Beat	10	(76)	F
2	20	How Am I Supposed To Live...	Michael Bolton	CBS	6	(1)	F
3	-	The Brits 1990	Various Artists	RCA	5		F L
4	-	Infinity	Guru Josh	Deconstruction	5		F L
5	-	Love Shack	B-52's	Reprise	8	(3)	
6	1	Nothing Compares 2 U	Sinead O'Connor	Ensign	10	(1)	F
7	-	Blue Savannah	Erasure	Mute	7		
8	-	That Sounds Good To Me	Jive Bunny & Mastermixers	Music Factory	3		
9	-	Moments In Soul	JT And The Big Family	Champion	4		F L
10	-	Lily Was Here	David A. Stewart Featuring Candy Dulfer	Anxious	7	(11)	F L
11	-	I'll Be Loving You (Forever)	New Kids On The Block	CBS	4	(1)	
12	16	Enjoy The Silence	Depeche Mode	Mute	6	(8)	
13	11	I Don't Know Anybody Else	Black Box	Deconstruction	5	(23)	
14	-	Strawberry Fields Forever	Candy Flip	Debut	7		F L
15	2	Get Up (Before The Night Is Over)	Technotronic Feat. Ya Kid K	Swanyard	7	(7)	
16	-	The Power	Snap	Arista	10	(2)	F
17	-	Elephant Stone	Stone Roses	Silvertone	2		
18	-	Downtown Train	Rod Stewart	Warner	4	(3)	
19	-	Black Betty	Ram Jam	Epic	3		L
20	-	Birdhouse In Your Soul	They Might Be Giants	Elektra	6		F L

April 1990

		Title	Artist	Label	Wks	(US Pos)	
1	-	Vogue	Madonna	Sire	10	(1)	
2	16	The Power	Snap	Arista	10	(2)	F
3	-	Black Velvet	Alannah Myles	Atlantic	8	(1)	F L
4	-	Kingston Town	UB40	Dep International	8		
5	-	Don't Miss The Partyline	Bizz Nizz	Cooltempo	5		F L
6	5	Love Shack	B-52's	Reprise	8	(3)	
7	-	Step On	Happy Mondays	Factory	7	(57)	
8	-	Hang On To Your Love	Jason Donovan	PWL	4		
9	-	All I Wanna Do Is Make Love To You	Heart	Capitol	8	(2)	
10	14	Strawberry Fields Forever	Candy Flip	Debut	7		F L
11	20	Birdhouse In Your Soul	They Might Be Giants	Elektra	6		F L
12	-	Opposites Attract	Paula Abdul (with The Wild Pair)	Siren	9	(1)	
13	-	Ghetto Heaven	Family Stand	Atlantic	8		F L
14	10	Lily Was Here	David A. Stewart/Candy Dulfer	Anxious	7	(11)	F L
15	7	Blue Savannah	Erasure	Mute	7		
16	-	This Beat Is Technotronic	Technotronic Feat. MC Eric	Swanyard	3		
17	-	Killer	Adamski	MCA	13		
18	-	Mamma Gave Birth To The Soul Children	Queen Latifah & De La Soul	Tommy Boy	4		F L
19	1	Dub Be Good To Me	Beats International/Lindy Layton	Go Beat	10	(76)	F
20	-	Everybody Needs Somebody To Love	Blues Brothers	Atlantic	3		F L

◆ Phil Collins' ...But Seriously sold a million in Britain in a record five weeks, topping the charts for 15 weeks. Oddly, for a week in February, Collins' 'I Wish It Would Rain Down' was the only male vocal record in the UK Top 10!

◆ The biggest recorded audience for a one act pop show was broken by Paul McCartney who attracted 184,000 to the Maracana Stadium in Brazil.

1990

This Mnth	Prev Mnth	Title	Artist	Label	Wks	(US 20 Pos)	
1	17	Killer	Adamski	MCA	13		
2	-	Dirty Cash	Adventures Of Stevie V	Mercury	9	(25)	F L
3	12	Opposites Attract	Paula Abdul (with The Wild Pair)	Siren	9	(1)	
4	1	Vogue	Madonna	Sire	10	(1)	
5	-	Better The Devil You Know	Kylie Minogue	PWL	6		
6	3	Black Velvet	Alannah Myles	Atlantic	8	(1)	F L
7	-	Cover Girl	New Kids On The Block	CBS	5	(2)	
8	-	A Dream's A Dream	Soul II Soul	Virgin	4	(85)	
9	4	Kingston Town	UB40	Dep International	8		
10	-	Hold On	En Vogue	Atlantic	6	(2)	F
11	2	The Power	Snap	Arista	10	(2)	F
12	9	All I Wanna Do Is Make Love To You	Heart	Capitol	8	(2)	
13	-	Won't Talk About It	Beats International	Go Beat	5	(76)	L
14	13	Ghetto Heaven	Family Stand	Atlantic	8		F L
15	-	Take Your Time	Mantronix Featuring Wondress	Capitol	4		L
16	7	Step On	Happy Mondays	Factory	7	(57)	
17	-	I Still Haven't Found What I'm Looking For	Chimes	CBS	5		F L
18	-	How Can We Be Lovers	Michael Bolton	CBS	4	(3)	
19	-	November Spawned A Monster	Morrissey	HMV	2		
20	-	Something Happened On The Way To Heaven	Phil Collins	Virgin	3	(4)	

This Mnth	Prev Mnth	Title	Artist	Label	Wks	(US 20 Pos)	
1	-	World In Motion	Englandneworder	Factory	9		L
2	1	Killer	Adamski	MCA	13		
3	-	Hear The Drummer (Get Wicked)	Chad Jackson	Big Wave	6		F L
4	-	Doin' The Doo	Betty Boo	Rhythm King	7		F
5	-	Sacrifice/Healing Hands	Elton John	Rocket	10	(18)	
6	-	Venus	Don Pablo's Animals	Rumour	6		F L
7	-	It Must Have Been Love	Roxette	EMI	9	(1)	
8	2	Dirty Cash	Adventures Of Stevie V	Mercury	9	(25)	F L
9	-	Step By Step	New Kids On The Block	CBS	3	(1)	
10	-	The Only One I Know	Charlatans	Situation Two	5		F
11	5	Better The Devil You Know	Kylie Minogue	PWL	6		
12	-	Oops Up	Snap	Arista	8	(35)	
13	-	Hold On	Wilson Phillips	SBK	7	(1)	F
14	-	Nessun Dorma	Luciano Pavarotti	Decca	6		F
15	10	Hold On	En Vogue	Atlantic	6	(2)	F L
16	17	I Still Haven't Found What I'm...	Chimes	CBS	5		F L
17	-	Star	Erasure	Mute	4		
18	-	The Only Rhyme That Bites	MC Tunes Versus 808 State	ZTT	6		F
19	-	Papa Was A Rolling Stone	Was (Not Was)	Fontana	3		
20	7	Cover Girl	New Kids On The Block	CBS	5	(2)	

◆ Stars at a Wembley show, celebrating the release of Nelson Mandela from a South African prison, included Tracy Chapman, Peter Gabriel, Patti Labelle, Simple Minds and Neil Young. An all-star John Lennon tribute show in Liverpool featured Natalie Cole, Terence Trent D'Arby, Roberta Flack, Daryll Hall & John Oates, Cyndi Lauper, Kylie Minogue and Wet Wet Wet. Headliners at a huge charity show at Knebworth included Phil Collins, Paul McCartney, Pink Floyd and Status Quo.

1990

July 1990

This Mnth	Prev Mnth	Title	Artist	Label	Wks	(US 20 Pos)	
1	5	Sacrifice/Healing Hands	Elton John	Rocket	10	(18)	
2	-	Mona	Craig McLachlan & Check 1-2	Epic	8		F
3	7	It Must Have Been Love	Roxette	EMI	9	(1)	
4	14	Nessun Dorma	Luciano Pavarotti	Decca	6		F
5	-	U Can't Touch This	M.C. Hammer	Capitol	11	(8)	F
6	-	Thunderbirds Are Go	FAB Featuring MC Parker	Brothers Org.	5		F L
7	12	Oops Up	Snap	Arista	8	(35)	
8	1	World In Motion	Englandneworder	Factory	9		L
9	-	Close To You	Maxi Priest	10	6	(1)	
10	-	Turtle Power	Partners In Kryme	SBK	8	(13)	F L
11	-	One Love	Stone Roses	Silvertone	4		
12	13	Hold On	Wilson Phillips	SBK	7	(1)	F
13	-	She Ain't Worth It	Glenn Medeiros Featuring Bobby Brown	London	4	(1)	L
14	-	Hanky Panky	Madonna	Sire	6	(10)	
15	18	The Only Rhyme That Bites	MC Tunes Versus 808 State	ZTT	6		F
16	-	I'm Free	Soup Dragons	Big Life	8	(79)	F L
17	-	Rockin' Over The Beat	Technotronic Featuring Ya Kid K	Swanyard	5	(95)	
18	-	Naked In The Rain	Blue Pearl	W.A.U.!Mr.Modo	9		F
19	-	Thinking Of You	Maureen	Urban	4		F L
20	4	Doin' The Doo	Betty Boo	Rhythm King	7		F

August 1990

This Mnth	Prev Mnth	Title	Artist	Label	Wks	(US 20 Pos)	
1	10	Turtle Power	Partners In Kryme	SBK	8	(13)	F L
2	-	Tom's Diner	DNA Featuring Suzanne Vega	A&M	7	(5)	F
3	18	Naked In The Rain	Blue Pearl	W.A.U.!Mr.Modo	9		F
4	5	U Can't Touch This	M.C. Hammer	Capitol	11	(8)	F
5	16	I'm Free	Soup Dragons	Big Life	8	(79)	F L
6	14	Hanky Panky	Madonna	Sire	6	(10)	
7	-	Tonight	New Kids On The Block	CBS	8	(7)	
8	-	Itsy Bitsy Teeny Weeny Yellow Polka Dot Bikini	Bombalurina	Carpet	8		F
9	1	Sacrifice/Healing Hands	Elton John	Rocket	10	(18)	
10	-	Thieves In The Temple	Prince	Paisley Park	3	(6)	
11	17	Rockin' Over The Beat	Technotronic Feat. Ya Kid K	Swanyard	5	(95)	
12	-	Listen To Your Heart/Dangerous	Roxette	EMI	5	(1)	
13	2	Mona	Craig McLachlan & Check 1-2	Epic	8		F
14	-	Hardcore Uproar	Together	Ffrr	4		F L
15	-	LFO	LFO	Warp	3		F L
16	-	Where Are You Baby?	Betty Boo	Rhythm King	6		
17	-	California Dreamin'/Carry The Blame	River City People	EMI	5		F L
18	-	Blaze Of Glory	Jon Bon Jovi	Vertigo	3	(1)	F L
19	3	It Must Have Been Love	Roxette	EMI	9	(1)	
20	-	Tricky Disco	Tricky Disco	Warp	3		F L

◆ Pink Floyd's *The Wall* show in Berlin drew 200,000 people and an estimated one billion saw it on TV. Among those appearing were Bryan Adams, The Band, Van Morrison, Sinead O'Connor and The Scorpions.

◆ Elton John's 'Sacrifice'/'Healing Hands' not only helped him equal Elvis Presley's American record of (at least) one Top 40 hit a year for 21 years, it also gave him his first British solo chart topper.

1990

This Mnth	Prev Mnth	Title	Artist	Label	Wks	(US 20 Pos)	
1	-	**The Joker**	Steve Miller Band	Capitol	7		L
2	-	**Groove Is In The Heart**	Deee-Lite	Elektra	8	(4)	F L
3	-	**Four Bacharach & David Songs (EP)**	Deacon Blue	CBS	6		
4	8	**Itsy Bitsy Teeny Weeny Yellow Polka Dot Bikini**	Bombalurina	Carpet	8		F
5	-	**What Time Is Love**	KLF/Children Of The Revolution	KLF Comms.	7	(57)	F
6	16	**Where Are You Baby?**	Betty Boo	Rhythm King	6		
7	7	**Tonight**	New Kids On The Block	CBS	8	(7)	
8	-	**Vision Of Love**	Mariah Carey	CBS	5	(1)	F
9	-	**The Space Jungle**	Adamski	MCA	4		L
10	-	**Show Me Heaven**	Maria McKee	Epic	9		F L
11	-	**Groovy Train**	Farm	Produce	5	(41)	F
12	-	**Praying For Time**	George Michael	Epic	4	(1)	
13	-	**Holy Smoke**	Iron Maiden	EMI	2		
14	3	**Naked In The Rain**	Blue Pearl	W.A.U.!Mr.Modo	9		F
15	-	**I've Been Thinking About You**	Londonbeat	Anxious	7	(1)	L
16	12	**Listen To Your Heart**	Roxette	EMI	5	(1)	
17	-	**Can Can You Party**	Jive Bunny & The Mastermixers	Music Factory	3		
18	-	**Rhythm Of The Rain**	Jason Donovan	PWL	2		
19	2	**Tom's Diner**	DNA Featuring Suzanne Vega	A&M	7	(5)	F
20	-	**Silhouettes**	Cliff Richard	EMI	4		

This Mnth	Prev Mnth	Title	Artist	Label	Wks	(US 20 Pos)	
1	10	**Show Me Heaven**	Maria McKee	Epic	9		F L
2	-	**Blue Velvet**	Bobby Vinton	Epic	8		L
3	-	**The Anniversary Waltz - Part 1**	Status Quo	Vertigo	6		
4	15	**I've Been Thinking About You**	Londonbeat	Anxious	7	(1)	L
5	-	**I Can't Stand It**	Twenty 4 Seven Featuring Captain Hollywood	BCM	6		F
6	-	**Megamix**	Technotronic	Swanyard	5		L
7	-	**A Little Time**	Beautiful South	Go! Discs	8		
8	-	**So Hard**	Pet Shop Boys	Parlophone	3	(62)	
9	-	**Have You Seen Her**	M.C. Hammer	Capitol	4	(4)	
10	2	**Fascinating Rhythm**	Bass-O-Matic	Virgin	5		F L
11	2	**Groove Is In The Heart**	Deee-Lite	Elektra	8	(4)	F L
12	1	**The Joker**	Steve Miller Band	Capitol	7		L
13	-	**It's A Shame (My Sister)**	Monie Love Feat. True Image	Cooltempo	4	(26)	
14	-	**Let's Try Again/Didn't I Blow Your Mind**	New Kids On The Block	CBS	3	(53)	
15	-	**I'm Your Baby Tonight**	Whitney Houston	Arista	6	(1)	
16	11	**Groovy Train**	Farm	Produce	5	(41)	F
17	-	**Unchained Melody**	Righteous Brothers	Verve	11	(13)	
18	-	**Kinky Afro**	Happy Mondays	Factory	4		
19	-	**From A Distance**	Cliff Richard	EMI	3		
20	-	**Cult Of Snap**	Snap	Arista	3		

◆ Steve Miller's 1974 US No. 1, 'The Joker', finally repeated that feat in the UK after it was heard in a TV advertisement for Levi jeans.

◆ Bobby Vinton's 1963 US chart topper, 'Blue Velvet', hit in Britain as Berlin's 'Take My Breath Away' returned. The Righteous Brothers' 'You've Lost That Lovin' Feeling' spent a record third time in the Top 10, and the duo's 25-year-old 'Unchained Melody' became the year's top seller.

November 1990

This Mnth	Prev Mnth	Title	Artist	Label	Wks	(US 20 Pos)	
1	17	Unchained Melody	Righteous Brothers	Verve	11	(13)	
2	7	A Little Time	Beautiful South	Go! Discs	8		
3	-	Don't Worry	Kim Appleby	Parlophone	8		F
4	-	Take My Breath Away	Berlin	CBS	6		L
5	-	Step Back In Time	Kylie Minogue	PWL	4		
6	-	(We Want) The Same Thing	Belinda Carlisle	MCA	5		
7	-	Fog On The Tyne (Revisited)	Gazza And Lindisfarne	Best	4		F L
8	-	Fantasy	Black Box	De Construction	6		
9	15	I'm Your Baby Tonight	Whitney Houston	Arista	6	(1)	
10	-	I'll Be Your Baby Tonight	Robert Palmer And UB40	EMI	6		
11	1	Show Me Heaven	Maria McKee	Epic	9		F L
12	-	Unbelievable	EMF	Parlophone	8	(1)	F
13	-	To Love Somebody	Jimmy Somerville	London	4		
14	-	Working Man	Rita McNeil	Polydor	4		F L
15	18	Kinky Afro	Happy Mondays	Factory	4		
16	-	Cubik/Olympic	808 State	ZTT	3		
17	-	Ice Ice Baby	Vanilla Ice	SBK	10	(1)	F
18	3	The Anniversary Waltz - Part 1	Status Quo	Vertigo	6		
19	-	Close To Me	Cure	Elektra	3	(97)	
20	2	Blue Velvet	Bobby Vinton	Epic	8		L

December 1990

This Mnth	Prev Mnth	Title	Artist	Label	Wks	(US 20 Pos)	
1	17	Ice Ice Baby	Vanilla Ice	SBK	10	(1)	F
2	12	Unbelievable	EMF	Parlophone	8	(1)	F
3	1	Unchained Melody	Righteous Brothers	Verve	11	(13)	
4	-	Saviour's Day	Cliff Richard	EMI	6		
5	-	Justify My Love	Madonna	Sire	6	(1)	
6	-	All Together Now	Farm	Produce	8		
7	3	Don't Worry	Kim Appleby	Parlophone	8		F
8	-	You've Lost That Lovin' Feeling/Ebb Tide	Righteous Brothers	Verve	6		L
9	-	Kinky Boots	Patrick MacNee & Honor Blackman	Deram	4		F L
10	-	Wicked Game	Chris Isaak	London	5	(6)	F
11	-	Mary Had A Little Boy	Snap	Arista	6		
12	-	Pray	M.C. Hammer	Capitol	7	(2)	
13	-	Sadness Part 1	Enigma	Virgin Int.	9	(5)	
14	-	It Takes Two	Rod Stewart & Tina Turner	Warner Bros.	4		
15	-	Falling	Julee Cruise	Warner Bros.	4		F L
16	-	This One's For The Children	New Kids On The Block	CBS	4	(7)	
17	8	Fantasy	Black Box	Deconstruction	6		
18	-	The Grease Megamix	John Travolta/O. Newton-John	Polydor	6		L
19	-	Just This Side Of Love	Malandra Burrows	YTV	4		F L
20	-	King Of The Road (EP)	Proclaimers	Chrysalis	3		L

◆ In October, for the first time since March 1986, there were no Stock Aitken & Waterman records in the Top 40. They had produced over 100 Top 75 entries.
◆ New Kids On The Block scored their seventh Top 10 single in 1990 equalling Bill Haley & The Comets' 1956 record.

NKOTB reportedly earned $115 million in 1990.
◆ Queen, who had not graced the American Top 20 since 1984, signed a $10 million deal with the Walt Disney-owned Hollywood label.

1991

January 1991

This Mnth	Prev Mnth	Title	Artist	Label	Wks	(US 20 Pos)	
1	13	**Sadness Part 1**	Enigma	Virgin Int.	9	(5)	
2	-	**Crazy**	Seal	ZTT	9	(8)	F
3	18	**The Grease Megamix**	John Travolta/O. Newton-John	Polydor	6		L
4	1	**Ice Ice Baby**	Vanilla Ice	SBK	10	(1)	F
5	-	**Bring Your Daughter...To The Slaughter**	Iron Maiden	EMI	3		
6	6	**All Together Now**	Farm	Produce	8		
7	-	**Gonna Make You Sweat**	C&C Music Factory/F. Williams	CBS	6	(1)	F
8	-	**3 A.M. Eternal**	KLF/Children Of The Revolution	KLF Comms.	8	(5)	
9	-	**(I've Had) The Time Of My Life**	Bill Medley & Jennifer Warnes	RCA	4		L
10	8	**You've Lost That Lovin' Feeling**	Righteous Brothers	Verve	6		L
11	12	**Pray**	M.C. Hammer	Capitol	7	(2)	
12	11	**Mary Had A Little Boy**	Snap	Arista	6		
13	-	**International Bright Young Thing**	Jesus Jones	Food	3		F L
14	-	**I Can't Take The Power**	Off-Shore	CBS	4		F L
15	5	**Justify My Love**	Madonna	Sire	6	(1)	
16	-	**Mercy Mercy Me - I Want You**	Robert Palmer	EMI	4	(16)	L
17	-	**Innuendo**	Queen	Parlophone	3		
18	4	**Saviour's Day**	Cliff Richard	EMI	6		
19	-	**The Total Mix**	Black Box	Deconstruction	4		
20	-	**All The Man That I Need**	Whitney Houston	Arista	3	(1)	

February 1991

1	-	**Do The Bartman**	Simpsons	Geffen	10		F
2	8	**3 A.M. Eternal**	KLF/Children Of The Revolution	KLF Comms.	8	(5)	
3	-	**Wiggle It**	2 In A Room	Big Life	6	(15)	F L
4	-	**(I Wanna Give You) Devotion**	Nomad/MC Mikee Freedom	Rumour	8		F
5	-	**What Do I Have To Do**	Kylie Minogue	PWL	5		
6	-	**Only You**	Praise	Epic	5		F L
7	-	**I Believe**	EMF	Parlophone	4		
8	-	**Hippychick**	Soho	S&M	5	(14)	F L
9	-	**Get Here**	Oleta Adams	Fontana	7	(5)	F L
10	-	**Cry For Help**	Rick Astley	RCA	5	(7)	L
11	2	**Crazy**	Seal	ZTT	9	(8)	F
12	-	**Play That Funky Music**	Vanilla Ice	SBK	4	(4)	L
13	17	**Innuendo**	Queen	Parlophone	3		
14	1	**Sadness Part 1**	Enigma	Virgin Int.	9	(5)	
15	-	**You Got The Love**	Source Featuring Candi Staton	Truelove	7		F
16	-	**G.L.A.D.**	Kim Appleby	Parlophone	3		
17	7	**Gonna Make You Sweat**	C&C Music Factory/F. Williams	CBS	6	(1)	F
18	-	**In Yer Face**	808 State	ZTT	4		
19	-	**All Right Now**	Free	Island	5		L
20	16	**Mercy Mercy Me - I Want You**	Robert Palmer	EMI	4	(16)	L

◆ Another spate of re-entries hit the UK Top 20 including records by Bill Medley & Jennifer Warnes, The Clash, Madonna, John Travolta & Olivia Newton-John and Free, while Patsy Cline's 1961 American hit, 'Crazy' made its UK debut.

◆ Eric Clapton played a record 24 nights at London's prestigious Royal Albert Hall.

◆ Michael Jackson, whose Bad album had now passed the 25 million sales mark globally, signed the world's biggest record deal (reportedly worth somewhere between $50 million and a billion!) with Sony.

March 1991

This Mnth	Prev Mnth	Title	Artist	Label	Wks	(US 20 Pos)	
1	-	Should I Stay Or Should I Go	Clash	CBS	6		
2	15	You Got The Love	Source Featuring Candi Staton	Truelove	7		F
3	1	Do The Bartman	Simpsons	Geffen	10		F
4	-	The Stonk	Hale & Pace & The Stonkers	London	5		F L
5	-	Crazy For You	Madonna	Sire	4		
6	-	Because I Love You (Postman Song)	Stevie B	LMR	6	(1)	F L
7	-	Move Your Body (Elevation)	Xpansions	Optimism	5		F L
8	-	Joyride	Roxette	EMI	7	(1)	
9	4	(I Wanna Give You) Devotion	Nomad/MC Mikee Freedom	Rumour	8		F
10	-	The One And Only	Chesney Hawkes	Chrysalis	6	(10)	F L
11	-	It's Too Late	Quartz Introducing Dina Carroll	Mercury	6		F L
12	-	Rhythm Of My Heart	Rod Stewart	Warner Bros.	8		
13	19	All Right Now	Free	Island	5		L
14	9	Get Here	Oleta Adams	Fontana	7	(5)	F L
15	-	Where The Streets Have No Name-Can't Take My Eyes Off You/How Can You Expect To Be Taken Seriously	Pet Shop Boys	EMI	4	(72)	
16	-	Love Rears It's Ugly Head	Living Colour	Epic	5		F L
17	2	3 A.M. Eternal	KLF/Children Of The Revolution	KLF Comms.	8	(5)	
18	-	Let There Be Love	Simple Minds	Virgin	4		
19	18	In Yer Face	808 State	ZTT	4		
20	-	Secret Love	Bee Gees	Warner Bros.	5		

April 1991

This Mnth	Prev Mnth	Title	Artist	Label	Wks	(US 20 Pos)	
1	-	Sit Down	James	Fontana	8		F
2	-	The Whole Of The Moon	Waterboys	Ensign	6		F L
3	10	The One And Only	Chesney Hawkes	Chrysalis	6	(10)	F L
4	12	Rhythm Of My Heart	Rod Stewart	Warner	8		
5	-	Rescue Me	Madonna	Sire	5	(9)	
6	-	The Size Of A Cow	Wonder Stuff	Polydor	5		
7	8	Joyride	Roxette	EMI	7	(1)	
8	-	Deep, Deep Trouble	Simpsons Feat. Bart & Homer	Geffen	5	(69)	L
9	-	Love & Kisses	Dannii Minogue	MCA	5		F
10	-	Human Nature	Gary Clail On-U Sound System	Perfecto	5		F L
11	-	Anthem	N-Joi	Deconstruction	5		F
12	20	Secret Love	Bee Gees	Warner	5		
13	-	I've Got News For You	Feargal Sharkey	Virgin	4		L
14	11	It's Too Late	Quartz Introducing Dina Carroll	Mercury	6		F L
15	18	Let There Be Love	Simple Minds	Virgin	4		
16	-	The Shoop Shoop Song (It's In His Kiss)	Cher	Geffen	11	(33)	
17	15	Where The Streets Have No Name...	Pet Shop Boys	EMI	4	(72)	
18	-	Snap Mega Mix	Snap	Arista	3		
19	-	Sailing On The Seven Seas	OMD	Virgin	8		
20	4	The Stonk	Hale & Pace & The Stonkers	London	5		F L

◆ Despite the fact that The Simpsons cartoon TV series was only seen by a minority of the British public who had satellite or cable TV, the single, 'Do The Bartman', took the quirky quintet to the top.

◆ New Kids On The Block ended their European tour at Wembley. They had played 31 dates and grossed $8.8 million.

1991

This Mnth	Prev Mnth	Title	Artist	Label	Wks	(US 20 Pos)	
1	16	**The Shoop Shoop Song** (It's In His...)	Cher	Geffen	11	(33)	
2	-	**Last Train To Trancentral**	KLF	KLF Comms.	7		
3	19	**Sailing On The Seven Seas**	OMD	Virgin	8		
4	-	**Senza Una Donna** (Without A Woman)	Zucchero & Paul Young	London	6		F
5	-	**Touch Me (All Night Long)**	Cathy Dennis	Polydor	6	(2)	
6	-	**Promise Me**	Beverley Craven	Epic	8		F L
7	-	**There's No Other Way**	Blur	Food	5	(82)	F
8	-	**Gypsy Woman (La Da Dee)**	Crystal Waters	A&M	6	(8)	F
9	-	**Get The Message**	Electronic	Factory	4		
10	-	**Born Free**	Vic Reeves/The Roman Numerals	Sense	4		F
11	1	**Sit Down**	James	Fontana	8		F
12	-	**Tainted Love**	Soft Cell/Marc Almond	Mercury	5		L
13	-	**Ring Ring Ring (Ha Ha Hey)**	De La Soul	Big Life	4		L
14	2	**The Whole Of The Moon**	Waterboys	Ensign	6		F L
15	-	**Future Love (EP)**	Seal	ZTT	3		
16	-	**Fading Like A Flower** (Every Time You Leave)	Roxette	EMI	3	(2)	
17	-	**I Wanna Sex You Up**	Color Me Badd	Giant	9	(2)	F
18	-	**Quadrophonia**	Quadrophonia	ARS	2		F L
19	-	**Anasthasia**	T99	Citybeat	2		F L
20	-	**Baby Baby**	Amy Grant	A&M	7	(1)	F

This Mnth	Prev Mnth	Title	Artist	Label	Wks	(US 20 Pos)	
1	17	**I Wanna Sex You Up**	Color Me Badd	Giant	9	(2)	F
2	1	**The Shoop Shoop Song** (It's In His Kiss)	Cher	Geffen	11	(33)	
3	20	**Baby Baby**	Amy Grant	A&M	7	(1)	F L
4	6	**Promise Me**	Beverley Craven	Epic	8		F L
5	-	**Shiny Happy People**	R.E.M.	Warner	6	(10)	
6	9	**Gypsy Woman (La Da Dee)**	Crystal Waters	A&M	6	(8)	F
7	-	**Thinking About Your Love**	Kenny Thomas	Cooltempo	8		
8	-	**Shocked**	Kylie Minogue	PWL	4		
9	-	**Any Dream Will Do**	Jason Donovan	Really Useful	9		
10	-	**Do You Want Me**	Salt-N-Pepa	ffrr	6	(21)	
11	12	**Tainted Love**	Soft Cell/Marc Almond	Mercury	5		L
12	-	**Light My Fire**	Doors	Elektra	3		L
13	-	**Only Fools (Never Fall In Love)**	Sonia	IQ	5		
14	-	**Holiday**	Madonna	Sire	3		
15	2	**Last Train To Trancentral**	KLF	KLF	7		
16	5	**Touch Me (All Night Long)**	Cathy Dennis	Polydor	6	(2)	
17	5	**Touch Me (All Night Long)**	Cathy Dennis	Polydor	6	(2)	
18	-	**Move That Body**	Technotronic Featuring Reggie	Ars	3		
19	-	**The Motown Song**	Rod Stewart	Warner Bros.	4	(10)	
20	-	**Success**	Dannii Minogue	MCA	3		

◆ As sister Dannii scored her second successive hit, Kylie Minogue became the first artist to see her first 13 hit singles all go into the Top 10.

◆ Small Faces' singer Steve Marriott died in a fire, and ex-Temptation David Ruffin died of drug-related causes.

◆ For the first time three consecutive No. 1s came from films. 'The One And Only' (*Buddy's Song*), 'The Shoop Shoop Song' (*Mermaids*) and 'I Wanna Sex You Up' (*New Jack City*).

1991

July 1991

This Mnth	Prev Mnth	Title	Artist	Label	Wks (US 20 Pos)	
1	-	(Everything I Do) I Do It For You	Bryan Adams	A&M	22 (1)	G
2	9	Any Dream Will Do	Jason Donovan	Really Useful	9	
3	-	Chorus	Erasure	Mute	6	
4	-	Rush Rush	Paula Abdul	Virgin	7 (1)	
5	7	Thinking About Your Love	Kenny Thomas	Cooltempo	8	
6	-	You Could Be Mine	Guns n' Roses	Geffen	7 (29)	
7	-	Now That We've Found Love	Heavy D. & The Boyz	MCA	8 (11)	F L
8	-	Always There	Incognito Featuring Jocelyn Brown	Talkin' Loud	5	F
9	1	I Wanna Sex You Up	Color Me Badd	Giant	9 (2)	F
10	10	Do You Want Me	Salt-N-Pepa	Ffrr	6 (21)	
11	-	Things That Make You Go Hmmmm....	C&C Music Factory	Columbia	7 (4)	L
12	-	7 Ways To Love	Cola Boy	Arista	4	F L
13	-	Pandora's Box	OMD	Virgin	5	L
14	-	Are You Mine?	Bros	Columbia	3	L
15	-	It Ain't Over 'Til It's Over	Lenny Kravitz	Virgin America	4 (2)	F
16					5	L
17	-	Love And Understanding	Cher	Geffen	5 (17)	L
18	-	I Touch Myself	Divinyls	Virgin America	5 (4)	F L
19	-	More Than Words	Extreme	A&M	8 (1)	
20	19	The Motown Song	Rod Stewart	Warner Bros	4 (10)	

August 1991

This Mnth	Prev Mnth	Title	Artist	Label	Wks (US 20 Pos)	
1	1	(Everything I Do) I Do It For You	Bryan Adams	A&M	22 (1)	G
2	19	More Than Words	Extreme	A&M	8 (1)	
3	-	I'm Too Sexy	Right Said Fred	Tug	12 (1)	F
4	-	Move Any Mountain	Shamen	One Little Indian	7 (38)	F
5	7	Now That We've Found Love	Heavy D. & The Boyz	MCA	8 (11)	F L
6	-	All For Love	Color Me Badd	Giant	6 (1)	L
7	-	Winter In July	Bomb The Bass	Rhythm King	5	L
8	-	Set Adrift On Memory Bliss	P.M. Dawn	Gee Street	5 (1)	F
9	11	Things That Make You Go Hmmmm....	C&C Music Factory	Columbia	7 (4)	L
10	-	Summertime	D.J. Jazzy Jeff & The Fresh Prince	Jive	5 (4)	F
11	-	Twist & Shout	Deacon Blue	Columbia	4	
12	13	Pandora's Box	OMD	Virgin	5	L
13	2	Any Dream Will Do	Jason Donovan	Really Useful	9	
14	-	Charly	Prodigy	XL	7	F
15	-	Enter Sandman	Metallica	Vertigo	2 (16)	
16	6	You Could Be Mine	Guns n' Roses	Geffen	7 (29)	
17	-	Sunshine On A Rainy Day	Zoe	M&G	9	F L
18	-	Jump To The Beat	Dannii Minogue	MCA	3	
19	-	Happy Together	Jason Donovan	PWL	4	
20	17	Love And Understanding	Cher	Geffen	5 (17)	

◆ Bryan Adams's recording of '(Everything I Do) I Do It For You' was the world's top selling single in 1991. It sold over three million in America and became the first million seller for six years in Britain, where it spent a record 16 successive weeks at the top.

◆ Of the current wave of new UK chart makers only EMF, Jesus Jones, The KLF, Cathy Dennis and Seal were selling well in the USA.

1991

This Mnth	Prev Mnth	Title	Artist	Label	Wks	(US 20 Pos)	
1	1	(Everything I Do) I Do It For You	Bryan Adams	A&M	22	(1)	G
2	3	I'm Too Sexy	Right Said Fred	Tug	11	(1)	F
3	-	Insanity	Oceanic	Dead Dead Good	11		F
4	14	Charly	Prodigy	XL	7		F
5	17	Sunshine On A Rainy Day	Zoe	M&G	9		F L
6	-	Let's Talk About Sex	Salt-N-Pepa	ffrr	9	(13)	
7	-	Gett Off	Prince/New Power Generation	Paisley Park	5	(21)	
8	-	What Can You Do For Me	Utah Saints	ffrr	7		F
9	-	I'll Be Back	Arnee & The Terminaters	Epic	4		F L
10	-	Love...Thy Will Be Done	Martika	Columbia	5	(10)	
11	-	Love To Hate You	Erasure	Mute	6		
12	-	Peace	Sabrina Johnson	East West	6		F L
13	8	Set Adrift On Memory Bliss	P.M. Dawn	Gee Street	5	(1)	F
14	-	Everybody's Free (To Feel Good)	Rozalla	Pulse 8	6	(37)	F
15	6	All For Love	Color Me Badd	Giant	6	(1)	L
16	-	20th Century Boy	Marc Bolan & T. Rex	Marc On Wax	4		L
17	-	Don't Cry	Guns N' Roses	Geffen	2	(10)	
18	2	More Than Words	Extreme	A&M	8	(1)	
19	-	Good Vibrations	Marky Mark & The Funky Bunch Featuring Loleatta Holloway	Interscope	3	(1)	F L
20	-	Something Got Me Started	Simply Red	East West	4	(23)	

This Mnth	Prev Mnth	Title	Artist	Label	Wks	(US 20 Pos)	
1	1	(Everything I Do) I Do It For You	Bryan Adams	A&M	22	(1)	G
2	-	Wind Of Change	Scorpions	Mercury	7	(4)	F L
3	3	Insanity	Oceanic	Dead Dead Good	11		F
4	6	Let's Talk About Sex	Salt-N-Pepa	ffrr	9	(13)	
5	-	Saltwater	Julian Lennon	Virgin	6		L
6	11	Love To Hate You	Erasure	Mute	6		
7	14	Everybody's Free (To Feel Good)	Rozalla	Pulse 8	6	(37)	F
8	-	Always Look On The Bright Side Of Life	Monty Python	Virgin	5		F L
9	-	World In Union	Kiri Te Kanawa	Columbia	7		F L
10	-	Get Ready For This	2 Unlimited	PWL Continental	8	(76)	F
11	12	Peace	Sabrina Johnson	East West	6		F L
12	5	Sunshine On A Rainy Day	Zoe	M&G	9		F L
13	2	I'm Too Sexy	Right Said Fred	Tug	11	(1)	F
14	-	Best Of You	Kenny Thomas	Cooltempo	3		
15	-	Such A Feeling	Bizarre Inc	Vinyl Solution	5		F
16	-	Change	Lisa Stansfield	Arista	4	(30)	
17	-	Live Your Life Be Free	Belinda Carlisle	Virgin	3		
18	-	Dizzy	Vic Reeves & The Wonder Stuff	Sense	8		
19	20	Something Got Me Started	Simply Red	East West	4	(23)	
20	-	Baby Love	Dannii Minogue	MCA	2		

◆ Opera singer Luciano Pavarotti topped the LP chart with Essential Pavarotti II. In America his In Concert album completed a year at the helm of the classical chart.

◆ In 1991, more singles charted than ever. Records tended to enter higher and have shorter chart life spans.

November 1991

This Mnth	Prev Mnth	Title	Artist	Label	Wks	(US 20 Pos)	
1	18	**Dizzy**	Vic Reeves & The Wonder Stuff	Sense	8		
2	10	**Get Ready For This**	2 Unlimited	PWL Continental	8	(76)	F
3	1	**(Everything I Do) I Do It For You**	Bryan Adams	A&M	22	(1)	G
4	-	**Rhythm Is A Mystery**	K-Klass	De Construction	4		F
5	-	**The Fly**	U2	Island	3	(58)	
6	-	**If You Were Here With Me Now**	Kylie Minogue/K. Washington	PWL	5		
7	9	**World In Union**	Kiri Te Kanawa	Columbia	7		F L
8	-	**Activ 8 (Come With Me)**	Altern 8	Network	5		F
9	-	**Is There Anybody Out There?**	Bassheads	Deconstruction	4		F
10	-	**Black Or White**	Michael Jackson	Epic	9	(1)	
11	-	**No Son Of Mine**	Genesis	Virgin	3	(12)	
12	-	**Playing With Knives**	Bizarre Inc	Vinyl Solution	3		
13	2	**Wind Of Change**	Scorpions	Mercury	7	(4)	F L
14	8	**Always Look On The Bright SideOf Life**	Monty Python	Virgin	5		F L
15	-	**American Pie**	Don McLean	Liberty	4		L
16	-	**Killer (EP)**	Seal	ZTT	3	(100)	
17	-	**When A Man Loves A Woman**	Michael Bolton	Columbia	3	(1)	
18	-	**Go**	Moby	Outer-Rhythm	4		F
19	3	**Insanity**	Oceanic	Dead Dead Good	11		F
20	-	**DJs Take Control/Way In My Brain**	SL2	XL	2		F

December 1991

This Mnth	Prev Mnth	Title	Artist	Label	Wks	(US 20 Pos)	
1	-	**Don't Let The Sun Go Down On Me**	George Michael/Elton John	Epic	6	(1)	
2	-	**When You Tell Me That You Love Me**	Diana Ross	EMI	9		
3	-	**Justified And Ancient**	KLF/Tammy Wynette	KLF Communications	9	(11)	
4	10	**Black Or White**	Michael Jackson	Epic	9	(1)	
5	-	**Driven By You**	Brian May	Parlophone	6		F
6	-	**Ride Like The Wind**	East Side Beat	Ffrr	7		F L
7	-	**Too Blind To See It**	Kym Sims	Atco	8	(38)	F
8	-	**Stars**	Simply Red	East West	6	(44)	
9	-	**Bohemian Rhapsody/These Are The Days Of Our Lives**	Queen	Parlophone	10	(2)	G
10	-	**Don't Talk Just Kiss**	Right Said Fred/Jocelyn Brown	Tug	7	(76)	
11	-	**Live And Let Die**	Guns n' Roses	Geffen	4	(33)	
12	8	**Activ 8 (Come With Me)**	Altern 8	Network	5		F
13	-	**Smells Like Teen Spirit**	Nirvana	DGC	3	(6)	F
14	-	**We Should Be Together**	Cliff Richard	EMI	3		
15	-	**Rocket Man (I Think It's Going To Be A Long Long Time)**	Kate Bush	Mercury	4		
16	1	**Dizzy**	Vic Reeves & WonderStuff	Sense	8		L
17	-	**If You Go Away**	New Kids On The Block	Columbia	2		L
18	-	**Addams Groove**	Hammer	Capitol	7	(7)	
19	-	**Sound**	James	Fontana	3		
20	-	**Bare Necessities Megamix**	UK Mixmasters	Connect	4		F L

◆ The Top 6 all came from different countries: Ireland, England, Holland, Canada, New Zealand and Germany.

◆ The Rolling Stones signed to Virgin for a $40 million advance, while Madonna's new deal guaranteed her at least $5 million per album.

◆ Freddie Mercury died. His group Queen ended the year as Britain's top album act and top singles group, and their Greatest Hits album was certified as a three million seller.

1992

This Mnth	Prev Mnth	Title	Artist	Label	Wks	(US 20 Pos)	
1	9	Bohemian Rhapsody/These Are The Days Of OurLives	Queen	Parlophone	10	(2)	G
2	3	Justified And Ancient	KLF/Tammy Wynette	KLF Communications	9	(11)	
3	7	Too Blind To See It	Kym Sims	Atco	8	(38)	F
4	19	Addams Groove	Hammer	Capitol	7	(7)	
5	10	Don't Talk Just Kiss	Right Said Fred/Jocelyn Brown	Tug	7	(76)	
6	-	Goodnight Girl	Wet Wet Wet	Precious	9		
7	-	Everybody In The Place (EP)	Prodigy	XL	5		
8	2	When You Tell Me That You Love Me	Diana Ross	EMI	9		
9	-	We Got A Love Thang	Ce Ce Peniston	A&M	5	(20)	F
10	17				5		F L
11	1	Don't Let The Sun Go Down On Me	George Michael/Elton John	Epic	6	(1)	
12	-	God Gave Rock & Roll To You II	Kiss	Interscope	5		L
13	11	Live And Let Die	Guns n' Roses	Geffen	4	(33)	
14	-	I Can't Dance	Genesis	Virgin	5	(7)	
15	5	Driven By You	Brian May	Parlophone	6		F
16	4	Black Or White	Michael Jackson	Epic	9	(1)	
17	-	Give Me Just A Little More Time	Kylie Minogue	PWL	5		
18	-	Different Strokes	Isotonik	Ffrreedom	2		F L
19	-	Feel So High	Des'ree	Dusted Sound	4		F
20	-	(Can You) Feel The Passion	Blue Pearl	Big Life	3		L

This	Prev	Title	Artist	Label	Wks	(US Pos)	
1	6	Goodnight Girl	Wet Wet Wet	Precious	9		
2	-	Stay	Shakespears Sister	London	14	(4)	
3	-	Twilight Zone	2 Unlimited	PWL Continental	7	(49)	
4	-	I'm Doing Fine Now	Pasadenas	Columbia	7		
5	-	I Wonder Why	Curtis Stigers	Arista	6	(9)	F
6	17	Give Me Just A Little More Time	Kylie Minogue	PWL	5		
7	-	Remember The Time	Michael Jackson	Epic	4	(3)	
8	-	My Girl	Temptations	Epic	8		L
9	1	Bohemian Rhapsody/These Are The Days Of Our Lives	Queen	Parlophone	10	(2)	G
10	-	The Bouncer	Kicks Like A Mule	Tribal Bass	4		F L
11	-	For Your Babies	Simply Red	East West	5		
12	12	God Gave Rock & Roll To You II	Kiss	Interscope	5		L
13	-	I Love Your Smile	Shanice	Motown	7	(2)	F L
14	14	I Can't Dance	Genesis	Virgin	5	(7)	
15	-	It's A Fine Day	Opus III	PWL Int	5		F L
16	7	Everybody In The Place (EP)	Prodigy	XL	5		
17	-	Thought I'd Died And Gone To Heaven	Bryan Adams	A&M	4	(13)	
18	-	Welcome To The Cheap Seats (EP)	Wonder StufF	Polydor	3		
19	-	Dixie-Narco (EP)	Primal Scream	Creation	2		
20	-	It Must Be Love	Madness	Virgin	5		L

◆ Following Freddie Mercury's death, Queen had the top 4 music videos and 'Bohemian Rhapsody' became the first record ever to top the charts twice (selling over a million on both occasions). Its double A-side, 'These Are The Days Of Our Lives', was voted Record of The Year at the Brit Awards.

◆ UK acts inducted into the *Rock And Roll Hall Of Fame* between 1989 and 1992 were Eric Clapton, The Kinks, Jimmy Page and The Who.

1992

March 1992

This Mnth	Prev Mnth	Title	Artist	Label	Wks	(US Pos)
1	2	**Stay**	Shakespears Sister	London	14	(4)
2	13	**I Love Your Smile**	Shanice	Motown	7	(2) F L
3	8	**My Girl**	Temptations	Epic	8	L
4	-	**America: What Time Is Love?**	KLF	KLF Communications	4	(57) L
5	-	**Weather With You**	Crowded House	Capitol	5	
6	15	**It's A Fine Day**	Opus III	PWL Int	5	
7	-	**November Rain**	Guns n' Roses	Geffen	3	(3)
8	-	**Tears In Heaven**	Eric Clapton	Reprise	5	(2) L
9	-	**Finally**	Ce Ce Peniston	A&M	6	(5)
10	-	**To Be With You**	Mr. Big	Atlantic	7	(1) F L
11	20	**It Must Be Love**	Madness	Virgin	5	L
12	-	**One**	U2	Island	2	
13	4	**I'm Doing Fine Now**	Pasadenas	Columbia	7	
14	-	**Deeply Dippy**	Right Said Fred	Tug	10	
15	-	**Come As You Are**	Nirvana	DGC	2	(32)
16	-	**Human Touch**	Bruce Springsteen	Columbia	2	(16) L
17	-	**I Know**	New Atlantic	3 Beat	4	F L
18	17	**Thought I'd Died And Gone To Heaven**	Bryan Adams	A&M	4	(13)
19	-	**Let's Get Rocked**	Def Leppard	Bludgeon Riffola	4	(15)
20	-	**Dragging Me Down**	Inspiral Carpets	Cow	3	

April 1992

This Mnth	Prev Mnth	Title	Artist	Label	Wks	(US Pos)
1	14	**Deeply Dippy**	Right Said Fred	Tug	10	
2	1	**Stay**	Shakespears Sister	London	14	(4)
3	10	**To Be With You**	Mr. Big	Atlantic	7	(1) F L
4	-	**Save The Best For Last**	Vanessa Williams	Polydor	7	(1) F L
5	-	**Joy**	Soul II Soul	Ten	4	L
6	9	**Finally**	Ce Ce Peniston	A&M	6	(5)
7	-	**Why**	Annie Lennox	RCA	5	(34) F
8	19	**Let's Get Rocked**	Def Leppard	Bludgeon Riffola	4	(15)
9	-	**Evapor 8**	Altern 8	Network	3	
10	-	**On A Ragga Tip**	SL2	XL	9	L
11	-	**You're All That Matters To Me**	Curtis Stigers	Arista	7	(98) L
12	-	**Breath Of Life**	Erasure	Mute	4	
13	-	**(I Want To Be) Elected**	Mr. Bean & Smear Campaign	London	3	F L
14	-	**Viva Las Vegas**	ZZ Top	Warner	4	
15	8	**Tears In Heaven**	Eric Clapton	Reprise	5	(2) L
16	-	**You**	Ten Sharp	Columbia	7	F L
17	-	**Be Quick Or Be Dead**	Iron Maiden	EMI	2	
18	-	**Take My Advice**	Kym Sims	Atco	2	(86) L
19	-	**Time To Make You Mine**	Lisa Stansfield	Arista	4	
20	-	**The Only Living Boy In New Cross**	Carter-USM	Big Cat	3	

◆ The KLF announced they were quitting the music business, on stage at the Brit Awards where they were voted Best British Group. Their 'Justified And Ancient' gave guest vocalist Tammy Wynette the highest placed US pop hit of her career.

◆ Bruce Springsteen's latest albums Human Touch and Lucky Town entered the UK chart in positions 1 and 2 (Nos. 2 and 3 in the USA) - the feat is more remarkable considering only three days' sales were taken into account - the albums were released on a Thursday rather than Monday as is usual in Britain.

1992

This Mnth	Prev Mnth	Title	Artist	Label	Wks	(US 20 Pos)	
1	-	Please Don't Go	KWS	Network	12	(6)	F
2	10	On A Ragga Tip	SL2	XL	9		L
3	-	Hang On In There Baby	Curiosity	RCA	6		L
4	1	Deeply Dippy	Right Said Fred	Tug	10		
5	-	The Days Of Pearly Spencer	Marc Almond	Some Bizzare	4		L
6	-	Workaholic	2 Unlimited	PWL Continental	4		
7	-	My Lovin'	En Vogue	East West America	5	(2)	
8	11	You're All That Matters To Me	Curtis Stigers	Arista	7	(98)	L
9	-	Everything About You	Ugly Kid Joe	Mercury	7	(9)	F
10	-	Nothing Else Matters	Metallica	Vertigo	3	(35)	
11	-	Knockin' On Heaven's Door	Guns N' Roses	Geffen	6		
12	-	Temple Of Love (1992)	Sisters Of Mercy	Merciful Release	3		
13	15	You	Ten Sharp	Columbia	7		F L
14	-	I Don't Care	Shakespears Sister	London	4	(55)	
15	-	In The Closet	Michael Jackson	Epic	3	(6)	
16	4	Save The Best For Last	Vanessa Williams	Polydor	7	(1)	F L
17	-	Beauty And The Beast	Celine Dion & Peabo Bryson	Epic	3	(9)	F
18	-	Keep On Walkin'	Ce Ce Peniston	A&M	3	(15)	
19	-	Song For Love	Extreme	A&M	3		
20	20	The Only Living Boy In New Cross	Carter-Unstoppable Sex Machine	Big Cat	3		

This Mnth	Prev Mnth	Title	Artist	Label	Wks	(US 20 Pos)	
1	1	Please Don't Go	KWS	Network	12	(6)	F
2	-	Hazard	Richard Marx	Capitol	10	(9)	
3	-	Jump	Kris Kross	Ruffhouse	6	(1)	F
4	-	Abba-Esque (EP)	Erasure	Mute	8		
5	-	Something Good	Utah Saints	ffrr	7	(98)	
6	-	Heartbeat	Nick Berry	Columbia	5		L
7	-	Toofunky	George Michael	Epic	5	(10)	
8	9	Everything About You	Ugly Kid Joe	Mercury	7	(9)	F
9	-	It Only Takes A Minute	Take That	RCA	6		F
10	11	Knockin' On Heaven's Door	Guns N' Roses	Geffen	6		
11	-	The One	Elton John	Rocket	5	(9)	
12	-	Friday, I'm In Love	Cure	Fiction	4	(18)	L
13	-	Blue Room	Orb	Big Life	3		F
14	2	On A Ragga Tip	SL2	XL	9		L
15	7	My Lovin'	En Vogue	East West America	5	(2)	
16	-	Midlife Crisis	Faith No More	Slash	2		F
17	-	Even Better Than The Real Thing	U2	Island	6	(32)	
18	-	Ain't 2 Proud 2 Beg	TLC	Arista	3	(6)	F
19	-	I'll Be There	Mariah Carey	Columbia	6	(1)	
20	14	I Don't Care	Shakespears Sister	London	4	(55)	

◆ Stars appearing in a successful tribute show for Freddie Mercury at Wembley included David Bowie, Def Leppard, Guns N' Roses, Elton John, Metallica, George Michael, Liza Minnelli, Robert Plant, Queen, Lisa Stansfield and U2.

◆ U2, who at times had seven albums on the UK chart, signed a £10 ($15) million publishing deal with Phonogram.
◆ Erasure's 17th Top 20 entry, the Abba tribute 'Abba-Esque', was their first chart topper. It also headed the list in Abba's homeland, Sweden.

1992

July 1992

This Mnth	Prev Mnth	Title	Artist	Label	Wks	(US 20 Pos)	
1	4	**Abba-Esque (EP)**	Erasure	Mute	8		
2	19	**I'll Be There**	Mariah Carey	Columbia	6	(1)	
3	-	**Rhythm Is A Dancer**	Snap	Arista	16	(5)	
4	-	**Ain't No Doubt**	Jimmy Nail	East West	9		
5	-	**Sesame's Treet**	Smart E's	Suburban Base	6	(60)	F L
6	2	**Hazard**	Richard Marx	Capitol	10	(9)	
7	-	**A Trip To Trumpton**	Urban Hype	Faze	5		F L
8	5	**Something Good**	Utah Saints	ffrr	7	(98)	
9	17	**Even Better Than The Real Thing**	U2	Island	6	(32)	
10	-	**One Shining Moment**	Diana Ross	EMI	6		
11	-	**Sexy MF/Strollin'**	Prince/New Power Generation	Paisley Park	4	(66)	
12	6	**Heartbeat**	Nick Berry	Columbia	5		L
13	-	**I Drove All Night**	Roy Orbison	MCA	6		
14	-	**Disappointed**	Electronic	Parlophone	2		L
15	-	**L.S.I.**	Shamen	One Little Indian	6		
16	1	**Please Don't Go**	KWS	Network	12	(6)	F L
17	7	**Toofunky**	George Michael	Epic	5	(10)	
18	-	**Shake Your Head**	Was (Not Was)	Fontana	8		L
19	-	**This Used To Be My Playground**	Madonna	Sire	6	(1)	
20	9	**It Only Takes A Minute**	Take That	RCA	6		F

August 1992

This Mnth	Prev Mnth	Title	Artist	Label	Wks	(US 20 Pos)	
1	3	**Rhythm Is A Dancer**	Snap	Arista	16	(5)	
2	4	**Ain't No Doubt**	Jimmy Nail	East West	9		
3	-	**Achy Breaky Heart**	Billy Ray Cyrus	Mercury	8	(4)	F L
4	-	**Barcelona**	Freddie Mercury & Montserrat Caballe	Polydor	5		
5	19	**This Used To Be My Playground**	Madonna	Sire	6	(1)	
6	18	**Shake Your Head**	Was (Not Was)	Fontana	8		L
7	-	**Just Another Day**	Jon Secada	SBK	10	(5)	F L
8	-	**The Best Things In Life Are Free**	Luther Vandross/Janet Jackson	Epic	10	(10)	L
9	-	**Don't You Want Me**	Felix	Deconstruction	8		F
10	15	**L.S.I.**	Shamen	One Little Indian	6		
11	5	**Sesame's Treet**	Smart E's	Suburban Base	6	(60)	F L
12	13	**I Drove All Night**	Roy Orbison	MCA	6		
13	-	**Baker Street**	Undercover	PWL International	11		F
14	-	**This Charming Man**	Smiths	WEA	2		
15	-	**Book Of Days**	Enya	WEA	3		
16	-	**Who Is It**	Michael Jackson	Epic	4	(14)	
17	-	**Rock Your Baby**	KWS	Network	4		L
18	-	**How Do You Do!**	Roxette	EMI	4	(58)	
19	-	**Magic Friend**	2 Unlimited	PWL Continental	4		
20	7	**A Trip To Trumpton**	Urban Hype	Faze	5		F L

◆ Elton John overtook The Beatles when he collected his 50th US Top 40 entry with 'The One'. Madonna's 'This Used To Be My Playground', not only gave her a (female) record 10th American No. 1, but also meant she had more UK Top 10 hits than The Beatles.

◆ Morrissey sold out the Hollywood Bowl in 23 minutes breaking another record set by The Beatles.
◆ Elvis Presley's estate received 110 gold and platinum records which went on display at Graceland.

1992

This Mnth	Prev Mnth	Title	Artist	Label	Wks	(US 20 Pos)	
1	1	Rhythm Is A Dancer	Snap	Arista	16	(5)	
2	-	Ebeneezer Goode	Shamen	One Little Indian	8		
3	13	Baker Street	Undercover	PWL Int.	11		F
4	8	The Best Things In Life Are Free	Luther Vandross/Janet Jackson	Epic	10	(10)	
5	-	Too Much Love Will Kill You	Brian May	Parlophone	6		
6	7	Just Another Day	Jon Secada	SBK	10	(5)	F L
7	-	It's My Life	Dr. Alban	Arista	9	(88)	F
8	-	My Destiny	Lionel Richie	Motown	9		L
9	3	Achy Breaky Heart	Billy Ray Cyrus	Mercury	8	(4)	F L
10	-	Walking On Broken Glass	Annie Lennox	RCA	5	(14)	
11	9	Don't You Want Me	Felix	Deconstruction	8		F
12	-	House Of Love	East 17	London	4		F
13	-	Theme From M*A*S*H/ (...) I Do It For You	Manic Street Preachers/ Fatima Mansions	Columbia	4		
14	-	Iron Lion Zion	Bob Marley & The Wailers	Tuff Gong	5		
15	17	Rock Your Baby	KWS	Network	4		L
16	-	Jam	Michael Jackson	Epic	2	(26)	
17	-	Take This Heart	Richard Marx	Capitol	2	(20)	
18	4	Barcelona	Freddie Mercury & Montserrat Caballe	Polydor	5		
19	-	Fire/Jericho	Prodigy	XL	2		
20	-	Rest In Peace	Extreme	A&M	2	(96)	

This Mnth	Prev Mnth	Title	Artist	Label	Wks	(US 20 Pos)	
1	-	Sleeping Satellite	Tasmin Archer	EMI	9	(32)	F
2	-	End Of The Road	Boyz II Men	Motown	12	(1)	F
3	7	It's My Life	Dr. Alban	Arista	9	(88)	F
4	2	Ebeneezer Goode	Shamen	One Little Indian	8		
5	-	I'm Gonna Get You	Bizarre Inc	Vinyl Solution	8	(47)	
6	3	Baker Street	Undercover	PWL International	11		
7	-	Erotica	Madonna	Maverick/sire	5	(3)	
8	-	Tetris	Doctor Spin	Carpet	5		F L
9	14	Iron Lion Zion	Bob Marley & The Wailers	Tuff Gong	5		L
10	-	A Million Love Songs (EP)	Take That	RCA	5		
11	8	My Destiny	Lionel Richie	Motown	9		L
12	-	Love Song/Alive And Kicking	Simple Minds	Virgin	3		L
13	-	Keep The Faith	Bon Jovi	Jambco	4	(29)	
14	-	My Name Is Prince	Prince & The New Power Generation	Paisley Park	3	(36)	
15	-	People Everyday	Arrested Development	Cooltempo	8	(8)	F
16	-	Sentinel	Mike Oldfield	WEA	3		L
17	1	Rhythm Is A Dancer	Snap	Arista	16	(5)	
18	4	The Best Things In Life Are Free	Luther Vandross & Janet Jackson	Epic	10	(10)	
19	5	Too Much Love Will Kill You	Brian May	Parlophone	6		
20	13	Theme From M*A*S*H/ (...) I Do It For You	Manic Street Preachers/ Fatima Mansions	Columbia	4		

◆ Motown hitmaker Mary Wells, reggae star Jackie Edwards and Tony Williams, the voice of The Platters, all died.

◆ American shows by Elton John, George Michael, Lionel Richie, Madonna and Billy Idol raised over $7 million for AIDS research. At the same time, Elton signed his publishing to Warner for a world record $26 million.

November 1992

This Mnth	Prev Mnth	Title	Artist	Label	Wks	(US 20 Pos)	
1	2	**End Of The Road**	Boyz II Men	Motown	12	(1)	F L
2	15	**People Everyday**	Arrested Development	Cooltempo	8	(8)	F
3	-	**Would I Lie To You?**	Charles & Eddie	Capitol	12	(13)	L
4	-	**Boss Drum**	Shamen	One Little Indian	5		
5	-	**Never Let Her Slip Away**	Undercover	PWL International	5		L
5	-	**Run To You**	Rage	Pulse 8	5		F L
7	-	**I Will Always Love You**	Whitney Houston	Arista	17	(1)	G
8	-	**Be My Baby**	Vanessa Paradis	Remark	6		L
9	-	**Supermarioland**	Ambassadors Of Funk/MC Mario	Living Beat	5		F L
10	5	**I'm Gonna Get You**	Bizarre Inc	Vinyl Solution	8	(47)	
11	-	**(Take A Little) Piece Of My Heart**	Erma Franklin	Epic	5		F L
12	-	**Temptation**	Heaven 17	Virgin	8		L
13	1	**Sleeping Satellite**	Tasmin Archer	EMI	9	(32)	F
14	-	**Invisible Touch (Live)**	Genesis	Virgin	2		L
15	-	**Who Needs Love (Like That)**	Erasure	Mute	3		
16	-	**Out Of Space/Ruff In The Jungle Bizness**	Prodigy	XL	9		
17	-	**Yesterdays/November Rain**	Guns n' Roses	Geffen	3	(3)	
18	-	**Montreux EP**	Simply Red	East West	7		
19	8	**A Million Love Songs (EP)**	Take That	RCA	5		
20	7	**Erotica**	Madonna	Maverick	5	(3)	

December 1992

This Mnth	Prev Mnth	Title	Artist	Label	Wks	(US 20 Pos)	
1	7	**I Will Always Love You**	Whitney Houston	Arista	17	(1)	G
2	-	**Heal The World**	Michael Jackson	Epic	8	(27)	
3	3	**Would I Lie To You?**	Charles & Eddie	Capitol	12	(13)	F L
4	-	**Tom Traubert's Blues (Waltzing Matilda)**	Rod Stewart	Warner Bros.	5		
5	-	**Slam Jam**	WWF Superstars	Arista	5		F
6	16	**Out Of Space/Ruff In The Jungle Bizness**	Prodigy	XL	9		
7	-	**Could It Be Magic**	Take That	RCA	9		
8	12	**Temptation**	Heaven 17	Virgin	8		L
9	-	**I Still Believe In You**	Cliff Richard	EMI	4		
10	-	**Deeper And Deeper**	Madonna	Maverick	5	(7)	
11	-	**Boney M Megamix**	Boney M	Arista	5		L
12	-	**In My Defence**	Freddie Mercury	Parlophone	4		L
13	-	**Phorever People**	Shamen	One Little Indian	7		
14	18	**Montreux EP**	Simply Red	East West	7		
15	-	**Step It Up**	Stereo MCs	Fourth & Broadway	7		
16	-	**If We Hold On Together**	Diana Ross	EMI	6		
17	1	**End Of The Road**	Boyz II Men	Motown	12	(1)	F
18	5	**Never Let Her Slip Away**	Undercover	PWL International	5		L
19	-	**Miami Hit Mix/Christmas Through Your Eyes**	Gloria Estefan	Epic	5		
20	2	**People Everyday**	Arrested Development	Cooltempo	8	(8)	F

◆ U2 grossed $64 million from their 1992 US tour; Barbra Streisand's new record contract with Columbia was slated to earn her a similar figure.

◆ Soon after the launch of her book, *Sex*, Madonna's equally controversial 'Erotica' single rocketed to No. 3 on both sides of the Atlantic and her album of the same name reached runner-up spot in the UK and USA.

1993

This Mnth	Prev Mnth	Title	Artist	Label	Wks	(US 20 Pos)	
1	1	I Will Always Love You	Whitney Houston	Arista	17	(1)	G
2	7	Could It Be Magic	Take That	RCA	9		
3	-	Exterminate!	Snap Featuring Niki Haris	Arista	8		
4	2	Heal The World	Michael Jackson	Epic	8	(27)	
5	13	Phorever People	Shamen	One Little Indian	7		
6	-	Mr. Wendal/Revolution	Arrested Development	Cooltempo	5	(6)	
7	3	Would I Lie To You?	Charles & Eddie	Capitol	12	(13)	F L
8	-	I'm Easy/Be Aggressive	Faith No More	Slash	5	(58)	
9	-	The Love I Lost	West End Featuring Sybil	PWL Sanctuary	9		F L
10	5	Slam Jam	WWF Superstars	Arista	5		F
11	-	We Are Family	Sister Sledge	Atlantic	4		
12	-	Open Your Mind	Usura	Deconstruction	5		F L
13	18	Miami Hit Mix/Christmas Through Your Eyes	Gloria Estefan	Epic	5		
14	-	Sweet Harmony	Beloved	East West	5		L
15	-	After All	Frank And Walters	Setanta	3		F L
16	11	Boney M Megamix	Boney M	Arista	5		L
17	6	Out Of Space/Ruff In The Jungle Bizness	Prodigy	XL	9		
18	-	Someday (I'm Coming Back)	Lisa Stansfield	Arista	5		
19	-	Steam	Peter Gabriel	Realworld	3	(32)	L
20	-	No Limit	2 Unlimited	PWL Continental	13		

This Mnth	Prev Mnth	Title	Artist	Label	Wks	(US 20 Pos)	
1	20	No Limit	2 Unlimited	PWL Continental	13		
2	1	I Will Always Love You	Whitney Houston	Arista	17	(1)	G
3	-	Deep	East 17	London	8		
4	9	The Love I Lost	West End Featuring Sybil	PWL Sanctuary	9		F L
5	-	Little Bird/Love Song For A Vampire	Annie Lennox	RCA	8	(49)	
6	-	Ordinary World	Duran Duran	Parlophone	6	(3)	
7	3	Exterminate!	Snap Featuring Niki Haris	Arista	8		
8	-	How Can I Love You More?	M People	Deconstruction	4		F
9	-	Why Can't I Wake Up With You?	Take That	RCA	4		
10	-	I'm Every Woman	Whitney Houston	Arista	6	(4)	
11	-	Stairway To Heaven	Rolf Harris	Vertigo	3		L
12	14	Sweet Harmony	Beloved	East West	5		L
13	12	Open Your Mind	Usura	Deconstruction	5		F L
14	-	Are You Gonna Go My Way	Lenny Kravitz	Virgin America	7		
15	11	We Are Family	Sister Sledge	Atlantic	4		
16	-	Independence	Lulu	Dome	3		
17	-	Give In To Me	Michael Jackson	Epic	6		
18	-	You're In A Bad Way	Saint Etienne	Heavenly	2		F
19	-	Ruby Tuesday	Rod Stewart	Warner Bros.	3		
20	-	I Feel You	Depeche Mode	Mute	2	(37)	

◆ Revivals enjoyed a revival with updated hits from such diverse acts as Take That, Faith No More, West End, Whitney Houston, Shaggy and Ugly Kid Joe, plus veterans Rolf Harris and Rod Stewart.

◆ Thirty-four years after his death, Buddy Holly's album Words of Love topped the UK chart.

March 1993

This Mnth	Prev Mnth	Title	Artist	Label	Wks	(US 20 Pos)	
1	1	**No Limit**	2 Unlimited	PWL Continental	13		
2	-	**Oh Carolina**	Shaggy	Greensleeves	12	(59)	F
3	17	**Give In To Me**	Michael Jackson	Epic	6		
4	5	**Little Bird/Love Song For A Vampire**	Annie Lennox	RCA	8	(49)	
5	14	**Are You Gonna Go My Way**	Lenny Kravitz	Virgin America	7		
6	-	**Mr. Loverman**	Shabba Ranks	Epic	8	(40)	
7	-	**Stick It Out**	Right Said Fred & Friends	Tug	5		L
8	10	**I'm Every Woman**	Whitney Houston	Arista	6	(4)	
9	-	**Animal Nitrate**	Suede	Nude	3		
10	-	**Informer**	Snow	East West America	11	(1)	F L
11	3	**Deep**	East 17	London	8		
12	-	**Too Young To Die**	Jamiroquai	Sony S^2	3		F
13	-	**Cat's In The Cradle**	Ugly Kid Joe	Mercury	6	(6)	L
14	-	**Shortsharpshock (EP)**	Therapy?	A&M	2		F
15	-	**Bad Girl**	Madonna	Maverick	3	(36)	
16	9	**Why Can't I Wake Up With You?**	Take That	RCA	4		
17	-	**Looking Through Patient Eyes**	PM Dawn	Gee Street	4	(6)	L
18	-	**Young At Heart**	Bluebells	London	8		L
19	-	**Fear Of The Dark (Live)**	Iron Maiden	EMI	2		
20	-	**Peace In Our Time**	Cliff Richard	EMI	2		

April 1993

This Mnth	Prev Mnth	Title	Artist	Label	Wks	(US 20 Pos)	
1	18	**Young At Heart**	Bluebells	London	8		L
2	10	**Informer**	Snow	East West America	11	(1)	F L
3	2	**Oh Carolina**	Shaggy	Greensleeves	12	(59)	F
4	-	**When I'm Good And Ready**	Sybil	PWL International	8		
5	6	**Mr. Loverman**	Shabba Ranks	Epic	8	(40)	
6	-	**Show Me Love**	Robin S.	Champion	6	(5)	F
7	-	**Don't Walk Away**	Jade	Giant	6	(4)	F
8	-	**Ain't No Love (Ain't No Use)**	Sub Sub Featuring Melanie Williams	Rob's	8		F L
9	1	**No Limit**	2 Unlimited	PWL Continental	13		
10	-	**U Got 2 Know**	Cappella	Internal	7		
11	13	**Cat's In The Cradle**	Ugly Kid Joe	Mercury	6	(6)	L
12	-	**Fever**	Madonna	Maverick	3		
13	-	**Regret**	New Order	London	3	(28)	
14	-	**Go Away**	Gloria Estefan	Epic	4		
15	-	**Wind It Up (Rewound)**	Prodigy	XL	3		
16	-	**Come Undone**	Duran Duran	Parlophone	4	(7)	
17	-	**Wrestlemania**	WWF Superstars	Arista	3		L
18	-	**Slow It Down**	East 17	London	3		
19	-	**I Have Nothing**	Whitney Houston	Arista	6	(4)	
20	-	**Jump They Say**	David Bowie	Arista	2		L

◆ At the end of March, for the first time reggae records held the top three places on the UK chart. They were 'Oh Carolina' by Shaggy, 'Informer' by white Canadian rapper Snow and 'Mr. Loverman' by Shabba Ranks.

◆ Depeche Mode, whose 'Walking in My Shoes' was their 21st Top 20 entry, entered the transatlantic charts at No. 1 with their album Songs Of Faith & Devotion.

1993

This Mnth	Prev Mnth	Title	Artist	Label	Wks	(US 20 Pos)	
1	-	Five Live (EP)	George Michael & Queen	Parlophone	7		
2	-	All That She Wants	Ace Of Base	London	12	(2)	F
3	-	Sweat (A La La La La Long)	Inner Circle	Magnet	8	(16)	F
4	-	That's The Way Love Goes	Janet Jackson	Virgin	6	(1)	
5	-	Tribal Dance	2 Unlimited	PWL Continental	7		
6	19	I Have Nothing	Whitney Houston	Arista	6	(4)	
7	-	Everybody Hurts	REM	Warner	8	(29)	
8	8	Ain't No Love (Ain't No Use)	Sub Sub Feat. Melanie Williams	Rob's	8		F L
9	2	Informer	Snow	East West	11	(1)	F L
10	1	Young At Heart	Bluebells	London	8		L
11	-	Housecall	Shabba Ranks Feat. Maxi Priest	Epic	5	(37)	
12	-	(I Can't Help) Falling In Love With You	UB40	Dep International	12	(1)	
13	10	U Got 2 Know	Cappella	Internal	7		
14	-	Believe In Me	Utah Saints	ffrr	3		L
15	4	When I'm Good And Ready	Sybil	PWL Int.	8		L
16	-	In These Arms	Bon Jovi	Jambco	3	(28)	
17	-	I Don't Wanna Fight	Tina Turner	Parlophone	5	(9)	
18	-	Jump Around	House Of Pain	Ruffness	4	(3)	F
19	6	Show Me Love	Robin S.	Champion	6	(5)	F
20	-	Express	Dina Carroll	A&M	3		

This Mnth	Prev Mnth	Title	Artist	Label	Wks	(US 20 Pos)	
1	12	(I Can't Help) Falling In Love With You	UB40	Dep International	12	(1)	
2	2	All That She Wants	Ace Of Base	London	12	(2)	F
3	-	Two Princes	Spin Doctors	Epic	10	(7)	F L
4	-	What Is Love	Haddaway	Arista	12	(11)	F
5	-	Three Little Pigs	Green Jelly	Zoo	5	(17)	F L
6	3	Sweat (A La La La La Long)	Inner Circle	Magnet	8	(16)	F
7	-	In All The Right Places	Lisa Stansfield	Arista	7		
8	-	Dreams	Gabrielle	Go.Beat	11	(32)	F
9	-	Shout	Louchie Lou & Michie One	ffrr	5		F L
10	-	Tease Me	Chaka Demus & Pliers	Mango	13		F
11	-	Can You Forgive Her?	Pet Shop Boys	Parlophone	3		
12	-	Do You See The Light (Looking For)	Snap Featuring Niki Haris	Arista	4		
13	5	Tribal Dance	2 Unlimited	PWL Continental	7		
14	-	Blow Your Mind	Jamiroquai	Sony S²	3		
15	17	I Don't Wanna Fight	Tina Turner	Parlophone	5	(9)	
16	1	Five Live (EP)	George Michael & Queen	Parlophone	7		
17	18	Jump Around	House Of Pain	Ruffness	4	(3)	F
18	4	That's The Way Love Goes	Janet Jackson	Virgin	6	(1)	
19	-	Have I Told You Lately	Rod Stewart	Warner Bros.	5	(5)	
20	-	One Night In Heaven	M People	Deconstruction	8		

◆ In April, nine of the British Top 10 were dance records, and at times only five of the Top 20 records were by British artists - two more firsts.

◆ Over 180,000 people saw France's top selling rock artist Johnny Halliday at the Parc Des Princes Stadium in Paris. To celebrate his 50th birthday a 40 CD box set was released – the biggest ever by a solo artist.

July 1993

This Mnth	Prev Mnth	Title	Artist	Label	Wks	(US 20 Pos)	
1	8	**Dreams**	Gabrielle	Go.Beat	11	(32)	F
2	4	**What Is Love**	Haddaway	Arista	12	(11)	F
3	10	**Tease Me**	Chaka Demus & Pliers	Mango	13		F
4	20	**One Night In Heaven**	M People	Deconstruction	8		
5	-	**What's Up**	4 Non Blondes	Interscope	11	(16)	F L
6	1	**(I Can't Help) Falling In Love With You**	UB40	Dep International	12	(1)	
7	-	**I Will Survive**	Gloria Gaynor	Polydor	6		L
8	-	**Pray**	Take That	RCA	7		
9	19	**Have I Told You Lately**	Rod Stewart	Warner Bros.	5	(5)	
10	3	**Two Princes**	Spin Doctors	Epic	10	(7)	F L
11	-	**Will You Be There**	Michael Jackson	Epic	4	(7)	
12	2	**All That She Wants**	Ace Of Base	London	12	(2)	F
13	-	**If I Can't Have You**	Kim Wilde	MCA	4		L
14	-	**Almost Unreal**	Roxette	EMI	5	(94)	
15	-	**This Is It**	Dannii Minogue	MCA	5		
16	7	**In All The Right Places**	Lisa Stansfield	Arista	7		
17	-	**Living On My Own**	Freddie Mercury	Parlophone	9		L
18	-	**Nothin' My Love Can't Fix**	Joey Lawrence	EMI	3	(19)	F L
19	-	**I Wanna Love You**	Jade	Giant	3	(16)	
20	-	**Can't Get Enough Of Your Love**	Taylor Dayne	Arista	3	(20)	L

August 1993

This Mnth	Prev Mnth	Title	Artist	Label	Wks	(US 20 Pos)	
1	17	**Living On My Own**	Freddie Mercury	Parlophone	9		L
2	-	**The Key The Secret**	Urban Cookie Collective	Pulse 8	10		F
3	5	**What's Up**	4 Non Blondes	Interscope	11	(16)	F L
4	-	**The River Of Dreams**	Billy Joel	Columbia	9	(3)	L
5	8	**Pray**	Take That	RCA	7		
6	-	**It Keeps Rainin' (Tears From My Eyes)**	Bitty McLean	Brilliant	9		F
7	3	**Tease Me**	Chaka Demus & Pliers	Mango	13		F
8	-	**Mr. Vain**	Culture Beat	Epic	11	(20)	F
9	-	**Nuff Vibes (EP)**	Apache Indian	Island	6		L
10	1	**Dreams**	Gabrielle	Go.Beat	11	(32)	F
11	-	**Rain**	Madonna	Maverick	4	(14)	
12	-	**Looking Up**	Michelle Gayle	RCA	4		F
13	14	**Almost Unreal**	Roxette	EMI	5	(94)	
14	-	**Higher Ground**	UB40	Dep International	5	(46)	
15	-	**Luv 4 Luv**	Robin S.	Champion	4		L
16	-	**I Will Always Love You**	Sarah Washington	Almighty	4		F L
17	2	**What Is Love**	Haddaway	Arista	12	(11)	F
18	-	**Dreamlover**	Mariah Carey	Columbia	6	(1)	
19	15	**This Is It**	Dannii Minogue	MCA	5		
20	-	**Right Here**	SWV	RCA	8	(2)	

◆ Several disco classics from the 1970s returned: 'If I Can't Have You' (Yvonne Elliman/Kim Wilde), 'This Is It' (Melba Moore/Dannii Minogue), 'Go West' (Village People/Pet Shop Boys), 'Disco Inferno' (Trammps/Tina Turner) and a remix of Gloria Gaynor's 'I Will Survive'.

◆ European music conglomerate Polygram bought Motown Records' 30,000 masters for $325 million, as the label re-signed Boyz II Men in a deal that could earn the act $30 million.

1993

This Mnth	Prev Mnth	Title	Artist	Label	Wks	(US 20 Pos)	
1	8	Mr. Vain	Culture Beat	Epic	11	(20)	F
2	6	It Keeps Rainin' (Tears From My Eyes)	Bitty McLean	Brilliant	9		F
3	20	Right Here	SWV	RCA	8	(2)	
4	4	The River Of Dreams	Billy Joel	Columbia	9	(3)	L
5	-	Boom! Shake The Room	Jazzy Jeff & Fresh Prince	Jive	10	(13)	F L
6	1	Living On My Own	Freddie Mercury	Parlophone	9		L
7	-	Faces	2 Unlimited	PWL Continental	4		
8	18	Dreamlover	Mariah Carey	Columbia	6	(1)	
9	-	Go West	Pet Shop Boys	Parlophone	6		
10	2	The Key The Secret	Urban Cookie Collective	Pulse 8	10		F
11	9	Nuff Vibes (EP)	Apache Indian	Island	6		L
12	14	Higher Ground	UB40	Dep International	5	(46)	
13	-	Heart-Shaped Box	Nirvana	Geffen	2		L
14	-	Creep	Radiohead	Parlophone	3	(34)	F
15	-	Slave To The Vibe	Aftershock	Virgin	5		F L
16	-	She Don't Let Nobody	Chaka Demus & Pliers	Mango	7		
17	-	Moving On Up	M People	Deconstruction	7		
18	-	Rubberband Girl	Kate Bush	EMI	2	(88)	L
19	-	Disco Inferno	Tina Turner	Parlophone	3		
20	-	It Must Have Been Love	Roxette	EMI	4		

This Mnth	Prev Mnth	Title	Artist	Label	Wks	(US 20 Pos)	
1	5	Boom! Shake The Room	Jazzy Jeff & Fresh Prince	Jive	10	(13)	F L
2	17	Moving On Up	M People	Deconstruction	7		
3	16	She Don't Let Nobody	Chaka Demus & Pliers	Mango	7		
4	-	I'd Do Anything For Love (But I Won't Do That)	Meat Loaf	Virgin	12	(1)	
5	-	Relight My Fire	Take That Featuring Lulu	RCA	5		
6	-	Stay	Eternal	EMI	6		F
7	-	Relax	Frankie Goes To Hollywood	ZTT	5		
8	-	Life	Haddaway	Logic	5	(83)	
9	9	Go West	Pet Shop Boys	Parlophone	6		
10	1	Mr. Vain	Culture Beat	Epic	11	(20)	F
11	-	U Got 2 Let The Music	Cappella	Internal	6		
12	-	One Love	Prodigy	XL	4		
13	-	Going Nowhere	Gabrielle	Go.Beat	4		
14	-	Don't Be A Stranger	Dina Carroll	A&M	11		
15	3	Right Here	SWV	RCA	8	(2)	
16	-	Here We Go	Stakka Bo	Polydor	4		F L
17	-	Please Forgive Me	Bryan Adams	A&M	9	(7)	
18	-	Play Dead	Bjork & David Arnold	Island	4		F
19	20	It Must Have Been Love	Roxette	EMI	4		
20	-	Both Sides Of The Story	Phil Collins	Virgin	2	(25)	

◆ UK acts Cream, Elton John, The Animals, John Lennon, Van Morrison and Rod Stewart joined other 1993 *Rock And Roll Hall Of Fame* inductees The Band, Ruth Brownl, Doors, Duane Eddy, Grateful Dead, Etta James, Frankie Lymon & The Teenagers, Bob Marley and Sly & The Family Stone.

◆ In the US, only 10 different singles made No. 1 in 1993 (a new low), and records, in general, stayed on the charts longer. In contrast, in Britain more records charted and a hit's life-span was shorter than ever. 1993 was the year of the American rock act, and the worst year for British artists in the US.

November 1993

This Mnth	Prev Mnth	Title	Artist	Label	Wks (US 20 Pos)	
1	4	I'll Do Anything For Love (But I Won't Do That)	Meat Loaf	Virgin	15 (1)	
2	17	Please Forgive Me	Bryan Adams	A&M	11 (7)	
3	14	Don't Be A Stranger	Dina Carroll	A&M	11	
4	-	Got To Get It	Culture Beat	Epic	5	
5	11	U Got 2 Let The Music	Cappella	Internal	6	
6	-	Give It Up	Goodmen	Fresh Fruit	5	F L
7	-	Hero	Mariah Carey	Columbia	10 (1)	
8	-	Feels Like Heaven	Urban Cookie Collective	Pulse 8	4	
9	-	Runaway Train	Soul Asylum	Columbia	5 (5)	F L
10	-	True Love	Elton John & Kiki Dee	Rocket	7 (56)	
11	-	Real Love '93	Time Frequency	Internal Affairs	3	L
12	-	Again	Janet Jackson	Virgin	8 (1)	
13	-	Feel Like Making Love	Pauline Henry	Sony	4	F L
14	-	Ain't It Fun	Guns N' Roses	Geffen	2	L
15	-	Little Fluffy Clouds	Orb	Big Life	2	
16	1	Boom! Shake That Room	Jazzy Jeff & Fresh Prince	Jive	10 (13)	F L
17	6	Stay	Eternal	EMI	6 (19)	F
18	-	Queen Of The Night	Whitney Houston	Arista	2	
19	-	Long Train Runnin'	Doobie Brothers	Warner Bros.	4	F L
20	20	Both Sides Of The Story	Phil Collins	Virgin	2 (25)	

December 1993

1	-	Mr. Blobby	Mr. Blobby	Destiny Music	7	F L
2	1	I'll Do Anything For Love (But I Won't Do That)	Meat Loaf	Virgin	15 (1)	
3	10	True Love	Elton John & Kiki Dee	Rocket	7 (56)	
4	-	For Whom The Bell Tolls	Bee Gees	Polydor	9	
5	2	Please Forgive Me	Bryan Adams	A&M	11 (7)	
6	3	Don't Be A Stranger	Dina Carroll	A&M	11	
7	-	It's Alright	East 17	London	10	
8	-	Babe	Take That	RCA	5	
9	-	Stay (Faraway, So Close!) /I've Got You Under My Skin	U2	Island	3	
10	-	Don't Look Any Further	M People	Deconstruction	6	
11	-	Twist And Shout	Chaka Demus & Pliers/ Jack Radics/Taxi Gang	Mango	9	L
12	12	Again	Janet Jackson	Virgin	8 (1)	
13	-	The Perfect Year	Dina Carroll	A&M	7	
14	19	Long Train Runnin'	Doobie Brothers	Warner Bros.	4	F L
15	-	Bat Out Of Hell	Meat Loaf	Epic	5	
16	-	Controversy	Prince	Paisley Park	2	
17	-	The Power Of Love	Frankie Goes To Hollywood	ZTT	4	
18	-	Y.M.C.A. '93 Remix	Village People	Bell	2	L
19	7	Hero	Mariah Carey	Columbia	10 (1)	
20	-	I Wouldn't Normally Do This Kind Of Thing	Pet Shop Boys	Parlophone	3	

◆ British teen idols Take That became the first act to have three successive singles enter at No. 1. They also had three of the country's Top 4 videos.
◆ Chaka Demus & Pliers, the first reggae act to have three successive Top 5 entries, took the song 'Twist And Shout' into the Top 10 for the fourth time.
◆ The year ended with the death of one of rock's true originals, Frank Zappa.

1994

This Mnth	Prev Mnth	Title	Artist	Label	Wks	(US 20 Pos)	
1	11	Twist And Shout	Chaka Demus & Pliers Feat. Jack Radics & Taxi Gang	Mango	9		
2	-	Things Can Only Get Better	D:ream	/Magnet	11		
3	-	Come Baby Come	K7	Tommy Boy	10	(18)	F
4	7	It's Alright	East 17	London	10		
5	1	Mr. Blobby	Mr. Blobby	Destiny Music	7		F L
6	-	All For Love	Bryan Adams/Rod Stewart/Sting	A&M	9	(1)	
7	8	Babe	Take That	RCA	5		
8	4	For Whom The Bell Tolls	Bee Gees	Polydor	9		
9	13	The Perfect Year	Dina Carroll	A&M	7		
10	-	Anything	Culture Beat	Epic	5		
11	-	Cornflake Girl	Tori Amos	East West	4		
12	-	I Miss You	Haddaway	Logic	8		
13	2	I'll Do Anything For Love (But I Won't Do That)	Meat Loaf	Virgin	15	(1)	
14	-	Save Our Love	Eternal	EMI	4		
15	15	Bat Out Of Hell	Meat Loaf	Epic	5		
16	-	Breathe Again	Toni Braxton	Laface	9	(3)	F
17	-	In Your Room	Depeche Mode	Mute	2		
18	-	Here I Stand	Bitty McLean	Brilliant	3		
19	-	A Whole New World (Aladdin's Theme)	Peabo Bryson & Regina Belle	Columbia	5	(1)	L
20	-	Return To Innocence	Enigma	Virgin	11	(4)	L

This Mnth	Prev Mnth	Title	Artist	Label	Wks	(US 20 Pos)	
1	2	Things Can Only Get Better	D:ream	/Magnet	11		
2	16	Breathe Again	Toni Braxton	Laface	9	(3)	F
3	20	Return To Innocence	Enigma	Virgin	11	(4)	L
4	6	All For Love	Bryan Adams/Rod Stewart/Sting	A&M	9	(1)	
5	-	The Power Of Love	Celine Dion	550 Music	6	(1)	
6	-	Without You	Mariah Carey	Columbia	9	(3)	
7	3	Come Baby Come	K7	Tommy Bo	10	(18)	F
8	-	A Deeper Love	Aretha Franklin	Arista	3	(63)	
9	-	Stay Together	Suede	Nude	3		
10	-	Come In Out Of The Rain	Wendy Moten	EMI USA	4		F L
11	11	Cornflake Girl	Tori Amos	East West	4		
12	-	Move On Baby	Cappella	Internal	4		
13	-	I Like To Move It	Reel 2 Real/The Mad Stuntman	Positiva	15	(89)	F
14	-	Let The Beat Control Your Body	2 Unlimited	PWL Continental	5		
15	10	Anything	Culture Beat	Epic	5		
16	-	The Sign	Ace Of Base	Arista	10	(1)	
17	-	Give It Away	Red Hot Chili Peppers	Warner	2	(73)	F
18	-	Sweet Lullaby	Deep Forest	Columbia	3	(78)	F
19	12	I Miss You	Haddaway	Logic/Arista	8		
20	1	Twist And Shout	Chaka Demus & Pliers Feat. Jack Radics & Taxi Gang	Mango	9		

◆ Newcomers Chaka Demus & Pliers became the fourth act to take 'Twist And Shout' into the Top 10 and their recording was also the 700th different single to head the UK chart.
◆ The classic ballad 'Without You' returned to the top, this time by Mariah Carey. Her transatlantic No. 1 was the first single by a female artist to enter the UK lists in pole position.
◆ Among the Brit Award winners were Sting, Dina Caroll, the Stereo MCs, M People and Take That.

March 1994

This Mnth	Prev Mnth	Title	Artist	Label	Wks	(US 20 Pos)		
1	6	**Without You**	Mariah Carey	Columbia	9	(3)		
2	16	**The Sign**	Ace Of Base	Arista	10	(1)		
3	-	**Doop**	Doop	Citybeat	7		F	L
4	3	**Return To Innocence**	Enigma	Virgin	11	(4		L
5	2	**Breathe Again**	Toni Braxton	Laface	9	(3)	F	
6	-	**Streets Of Philadelphia**	Bruce Springsteen	Columbia	8	(9)		L
7	-	**Renaissance**	M People	Deconstruction	3			
8	13	**I Like To Move It**	Reel 2 Real/The Mad Stuntman	Positiva	15	(89)	F	
9	-	**Girls And Boys**	Blur	Food	4	(59)		
10	14	**Let The Beat Control Your Body**	2 Unlimited	PWL Continental	5			
11	1	**Things Can Only Get Better**	D:ream	Magnet	11			
12	-	**U R The Best Thing**	D:ream	Magnet	5			
13	-	**Don't Go Breaking My Heart**	Elton John & RuPaul	Rocket	3			
14	-	**Rocks/Funky Jam**	Primal Scream	Creation	2			
15	12	**Move On Baby**	Cappella	Internal	4			
16	-	**Whatta Man**	Salt-N-Pepa Featuring En Vogue	Next Plateau	6	(3)		
17	-	**Pretty Good Year**	Tori Amos	East West	1			
18	-	**Shine On**	Degrees Of Motion	ffrr	5		F	L
19	-	**The More You Ignore Me, The Closer I Get**	Morrissey	Parlophone	1	(46)		L
20	4	**All For Love**	Bryan Adams/Rod Stewart/Sting	A&M	9	(1)		

April 1994

This Mnth	Prev Mnth	Title	Artist	Label	Wks	(US 20 Pos)		
1	6	**Streets Of Philadelphia**	Bruce Springsteen	Columbia	8	(9)		L
2	-	**The Most Beautiful Girl In The World**	TAFKAP	NPG	9	(3)		
3	-	**Everything Changes**	Take That	RCA	5			
4	3	**Doop**	Doop	Citybeat	7		F	L
5	8	**I Like To Move It**	Reel 2 Real/The Mad Stuntman	Positiva	15	(89)	F	
6	2	**The Sign**	Ace Of Base	Arista	10	(1)		
7	-	**The Real Thing**	Tony Di Bart	Cleveland City	8		F	L
8	12	**U R The Best Thing**	D:ream	Magnet	5			
9	-	**Mmm Mmm Mmm Mmm**	Crash Test Dummies	Arista	6	(4)	F	L
10	16	**Whatta Man**	Salt-N-Pepa Featuring En Vogue	Next Plateau	6	(3)		
11	-	**Dedicated To The One I Love**	Bitty McLean	Brilliant	6			L
12	-	**I'll Remember**	Madonna	Maverick	4	(2)		
13	-	**Rock My Heart**	Haddaway	Logic	5			
14	1	**Without You/Never Forget You**	Mariah Carey	Columbia	9	(3)		
15	-	**Sweets For My Sweet**	CJ Lewis	Black Market	8		F	
16	18	**Shine On**	Degrees Of Motion	ffrr	5		F	L
17	-	**Dry County**	Bon Jovi	Vertigo	2			
18	-	**I'll Stand By You**	Pretenders	WEA	4	(16)		L
19	-	**Light My Fire**	Clubhouse Featuring Carl	PWL International	5			L
20	-	**Hung Up**	Paul Weller	Go! Discs	1			

◆ A record number of European artists reached the chart this quarter and for the first time since the late 1950s, 7" vinyl singles accounted for less than 10% of the market.

◆ 'Everything Changes' gave Take That a record fourth entry at No. 1; the single had logged up 300,000 advance orders. They were the first act since The Beatles to take four successive singles to the top. Also, group member Gary Barlow was named Songwriter of the Year at the Ivor Novello Awards.

1994

This Mnth	Prev Mnth	Title	Artist	Label	Wks	(US 20 Pos)	
1	-	Come On You Reds	Manchester United Squad	Polygram TV	10		
2	-	Inside	Stiltskin	White Water	8		F L
3	7	The Real Thing	Tony Di Bart	Cleveland City	8		F L
4	15	Sweets For My Sweet	CJ Lewis	Black Market	8		F
5	2	The Most Beautiful Girl In The World	TAFKAP	NPG	9	(3)	
6	9	Mmm Mmm Mmm Mmm	Crash Test Dummies	Arista	6	(4)	F L
7	-	Around The World	East 17	London	7		
8	-	Love Is All Around	Wet Wet Wet	Precious	21	(45)	G
9	-	Just A Step From Heaven	Eternal	EMI	6		
10	19	Light My Fire	Clubhouse Featuring Carl	PWL International	5		L
11	-	Always	Erasure	Mute	5	(20)	L
12	-	Get-A-Way	Maxx	Pulse 8	7		F
13	-	The Real Thing	2 Unlimited	PWL	4		
14	-	More To This World	Bad Boys Inc	A&M	4		
15	11	Dedicated To The One I Love	Bitty McLean	Brilliant	6		L
16	5	I Like To Move It	Reel 2 Real/The Mad Stuntman	Positiva	15	(89)	F
17	-	No Good (Start The Dance)	Prodigy	XL	8		
18	18	I'll Stand By You	Pretenders	WEA	4	(16)	L
19	-	Carry Me Home	Gloworm	Go! Discs	6		L
20	-	Under The Bridge	Red Hot Chili Peppers	Warner	3	(2)	

This Mnth	Prev Mnth	Title	Artist	Label	Wks	(US 20 Pos)	
1	8	Love Is All Around	Wet Wet Wet	Precious	21	(45)	G
2	-	Baby I Love Your Way	Big Mountain	RCA	10	(6)	F L
3	1	Come On You Reds	Manchester United Football Squad	Polygram TV	10		
4	17	No Good (Start The Dance)	Prodigy	XL	8		
5	12	Get-A-Way	Maxx	Pulse 8	7		F
6	7	Around The World	East 17	London	7		
7	-	You Don't Love Me (No, No, No)	Dawn Penn	Big Beat	7	(58)	F L
8	-	Swamp Thing	Grid	Deconstruction	12		F
9	-	Don't Turn Around	Ace Of Base	Arista	7	(4)	
10	-	Absolutely Fabulous	Absolutely Fabulous	Spaghetti	3		F L
11	2	Inside	Stiltskin	White Water	8		F L
12	-	Anytime You Need A Friend	Mariah Carey	Columbia	3	(12)	
13	-	I Swear	All-4-One	Blitzz	14	(1)	F L
14	19	Carry Me Home	Gloworm	Go! Discs	6		L
15	4	Sweets For My Sweet	CJ Lewis	Black Market	8		F
16	-	Since I Don't Have You	Guns N' Roses	Geffen	2	(69)	
17	-	Everybody's Talkin'	Beautiful South	Go! Discs	4		
18	13	The Real Thing	2 Unlimited	PWL	4		
19	-	No More Tears (Enough Is Enough)	Kym Mazelle & Jocelyn Brown	Bell	3		L
20	14	More To This World	Bad Boys Inc	A&M	4		

◆ Prince changed his name to a symbol, and released his first single away from Warner Brothers. The record, 'The Most Beautiful Girl In The World', gave him his first British No. 1.

◆ Danish-born Whigfield became the first artist to make their UK chart debut at No. 1. 'Saturday Night', one of Europe's biggest summertime hits, sold over half a million in just three weeks.

July 1994

This Mnth	Prev Mnth	Title	Artist	Label	Wks	(US 20 Pos)	
1	1	Love Is All Around	Wet Wet Wet	Precious	21	(45)	G
2	13	I Swear	All-4-One	Blitzz	14	(1)	F L
3	8	Swamp Thing	Grid	Deconstruction	12		F
4	-	(Meet) The Flintstones	BC-52s	MCA	9	(33)	L
5	2	Baby I Love Your Way	Big Mountain	RCA	10	(6)	F L
6	-	Love Ain't Here Anymore	Take That	RCA	4		
7	-	Shine	Aswad	Bubblin'	9		L
8	-	Crazy For You	Let Loose	Mercury	13		F
9	7	You Don't Love Me (No, No, No)	Dawn Penn	Big Beat	7	(58)	F L
10	-	Go On Move	Reel 2 Real/Mad Stuntman	Positiva	4		
11	9	Don't Turn Around	Ace Of Base	Arista	7	(4)	
12	-	Everybody Gonfi Gon	Two Cowboys	ffrreedom	5		F L
13	-	Regulate	Warren G & Nate Dogg	Death Row	10	(2)	F
14	-	Word Up	Gun	A&M	4		F
15	4	No Good (Start The Dance)	Prodigy	XL	8		
16	-	Run To The Sun	Erasure	Mute	2		
17	-	Searching	China Black	Wild Card	10		F
18	-	U & Me	Cappella	Internal	3		
19	-	Everything Is Alright (Uptight)	CJ Lewis	Black Market	4		
20	-	Shakermaker	Oasis	Creation	2		F

August 1994

This Mnth	Prev Mnth	Title	Artist	Label	Wks	(US Pos)	
1	1	Love Is All Around	Wet Wet Wet	Precious	21	(45)	G
2	8	Crazy For You	Let Loose	Mercury	13		F
3	2	I Swear	All-4-One	Blitzz	14	(1)	F L
4	17	Searching	China Black	Wild Card	10		F
5	-	Compliments On Your Kiss	Red Dragon With Brian/Tony Gold	Mango	9		F L
6	4	(Meet) The Flintstones	BC-52s	MCA	9	(33)	L
7	13	Regulate	Warren G & Nate Dogg	Death Row	10	(2)	F
8	-	7 Seconds	Youssou N'dour/Neneh Cherry	Columbia	9	(98)	F L
9	-	What's Up	DJ Miko	Systematic	6		F L
10	-	No More (I Can't Stand It)	Maxx	Pulse 8	4		L
11	-	Let's Get Ready To Rumble	PJ And Duncan	XSrhythm/	7		F
12	7	Shine	Aswad	Bubblin'	9		L
13	-	Trouble	Shampoo	Food	7		F L
14	3	Swamp Thing	Grid	Deconstruction/RCA	12	F	
15	-	Eighteen Strings	Tinman	ffrr	4		F L
16	-	Live Forever	Oasis	Creation	3		
17	19	Everything Is Alright (Uptight)	CJ Lewis	Black Market	4		
18	-	Black Hole Sun	Soundgarden	A&M	2		L
19	-	Midnight At The Oasis	Brand New Heavies	Acid Jazz	3		
20	-	So Good	Eternal	EMI	3		

◆ Sweden's latest hit making machine, Ace Of Base, reached the Top 5 in 30 countries with their album The Sign (aka Happy Nation). Their current transatlantic hit ,'Don't Turn Around' was one of a record seven reggae-styled tracks in the UK Top 30.

◆ In Britain Wet Wet Wet held the top rung for a staggering 15 weeks with a revival of The Troggs' 'Love Is All Around', whilst in the USA 'I'll Make Love To You' by Boyz II Men hogged the No. 1 position for an unprecedented 14 weeks.

1994

This Mnth	Prev Mnth	Title	Artist	Label	Wks	(US 20 Pos)	
1	1	**Love Is All Around**	Wet Wet Wet	Precious	21	(45)	G
2	8	**7 Seconds**	Youssou N'dour/Neneh Cherry	Columbia	9	(98)	F L
3	5	**Compliments On Your Kiss**	Red Dragon With Brian & Tony Gold	Mango	9		F L
4	-	**Confide In Me**	Kylie Minogue	Deconstruction	4		
5	-	**I'll Make Love To You**	Boyz II Men	Motown	7	(1)	
6	-	**The Rhythm Of The Night**	Corona	WEA	8	(11)	F
7	-	**Saturday Night**	Whigfield	Systematic	12		F G
8	2	**Crazy For You**	Let Loose	Mercury	13		F
9	-	**Endless Love**	Luther Vandross/Mariah Carey	Columbia	5	(2)	
10	4	**Searching**	China Black	Wild Card	10		F
11	7	**Regulate**	Warren G & Nate Dogg	Death Row	10	(2)	F
12	3	**I Swear**	All-4-One	Blitzz	14	(1)	F L
13	-	**Incredible**	M-Beat feat General Levy	Renk	5		F
14	-	**Always**	Bon Jovi	Mercury	12	(4)	
15	9	**What's Up**	DJ Miko	Systematic	6		F L
16	-	**What's The Frequency, Kenneth?**	REM	Warner Bros.	3	(21)	
17	-	**Parklife**	Blur	Food	3		
18	-	**Hey Now (Girls Just Want To Have Fun)**	Cyndi Lauper	Epic	9	(87)	L
19	-	**Right Beside You**	Sophie B. Hawkins	Columbia	6	(56)	L
20	15	**Eighteen Strings**	Tinman	ffrr	4		F L

This Mnth	Prev Mnth	Title	Artist	Label	Wks	(US 20 Pos)	
1	7	**Saturday Night**	Whigfield	Systematic	12		F G
2	14	**Always**	Bon Jovi	Mercury	12	(4)	
3	-	**Baby Come Back**	Pato Banton	Virgin	15		F
4	18	**Hey Now (Girls Just Want To Have Fun)**	Cyndi Lauper	Epic	9	(87)	L
5	6	**The Rhythm Of The Night**	Corona	WEA	8	(11)	F
6	-	**Sure**	Take That	RCA	4		
7	-	**Sweetness**	Michelle Gayle	RCA	10		
8	-	**Stay**	Lisa Loeb & Nine Stories	RCA	9	(1)	F L
9	9	**Endless Love**	Luther Vandross & Mariah Carey	Columbia	5	(2)	
10	-	**Secret**	Madonna	Maverick	5	(3)	
11	-	**Steam**	East 17	London	4		
12	-	**Welcome To Tomorrow**	Snap Featuring Summer	Arista	7		
13	-	**She's Got That Vibe**	R. Kelly	Jive	6	(59)	
14	-	**Cigarettes & Alcohol**	Oasis	Creation	2		
15	-	**Circle Of Life**	Elton John	Rocket	6	(18)	
16	5	**I'll Make Love To You**	Boyz II Men	Motown	7	(1)	
17	1	**Love Is All Around**	Wet Wet Wet	Precious	21	(45)	G
18	13	**Incredible**	M-Beat Featuring General Levy	Renk	5		F
19	-	**When We Dance**	Sting	A&M	3	(38)	
20	-	**Seventeen**	Let Loose	Mercury	3		

◆ Record piracy rocketed to new heights, sales were up 17% in the UK and 20% in the USA. Interestingly, there had been only nine US No. 1 singles in 1994, fewer than any year since 1955.

◆ In a year when the remaining members of Led Zeppelin reportedly refused $100 million to reform, tours by fellow UK veterans The Rolling Stones and Pink Floyd both surpassed $100 million in ticket sales alone.

November 1994

This Mnth	Prev Mnth	Title	Artist	Label	Wks	(US 20 Pos)	
1	3	**Baby Come Back**	Pato Banton	Virgin	15		F
2	2	**Always**	Bon Jovi	Mercury	12	(4)	
3	-	**Another Night**	(MC Sar &) the Real McCoy	Arista	10	(3)	F
4	13	**She's Got That Vibe**	R. Kelly	Jive	6	(59)	
5	-	**Oh Baby I**	Eternal	EMI	7		
6	1	**Saturday Night**	Whigfield	Systematic	12		F G
7	-	**All I Wanna Do**	Sheryl Crow	A&M	6	(2)	F
8	-	**Let Me Be Your Fantasy**	Baby D	Systematic	9		F
9	7	**Sweetness**	Michelle Gayle	RCA	10		
10	12	**Welcome To Tomorrow**	Snap Featuring Summer	Arista	7		
11	-	**We Have All The Time In The World**	Louis Armstrong	EMI	7		L
12	-	**Sight For Sore Eyes**	M People	Deconstruction	5		
13	-	**Some Girls**	Ultimate Kaos	Wild Card	5		F
14	4	**Hey Now (Girls Just Want To Have Fun)**	Cyndi Lauper	Epic	9	(87	L
15	-	**True Faith - 94**	New Order	Centredate Co.	3		
16	-	**Crocodile Shoes**	Jimmy Nail	East West	8		
17	-	**If I Only Knew**	Tom Jones	ZTT	3		L
18	8	**Stay**	Lisa Loeb & Nine Stories	RCA	9	(1)	F L
19	-	**Spin The Black Circle**	Pearl Jam	Epic	1	(18)	L
20	-	**This D.J.**	Warren G	Violator	2	(9)	F

December 1994

		Title	Artist	Label	Wks	(US 20 Pos)	
1	-	**Stay Another Day**	East 17	London	9		
2	-	**All I Want For Christmas Is You**	Mariah Carey	Columbia	5		
3	8	**Let Me Be Your Fantasy**	Baby D	Systematic	9		F
4	11	**We Have All The Time In The World**	Louis Armstrong	EMI	7		L
5	16	**Crocodile Shoes**	Jimmy Nail	East West	8		
6	-	**Love Me For A Reason**	Boyzone	Polydor	9		F
7	-	**Think Twice**	Celine Dion	Epic	20	(95)	G
8	-	**Power Rangers**	Mighty Morph'n Power Rangers	RCA	5		F L
9	3	**Another Night**	(MC Sar &) the Real McCoy	Arista	10	(3)	F
10	-	**Love Spreads**	Stone Roses	Geffen	2		
11	1	**Baby Come Back**	Pato Banton	Virgin	15		F
12	-	**Cotton Eye Joe**	Rednex	Internal Affairs	12	(25)	F
13	-	**Please Come Home For Christmas**	Bon Jovi	Jambco	4		
14	-	**Whatever**	Oasis	Creation	6		
15	-	**Hold Me, Thrill Me, Kiss Me**	Gloria Estefan	Epic	6		
16	-	**Another Day**	Whigfield	Systematic	6		
17	-	**Them Girls Them Girls**	Zig And Zag	RCA	5		F L
18	7	**All I Wanna Do**	Sheryl Crow	A&M	6	(2)	F
19	-	**Eternal Love**	PJ And Duncan	XSrhythm	6		
20	12	**Sight For Sore Eyes**	M People	Deconstruction	5		

◆ As the ground breaking ceremony took place for the National Black Music Hall Of Fame in New Orleans, a survey pointed out that black American artists were seven times more likely to get a British hit than white ones.

◆ 1994 was a year of unrest for major superstars with George Michael, Prince and Metallica taking legal action against their record companies.

1995

This Mnth	Prev Mnth	Title	Artist	Label	Wks	(US 20 Pos)	
1	12	**Cotton Eye Joe**	Rednex	Internal Affairs	12	(25)	F
2	7	**Think Twice**	Celine Dion	Epic	20	(95)	G
3	6	**Love Me For A Reason**	Boyzone	Polydor	9		F
4	1	**Stay Another Day**	East 17	London	9		
5	-	**Here Comes The Hotstepper**	Ini Kamoze	Columbia	11	(1)	F L
6	-	**Set You Free**	N-Trance	All Around The World	10		F
7	-	**Tell Me When**	Human League	East West	6	(31)	
8	14	**Whatever**	Oasis	Creation	6		
9	-	**Total Eclipse Of The Heart**	Nicki French	Bags of Fun	8	(2)	F L
10	17	**Them Girls Them Girls**	Zig And Zag	RCA	5		F L
11	16	**Another Day**	Whigfield	Systematic	6		
12	-	**Bump N' Grind**	R. Kelly	Jive	6	(1)	
13	-	**Basket Case**	Green Day	Reprise	3		
14	-	**Sympathy For The Devil**	Guns N' Roses	Geffen	2	(55)	
15	5	**Crocodile Shoes**	Jimmy Nail	East West	8		
16	2	**All I Want For Christmas Is You**	Mariah Carey	Columbia	5		
17	-	**Riverdance**	Bill Whelan	Son	9		F L
18	-	**She's A River**	Simple Minds	Virgin	2	(52)	
19	-	**Glory Box**	Portishead	Go Beat	3		F
20	8	**Power Rangers**	Mighty Morph'n Power Rangers	RCA	5		F L

This Mnth	Prev Mnth	Title	Artist	Label	Wks	(US 20 Pos)	
1	2	**Think Twice**	Celine Dion	Epic	20	(95)	G
2	6	**Set You Free**	N-Trance	All Around The World	10		F
3	1	**Cotton Eye Joe**	Rednex	Internal Affairs	12	(25)	F
4	-	**I've Got A Little Something For You**	MN8	Columbia	8		F
5	5	**Here Comes The Hotstepper**	Ini Kamoze	Columbia	11	(1)	F L
6	9	**Total Eclipse Of The Heart**	Nicki French	Bags of Fun	8	(2)	F L
7	-	**No More 'I Love You's**	Annie Lennox	RCA	5	(23)	
8	-	**Run Away**	Real McCoy	Arista	7	(3)	
9	-	**Reach Up (Papa's Got A Brand New Pig Bag)**	Perfecto Allstarz	Perfecto	7		F L
10	-	**Don't Give Me Your Life**	Alex Party	Systematic	9		F L
11	-	**Bedtime Story**	Madonna	Maverick	2	(42)	
12	17	**Riverdance**	Bill Whelan	Son	9		F L
13	-	**Open Your Heart**	M People	Deconstruction	3		
14	13	**Basket Case**	Green Day	Reprise	3		
15	-	**Call It Love**	Deuce	London	5		F
16	-	**Independent Love Song**	Scarlet	WEA	7		F L
17	-	**Someday I'll Be Saturday Night**	Bon Jovi	Jambco	3		
18	7	**Tell Me When**	Human League	East West	6	(31)	
19	12	**Bump N' Grind**	R. Kelly	Jive	6	(1)	
20	-	**One Night Stand**	Let Loose	Mercury	3		

◆ A survey of 1994 showed that for the first time there were more European than American artists among the UK's Top 100 singles acts. British acts were having their worst spell on the US charts since the start of the Beat Boom, 32 years earlier.

◆ Celine Dion's minor US hit 'Think Twice' was one of the year's biggest sellers in Britain. Canadian Dion held the top single and album positions for five consecutive weeks, a feat last performed by The Beatles.

March 1995

This Mnth	Prev Mnth	Title	Artist	Label	Wks	(US 20 Pos)	
1	1	**Think Twice**	Celine Dion	Epic	20	(95)	G
2	10	**Don't Give Me Your Life**	Alex Party	Systematic	9		F L
3	-	**Push The Feeling On**	Nightcrawlers	ffrr	7		F
4	4	**I've Got A Little Something For You**	MN8	Columbia	8		F
5	-	**Love Can Build A Bridge**	Cher/Chrissie Hynde/ Neneh Cherry/Eric Clapton	London	5		L
6	-	**The Bomb! (These Sounds Fall Into My Mind)**	Bucketheads	Positiva	9	(49)	F L
7	7	**No More 'I Love You's**	Annie Lennox	RCA	5	(23)	
8	-	**Don't Stop (Wiggle Wiggle)**	Outhere Brothers	Eternal	11		F
9	-	**Turn On, Tune In, Cop Out**	Freak Power	4th & Broadway	5		F L
10	-	**Axel F/Keep Pushin'**	Clock	Media	5		F
11	9	**Reach Up (Papa's Got A Brand New Pig Bag)**	Perfecto Allstarz	Perfecto	7		F L
12	2	**Set You Free**	N-Trance	All Around The World	10	F	
13	-	**Julia Says**	Wet Wet Wet	Precious	5		
14	-	**Wake Up Boo!**	Boo Radleys	Creation	3		F L
15	17	**Someday I'll Be Saturday Night**	Bon Jovi	Jambco	3		
16	-	**Whoops Now/What'll I Do**	Janet Jackson	Virgin	4		
17	5	**Here Comes The Hotstepper**	Ini Kamoze	Columbia	11	(1)	F L
18	11	**Bedtime Story**	Madonna	Maverick	2	(42)	
19	-	**Over My Shoulder**	Mike + The Mechanics	Virgin	3		L
20	3	**Cotton Eye Joe**	Rednex	Internal Affairs	12	(25)	F

April 1995

This Mnth	Prev Mnth	Title	Artist	Label	Wks	(US 20 Pos)	
1	8	**Don't Stop (Wiggle Wiggle)**	Outhere Brothers	Eternal	11		F
2	-	**Back For Good**	Take That	Arista	8	(7)	
3	-	**Two Can Play The Game**	Bobby Brown	MCA	8		
4	-	**U Sure Do**	Strike	Fresh	5		F L
5	13	**Julia Says**	Wet Wet Wet	Precious	5		
6	-	**Baby Baby**	Corona	Eternal	5	(57)	
7	5	**Love Can Build A Bridge**	Cher/Chrissie Hynde/ Neneh Cherry/Eric Clapton	London	5		L
8	-	**Not Over Yet**	Grace	Perfecto	4		F L
9	-	**Have You Ever Really Loved A Woman?**	Bryan Adams	A&M	4	(1)	
10	1	**Think Twice**	Celine Dion	Epic	20	(95)	G
11	-	**If You Love Me**	Brownstone	MJJ	6	(8)	F
12	-	**Chains**	Tina Arena	Columbia	8	(38)	F L
13	-	**Key To My Life**	Boyzone	Polydor	4		
14	6	**The Bomb! (These Sounds Fall Into My Mind)**	Bucketheads	Positiva	9	(49)	F L
15	2	**Don't Give Me Your Life**	Alex Party	Systematic	9		F L
16	-	**Baby It's You**	Beatles	Apple	2	(67)	L
17	-	**If You Only Let Me In**	MN8	Columbia	3		
18	9	**Turn On, Tune In, Cop Out**	Freak Power	4th & Broadway	5		F L
19	-	**Best In Me**	Let Loose	Mercury	2		L
20	-	**Let It Rain**	East 17	London	3		

◆ At times re-mixes of singles that flopped when first released hogged half of the UK Top 10. TV actors Robson Green & Jerome Flynn became the first UK act to make their chart debut at No. 1. Their version of the oft-recorded 'Unchained Melody' sold a million in three weeks!

1995

This Mnth	Prev Mnth	Title	Artist	Label	Wks	20	(US Pos)	
1	-	**Guaglione**	Perez 'Prez' Prado	RCA	8			L
2	-	**Some Might Say**	Oasis	Creation	4			
3	-	**Dreamer**	Livin' Joy	Undiscovered	5	(72)		L
4	2	**Back For Good**	Take That	Arista	8	(7)		
5	-	**Scatman (Ski-Ba-Bop-Ba-Dop-Bop)**	Scatman John	RCA	8	(60)		F
6	-	**Unchained Melody/ White Cliffs ...**	Robson Green/Jerome Flynn	RCA	11			F G
7	13	**Key To My Life**	Boyzone	Polydor	4			
8	12	**Chains**	Tina Arena	Columbia	8	(38)		F L
9	3	**Two Can Play The Game**	Bobby Brown	MCA	8			
10	1	**Don't Stop (Wiggle Wiggle)**	Outhere Brothers	Eternal	11			F
11	-	**We're Gonna Do It Again**	Manchester United FC	PolyGram TV	3			L
12	-	**Love City Groove**	Love City Groove	Planet3	6			F L
13	-	**That Look In Your Eye**	Ali Campbell	Kuff	6			F L
14	-	**Your Loving Arms**	Billie Ray Martin	Magnet	6			F L
15	-	**Only One Road**	Celine Dion	Epic	3	(93)		
16	17	**If You Only Let Me In**	MN8	Columbia	3			
17	-	**Surrender Your Love**	Nightcrawlers/John Reid	Final Vinyl	4			
18	-	**The Changingman**	Paul Weller	Go! Discs	1			
19	9	**Have You Ever Really Loved A Woman?**	Bryan Adams	A&M	4	(1)		
20	-	**This Is How We Do It**	Montell Jordan	Def Jam	5	(1)		F

This Mnth	Prev Mnth	Title	Artist	Label	Wks	20	(US Pos)	
1	6	**Unchained Melody/ White Cliffs ...**	Robson Green/Jerome Flynn	RCA	11			F G
2	-	**Common People**	Pulp	Island	7			
3-	-	**(Everybody's Got To Learn Sometime) I Need Your....**	Baby D	Systematic	6			
4	1	**Guaglione**	Perez 'Prez' Prado	RCA	8			L
5	-	**Scream**	Michael & Janet Jackson	Epic	5	(5)		
6	5	**Scatman (Ski-Ba-Bop-Ba-Dop-Bop)**	Scatman John	RCA	8	(60)		F
7	-	**Hold Me, Thrill Me, Kiss Me, Kill Me**	U2	Island	10	(16		
8	13	**That Look In Your Eye**	Ali Campbell	Kuff	6			F L
9	-	**This Ain't A Love Song**	Bon Jovi	Mercury	3	(14)		
10	-	**Think Of You**	Whigfield	Systematic	6			
11	-	**Boom Boom Boom**	Outhere Brothers	Eternal	11	(65)		
12	-	**Don't Want To Forgive Me Now**	Wet Wet Wet	Precious	3			
13	14	**Your Loving Arms**	Billie Ray Martin	Magnet	6			F L
14	17	**Surrender Your Love**	Nightcrawlers/John Reid	Final Vinyl	4			
15	-	**Yes**	McAlmont & Butler	Hut	3			F
16	-	**Right In The Night (Fall In Love With Music)**	Jam & Spoon Feat Plavka	Epic	5			F L
17	-	**A Girl Like You**	Edwyn Collins	Setanta	9	(32)		F L
18	-	**Reverend Black Grape**	Black Grape	Radioactive	1			F
19	-	**Search For The Hero**	M People	Deconstruction	3			
20	3	**Dreamer**	Livin' Joy	Undiscovered	5	(72)		L

◆ Take That's 'Back For Good' sold half a million in two weeks and their LP Nobody Else went double platinum in three days.

◆ Soon after Blur won a record four Brit Awards, arch rivals Oasis clocked up their first chart No. 1, 'Some Might Say' and five of their old singles re-charted.

1995

July 1995

This Mnth	Prev Mnth	Title	Artist	Label	Wks	(US 20 Pos)	
1	11	Boom Boom Boom	Outhere Brothers	Eternal	11	(65)	
2	1	Unchained Melody/ White Cliffs Of Dover	Robson Green/Jerome Flynn	RCA	11		F G
3	-	Shy Guy	Diana King	Work	9	(13)	F
4	7	Hold Me, Thrill Me, Kiss Me, Kill Me	U2	Island	10	(16)	
5	17	A Girl Like You	Edwyn Collins	Setanta	9	(32)	F L
6	-	Alright/Time	Supergrass	Parlophone	7		
7	-	Whoomph! (There It Is)	Clock	Media	5		
8	-	In The Summertime	Shaggy Featuring Rayvon	Virgin	7	(3)	
9	-	I'm A Believer	EMF/Reeves And Mortimer	Parlophone	3		L
10	-	Kiss From A Rose	Seal	ZTT	9	(1)	
11	10	Think Of You	Whigfield	Systematic	6		
12	3	(Everybody's Got To Learn Sometime) I Need Your...	Baby D	Systematic	6		
13	-	This Is A Call	Foo Fighters	Roswell	1		F
14	-	Shoot Me With Your Love	D:ream	Magnet	2		
15	-	Humpin' Around	Bobby Brown	MCA	2		
16	-	3 Is Family	Dana Dawson	EMI	4		F L
17	-	Try Me Out	Corona	Eternal	8		
18	-	Happy	MN8	Columbia	3		L
19	5	Scream	Michael Jackson/Janet Jackson	Epic	5	(5)	
20	-	Stillness In Time	Jamiroquai	Sony	2		

August 1995

This Mnth	Prev Mnth	Title	Artist	Label	Wks	(US 20 Pos)	
1	-	Never Forget	Take That	RCA	6		
2	10	Kiss From A Rose	Seal	ZTT	9	(1)	
3	3	Shy Guy	Diana King	Work	9	(13)	F
4	1	Boom Boom Boom	Outhere Brothers	Eternal	11	(65)	
5	-	Waterfalls	TLC	Laface	10	(1)	
6	17	Try Me Out	Corona	Eterna	8		L
7	-	I Luv U Baby	Original	Ore	5		F L
8	-	So Good	Boyzone	Polydor	3		
9	6	Alright/Time	Supergrass	Parlophone	7		
10	-	Country House	Blur	Food	6		
11	-	Roll With It	Oasis	Creation	4		
12	-	Son Of A Gun	JX	Ffrreedom	3		L
13	-	I'm Only Sleeping/ Off On Holiday	Suggs	WEA	3		F
14	4	Hold Me, Thrill Me, Kiss Me, Kill Me	U2	Island	10	(16)	
15	-	Everybody	Clock	Media	3		
16	-	In The Name Of The Father	Black Grape	Radioactive	2		
17	8	In The Summertime	Shaggy Featuring Rayvon	Virgin	7	(3)	
18	-	Human Nature	Madonna	Maveric	1		
19	-	Don't You Want Me	Felix	Deconstruction	2		
20	5	A Girl Like You	Edwyn Collins	Setanta	9	(32)	F L

◆ For the first time in years, a battle for the top of the charts made the national press, when Oasis and Blur released new singles simultaneously. Blur's 'Country House' came in at No. 1 and 'Roll With It' by Oasis entered in runner-up position.

◆ Records were spending less time on the UK Top 20 than ever before. It was now quite normal for singles to peak in their first chart week and to spend less than three weeks on the Top 20.

1995

This Mnth	Prev Mnth	Title	Artist	Label	Wks	(US 20 Pos)	
1	-	**You Are Not Alone**	Michael Jackson	Epic	10	(1)	
2	-	**I'll Be There For You**	Rembrandts	East West	8	(17)	F L
3	10	**Country House**	Blur	Food	6		
4	-	**The Sunshine After The Rain**	Berri	Ffrreedom	6		F
5	-	**Stayin' Alive**	N-Trance Featuring Ricardo Da Force	All Around The World	6		
6	11	**Roll With It**	Oasis	Creation	4		
7	-	**Boombastic**	Shaggy	Virgin	8	(3)	
8	7	**I Luv U Baby**	Original	Ore	5		F L
9	-	**Who The F**k Is Alice?**	Smokie/Roy Chubby Brown	Now	10		L
10	5	**Waterfalls**	TLC	Laface	10	(1)	
11	-	**Fantasy**	Mariah Carey	Columbia	7	(1)	
12	-	**Fairground**	Simply Red	East West	9		
13	-	**Can I Touch You...There?**	Michael Bolton	Columbia	4	(27)	L
14	-	**Hideaway**	De'lacy	Slip'n'slide	4		F L
15	-	**Runaway**	Janet Jackson	Epic	3	(3)	
16	-	**Tu M'Aimes Encore (To Love Me Again)**	Celine Dion	Epic	3		
17	-	**La La La Hey Hey**	Outhere Brothers	Eternal	3		
18	-	**Scatman's World**	Scatman John	RCA	4		L
19	1	**Never Forget**	Take That	RCA	6		
20	-	**I Feel Love**	Donna Summer	Manifesto	2		L

This Mnth	Prev Mnth	Title	Artist	Label	Wks	(US 20 Pos)	
1	12	**Fairground**	Simply Red	East West	9		
2	7	**Boombastic**	Shaggy	Virgin	8	(3)	
3	9	**Who The F**k Is Alice?**	Smokie/Roy Chubby Brown	Now	10		L
4	-	**Mis-Shapes/Sorted For Es & Wizz**	Pulp	Island	4		
5	1	**You Are Not Alone**	Michael Jackson	Epic	10	(1)	
6	-	**When Love & Hate Collide**	Def Leppard	Bludgeon Riffola	6		L
7	11	**Fantasy**	Mariah Carey	Columbia	7	(1)	
8	-	**Gangsta's Paradise**	Coolio Featuring L.V.	Tommy Boy	17	(1)	G
9	-	**I'd Lie For You (And That's The Truth)**	Meat Loaf	MCA	5	(13)	L
10	-	**Power Of A Woman**	Eternal	EMI	4		
11	-	**Light Of My Life**	Louise	EMI	4		F
12	-	**Somewhere Somehow**	Wet Wet Wet	Precious	4		
13	5	**Stayin' Alive**	N-Trance Featuring Ricardo Da Force	All Around The World	6		
14	-	**Higher State Of Consciousness**	Josh Wink	Manifesto	3		F L
15	2	**I'll Be There For You**	Rembrandts	East West	8	(17)	F L
16	-	**Something For The Pain**	Bon Jovi	Mercury	3		
17	-	**Missing**	Everything But The Girl	Blanco Y Negro	16	(2)	
18	-	**Man On The Edge**	Iron Maiden	EMI	1		L
19	-	**Renegade Master**	Wildchild	Hi-Life	2		F L
20	-	**Walking In Memphis**	Cher	WEA	2		

◆ The Beatles' 'Free As A Bird' just failed to give them their 18th UK No. 1, which would have topped Elvis Presley's total. Their Anthology I double album sold an unprecedented 500,000 on its first day in America, and the first *Beatles Anthology* TV show attracted 47 million US viewers, double the amount of its nearest competitor.

November 1995

This Mnth	Prev Mnth	Title	Artist	Label	Wks	(US 20 Pos)	
1	8	**Gangsta's Paradise**	Coolio Featuring L.V.	Tommy Boy	17	(1)	G
2	-	**I Believe/Up On The Roof**	Robson Green & Jerome Flynn	RCA	10		G
3	17	**Missing**	Everything But The Girl	Blanco Y Negro	16	(2)	
4	-	**Wonderwall**	Oasis	Creation	13	(8)	
5	-	**Heaven For Everyone**	Queen	Parlophone	4		
6	-	**Thunder**	East 17	London	8		
7	9	**I'd Lie For You (And That's The Truth)**	Meat Loaf	MCA	5	(13)	L
8	-	**You'll See**	Madonna	Maverick	8	(8)	
9	-	**Fairground**	Simply Red	East West	9		
10	6	**When Love & Hate Collide**	Def Leppard	Bludgeon Riffola	6		L
11	-	**The Universal**	Blur	Food/Parlophone	3		
12	-	**Anywhere Is**	Enya	WEA	7		L
13	-	**I Believe**	Happy Clappers	Shindig/PWL	2		F L
14	3	**Who The F**k Is Alice?**	Smokie/Roy Chubby Brown	Now	10		L
15	-	**Father And Son**	Boyzone	Polydor	11		
16	10	**Power Of A Woman**	Eternal	EMI	4		
17	-	**It's Oh So Quiet**	Bjork	One Little Indian	9		
18	2	**Boombastic**	Shaggy	Virgin	8	(3)	
19	-	**Goldeneye**	Tina Turner	Parlophone	2		L
20	-	**He's On The Phone**	Saint Etienne	Heavenly	2		L

December 1995

		Title	Artist	Label	Wks		
1	15	**Father And Son**	Boyzone	Polydor	11		
2	-	**Earth Song**	Michael Jackson	Epic	11		G
3	2	**I Believe/Up On The Roof**	Robson Green/Jerome Flynn	RCA	10		G
4	1	**Gangsta's Paradise**	Coolio Featuring L.V.	Tommy Boy	17	(1)	G
5	3	**Missing**	Everything But The Girl	Blanco Y Negro	16	(2)	
6	17	**It's Oh So Quiet**	Bjork	One Little Indian	9		
7	4	**Wonderwall**	Oasis	Creation	13	(8)	
8	-	**Free As A Bird**	Beatles	Apple	4	(6)	
9	-	**One Sweet Day**	Mariah Carey & Boyz II Men	Columbia	6	(1)	
10	12	**Anywhere Is**	Enya	WEA	7		L
11	-	**Wonderwall**	Mike Flowers Pops	London	3		F L
12	-	**Disco 2000**	Pulp	Island	6		
13	-	**Miss Sarajevo**	Passengers	Island	3		F L
14	-	**A Winter's Tale**	Queen	Parlophone	2		L
15	-	**The Gift Of Christmas**	Childliners	London	4		F L
16	-	**I Am Blessed**	Eternal	EMI	7		
17	-	**The Best Things In Life Are Free**	Luther Vandross/Janet Jackson	A&M	3		
18	8	**You'll See**	Madonna	Maverick/Sire	8	(8)	
19	-	**Gold**	TAFKAP	Warner	5		
20	-	**Lie To Me**	Bon Jovi	Mercury	2		

◆ In Christmas week, a record-shattering 10.6 million albums were sold in the UK. The biggest seller was Robson & Jerome's eponymous debut LP which sold a record-breaking 2 million copies in just seven weeks. The duo also clocked up their second No. 1 single, 'I Believe', which had amassed 600,000 advance orders.

1996

This Mnth	Prev Mnth	Title	Artist	Label	Wks	(US 20 Pos)	
1	2	**Earth Song**	Michael Jackson	Epic	11		G
2	1	**Father And Son**	Boyzone	Polydor	11		
3	5	**Missing**	Everything But The Girl	Blanco Y Negro	16	(2)	
4	7	**Wonderwall**	Oasis	Creation	13	(8)	
5	-	**Jesus To A Child**	George Michael	Virgin	4	(7)	
6	-	**So Pure**	Baby D	Systematic	4		L
7	-	**Spaceman**	Babylon Zoo	EMI	7		G L
8	6	**It's Oh So Quiet**	Bjork	One Little Indian	9		
9	11	**Wonderwall**	Mike Flowers Pops	London	3		F L
10	4	**Gangsta's Paradise**	Coolio Featuring L.V.	Tommy Boy	17	(1)	F
11	16	**I Am Blessed**	Eternal	EMI	7		
12	-	**Whole Lotta Love**	Goldbug	Acid Jazz	3		F L
13	-	**Creep '96**	TLC	Laface	3		L
14	-	**Anything**	3T	MJJ	9	(15)	F
15	-	**One By One**	Cher	WEA	5		L
16	-	**If You Wanna Party**	Molella Featuring The Outhere Brothers	Eternal	6		F L
17	-	**Sandstorm**	Cast	Polydor	2		
18	3	**I Believe/Up On The Roof**	Robson Green/ Jerome Flynn	RCA	10		G
19	-	**Too Hot**	Coolio	Tommy Boy	2		
20	-	**Why You Treat Me So Bad**	Shaggy Featuring Grand Puba	Virgin	2		

This Mnth	Prev Mnth	Title	Artist	Label	Wks	(US 20 Pos)	
1	7	**Spaceman**	Babylon Zoo	EMI	7		G L
2	14	**Anything**	3T	MJJ	9		F
3	-	**Slight Return**	Bluetones	Superior Quality	4		
4	-	**Lifted**	Lighthouse Family	Wild Card	6		F
5	-	**I Got 5 On It**	Luniz	Noo Trybe	7	(8)	F L
6	6	**I Just Want To Make Love To You**	Etta James	/MCA	4		F L
7	-	**One Of Us**	Joan Osborne	Blue Gorilla	4	(4)	F L
8	5	**Jesus To A Child**	George Michael	Virgin	4	(7)	
9	-	**I Wanna Be A Hippy**	Technohead	Mokum	9		F L
10	-	**Children**	Robert Miles	Deconstruction	13	(54)	F
11	-	**Do U Still?**	East 17	London	3		
12	-	**Open Arms**	Mariah Carey	Columbia	2		
13	-	**Not A Dry Eye In The House**	Meat Loaf	Virgin	3		
14	15	**One By One**	Cher	WEA	5		L
15	-	**Street Spirit (Fade Out)**	Radiohead	Parlophone	1		
16	12	**Whole Lotta Love**	Goldbug	Acid Jazz	3		F L
17	-	**Stereotypes**	Blur	Food	2		
18	-	**No Fronts - The Remixes**	Dog Eat Dog	Roadrunner	2		F
19	-	**Hyperballad**	Bjork	One Little Indian	1		L
20	-	**Change Your Mind**	Upside Down	World	3		F L

◆ The Brit Awards attracted massive media coverage when Jarvis Cocker of Pulp semi-sabotaged Michael Jackson's performance of 'Earth Song'.

◆ The Beatles, whose Anthology I passed the 10 million mark world-wide, ended this last quarter with Anthology 2 at the top.

◆ Take That, Britain's top act of the 1990s, disbanded. Their final single, 'How Deep Is Your Love' giving them eight No.1s from their last nine releases.

March 1996

This Mnth	Prev Mnth	Title	Artist	Label	Wks	(US 20 Pos)	
1	10	Children	Robert Miles	Deconstruction	13	(54)	F
2	-	Don't Look Back In Anger	Oasis	Creation	8		
3	-	How Deep Is Your Love	Take That	RCA	7		L
4	-	Coming Home Now	Boyzone	Polydor	4		
5	-	Give Me A Little More Time	Gabrielle	Go!discs	10		
6	9	I Wanna Be A Hippy	Technohead	Mokum	9		F L
7	2	Anything	3T	MJJ	9		F
8	-	Return Of The Mack	Mark Morrison	WEA	*10		
9	-	I Got 5 On It	Luniz	Noo Trybe	7	(8)	F L
10	-	Firestarter	Prodigy	XL	6		
11	-	Real Love	Beatles	Apple	2	(11)	
12	-	Stupid Girl	Garbage	Mushroom	2		
13	-	The X Files	Mark Snow	Warner	6		F L
14	-	Passion	Gat Decor	Way Of Life	3		F L
15	-	Spaceman	Babylon Zoo	EMI	7		G L
16	-	Going Out	Supergrass	Parlophone	3		L
17	-	Falling Into You	Celine Dion	Epic	5		
18	-	Perseverance	Terrorvision	Total Vegas	1		F L
19	-	These Days	Bon Jovi	Mercury	2		
20	4	Lifted	Lighthouse Family	Wild Card	6		F

April 1996

		Title	Artist	Label	Wks	(US Pos)	
1	8	Return Of The Mack	Mark Morrison	WEA	14	(2)	
2	10	Firestarter	Prodigy	XL	6	(30)	
3	-	Ooh Aah...Just A Little Bit	Gina G	Eternal/WEA	11	(12)	F
4	13	The X Files	Mark Snow	Warner	6		F L
5	1	Children	Robert Miles	Deconstruction	14	(21)	F
6	5	Give Me A Little More Time	Gabrielle	Go!Discs	10		
7	-	They Don't Care About Us	Michael Jackson	Epic	5	(30)	
8	-	A Design For Life	Manic Street Preachers	Epic	5		
9	-	California Love	2 Pac Feat Dr Dre	Death Row/Island	3	(1)	F
10	-	Cecilia	Suggs	WEA	8		L
11	-	X-Files	DJ Dado	ZYX	3		F L
12	-	Walking Wounded	Everything But The Girl	Virgin	2		
13	-	Goldfinger	Ash	Infectious	2		
14	-	Peaches	Presidents Of The United States	Columbia	3	(29)	
15	3	How Deep Is Your Love	Take That	RCA	7		L
16	-	You've Got It Bad	Ocean Colour Scene	MCA	2		
17	-	Keep On Jumpin'	Lisa Marie Experience	3 Beat/ffrr	4		F L
18	-	Bulls On Parade	Rage Against The Machine	Epic	1		L
19	2	Don't Look Back In Anger	Oasis	Creation	8	(55)	
20	-	Something Changed	Pulp	Island	1		

◆ Prodigy's tenth Top 20 single, 'Firestarter', took them to new heights. It not only gave the group their first UK No. 1, but it also helped propel their album, The Fat Of The Land, to the top of the charts in many other parts of the world including the USA.

◆ In its 10th month on the chart the album Jagged Little Pill by Canadian Alanis Morissette passed the million sales mark and finally reached No. 1. It headed the UK chart for 10 weeks, a female record which was previously held by Madonna, who owned Morissette's US label!

1996

This Mnth	Prev Mnth	Title	Artist	Label	Wks	(US 20 Pos)	
1	-	Fastlove	George Michael	Virgin	7	(8)	
2	3	Ooh Aah...Just A Little Bit	Gina G	Eternal	11	(12)	F
3	1	Return Of The Mack	Mark Morrison	WEA	14	(2)	
4	10	Cecilia	Suggs	WEA	8		L
5	-	Move Move Move (The Red Tribe)	Manchester United FA Cup Squad	Music Collection	5		L
6	8	A Design For Life	Manic Street Preachers	Epic	5		
7	-	There's Nothing I Won't Do	JX	Ffrreedom	8		
8	-	Charmless Man	Blur	Food/Parlophone	3		
9	-	Pass & Move (It's The Liverpool Groove)	Liverpool FC & The Boot Room Boys	Telstar	2		L
10	-	Nobody Knows	Tony Rich Project	Lafac	10	(2)	F L
11	7	They Don't Care About Us	Michael Jackson	Epic	5	(30)	
12	-	Tonight, Tonight	Smashing Pumpkins	Virgin	2	(36)	
13	-	Cut Some Rug/Castle Rock	Bluetones	Superior Quality	1		
14	-	Before	Pet Shop Boys	Parlophone	1		
15	-	Woo-Hah!! Got You All In Check	Busta Rhymes	Elektra	2	(8)	F
16	17	Keep On Jumpin'	Lisa Marie Experience	/ffrr	4		F L
17	-	Klubbhopping	Klubbheads	AM:PM	3		F L
18	-	24/7	3T	MJJ	3		
19	-	Blue Moon/Only You	John Alford	Love This	2		L
20	-	Sale Of The Century	Sleeper	Indolent	2		

This Mnth	Prev Mnth	Title	Artist	Label	Wks	(US 20 Pos)	
1	-	Three Lions (Official Song Of The England Team)	Baddiel & Skinner & Lightning Seeds	Epic	10		F L
2	-	Mysterious Girl	Peter Andre Feat Bubbler Ranx	Mushroom	13		
3	-	Killing Me Softly	Fugees	Columbia	12		F G
4	-	Because You Loved Me	Celine Dion	Epic	10	(1)	
5	10	Nobody Knows	Tony Rich Project	Laface/Arista	10	(2)	F L
6	2	Ooh Aah...Just A Little Bit	Gina G	Eternal/WEA	11	(12)	F
7	-	Don't Stop Movin'	Livin' Joy	Undiscovered/MCA	9	(67)	
8	-	The Day We Caught The Train	Ocean Colour Scene	MCA	5		
9	-	Always Be My Baby	Mariah Carey	Columbia	5	(1)	
10	7	There's Nothing I Won't Do	JX	Ffrreedom	8		
11	-	Blurred	Pianoman	Ffrreedom	4		F L
12	-	Naked	Louise	1st Avenue/EMI	3		
13	-	Until It Sleeps	Metallica	Vertigo	2	(10)	
14	1	Fastlove	George Michael	Virgin	7	(8)	
15	-	The Only Thing That Looks Good On Me Is You	Bryan Adams	A&M	2	(52)	
16	-	Fable	Robert Miles	Deconstruction	2		
17	-	Theme From 'Mission: Impossible'	Adam Clayton & Larry Mullen	Mother	7	(7)	F L
18	-	Make It With You	Let Loose	Mercury	2		L
19	-	England's Irie	Black Grape Featuring Joe Strummer & Keith Allen	Radioactive	2		L
20	3	Return Of The Mack	Mark Morrison	WEA	14	(2)	

◆ As Phil Collins departed Genesis, Australasian act Crowded House (whose Very Best Of album topped the chart soon after) announced they were disbanding and The Sex Pistols re-united after 18 years for the Filthy Lucre Tour - the group members netting £750,000 each. The most popular football song of all time, 'Three Lions' by Baddiel & Skinner and The Lightning Seeds, topped the chart and was heard throughout the Euro 96 competition.

July 1996

This Mnth	Prev Mnth	Title	Artist	Label	Wks	(US 20 Pos)	
1	3	**Killing Me Softly**	Fugees	Columbia	12		F G
2	1	**Three Lions (Official Song Of The England Team)**	Baddiel & Skinner & Lightning Seeds	Epic	10		F L
3	2	**Mysterious Girl**	Peter Andre Feat Bubbler Ranx	Mushroom	13		
4	-	**Born Slippy**	Underworld	Junior Boy's Own	10		F L
5	4	**Because You Loved Me**	Celine Dion	Epic	10	(1)	
6	-	**Wannabe**	Spice Girls	Virgin	13	(1)	F
7	-	**Forever Love**	Gary Barlow	RCA	4		F
8	7	**Don't Stop Movin'**	Livin' Joy	Undiscovered	9	(67)	
9	-	**Tattva**	Kula Shaker	Columbia	3		F
10	-	**You're Makin' Me High**	Toni Braxton	Laface	4	(1)	
11	-	**In Too Deep**	Belinda Carlisle	Chrysalis	2		
12	-	**Jazz It Up**	Reel 2 Real	Positiva	3		L
13	-	**Oh Yeah**	Ash	Infectious	2		
14	-	**Crazy**	Mark Morrison	WEA	3		
15	-	**Macarena (Bayside Boys Mix)**	Los Del Rio	RCA	11	(1)	F L
16	-	**Keep On Jumpin'**	Todd Terry Featuring Martha Wash & Jocelyn Brown	Manifesto	3		F
17	-	**Higher State Of Consciousness '96**	Wink	Manifesto	5		F L
18	-	**Where Love Lies**	Alison Limerick	Arista	2		L
19	9	**Always Be My Baby**	Mariah Carey	Columbia	5	(1)	
20	-	**Bad Actress**	Terrorvision	Total Vegas	1		

August 1996

This Mnth	Prev Mnth	Title	Artist	Label	Wks	(US 20 Pos)	
1	6	**Wannabe**	Spice Girls	Virgin	13	(1)	F
2	15	**Macarena (Bayside Boys Mix)**	Los Del Rio	RCA	11	(1)	F L
3	1	**Killing Me Softly**	Fugees	Columbia	12		F G
4	-	**Why**	3T Featuring Michael Jackson	MJJ	3		
5	-	**Good Enough**	Dodgy	A&M	5		
6	-	**Freedom**	Robbie Williams	RCA	3		F
7	3	**Mysterious Girl**	Peter Andre Feat Bubbler Ranx	Mushroom	13		
8	-	**How Bizarre**	OMC	Polydor	10		F L
9	4	**Born Slippy**	Underworld	Junior Boy's Own	10		F L
10	-	**We've Got It Goin' On**	Backstreet Boys	Jive	4	(69)	
11	-	**Someday**	Eternal	EMI	3		
12	-	**Trash**	Suede	Nude	2		
13	-	**Spinning The Wheel**	George Michael	Virgin	4		
14	-	**Tha Crossroads**	Bone Thugs N Harmony	Epic	5	(1)	F
15	-	**Virtual Insanity**	Jamiroquai	Sony S^2	7		
16	-	**E-Bow The Letter**	REM	Warner Bros.	2	(49)	
17	17	**Higher State Of Consciousness '96**	Wink	Manifesto	5		F L
18	-	**Everything Must Go**	Manic Street Preachers	Epic	2		
19	-	**Undivided Love**	Louise	EMI	3		
20	-	**Peacock Suite**	Paul Weller	Go! Discs	1		

◆ Newcomers the Spice Girls notched up the first of a record shattering six successive UK No. 1 singles with 'Wannabe'. The track, which was the first ever by an all-British girl group to reach the top, went on to top the charts in more than 30 countries and became the biggest selling debut record by a British act.

◆ Veteran duo Los Del Rio scored the biggest ever hit from Spain with 'Macarena', which spent a record breaking 60 weeks on the US Top 100.

1996

This Mnth	Prev Mnth	Title	Artist	Label	Wks	(US 20 Pos)		
1	1	**Wannabe**	Spice Girls	Virgin	13	(1)	F	G
2	-	**Ready Or Not**	Fugees	Columbia	7			
3	-	**Flava**	Peter Andre	Mushroom	5			
4	-	**I've Got A Little Puppy**	Smurfs	EMI TV	5			
5	15	**Virtual Insanity**	Jamiroquai	Sony S^2	7			
6	-	**Hey Dude**	Kula Shaker	Columbia	3			
7	-	**Breakfast At Tiffany's**	Deep Blue Something	Interscope	8	(5)	F L	
8	-	**One To Another**	Charlatans	Beggars Banquet	2			
9	-	**I'm Alive**	Stretch & Vern Present Maddog	ffrr	4		F L	
10	8	**How Bizarre**	OMC	Polydor	10		F L	
11	2	**Macarena**	Los Del Rio	RCA	11	(1)	F L	
12	-	**Escaping**	Dina Carroll	A&M	4		L	
13	13	**Spinning The Wheel**	George Michael	Virgin	4			
14	-	**Seven Days And One Week**	BBE	Positiva	5		F	
15	-	**The Circle**	Ocean Colour Scene	MCA	2			
16	-	**I Love You Always Forever**	Donna Lewis	Atlantic	9	(2)	F L	
17	-	**Marblehead Johnson**	Bluetones	Superior Quality	2			
18	-	**Me And You Versus The World**	Space	Gut	3			
19	-	**Always Breaking My Heart**	Belinda Carlisle	Chrysalis	2			
20	-	**Oh What A Night**	Clock	MCA	7			

This Mnth	Prev Mnth	Title	Artist	Label	Wks	(US 20 Pos)		
1	7	**Breakfast At Tiffany's**	Deep Blue Something	Interscope	8	(5)	F L	
2	-	**It's All Coming Back To Me Now**	Celine Dion	Epic	7	(2)		
3	-	**Setting Sun**	Chemical Brothers	Virgin	3			
4	16	**I Love You Always Forever**	Donna Lewis	Atlantic	9	(2)	F L	
5	14	**Seven Days And One Week**	BBE	Positiva	5		F	
6	-	**You're Gorgeous**	Baby Bird	Echo	8		F	
7	-	**Words**	Boyzone	Polydor	6			
8	2	**Ready Or Not**	Fugees	Columbia	7			
9	-	**Rotterdam**	Beautiful South	Go! Discs	4			
10	12	**Escaping**	Dina Carroll	A&M	4		L	
11	-	**Say You'll Be There**	Spice Girls	Virgin	11	(3)		
12	-	**Insomnia**	Faithless	Cheeky	6		F	
13	-	**Loungin'**	LL Cool J	Def Jam	4	(3)		
14	-	**Flying**	Cast	Polydor	2			
15	-	**Trippin'**	Mark Morrison	WEA	2			
16	3	**Flava**	Peter Andre	Mushroom	5			
17	-	**No Diggity**	Blackstreet Featuring Dr Dre	Interscope	3	(1)	F	
18	-	**Beautiful Ones**	Suede	Nude	2			
19	-	**Dance Into The Light**	Phil Collins	Face Value	2	(45)	L	
20	-	**Kevin Carter**	Manic Street Preachers	Epic	1			

◆ As America's Backstreet Boys and 3T joined the boy band elite, Gary Barlow and Robbie Williams reached the Top 3 with their first solo singles since leaving the 1990s top boy band, Take That.

◆ The Fugees and Deep Blue Something helped keep the flag flying for American groups. The former achieved two No. 1s in three months, with their million selling revival of Roberta Flack's 1973 hit 'Killing Me Softly' and 'Ready Or Not', which was based a 1968 track by The Delfonics. Deep Blue Something were the first US rock band to top the UK chart with a self-penned debut hit since Buddy Holly & The Crickets in 1957.

1996

November 1996

This Mnth	Prev Mnth	Title	Artist	Label	Wks	(US 20 Pos)	
1	11	**Say You'll Be There**	Spice Girls	Virgin	11	(3)	
2	-	**If You Ever**	East 17 Featuring Gabrielle	London	10		
3	-	**What Becomes Of The Broken Hearted**	Robson Green & Jerome Flynn	RCA	6		L
4	-	**Un-Break My Heart**	Toni Braxton	Laface	14	(1)	
5	-	**Breathe**	Prodigy	XL	10		
6	-	**What's Love Got To Do t With I**	Warren G Featuring Adina Howard	Interscope	6		
7	7	**Words**	Boyzone	Polydor	6		
8	12	**Insomnia (remix)**	Faithless	Cheeky	6		F
9	-	**Hillbilly Rock Hillbilly Roll**	Woolpackers	RCA	9		F L
10	6	**You're Gorgeous**	Baby Bird	Echo	8		F
11	-	**One & One**	Robert Miles Featuring Maria Nayler	Deconstruction	10	(54)	
12	-	**Stranger In Moscow**	Michael Jackson	Epic	3	(91)	
13	-	**No Woman No Cry**	Fugees	Columbia	3		
14	-	**Angel**	Simply Red	East West	2		
15	-	**Child**	Mark Owen	RCA	3		F
16	-	**I Belong To You**	Gina G	Eternal/WEA	3		
17	-	**Place Your Hands**	Reef	Sony	3		
18	2	**It's All Coming Back To Me Now**	Celine Dion	Epic	7	(2)	
19	-	**Govinda**	Kula Shaker	Columbia	3		
20	-	**I'll Never Break Your Heart**	Backstreet Boys	Jive	2		

December 1996

This Mnth	Prev Mnth	Title	Artist	Label	Wks	(US 20 Pos)	
1	4	**Un-Break My Heart**	Toni Braxton	Laface	14	(1)	
2	5	**Breathe**	Prodigy	XL	10		
3	11	**One & One**	Robert Miles Featuring Maria Nayler	Deconstruction	10	(54)	
4	-	**A Different Beat**	Boyzone	Polydor	5		
5	-	**Knockin' On Heaven's Door/ Throw These Guns Away**	Dunblane	BMG	4		F L
6	-	**I Feel You**	Peter Andre	Mushroom	3		
7	-	**I Need You**	3T	Epic	6		
8	-	**2 Becomes 1**	Spice Girls	Virgin	9	(4)	
9	-	**Forever**	Damage	Big Life	5		
10	-	**Horny**	Mark Morrison	WEA	5		
11	-	**Don't Cry For Me Argentina**	Madonna	Warner Bros.	6	(8)	
12	-	**All By Myself**	Celine Dion	Epic	4	(4)	
13	-	**Don't Marry Her**	Beautiful South	Go! Discs	5		L
14	-	**Cosmic Girl**	Jamiroquai	Sony S^2	6		
15	6	**What's Love Got To Do With It**	Warren G Featuring Adina Howard	Interscope	6		
16	9	**Hillbilly Rock Hillbilly Roll**	Woolpackers	RCA	9		F L
17	-	**Your Christmas Wish**	Smurfs	EMI TV	3		L
18	2	**If You Ever**	East 17 Featuring Gabrielle	London	10		
19	-	**Australia**	Manic Street Preachers	Epic	1		L
20	13	**No Woman No Cry**	Fugees	Columbia	3		

◆ The debut album by the Spice Girls, Spice, went platinum in the UK after just five days . It became the biggest selling and fastest selling debut album ever by a British act. It also topped the chart in over a dozen other countries and sold close to 20 million copies worldwide. The quintet also won the battle for the Christmas No. 1 with 2 Become 1, which amassed over 700,000 advance orders. It was the fastest selling single since Band Aid.

1997

This Mnth	Prev Mnth	Title	Artist	Label	Wks	(US 20 Pos)	
1	8	**2 Become 1**	Spice Girls	Virgin	9	(4)	
2	-	**Professional Widow**					
		(It's Got To Be Big)	Tori Amos	East West	5		L
3	1	**Un-Break My Heart**	Toni Braxton	Laface/Arista	14	(1)	
4	11	**Don't Cry For Me Argentina**	Madonna	Warner Bros.	6	(8)	
5	-	**Quit Playing Games**					
		(With My Heart)	Backstreet Boys	Jive	6	(2)	
6	3	**One & One**	Robert Miles				
			Featuring Maria Nayler	Deconstruction	10	(54)	
7	-	**Say What You Want**	Texas	Mercury	6		
8	-	**Don't Let Go (Love)**	En Vogue	East West America	10	(2)	
9	-	**Your Woman**	White Town	Chrysalis	5	(23)	F L
10	-	**Satan**	Orbital	Internal	2		
11	5	**Knockin' On Heaven's Door-**					
		Throw These Guns Away	Dunblane	BMG	4		F L
12	-	**Hey Child**	East 17	London	2		L
13	-	**People Hold On**	Lisa Stansfield Vs				
		(The Bootleg Mixes)	The Dirty Rotten Scoundrels	Arista	2		
14	2	**Breathe**	Prodigy	XL	10		
15	-	**Where Do You Go**	No Mercy	Arista	12	(5)	F
16	10	**Horny**	Mark Morrison	WEA	5		
17	4	**A Different Beat**	Boyzone	Polydor	5		
18	-	**Saturday Night**	Suede	Nude	1		
19	-	**I Can Make You Feel Good**	Kavana	Nemesis	3		F
20	-	**Come Back Brighter**	Reef	Sony	2		

This Mnth	Prev Mnth	Title	Artist	Label	Wks	(US 20 Pos)	
1	15	**Where Do You Go**	No Mercy	Arista	12	(5)	F
2	9	**Your Woman**	White Town	Chrysalis	5	(23)	F L
3	-	**Ain't Nobody**	LL Cool J	Geffen	4	(46)	
4	8	**Don't Let Go (Love)**	En Vogue	East West America	10	(2)	
5	-	**Discotheque**	U2	Island	3	(10)	
6	-	**Beetlebum**	Blur	Food	2		
7	7	**Say What You Want**	Texas	Mercury	6		
8	-	**Don't Speak**	No Doubt	Interscope	11		F
9	-	**Older/I Can't Make You Love Me**	George Michael	Virgin	2		
10	-	**Nancy Boy**	Placebo	Elevator Music	3		F
11	-	**Clementine**	Mark Owen	RCA	3		L
12	-	**Remember Me**	Blue Boy	Pharm	8		F L
13	-	**I Shot The Sheriff**	Warren G	Def Jam	3	(20)	
14	-	**Toxygene**	Orb	Island	2		
15	-	**The Day We Find Love**	911	Ginga	2		
16	-	**Barrel Of A Gun**	Depeche Mode	Mute	1		
17	-	**Do You Know**	Michelle Gayle	RCA	2		
18	-	**Walk On By**	Gabrielle	Go. Beat	2		L
19	-	**Ain't Talkin' 'Bout Dub**	Apollo Four Forty	Stealth Sonic	3		F L
20	-	**Da Funk/Musique**	Daft Punk	Virgin	2	(61)	F

◆ Madonna took the song 'Don't Cry For Me Argentina' into the UK Top 5 for the third time, and all the way to the top of the European chart. It was, perhaps surprisingly, the first recording of an Andrew Lloyd Webber song to reach the US Top 10. The track was taken from the soundtrack album to her film Evita, which gave the recent mum her fifth UK No. 1.

◆ Among the acts returning to the Top 20 singles chart after a notable absence were British bands Texas, Depeche Mode and the Bee Gees.

1997

March 1997

This Mnth	Prev Mnth	Title	Artist	Label	Wks	(US 20 Pos)	
1	8	Don't Speak	No Doubt	Interscope	11		F
2	-	Encore Une Fois	Sash!	Multiply	10		F
3	-	Mama/Who Do You Think You Are	Spice Girls	Virgin	7		
4	1	Where Do You Go	No Mercy	Arista	12	(5)	F
5	-	Alone	Bee Gees	Polydor	5	(28)	
6	-	Hush	Kula Shaker	Columbia	3		L
7	-	Rumble In The Jungle	Fugees	Mercury	4		L
8	-	You Got The Love	Source Featuring Candi Staton	React	3		L
9	-	Don't You Love Me	Eternal	EMI	3		
10	-	Isn't It A Wonder	Boyzone	Polydor	3		
11	-	If I Never See You Again	Wet Wet Wet	Precious Org.	3		
12	-	I Believe I Can Fly	R. Kelly	Jive	11	(2)	
13	4	Don't Let Go (Love)	En Vogue	East West America	10	(2)	
14	-	Fresh	Gina G	Eternal	3		
15	-	Anywhere For You	Backstreet Boys	Jive	2		
16	12	Remember Me	Blue Boy	Pharm	8		F L
17	-	Flash	BBE	Positiva	2		L
18	-	Natural	Peter Andre	Mushroom	2		
19	-	Swallowed	Bush	Interscope	2		F L
20	-	Love Guaranteed	Damage	Big Life	2		

April 1997

This Mnth	Prev Mnth	Title	Artist	Label	Wks	(US 20 Pos)	
1	12	I Believe I Can Fly	R. Kelly	Jive	11	(2)	
2	1	Don't Speak	No Doubt	Interscope	11		F
3	-	Belissima	DJ Quicksilver	Positiva	12		F
4	3	Mama/Who Do You Think You Are	Spice Girls	Virgin	7		
5	-	Block Rockin' Beats	Chemical Brothers	Virgin	3		
6	-	Richard III	Supergrass	Parlophone	2		
7	-	Song 2	Blur	Food	2		
8	-	The Saint	Orbital	ffrr	2		L
9	-	Underwater Love	Smoke City	Jive	3		F L
10	-	Old Before I Die	Robbie Williams	RCA	3		
11	-	North Country Boy	Charlatans	Beggars Banquet	2		
12	-	Ready Or Not	Course	The Brothers	4		F
13	-	Staring At The Sun	U2	Island	2	(26)	
14	-	It's No Good	Depeche Mode	Mute	2	(38)	L
15	2	Encore Une Fois	Sash!	Multiply	10		F
16	-	You Might Need Somebody	Shola Ama	WEA	8		F
17	-	Around The World	Daft Punk	Virgin	2	(61)	L
18	-	Don't Leave Me	Blackstreet	Interscope	5		
19	-	Free Me	Cast	Polydor	2		
20	-	Hit 'Em High (The Monstars' Anthem)	B Real/Busta Rhymes/Coolio/LL Cool J/M. Man	Atlantic	2		F L

◆ It was announced that producer Frank Farian had sold over 80 million records around the globe. The German, who had previously given the world Boney M and Milli Vanilli, was now producing the Cuban-American pop trio, No Mercy.

◆ Jyoti Mishra (aka White Town) was the first British-based solo artist to enter the chart at No. 1 with a debut hit. The Indian born Mishra, who recorded 'Your Woman' in his bedroom, was unkindly tagged "The nerd from nowhere" by the media.

1997

This Mnth	Prev Mnth	Title	Artist	Label	Wks (US 20 Pos)	
1	-	Lovefool	Cardigans	Stockholm	7	F L
2	1	I Believe I Can Fly	R. Kelly	Jive	11 (2)	
3	16	You Might Need Somebody	Shola Ama	WEA	8	F
4	-	You Are Not Alone	Olive	RCA	6 (56)	F
5	3	Belissima	DJ Quicksilver	Positiva	12	F
6	-	Love Won't Wait	Gary Barlow	RCA	3	
7	-	Wonderful Tonight	Damage	Big Life	4	L
8	-	Time To Say Goodbye (Con Te Partiro)	Sarah Brightman & Andrea Bocelli	Coalition	8	L
9	-	Blood On The Dance Floor	Michael Jackson	Epic	2 (42)	
10	-	Love Shine A Light	Katrina & The Waves	Eternal	4	L
11	-	Bodyshakin'	911	Virgin	4	
12	-	Star People '97	George Michael	Virgin	2	
13	-	I Wanna Be The Only One	Eternal Featuring Bebe Winans	EMI	10	
14	-	Love Is The Law	Seahorses	Geffen	2	F
15	-	Please Don't Go	No Mercy	Arista	3 (21)	
16	-	I'll Be There For You	Rembrandts	East West	5 (17)	L
17	-	Closer Than Close	Rosie Gaines	Big Bang	7	F L
18	-	I'm A Man Not A Boy	North & South	RCA	3	F
19	-	Alright	Jamiroquai	Sony S^2	2 (78)	
20	18	Don't Leave Me	Blackstreet	Interscope	5	

1	-	Mmmbop	Hanson	Mercury	8 (1)	F
2	13	I Wanna Be The Only One	Eternal Featuring Bebe Winans	EMI	10	
3	8	Time To Say Goodbye (Con Te Partiro)	Sarah Brightman & AndreaBocelli	Coalition	8	L
4	17	Closer Than Close	Rosie Gaines	Big Bang	7	F L
5	-	Free	Ultra Naté	AM:PM	12 (75)	F
6	-	Paranoid Android	Radiohead	Parlophone	2	
7	-	I'll Be Missing You	Puff Daddy & Faith Evans	Puff Daddy	15 (1)	G
8	-	Bitter Sweet Symphony	Verve	Hut	7 (12)	F
9	-	Midnight In Chelsea	Jon Bon Jovi	Mercury	2	
10	-	Coco Jamboo	Mr. President	WEA	6 (21)	F L
11	16	I'll Be There For You	Rembrandts	East West	5 (17)	L
12	-	Hundred Mile High City	Ocean Colour Scene	MCA	3	
13	4	You Are Not Alone	Olive	RCA	6 (56)	F
14	-	On Your Own	Blur	Food	1	
15	-	Love Rollercoaster	Red Hot Chili Peppers	Geffen	3	L
16	-	How High	Charlatans	Beggars Banquet	1	
17	-	Hard To Say I'm Sorry	Az Yet	Laface	2 (8)	F L
18	1	Lovefool	Cardigans	Stockholm	7	F L
19	-	Nothing Lasts Forever	Echo & The Bunnymen	London	3	L
20	-	I'll Be	Foxy Brown Featuring Jay Z	Def Jam	1 (7)	

◆ More records entered the UK Top 10 in their first week than ever before (on one week alone there were seven new entries!), and the average single only spent two weeks in the Top 20, another record. For 11 consecutive weeks a new single entered at No. 1.

◆ Among the quarter's No. 1 albums was **OK Computer** by the critically acclaimed Radiohead (it included the hit single 'Paranoid Android'), which sold over 135,000 in its first week, and the US chart topper, **Wu-Tang Forever**, by the Wu-Tang Clan.

1997

This Mnth	Prev Mnth	Title	Artist	Label	Wks	(US 20 Pos)	
1	7	I'll Be Missing You	Puff Daddy & Faith Evans	Puff Daddy	15	(1)	G
2	-	Ecuador	Sash! Featuring Rodriguez	Multiply	7		
3	5	Free	Ultra Naté	AM:PM	12	(75)	F
4	-	D'You Know What I Mean?	Oasis	Creation	6		
5	8	Bitter Sweet Symphony	Verve	Virgin	7	(12)	F
6	1	Mmmbop	Hanson	Mercury	8	(1)	F
7	-	Freed From Desire	Gala	Big Life	10		F
8	-	C U When U Get There	Coolio Featuring 40 Thevz	Tommy Boy	7	(12)	
9	-	Just A Girl	No Doubt	Interscope	3	(23)	
10	-	The Journey	911	Virgin	2		
11	-	Something Goin' On	Todd Terry	Manifesto	5		
12	-	History/Ghosts	Michael Jackson	Epic	3		L
13	2	I Wanna Be The Only One	Eternal Featuring Bebe Winans	EMI	10		
14	-	Piece Of My Heart	Shaggy Featuring Marsha	Virgin	3	(72)	L
15	-	Ain't Nobody	Course	The Brothers	2		L
16	-	Blinded By The Sun	Seahorses	Geffen	2		
17	-	Gotham City	R. Kelly	Jive	3	(9)	L
18	10	Coco Jamboo	Mr. President	WEA	6	(21)	F L
19	-	A Change Would Do You Good	Sheryl Crow	A&M	1		
20	-	Lazy Days	Robbie Williams	Chrysalis	1		

This	Prev	Title	Artist	Label	Wks	(US Pos)	
1	1	I'll Be Missing You	Puff Daddy & Faith Evans	Puff Daddy	15	(1)	G
2	7	Freed From Desire	Gala	Big Life	10		F
3	-	Everybody (Backstreet's Back)	Backstreet Boys	Jive	7	(8)	
4	-	Men In Black	Will Smith	Columbia	11		F L
5	-	Picture Of You	Boyzone	Polydor	5		
6	-	Bitch	Meredith Brooks	Capitol	6	(2)	FL
7	-	Mo Money Mo Problems	Notorious B.I.G. Featuring Puff Daddy & Mase	Puff Daddy	5	(1)	L
8	-	Tubthumping	Chumbawamba	EMI	14	(6)	F L
9	8	C U When U Get There	Coolio Featuring 40 Thevz	Tommy Boy	7	(12)	
10	-	All About Us	Peter Andre	Mushroom	3		
11	-	All I Wanna Do	Dannii Minogue	Eternal	4		
12	4	D'You Know What I Mean?	Oasis	Creation	6		
13	-	Yesterday	Wet Wet Wet	Precious Org.	3		L
14	-	Everything	Mary J. Blige	MCA	3	(24)	
15	-	You're The One I Love	Shola Ama	WEA	3		
16	3	Free	Ultra Naté	AM:PM	12	(75)	F
17	-	Black Eyed Boy	Texas	Mercury	3		
18	-	California Dreamin	Mamas & The Papas	MCA	3		L
19	-	Never Gonna Let You Go	Tina Moore	Delirious	9		F
20	-	Filmstar	Suede	Nude	1		L

◆ For the first time since 1981 the UK won the Eurovision Song Contest, and for the first time the singer was American born. 'Love Shine A Light' by British-based Katrina (Leskanich) & The Waves collected the most votes ever and outsold all the other winners from the 1990s.

◆ 'Mmmbop', the debut single from young long-haired American family trio Hanson topped the charts in the UK, US and many other territories including Australia (where they were the first act to enter at No. 1 with their debut single!). In the UK it sold more than 500,000 copies in just four weeks.

1997

This Mnth	Prev Mnth	Title	Artist	Label	Wks	(US 20 Pos)	
1	4	**Men In Black**	Will Smith	Columbia	11		F L
2	8	**Tubthumping**	Chumbawamba	EMI	14	(6)	F L
3	-	**The Drugs Don't Work**	Verve	Hut	7		
4	-	**Candle In The Wind 1997/ Something About The...**	Elton John	Rocket	17	(1)	P L
5	-	**I Know Where It's At**	All Saints	London	4	(36)	F L
6	1	**I'll Be Missing You**	Puff Daddy & Faith Evans	Puff Daddy	15	(1)	G
7	-	**Honey**	Mariah Carey	Columbia	4	(1)	L
8	-	**You Have Been Loved/The Strangest Thing '97**	George Michael	Virgin	3		L
9	-	**Where's The Love**	Hanson	Mercury	4		
10	-	**Sunchyme**	Dario G	Eternal	8		F L
11	19	**Never Gonna Let You Go**	Tina Moore	Delirious	9		F
12	-	**(Un, Dos, Tres) Maria**	Ricky Martin	Virgin	3		F L
13	-	**Travellers Tune**	Ocean Colour Scene	MCA	2		
14	-	**Free**	DJ Quicksilver	Positiva	2		L
15	-	**Fix**	Blackstreet	Interscope	2	(58)	
16	-	**Live The Dream**	Cast	Polydor	1		
17	2	**Freed From Desire**	Gala	Big Life	10		F
18	-	**Samba De Janeiro**	Bellini	Virgin	3		F L
19	-	**Karma Police**	Radiohead	Parlophone	1		
20	-	**All Mine**	Portishead	Go Beat	1		L

This Mnth	Prev Mnth	Title	Artist	Label	Wks	(US 20 Pos)	
1	4	**Candle In The Wind 1997/ Something About The...**	Elton John	Rocket	17	(1)	P L
2	10	**Sunchyme**	Dario G	Eternal	8		F L
3	-	**As Long As You Love Me**	Backstreet Boys	Jive	9		L
4	2	**Tubthumping**	Chumbawamba	EMI	14	(6)	F L
5	-	**Stand By Me**	Oasis	Creation	3		
6	-	**Angel Of Mine**	Eternal	EMI	6		L
7	-	**Stay**	Sash! Featuring La Trec	Multiply	6		
8	-	**Got 'Til It's Gone**	Janet Featuring Q-Tip And Joni Mitchell	Virgin	4		L
9	-	**Arms Around The World**	Louise	EMI	3		
10	-	**Spice Up Your Life**	Spice Girls	Virgin	6	(18)	
11	-	**Barbie Girl**	Aqua	Universal	13	(7)	FGL
12	-	**Raincloud**	Lighthouse Family	Wild Card	3		L
13	1	**Men In Black**	Will Smith	Columbia	11		F L
14	-	**On Her Majesty's Secret Service**	Propellerheads/David Arnold	East West	2		F
15	-	**Just For You**	M People	M People	3		L
16	-	**Please**	U2	Island	1		
17	-	**You've Got A Friend**	Brand New Heavies	London	4		L
18	11	**Never Gonna Let You Go**	Tina Moore	Delirious	9		F
19	3	**The Drugs Don't Work**	Verve	Hut	7		
20	-	**U Sexy Thing**	Clock	Media	5		

◆ Sean 'Puff Daddy' Coombs produced five of America's 10 No. 1 hits in 1997 and co-wrote and performed on three of them. He was the producer and artist on the most successful rap single ever, 'I'll Be Missing You', which sold over seven million worldwide.

◆ European dance acts continued to clock up major UK hit singles. Among the current chart makers were: German group Mr. President, fellow German Sash!, Italian act Gala, the Course from Holland, Turkish-born DJ Quicksilver and the multi-national group Bellini.

November 1997

This Mnth	Prev Mnth	Title	Artist	Label	Wks	(US 20 Pos)	
1	11	**Barbie Girl**	Aqua	Universal	13	(7)	F G
2	-	**Torn**	Natalie Imbruglia	RCA	13		F
3	1	**Candle In The Wind 1997/ Something About The...**	Elton John	Rocket	17	(1)	P L
4	10	**Spice Up Your Life**	Spice Girls	Virgin	6	(18)	
5	-	**Tell Him**	Barbra Streisand & Celine Dion	Epic	8		L
6	7	**Stay**	Sash! Featuring La Trec	Multiply	6		
7	3	**As Long As You Love Me**	Backstreet Boys	Jive	9		L
8	-	**Never Ever**	All Saints	London	17		G L
9	-	**Perfect Day**	Various	Chrysalis	11		FGL
10	-	**Do Ya Think I'm Sexy?**	N-Trance Featuring Rod Stewart	All Around The World	4		L
11	2	**Sunchyme**	Dario G	Eternal	8		F L
12	-	**Wind Beneath My Wings**	Steven Houghton	RCA	7		F L
13	-	**Choose Life**	PF Project Featuring Ewan McGregor	Positiva	4		F L
14	-	**Party People...Friday Night**	911	Ginga	2		L
15	-	**I Will Come To You**	Hanson	Mercury	2	(9)	L
16	-	**You Sexy Thing**	Hot Chocolate	EMI	3		L
17	-	**Ain't That Just The Way**	Lutricia McNeal	Wildstar	7	(63)	F L
18	-	**Lonely**	Peter Andre	Mushroom	1		
19	-	**Open Road**	Gary Barlow	RCA	2		L
20	-	**James Bond Theme**	Moby	Mute	2		L

December 1997

This Mnth	Prev Mnth	Title	Artist	Label	Wks	(US 20 Pos)	
1	9	**Perfect Day**	Various	Chrysalis	11		FGL
2	1	**Barbie Girl**	Aqua	Universal	13	(7)	F G
3	-	**Teletubbies Say Eh-Oh!**	Teletubbies	BBC Worldwide	6		FGL
4	-	**Baby Can I Hold You/Shooting Star**	Boyzone	Polydor	8		L
5	8	**Never Ever**	All Saints	London	17		L G
6	12	**Wind Beneath My Wings**	Steven Houghton	RCA	7		F L
7	2	**Torn**	Natalie Imbruglia	RCA	13		F
8	-	**Together Again**	Janet Jackson	Virgin	13	(1)	
9	-	**Angels**	Robbie Williams	Chrysalis	14		
10	-	**Too Much**	Spice Girls	Virgin	5	(9)	
11	5	**Tell Him**	Barbra Streisand & Celine Dion	Epic	8		L
12	3	**Candle In The Wind 1997/ Something About The...**	Elton John	Rocket	17	(1)	P L
13	17	**Ain't That Just The Way**	Lutricia McNeal	Wildstar	7	(63)	F L
14	-	**Lucky Man**	Verve	Hut	1		L
15	-	**Slam Dunk (Da Funk)**	5	RCA	5		F L
16	-	**Sing Up For The Champions**	Reds United	Music Collection	5		F L
17	-	**Feel So Good**	Mase	Puff Daddy	3	(5)	L
18	-	**The Reason**	Celine Dion	Epic	3		
19	-	**Let A Boy Cry**	Gala	Big Life	1		L
20	-	**If God Will Send His Angels**	U2	Island	1		L

◆ No single in history has sold as many copies as Elton John's tribute to Diana, Princess Of Wales, 'Candle In The Wind 1997'. Within three months of its release, it topped the chart in every corner of the world, and over 33 million copies were shipped out. It smashed sales records all over the globe; in the UK, 4.9 million copies were sold and in the US (where it was No. 1 longer than any previous UK recording) it was credited with a record shattering 8 million sales. By mid-December the record had earned £20 million.

1998

This Mnth	Prev Mnth	Title	Artist	Label	Wks	(US 20 Pos)	
1	5	Never Ever	All Saints	London	17		G L
2	1	Perfect Day	Various	Chrysalis	11		FGL
3	8	Together Again	Janet Jackson	Virgin	13	(1)	
4	10	Too Much	Spice Girls	Virgin	5	(9)	
5	9	Angels	Robbie Williams	Chrysalis	14		
6	-	High	Lighthouse Family	Polydor	8		L
7	-	Bamboogie	Bamboo	VC	5		FL
8	-	Renegade Master 98	Wildchild	Hi-Life	5		L
9	-	All Around The World	Oasis	Creation	3		L
10	3	Teletubbies Say Eh-Oh!	Teletubbies	BBC Worldwide	6		FGL
11	-	You Make Me Wanna	Usher	Laface	5	(2)	FL
12	7	Torn	Natalie Imbruglia	RCA	13		F
13	-	Avenging Angels	Space	Gut	3		
14	-	Mulder And Scully	Catatonia	Blanco Y Negro	4		FL
15	-	No Surprises	Radiohead	Parlophone	1		L
16	-	My Star	Ian Brown	Polydor	2		F L
17	2	Barbie Girl	Aqua	Universal	13	(7)	F G
18	4	Baby Can I Hold You/ Shooting Star	Boyzone	Polydor	8		L
19	12	Candle In The Wind 1997/ Something About The...	Elton John	Rocket	17	(1)	P L
20	-	Amnesia	Chumbawamba	EMI	2		L

This Mnth	Prev Mnth	Title	Artist	Label	Wks	(US 20 Pos)	
1	-	Doctor Jones	Aqua	Universal	7		L
2	1	Never Ever	All Saints	London	17		G L
3	-	Gettin' Jiggy Wit It	Will Smith	Columbia	6	(1)	L
4	5	Angels	Robbie Williams	Chrysalis	14		
5	11	You Make Me Wanna	Usher	Laface	5	(2)	F L
6	-	My Heart Will Go On	Celine Dion	Epic	14	(1)	G L
7	-	All I Have To Give	Backstreet Boys	Jive	3		L
8	-	Cleopatra's Theme	Cleopatra	WEA	4		F L
9	6	High	Lighthouse Family	Polydor	8		L
10	-	Brimful Of Asha	Cornershop	Wiiija	8		F L
11	-	Let Me Show You	Camisra	VC	3		F L
12	-	Truly Madly Deeply	Savage Garden	Columbia	*14	(1)	L
13	3	Together Again	Janet Jackson	Virgin	13	(1)	
14	-	When I Need You	Will Mellor	Unity	2		F L
15	14	Mulder And Scully	Catatonia	Blanco Y Negro	4		F L
16	-	Be Alone No More	Another Level	Northwestside	3		F L
17	-	Crazy Little Party Girl	Aaron Carter	Ultra Pop	2		F L
18	7	Bamboogie	Bamboo	VC	5		F L
19	-	You're Still The One	Shania Twain	Mercury	4	(2)	F L
20	-	Solomon Bites The Worm	Bluetones	Superior Quality	1		L

◆ 1998 Brit winners included Finley Quaye, Shola Ama, the Verve (three awards including Best Album for Urban Hymns), the Prodigy, U2, the Stereophonics and Chumbawamba, whose Danbert Nobacon (AKA Nigel Hunter) threw a bucket of iced water over deputy Prime Minister, John Prescott.

◆ Celine Dion became the first woman to sell over a million copies of two separate singles in the UK. The latest, 'My Heart Will Go On', topped the charts in most territories. It was featured on her No. 1 album, **Let's Talk About Love**, (her second in a row to sell over 20 million copies globally) and on the record breaking **Titanic** soundtrack.

1998

March 1998

This Mnth	Prev Mnth	Title	Artist	Label	Wks (US 20 Pos)	
1	6	My Heart Will Go On	Celine Dion	Epic	14 (1)	G L
2	-	Frozen	Madonna	Maverick	7 (2)	L
3	10	Brimful Of Asha	Cornershop	Wiiija	8	F L
4	-	It's Like That	Run-DMC Vs Jason Nevins	Sm:)e Communications	10	G L
5	12	Truly Madly Deeply	Savage Garden	Columbia	*14 (1)	L
6	-	Stop	Spice Girls	Virgin	6	L
7	-	Big Mistake	Natalie Imbruglia	RCA	3	L
8	-	The Ballad Of Tom Jones	Space With Cerys Of Catatonia	Gut	3	L
9	-	When The Lights Go Out	5	RCA	4	L
10	-	How Do I Live	Leann Rimes	Curb	*13 (2)	F L
11	-	Say What You Want/Insane	Texas Featuring Wu Tang Clan	Mercury	2	L
12	1	Doctor Jones	Aqua	Universal	7	L
13	-	Let Me Entertain You	Robbie Williams	Chrysalis	5	L
14	-	Everlasting Love	Cast From Casualty	Warner.esp	2	F L
15	-	No, No, No	Destiny's Child	Columbia	3 (3)	F L
16	-	Here's Where The Story Ends	Tin Tin Out Featuring Shelley Nelson	VC	5	L
17	-	Show Me Love	Robyn	RCA	2 (7)	F L
18	16	Be Alone No More	Another Level	Northwestside	3	F L
19	-	Angel St	M People	M People	2	L
20	-	Uh La La La	Alexia	Dance Pool	3	F L

April 1998

This	Prev	Title	Artist	Label	Wks (US 20 Pos)	
1	4	It's Like That	Run-DMC Vs Jason Nevins	Sm:)e Communications	10	G L
2	1	My Heart Will Go On	Celine Dion	Epic	14 (1)	G L
3	-	La Primavera	Sash!	Multiply	5	L
4	5	Truly Madly Deeply	Savage Garden	Columbia	*14 (1)	L
5	-	Turn It Up/Fire It Up	Busta Rhymes	Elektra	5	L
6	-	Kiss The Rain	Billie Myers	Universal	5 (15)	F L
7	13	Let Me Entertain You	Robbie Williams	Chrysalis	5	L
8	10	How Do I Live	Leann Rimes	Curb	*14 (2)	F L
9	-	All I Want Is You	911	Virgin	3	L
10	-	I Get Lonely	Janet Jackson	Virgin	4	L
11	6	Stop	Spice Girls	Virgin	6	L
12	-	Feel It	Tamperer Featuring Maya	Pepper	*6	F L
13	-	Found A Cure	Ultra Nate	AM:PM	3	L
14	-	Give A Little Love	Daniel O'Donnell	Ritz	2	L
15	16	Here's Where The Story Ends	Tin Tin Out Featuring Shelley Nelson	VC	5	L
16	-	All My Life	K-Ci & Jojo	MCA	4 (1)	F L
17	15	No, No, No	Destiny's Child	Columbia	3 (3)	F L
18	-	Kung-Fu	187 Lockdown	East West	1	L
19	-	Say You Do	Ultra	East West	2	F L
20	-	All That Matters	Louise	EMI	2	L

◆ First the good news: Elton John received a knighthood from the Queen and Petula Clark was awarded a CBE. Then the bad: recent deaths included former hitmakers Michael Hutchence (INXS), John Denver, Austria's biggest star Falco, pianist Floyd Cramer, the 1950s top songwriter Bob Merrill and R&R legend Carl Perkins. Also Carl Wilson (Beach Boys), drummer Cozy Powell, Sonny Bono (Sonny & Cher), Linda McCartney, reggae rude boy Judge Dread and "The First Lady of Country Music", Tammy Wynette.

Listings by ARTIST

Code to Nationalities

A Austria
Aus Australia
B Belgium
Bra Brazil
C Canada
Cz Czechoslavakia

D Denmark
F France
G Germany
Gre Greece
H Holland
I Ireland

Ice Iceland
Isr Israel
Ita Italy
Jap Japan
Ken Kenya

N Norway
NZ New Zealand
R Romania
S Sweden
SA South Africa
Sen Senegal

Spa Spain
Swi Switzerland
UK United Kingdom
US United States
WI West Indies
Y Yugoslavia

Zim Zimbabwe
❖ Shared hit
★ Reissue

Aaliyah to Peter Andre

	UK Top 20 Ent
ABBA (S/N)	
Angel Eyes/Voulez Vous	8/79
Chiquitita	2/79
Dancing Queen	9/76
Does Your Mother Know	5/79
Fernando	4/76
Gimme Gimme Gimme (A Man After Midnight)	10/79
I Have A Dream	12/79
Knowing Me Knowing You	3/77
Lay All Your Love On Me	7/81
Mamma Mia	1/76
Money Money Money	12/76
The Name Of The Game	11/77
One Of Us	12/81
S.O.S.	10/75
Summer Night City	9/78
Super Trouper	11/80
Take A Chance On Me	2/78
Waterloo	4/74
The Winner Takes It All	8/80
Russ ABBOT (UK)	
Atmosphere	1/85
Gregory ABBOTT (US)	
Shake You Down	12/86
ABC (UK)	
All Of My Heart	9/82
The Look Of Love (Part 1)	5/82
Poison Arrow	3/82
When Smokey Sings	6/87
Paula ABDUL (US)	
Rush Rush	7/91
Straight Up	3/89
Paula ABDUL (duet with The Wild Pair) (US)	
Opposites Attract	4/90
Colonel ABRAMS (US)	
Trapped	10/85
ABSOLUTELY FABULOUS (UK)	
Absolutely Fabulous	6/94
AC/DC (Aus/UK)	
Heatseeker	1/88
Let's Get It Up	2/82
Rock 'n' Roll Ain't Noise Pollution	12/80
ACE OF BASE (S)	
All That She Wants	5/93
Don't Turn Around	6/94
The Sign	2/94
ADAM & THE ANTS (UK)	
Ant Rap	12/81
Antmusic	12/80
Deutscher Girls	3/82
Dog Eat Dog	11/80
Kings Of The Wild Frontier	3/81
Prince Charming	9/81
Stand And Deliver	5/81
Young Parisians	2/81

	UK Top 20 Ent
ADAM ANT (UK)	
Friend Or Foe	10/82
Goody Two Shoes	5/82
Puss 'n Boots	11/83
Bryan ADAMS (C)	
Can't Stop This Thing We Started	10/91
(Everything I Do) I Do It For You	7/91
Have You Ever Really Loved A Woman?	4/95
The Only Thing That Looks Good On Me Is You	6/96
Please Forgive Me	10/93
Run To You	2/85
Thought I'd Died And Gone To Heaven	2/92
Bryan ADAMS/Rod Stewart/Sting (C/US)	
All For Love	1/94
Oleta ADAMS (US)	
Get Here	2/91
ADAMSKI (UK)	
Killer	4/90
The Space Jungle	9/90
ADVENTURES OF STEVIE V (UK)	
Dirty Cash	5/90
AFTERSHOCK (US)	
Slave To The Vibe	9/93
A-HA (N)	
Cry Wolf	12/86
Hunting High And Low	6/86
I've Been Losing You	10/86
The Living Daylights	7/87
Stay On These Roads	4/88
The Sun Always Shines On T.V.	1/86
Take On Me	10/85
Touchy!	9/88
Train Of Thought	4/86
You Are The One	1/89
AIR SUPPLY (Aus/UK)	
All Out Of Love	11/80
Morris ALBERT (Bra)	
Feelings	10/75
ALESSI (US)	
Oh Lori	7/77
ALEXIA (Ita)	
Uh La La La	3/98
John ALFORD (UK)	
Blue Moon/Only You	5/96
ALL ABOUT EVE (UK)	
Martha's Harbour	8/88
ALL-4-ONE (US)	
I Swear	6/94
ALL Saints (UK/C)	
I Know Where It's At	9/97
Never Ever	11/97
Donna ALLEN (US)	
Serious	6/87
ALLISONS (UK)	
Are You Sure	3/61

	UK Top 20 Ent
Marc ALMOND (UK)	
The Days Of Pearly Spencer	5/92
❖ with *Bronski Beat* I Feel Love	4/85
Marc ALMOND featuring Gene Pitney (UK/US)	
Something's Gotten Hold Of My Heart	1/89
Herb ALPERT (US)	
Spanish Flea	1/66
A Taste Of Honey	11/65
This Guy's In Love With You	7/68
ALPHAVILLE (G)	
Big In Japan	9/84
ALTERED IMAGES (UK)	
Don't Talk To Me About Love	4/83
Happy Birthday	10/81
I Could Be Happy	1/82
See Those Eyes	4/82
ALTERN 8 (UK)	
Activ 8 (Come With Me)	11/91
Evapor 8	4/92
ALTHIA AND DONNA (J)	
Uptown Top Ranking	1/78
Shola AMA (UK)	
You Might Need Somebody	4/97
You're The One I Love	8/97
AAMAZULU (UK)	
Excitable	8/85
Montego Bay	10/86
Too Good To Be Forgotten	6/86
AMBASSADORS OF FUNK featuring MC Mario (US)	
Supermarioland	11/92
AMEN CORNER (UK)	
Bend Me Shape Me	2/68
Gin House Blues	8/67
Hello Susie	7/69
High In The Sky	8/68
(If Paradise Is) Half As Nice	2/69
AMERICA (US)	
A Horse With No Name	1/72
AMES BROTHERS (US)	
The Naughty Lady Of Shady Lane	2/55
Tori AMOS (US)	
Cornflake Girl	1/94
Professional Widow (It's Got To Be Big)	1/97
Pretty Good Year	3/94
Angry ANDERSON (Aus)	
Suddenly	12/88
Laurie ANDERSON (US)	
O Superman	10/81
Lynn ANDERSON (US)	
Rose Garden	3/71
Peter ANDRE (UK)	
All About Us	8/97
Flava	9/96
I Feel You	12/96

	UK Top 20 Ent
You Keep It All In	10/89
Gilbert BECAUD (F)	
A Little Love And Understanding	5/75
BECK (US)	
Loser	3/94
Jeff BECK (UK)	
❖ with Donovan Goo Goo	
Barabajagal (Love Is Hot)	8/69
Hi-Ho Silver Lining	5/67
Robin BECK (US)	
The First Time	11/88
BEE GEES (UK)	
Alone	3/97
Don't Forget To Remember	9/69
First Of May	3/69
For Whom The Bell Tolls	12/93
How Deep Is Your Love	11/77
I've Gotta Get A Message To You	8/68
Jive Talkin'	7/75
(The Lights Went Out In) Massachusetts	
	10/67
Love You Inside Out	5/79
New York Mining Disaster	5/67
Night Fever	4/78
Run To Me	8/72
Secret Love	3/91
Stayin' Alive	3/78
Too Much Heaven	12/78
Tragedy	2/79
Words	2/68
World	12/67
You Should Be Dancing	8/76
You Win Again	10/87
BEGGAR & CO (UK)	
(Somebody) Help Me Out	3/81
Harry BELAFONTE (US)	
Banana Boat (Day-O)	3/57
Island In The Sun	6/57
Mary's Boy Child	11/57
★ Mary's Boy Child	12/58
Archie BELL & The Drells (US)	
Here I Go Again	11/72
Freddie BELL & THE BELLBOYS (US)	
Giddy-Up-A-Ding-Dong	10/56
Maggie BELL (UK) See B.A.	
Robertson & Maggie Bell	
William BELL (US)	
❖ with Judy Clay Private Number	
	12/68
BELLAMY BROTHERS (US)	
If I Said You Had A Beautiful Body	
Would You Hold It Against Me	9/79
Let Your Love Flow	6/76
BELLE & The Devotions (UK)	
Love Games	5/84
BELLE STARS (UK)	
The Clapping Song	8/82
Sign Of The Times	2/83
Regina BELLE (US) See Peabo	
Bryson & Regina Belle	
BELLINI (V)	
Samba De Janeiro	9/97
BELOVED (UK)	
Sweet Harmony	1/93
Cliff BENNETT & The Rebel Rousers (UK)	
Got To Get You Into My Life	9/66
One Way Love	10/64
Tony BENNETT (US)	
Stranger In Paradise	4/55

	UK Top 20 Ent
George BENSON (US)	
Give Me The Night	8/80
In Your Eyes	10/83
Lady Love Me (One More Time)	6/83
BERLIN (US)	
Take My Breath Away	11/86
★ Take My Breath Away	11/90
Elmer BERNSTEIN (US)	
Staccato's Theme	12/59
BERRI (US)	
The Sunshine After The Rain	9/95
Chuck BERRY (US)	
Memphis Tennessee	10/63
My Ding-A-Ling	11/72
No Particular Place To Go	6/64
Dave BERRY (UK)	
The Crying Game	9/64
Little Things	4/65
Mama	8/66
Mike BERRY (UK)	
Don't You Think It's Time	1/63
Sunshine Of Your Smile	8/80
Nick BERRY (UK)	
Every Loser Wins	10/86
Heartbeat	6/92
BEVERLEY SISTERS (UK)	
I Saw Mommy Kissing Santa Claus	
	1/54
Little Donkey	12/59
The Little Drummer Boy	2/59
B-52'S (US)	
Love Shack	3/90
BC-52S (US)	
(Meet) The Flintstones	7/94
BIG AUDIO DYNAMITE (UK)	
E=MC^2	4/86
BIG BEN BANJO BAND (UK)	
Let's Get Together No. 1	12/54
BIG BOPPER (US)	
Chantilly Lace	1/59
BIG COUNTRY (UK)	
Chance	9/83
Fields Of Fire (400 Miles)	4/83
Look Away	4/86
Wonderland	1/84
BIG FUN (UK)	
Blame It On The Boogie	8/89
Can't Shake The Feeling	12/89
BIG MOUNTAIN (US)	
Baby I Love Your Way	6/94
Barry BIGGS (J)	
Side Show	1/77
Acker BILK (UK)	
Aria	9/76
Buona Sera	1/61
Lonely	10/62
Stranger On The Shore	8/62
Summer Set	2/60
That's My Home	8/61
BIMBO JET (F)	
El Bimbo	8/75
Jane BIRKIN & Serge Gainsbourg (UK/F)	
Je T'Aime...Moi Non Plus	9/69
BIZARRE INC (UK)	
Playing With Knives	11/91
Such A Feeling	3/91
BIZARRE INC featuring Angie Brown (UK)	
I'm Gonna Get You	10/92
BIZZ NIZZ (US/B)	
Don't Miss The Partyline	4/90

	UK Top 20 Ent
BJORK (Ice)	
Hyperballad	2/96
It's Oh So Quiet	11/95
BJORK & David Arnold (Ice/UK)	
Play Dead	10/93
BLACK (UK)	
Sweetest Smile	7/87
Wonderful Life	9/87
Cilla BLACK (UK)	
Alfie	4/66
Anyone Who Had A Heart	2/64
Conversations	8/69
Don't Answer Me	6/66
A Fool Am I	11/66
It's For You	8/64
Love's Just A Broken Heart	2/66
Something Tells Me (Something Is Gonna Happen Tonight)	12/71
Step Inside Love	4/68
Surround Yourself With Sorrow	3/69
You're My World	5/64
You've Lost That Lovin' Feelin'	1/65
BLACK BOX (Ita)	
Fantasy	11/90
I Don't Know Anybody Else	2/90
Ride On Time	8/89
The Total Mix	1/91
BLACKFOOT SUE (UK)	
Standing In The Road	9/72
BLACK GRAPE (UK)	
In The Name Of The Father	8/95
Reverend Black Grape	6/95
BLACK LACE (UK)	
Agadoo	8/84
Do The Conga	12/84
Superman (Gioca Jouer)	10/83
BLACK SABBATH (UK)	
Paranoid	10/70
BLACK SLATE (UK/J)	
Amigo	10/80
BLACK GRAPE featuring Joe Strummer & Keith Allen (UK)	
England's Irie	6/96
BLACKSTREET (US)	
Don't Leave Me	4/97
Fix	9/97
BLACKSTREET featuring Dr Dre (US)	
No Diggity	10/96 F
Band Of The BLACK WATCH (UK)	
Scotch On The Rocks	10/75
BLANCMANGE (UK)	
Blind Vision	5/83
Don't Tell Me	4/84
Living On The Ceiling	11/82
Mary J. BLIGE (US)	
Everything	8/97
Billy BLAND (US)	
Let The Little Girl Dance	5/60
BLONDIE (US)	
Atomic	2/80
Call Me	4/80
Denis	3/78
Dreaming	10/79
Hanging On The Telephone	11/78
Heart Of Glass	1/79
(I'm Always Touched By Your) Presence Dear	5/78
Island Of Lost Souls	6/82
Picture This	9/78
Rapture	2/81

	UK Top 20 Ent
On Bended Knee	11/94
❖ with Mariah Carey One Sweet Day	12/95
BOYZONE (I)	
Baby Can I Hold You/Shooting Star	12/97
A Different Beat	12/96
Isn't It A Wonder	3/97
Picture Of You	8/97
Words	10/96
Coming Home Now	3/96
Father And Son	11/95
Key To My Life	4/95
Love Me For A Reason	12/94
So Good	8/95
Billy BRAGG with Cara Tivey (UK)	
She's Leaving Home	5/88
BRAND NEW HEAVIES (UK/US)	
Midnight At The Oasis	8/94
You've Got A Friend	10/97
Johnny BRANDON (UK)	
Tomorrow	3/55
Laura BRANIGAN (US)	
Gloria	2/83
Self Control	8/84
Los BRAVOS (Spa/G)	
Black Is Black	7/66
Toni BRAXTON (US)	
Un-Break My Heart	11/96
You're Makin' Me High	7/96
Breathe Again	1/94
BREAD (US)	
Baby I'm A Want You	2/72
Make It With You	9/70
BREAK MACHINE (US)	
Break Dance Party	5/84
Street Dance	3/84
BREATHE (UK)	
Hands To Heaven	8/88
BRENDON (UK)	
Gimme Some	4/77
Tony BRENT (UK)	
Cindy Oh Cindy	12/56
Girl Of My Dreams	9/58
Three Coins In The Fountain	8/54
Bernard BRESSLAW (UK)	
Mad Passionate Love	9/58
Teresa BREWER (US)	
Let Me Go, Lover!	2/55
A Sweet Old Fashioned Girl	8/56
A Tear Fell	4/56
BRIAN & MICHAEL (UK)	
Matchstalk Men And Matchstalk Cats And Dogs	3/78
BRIGHOUSE AND RASTRICK BRASS BAND (UK)	
The Floral Dance	12/77
Sarah BRIGHTMAN (UK)	
❖ with Cliff Richard All I Ask Of You	10/86
Wishing You Were Somehow Here Again	2/87
Sarah BRIGHTMAN & Andrea Bocelli (UK/I)	
Time To Say Goodbye (Con Te Partiro)	5/97
Sarah BRIGHTMAN & Hot Gossip (UK)	
I Lost My Heart To A Starship Trooper	12/78

	UK Top 20 Ent
Sarah BRIGHTMAN & Paul Miles-Kingston (UK)	
Pie Jesu	3/85
Sarah BRIGHTMAN & Steve Harley (UK)	
The Phantom Of The Opera	2/86
Johnny BRISTOL (US)	
Hang On In There Baby	9/74
BRONSKI BEAT (UK)	
Hit That Perfect Beat	12/85
Smalltown Boy	6/84
Why?	10/84
BRONSKI BEAT & Marc Almond (UK)	
I Feel Love	4/85
BROOK BROTHERS (UK)	
Warpaint	4/61
Elkie BROOKS (UK)	
Don't Cry Out Loud	12/78
No More The Fool	1/87
Pearl's A Singer	4/77
Sunshine After The Rain	10/77
Meredith BROOKS (US)	
Bitch	8/97
BROS (UK)	
Are You Mine?	7/91
Cat Among The Pigeons/Silent Night	2/88
Chocolate Box	10/89
Drop The Boy	3/88
I Owe You Nothing	6/88
I Quit	9/88
Sister	12/89
Too Much	8/89
When Will I Be Famous	1/88
BROTHER BEYOND (UK)	
The Harder I Try	8/88
He Ain't No Competiition	11/88
BROTHERHOOD OF MAN (UK)	
Angelo	7/77
Figaro	1/78
Oh Boy	4/77
Save Your Kisses For Me	3/76
United We Stand	2/70
BROTHERS JOHNSON (US)	
Stomp!	4/80
BROTHERS (UK)	
Sing Me	2/77
Crazy World Of Arthur BROWN (UK)	
Fire	7/68
Bobby BROWN (US)	
Don't Be Cruel	4/89
Every Little Step	5/89
Humpin' Around	7/95
My Prerogative	2/89
On Our Own	7/89
❖ with Glenn Medeiros She Ain't Worth It	7/90
Two Can Play The Game	4/95
Roy Chubby BROWN (US) See Smokie	
James BROWN (US)	
Living In America	2/86
Jocelyn BROWN (US)	
❖ with Incognito Always There	7/91
❖ with Right Said Fred Don't Talk Just Kiss	12/91
❖ with Kym Mazelle No More Tears (Enough Is Enough)	6/94
Somebody Else's Guy	5/84
Joe BROWN & The Bruvvers (UK)	
It Only Took A Minute	12/62
A Picture Of You	6/62
That's What Love Will Do	2/63

	UK Top 20 Ent
Foxy BROWN featuring Jay Z (US)	
I'll Be	6/97
Ian BROWN (UK)	
My Star	1/98
Sam BROWN (UK)	
Stop	2/89
Jackson BROWNE (US)	
Stay	8/78
Tom BROWNE (US)	
Funkin' For Jamaica (N.Y.)	8/80
BROWNS (US)	
The Three Bells	9/59
BROWNSTONE (US)	
If You Love Me	4/95
Dave BRUBECK QUARTET (US)	
Take Five	11/61
Tommy BRUCE & The Bruisers (UK)	
Ain't Misbehavin'	6/60
Dora BRYAN (UK)	
All I Want For Christmas Is A Beatle	12/63
Peabo BRYSON (US)	
❖ with Celine Dion Beauty And The Beast	5/92
Peabo BRYSON & Regina Belle (US)	
A Whole New World (Aladdin's Theme)	1/94
Peabo BRYSON & Roberta Flack (US)	
Tonight I Celebrate My Love	9/83
BUCKETHEADS (US)	
The Bomb! (These Sounds Fall Into My Mind)	3/95
BUCKS FIZZ (UK)	
If You Can't Stand The Heat	1/83
Land Of Make Believe	12/81
Making Your Mind Up	4/81
My Camera Never Lies	4/82
New Beginning (Mamba Seyra)	6/86
Now Those Days Are Gone	7/82
Piece Of The Action	7/81
When We Were Young	7/83
BUGGLES (UK)	
Video Killed The Radio Star	10/79
B. BUMBLE & The Stingers (US)	
Nut Rocker	4/62
Johnny BURNETTE (US)	
Dreamin'	10/60
You're Sixteen	1/61
Ray BURNS (UK)	
Mobile	2/55
That's How A Love Song Was Born	9/55
Malandra BURROWS (UK)	
Just This Side Of Love	12/90
BUSH (UK)	
Swallowed	3/97
Lou BUSCH (US)	
Zambesi	2/56
Kate BUSH (UK)	
Babooshka	7/80
❖ with Peter Gabriel Don't Give Up	11/86
Kate Bush On Stage E.P.	10/79
Man With The Child In His Eyes	7/78
Rocket Man (I Think It's Going To Be A Long Long Time)	12/91
Rubberband Girl	9/93
Running Up That Hill	8/85
Sat In Your Lap	7/81
Wow	4/79
Wuthering Heights	3/78

281

	UK Top 20 Ent
❖ with Barbra Streisand You Don't Bring Me Flowers	12/78
DIAMONDS (C)	
The Church Bells May Ring	6/56
Little Darlin'	6/57
DICKIES (US)	
Banana Splits (Tra La La Song)	5/79
Barbara DICKSON (UK)	
❖ with Elaine Paige I Know Him So Well	1/85
January February	4/80
DION (US)	
Runaround Sue	11/61
The Wanderer	3/62
Celine DION (C)	
All By Myself	12/96
Because You Loved Me	6/96
It's All Coming Back To Me Now	10/96
My Heart Will Go On	2/98
The Reason	12/97
Falling Into You	3/96
Only One Road	5/95
The Power Of Love	1/94
Think Twice	12/94
Tu M'Aimes Encore (To Love Me Again)	9/95
Where Does My Heart Beat Now	2/91
Celine DION & Peabo Bryson (C/US)	
Beauty And The Beast	5/92
DIRE STRAITS (UK)	
Money For Nothing	8/85
Sultans Of Swing	4/79
Walk Of Life	1/86
DISCO TEX & The Sex-O-Lettes (US)	
Get Dancin'	12/74
I Wanna Dance Wit Choo'	5/75
Sacha DISTEL (F)	
Raindrops Keep Fallin' On My Head	3/70
DIVINYLS (Aus)	
I Touch Myself	7/91
DJ DADO (Ita)	
X-Files	4/96
DJ QUICKSILVER (T)	
Belissima	4/97
Free	9/97
DNA featuring Suzanne Vega (UK/US)	
Tom's Diner	8/90
Anita DOBSON (UK)	
Anyone Can Fall In Love	8/86
DOCTOR & The Medics (UK)	
Spirit In The Sky	5/86
DR. ALBAN (S)	
It's My Life	9/92
DR. FEELGOOD (UK)	
Milk And Alcohol	2/79
DR. HOOK (US)	
Better Love Next Time	1/80
If Not You	11/76
A Little Bit More	7/76
More Like The Movies	4/78
Sexy Eyes	4/80
Sylvia's Mother	7/72
When You're In Love With A Beautiful Woman	10/79
DOCTOR SPIN (UK)	
Tetris	10/92
Ken DODD (UK)	
Let Me Cry On Your Shoulder	2/67
Love Is Like A Violin	9/60
Promises	5/66

	UK Top 20 Ent
The River	12/65
Tears	9/65
DODGY (UK)	
Good Enough	8/96
DOG EAT DOG (US)	
No Fronts - The Remixes	2/96
Nate DOGG (US) See Warren G & Nate Dogg	
Joe DOLAN (UK)	
Make Me An Island	8/69
You're Such A Good Looking Woman	4/70
Joe DOLCE MUSIC THEATRE (US)	
Shaddup You Face	2/81
DOLLAR (UK)	
Give Me Back My Heart	4/82
Love's Gotta Hold On Me	9/79
Mirror Mirror (Mon Amour)	12/81
O L'Amour	2/88
Fats DOMINO (US)	
Be My Guest	1/60
Blueberry Hill	1/57
I'm In Love Again	9/56
DON PABLO'S ANIMALS (US)	
Venus	6/90
Lonnie DONEGAN (UK)	
Battle Of New Orleans	6/59
Bring A Little Water Sylvie/Dead Or Alive	9/56
The Comancheros	2/62
Cumberland Gap	4/57
Does Your Chewing Gum Lose It's Flavour	2/59
Don't You Rock Me Daddy-O	1/57
Fort Worth Jail	5/59
Gamblin' Man/Putting On The Style	6/57
Grand Coolie Dam	5/58
Have A Drink On Me	6/61
I Wanna Go Home	6/60
Jack O' Diamonds	1/58
Lively	12/60
Lost John/Stewball	5/56
Michael Row The Boat	9/61
My Dixie Darling	10/57
My Old Man's A Dustman	3/60
The Party's Over	5/62
Pick A Bale Of Cotton	9/62
Rock Island Line	1/56
Sal's Got A Sugar Lip	9/59
Sally Don't You Grieve/Betty, Betty, Betty	7/58
Tom Dooley	11/58
DONOVAN (UK)	
Catch The Wind	4/65
Colours	6/65
Hurdy Gurdy Man	6/68
Jennifer Juniper	3/68
Mellow Yellow	2/67
Sunshine Superman	12/66
There Is A Mountain	11/67
DONOVAN & The Jeff Beck Group (UK)	
Goo Goo Barabajagal (Love Is Hot)	8/69
Jason DONOVAN (Aus)	
Any Dream Will Do	6/91
❖ with Kylie Minogue Especially For You	12/88
Every Day (I Love You More)	9/89
Hang On To Your Love	4/90
Happy Together	8/91

	UK Top 20 Ent
Nothing Can Divide Us	9/88
Rhythm Of The Rain	9/90
Sealed With A Kiss	6/89
Too Many Broken Hearts	3/89
When You Come Back To Me	12/89
DOOBIE BROTHERS (US)	
Long Train Running	11/93
DOOLEYS (UK)	
The Chosen Few	10/79
Love Of My Life	12/77
A Rose Has To Die	10/78
Wanted	7/79
Val DOONICAN (I)	
Elusive Butterfly	4/66
If The Whole World Stopped Loving	11/67
Memories Are Made Of This	3/67
Morning	1/72
The Special Years	2/65
Walk Tall	12/64
What Would I Be	11/66
DOOP (H)	
Doop	3/94
DOORS (US)	
Hello, I Love You	10/68
Light My Fire	6/91
Lee DORSEY (US)	
Holy Cow	11/66
Working In The Coal Mine	9/66
Tommy DORSEY ORCHESTRA (US)	
Tea For Two Cha Cha	11/58
DOUBLE TROUBLE (UK)	
❖ with The Rebel MC.Street Tuff	10/89
DOUBLE TROUBLE & Rebel MC (UK)	
Just Keep Rockin'	6/89
DOUBLE (Swi)	
The Captain Of Her Heart	2/86
Carl DOUGLAS (UK)	
Kung Fu Fighting	9/74
Craig DOUGLAS (UK)	
Heart Of A Teenage Girl	5/60
A Hundred Pounds Of Clay	4/61
Oh Lonesome Me	11/62
Only Sixteen	8/59
Our Favourite Melodies	7/62
Pretty Blue Eyes	2/60
A Teenager In Love	6/59
Time	7/61
When My Little Girl Is Smiling	4/62
Charlie DRAKE (UK)	
Mr. Custer	11/60
My Boomerang Won't Come Back	10/61
Splish Splash	8/58
DREAM WEAVERS (US)	
It's Almost Tomorrow	2/56
DRIFTERS (US)	
At The Club/Saturday Night At The Movies	5/72
Can I Take You Home Little Girl	1/76
Come On Over To My Place	9/72
Down On The Beach Tonight	11/74
Hello Happiness	4/76
Kissin' In The Back Row Of The Movies	7/74
Like Sister And Brother	9/73
Save The Last Dance For Me	11/60
There Goes My First Love	9/75
You're More Than A Number In My Little Red Book	1/77

UK Top
20 Ent

Julie DRISCOLL, Brian Auger & The Trinity (UK)
This Wheel's On Fire 6/68
DRIVER 67 (UK)
Car 67 1/79
DUNBLANE (UK)
Knockin' On Heaven's Door-Throw
These Guns Away 12/96
DUBLINERS (I)
Black Velvet Band 10/67
❖ with The Pogues The Irish
Rover 4/87
Seven Drunken Nights 5/67
Stephen 'Tin Tin' DUFFY (UK)
Kiss Me 3/85
Candy DULFER (H) See David A.
Stewart introducing Candy Dulfer.
Johnny DUNCAN & The Blue Grass Boys (US)
Last Train To San Fernando 8/57
David DUNDAS (UK)
Jeans On 8/76
Erroll DUNKLEY (J)
O.K. Fred 10/79
Clive DUNN (UK)
Grandad 12/70
Simon DUPREE & The Big Sound (UK)
Kites 12/67
DURAN DURAN (UK)
All She Wants Is 1/89
Come Undone 4/93
Girls On Film 8/81
Hungry Like The Wolf 6/82
Is There Something I Should Know
3/83
New Moon On Monday 2/84
Notorious 11/86
Ordinary World 2/93
The Reflex 4/84
Rio 11/82
Save A Prayer 8/82
Union Of The Snake 11/83
A View To Kill 5/85
The Wild Boys 11/84
Ian DURY & The Blockheads (UK)
Hit Me With Your Rhythm Stick 1/79
Reasons To Be Cheerful (Pt 3) 8/79
What A Waste 6/78
Slim DUSTY (Aus)
A Pub With No Beer 2/59
Bob DYLAN (US)
Baby Stop Crying 8/78
I Want You 8/66
Lay Lady Lay 10/69
Like A Rolling Stone 9/65
Positively 4th Street 11/65
Rainy Day Women #12 & 35 5/66
Subterranean Homesick Blues 5/65
Times They Are A-Changin' 4/65
EAGLES (US)
Hotel California 5/77
Robert EARL (UK)
I May Never Pass This Way Again
5/58
Wonderful Secret Of Love 3/59
EARTH, WIND & FIRE (US)
After The Love Has Gone 8/79
Fantasy 3/78
Let's Groove 11/81
September 1/79

EARTH, WIND & FIRE With The Emotions (US)
Boogie Wonderland 6/79
EAST OF EDEN (UK)
Jig A Jig 5/71
EAST 17 (UK)
Around The World 5/94
Do U Still? 2/96
Deep 2/93
House Of Love 9/92
It's Alright 12/93
Let It Rain 4/95
Slow It Down 4/93
Stay Another Day 12/94
Steam 10/94
Thunder 11/95
Hey Child 1/97
EAST 17 featuring Gabrielle (UK)
If You Ever 11/96
EAST SIDE BEAT (Ita/UK)
Ride Like The Wind 12/91
Sheena EASTON (UK)
For Your Eyes Only 8/81
Modern Girl 9/80
9 To 5 (Morning Train) 8/80
EASYBEATS (Aus)
Friday On My Mind 12/66
ECHO & THE BUNNYMEN (UK)
Nothing Lasts Forever 6/97
The Cutter 2/83
The Killing Moon 2/84
Billy ECKSTINE (US)
Gigi 2/59
No One But You 11/54
EDDIE & The Hot Rods (UK) see The Rods
Duane EDDY (US)
Ballad Of Paladin 9/62
Because They're Young 8/60
Bonnie Came Back 3/60
(Dance With The) Guitar Man 11/62
Forty Miles Of Bad Road 9/59
Kommotion 11/60
Pepe 11/60
❖ with The Art Of Noise Peter Gunn
4/86
Peter Gunn Theme 6/59
Shazam 5/60
Some Kind-A Earthquake 1/60
Theme From Dixie 5/61
Duane EDDY & The Rebelettes (US)
Play Me Like You Play Your Guitar
4/75
EDELWEISS (Swi)
Bring Me Edelweiss 5/89
EDISON LIGHTHOUSE (UK)
Love Grows (Where My Rosemary
Goes) 1/70
Dave EDMUNDS (UK)
Baby I Love You 2/73
Born To Be With You 7/73
Girls Talk 7/79
I Hear You Knocking 11/70
Queen Of Hearts 10/79
Rupie EDWARDS (J)
Ire Feelings (Skanga) 12/74
Tommy EDWARDS (US)
It's All In The Game 10/58
808 STATE (UK)
Cubik/Olympic 11/90
In Yer Face 2/91

❖ with MC Tunes The Only Rhyme
That Bites 6/90
Pacific 12/89
EIGHTH WONDER (UK)
I'm Not Scared 4/88
Donnie ELBERT (US)
I Can't Help Myself 3/72
Where Did Our Love Go 1/72
ELECTRIC LIGHT ORCHESTRA (UK)
Confusion/Last Train To London
12/79
The Diary Of Horace Wimp 8/79
Don't Bring Me Down 9/79
Evil Woman 2/76
Hold On Tight 8/81
Livin' Thing 12/76
Mr. Blue Sky 2/78
10538 Overture 8/72
Rock 'n' Roll Is King 7/83
Rockaria 3/77
Roll Over Beethoven 2/73
Shine A Little Love 6/79
Showdown 10/73
Sweet Talkin' Woman 10/78
Telephone Line 6/77
Wild West Hero 7/78
❖ with Olivia Newton-John Xanadu
7/80
ELECTRONIC (UK)
Disappointed 7/92
Get The Message 5/91
ELGINS (US)
Heaven Must Have Sent You 5/71
ELIAS & His Zigzag Jive Flutes (SA)
Tom Hark 5/58
Yvonne ELLIMAN (US)
If I Can't Have You 5/78
Love Me 12/76
Duke ELLINGTON (US)
Skin Deep 3/54
Shirley ELLIS (US)
The Clapping Song 5/65
EMERSON, LAKE & PALMER (UK)
Fanfare For The Common Man 6/77
EMF (UK)
I Believe 2/91
Unbelievable 11/90
EMF/Reeves And Mortimer (UK)
I'm A Believer 7/95
EMOTIONS (US)
Best Of My Love 9/77
❖ with Earth, Wind & Fire Boogie
Wonderland 6/79
EN VOGUE (US)
Don't Let Go (Love) 1/97
Free Your Mind 11/92
Giving Him Something He Can Feel
11/92
Hold On 5/90
My Lovin' (You're Never Gonna Get It)
5/92
❖ with Salt-N-Pepa Whatta Man
3/94
Harry ENFIELD (UK)
Loadsamoney (Doin' Up The House)
5/88
ENGLAND WORLD CUP SQUAD (UK)
Back Home 5/70
This Time (We'll Get It Right)/
England We'll Fly The Flag 5/82

	UK Top 20 Ent
ENGLANDNEWORDER (UK)	
World In Motion...	6/90
Scott ENGLISH (US)	
Brandy	11/71
ENIGMA (UK)	
Ain't No Stoppin'	6/81
ENIGMA (R/G)	
Return To Innocence	1/94
Sadeness Part 1	12/90
ENYA (I)	
Anywhere Is	11/95
Book Of Days	8/92
Orinoco Flow	10/88
EQUALS (UK/Guy)	
Baby Come Back	6/68
Black Skin Blue Eyed Boys	1/71
Viva Bobbie Joe	8/69
ERASURE (UK)	
Abba-Esque (E.P.)	6/92
Always	5/94
Blue Savannah	3/90
Breath Of Life	4/92
Chains Of Love	6/88
Chorus	6/91
The Circus	10/87
Crackers International (E.P.)	12/88
Drama!	10/89
It Doesn't Have To Be	3/87
A Little Respect	10/88
Love To Hate You	9/91
Run To The Sun	7/94
Ship Of Fools	3/88
Sometimes	12/86
Star	6/90
Victim Of Love	6/87
Who Needs Love (Like That)	11/92
ERUPTION (US)	
I Can't Stand The Rain	3/78
One Way Ticket	5/79
David ESSEX (UK)	
Gonna Make You A Star	10/74
Hold Me Close	9/75
If I Could	1/76
Lamplight	12/73
Oh What A Circus	9/78
Rock On	9/73
Rollin' Stone	7/75
Silver Dream Machine (Pt. 1)	4/80
Stardust	1/75
Tahiti (From Mutiny On The Bounty)	10/83
A Winter's Tale	12/82
Gloria ESTEFAN (US)	
Don't Wanna Lose You	7/89
Go Away	4/93
Hold Me, Thrill Me, Kiss Me	12/94
Miami Hit Mix/Christmas Through Your Eyes	12/92
Gloria ESTEFAN & The Miami Sound Machine (US)	
Anything For You	9/88
Can't Stay Away From You	3/89
Dr. Beat	9/84
1-2-3	11/88
ETERNAL (UK)	
I Am Blessed	12/95
Just A Step From Heaven	5/94
Oh Baby I...	11/94
Power Of A Woman	10/95
Save Our Love	1/94
So Good	8/94

	UK Top 20 Ent
Stay	10/93
Angel Of Mine	10/97
Don't You Love Me	3/97
Someday	8/96
ETERNAL featuring Bebe Winans (UK/US)	
I Wanna Be The Only One	5/97
EUROPE (S)	
The Final Countdown	11/86
EURYTHMICS (UK)	
Here Comes The Rain Again	2/84
It's Alright (Baby's Coming Back)	1/86
Love Is A Stranger	4/83
Right By Your Side	12/83
Sexcrime (Nineteen Eighty Four)	11/84
Sweet Dreams (Are Made Of This)	3/83
There Must Be An Angel (Playing With My Heart)	7/85
Thorn In My Side	9/86
Who's That Girl	7/83
EURYTHMICS & Aretha Franklin (UK/US)	
Sisters Are Doin' It For Themselves	11/85
Maureen EVANS (UK)	
Like I Do	1/63
Paul EVANS (US)	
Hello This Is Joannie (The Telephone Answering Machine Song)	1/79
Paul EVANS & The Curls (US)	
Seven Little Girls Sitting In The Back Seat	11/59
Kenny EVERETT (UK)	
Snot Rap	4/83
EVERLY BROTHERS (US)	
All I Have To Do Is Dream	6/58
Bird Dog	9/58
Bye Bye Love	7/57
Cathy's Clown	4/60
Cryin' In The Rain	1/62
Love Is Strange	11/65
No One Can Make My Sunshine Smile	11/62
Poor Jenny	7/59
The Price Of Love	6/65
Problems	1/59
So Sad (To Watch Good Love Go Bad)	10/60
Temptation	6/61
('Til) I Kissed You	9/59
Wake Up Little Susie	11/57
Walk Right Back	2/61
When Will I Be Loved	7/60
Phil EVERLY & Cliff Richard (US/UK)	
She Means Nothing To Me	3/83
EVERYTHING BUT THE GIRL (UK)	
I Don't Want To Talk About It	7/88
Missing	10/95
Walking Wounded	4/96
EXILE (US)	
Kiss You All Over	9/78
EXTREME (US)	
More Than Words	7/91
Rest In Peace	9/92
Song For Love	5/92
FAB featuring MC Parker (UK)	
Thunderbirds Are Go	7/90
FACES (UK)	
Cindy Incidentally	2/73
Pool Hall Richard/I Wish It Would	

	UK Top 20 Ent
Rain	1/74
Stay With Me	1/72
Rod STEWART & The Faces (UK)	
You Can Make Me Dance Sing Or Anything	12/74
Joe FAGIN (UK)	
That's Living (Alright)	1/84
Yvonne FAIR (US)	
It Should Have Been Me	2/76
FAIRGROUND ATTRACTION (UK)	
Find My Love	8/88
Perfect	5/88
FAIR WEATHER (UK)	
Natural Sinner	8/70
Andy FAIRWEATHER-LOW (UK)	
Reggae Tune	10/74
Wide Eyed And Legless	12/75
FAITH NO MORE (US)	
I'm Easy/Be Aggressive	1/93
Midlife Crisis	6/92
Adam FAITH (UK)	
As You Like It	5/62
Don't That Beat All	9/62
Don't You Know It	7/61
Easy Going Me	5/61
The First Time	10/63
How About That	9/60
Lonely Pup (In A Christmas Shop)	12/60
Lonesome	2/62
Made You	7/60
Message To Martha (Kentucky Bluebird)	12/64
Poor Me	2/60
Someone Else's Baby	4/60
The Time Has Come	11/61
We Are In Love	1/64
What Do You Want	11/59
When Johnny Comes Marching Home	7/60
Who Am I/This Is It	2/61
Horace FAITH (J)	
Black Pearl	10/70
Percy FAITH (US)	
Theme From 'A Summer Place'	3/60
Marianne FAITHFULL (UK)	
As Tears Go By	9/64
Come And Stay With Me	3/65
Summer Nights	8/65
This Little Bird	5/65
FAITHLESS (UK)	
Insomnia	10/96
FALCO (A)	
Rock Me Amadeus	4/86
Vienna Calling	6/86
Harold FALTERMEYER (G)	
Axel F	6/85
FAME AND PRICE TOGETHER (UK)	
Rosetta	5/71
Georgie FAME (UK)	
The Ballad Of Bonnie And Clyde	1/68
Get Away	7/66
Sittin' In The Park	1/67
Sunny	10/66
Yeh Yeh	1/65
FAMILY STAND (US)	
Ghetto Heaven	4/90
FAMILY (UK)	
Burlesque	11/72
In My Own Time	8/71
Strange Band	10/70

	UK Top 20 Ent
[Four Tops]	
I Can't Help Myself	4/70
If I Were A Carpenter	3/68
It's All In The Game	6/70
Loco In Acapulco	12/88
Reach Out I'll Be There	10/66
★ Reach Out I'll Be There	8/88
❖ with The Supremes River Deep-Mountain High	7/71
Seven Rooms Of Gloom	7/67
Simple Game	10/71
Standing In The Shadows Of Love	1/67
Still Water (Love)	10/70
Walk Away Renee	12/67
When She Was My Girl	11/81
FOURMOST (UK)	
Hello Little Girl	10/63
A Little Loving	5/64
FOX (UK)	
Only You Can	3/75
S-S-S-Single Bed	4/76
Samantha FOX (UK)	
Do Ya Do Ya (Wanna Please Me)	7/86
Nothing's Gonna Stop Me Now	6/87
Touch Me (I Want Your Body)	3/86
FPI PROJECT (Ita)	
Going Back To My Roots/Rich In Paradise	1/90
Peter FRAMPTON (UK)	
Show Me The Way	6/76
Connie FRANCIS (US)	
Among My Souvenirs	12/59
Breakin' In A Brand New Broken Heart	7/61
Carolina Moon/Stupid Cupid	8/58
Everybody's Somebody's Fool	8/60
I'm Sorry I Made You Cry	7/58
Lipstick On Your Collar	7/59
Mama	5/60
Many Tears Ago	2/61
My Happiness	2/59
x	11/60
Robot Man	6/60
Together	9/61
Vacation	8/62
Where The Boys Are	4/61
Who's Sorry Now	4/58
You Always Hurt The One You Love	1/59
FRANK AND WALTERS (I)	
After All	1/93
FRANKIE GOES TO HOLLYWOOD (UK)	
The Power Of Love	12/84
★ The Power Of Love	12/93
Rage Hard	9/86
Relax	1/84
★ Relax	10/93
Two Tribes	6/84
Welcome To The Pleasure Dome	4/85
Aretha FRANKLIN (US)	
Bridge Over Troubled Water/Brand New Me	5/71
A Deeper Love	2/94
Don't Play That Song	9/70
I Say A Little Prayer	8/68
Respect	7/67
❖ with Eurythmics Sisters Are Doin' It For Themselves	11/85
Who's Zoomin' Who	1/86

	UK Top 20 Ent
Aretha FRANKLIN & George Michael (US/UK)	
I Knew You Were Waiting (For Me)	1/87
Rodney FRANKLIN (US)	
The Groove	5/80
FRANTIQUE (US)	
Strut Your Funky Stuff	9/79
FREAK POWER (UK/C)	
Turn On, Tune In, Cop Out	3/95
Stan FREBERG (US)	
Sh-Boom	11/54
John FRED & His Playboy Band (US)	
Judy In Disguise (With Glasses)	1/68
FREDDIE & The Dreamers (UK)	
I Understand	12/64
I'm Telling You Now	8/63
If You Gotta Make A Fool Of Somebody	6/63
Over You	3/64
You Were Made For Me	11/63
FREE (UK)	
All Right Now	6/70
★ All Right Now	8/73
★ All Right Now	2/91
Free (E.P.)	3/78
Little Bit Of Love	7/72
My Brother Jake	5/71
Wishing Well	1/73
FREEEZ (UK)	
I.O.U.	7/83
Southern Freeez	3/81
FREIHEIT (G)	
Keeping The Dream Alive	1/89
Nicki FRENCH (UK)	
Total Eclipse Of The Heart 5/95	1/95
FRESH 4 featuring Lizz E (UK)	
Wishing On A Star	10/89
Doug E. FRESH & The Get Fresh Crew (US)	
The Show	11/85
Glenn FREY (US)	
The Heat Is On	4/85
Dean FRIEDMAN (US)	
Lucky Stars	10/78
FRIJID PINK (US)	
House Of The Rising Sun	5/70
FUGEES (US)	
Killing Me Softly	6/96
No Woman No Cry	11/96
Ready Or Not	9/96
Rumble In The Jungle	3/97
FULL FORCE (US)	
Alice I Want You Just For Me	1/86
FUN BOY THREE (UK)	
Our Lips Are Sealed	5/83
❖ with Bananarama Really Saying Something	5/82
The Tunnel Of Love	2/83
FUN BOY THREE & Bananarama (UK)	
It Ain't What You Do It's The Way That You Do It	3/82
FARLEY 'JACKMASTER' FUNK (US)	
Love Can't Turn Around	9/86
FUNKADELIC (US)	
One Nation Under A Groove (Pt. 1)	1/79
FUNK MASTERS (UK)	
It's Over	7/83
FUNKY WORM (UK)	
Hustle! (To The Music...)	8/88

	UK Top 20 Ent
FUREYS & Davey Arthur (UK)	
When You Were Sweet Sixteen	11/81
Billy FURY (UK)	
Halfway To Paradise	6/61
I Will	5/64
I'd Never Find Another You	12/61
In Summer	8/63
In Thoughts Of You	8/65
It's Only Make Believe	8/64
Jealousy	9/61
Last Night Was Made For Love	5/62
Like I've Never Been Gone	3/63
Once Upon A Dream	8/62
When Will You Say I Love You	5/63
FUZZBOX (UK)	
International Rescue	4/89
Gina G (Aus)	
Fresh	3/97
I Belong To You	11/96
Ooh Aah...Just A Little Bit	4/96
Warren G (US)	
I Shot The Sheriff	2/97
Warren G featuring Adina Howard (US)	
What's Love Got To Do With It	11/96
This D.J.	11/94
Warren G & Nate Dogg (US)	
Regulate	7/94
Peter GABRIEL (UK)	
Big Time	4/87
Games Without Frontiers	3/80
Sledgehammer	5/86
Solsbury Hill	5/77
Steam	1/93
Peter GABRIEL & Kate Bush (UK)	
Don't Give Up	11/86
GABRIELLE (UK)	
Dreams	6/93
Give Me A Little More Time	3/96
Going Nowhere	10/93
Walk On By	2/97
Rosie GAINES (US)	
Closer Than Close	5/97
GALA (Ita)	
Freed From Desire	7/97
Let A Boy Cry	12/97
GALAXY (UK) See Phil Fearon & Galaxy	5/83
GALLAGHER & LYLE (UK)	
Heart On My Sleeve	6/76
I Wanna Stay With You	3/76
Patsy GALLANT (C)	
From New York To L.A.	10/77
James GALWAY (UK)	
Annie's Song	6/78
GAP BAND (US)	
Big Fun	12/86
Oops Upside Your Head	8/80
GARBAGE (US/UK)	
Stupid Girl	3/96
Boris GARDINER (J)	
I Want To Wake Up With You	8/86
Art GARFUNKEL (US)	
Bright Eyes	4/79
I Only Have Eyes For You	9/75
Leif GARRETT (US)	
I Was Made For Dancin'	2/79
GARY'S GANG (US)	
Keep On Dancin'	3/79
GAT DECOR (UK)	
Passion	3/96

UK Top
20 Ent

Marvin GAYE (US)
Abraham Martin & John — 6/70
Got To Give It Up (Pt.1) — 5/77
I Heard It Through The Grapevine — 3/69
★ I Heard It Through The Grapevine — 5/86
Inner City Blues (Makes Me Wanna Holler) — 11/71
Sexual Healing — 11/82
Too Busy Thinking About My Baby — 8/69

❖ with Diana Ross You Are Everything — 4/74
Marvin GAYE & Tammi Terrell (US)
If I Could Build My Whole World Around You — 1/68
Onion Song — 12/69
Crystal GAYLE (US)
Don't It Make My Brown Eyes Blue — 1/78
Talking In Your Sleep — 10/78
Michelle GAYLE (UK)
Do You Know — 2/97
Looking Up — 8/93
Sweetness — 10/94
Gloria GAYNOR (US)
I Will Survive — 2/79
★ I Will Survive — 7/93
Never Can Say Goodbye — 1/75
Reach Out I'll Be There — 4/75
GAZZA And Lindisfarne (UK)
Fog On The Tyne (Revisited) — 11/90
J. GEILS BAND (US)
Centerfold — 2/82
GENERATION X (UK)
King Rocker — 2/79
GENESIS (UK)
Abacab — 9/81
Follow You Follow Me — 4/78
I Can't Dance — 1/92
Invisible Touch (Live) — 11/92
Land Of Confusion — 12/86
Mama — 9/83
No Son Of Mine — 11/91
Spot The Pigeon (E.P.) — 6/77
That's All! — 12/83
3 X 3 (E.P.) — 6/82
Turn It On Again — 4/80
Bobbie GENTRY (US)
I'll Never Fall In Love Again — 9/69
Ode To Billie Joe — 10/67
Bobbie GENTRY & Glen Campbell (US)
All I Have To Do Is Dream — 12/69
GEORDIE (UK)
All Because Of You — 4/73
Can You Do It — 7/73
Sophia GEORGE (J)
Girlie Girlie — 1/86
Danyel GERARD (F)
Butterfly — 10/71
GERRY & The Pacemakers (UK)
Don't Let The Sun Catch You Crying — 5/64
Ferry Across The Mersey — 1/65
How Do You Do It? — 3/63
I Like It — 6/63
I'll Be There — 4/65
I'm The One — 1/64
You'll Never Walk Alone — 10/63

Stan GETZ & Charlie Byrd (US)
Desafinado — 1/63
Andy GIBB (UK)
An Everlasting Love — 9/78
Robin GIBB (UK)
Saved By The Bell — 7/69
Steve GIBBONS BAND (US)
Tulane — 9/77
Debbie GIBSON (US)
Electric Youth — 5/89
Foolish Beat — 7/88
Only In My Dreams — 4/88
Shake Your Love — 2/88
GIBSON BROTHERS (F)
Cuba/Better Do It Salsa — 3/80
Mariana — 8/80
Ooh! What A Life — 9/79
Que Sera Mi Vida (If You Should Go) — 12/79
GIDEA PARK (UK)
Beach Boy Gold — 8/81
Stuart GILLIES (UK)
Amanda — 4/73
Jim GILSTRAP (US)
Swing Your Daddy — 4/75
Gary GLITTER (UK)
Always Yours — 6/74
Another Rock And Roll Christmas — 12/84
Do You Wanna Touch Me (Oh Yeah) — 1/73
Doing Alright With The Boys — 6/75
Hello Hello I'm Back Again — 4/73
I Didn't Know I Loved You (Till I Saw You Rock'n'Roll) — 10/72
I Love You Love Me Love — 11/73
I'm The Leader Of The Gang (I Am) — 7/73
Oh Yes! You're Beautiful — 11/74
Remember Me This Way — 4/74
Rock And Roll Part 2 — 6/72
GLITTER BAND (UK)
Angel Face — 4/74
Goodbye My Love — 2/75
Just For You — 8/74
Let's Get Together Again — 11/74
Love In The Sun — 8/74
People Like You And People Like Me — 3/76
The Tears I Cried — 5/75
GLOWORM (UK/US)
Carry Me Home — 5/94
GO WEST (UK)
Call Me — 6/85
Don't Look Down-The Sequel — 12/85
We Close Our Eyes — 3/85
GODLEY & CREME (UK)
Under Your Thumb — 10/81
Wedding Bells — 12/81
Andrew GOLD (US)
Lonely Boy — 5/77
Never Let Her Slip Away — 4/78
Brian & Tony GOLD (J) See Red Dragon featuring Brian & Tony Gold
GOLDBUG (UK)
Whole Lotta Love — 1/96
GOLDEN EARRING (H)
Radar Love — 1/74
GOLDIE (UK)
Making Up Again — 6/78

Bobby GOLDSBORO (US)
Honey — 5/68
★ Honey — 4/75
Summer (The First Time) — 8/73
GOODIES (UK)
Funky Gibbon/Sick Man Blues — 4/75
The In Betweenies/Father Christmas Do Not Touch Me — 12/74
GOOMBAY DANCE BAND (G/UK)
Seven Tears — 3/82
GOONS (UK)
Bloodnok's Rock 'n' Roll Call/Ying Tong Song — 9/56
I'm Walking Backwards For Christmas/Bluebottle Blues — 7/56
★ Ying Tong Song — 8/73
Lonnie GORDON (US)
Happenin' All Over Again — 2/90
Lesley GORE (US)
It's My Party — 6/63
Eydie GORME (US)
❖ with Steve Lawrence I Want To Stay Here — 9/63
Yes My Darling Daughter — 7/62
GRACE (UK)
Not Over Yet — 4/95
Charlie GRACIE (US)
Butterfly — 5/57
Fabulous — 6/57
Wanderin' Eyes/I Love You So Much It Hurts — 9/57
Jaki GRAHAM (UK)
❖ with David Grant Could It Be I'm Falling In Love — 4/85
Round And Round — 7/85
Set Me Free — 6/86
GRAND PUBA (US) See Shaggy featuring Grand Puba
GRANDMASTER FLASH, Melle Mel & The Furious Five (US)
The Message — 9/82
White Lines (Don't Don't Do It) — 7/84
GRANDMASTER MELLE MEL & The Furious Five (US)
Step Off (Pt. 1) — 1/85
GRANGE HILL CAST (UK)
Just Say No — 4/86
Amy GRANT (US)
Baby Baby — 5/91
David GRANT (UK)
Watching You Watching Me — 8/83
David GRANT & Jaki Graham (UK)
Could It Be I'm Falling In Love — 4/85
Eddy GRANT (Guy)
Do You Feel My Love — 12/80
Electric Avenue — 1/83
Gimme Hope Jo'anna — 2/88
I Don't Wanna Dance — 11/82
Living On The Front Line — 7/79
Gogi GRANT (US)
The Wayward Wind — 7/56
GREEN DAY (US)
Basket Case — 1/95
GREEN JELLY (US)
Three Little Pigs — 6/93
Al GREEN (US)
Let's Stay Together — 1/72
Tired Of Being Alone — 11/71
Robson GREEN & Jerome Flynn (UK)
I Believe/Up On The Roof — 11/95

	UK Top 20 Ent

HUMBLE PIE (UK)
Natural Born Bugie — 9/69

Engelbert HUMPERDINCK (UK)
Am I That Easy To Forget — 1/68
Another Time Another Place — 10/71
I'm A Better Man — 9/69
The Last Waltz — 9/67
Les Bicyclettes De Belsize — 10/68
A Man Without A Love — 5/68
Release Me (And Let Me Love Again) — 2/67
There Goes My Everything — 6/67
The Way It Used To Be — 2/69
Winter World Of Love — 12/69

Tab HUNTER (US)
Ninety-Nine Ways — 4/57
Young Love — 2/57

Steve 'Silk' HURLEY (US)
Jack Your Body — 1/87

Brian HYLAND (US)
Ginny Come Lately — 6/62
Itsy Bitsy Teenie Weenie Yellow Polka Dot Bikini — 7/60
Sealed With A Kiss — 8/62
★ Sealed With A Kiss — 7/75

Dick HYMAN (US)
Moritat (A Theme From 'The Three Penny Opera') — 3/56

Chrissie HYNDE (US)
❖ with UB40 Breakfast In Bed — 7/88
❖ with UB40 I Got You Babe — 8/85
❖ with Cher, Neneh Cherry & Eric Clapton Love Can Build A Bridge — 3/95

Billy IDOL (UK)
Hot In The City — 2/88
Mony Mony — 10/87
Rebel Yell — 10/85
White Wedding — 8/85

Frank IFIELD (UK)
Confessin' — 6/63
Don't Blame Me — 2/64
I Remember You — 7/62
Lovesick Blues — 10/62
Nobody's Darlin' But Mine — 4/63
Wayward Wind — 2/63

Julio IGLESIAS (Spa)
Begin The Beguine (Volver A Empezar) — 11/81
Quiereme Mucho (Yours) — 3/82

Julio IGLESIAS (featuring Stevie Wonder) (Spa/US)
My Love — 8/88

IMAGINATION (UK)
Body Talk — 7/81
Just An Illusion — 3/82
Music And Lights — 7/82

Natalie IMBRUGLIA (Aus)
Big Mistake — 3/98
Torn — 11/97

INCANTATION (UK)
Cacharpaya (Andes Pumpsa Daesi) — 1/83

INCOGNITO featuring Jocelyn Brown (F/UK/US)
Always There — 7/91

INDEEP (US)
Last Night A D.J. Saved My Life — 2/83

Los INDIOS TABAJARAS (Bra)
Maria Elena — 11/63

James INGRAM (US)
❖ with Patti Austin Baby Come To Me — 3/83
❖ with Quincy Jones One Hundred Ways — 4/82
❖ with Linda Ronstadt Somewhere Out There — 8/87

JAMES INGRAM & Michael McDonald (US)
Yah Mo B There — 2/85

INK SPOTS (US)
Melody Of Love — 5/55

INNER CIRCLE (J)
Sweat (A La La La La Long) — 5/93

INNER CITY (US)
Big Fun — 9/88
Good Life — 12/88

INSPIRAL CARPETS (UK)
Dragging Me Down — 3/92

INXS (Aus)
Need You Tonight — 11/88

IRON MAIDEN (UK)
Be Quick Or Be Dead — 4/92
Bring Your Daughter To The Slaughter — 1/91
Can I Play With Madness — 3/88
The Clairvoyant — 11/88
The Evil That Men Do — 8/88
Fear Of The Dark (Live) — 3/93
Holy Smoke — 9/90
Infinite Dreams — 11/89
Run To The Hills — 3/82
The Trooper — 7/83

Big Dee IRWIN (US)
Swinging On A Star — 12/63

Chris ISAAK (US)
Wicked Game — 12/90

ISLEY BROTHERS (US)
Behind A Painted Smile — 5/69
Harvest For The World — 8/76
I Guess I'll Always Love You — 10/73
That Lady — 10/73
This Old Heart Of Mine — 11/68

ISOTONIK (UK)
Different Strokes — 1/92

IT BITES (UK)
Calling All The Heroes — 8/86

Burl IVES (US)
A Little Bitty Tear — 2/62

IVY LEAGUE (UK)
Funny How Love Can Be — 2/65
Tossing And Turning — 7/65

JACK 'N' CHILL (UK)
The Jack That House Built — 2/88

Terry JACKS (US)
If You Go Away — 7/74
Seasons In The Sun — 3/74

Chad JACKSON (UK)
Hear The Drummer (Get Wicked) — 6/90

Dee D. JACKSON (UK)
Automatic Lover — 5/78

Janet featuring Q-Tip And Joni Mitchell (US)
Got 'til It's Gone — 10/97

Janet JACKSON (US)
Again — 11/93
Any Time, Any Place/And On And On — 6/94
Because Of Love — 3/94

❖ with Luther Vandross The Best Things In Life Are Free — 8/92
★ ❖ with Luther Vandross The Best Things In Life Are Free — 12/95
I Get Lonely — 4/98
Let's Wait Awhile — 4/87
Runaway — 9/95
❖ with Michael Jackson Scream — 6/95
That's The Way Love Goes — 5/93
Together Again — 12/97
What Have You Done For Me Lately — 4/86
When I Think Of You — 9/86
Whoops Now/What'll I Do — 3/95

Jermaine JACKSON (US)
Do What You Do — 3/85
Let's Get Serious — 6/80

Joe JACKSON (UK)
It's Different For Girls — 2/80
Steppin' Out — 1/83

Michael JACKSON (US)
Ain't No Sunshine — 9/72
Bad — 9/87
Beat It — 4/83
Ben — 12/72
Billie Jean — 2/83
Black Or White — 11/91
Blood On The Dance Floor — 5/97
History/Ghosts — 7/97
Stranger In Moscow — 11/96
They Don't Care About Us — 4/96
Dirty Diana — 7/88
Don't Stop Till You Get Enough — 10/79
Earth Song — 12/95
Farewell My Summer Love — 6/84
Give In To Me — 2/93
Got To Be There — 2/72
Heal The World — 12/92
I Just Can't Stop Loving You — 8/87
In The Closet — 5/92
Jam — 9/92
Leave Me Alone — 2/89
Off The Wall — 12/79
One Day In Your Life — 6/81
P.Y.T. (Pretty Young Thing) — 4/84
Remember The Time — 2/92
Rock With You — 2/80
Rockin' Robin — 6/72
❖ with Paul McCartney Say Say Say — 11/83
She's Out Of My Life — 5/80
Smooth Criminal — 12/88
Thriller — 12/83
Wanna Be Startin' Something — 6/83
The Way You Make Me Feel — 12/87
Who Is It — 8/92
Will You Be There — 7/93
You Are Not Alone — 9/95

Michael JACKSON & Janet Jackson (US)
Scream/Childhood — 6/95

Michael JACKSON & Paul McCartney (US/UK)
The Girl Is Mine — 11/82

Michael JACKSON with The Jackson Five (US)
I Want You Back '88 — 4/88

JACKSON FIVE (US) also see Jacksons
ABC — 6/70

	UK Top 20 Ent
Daughter Of Darkness	5/70
Delilah	3/68
Detroit City	3/67
Funny Familiar Forgotten Feelings	5/67
Green Green Grass Of Home	11/66
Help Yourself	8/68
If I Only Knew	11/94
I'll Never Fall In Love Again9/69	8/67
I'm Comin' Home	12/67
It's Not Unusual	3/65
❖ with The Art Of Noise Kiss	11/88
Love Me Tonight	5/69
A Minute Of Your Time	12/68
She's A Lady	2/71
Till	11/71
What's New Pussycat?	9/65
With These Hands	8/65
Without Love (There Is Nothing)12/69	
The Young New Mexican Puppeteer	4/72

Montell JORDAN (US)
| This Is How We Do It | 5/95 |

JOY DIVISION (UK)
| Love Will Tear Us Apart | 7/80 |

JT & The Big Family (Ita)
| Moments In Soul | 3/90 |

JUDAS PRIEST (UK)
| Breaking The Law | 6/80 |
| Living After Midnight | 4/80 |

JUDGE DREAD (UK)
Big Eight	5/73
Big Seven	1/73
Big Six	10/72
Big Ten	10/75
Je T'Aime (Moi Non Plus)	7/75

Rosemary JUNE (US)
| Apple Blossom Time | 2/59 |

JUNIOR (UK)
| ❖ with Kim Wilde Another Step (Closer To You) | 5/87 |
| Mama Used To Say | 6/82 |

Jimmy JUSTICE (UK)
| Ain't That Funny | 6/62 |
| When My Little Girl Is Smiling | 4/62 |

Bill JUSTIS (US)
| Raunchy | 2/58 |

JX (UK)
| Son Of A Gun | 8/95 |
| There's Nothing I Won't Do | 5/96 |

K-KLASS (UK)
| Rhythm Is A Mystery | 11/91 |

K7 (US)
| Come Baby Come | 1/94 |

KAJAGOOGOO (UK)
Big Apple	10/83
Hang On Now	6/83
Ooh To Be Ah	4/83
Too Shy	2/83

KALIN TWINS (US)
| When | 8/58 |

Kitty KALLEN (US)
| Little Things Mean A Lot | 7/54 |

Nick KAMEN (UK)
| Each Time You Break My Heart11/86 | |

Ini KAMOZE (J)
| Here Comes The Hotstepper | 1/95 |

Kiri Te KANAWA (NZ)
| World In Union | 10/91 |

KANDIDATE (UK)
| I Don't Wanna Lose You | 4/79 |

	UK Top 20 Ent
Eden KANE (UK)	
Boys Cry	3/64
Forget Me Not	1/62
Get Lost	9/61
I Don't Know Why	5/62
Well I Ask You	6/61

KANE GANG (UK)
| Closest Thing To Heaven | 8/84 |

KAOMA (F)
| Lambada | 12/89 |

KATRINA & The Waves (US/UK)
| Love Shine A Light | 5/97 |
| Walking On Sunshine | 6/85 |

Janet KAY (UK)
| Silly Games | 7/79 |

KAVANA (UK)
| I Can Make You Feel Good | 1/97 |

KAYE SISTERS (UK)
❖ with Frankie Vaughan Come Softly To Me	5/59
❖ with Frankie Vaughan Gotta Have Something In The Bank Frank	11/57
Paper Roses	8/60

K-CI & Jojo (US)
| All My Life | 4/98 |

KC & THE SUNSHINE BAND (US)
Give It Up	8/83
Please Don't Go	1/80
Queen Of Clubs	9/74
That's The Way (I Like It)	8/75

Jerry KELLER (US)
| Here Comes Summer | 9/59 |

R. KELLY (US)
Gotham City	7/97
I Believe I Can Fly	3/97
Bump N' Grind	2/95
She's Got That Vibe	10/94
Your Body's Callin'	5/94

KENNY (UK)
Baby I Love You, OK	6/75
The Bump	1/75
Fancy Pants	3/75
Heart Of Stone	3/73
Julie Ann	9/75

Nik KERSHAW (UK)
Dancing Girls	5/84
Don Quixote	8/85
I Won't Let The Sun Go Down On Me	6/84
The Riddle	11/84
Wide Boy	3/85
Wouldn't It Be Good	2/84

Chaka KHAN (US) also see Rufus & Chaka Khan
I Feel For You	10/84
I'm Every Woman	1/79
★ I'm Every Woman	5/89

KICKS LIKE A MULE (UK)
| The Bouncer | 2/92 |

Johnny KIDD & The Pirates (UK)
| I'll Never Get Over You | 8/63 |
| Shakin' All Over | 7/60 |

KIDS FROM 'FAME' (US)
Friday Night (Live Version)	5/83
Hi-Fidelity	9/82
Starmaker	10/82

Andy KIM (US)
| Rock Me Gently | 9/74 |

KING (UK)
| Alone Without You | 8/85 |

	UK Top 20 Ent
Love & Pride	1/85
The Taste Of Your Tears	11/85
B.B. KING (US)	
❖ with U2 When Love Comes To Town	4/89

Ben E. KING (US)
| ★ Stand By Me | 2/87 |

Carole KING (US)
| It Might As Well Rain Until September | 9/62 |
| It's Too Late/I Feel The Earth Move | 9/71 |

Dave KING (UK)
| Memories Are Made Of This | 2/56 |
| You Can't Be True To Two | 4/56 |

Diana KING (J)
| Shy Guy | 7/95 |

Evelyn 'Champagne' KING (US)
| Love Come Down | 10/82 |

Jonathan KING (UK)
| Everyone's Gone To The Moon8/65 | |
| Una Paloma Blanca | 10/75 |

Solomon KING (US)
| She Wears My Ring | 1/68 |

KING BROTHERS (UK)
Mais Oui	8/60
Standing On The Corner	4/60
A White Sport Coat	6/57

KINGSTON TRIO (US)
| Tom Dooley | 12/58 |

KINKS (UK)
All Day And All Of The Night	11/64
Ape Man	1/71
Autumn Almanac	11/67
Days	8/68
Dead End Street	12/66
Dedicated Follower Of Fashion3/66	
Everybody's Gonna Be Happy	4/65
Lola	7/70
See My Friend	9/65
Set Me Free	6/65
Sunny Afternoon	6/66
Till The End Of The Day	1/66
Tired Of Waiting For You	2/65
Waterloo Sunset	5/67
You Really Got Me	8/64

Fern KINNEY (US)
| Together We Are Beautiful | 3/80 |

Kathy KIRBY (UK)
Dance On	9/63
Let Me Go, Lover	3/64
Secret Love	11/63

Bo KIRKLAND & Ruth Davis (US)
| You're Gonna Get Next To Me | 7/77 |

KISS (US)
| Crazy Crazy Nights | 10/87 |
| God Gave Rock & Roll To You II | 1/92 |

Mac & Katie KISSOON (UK)
| Don't Do It Baby | 5/75 |
| Sugar Candy Kisses | 2/75 |

Eartha KITT (US)
| Under The Bridges Of Paris | 4/55 |

KLF (UK)
| America: What Time Is Love? | 3/92 |

KLF featuring The Children Of The Revolution (UK)
Last Train To Trancentral	5/91
3 A.M. Eternal	1/91
What Time Is Love	9/90

295

	UK Top 20 Ent
KLF featuring Tammy Wynette (UK/US)	
Justified And Ancient	12/91
KLF (AKA THE TIMELORDS) (UK)	
Doctorin' The Tardis	6/88
KLUBBHEADS (H)	
Klubbhopping	5/96
KNACK (US)	
My Sharona	7/79
Gladys KNIGHT (US)	
Licence To Kill	7/89
Gladys KNIGHT & The Pips (US)	
Baby Don't Change Your Mind	6/77
Best Thing That Ever Happened To Me	8/75
Come Back And Finish What You Started	8/78
Help Me Make It Through The Night	12/72
IMidnight Train To Georgia	6/76
The Way We Were/Try To Remember (Medley)	5/75
Robert KNIGHT (US)	
Love On A Mountain Top	1/74
KON KAN (C)	
I Beg Your Pardon	4/89
John KONGOS (SA)	
He's Gonna Step On You Again	6/71
Tokoloshe Man	12/71
KOOL & THE GANG (US)	
Celebration	11/80
Cherish	6/85
Fresh	12/84
Get Down On It	1/82
Joanna	3/84
Ladies Night	11/79
Ooh La La La (Let's Go Dancing)	11/82
Tonight	3/84
(When You Say You Love Somebody) In The Heart	4/84
KORGIS (UK)	
Everybody's Got To Learn Sometime	6/80
KRAFTWERK (G)	
Autobahn	6/75
The Model/Computer Love	1/82
Billy J. KRAMER & The Dakotas (UK)	
Bad To Me	8/63
Do You Want To Know A Secret	5/63
From A Window	8/64
I'll Keep You Satisfied	11/63
Little Children	3/64
Trains And Boats And Planes	6/65
Lenny KRAVITZ (US)	
Are You Gonna Go My Way	2/93
It Ain't Over 'Til It's Over	7/91
KRIS KROSS (US)	
Jump	6/92
KRUSH (UK)	
House Arrest	1/88
KULA SHAKER (UK)	
Govinda	11/96
Hey Dude	9/96
Hush	3/97
Tattva	7/96
KURSAAL FLYERS (UK)	
Little Does She Know	12/76
KWS (UK)	
Please Don't Go	5/92
Rock Your Baby	8/92

	UK Top 20 Ent
L.A. MIX (UK)	
Check This Out	6/88
L.L. COOL J (US)	
Ain't Nobody	2/97
Loungin'	10/96
Hey Lover	1/96
I Need Love	10/87
LA BELLE EPOQUE (F)	
Black Is Black	10/77
Patti LABELLE & Michael McDonald (US)	
On My Own	5/86
Cleo LAINE (UK)	
You'll Answer To Me	9/61
Frankie LAINE (US)	
Answer Me	1/54
Blowing Wild	1/54
Cool Water	6/55
Granada	3/54
Hawkeye	12/55
The Kid's Last Fight	4/54
Moonlight Gambler	12/56
My Friend	8/54
Rain Rain Rain	10/54
Rawhide	12/59
Sixteen Tons	1/56
Some Day	9/54
Strange Lady In Town	7/55
There Must Be A Reason	10/54
A Woman In Love	9/56
Greg LAKE (UK)	
I Believe In Father Christmas	12/75
LAMBRETTAS (UK)	
D-a-a-ance	6/80
Poison Ivy	4/80
LANDSCAPE (UK)	
Einstein A Go-Go	4/81
Ronnie LANE (UK)	
How Come	2/74
Don LANG (UK)	
Witch Doctor	6/58
Mario LANZA (US)	
Drinking Song	2/55
Denise LA SALLE (US)	
My Toot Toot	7/85
LATINO RAVE (Various)	
Deep Heat '89	1/90
Stacy LATTISAW (US)	
Jump To The Beat	7/80
Cyndi LAUPER (US)	
Girls Just Want To Have Fun	2/84
Hey Now (Girls Just Want To Have Fun)	9/94
I Drove All Night	6/89
Time After Time	7/84
True Colors	10/86
LAUREL & HARDY with The Avalon Boys (US)	
The Trail Of The Lonesome Pine	12/75
Joey LAWRENCE (US)	
Nothin' My Love Can't Fix	7/93
Lee LAWRENCE (UK)	
Crying In The Chapel	1/54
Suddenly There's A Valley	12/55
Steve LAWRENCE (US)	
Footsteps	4/60
Steve LAWRENCE & Eydie Gorme (US)	
I Want To Stay Here	9/63
Lindy LAYTON (UK) See Beats International featuring Lindy Layton	

	UK Top 20 Ent
Vicky LEANDROS (Gre)	
Come What May	4/72
Brenda LEE (US)	
All Alone Am I	2/63
As Usual	1/64
Here Comes That Feeling	6/62
I'm Sorry	8/60
It Started All Over Again	10/62
Let's Jump The Broomstick	3/61
Losing You	5/63
Rockin' Around The Christmas Tree	12/62
Speak To Me Pretty	4/62
Sweet Nothin's	4/60
Dee C. LEE (UK)	
See The Day	11/85
Jackie LEE (US)	
Rupert	2/71
Leapy LEE (UK)	
Little Arrows	9/68
Peggy LEE (US)	
Fever	8/58
Mr. Wonderful	5/57
LEEDS UNITED F.C. (UK)	
Leeds United	5/72
LEMON PIPERS (US)	
Green Tambourine	3/68
John LENNON/Yoko Ono/Plastic Ono Band (UK/Jap)	
Cold Turkey	11/69
Give Peace A Chance	7/69
Happy Xmas (War Is Over)	12/72
★ Happy Xmas (War Is Over)	12/80
Imagine	11/75
★ Imagine	1/81
Instant Karma (We All Shine On)	2/70
(Just Like) Starting Over	11/80
Nobody Told Me	1/84
Power To The People	3/71
Woman	1/81
Julian LENNON (UK)	
Saltwater	10/91
Too Late For Goodbyes	11/84
Annie LENNOX (UK)	
Little Bird/Love Song For A Vampire	2/93
No More 'I Love You's'	2/95
Walking On Broken Glass	9/92
Why	4/92
Ketty LESTER (US)	
Love Letters	4/62
LET LOOSE (UK)	
Make It With You	6/96
Best In Me	4/95
Crazy For You	7/94
One Night Stand	2/95
Seventeen	10/94
LEVEL 42 (UK)	
It's Over	9/87
Lessons In Love	5/86
Running In The Family	2/87
Something About You	11/85
The Sun Goes Down (Living It Up)	9/83
To Be With You Again	5/87
LEVERT (US)	
Casanova	9/87
GENERAL LEVY (UK) See M-Beat featuring General Levy	
Jona LEWIE (UK)	
Stop The Cavalry	12/80

	UK Top 20 Ent
Lena MARTELL (UK)	
One Day At A Time	10/79
MARTHA & THE MUFFINS (C)	
Echo Beach	4/80
MARTHA (REEVES) & The Vandellas (US)	
Dancing In The Street	2/69
Forget Me Not	3/71
MARTIKA (US)	
I Feel The Earth Move	11/89
Love...Thy Will Be Done	9/91
Toy Soldiers	8/89
Billie Ray MARTIN (G)	
Your Loving Arms	5/95
Dean MARTIN (US)	
Everybody Loves Somebody	9/64
Gentle On My Mind	3/69
Let Me Go, Lover	3/55
Mambo Italiano	2/55
Memories Are Made Of This	2/56
Naughty Lady Of Shady Lane	2/55
Return To Me	8/58
Sway	10/54
That's Amore	1/54
Under The Bridges Of Paris	4/55
Volare	9/58
Juan MARTIN (Spa)	
Love Theme From 'The Thorn Birds'	2/84
Ray MARTIN (UK)	
Swedish Rhapsody	1/54
Tony MARTIN (US)	
Stranger In Paradise	4/55
Walk Hand In Hand	7/56
Ricky MARTIN (US)	
(Un, Dos, Tres) Maria	9/97
Wink MARTINDALE (US)	
Deck Of Cards	5/63
Al MARTINO (US)	
Spanish Eyes	8/73
The Story Of Tina	10/54
Wanted	6/54
Lee MARVIN (US)	
Wand'rin' Star	2/70
Richard MARX (US)	
Hazard	6/92
Now And Forever	1/94
Right Here Waiting	9/89
Take This Heart	9/92
MASH (US)	
Theme From M*A*S*H (Suicide Is Painless)	5/80
MASE (US)	
Feel So Good	12/97
MATCHBOX (UK)	
Midnite Dynamos	6/80
When You Ask About Love	10/80
MATCHROOM MOB with Chas & Dave (UK)	
Snooker Loopy	5/86
Johnny MATHIS (US)	
A Certain Smile	10/58
I'm Stone In Love With You	3/75
Misty	2/60
My Love For You	10/60
Someone	8/59
When A Child Is Born (Soleado)	12/76
Johnny MATHIS & Deniece Williams (US)	
Too Much, Too Little, Too Late	4/78
MATT BIANCO (UK)	
Don't Blame It On That Girl/Wap	

	UK Top 20 Ent
Bam Boogie	7/88
MATTHEWS SOUTHERN COMFORT (UK)	
Woodstock	10/70
Susan MAUGHAN (UK)	
Bobby's Girl	11/62
MAUREEN (UK)	
Thinking Of You	7/90
Paul MAURIAT (F)	
Love Is Blue	4/68
MAXX (UK/S/G)	
Get-A-Way	5/94
No More (I Can't Stand It)	8/94
Billy MAY (US)	
Main Title Theme From The Man With The Golden Arm	5/56
Brian MAY (UK)	
Driven By You	12/91
Too Much Love Will Kill You	9/92
Simon MAY (UK)	
Summer Of My Life	10/76
Curtis MAYFIELD (US)	
Wait	2/89
Kym MAZELLE (US)	
❖ with Robert Howard Wait	2/89
Kym MAZELLE & Jocelyn Brown (US)	
No More Tears (Enough Is Enough)	6/94
MC HAMMER (US) See Hammer	
MC MIKER 'G' & Deejay Sven (H)	
Holiday Rap	9/86
MC TUNES Versus 808 State (UK)	
The Only Rhyme That Bites	6/90
McALMONT & BUTLER (UK)	
Yes	6/95
C.W. McCALL (US)	
Convoy	2/76
Paul McCARTNEY/Wings (UK)	
Another Day/Oh Woman Oh Why Oh Why	3/71
Band On The Run	7/74
Coming Up (Live At Glasgow)	4/80
❖ with The Christians, Holly Johnson, Gerry Marsden & Stock Aitken Waterman Ferry 'Cross The Mersey	5/89
❖ with Michael Jackson The Girl Is Mine	11/82
Goodnight Tonight	5/79
Helen Wheels	12/73
Hi, Hi, Hi/C Moon	1/73
Jet	3/74
Let 'Em In	8/76
Listen To What The Man Said	6/75
Live And Let Die	6/73
Mary Had A Little Lamb	6/72
Mull Of Kintyre/Girls School	11/77
My Love	4/73
No More Lonely Nights (Ballad)	10/84
Once Upon A Long Ago	12/87
Pipes Of Peace	1/84
Silly Love Songs	6/76
Spies Like Us	12/85
Waterfalls	7/80
With A Little Luck	4/78
Wonderful Christmastime	12/79
Paul McCARTNEY & The Frog Chorus (UK)	
We All Stand Together	12/84

	UK Top 20 Ent
PAUL McCARTNEY & Michael Jackson (UK/US)	
Say Say Say	11/83
Paul McCARTNEY & Stevie Wonder (UK/US)	
Ebony And Ivory	4/82
Marilyn McCOO & Billy Davis Jr (US)	
You Don't Have To Be A Star (To Be In My Show)	4/77
Van McCOY (US)	
The Hustle	6/75
The Shuffle	5/77
McCOYS (US)	
Hang On Sloopy	10/65
George McCRAE (US)	
I Can't Leave You Alone	10/74
It's Been So Long	8/75
Rock Your Baby	7/74
Chas McDEVITT SKIFFLE GROUP (UK)	
Freight Train	4/57
Michael McDONALD (US)	
❖ with Patti Labelle On My Own	5/86
Sweet Freedom	9/86
❖ with James Ingram Yah Mo B There	2/85
McFADDEN & WHITEHEAD (US)	
Ain't No Stoppin' Us Now	6/79
Bobby McFERRIN (US)	
Don't Worry Be Happy	10/88
Maureen McGOVERN (US)	
The Morning After (Song From The Poseidon Adventure)	
Freddie McGREGOR (J)	
Just Don't Want To Be Lonely	8/87
McGUINNESS FLINT (UK)	
Malt And Barley Blues	5/71
When I'm Dead And Gone	12/70
McGUIRE SISTERS (US)	
May You Always	5/59
Sincerely	7/55
Sugartime	2/58
Barry McGUIRE (US)	
Eve Of Destruction	9/65
Maria McKEE (US)	
Show Me Heaven	9/90
Scott McKENZIE (US)	
San Francisco (Be Sure To Wear Some Flowers In Your Hair)	7/67
Craig McLACHLAN & Check 1-2 (Aus)	
Mona	7/90
Malcolm McLAREN (UK)	
Double Dutch	7/83
Madame Butterfly	9/84
Malcolm McLAREN & The World's Famous Supreme Team (UK/US)	
Buffalo Gals	1/83
Bitty McLEAN (UK)	
Dedicated To The One I Love	4/94
Here I Stand	1/94
It Keeps Rainin' (Tears From My Eyes)	8/93
Don McLEAN (US)	
American Pie (Pts 1 & 2)	2/72
★ American Pie	11/91
Crying	6/80
Vincent/Castles In The Air	6/72
Lutricia McNEAL (US)	
Ain't That Just	11/97
Rita McNEIL (C)	
Working Man	11/90

	UK Top 20 Ent
NOTORIOUS B.I.G. featuring Puff Daddy & Mase (US)	
Mo Money Mo Problems	8/97 F
NU SHOOZ (US)	
I Can't Wait	6/86
Gary NUMAN (UK)	
Cars	9/79
Complex	12/79
I Die:You Die	9/80
She's Got Claws	9/81
We Are Glass	5/80
We Take Mystery (To Bed)	6/82
Gary NUMAN (UK) (TUBEWAY ARMY)	
Are 'Friends' Electric	6/79
OASIS (UK)	
All Around The World	1/98
D'You Know What I Mean?	7/97
Stand By Me	10/97
Cigarettes & Alcohol	10/94
Don't Look Back In Anger	3/96
Live Forever	8/94
Roll With It	8/95
Shakermaker	7/94
Some Might Say	5/95
Whatever	12/94
Wonderwall	11/95
OBERNKIRCHEN CHILDREN'S CHOIR (G)	
Happy Wanderer	1/54
Billy OCEAN (UK)	
The Circle	9/96
The Day We Caught The Train	6/96
Hundred Mile High City	6/97
Travellers Tune	9/97
You've Got It Bad	4/96
Caribbean Queen (No More Love On The Run)	11/84
Get Outta My Dreams Get Into My Car	2/88
Love Really Hurts Without You	3/76
Loverboy	2/85
Red Light Spells Danger	4/77
Stop Me (If You've Heard It All Before)	12/76
Suddenly	6/85
There'll Be Sad Songs (To Make You Cry)	5/86
When The Going Gets Tough, The Tough Get Going	1/86 2/86
OCEANIC (UK)	
Insanity	9/91
Des O'CONNOR (UK)	
Careless Hands	12/67
I Pretend	6/68
One Two Three O'Leary	12/68
❖ with Roger Whittaker The Skye Boat Song	12/86
Hazel O'CONNOR (UK)	
D-Days	4/81
Eighth Day	9/80
Will You	6/81
Sinead O'CONNOR (I)	
Nothing Compares 2 U	1/90
Daniel O'DONNELL (I)	
Give A Little Love	4/98
OLIVE (UK)	
You Are Not Alone	5/97
ODYSSEY (US)	
Going Back To My Roots	6/81
If You're Lookin' For A Way Out	10/80

	UK Top 20 Ent
Inside Out	6/82
Native New Yorker	1/78
Use It Up And Wear It Out	7/80
ESTHER & ABI OFARIM (Isr)	
Cinderella Rockafella	2/68
One More Dance	7/68
OFF-SHORE (G)	
I Can't Take The Power	1/91
OHIO EXPRESS (US)	
Yummy Yummy Yummy	7/68
O'JAYS (US)	
I Love Music (Pt. 1)	3/76
Love Train	4/73
Use Ta Be My Girl	7/78
Mike OLDFIELD (UK)	
In Dulce Jubilo/On Horseback	1/76
Moonlight Shadow	7/83
Portsmouth	12/76
Sentinel	10/92
OLIVER (US)	
Good Morning Starshine	9/69
OLLIE & JERRY (US)	
Breakin'...There's No Stopping Us	7/84
OLYMPICS (US)	
Western Movies	10/58
OMC (NZ)	
How Bizarre	8/96
ORB (UK)	
Toxygene	2/97
OMD (UK) See Orchestral Manoeuvres In The Dark	
ONE HUNDRED TON & A FEATHER (UK)	
It Only Takes A Minute	7/76
Alexander O'NEAL (US)	
Criticize	11/87
❖ with Cherelle Saturday Love	1/86
OPUS III (UK)	
It's A Fine Day	2/92
OPUS (A)	
Live Is Life	7/85
ORANGE JUICE (UK)	
Rip It Up	3/83
ORB (UK)	
Blue Room	6/92
Little Fluffy Clouds	11/93
Roy ORBISON (US)	
Blue Angel	12/60
Blue Bayou	10/63
Dream Baby	3/62
Falling	6/63
Goodnight	3/65
I Drove All Night	7/92
In Dreams	4/63
It's Over	5/64
Lana	7/66
Oh Pretty Woman	9/64
Only The Lonely	9/60
Pretty Paper	12/64
Running Scared	6/61
There Won't Be Many Coming Home	12/66
Too Soon To Know	9/66
You Got It	1/89
ORBITAL (UK)	
The Saint	4/97
Satan	1/97
187 LOCKDOWN (UK)	
Kung-Fu	4/98

	UK Top 20 Ent
ORCHESTRAL MANOEUVRES IN THE DARK (UK)	
Enola Gay	11/80
(Forever) Live And Die	10/86
If You Leave	5/86
Joan Of Arc	11/81
Locomotion	5/84
Maid Of Orleans (The Waltz Joan Of Arc)	2/82
Messages	6/80
Pandora's Box	7/91
Sailing On The Seven Seas	4/91
Souvenir	9/81
Talking Loud And Clear	7/84
ORIGINAL (US)	
I Luv U Baby	8/95
Tony ORLANDO (US) also see Dawn	
Bless You	10/61
Jeffrey OSBORNE (US)	
On The Wings Of Love	8/84
You Should Be Mine (The Woo Woo Song)	8/86
Joan OSBORNE (US)	
One Of Us	2/96
Ozzy OSBOURNE (UK) See Lita Ford (& Ozzy Osbourne)	
Donny OSMOND (US)	
Are You Lonesome Tonight/When I Fall In Love	11/73
Puppy Love	7/72
Too Young	9/72
The Twelfth Of Never	3/73
Why/Lonely Boy	11/72
Young Love	8/73
Donny & Marie OSMOND (US)	
I'm Leaving It (All) Up To You	8/74
Morning Side Of The Mountain	1/75
Little Jimmy OSMOND (US)	
I'm Gonna Knock On Your Door	4/74
Long Haired Lover From Liverpool	12/72
Tweedle Dee	4/73
Marie OSMOND (US)	
Paper Roses	11/73
OSMONDS (US)	
Crazy Horses	11/72
Going Home	7/73
I Can't Stop	5/74
Let Me In	11/73
Love Me For A Reason	8/74
The Proud One	6/75
Gilbert O'SULLIVAN (I)	
Alone Again (Naturally)	3/72
Clair	10/72
Get Down	3/73
No Matter How I Try	12/71
Nothing Rhymed	12/70
Ooh-Wakka-Doo-Wakka-Day	7/72
Why Oh Why Oh Why	12/73
Johnny OTIS SHOW (US)	
Ma He's Making Eyes At Me	11/57
OTTAWAN (F)	
D.I.S.C.O.	10/80
Hands Up (Give Me Your Heart)	9/81
OUR KID (UK)	
You Just Might See Me Cry	6/76
OUTHERE BROTHERS (US)	
Boom Boom Boom	6/95
Don't Stop (Wiggle Wiggle)	3/95
❖ with Molella If You Wanna Party	1/96

	UK Top 20 Ent
Robert PLANT (UK)	
Big Log	8/83
PLASTIC BERTRAND (B)	
Ca Plane Pour Moi	6/78
PLASTIC ONO BAND (UK) See John Lennon	
PLASTIC PENNY (UK)	
Everything I Am	1/68
PLATTERS (US)	
The Great Pretender	9/56
Harbor Lights	2/60
My Prayer	11/56
Only You	9/56
Smoke Gets In Your Eyes	1/59
Twilight Time	6/58
PLAVKA (G) See Jam & Spoon featuring Plavka	
PLAYERS ASSOCIATION (US)	
Turn The Music Up	4/79
POGUES & The Dubliners (I/UK)	
The Irish Rover	4/87
POGUES featuring Kirsty MacColl (I/UK)	
Fairytale Of New York	12/87
POINTER SISTERS (US)	
Automatic	5/84
I'm So Excited	11/84
Jump (For My Love)	7/84
Slow Hand	9/81
POISON (US)	
Every Rose Has Its Thorn	3/89
Your Mama Don't Dance	5/89
POLICE (UK/US)	
Can't Stand Losing You	8/79
De Do Do Do, De Da Da Da	12/80
Don't Stand So Close To Me	9/80
Every Breath You Take	5/83
Every Little Thing She Does Is Magic	11/81
Invisible Sun	10/81
Message In A Bottle	9/79
Roxanne	5/79
So Lonely	3/80
Spirits In The Material World	12/81
Walking On The Moon	12/79
Wrapped Around Your Finger	7/83
SU POLLARD (UK)	
Starting Together	2/86
PONI-TAILS (US)	
Born Too Late	9/58
Brian POOLE & The Tremeloes (UK)	
Candy Man	2/64
Do You Love Me	9/63
Someone Someone	6/64
Twist And Shout	7/63
POPPY FAMILY (C)	
Which Way You Goin' Billy	9/70
PORTISHEAD (UK)	
All Mine	9/97
Glory Box	1/95
Cozy POWELL (UK)	
Dance With The Devil	1/74
Na Na Na	9/74
Perez PRADO (US)	
Cherry Pink And Apple Blossom White	4/55
Guaglione	5/95
Patricia	8/58
PRAISE (UK)	
Only You	2/91
PREFAB SPROUT (UK)	
The King Of Rock 'n' Roll	5/88

	UK Top 20 Ent
Elvis PRESLEY (US)	
All Shook Up	6/57
Always On My Mind	1/73
An American Trilogy	7/72
Are You Lonesome Tonight ?	1/61
Big Hunk O' Love	7/59
Blue Christmas	12/64
Blue Moon	11/56
Blue Suede Shoes	6/56
Burning Love	10/72
Can't Help Falling In Love	2/62
Crying In The Chapel	6/65
Don't Cry Daddy/Rubberneckin'	3/70
Don't/I Beg Of You	3/58
Follow That Dream E.P.	6/62
A Fool Such As I	4/59
Girl Of My Best Friend	8/60
★ Girl Of My Best Friend	10/76
Good Luck Charm	5/62
Hard Headed Woman	7/58
Heartbreak Hotel	5/56
★ Heartbreak Hotel	8/71
Hound Dog/Don't Be Cruel	8/56 / 9/56
I Got Stung	1/59
I Just Can't Help Believing	1/72
I Need Your Love Tonight	4/59
I Want You, I Need You, I Love You	9/56
I've Lost You	11/70
If Every Day Was Like Christmas	12/66
If I Can Dream	3/69
In The Ghetto	6/69
It's Now Or Never	11/60
It's Only Love/Beyond The Reef	11/80
Jailhouse Rock	1/58
Kid Galahad E.P.	11/62
King Creole	10/58
Kiss Me Quick	1/64
Kissin' Cousins	7/64
Love Letters	7/66
Love Me Tender	12/56
(Marie's The Name) His Latest Flame	11/61
A Mess Of Blues	8/60
Moody Blue	3/77
My Boy	12/74
My Way	12/77
One Broken Heart For Sale	3/63
One Night	1/59
Paralysed	9/57
Party	10/57
Promised Land	2/75
Rags To Riches	6/71
Return To Sender	11/62
Rock-A-Hula-Baby	2/62
Santa Bring My Baby Back To Me	11/57
She's Not You	9/62
Stuck On You	4/60
Such A Night	9/64
Surrender	5/61
Suspicion	2/77
Suspicious Minds	12/69
Teddy Bear	7/57
Tell Me Why	12/65
There Goes My Everything	4/71
Too Much	5/57
Until It's Time For You To Go	4/72
Viva Las Vegas	4/64
Way Down	8/77

	UK Top 20 Ent
Wear My Ring Around Your Neck	5/58
Wild In The Country	9/61
The Wonder Of You/Mama Liked The Roses	7/70
Wooden Heart	3/61
You Don't Have To Say You Love Me/ Patch It Up	1/71
(You're The) Devil In Disguise	7/63
PRESIDENTS OF THE UNITED STATES (US)	
Peaches	4/96
Billy PRESTON (US)	
❖ with The Beatles Get Back	4/69
That's The Way God Planned It	7/69
Billy PRESTON & Syreeta (US)	
With You I'm Born Again	1/80
Johnny PRESTON (US)	
Cradle Of Love	5/60
Running Bear	2/60
Mike PRESTON (UK)	
Mr. Blue	11/59
PRETENDERS (UK/US)	
Brass In Pocket	12/79
Don't Get Me Wrong	11/86
Hymn To Her	1/87
I Go To Sleep	11/81
I'll Stand By You	4/94
Message Of Love	2/81
Talk Of The Town	4/80
PRETTY THINGS (UK)	
Don't Bring Me Down	11/64
Honey I Need	3/65
Alan PRICE (UK)	
Jarrow Song	6/74
❖ with Georgie Fame Rosetta	5/71
Alan PRICE SET (UK)	
Don't Stop The Carnival	2/68
Hi-Lili-Hi-Lo	8/66
The House That Jack Built	8/67
I Put A Spell On You	4/66
Simon Smith & His Amazing Dancing Bear	3/67
Lloyd PRICE (US)	
Personality	7/59
Stagger Lee	3/59
Maxi PRIEST (UK)	
Close To You	7/90
❖ with Shabba Ranks Housecall	5/93
Some Guys Have All The Luck	12/87
Wild World	6/88
PRIMAL SCREAM (UK)	
Dixie-Narco (EP)	2/92
Rocks/Funky Jam	3/94
PRIMITIVES (UK)	
Crash	3/88
PRINCE (US)	
Alphabet Street	5/88
Batdance	6/89
Controversy	12/93
Gett Off	9/91
Gold	12/95
I Hate U	9/95
Kiss	3/86
Let's Go Crazy	3/85
Little Red Corvette	1/85
The Most Beautiful Girl In The World	4/94
My Name Is Prince	10/92
1999	1/85

	UK Top 20 Ent
Purple Rain	10/84
Sexy MF/Strollin'	7/92
Sign 'O' The Times	3/87
Thieves In The Temple	8/90
U Got The Look	9/87
When Doves Cry	7/84
PRINCESS (UK)	
Say I'm Your No. 1	8/85
P.J. PROBY (US)	
Hold Me	7/64
I Apologise	3/65
Maria	12/65
Somewhere	12/64
Together	10/64
PROCLAIMERS (UK)	
I'm Gonna Be (500 Miles)	9/88
King Of The Road (E.P.)	12/90
Letter From America	12/87
PROCOL HARUM (UK)	
Homburg	10/67
A Whiter Shade Of Pale	6/67
★ A Whiter Shade Of Pale	6/72
PRODIGY (UK)	
Breathe	11/96
Charly	8/91
Everybody In The Place (EP)	1/92
Fire/Jericho	9/92
Firestarter	3/96
No Good (Start The Dance)	5/94
One Love	10/93
Out Of Space/Ruff In The Jungle Bizness	11/92
Wind It Up (Rewound)	4/93
PROPELLERHEADS/David Arnold (UK)	
On Her Majesty's Secret Service	10/97
Dorothy PROVINE (US)	
Don't Bring Lulu	12/61
PSEUDO ECHO (Aus)	
Funky Town	8/87
PUBLIC IMAGE LTD. (UK)	
Public Image	11/78
Rise	2/86
This Is Not A Love Song	10/83
Gary PUCKETT & The Union Gap (US)	
Lady Willpower	9/68
Young Girl	5/68
★ Young Girl	7/74
PUFF DADDY & Faith Evans (US)	
I'll Be Missing You	6/97
PULP (UK)	
Common People	6/95
Disco 2000	12/95
Mis-Shapes/Sorted For Es & Wizz	10/95
Something Changed	4/96
PUSSYCAT (H)	
Mississippi	9/76
PYTHON LEE JACKSON (Aus)	
In A Broken Dream	10/72
QUADROPHONIA (B)	
Quadrophonia	5/91
QUANTUM JUMP (UK)	
The Lone Ranger	6/79
QUARTZ Introducing Dina Carroll (UK)	
It's Too Late	3/91
Suzi QUATRO (US)	
Can The Can	5/73
Devil Gate Drive	2/74
48 Crash	8/73
If You Can't Give Me Love	4/78

	UK Top 20 Ent
She's In Love With You	11/79
The Wild One	11/74
QUEEN LATIFAH & De La Soul (US)	
Mamma Gave Birth To The Soul Children	4/90
QUEEN (UK)	
Another One Bites The Dust	9/80
Bicycle Race/Fat Bottomed Girls	11/78
Bohemian Rhapsody	11/75
★ Bohemian Rhapsody/These Are The Days Of Our Lives	12/91
Breakthru'	7/89
Crazy Little Thing Called Love	11/79
Don't Stop Me Now	3/79
❖ with George Michael Five Live (EP)	5/93
Flash	12/80
Heaven For Everyone	11/95
I Want It All	5/89
I Want To Break Free	4/84
Innuendo	1/91
It's A Hard Life	8/84
Killer Queen	11/74
A Kind Of Magic	4/86
Now I'm Here	2/75
One Vision	11/85
Radio Ga Ga	2/84
Seven Seas Of Rhye	4/74
Somebody To Love	11/76
We Are The Champions	11/77
A Winter's Tale	12/95
You're My Best Friend	7/76
QUEEN & David Bowie (UK)	
Under Pressure	11/81
RACEY (UK)	
Lay Your Love On Me	12/78
Some Girls	4/79
RADHA KRISHNA TEMPLE (UK)	
Hare Krishna	10/69
RADIOHEAD (UK)	
Creep	9/93
Karma Police	9/97
No Surprises	1/98
Paranoid Android	6/97
Street Spirit (Fade Out)	2/96
Gerry RAFFERTY (UK)	
Baker Street	3/78
Night Owl	6/79
RAGE (UK)	
Run To You	11/92
RAGE Against The Machine (US)	
Bulls On Parade	4/96
RAH BAND (UK)	
Clouds Across The Moon	4/85
The Crunch	8/77
RAINBOW (UK)	
All Night Long	3/80
I Surrender	2/81
Since You've Been Gone	10/79
Marvin RAINWATER (US)	
Whole Lotta Woman	3/58
RAM JAM (US)	
Black Betty	10/77
★ Black Betty	3/90
RAMBLERS (UK)	
The Sparrow	11/79
RAMRODS (US)	
Riders In The Sky	2/61
Shabba RANKS (J)	
Mr. Loverman	3/93

	UK Top 20 Ent
Shabba RANKS featuring Maxi Priest (J/UK)	
Housecall	5/93
RASCALS (US)	
Groovin'	6/67
RATTLES (G)	
The Witch	11/70
Lou RAWLS (US)	
You'll Never Find Another Love Like Mine	8/76
Johnnie RAY (US)	
Build Your Love	9/57
Destiny	8/54
Hernando's Hideaway	10/55
Hey There	10/55
If You Believe	5/55
Just Walking In The Rain	10/56
Look Homeward Angel	4/57
Song Of The Dreamer	11/55
Such A Night	4/54
Yes Tonight Josephine	5/57
You Don't Owe Me A Thing	2/57
RAYDIO (US) See Ray Parker Jr. & Raydio	
Chris REA (UK)	
Let's Dance	7/87
The Road To Hell (Pt. 2)	10/89
REAL McCOY (G/US)	
Run Away	2/95
REAL ROXANNE with Hitman Howie Tee (US)	
(Bang Zoom) Let's Go Go	7/86
REAL THING (UK)	
Can You Feel The Force	3/79
Can't Get By Without You	9/76
★ Can't Get By Without You	6/86
You To Me Are Everything	6/76
★ You To Me Are Everything	4/86
REBEL MC (UK)	
❖ with Double Trouble Just Keep Rockin'	6/89
REBEL MC & Double Trouble (UK)	
Street Tuff	10/89
RED BOX (UK)	
For America	11/86
Lean On Me (Ah-Li-Ayo)	9/85
Love Rollercoaster	6/97
RED DRAGON with Brian & Tony Gold (J)	
Compliments On Your Kiss	8/94
RED HOT CHILI PEPPERS (US)	
Give It Away	2/94
Under The Bridge	5/94
REDBONE (US)	
Witch Queen Of New Orleans	10/71
REDS UNITED (UK)	
Sing Up For The Champions	12/97
Otis REDDING (US)	
Hard To Handle	9/68
My Girl	1/66
(Sittin' On) The Dock Of The Bay	3/68
Helen REDDY (Aus)	
Angie Baby	2/75
REDHEAD KINGPIN & The FBI (US)	
Do The Right Thing	8/89
REDNEX (S)	
Cotton Eye Joe	12/94
Lou REED (US)	
Walk On The Wild Side	6/73
Michael REED ORCHESTRA (UK) See Richard Hartley/Michael Reed Orchestra	

	UK Top 20 Ent
REEF (UK)	
Come Back Brighter	1/97
Place Your Hands	11/96
REEL 2 Real (US)	
Jazz It Up	7/96
REEL 2 REAL featuring The Mad Stuntman (US)	
Go On Move	7/94
I Like To Move It	2/94
Jim REEVES (US)	
Distant Drums	9/66
He'll Have To Go	6/60
I Love You Because	3/64
I Won't Come In While He's There	2/67
I Won't Forget You	7/64
It Hurts So Much	2/65
There's A Heartache Following Me	11/64
Welcome To My World	7/63
Martha REEVES (US) See Martha & The Vandellas	
VIC REEVES & Mortimer	
❖ with EMF I'm A Believer	7/95
Vic REEVES & The Roman Numerals (UK)	
Born Free	5/91
VIC REEVES & The Wonder Stuff (UK)	
Dizzy	10/91
Joan REGAN (UK)	
If I Give My Heart To You	10/54
May You Always	6/59
Prize Of Gold	4/55
Ricochet	1/54
Someone Else's Roses	5/54
REGENTS (US)	
7 Teen	2/80
John REID (UK) See Nightcrawlers featuring John Reid	
Mike REID (UK)	
The Ugly Duckling	4/75
Neil REID (UK)	
Mother Of Mine	1/72
R.E.M. (US)	
E-Bow The Letter	8/96
Everybody Hurts	5/93
Shiny Happy People	6/91
What's The Frequency, Kenneth	9/94
REMBRANDTS (US)	
I'll Be There For You/This House Is Not A Home	9/95
I'll Be There For You	5/97
RENAISSANCE (UK)	
Northern Lights	8/78
RENEE AND RENATO (UK/Ita)	
Save Your Love	12/82
REO SPEEDWAGON (US)	
Keep On Loving You	5/81
REPERATA & The Delrons (US)	
Captain Of Your Ship	4/68
REYNOLDS GIRLS (UK)	
I'd Rather Jack	3/89
Debbie REYNOLDS (US)	
Tammy	9/57
Charlie RICH (US)	
The Most Beautiful Girl	3/74
Tony RICH Project (US)	
Nobody Knows	5/96
Cliff RICHARD (UK)	
All My Love	12/67
Bachelor Boy	12/62

	UK Top 20 Ent
The Best Of Me	6/89
Big Ship	6/69
Carrie	2/80
Congratulations	4/68
Constantly	5/64
Daddy's Home	12/81
The Day I Met Marie	9/67
Devil Woman	6/76
Do You Wanna Dance	6/62
Don't Talk To Him	11/63
Dreaming	9/80
Fall In Love With You	4/60
From A Distance	10/90
Gee Whiz It's You	4/61
A Girl Like You	6/61
Good Times (Better Times)	3/69
Goodbye Sam Hello Samantha	6/70
High Class Baby	12/58
I Could Easily Fall	12/64
I Just Don't Have The Heart	9/89
I Love You	12/60
I Still Believe In You	12/92
I'm Looking Out The Window	5/62
I'm The Lonely One	2/64
In The Country	1/67
It'll Be Me	9/62
It's All In The Game	8/63
It's All Over	4/67
Living Doll	7/59
Living In Harmony	9/72
Lucky Lips	5/63
Mean Streak	5/59
The Minute You're Gone	3/65
Miss You Nights	3/76
Mistletoe And Wine	12/88
Move It	10/58
My Pretty One	7/87
The Next Time	12/62
Nine Times Out Of Ten	9/60
On My Word	7/65
On The Beach	7/64
The Only Way Out	8/82
Peace In Our Time	3/93
Please Don't Fall In Love	12/83
Please Don't Tease	7/60
Power To All Our Friends	3/73
Saviour's Day	12/90
❖ with Phil Everly She Means Nothing To Me	3/83
Silhouettes	9/90
Sing A Song Of Freedom	12/71
Some People	9/87
Summer Holiday	2/63
Theme For A Dream	3/61
Throw Down A Line	9/69
Time Drags By	11/66
Travellin' Light	10/59
True Love Ways	5/83
The Twelfth Of Never	10/64
Visions	8/66
Voice In The Wilderness	1/60
We Don't Talk Anymore	8/79
We Should Be Together	12/91
When The Girl In Your Arms Is The Girl In Your Heart	10/61
Wind Me Up (Let Me Go)	11/65
Wired For Sound	9/81
The Young Ones	1/62
Cliff RICHARD & Sarah Brightman (UK)	
All I Ask Of You	10/86

	UK Top 20 Ent
Cliff RICHARD & The Young Ones (UK)	
Living Doll	3/86
Lionel RICHIE (US)	
All Night Long (All Night)	10/83
Dancing On The Ceiling	8/86
❖ with Diana Ross Endless Love	9/81
Hello	3/84
My Destiny	9/92
Running With The Night	1/84
Say You, Say Me	12/85
Stuck On You	7/84
Truly	12/82
Jonathan RICHMAN & The Modern Lovers (US)	
Egyptian Reggae	12/77
Roadrunner	8/77
Stan RIDGWAY (US)	
Camouflage	7/86
RIGHT SAID FRED (UK)	
Deeply Dippy	3/92
I'm Too Sexy	8/91
RIGHT SAID FRED & Friends (UK)	
Stick It Out	3/93
RIGHT SAID FRED featuring Jocelyn Brown (UK/US)	
Don't Talk Just Kiss	12/91
RIGHTEOUS BROTHERS (US)	
Unchained Melody	9/65
★ Unchained Melody	10/90
You've Lost That Lovin' Feelin'	1/65
★ You've Lost That Lovin' Feelin'	3/69
★ You've Lost That Lovin' Feelin'/Ebb Tide	12/90
Jeannie C. RILEY (US)	
Harper Valley P.T.A.	12/68
Leann RIMES (US)	
How Do I Live	3/98
Waldo De Los RIOS (Bra)	
Mozart Symphony No. 40 In G Minor	4/71
Minnie RIPERTON (US)	
Lovin' You	4/75
RITCHIE FAMILY (US)	
The Best Disco In Town	10/76
Tex RITTER (US)	
Wayward Wind	7/56
RIVER CITY PEOPLE (UK)	
California Dreamin'/Carry The Blame	8/90
ROACHFORD (UK)	
Cuddly Toy	1/89
ROB 'N' RAZ featuring Leila K (S)	
Got To Get	12/89
Kate ROBBINS & Beyond (UK)	
More Than In Love	6/81
Marty ROBBINS (US)	
Devil Woman	11/62
A White Sport Coat (And A Pink Carnation)	5/57
Malcolm ROBERTS (UK)	
Love Is All	12/69
May I Have The Next Dream With You	12/68
B.A. ROBERTSON (UK)	
Bang Bang	8/79
Knocked It Off	11/79
To Be Or Not To Be	7/80
B.A. ROBERTSON & Maggie Bell (UK)	
Hold Me	11/81

	UK Top 20 Ent
Don ROBERTSON (US)	
The Happy Whistler	5/56
Floyd ROBINSON (US)	
Makin' Love	10/59
Smokey ROBINSON (US) also see The Miracles	
Being With You	6/81
Tom ROBINSON BAND (UK)	
2-4-6-8 Motorway	11/77
War Baby	7/83
ROBYN (S)	
Show Me Love	3/98
ROCK FOLLIES (UK)	
O.K.	6/77
ROCKER'S REVENGE (US)	
Walking On Sunshine	9/82
ROCKIN' BERRIES (UK)	
He's In Town	11/64
Poor Man's Son	5/65
Lord ROCKINGHAM'S XI (UK)	
Hoots Mon	10/58
ROCKSTEADY CREW (US)	
(Hey You) The Rocksteady Crew	10/83
ROCKWELL (US)	
Somebody's Watching Me	2/84
Clodagh RODGERS (I)	
Come Back And Shake Me	4/69
Goodnight Midnight	8/69
Jack In The Box	3/71
Jimmie RODGERS (US)	
English Country Garden	7/62
Kisses Sweeter Than Wine	1/58
RODS (UK)	
Do Anything You Wanna Do	9/77
Tommy ROE (US)	
Dizzy	5/69
Everybody	10/63
The Folk Singer	4/63
Sheila	9/62
Julie ROGERS (UK)	
The Wedding	9/64
Kenny ROGERS/First Edition (US)	
Coward Of The County	2/80
Just Dropped In (To See What Condition	
Lady	12/80
Lucille	5/77
Ruby, Don't Take Your Love To Town	11/69
Something's Burning	3/70
Kenny ROGERS & Dolly Parton (US)	
Islands In The Stream	12/83
ROLLING STONES (UK)	
Angie	9/73
Brown Sugar	5/71
Emotional Rescue	7/80
Fool To Cry	5/76
Get Off Of My Cloud	11/65
Have You Seen Your Mother Baby Standing In The Shadow?	10/66
Honky Tonk Women	7/69
(I Can't Get No) Satisfaction	9/65
I Wanna Be Your Man	12/63
It's All Over Now	7/64
It's Only Rock 'n Roll (But I Like It)	8/74
Jumpin' Jack Flash	6/68
The Last Time	3/65
Let's Spend The Night Together/ Ruby Tuesday	2/67

	UK Top 20 Ent
Little Red Rooster	11/64
Miss You	6/78
19th Nervous Breakdown	2/66
Not Fade Away	3/64
Paint It, Black	5/66
Start Me Up	9/81
Tumbling Dice	5/72
Undercover Of The Night	11/83
We Love You/Dandelion	9/67
Max ROMEO (J)	
Wet Dream	8/69
RONETTES (US)	
Baby I Love You	2/64
Be My Baby	10/63
Linda RONSTADT & James Ingram (US)	
Somewhere Out There	8/87
Linda RONSTADT (featuring Aaron Neville) (US)	
Don't Know Much	11/89
ROOFTOP SINGERS (US)	
Walk Right In	2/63
ROSE ROYCE (US)	
Car Wash	2/77
Is It Love You're After	1/80
Love Don't Live Here Anymore	9/78
Wishing On A Star	2/78
Diana ROSS (US) also see the Supremes	
Ain't No Mountain High Enough	10/70
All Of My Life	2/74
Chain Reaction	2/86
Doobedood'ndoobe Doobedood'ndoobe	6/72
I'm Still Waiting	8/71
If We Hold On Together	12/92
Love Hangover	5/76
My Old Piano	10/80
One Shining Moment	7/92
Remember Me	5/71
Surrender	11/71
Theme From Mahogany (Do You Know Where You're Going To)	4/76
Touch Me In The Morning	8/73
Upside Down	8/80
When You Tell Me That You Love Me	12/91
Why Do Fools Fall In Love	11/81
Work That Body	6/82
Diana ROSS & Lionel Richie (US)	
Endless Love	9/81
Diana ROSS & Marvin Gaye (US)	
You Are Everything	4/74
Nini ROSSO (Ita)	
Il Silenzio	9/65
Demis ROUSSOS (Gre)	
Happy To Be On An Island In The Sun	12/75
The Roussos Phenomenon E.P.	7/76
When Forever Has Gone	10/76
John ROWLES (UK)	
Hush Not A Word To Mary	7/68
If I Only Had Time	4/68
ROXETTE (S)	
Almost Unreal	7/93
Dangerous	8/90
Fading Like A Flower (Every Time You Leave)	5/91
How Do You Do!	8/92
It Must Have Been Love	6/90
★ It Must Have Been Love	9/93
Joyride	3/91

	UK Top 20 Ent
Listen To Your Heart	8/90
The Look	5/89
ROXY MUSIC (UK)	
All I Want Is You	11/74
Angel Eyes	8/79
Dance Away	5/79
Jealous Guy	2/81
Love Is The Drug	11/75
More Than This	4/82
Oh Yeah (On The Radio)	8/80
Over You	5/80
Pyjamarama	4/73
The Same Old Scene	11/80
Street Life	12/73
Virginia Plain	9/72
★ Virginia Plain	11/77
ROYAL GUARDSMEN (US)	
Snoopy Vs. The Red Baron	2/67
ROYAL PHILHARMONIC ORCHESTRA (UK)	
Hooked On Classics	8/81
ROYAL SCOTS DRAGOON GUARDS (UK)	
Amazing Grace	4/72
Little Drummer Boy	12/72
ROZALLA (Zim)	
Everybody's Free (To Feel Good)	9/91
RUBETTES (UK)	
Baby I Know	3/77
I Can Do It	3/75
Juke Box Jive	11/74
Sugar Baby Love	5/74
Tonight	8/74
Bruce RUFFIN (J)	
Mad About You	7/72
David RUFFIN (US)	
Walk Away From Love	2/76
Jimmy RUFFIN (US)	
Farewell Is A Lonely Sound	4/70
Hold On To My Love	5/80
I'll Say Forever My Love	8/70
It's Wonderful	11/70
What Becomes Of The Brokenhearted	12/66
★ What Becomes Of The Brokenhearted	8/74
RUFUS & Chaka Khan (US)	
Ain't Nobody	4/84
★ Ain't Nobody	7/89
RUN D.M.C. (US)	
Walk This Way	9/86
RUN-DMC Vs Jason Nevins (US)	
It's Like That	3/98
RuPAUL (US) See Rlton John & RuPaul	
Jennifer RUSH (US)	
The Power Of Love	10/85
Patrice RUSHEN (US)	
Forget Me Nots	5/82
RUTS (UK)	
Babylon's Burning	7/79
Barry RYAN (UK)	
Eloise	11/68
Marion RYAN (UK)	
Love Me Forever	2/58
Paul & Barry RYAN (UK)	
Don't Bring Me Your Heartaches	12/65
Bobby RYDELL (US)	
Forget Him	6/63

	UK Top 20 Ent
SPACE (F)	
Magic Fly	9/77
SPAGNA (Ita)	
Call Me	8/87
SPANDAU BALLET (UK)	
Chant No.1 (I Don't Need This Pressure On)	7/81
Communication	3/83
Gold	8/83
I'll Fly For You	9/84
Instinction	5/82
Lifeline	10/82
Musclebound/Glow	5/81
Only When You Leave	6/84
Through The Barricades	11/86
To Cut A Long Story Short	12/80
True	4/83
SPARKS (US)	
Amateur Hour	8/74
Beat The Clock	8/79
Never Turn Your Back On Mother Earth	11/74
This Town Ain't Big Enough For Both Of Us	5/74
Billie Jo SPEARS (US)	
Blanket On The Ground	8/75
What I've Got In Mind	8/76
SPECIAL AKA (UK)	
Nelson Mandela	4/84
SPECIALS (UK)	
Do Nothing/Maggie's Farm	1/81
Gangsters	8/79
Ghost Town	6/81
A Message To You Rudy/Nite Klub	11/79
Rat Race/Rude Boys Outa Jail	6/80
Stereotype/International Jet Set	10/80
Too Much Too Young E.P.	2/80
Chris SPEDDING (UK)	
Motor Biking	9/75
Johnny SPENCE (UK)	
Dr. Kildare Theme	4/62
SPICE GIRLS (UK)	
2 Become 1	12/96
Mama/Who Do You Think You Are	3/97
Say You'll Be There	10/96
Spice Up Your Life	10/97
Stop	3/98
Too Much	12/97
Wannabe	7/96
SPIN DOCTORS (US)	
Two Princes	6/93
(DETROIT) SPINNERS (US)	
Cupid-I've Loved You For A Long Time (Medley)	7/80
Ghetto Child	10/73
Working My Way Back To You-Forgive Me, Girl	3/80
SPITTING IMAGE (UK)	
The Chicken Song	5/86
SPLODGENESSABOUNDS (UK)	
Simon Templar/Two Pints Of Lager And A Packet Of Crisps Please	6/80
Dusty SPRINGFIELD (UK)	
All I See Is You	10/66
Goin' Back	7/66
I Close My Eyes And Count To Ten	7/68
I Just Don't Know What To Do With Myself	7/64

	UK Top 20 Ent
I Only Want To Be With You	11/63
In Private	12/89
In The Middle Of Nowhere	7/65
Losing You	12/64
Some Of Your Lovin'	10/65
Son-Of-A Preacher Man	1/69
Stay Awhile	3/64
❖ with Pet Shop Boys What Have I Done To Deserve This	8/87
You Don't Have To Say You Love Me	4/66
SPRINGFIELDS (UK)	
Island Of Dreams	2/63
Say I Won't Be There	4/63
Bruce SPRINGSTEEN (US)	
Born In The U.S.A.	7/85
Dancing In The Dark	2/85
Human Touch/Better Days	3/92
I'm On Fire	7/85
My Hometown	12/85
Santa Claus Is Comin' To Town/My Hometown	12/85
Streets Of Philadelphia	3/94
Tougher Than The Rest	7/88
SPRINGWATER (UK)	
I Will Return	11/71
SQUEEZE (UK)	
Cool For Cats	4/79
Labelled With Love	11/81
Up The Junction	6/79
Jim STAFFORD (US)	
Spiders & Snakes	5/74
Jo STAFFORD (US)	
Make Love To Me!	5/54
Suddenly There's A Valley	12/55
STAKKA BO (S)	
Here We Go	10/93
Lisa STANSFIELD (UK)	
All Around The World	11/89
Change	10/91
In All The Right Places	6/93
Live Together	2/90
❖ with Coldcut People Hold On	4/89
Someday (I'm Coming Back)	1/93
Time To Make You Mine	4/92
Lisa STANSFIELD Vs The Dirty Rotten Scoundrels (UK)	
People Hold On (Bootleg Mixes)	1/97
Cyril STAPLETON (UK)	
Blue Star	9/55
Alvin STARDUST (UK)	
I Feel Like Buddy Holly	6/84
I Won't Run Away	12/84
Jealous Mind	2/74
My Coo-Ca-Choo	12/73
Pretend	9/81
Red Dress	5/74
You You You	9/74
STARGAZERS (UK)	
Close The Door	9/55
Crazy Otto Rag	6/55
Happy Wanderer	4/54
I See The Moon	2/54
Twenty Tiny Fingers	11/55
STARLIGHT (Ita)	
Numero Uno	9/89
Edwin STARR (US)	
Contact	2/79
H.A.P.P.Y. Radio	6/79
Stop Her On Sight (SOS)/Headline News	1/69

	UK Top 20 Ent
War	11/70
Freddie STARR (UK)	
It's You	3/74
Kay STARR (US)	
Changing Partners	3/54
Rock And Roll Waltz	2/56
Ringo STARR (UK)	
Back Off Boogaloo	4/72
It Don't Come Easy	5/71
Photograph	11/73
You're Sixteen	3/74
STARSHIP (US)	
Nothing's Gonna Stop Us Now	5/87
We Built This City	12/85
STARSOUND (H)	
Stars On 45 (Medley)	5/81
Stars On 45 (Vol 2)	7/81
STAR TURN ON 45 PINTS (UK)	
Pump Up The Bitter	5/88
Candi STATON (US)	
Nights On Broadway	8/77
❖ with The Source You Got The Love	2/91
Young Hearts Run Free	6/76
STATUS QUO (UK)	
Again And Again	9/78
The Anniversary Waltz - Part 1	10/90
Break The Rules	5/74
Burning Bridges (On And Off And On Again)	12/88
Caroline	10/73
Caroline (Live At The N.E.C.)	11/82
Dear John	4/82
Down Down	12/74
Down The Dustpipe	6/70
Ice In The Sun	10/68
In The Army Now	10/86
Lies/Don't Drive My Car	12/80
Marguerita Time	12/83
Mystery Song	8/76
Ol' Rag Blues	9/83
Paper Plane	2/73
Pictures Of Matchstick Men	2/68
Rain	2/76
Rock 'n' Roll	12/81
Rockin' All Over The World	10/77
Roll Over Lay Down	6/75
Rolling Home	5/86
Something 'Bout You Baby I Like	3/81
The Wanderer	11/84
What You're Proposing	10/80
Whatever You Want	10/79
Wild Side Of Life	1/77
STEALER'S WHEEL (UK)	
Stuck In The Middle With You	6/73
STEAM (US)	
Na Na Hey Hey Kiss Him Goodbye	3/70
Anthony STEEL & The Radio Revellers (UK)	
West Of Zanzibar	9/54
Tommy STEELE (UK)	
Butterfingers	5/57
Come On Let's Go	11/58
Little White Bull	12/59
Nairobi	3/58
Shiralee	9/57
Singing The Blues	1/57
Tallahassee Lassie	8/59
Water Water/Handful Of Songs	9/57

	UK Top 20 Ent
Tammi TERRELL (US) See Marvin Gaye & Tammi Terrell	
TERRORVISION (UK)	
Perseverance	3/96
Joe TEX (US)	
Ain't Gonna Bump No More (With No Big Fat Woman)	5/77
TEXAS (UK)	
Black Eyed Boy	8/97
I Don't Want A Lover	3/89
Say What You Want	1/97
TEXAS featuring Wu Tang Clan (UK/US)	
Say What You Want/Insane	3/98
THEM (UK)	
Baby Please Don't Go	1/65
Here Comes The Night	4/65
THEN JERICO (UK)	
Big Area	2/89
THERAPY? (UK)	
Shortsharpshock (EP)	3/93
TERRORVISION (UK)	
Bad Actress	7/96
THEY MIGHT BE GIANTS (US)	
Birdhouse In Your Soul	3/90
THIN LIZZY (I/UK)	
The Boys Are Back In Town	7/76
Dancin' In The Moonlight (It's Caught Me In The Spotlight)	9/77
Don't Believe A Word	2/77
Killer On The Loose	10/80
Waiting For An Alibi	3/79
Whisky In The Jar	2/73
THIRD WORLD (J)	
Dancing On The Floor (Hooked On Love)	7/81
Now That We've Found Love	10/78
Evelyn THOMAS (US)	
High Energy	6/84
Kenny THOMAS (US)	
Best Of You	10/91
Thinking About Your Love	6/91
Nicky THOMAS (J)	
Love Of The Common People	7/70
Timmy THOMAS (US)	
Why Can't We Live Together	4/73
THOMPSON TWINS (UK/NZ)	
Doctor! Doctor!	2/84
Hold Me Now	12/83
Love On Your Side	3/83
Sister Of Mercy	7/84
We Are Detective	5/83
You Take Me Up	4/84
Theme From 'The Legion's Last Patrol'	8/63
3T (US)	
24/7	5/96
I Need You	12/96
3T featuring Michael Jackson (US)	
Why	8/96
THREE DEGREES (US)	
Givin' Up Givin' In	11/78
My Simple Heart	12/79
The Runner	4/79
Take Good Care Of Yourself	5/75
When Will I See You Again	7/74
Women In Love	1/79
THREE DOG NIGHT (US)	
Mama Told Me (Not To Come)	9/70
THUNDERCLAP NEWMAN (UK)	
Something In The Air	6/69

	UK Top 20 Ent
Bobby THURSTON (US)	
Check Out The Groove	5/80
TIFFANY (US)	
Could've Been	3/88
I Saw Him Standing There	6/88
I Think We're Alone Now	1/88
TIGHT FIT (UK)	
Back To The Sixties	8/81
Fantasy Island	5/82
The Lion Sleeps Tonight	2/82
Tanita TIKARAM (UK)	
Good Tradition	8/88
Johnny TILLOTSON (US)	
Poetry In Motion	12/60
TIME FREQUENCY (UK)	
Real Love '93	11/93
TIMELORDS (UK) see KLF	
TINMAN (UK)	
Eighteen Strings	8/94
TIN TIN OUT featuring Shelley Nelson(UK)	
Here's Where The Story Ends	3/98
TITANIC (N/UK)	
Sultana	10/71
TLC (US)	
Ain't Too Proud 2 Beg	6/92
Creep	1/96
Diggin' On You	11/95
Red Light Special	4/95
Waterfalls	8/95
Todd TERRY (US)	
Something Goin' On	7/97
Todd TERRY featuring Martha Wash & Jocelyn Brown (US)	
Keep On Jumpin'	7/96
TOGETHER (US)	
Hardcore Uproar	8/90
TOKENS (US)	
The Lion Sleeps Tonight	1/62
TOM TOM CLUB (US)	
Wordy Rappinghood	7/81
TONIGHT (UK)	
Drummer Man	2/78
TOPOL (Isr)	
If I Were A Rich Man	7/67
Mel TORME (US)	
Coming Home Baby	1/63
Mountain Greenery	5/56
TORNADOS (UK)	
Globetrotter	1/63
The Ice Cream Man	6/63
Robot	4/63
Telstar	9/62
Mitchell TOROK (US)	
When Mexico Gave Up The Rumba	10/56
TOTO (US)	
Africa	2/83
TOTO COELO (UK)	
I Eat Cannibals Pt. 1	8/82
TOTTENHAM HOTSPUR F.A. CUP FINAL SQUAD (UK)	
Ossie's Dream (Spurs Are On Their Way To Wembley)	5/81
TOURISTS (UK)	
I Only Want To Be With You	12/79
So Good To Be Back Home Again	3/80
TOXIC TWO (US)	
Rave Generator	3/92

	UK Top 20 Ent
TOY DOLLS (UK)	
Nellie The Elephant	12/84
TOYAH (UK)	
Four From Toyah E.P.	3/81
Four More From Toyah E.P.	12/81
I Want To Be Free	5/81
Thunder In Mountains	10/81
TOYS (US)	
A Lovers Concerto	11/65
T'PAU (UK)	
China In Your Hand	11/87
Heart And Soul	9/87
Valentine	2/88
TRACIE (UK)	
The House That Jack Built	4/83
TRAFFIC (UK)	
Here We Go Round The Mulberry Bush	12/67
Hole In My Shoe	9/67
Paper Sun	6/67
TRAMMPS (US)	
Hold Back The Night	11/75
TRANSVISION VAMP (UK)	
Baby I Don't Care	4/89
I Want Your Love	7/88
TRANS-X (C)	
Living On Video	7/85
John TRAVOLTA (US)	
Greased Lightning	12/78
Sandy	10/78
John TRAVOLTA & Olivia Newton-John (US/UK)	
The Grease Megamix	12/90
Summer Nights	9/78
You're The One That I Want	6/78
TREMELOES (UK) also see Brian Poole	
(Call Me) Number One	11/69
Even The Bad Times Are Good	8/67
Helule Helule	6/68
Here Comes My Baby	2/67
Me And My Life	10/70
My Little Lady	10/68
Silence Is Golden	5/67
Suddenly You Love Me	2/68
Jackie TRENT (UK)	
Where Are You Now (My Love)	5/65
TRICKY DISCO (UK)	
Tricky Disco	8/90
TRIO (G)	
Da Da Da	7/82
TROGGS (UK)	
Any Way That You Want Me	1/67
Give It To Me	3/67
I Can't Control Myself	10/66
Love Is All Around	11/67
Wild Thing	5/66
With A Girl Like You	7/66
Andrea TRUE CONNECTION (US)	
More, More, More (Pt. 1)	5/76
TUBEWAY ARMY (UK) See Gary Numan	
Ike & Tina TURNER (US)	
Nutbush City Limits	10/73
River Deep Mountain High	6/66
Tina TURNER (US) also see Ike & Tina TURNER	
The Best	9/89
Disco Inferno	9/93
Goldeneye	11/95
I Don't Wanna Fight	5/93

Listing by artist: Frankie Vaughan to Barry White

	UK Top 20 Ent
Garden Of Eden	1/57
Green Door	11/56
Happy Days And Lonely Nights	2/55
The Heart Of A Man	8/59
Heartless	5/54
Kewpie Doll	5/58
Kisses Sweeter Than Wine	1/58
Loop De Loop	2/63
Man On Fire/Wanderin' Eyes	10/57
There Must Be A Way	9/67
Tower Of Strength	11/61

Frankie VAUGHAN & The Kaye Sisters (UK)

| Come Softly To Me | 5/59 |
| Gotta Have Something In The Bank Frank | 11/57 |

Malcolm VAUGHAN (UK)

Chapel Of The Roses	5/57
Every Day Of My Life	7/55
More Than Ever (Come Prima)	10/58
My Special Angel	12/57
St. Therese Of The Roses	11/56
To Be Loved	4/58
Wait For Me	4/59

Sarah VAUGHAN (US)

| Broken-Hearted Melody | 10/59 |

Billy VAUGHN (US)

| The Shifting Whispering Sands (Pts 1 & 2) | 10/55 |
| Theme From 'The Threepenny Opera' | 4/56 |

Bobby VEE (US)

A Forever Kind Of Love	11/62
How Many Tears	9/61
More Than I Can Say	5/61
The Night Has A Thousand Eyes	2/63
Rubber Ball	2/61
Run To Him	1/62
Take Good Care Of My Baby	11/61

Suzanne VEGA (US)

| ❖ with DNA Tom's Diner | 8/90 |

VENTURES (US)

| Perfidia | 12/60 |
| Walk-Don't Run | 9/60 |

VERVE (UK)

Bitter Sweet Symphony	6/97
The Drugs Don't Work	9/97
Lucky Man	12/97

Maria VIDAL (US)

| Body Rock | 9/85 |

VILLAGE PEOPLE (US)

Can't Stop The Music	9/80
In The Navy	3/79
Y.M.C.A.	12/78
★ Y.M.C.A.	12/93

Bobby VINTON (US)

| Blue Velvet | 10/90 |
| Roses Are Red (My Love) | 8/62 |

VIPERS SKIFFLE GROUP (UK)

| Cumberland Gap | 4/57 |
| Don't You Rock Me Daddy-O | 2/57 |

VISAGE (UK)

Damned Don't Cry	4/82
Fade To Grey	2/81
Mind Of A Toy	4/81
Night Train	7/82

WAH! (UK)

| The Story Of The Blues | 1/83 |

John WAITE (UK)

| Missing You | 10/84 |

Johnny WAKELIN & The Kinshasa Band (UK)

| Black Superman (Muhammad Ali) | 2/75 |
| In Zaire | 8/76 |

WALKER BROTHERS (US)

Another Tear Falls	10/66
Make It Easy On Yourself	9/65
My Ship Is Coming In	12/65
No Regrets	2/76
The Sun Ain't Gonna Shine Anymore	3/66

Jr. WALKER & The All Stars (US)

| (I'm A) Road Runner | 5/69 |
| What Does It Take To Win Your Love | 11/69 |

Scott WALKER (US)

| Joanna | 5/68 |
| Lights Of Cincinatti | 7/69 |

Trevor WALTERS (J)

| Stuck On You | 8/84 |

WAR (US)

| Low Rider | 2/76 |

Anita WARD (US)

| Ring My Bell | 6/79 |

Billy WARD & His Dominoes (US)

| Stardust | 9/57 |

Clifford T. WARD (UK)

| Gaye | 7/73 |

Jennifer WARNES (US)

❖ with Bill Medley (I've Had) The Time Of My Life	11/87
★ ❖ with Bill Medley (I've Had) The Time Of My Life	1/91
❖ with Joe Cocker Up Where We Belong	2/83

Dionne WARWICK (US)

All The Love In The World	1/83
Do You Know The Way To San Jose	6/68
Heartbreaker	11/82
Walk On By	5/64

WAS (NOT WAS) (US)

Papa Was A Rolling Stone	6/90
Shake Your Head	7/92
Walk The Dinosaur	10/87

Keith WASHINGTON (US) See Kylie Minogue

Sarah WASHINGTON (UK)

| I Will Always Love You | 8/93 |

WATERBOYS (UK)

| The Whole Of The Moon | 4/91 |

Dennis WATERMAN (UK)

| I Could Be So Good For You | 11/80 |

Crystal WATERS (US)

| Gypsy Woman (She's Homeless) | 5/91 |
| 100% Pure Love | 4/94 |

Jody WATLEY (US)

| Looking For A New Love | 6/87 |

WAX (UK)

| Bridge To Your Heart | 9/87 |

Jeff WAYNE (UK)

| Eve Of The War (Ben Liebrand Remix) | 12/89 |

WEATHER GIRLS (US)

| It's Raining Men | 3/84 |

Marti WEBB (UK)

Always There	10/86
Ben	6/85
Take That Look Of Your Face	3/80

Fred WEDLOCK (UK)

| Oldest Swinger In Town | 2/81 |

WEE PAPA GIRL RAPPERS (UK)

| Wee Rule | 10/88 |

Bert WEEDON (UK)

| Guitar Boogie Shuffle | 5/59 |

Frank WEIR (UK)

The Happy Wanderer	6/54
The Little Shoemaker	7/54
Never Never Land	7/54

Paul WELLER (UK)

Peacock Suite	8/96
The Changingman	5/95
Hung Up	4/94

Mary WELLS (US)

| My Guy | 6/64 |

WEST END featuring Sybil (UK/US)

| The Love I Lost | 1/93 |

Keith WEST (UK)

| Excerpt From A Teenage Opera | 9/67 |

WET WET WET (UK)

Angel Eyes (Home And Away)	1/88
Don't Want To Forgive Me Now	6/95
Goodnight Girl	1/92
Julia Says	3/95
If I Never See You Again	3/97
Yesterday	8/97
Love Is All Around	5/94
Somewhere Somehow	10/95
Sweet Little Mystery	8/87
Sweet Surrender	10/89
Wishing I Was Lucky	6/87
With A Little Help From My Friends	5/88

WHAM! (UK)

Bad Boys	5/83
Club Tropicana	8/83
The Edge Of Heaven	6/86
Everything She Wants	12/84
Freedom	10/84
I'm Your Man	11/85
Last Christmas/Everything She Wants	12/84
★ Last Christmas	12/85
Wake Me Up Before You Go-Go	5/84
Wham Rap	2/83
Young Guns (Go For It)	11/82

Caron WHEELER (UK) See Soul II Soul

Bill WHELAN (I)

| Riverdance | 1/95 |

WHIGFIELD (D)

Another Day	12/94
Saturday Night	9/94
Think Of You	6/95

WHISPERS (US)

| And The Beat Goes On | 2/80 |
| It's A Love Thing | 4/81 |

WHISTLE (US)

| (Nothin' Serious) Just Buggin' | 3/86 |

Barry WHITE (US)

Can't Get Enough Of Your Love, Babe	9/74
I'm Gonna Love You Just A Little More Baby	5/73
It's Ecstasy When You Lay Down Next To Me	10/77
Just The Way You Are	2/79
Let The Music Play	1/76
Never, Never Gonna Give Ya Up	3/74

317

	UK Top 20 Ent
What Am I Gonna Do With You	3/75
You See The Trouble With Me	3/76
You're The First, The Last, My Everything	11/74
Karyn WHITE (US)	
Superwoman	7/89
Snowy WHITE (UK)	
Bird Of Paradise	1/84
WHITE PLAINS (UK)	
Julie, Do Ya Love Me	11/70
My Baby Loves Lovin'	2/70
When You Are A King	7/71
WHITESNAKE (UK)	
Here I Go Again	11/87
Is This Love	6/87
WHITE TOWN (UK)	
Your Woman	1/97
David WHITFIELD (UK)	
Adoration Waltz	2/57
Answer Me	1/54
Beyond The Stars	2/55
The Book	2/54
Cara Mia	6/54
Ev'rywhere	7/55
Mama	8/55
My September Love	4/56
On The Street Where You Live	7/58
Rags To Riches	1/54
Santo Natale	11/54
When You Lose The One You Love	12/55
Slim WHITMAN (US)	
China Doll	9/55
I'll Take You Home Again Kathleen	4/57
Indian Love Call	8/55
Rose Marie	7/55
Serenade	8/56
Roger WHITTAKER (Ken)	
Durham Town (The Leavin')	12/69
I Don't Believe In If Anymore	5/70
The Last Farewell	8/75
Roger WHITTAKER & Des O'Connor (Ken/UK)	
The Skye Boat Song	12/86
WHO (UK)	
Anyway Anyhow Anywhere	6/65
Happy Jack	1/67
I Can See For Miles	11/67
I Can't Explain	4/65
I'm A Boy	9/66
Join Together	7/72
My Generation	11/65
Pictures Of Lily	5/67
Pinball Wizard	4/69
Squeeze Box	2/76
Substitute	4/66
★ Substitute	11/76
Won't Get Fooled Again	8/71
You Better You Bet	3/81
Jane WIEDLIN (US)	
Rush Hour	9/88
WIGAN'S CHOSEN FEW (UK)	
Footsee	2/75
WIGAN'S OVATION (UK)	
Skiing In The Snow	4/75
WILD CHERRY (US)	
Play That Funky Music	11/76
WILDCHILD (UK)	
Renegade Master	10/95
Renegade Master 98	1/98

	UK Top 20 Ent
Kim WILDE (UK)	
Cambodia	12/81
Chequered Love	5/81
Four Letter Word	1/89
If I Can't Have You	7/93
Kids In America	3/81
Never Trust A Stranger	10/88
Water On Glass/Boys	8/81
You Came	7/88
You Keep Me Hangin' On	11/86
Kim WILDE & Junior (UK)	
Another Step (Closer To You)	5/87
Kim WILDE & Mel Smith (UK) (MEL & KIM)	
Rockin' Around The Christmas Tree	12/87
Marty WILDE (UK)	
Bad Boy	1/60
Donna	4/59
Endless Sleep	7/58
Rubber Ball	2/61
Sea Of Love	10/59
A Teenager In Love	6/59
Matthew WILDER (US)	
Break My Stride	2/84
WILL TO POWER (US)	
Baby I Love Your Way/Freebird Medley	1/89
Alyson WILLIAMS (US)	
I Need Your Lovin'	9/89
Andy WILLIAMS (US)	
Almost There	10/65
Butterfly	5/57
Can't Get Used To Losing You	4/63
Can't Help Falling In Love	3/70
Can't Take My Eyes Off You	4/68
Home Lovin' Man	12/70
I Like Your Kind Of Love	7/57
It's So Easy	9/70
Solitaire	1/74
(Where Do I Begin) Love Story	4/71
Danny WILLIAMS (UK)	
Moon River	11/61
Wonderful World Of The Young	4/62
Deniece WILLIAMS (US)	
Free	4/77
Let's Hear It For The Boy	4/84
That's What Friends Are For	8/77
❖ with Johnny Mathis Too Much, Too Little, Too Late	4/78
Larry WILLIAMS (US)	
Bony Moronie/You Bug Me, Baby	2/58
Mason WILLIAMS (US)	
Classical Gas	9/68
Maurice WILLIAMS & The Zodiacs (US)	
Stay	1/61
Robbie WILLIAMS (UK)	
Angels	12/97
Freedom	8/96
Lazy Days	7/97
Let Me Entertain You	3/98
Old Before I Die	4/97
Vanessa WILLIAMS (US)	
Save The Best For Last	4/92
Vesta WILLIAMS (US)	
Once Bitten Twice Shy	2/87
Bruce WILLIS (US)	
Respect Yourself	3/87
Under The Boardwalk	6/87

	UK Top 20 Ent
Viola WILLS (US)	
Gonna Get Along Without You Now	11/79
WILSON PHILLIPS (US)	
Hold On	6/90
Ann WILSON (US)	
❖ with Mike Reno Almost Paradise	
J. Frank WILSON & The Cavaliers (US)	
Last Kiss	10/64
Jackie WILSON (US)	
I Get The Sweetest Feeling	9/72
★ I Get The Sweetest Feeling	3/87
Reet Petite	12/57
★ Reet Petite	12/86
Higher And Higher	6/69
Mari WILSON (UK)	
Just What I Always Wanted	10/82
Meri WILSON (US)	
Telephone Man	9/77
Pete WINGFIELD (UK)	
Eighteen With A Bullet	7/75
WINGS (UK) see Paul McCartney	
Josh WINK (US)	
Higher State Of Consciousness	0/95
WINK (US)	
Higher State Of Consciousness '96	7/96
Ruby WINTERS (US)	
Come To Me	6/78
I Will	12/77
Steve WINWOOD (UK)	
Higher Love	7/86
Norman WISDOM (UK)	
Don't Laugh At Me	2/54
Wisdom Of A Fool	3/57
Bill WITHERS (US)	
Lovely Day	1/78
★ Lovely Day	9/88
WIZZARD (UK)	
Angel Fingers	9/73
Are You Ready To Rock	1/75
Ball Park Incident	1/73
I Wish It Could Be Christmas Everyday	12/73
Rock 'n Roll Winter	5/74
See My Baby Jive	5/73
WOMACK & WOMACK (US)	
Teardrops	9/88
WOMBLES (UK)	
Banana Rock	7/74
Remember You're A Womble	4/74
The Wombling Song	2/74
Wombling Merry Christmas	12/74
WONDER STUFF (UK)	
❖ with Vic Reeves Dizzy	10/91
The Size Of A Cow	4/91
Welcome To The Cheap Seats (EP)	2/92
Stevie WONDER (US)	
Boogie On Reggae Woman	2/75
Do I Do	6/82
❖ with Paul McCartney Ebony And Ivory	4/82
For Once In My Life	1/69
Happy Birthday	8/81
He's Misstra Know It All	5/74
I Ain't Gonna Stand For It	1/81
I Just Called To Say I Love You	8/84
I Was Made To Love Her	8/67
I Wish	1/77

	UK Top 20 Ent
Lately	3/81
Master Blaster (Jammin')	9/80
My Cherie Amour	8/69
❖ with *Julio Iglesias* My Love	8/88
Never Had A Dream Come True	4/70
Part Time Lover	9/85
Signed Sealed Delivered I'm Yours	8/70
Sir Duke	4/77
Superstition	2/73
Yester-Me, Yester-You, Yesterday	11/69
You Are The Sunshine Of My Life	6/73
Brenton WOOD (US)	
Gimme Little Sign	2/68
Roy WOOD (UK)	
Forever	12/73
Going Down The Road	7/74
Oh What A Shame	6/75
Sheb WOOLEY (US)	
The Purple People Eater	7/58
WOOLPACKERS (UK)	
Hillbilly Rock Hillbilly Roll	11/96
Charles WRIGHT & The Watts 103rd Street Rhythm Ruby WRIGHT (US)	
Bimbo	4/54
WURZELS (UK)	
Combine Harvester (Brand New Key)	5/76
I Am A Cider Drinker (Paloma Blanca)	9/76
WWF SUPERSTARS (US)	
Slam Jam	12/92
Wrestlemania	4/93
Tammy WYNETTE (US)	
D.I.V.O.R.C.E.	7/75
❖ with *KLF* Justified And Ancient	12/91
Stand By Your Man	5/75
Mark WYNTER (UK)	
Go Away Little Girl	1/63
It's Almost Tomorrow	11/63
Venus In Blue Jeans	10/62

	UK Top 20 Ent
XPANSIONS (UK)	
Move Your Body (Elevation)	3/91
XTC (UK)	
Senses Working Overtime	2/82
YARBROUGH & PEOPLES (US)	
Don't Stop The Music	1/81
YARDBIRDS (UK)	
Evil Hearted You/Still I'm Sad	10/65
For Your Love	4/65
Heart Full Of Soul	7/65
Over Under Sideways Down	8/66 6/66
Shapes Of Things	3/66
YAZOO (UK)	
Don't Go	7/82
Nobody's Diary	5/83
Only You	5/82
The Other Side Of Love	12/82
YAZZ (UK)	
Fine Time	2/89
Stand Up For Your Love Rights	11/88
Where Has All The Love Gone	5/89
YAZZ & The Plastic Population (UK)	
❖ with *Coldcut* Doctorin' The House	3/88
The Only Way Is Up	8/88
YELL! (UK)	
Instant Replay	2/90
YELLO (Swi)	
The Race	9/88
YELLOW DOG (UK)	
Just One More Night	2/78
YES (UK/SA)	
Wonderous Stories	9/77
YOUNG ONES (UK) See Cliff Richard & The Young Ones	
Faron YOUNG (US)	
It's Four In The Morning	8/72
Jimmy YOUNG (UK)	
Chain Gang	3/56
Little Things Mean A Lot	9/54
The Man From Laramie	9/55
More	10/56
Someone On Your Mind	1/56
Unchained Melody	5/55

	UK Top 20 Ent
John Paul YOUNG (Aus)	
Love Is In The Air	5/78
Karen YOUNG (UK)	
Nobody's Child	10/69
Neil YOUNG (CAN)	
Heart Of Gold	4/72
Paul YOUNG (UK)	
Come Back And Stay	9/83
Everything Must Change	12/84
Everytime You Go Away	3/85
I'm Gonna Tear Your Playhouse Down	10/84
Love Of The Common People	11/83
❖ with *Zucchero* Senza Una Donna	5/91
Wherever I Lay My Hat (That's My Home)	7/83
Sydney YOUNGBLOOD (US)	
If Only I Could	9/89
Helmut ZACHARIAS ORCHESTRA (G)	
Tokyo Melody	11/64
ZAGER & EVANS (US)	
In The Year 2525 (Exordium & Terminus)	8/69
Michael ZAGER BAND (US)	
Let's All Chant	5/78
Georghe ZAMFIR (R)	
(Light Of Experience) Doina De Jale	9/76
Lena ZAVARONI (UK)	
Ma He's Making Eyes At Me	3/74
ZOE (UK)	
Sunshine On A Rainy Day	8/91
ZOMBIES (UK)	
She's Not There	9/64
ZUCCHERO/Paul Young (Ita/UK)	
Senza Una Donna (Without A Woman)	5/91
ZZ TOP (US)	
Gimme All Your Lovin'	11/84
Viva Las Vegas	4/92

Listings by TITLE

Listing by title: Abacab to Another Day

Title	Artist
Abacab	Genesis
Abba-Esque (EP)	Erasure
ABC	Jackson Five
Abracadabra	Steve Miller Band
Abraham Martin & John	Marvin Gaye
Absolute Beginners	David Bowie
Absolute Beginners	Jam
Absolutely Fabulous	Absolutely Fabulous
Achy Breaky Heart	Billy Ray Cyrus
Activ 8 (Come With Me)	Altern 8
Addams Groove	Hammer
Addicted To Love	Robert Palmer
Adoration Waltz	David Whitfield
Africa	Toto
African Waltz	Johnny Dankworth
After All	Frank And Walters
After The Love Has Gone	Earth, Wind & Fire
Agadoo	Black Lace
Again	Janet Jackson
Again And Again	Status Quo
Against All Odds (Take A Look At Me Now)	Phil Collins
Ain't Gonna Bump No More (With No Big Fat Woman)	Joe Tex
Ain't Gonna Kiss Ya (E.P.)	Searchers
Ain't Got No - I Got Life	Nina Simone
Ain't It Fun	Guns N' Roses
Ain't Misbehavin'	Tommy Bruce & The Bruisers
Ain't No Doubt	Jimmy Nail
Ain't No Love (Ain't No Use)	Sub Sub Featuring Melanie Williams
Ain't No Mountain High Enough	Diana Ross
Ain't No Pleasing You	Chas & Dave
Ain't No Stoppin'	Enigma
Ain't No Stoppin' Us Now	McFadden & Whitehead
Ain't No Sunshine	Michael Jackson
Ain't No Nobody	Course
Ain't No Nobody	LL Cool J
Ain't No Nobody	Rufus & Chaka Khan
Ain't No Nothin' But A Houseparty	Showstoppers
Ain't Nothing Goin' On But The Rent	Gwen Guthrie
Ain't Talkin' 'Bout Dub	Apollo Four Forty
Ain't That A Shame	Pat Boone
Ain't That Funny	Jimmy Justice
Ain't That Just The Way	Lutricia McNeal
Ain't 2 Proud 2 Beg	TLC
The Air That I Breathe	Hollies
Airport	Motors
Albatross	Fleetwood Mac
Alfie	Cilla Black
Alice I Want You Just For Me	Full Force
Alive And Kicking	Simple Minds
All About Us	Peter Andre
All Alone Am I	Brenda Lee
All Along The Watchtower	Jimi Hendrix Experience
All Around My Hat	Steeleye Span
All Around The World	Oasis
All Around The World	Lisa Stansfield
All Because Of You	Geordie
All By Myself	Celine Dion
All Cried Out	Alison Moyet

Title	Artist
All Day And All Of The Night	Kinks
All Day And All Of The Night	Stranglers
All For Love	Bryan Adams/Rod Stewart/Sting
All For Love	Color Me Badd
All I Ask Of You	Cliff Richard
All I Ever Need Is You	Sonny & Cher
All I Have To Do Is Dream	Everly Brothers
All I Have To Do Is Dream	Bobbie Gentry & Glen Campbell
All I Have To Give	Backstreet Boys
All I Really Want To Do	Byrds
All I Really Want To Do	Cher
All I See Is You	Dusty Springfield
All I Wanna Do	Sheryl Crow
All I Wanna Do	Dannii Minogue
All I Wanna Do Is Make Love To You	Heart
All I Want For Christmas Is A Beatle	Dora Bryan
All I Want For Christmas Is You	Mariah Carey
All I Want Is You	911
All I Want Is You	Roxy Music
All I Want Is You	U2
All Kinds Of Everything	Dana
All Mine	Portishead
All My Life	K-Ci & Jojo
All My Love	Cliff Richard
All Night Long	Rainbow
All Night Long (All Night)	Lionel Richie
(All Of A Sudden) My Heart Sings	Paul Anka
All Of Me Loves All Of You	Bay City Rollers
All Of My Heart	ABC
All Of My Life	Diana Ross
All Or Nothing	Small Faces
All Out Of Love	Air Supply
All Right Now	Free
All She Wants Is	Duran Duran
All Shook Up	Elvis Presley
All Star Hit Parade	Various Artists
All Stood Still	Ultravox
All That Matters	Louise
All That She Wants	Ace Of Base
All The Love In The World	Dionne Warwick
All The Man That I Need	Whitney Houston
All The Things She Said	Simple Minds
All The Way	Frank Sinatra
All The Way From Memphis	Mott The Hoople
All The Young Dudes	Mott The Hoople
All Together Now	Farm
All You Need Is Love	Beatles
Ally's Tartan Army	Andy Cameron
Almaz	Randy Crawford
Almost There	Andy Williams
Almost Unreal	Roxette
Alone	Bee Gees
Alone	Petula Clark
Alone	Heart
Alone Again (Naturally)	Gilbert O'Sullivan
Alone Without You	King
Alphabet Street	Prince
Alright	Jamiroquai
Alright	Supergrass

Title	Artist
Alright Alright Alright	Mungo Jerry
Also Sprach Zarathustra (2001)	Deodata
Alternate Title	Monkees
Always	Atlantic Starr
Always	Bon Jovi
Always	Erasure
Always And Forever	Heatwave
Always Be My Baby	Mariah Carey
Always Breaking My Heart	Belinda Carlisle
Always Look On The Bright Side	Monty Python
Always On My Mind	Pet Shop Boys
Always On My Mind	Elvis Presley
Always There	Incognito Featuring Jocelyn Brown
Always There	Marti Webb
Always Yours	Gary Glitter
Am I That Easy To Forget	Engelbert Humperdinck
Amanda	Stuart Gillies
Amateur Hour	Sparks
Amazing Grace	Judy Collins
Amazing Grace	Royal Scots Dragoon Guards
America: What Time Is Love?	KLF
American Pie	Don McLean
An American Trilogy	Elvis Presley
Americanos	Holly Johnson
Amigo	Black Slate
Amityville (The House On The Hill)	Lovebug Starski
Amnesia	Chumbawamba
Among My Souvenirs	Connie Francis
Amoureuse	Kiki Dee
Anasthasia	T99
And I Love You So	Perry Como
And The Bands Played On	Saxon
And The Beat Goes On	Whispers
And The Heavens Cried	Anthony Newley
Anfield Rap (Red Machine In Full Effect)	Liverpool F.C.
Angel	Madonna
Angel	Simply Red
Angel	Rod Stewart
Angel Eyes	Abba
Angel Eyes	Roxy Music
Angel Eyes (Home And Away)	Wet Wet Wet
Angel Face	Glitter Band
Angel Fingers	Wizzard
Angel Of Harlem	U2
Angel Of Mine	Eternal
Angel St	M People
Angela Jones	Michael Cox
Angelo	Brotherhood Of Man
Angels	Robbie Williams
Angie	Rolling Stones
Angie Baby	Helen Reddy
Animal	Def Leppard
Animal Nitrate	Suede
Annie I'm Not Your Daddy	Kid Creole & The Coconuts
Annie's Song	John Denver
Annie's Song	James Galway
The Anniversary Waltz - Part 1	Status Quo
Another Brick In The Wall (Pt. 2)	Pink Floyd
Another Day	Paul McCartney

Title	Artist
Another Day	Whigfield
Another Day In Paradise	Phil Collins
Another One Bites The Dust	Queen
Another Rock And Roll Christmas	
	Gary Glitter
Another Step (Closer To You)	
	Kim Wilde & Junior
Another Tear Falls	Walker Brothers
Another Time Another Place	Engelbert
	Humperdinck
Answer Me	Frankie Laine
Answer Me	David Whitfield
Ant Rap	Adam & The Ants
Anthem	N-Joi
Antmusic	Adam & The Ants
Any Dream Will Do	Jason Donovan
Any Time, Any Place	Janet Jackson
Any Way That You Want Me	Troggs
Anyone Can Fall In Love	Anita Dobson
Anyone Who Had A Heart	Cilla Black
Anything	3T
Anything	Culture Beat
Anything For You	Gloria Estefan
& The Miami Sound Machine	
Anytime You Need A Friend	
	Mariah Carey
Anyway Anyhow Anywhere	Who
Anywhere For You	Backstreet Boys
Anywhere Is	Enya
Apache	Shadows
Ape Man	Kinks
Apple Blossom Time	Rosemary June
Applejack	Jet Harris & Tony Meehan
April Love	Pat Boone
April Skies	Jesus And Mary Chain
Are 'Friends' Electric	Tubeway Army
Are You Gonna Go My Way	
	Lenny Kravitz
Are You Lonesome Tonight ?	
	Elvis Presley
Are You Mine?	Bros
Are You Ready To Rock	Wizzard
Are You Sure	Allisons
Argentine Melody (Cancion De	
Argentina)	San Jose
Aria	Acker Bilk
Arms Around The World	Louise
Arms Of Mary	Sutherland Brothers
	And Quiver
Army Game	TV Cast
Around The World	Bing Crosby
Around The World	Daft Punk
Around The World	East 17
Around The World	Gracie Fields
Around The World	Ronnie Hilton
Art For Art's Sake	10cc
Arthur Daley ('E's Alright)	Firm
Arthur's Theme (Best That You Can Do)	
	Christopher Cross
As I Love You	Shirley Bassey
As Long As He Needs Me	
	Shirley Bassey
As Long As You Love Me	Backstreet
	Boys
As Tears Go By	Marianne Faithfull
As Usual	Brenda Lee
As You Like It	Adam Faith
Ashes To Ashes	David Bowie
At The Club	Drifters
At The Hop	Danny & The Juniors
Atlantis	Shadows
Atmosphere	Russ Abbot
Atomic	Blondie
Attention To Me	Nolans
Australia	Manic Street Preachers

Title	Artist
Autobahn	Kraftwerk
Automatic	Pointer Sisters
Automatic Lover	Dee D. Jackson
Automatically Sunshine	Supremes
Autumn Almanac	Kinks
Avenging Angels	Space
Axel F	Clock
Axel F	Harold Faltermeyer
Ay Ay Ay Ay Moosey	Modern Romance
Babe	Styx
Babe	Take That
Babooshka	Kate Bush
Baby Baby	Corona
Baby Baby	Amy Grant
Baby Baby	Frankie Lymon
	& The Teenagers
Baby Can I Hold You	Boyzone
Baby Come Back	Pato Banton
Baby Come Back	Equals
Baby, Come To Me	Patti Austin
	(duet with James Ingram)
Baby Don't Change Your Mind	Gladys
	Knight & The Pips
Baby Don't Go	Sonny & Cher
Baby Face	Little Richard
Baby I Don't Care	Buddy Holly
Baby I Don't Care	Transvision Vamp
Baby I Know	Rubettes
Baby I Love You	Dave Edmunds
Baby I Love You	Ronettes
Baby I Love You, OK	Kenny
Baby I Love You Way	Big Mountain
Baby I'm A Want You	Bread
Baby It's You	Beatles
Baby Jane	Rod Stewart
Baby Jump	Mungo Jerry
Baby Love	Dannii Minogue
Baby Love	Supremes
Baby Lover	Petula Clark
Baby Make It Soon	Marmalade
Baby, Now That I Found You	
	Foundations
Baby Please Don't Go	Them
Baby Sittin' Boogie	Buzz Clifford
Baby Stop Crying	Bob Dylan
Babylon's Burning	Ruts
Bachelor Boy	Cliff Richard
Back And Forth	Cameo
Back For Good	Take That
Back Home	England World Cup Squad
Back Off Boogaloo	Ringo Starr
Back Street Luv	Curved Air
Back To Life (However Do You Want	
Me)	Soul II Soul (featuring Caron
	Wheeler)
Back To The Sixties	Tight Fit
Back Together Again	Roberta Flack &
	Donny Hathaway
Backstage	Gene Pitney
Bad	Michael Jackson
Bad Actress	Terrorvision
Bad Bad Boy	Nazareth
Bad Boy	Marty Wilde
Bad Boys	Wham!
Bad Girl	Madonna
Bad Moon Rising	Creedence
	Clearwater Revival
Bad Old Days	Coco
Bad To Me	Billy J. Kramer
	& The Dakotas
Baggy Trousers	Madness
Baker Street	Gerry Rafferty
Baker Street	Undercover
Ball Of Confusion	Temptations
Ball Park Incident	Wizzard

Title	Artist
Ballad Of Bonnie & Clyde	Georgie
	Fame
The Ballad Of Davy Crockett	
	Tennessee Ernie Ford
The Ballad Of Davy Crockett	Bill Hayes
Ballad Of John And Yoko	Beatles
Ballad Of Paladin	Duane Eddy
The Ballad Of Tom Jones	Space With
	Cerys Of Catatonia
Ballroom Blitz	Sweet
Bamboogie	Bamboo
Banana Boat Song	Shirley Bassey
Banana Boat Song	Harry Belafonte
Banana Republic	Boomtown Rats
Banana Rock	Wombles
Banana Splits (Tra La La Song)	
	Dickies
Band Of Gold	Don Cherry
Band Of Gold	Freda Payne
Band On The Run	Paul McCartney
Get It On	T. Rex
Bang Bang	B.A. Robertson
Bang Bang (My Baby Shot Me Down)	
	Cher
(Bang Zoom) Let's Go Go	Real Roxanne
	With Hitman Howie
Bangin' Man	Slade
Bangla Desh	George Harrison
Bank Robber	Clash
Banks Of The Ohio	Olivia Newton-John
Banner Man	Blue Mink
Barbados	Typically Tropical
Barbara Ann	Beach Boys
Barbie Girl	Aqua
Barcelona	Monserrat Caballe
Barcelona	Freddie Mercury
	& Monserrat Caballe
Barrel Of A Gun	Depeche Mode
Basket Case	Green Day
Batdance	Prince
Battle Of New Orleans	Lonnie Donegan
Be Aggressive	Faith No More
Be Alone No More	Another Level
Be Mine	Lance Fortune
Be My Baby	Vanessa Paradis
Be My Baby	Ronettes
Be My Girl	Jim Dale
Be My Guest	Fats Domino
Be Quick Or Be Dead	Iron Maiden
Beach Baby	First Class
Beach Boy Gold	Gidea Park
Beat Dis	Bomb The Bass
Beat It	Michael Jackson
Beat Surrender	Jam
Beat The Clock	Sparks
Beatles Movie Medley	Beatles
Beatnik Fly	Johnny & The Hurricanes
Beautiful Noise	Neil Diamond
Beautiful Ones	Suede
Beauty & The Beast	Celine Dion
	& Peabo Bryson
Because I Love You (The Postman	
Song)	Stevie B
Because Of Love	Janet Jackson
Because The Night	Patti Smith Group
Because They're Young	Duane Eddy
Because You Loved Me	Celine Dion
Bed Sitter	Soft Cell
Beds Are Burning	Midnight Oil
Bedtime Story	Madonna
Beetlebum	Blur
Before	Pet Shop Boys
Beg Steal Or Borrow	New Seekers
Begin The Beguine (Volver A Empezar)	
	Julio Iglesias

Title	Artist
Bring It On Home To Me	Animals
Bring It On Home To Me	Rod Stewart
Bring Me Edelweiss	Edelweiss
Bring Your Daughter To The Slaughter	Iron Maiden
Bringing On Back The Good Times	Love Affair
British Hustle	Hi Tension
The BRITS 1990	Various Artists
Broken Down Angel	Nazareth
Broken Wings	Mr. Mister
Broken Hearted Melody	Sarah Vaughan
Brontosaurus	Move
Brother Louie	Hot Chocolate
Brother Louie	Modern Talking
Brown Eyed Handsome Man	Buddy Holly
Brown Girl In The Ring	Boney M
Brown Sugar	Rolling Stones
Buddy	De La Soul
Buffalo Gals	Malcolm McLaren & The World's Famous Sup
Buffalo Soldier	Bob Marley & The Wailers
Buffalo Stance	Neneh Cherry
Build Me Up Buttercup	Foundations
Build Your Love	Johnnie Ray
Bulls On Parade	Rage Against The Machine
The Bump	Kenny
Bump N' Grind	R. Kelly
Buona Sera	Acker Bilk
Burlesque	Family
Burn It Up	Beatmasters With P.P. Arnold
Burning Bridges (On And Off And On Again)	Status Quo
Burning Heart	Survivor
Burning Love	Elvis Presley
Bus Stop	Hollies
But I Do	Clarence 'Frogman' Henry
Butterfingers	Tommy Steele
Butterfly	Danyel Gerrard
Butterfly	Charlie Gracie
Butterfly	Andy Williams
By The Light Of The Silvery Moon	Little Richard
Bye Bye Baby	Bay City Rollers
Bye Bye Love	Everly Brothers
C Moon	Paul McCartney
C U When U Get There	Coolio Featuring 40 Thevz
Ca Plane Pour Moi	Plastic Bertrand
Cacharpaya (Andes Pumpsa Daesi)	Incantation
Calendar Girl	Neil Sedaka
California Dreamin	Mamas & The Papas
California Dreamin'	River City People
California Love	2 Pac Feat Dr Dre
California Man	Move
Call It Love	Deuce
Call Me	Blondie
Call Me	Go West
Call Me	Spagna
(Call Me) Number One	Tremeloes
Call Rosie On The Phone	Guy Mitchell
Call Up The Groups	Barron Knights
Calling All The Heroes	It Bites
Calling Occupants Of Interplanetary Craft	Carpenters
Calling Your Name	Marilyn
Cambodia	Kim Wilde
Camouflage	Stan Ridgway
Can Can	Bad Manners

Title	Artist
Can Can You Party	Jive Bunny & The Mastermixers
Can I Play With Madness	Iron Maiden
Can I Take You Home Little Girl	Drifters
Can I Touch You...There?	Michael Bolton
Can The Can	Suzi Quatro
Can You Do It	Geordie
(Can You) Feel The Passion	Blue Pearl
Can You Feel It	Jacksons
Can You Feel The Force	Real Thing
Can You Feel The Love Tonight	Elton John
Can You Forgive Her?	Pet Shop Boys
Can't Be Without You Tonight	Judy Boucher
Can't Buy Me Love	Beatles
Can't Get Along Without You	Frankie Vaughan
Can't Get By Without You	Real Thing
Can't Get Enough Of Your Love	Taylor Dayne
Can't Get Enough Of Your Love, Babe	Barry White
Can't Get Used To Losing You	Beat
Can't Get Used To Losing You	Andy Williams
Can't Give You Anything (But My Love)	Stylistics
(I Can't Help) Falling In Love	UB40
Can't Help Falling In Love	Elvis Presley
Can't Help Falling In Love	Stylistics
Can't Help Falling In Love	Andy Williams
Can't Keep It In	Cat Stevens
Can't Shake The Feeling	Big Fun
Can't Stand Losing You	Police
Can't Stay Away From You	Gloria Estefan & The Miami Sound Machine
Can't Stop The Music	Village People
Can't Take My Eyes Off You	Boystown Gang
Can't Take My Eyes Off You	Pet Shop Boys
Can't Take My Eyes Off You	Andy Williams
Can't Wait Another Minute	Five Star
Can't You See That She's Mine	Dave Clark Five
Candida	Dawn
Candle In The Wind	Elton John
Candle In The Wind (Live)	Elton John
Candle In The Wind 1997	Elton John
Candy Girl	New Edition
Candy Man	Brian Poole & The Tremeloes
Cantina Band	Meco
Capstick Comes Home	Tony Capstick
Captain Beaky	Keith Michel
The Captain Of Her Heart	Double
Captain Of Your Ship	Reperata & The Delrons
Car 67	Driver 67
Car Wash	Rose Royce
Cara Mia	David Whitfield
Caravan Of Love	Housemartins
Cardiac Arrest	Madness
Careless Hands	Des O'Connor
Careless Whisper	Wham! Featuring George Michael
Caribbean Disco	Lobo
Caribbean Queen (No More Love On The Run)	Billy Ocean
The Carnival Is Over	Seekers
Carolina Moon	Connie Francis

Title	Artist
Caroline	Status Quo
Caroline (Live At The N.E.C.)	Status Quo
Carrie	Cliff Richard
Carrie-Anne	Hollies
Carry Me Home	Gloworm
Carry The Blame	River City People
Cars	Gary Numan
Casanova	Coffee
Casanova	Levert
Cast Your Fate To The Wind	Sounds Orchestral
Castle Rock	Bluetones
Cat Among The Pigeons	Bros
The Cat Crept In	Mud
Cat's In The Cradle	Ugly Kid Joe
Catch A Falling Star	Perry Como
Catch The Wind	Donovan
Catch Us If You Can	Dave Clark Five
Cathy's Clown	Everly Brothers
Causing A Commotion	Madonna
Cecilia	Suggs
Celebration	Kool & The Gang
Centrefold	J. Geils Band
A Certain Smile	Johnny Mathis
C'est La Vie	Robbie Nevil
Chain Gang	Sam Cooke
Chain Gang	Jimmy Young
Chain Reaction	Diana Ross
Chains	Tina Arena
Chains Of Love	Erasure
Chance	Big Country
Change	Lisa Stansfield
Change	Tears For Fears
A Change Would Do You Good	Sheryl Crow
Change Your Mind	Upside Down
Changing Partners	Bing Crosby
Changing Partners	Kay Starr
The Changingman	Paul Weller
Chanson D'amour	Manhattan Transfer
Chant No. 1 (I Don't Need This Pressure On)	Spandau Ballet
Chantilly Lace	Big Bopper
Chapel Of The Roses	Malcolm Vaughan
Chariots Of Fire - Titles	Vangelis
Charleston	Winifred Atwell
Charlie Brown	Coasters
Charly	Prodigy
Charmaine	Bachelors
Charmless Man	Blur
Check Out The Groove	Bobby Thurston
Check This Out	L.A. Mix
Chequered Love	Kim Wilde
Cherish	David Cassidy
Cherish	Kool & The Gang
Cherish	Madonna
Cherry Oh Baby	UB40
Cherry Pink And Apple Blossom White	Eddie Calvert
Cherry Pink And Apple Blossom White	Perez Prado
Chi Mai Theme	Ennio Morricone
The Chicken Song	Spitting Image
Chika Boom	Guy Mitchell
Child	Mark Owen
A Child's Prayer	Hot Chocolate
Children	Robert Miles
Children Of The Revolution	T. Rex
China Doll	Slim Whitman
China Girl	David Bowie
China In Your Hand	T'Pau
China Tea	Russ Conway
Chiquitita	Abba

Title	Artist
Dancing In The Dark	Bruce Springsteen
Dancing In The Street	David Bowie
Dancing In The Street	Mick Jagger & David Bowie
Dancing In The Street	Martha & The Vandellas
(Dancing) On A Saturday Night	Barry Blue
Dancing On The Ceiling	Lionel Richie
Dancing On The Floor (Hooked On Love)	Third World
Dancing Queen	Abba
Dancing Tight	Galaxy Featuring Phil Fearon
Dancing With Tears In My Eyes	Ultravox
Dancing With The Captain	Paul Nicholas
Dandelion	Rolling Stones
Danger Games	Pinkees
Dangerous	Roxette
Daniel	Elton John
Dark Is The Night	Shakatak
Darlin'	Beach Boys
Darlin'	Frankie Miller
Dat	Pluto Shervington
Daughter Of Darkness	Tom Jones
Davy's On The Road Again	Manfred Mann's Earth Band
Day After Day	Badfinger
The Day I Met Marie	Cliff Richard
The Day The Rains Came	Jane Morgan
Day Trip To Bangor (Didn't We Have A Lovely Time)	Fiddler's Dram
Day Tripper	Beatles
The Day We Caught The Train	Ocean Colour Scene
The Day We Find Love	911
A Day Without Love	Love Affair
Daydream	Lovin' Spoonful
Daydream Believer	Monkees
Daydreamer	David Cassidy
Days	Kinks
Days	Kirsty MacColl
The Days Of Pearly Spencer	Marc Almond
De Do Do Do, De Da Da Da	Police
Dead End Street	Kinks
Dead Giveaway	Shalamar
Dead Or Alive	Lonnie Donegan
Dead Ringer For Love	Meat Loaf
Deadwood Stage	Doris Day
The Dean And I	10cc
Dear Jessie	Madonna
Dear John	Status Quo
Dear Prudence	Siouxsie & The Banshees
Death Of A Clown	Dave Davies
Debora	Tyrannosaurus Rex
December '63 (Oh What A Night)	Four Seasons
Deck Of Cards	Max Bygraves
Deck Of Cards	Wink Martindale
Dedicated Follower Of Fashion	Kinks
Dedicated To The One I Love	Mamas & The Papas
Dedicated To The One I Love	Bitty McLean
Deep	East 17
Deep, Deep Trouble	Simpsons
Deep Down Inside	Donna Summer
Deep Heat '89	Latino Rave
Deeper And Deeper	Madonna
A Deeper Love	Aretha Franklin
Deeply Dippy	Right Said Fred
Delaware	Perry Como

Title	Artist
Delilah	Sensational Alex Harvey Band
Delilah	Tom Jones
Delta Lady	Joe Cocker
Denis	Blondie
Desafinado	Stan Getz & Charlie Byrd
Desiderata	Les Crane
A Design For Life	Manic Street Preachers
Desire	U2
Destiny	Johnnie Ray
Detroit City	Tom Jones
Deutscher Girls	Adam & The Ants
Devil Gate Drive	Suzi Quatro
Devil Woman	Cliff Richard
Devil Woman	Marty Robbins
Devil's Answer	Atomic Rooster
Diamonds	Jet Harris & Tony Meehan
Diana	Paul Anka
Diane	Bachelors
The Diary Of Horace Wimp	Electric Light Orchestra
Did You Ever	Nancy Sinatra & Lee Hazlewood
Didn't I Blow Your Mind	New Kids On The Block
A Different Beat	Boyzone
A Different Corner	George Michael
Different Strokes	Isotonik
Diggin' On You	TLC
Digging Your Scene	Blow Monkeys
Dime And A Dollar	Guy Mitchell
Dippety Day	Father Abraham & The Smurfs
Dirty Cash	Adventures Of Stevie V
Dirty Diana	Michael Jackson
Disappointed	Electronic
D.I.S.C.O.	Ottawan
Disco 2000	Pulp
Disco Connection	Isaac Hayes
Disco Duck	Rick Dees & His Cast Of Idiots
Disco Inferno	Tina Turner
Disco Queen	Hot Chocolate
Disco Stomp	Hamilton Bohannon
Discoteque	U2
Distant Drums	Jim Reeves
Divine Emotions	Narada
D.I.V.O.R.C.E.	Billy Connolly
D.I.V.O.R.C.E.	Tammy Wynette
Dixie-Narco (EP)	Primal Scream
Dixieland	Winifred Atwell
Dizzy	Vic Reeves & The Wonder Stuff
Dizzy	Tommy Roe
DJs Take Control	SL2
Do Anything You Wanna Do	Rods
Do Anything You Want To	Thin Lizzy
Do I Do	Stevie Wonder
Do It Again	Beach Boys
Do It Again	Raffaella Carra
Do Nothing	Specials
Do That To Me One More Time	Captain & Tennille
Do The Bartman	Simpsons
Do The Conga	Black Lace
(Do) The Hucklebuck	Coast To Coast
Do The Right Thing	Redhead Kingpin & The FBI
(Do The) Spanish Hustle	Fatback Band
Do They Know It's Christmas	Band Aid
Do They Know It's Christmas?	Band Aid 11
Do U Still?	East 17
Do Wah Diddy Diddy	Manfred Mann
Do What You Do	Jermaine Jackson
Do What You Gotta Do	Four Tops
Do What You Gotta Do	Nina Simone

Title	Artist
Do What You Wanna Do	T-Connection
Do Ya Do Ya (Wanna Please Me)	Samantha Fox
Do Ya Think I'm Sexy?	N-Trance Featuring Rod Stewart
Do You Believe In Love	Huey Lewis & The News
Do You Feel My Love	Eddy Grant
Do You Know	Michelle Gayle
Do You Know The Way To San Jose	Dionne Warwick
Do You Love Me	Brian Poole & The Tremeloes
Do You Mind	Anthony Newley
Do You Really Want To Hurt Me	Culture Club
Do You See The Light (Looking For)	Snap
Do You Wanna Dance	Barry Blue
Do You Wanna Dance	Cliff Richard
Do You Wanna Touch Me (Oh Yeah)	Gary Glitter
Do You Want Me	Salt-N-Pepa
Do You Want To Know A Secret	Billy J. Kramer & The Dakotas
Dr. Beat	Miami Sound Machine
Doctor Doctor	Thompson Twins
Doctor Jones	Aqua
Dr. Kildare Theme	Johnny Spence
Dr. Love	Tina Charles
Doctor My Eyes	Jackson Five
Doctor's Orders	Sunny
Doctorin' The House	Coldcut Featuring Yazz & The Plastic Population
Doctorin' The Tardis	Timelords
Does Your Chewing Gum Lose Its Flavour	Lonnie Donegan
Does Your Mother Know	Abba
Dog Eat Dog	Adam & The Ants
Doin' The Doo	Betty Boo
Doing Alright With The Boys	Gary Glitter
Dolce Vita	Ryan Paris
Dolly My Love	Moments
Dominique	Singing Nun (Soeur Sourire)
Domino Dancing	Pet Shop Boys
Don Quixote	Nik Kershaw
Don't	Elvis Presley
Don't Answer Me	Cilla Black
Don't Be Cruel	Bobby Brown
Don't Believe A Word	Thin Lizzy
Don't Blame It On That Girl	Matt Bianco
Don't Blame Me	Frank Ifield
Don't Break My Heart	UB40
Don't Bring Lulu	Dorothy Provine
Don't Bring Me Down	Animals
Don't Bring Me Down	Electric Light Orchestra
Don't Bring Me Down	Pretty Things
Don't Bring Me Your Heartaches	Paul & Barry Ryan
Don't Cry	Guns N' Roses
Don't Cry Daddy	Elvis Presley
Don't Cry For Me Argentina	Julie Covington
Don't Cry For Me Argentina	Madonna
Don't Cry For Me Argentina	Shadows
Don't Cry Out Loud	Elkie Brooks
Don't Do It Baby	Mac & Katie Kissoon
Don't Drive My Car	Status Quo
Don't Ever Change	Crickets
Don't Forbid Me	Pat Boone
Don't Forget To Remember	Bee Gees
Don't Get Me Wrong	Pretenders
Don't Give Me Your Life	Alex Party

Title	Artist
Don't Give Up	Peter Gabriel & Kate Bush
Don't Give Up On Us	David Soul
Don't Go	Yazoo
Don't Go Breaking My Heart	Elton John & Rupaul
Don't Go Breaking My Heart	Elton John & Kiki Dee
Don't It Make My Brown Eyes Blue	Crystal Gayle
Don't Knock The Rock	Bill Haley & His Comets
Don't Know Much	Linda Ronstadt (featuring Aaron Neville)
Don't Laugh At Me	Norman Wisdom
Don't Leave Me	Blackstreet
Don't Leave Me This Way	Communards
Don't Leave Me This Way	Thelma Houston
Don't Leave Me This Way	Harold Melvin & The Blue Notes
Don't Let Go (Love)	En Vogue
Don't Let It Die	Hurricane Smith
Don't Let Me Be Misunderstood	Animals
Don't Let The Sun Catch You Crying	Gerry & The Pacemakers
Don't Let The Sun Go Down On Me	George Michael/Elton John
Don't Look Any Further	M People
Don't Look Back In Anger	Oasis
Don't Look Down-The Sequel	Go West
Don't Make Me Wait	Bomb The Bass
Don't Make My Baby Blue	Shadows
Don't Make Waves	Nolans
Don't Marry Her	Beautiful South
Don't Miss The Partyline	Bizz Nizz
Don't Play That Song	Aretha Franklin
Don't Play Your Rock 'n' Roll To Me	Smokey
Don't Push It, Don't Force It	Leon Haywood
Don't Sleep In The Subway	Petula Clark
Don't Speak	No Doubt
Don't Stand So Close To Me	Police
Don't Stay Away Too Long	Peters & Lee
Don't Stop (Wiggle Wiggle)	Outhere Brothers
Don't Stop It Now	Hot Chocolate
Don't Stop Me Now	Queen
Don't Stop Movin'	Livin' Joy
Don't Stop The Carnival	Alan Price Set
Don't Stop The Music	Yarbrough & Peoples
Don't Stop Till You Get Enough	Michael Jackson
Don't Take Away The Music	Tavares
Don't Talk Just Kiss	Right Said Fred/Jocelyn Brown
Don't Talk To Him	Cliff Richard
Don't Talk To Me About Love	Altered Images
Don't Tell Me	Blancmange
Don't That Beat All	Adam Faith
Don't Throw Your Love Away	Searchers
Don't Treat Me Like A Child	Helen Shapiro
Don't Turn Around	Ace Of Base
Don't Turn Around	Aswad
Don't Turn Around	Merseybeats
Don't Walk Away	Jade
Don't Wanna Lose You	Gloria Estefan
Don't Want To Forgive Me Now	Wet Wet Wet
Don't Waste My Time	Paul Hardcastle

Title	Artist
Don't Worry	Kim Appleby
Don't Worry Be Happy	Bobby McFerrin
Don't You (Forget About Me)	Simple Minds
Don't You Know It	Adam Faith
Don't You Love Me	Eternal
Don't You Rock Me Daddy-O	Lonnie Donegan
Don't You Rock Me Daddy-O	Vipers Skiffle Group
Don't You Think It's Time	Mike Berry
Don't You Want Me	Felix
Don't You Want Me	Human League
Donald Where's Your Troosers	Andy Stewart
Donna	10cc
Donna	Marty Wilde
Doobedood'ndoobe	
Doobedood'ndoobe	Diana Ross
Doop	Doop
Double Barrel	Dave & Ansil Collins
Double Dutch	Malcolm McLaren
Down Down	Status Quo
Down On The Beach Tonight	Drifters
Down On The Street	Shakatak
Down The Dustpipe	Status Quo
Down To Earth	Curiosity Killed The Cat
Down Under	Men At Work
Down Yonder	Johnny & The Hurricanes
Downtown	Petula Clark
Downtown Train	Rod Stewart
Dr Kiss Kiss	5000 Volts
Dragging Me Down	Inspiral Carpets
Dragnet	Ray Anthony
Dragnet	Ted Heath
Drama!	Erasure
Dreadlock Holiday	10cc
Dream A Lie	UB40
Dream A Little Dream Of Me	Mama Cass
Dream Baby	Roy Orbison
Dream Lover	Bobby Darin
A Dream's A Dream	Soul II Soul
Dreamboat	Alma Cogan
Dreamer	Supertramp
Dreamin'	Johnny Burnette
Dreaming	Blondie
Dreaming	Cliff Richard
Dreamlover	Mariah Carey
Dreams	Gabrielle
Dreams Can Tell A Lie	Nat 'King' Cole
Dress You Up	Madonna
Drinking Song	Mario Lanza
Drive	Cars
Drive-In Saturday	David Bowie
Driven By You	Brian May
Driving My Car	Madness
Drop The Boy	Bros
Drowning In Berlin	Mobiles
The Drugs Don't Work	Verve
Drummer Man	Tonight
Dry County	Bon Jovi
Dub Be Good To Me	Beats International
Duke Of Earl	Darts
Durham Town (The Leavin')	Roger Whittaker
Dyna-Mite	Mud
E=mc2	Big Audio Dynamite
E-Bow The Letter	REM
Each Time You Break My Heart	Nick Kamen
Early In The Morning	Vanity Fare
Earth Angel	Crew-Cuts
The Earth Dies Screaming	UB40
Earth Song	Michael Jackson
Easier Said Than Done	Shakatak

Title	Artist
Easy	Commodores
Easy Going Me	Adam Faith
Easy Lover	Philip Bailey & Phil Collins
Ebb Tide	Frank Chacksfield
Ebeneezer Goode	Shamen
Ebony And Ivory	Paul McCartney & Stevie Wonder
Echo Beach	Martha & The Muffins
Ecuador	Sash! Featuring Rodriguez
Edelweiss	Vince Hill
The Edge Of Heaven	Wham!
Egyptian Reggae	Jonathan Richman & The Modern Lovers
18 And Life	Skid Row
Eighteen Strings	Tinman
Eighteen With A Bullet	Pete Wingfield
Eighth Day	Hazel O'Connor
Einstein A Go-Go	Landscape
El Bimbo	Bimbo Jet
El Lute	Boney M
Eleanor Rigby	Beatles
Elected	Alice Cooper
Election Day	Arcadia
Electric Avenue	Eddy Grant
Electric Youth	Debbie Gibson
Elenore	Turtles
Elephant Stone	Stone Roses
Eloise	Damned
Eloise	Barry Ryan
Elusive Butterfly	Val Doonican
Elusive Butterfly	Bob Lind
Embarrassment	Madness
Emma	Hot Chocolate
Emotions	Samantha Sang
Emotional Rescue	Rolling Stones
Encore Une Fois	Sash!
End Of The Road	Boyz II Men
Endless Love	Diana Ross & Lionel Richie
Endless Love	Luther Vandross & Mariah Carey
Endless Sleep	Marty Wilde
England We'll Fly The Flag	England World Cup Squad
England's Irie	Black Grape Featuring Joe Strummer & Keith Allen
English Country Garden	Jimmie Rodgers
Enjoy The Silence	Depeche Mode
Enola Gay	Orchestral Manoeuvres In The Dark
Enter Sandman	Metallica
Ernie (The Fastest Milk Man In The West)	Benny Hill
Erotica	Madonna
Escaping	Dina Carroll
Especially For You	Kylie Minogue & Jason Donovan
Et Les Oiseaux Chantaient (And The Birds Were Singing)	Sweet People
Eternal Flame	Bangles
Eternal Love	PJ And Duncan
The Eton Rifles	Jam
European Female	Stranglers
Ev'ry Time We Say Goodbye	Simply Red
Ev'rybody's Twistin'	Frank Sinatra
Ev'rywhere	David Whitfield
Evapor 8	Altern 8
Eve Of Destruction	Barry McGuire
Eve Of The War (Ben Liebrand Remix)	Jeff Wayne
Even Better Than The Real Thing	U2
Even The Bad Times Are Good	Tremeloes
Ever Fallen In Love	Fine Young Cannibals

Title	Artist
Evergreen (Love Theme From 'A Star Is Born')	Barbra Streisand
An Everlasting Love	Andy Gibb
Everlasting Love	Cast From Casualty
Everlasting Love	Love Affair
Evermore	Ruby Murray
Every Beat Of My Heart	Rod Stewart
Every Breath You Take	Police
Every Day Hurts	Sad Cafe
Every Day (I Love You More)	Jason Donovan
Every Day Of My Life	Malcolm Vaughan
Every Little Step	Bobby Brown
Every Little Thing She Does Is Magic	Police
Every Loser Wins	Nick Berry
Every 1's A Winner	Hot Chocolate
Every Rose Has Its Thorn	Poison
Everybody	Clock
Everybody	Tommy Roe
Everybody (Backstreet's Back)	Backstreet Boys
Everybody Dance	Chic
Everybody Get Together	Dave Clark Five
Everybody Gonfi Gon	Two Cowboys
Everybody Hurts	R.E.M.
Everybody In The Place (EP)	Prodigy
Everybody Knows	Dave Clark Five
Everybody Loves Somebody	Dean Martin
Everybody Needs Somebody To Love	Blues Brothers
Everybody Salsa	Modern Romance
Everybody Wants To Rule The World	Tears For Fears
Everybody Wants To Run The World	Tears For Fears
(Everybody's Got To Learn Sometime) I Need Your Loving	Baby D
Everybody's Free (To Feel Good)	Rozalla
Everybody's Gonna Be Happy	Kinks
Everybody's Got To Learn Sometime	Korgis
Everybody's Laughing	Phil Fearon & Galaxy
Everybody's Somebody's Fool	Connie Francis
Everybody's Talkin'	Beautiful South
Everyday	Slade
Everyday Is Like Sunday	Morrissey
Everyone's Gone To The Moon	Jonathan King
Everything	Mary J. Blige
Everything About You	Ugly Kid Joe
Everything Changes	Take That
Everything Counts	Depeche Mode
(Everything I Do) I Do It For You	Bryan Adams
Everything I Am	Plastic Penny
Everything I Own	Ken Boothe
Everything I Own	Boy George
Everything Is Alright (Uptight)	CJ Lewis
Everything Is Beautiful	Ray Stevens
Everything Must Change	Paul Young
Everything Must Go	Manic Street Preachers
Everything She Wants	Wham!
Everything's Alright	Mojos
Everything's Tuesday	Chairmen Of The Board
Everytime You Go Away	Paul Young
Everywhere	Fleetwood Mac

Title	Artist
Evil Hearted You	Yardbirds
The Evil That Men Do	Iron Maiden
Evil Woman	Electric Light Orchestra
Excerpt From A Teenage Opera	Keith West
Excitable	Amazulu
Exhale (Shoop Shoop)	Whitney Houston
Exodus	Ferrante & Teicher
Experiments With Mice	Johnny Dankworth
Express	Dina Carroll
Express Yourself	Madonna
Extended Play E.P.	Bryan Ferry
Exterminate!	Snap Featuring Niki Haris
Eye Level	Simon Park Orchestra
Eye Of The Tiger	Survivor
Fable	Robert Miles
Fabulous	Charlie Gracie
Faces	2 Unlimited
Fade To Grey	Visage
Fading Like A Flower (Every Time You Leave)	Roxette
Fairground	Simply Red
Fairytale	Dana
Fairytale Of New York	Pogues
Faith	George Michael
Fall In Love With You	Cliff Richard
Falling	Julee Cruise
Falling	Roy Orbison
Falling Apart At The Seams	Marmalade
Falling Into You	Celine Dion
Fame	Irene Cara
Fancy Pants	Kenny
Fanfare For The Common Man	Emerson, Lake & Palmer
Fantastic Day	Haircut 100
Fantasy	Black Box
Fantasy	Mariah Carey
Fantasy	Earth, Wind & Fire
Fantasy Island	Tight Fit
Far Far Away	Slade
Farewell	Rod Stewart
Farewell Is A Lonely Sound	Jimmy Ruffin
Farewell My Summer Love	Michael Jackson
Fascinating Rhythm	Bass-O-Matic
Fashion	David Bowie
Fast Car	Tracy Chapman
Fastlove	George Michael
Fat Bottomed Girls	Queen
Father And Son	Boyzone
Father Christmas Do Not Touch Me	Goodies
Fattie Bum-Bum	Carl Malcolm
Favourite Shirts (Boy Meets Girl)	Haircut 100
F.B.I.	Shadows
Fear Of The Dark (Live)	Iron Maiden
Feel It	Tamperer Featuring Maya
Feel Like Making Love	Pauline Henry
Feel So Good	Mase
Feel So High	Des'ree
Feel So Real	Steve Arrington
Feel The Need In Me	Detroit Emeralds
Feel The Need In Me	Detroit Emeralds
Feelings	Morris Albert
(Feels Like) Heaven	Fiction Factory
Feels Like Heaven	Urban Cookie Collective
Feels Like I'm In Love	Kelly Marie
Fernando	Abba
Ferry 'cross The Mersey	Marsden/McCartney/Johnson/Christians
Ferry Across The Mersey	Gerry & The Pacemakers
Fever	Peggy Lee

Title	Artist
Fever	Madonna
Fields Of Fire (400 Miles)	Big Country
Figaro	Brotherhood Of Man
Filmstar	Suede
The Final Countdown	Europe
Finally	Ce Ce Peniston
Finchley Central	New Vaudeville Band
Find My Love	Fairground Attraction
Find The Time	Five Star
Fine Time	New Order
Fine Time	Yazz
Finger Of Suspicion	Dickie Valentine
Fings Ain't What They Used T'be	Max Bygraves
Fire	Crazy World Of Arthur Brown
Fire	Prodigy
Fire Brigade	Move
Fire It Up	Busta Rhymes
Fireball	Deep Purple
Firestarter	Prodigy
First Cut Is The Deepest	Rod Stewart
First Of May	Bee Gees
The First Time	Robin Beck
The First Time	Adam Faith
5-4-3-2-1	Manfred Mann
Five Live (EP)	George Michael & Queen
5-7-0-5	City Boy
Fix	Blackstreet
Flash	Bbe
Flash	Queen
Flashdance....What A Feeling	Irene Cara
Flava	Peter Andre
F.L.M.	Mel & Kim
Float On	Floaters
The Floral Dance	Brighouse And Rastrick
Flowers In The Rain	Move
Floy Joy	Supremes
The Fly	U2
Flying	Cast
Fog On The Tyne (Revisited)	Gazza And Lindisfarne
The Folk Singer	Tommy Roe
Follow That Dream (E.P.)	Elvis Presley
Follow You Follow Me	Genesis
Food For Thought	UB40
A Fool Am I	Cilla Black
A Fool Such As I	Elvis Presley
Fool To Cry	Rolling Stones
Fool's Gold	Stone Roses
Foolish Beat	Debbie Gibson
Fools Rush In	Rick Nelson
Foot Tapper	Shadows
Footloose	Kenny Loggins
Footsee	Wigan's Chosen Few
Footsteps	Steve Lawrence
For All We Know	Shirley Bassey
For America	Red Box
For Once In My Life	Stevie Wonder
For The Good Times	Perry Como
For Whom The Bell Tolls	Bee Gees
For You	Rick Nelson
For Your Babies	Simply Red
For Your Eyes Only	Sheena Easton
For Your Love	Yardbirds
Forever	Damage
Forever	Roy Wood
Forever & Ever	Slik
Forever Autumn	Justin Hayward
A Forever Kind Of Love	Bobby Vee
(Forever) Live And Die	Orchestral Manoeuvres In The Dark
Forever Love	Gary Barlow
Forget About You	Motors
Forget Him	Bobby Rydell

Title	Artist
Forget Me Not	Eden Kane
Forget Me Not	Martha & The Vandellas
Forget Me Nots	Patrice Rushen
Forgive Me, Girl	Spinners
Fort Worth Jail	Lonnie Donegan
48 Crash	Suzi Quatro
40 Miles Of Bad Road	Duane Eddy
Found A Cure	Ultra Nate
Four Bacharach & David Songs (EP)	
	Deacon Blue
Four From Toyah E.P.	Toyah
Four Letter Word	Kim Wilde
Four More From Toyah E.P.	Toyah
Fox On The Run	Manfred Mann
Fox On The Run	Sweet
Frankie	Sister Sledge
Free	Dj Quicksilver
Free	Ultra Nate
Free	Deniece Williams
Free As A Bird	Beatles
Free E.P.	Free
Free Me	Cast
Free Your Mind	En Vogue
Freebird	Will To Power
Freed From Desire	Gala
Freedom	Wham!
Freedom	Robbie Williams
Freedom Come Freedom Go	Fortunes
Freek'n You	Jodeci
Freight Train	Chas McDevitt Skiffle Group
French Kiss	Lil Louis
French Kissin' In The USA	Debbie Harry
Fresh	Gina G
Fresh	Kool & The Gang
Friday, I'm In Love	Cure
Friday Night (Live Version)	Kids From 'Fame'
Friday On My Mind	Easybeats
Friend Or Foe	Adam Ant
Friendly Persuasion	Pat Boone
Friends	Arrival
Friends	Shalamar
Friends	Amii Stewart
Friends And Neighbours	Max Bygraves & The Tanner Sisters
Friends And Neighbours	Billy Cotton & His Band
Friggin' In The Riggin'	Sex Pistols
Frightened City	Shadows
From A Distance	Cliff Richard
From A Jack To A King	Ned Miller
From A Window	Billy J. Kramer & The Dakotas
From Here To Eternity	Frank Sinatra
From Me To You	Beatles
From New York To L.A.	Patsy Gallant
From The Underworld	Herd
Frozen	Madonna
Frozen Orange Juice	Peter Sarstedt
Full Metal Jacket (I Wanna Be Your Drill Instructor)	Abigail Mead & Nigel Goulding
Funeral Pyre	Jam
Funkin' For Jamaica (N.Y.)	Tom Browne
Funky Gibbon	Goodies
Funky Jam	Primal Scream
Funky Moped	Jasper Carrott
Funky Town	Pseudo Echo
Funky Weekend	Stylistics
Funkytown	Lipps Inc.
Funny Familiar Forgotten Feeling	Tom Jones
Funny Funny	Sweet
Funny How Love Can Be	Ivy League
Future Love (EP)	Seal
Gal With The Yaller Shoes	Michael Holliday
Galveston	Glen Campbell
Gambler	Madonna
Gamblin' Man	Lonnie Donegan
Game Of Love	Wayne Fontana & The Mindbenders
Games People Play	Joe South
Games Without Frontiers	Peter Gabriel
Gangsta's Paradise	Coolio Featuring L.V.
Gangsters	Specials
Garden Of Eden	Gary Miller
Garden Of Eden	Frankie Vaughan
Gasoline Alley Bred	Hollies
Gaye	Clifford T. Ward
Gee Baby	Peter Shelley
Gee Whiz It's You	Cliff Richard
Geno	Dexy's Midnight Runners
Gentle On My Mind	Dean Martin
Georgy Girl	Seekers
Geronimo	Shadows
Get A Life	Soul II Soul
Get Away	Georgie Fame
Get Back	Beatles
Get Back	Rod Stewart
Get Dancing	Disco Tex & The Sex-O-Lettes
Get Down	Gene Chandler
Get Down	Gilbert O'Sullivan
Get Down And Get With It	Slade
Get Down On It	Kool & The Gang
Get Here	Oleta Adams
Get It	Darts
Get Lost	Eden Kane
Get Off Of My Cloud	Rolling Stones
Get Outta My Dreams Get Into My Car	Billy Ocean
Get Ready	Temptations
Get Ready For This	2 Unlimited
Get The Message	Electronic
Get Up And Boogie (That's Right)	Silver Convention
Get Up (Before The Night Is Over)	Technotronic
Get-A-Way	Maxx
Gett Off	Prince
Gettin' Jiggy Wit It	Will Smith
Ghetto Child	Detroit Spinners
Ghetto Heaven	Family Stand
Ghost Town	Specials
Ghostbusters	Ray Parker Jr.
Ghosts	Michael Jackson
Ghosts	Japan
Giddy-Up-A-Ding-Dong	Freddie Bell & The Bellboys
The Gift Of Christmas	Childliners
Gigi	Billy Eckstine
Gilly Gilly Ossenfeffer Katzenellen Bogen By The Sea	Max Bygraves
Gimme All Your Lovin'	ZZ Top
Gimme Dat Ding	Pipkins
Gimme Gimme Gimme (A Man After Midnight)	Abba
Gimme Gimme Good Lovin'	Crazy Elephant
Gimme Hope Jo'anna	Eddy Grant
Gimme Little Sign	Brenton Wood
Gimme Some	Brendon
Gimme Some Loving	Spencer Davis Group
Gin House Blues	Amen Corner
Ginny Come Lately	Brian Hyland
Girl	St. Louis Union
The Girl Can't Help It	Darts
The Girl Can't Help It	Little Richard
Girl Crazy	Hot Chocolate
Girl Don't Come	Sandie Shaw
Girl I'm Gonna Miss You	Milli Vanilli
The Girl Is Mine	Michael Jackson
The Girl Is Mine	Paul McCartney & Michael Jackson
A Girl Like You	Edwyn Collins
A Girl Like You	Cliff Richard
Girl Of My Best Friend	Elvis Presley
Girl Of My Dreams	Tony Brent
Girl You Know It's True	Milli Vanilli
Girlfriend	Pebbles
Girlie Girlie	Sophia George
Girls	Moments And Whatnauts
Girls And Boys	Blur
Girls Girls Girls	Sailor
Girls Just Want To Have Fun	Cyndi Lauper
Girls On Film	Duran Duran
Girls Talk	Dave Edmunds
Give A Little Love	Aswad
Give A Little Love	Bay City Rollers
Give A Little Love	Daniel O'donnell
Give In To Me	Michael Jackson
Give It Away	Red Hot Chili Peppers
Give It To Me	Troggs
Give It Up	Goodmen
Give It Up	KC & The Sunshine Band
Give Me A Little More Time	Gabrielle
Give Me Back My Heart	Dollar
Give Me Just A Little More Time	Chairmen Of The Board
Give Me Just A Little More Time	Kylie Minogue
Give Me Love (Give Me Peace On Earth)	George Harrison
Give Me The Night	George Benson
Give Me Your Heart Tonight	Shakin' Stevens
Give Me Your Word	Tennessee Ernie Ford
Give Peace A Chance	Plastic Ono Band
Givin' Up Givin' In	Three Degrees
Giving It All Away	Roger Daltrey
G.L.A.D.	Kim Appleby
Glad All Over	Dave Clark Five
Glad It's All Over	Captain Sensible
Glass Of Champagne	Sailor
Globetrotter	Tornados
Gloria	Laura Branigan
Glory Box	Portishead
Glory Of Love	Peter Cetera
Glow	Spandau Ballet
Go	Moby
Go Away	Gloria Estefan
Go Away Little Girl	Mark Wynter
Go (Before You Break My Heart)	Gigliola Cinquetti
Go Buddy Go	Stranglers
Go Now!	Moody Blues
Go On By	Alma Cogan
Go On Move	Reel 2 Real
Go West	Pet Shop Boys
Go Wild In The Country	Bow Wow Wow
God Gave Rock & Roll To You II	Kiss
God Only Knows	Beach Boys
God Save The Queen	Sex Pistols
Goin' Back	Dusty Springfield
Going Back To My Roots	FPI Project
Going Back To My Roots	Odyssey
Going Down The Road	Roy Wood
Going Home	Osmonds
Going In With My Eyes Open	David Soul

Title	Artist
Going Nowhere	Gabrielle
Going Out	Supergrass
Going Underground	Jam
Gold	TAFKAP
Gold	Spandau Ballet
Golden Brown	Stranglers
Golden Years	David Bowie
The Golden Years E.P.	Motorhead
Goldeneye	Tina Turner
Goldfinger	Ash
Gonna Get Along Without You Now	Viola Wills
Gonna Make You A Star	David Essex
Gonna Make You An Offer You Can't Refuse	Jimmy Helms
Gonna Make You Sweat	C&C Music Factory Feat. Freedom Williams
Goo Goo Barabajagal (Love Is Hot)	Donovan & Jeff Beck Group
Good Enough	Dodgy
Good Golly Miss Molly	Little Richard
Good Golly Miss Molly	Swinging Blue Jeans
A Good Heart	Feargal Sharkey
Good Life	Inner City
Good Luck Charm	Elvis Presley
Good Morning Freedom	Blue Mink
Good Morning Judge	10cc
Good Morning Starshine	Oliver
Good Old Rock 'n' Roll	Dave Clark Five
The Good, The Bad And The Ugly	Hugo Montenegro & His Orchestra
Good Thing	Fine Young Cannibals
Good Thing Going (We've Got A Good Thing Going)	Sugar Minott
Good Times	Chic
Good Times (Better Times)	Jimmy Jones
Good Timin'	Jimmy Jones
Good Tradition	Tanita Tikaram
Good Vibrations	Beach Boys
Good Vibrations	Marky Mark & The Funky Bunch
A Good Year For The Roses	Elvis Costello
Goodbye	Mary Hopkin
Goodbye Jimmy, Goodbye	Ruby Murray
Goodbye My Love	Glitter Band
Goodbye My Love	Searchers
Goodbye Sam Hello Samantha	Cliff Richard
Goodbye Stranger	Pepsi & Shirlie
Goodbye To Love	Carpenters
Goodbye Yellow Brick Road	Elton John
Goodness Gracious Me	Peter Sellers & Sophia Loren
Goodnight	Roy Orbison
Goodnight Girl	Wet Wet Wet
Goodnight Midnight	Clodagh Rodgers
Goodnight Tonight	Paul McCartney
Goody Two Shoes	Adam Ant
Google Eye	Nashville Teens
Got 'til It's Gone	Janet Featuring Q-Tip And Joni Mitchell
Got My Mind Set On You	George Harrison
Got To Be Certain	Kylie Minogue
Got To Be There	Michael Jackson
Got To Get	Rob 'n' Raz Featuring Leila K
Got To Get It	Culture Beat
Got To Get You Into My Life	Cliff Bennett & The Rebel Rousers
Got To Give It Up	Marvin Gaye
Got To Have Your Love	Mantronix Featuring Wondress
Gotham City	R. Kelly
Gotta Go Home	Boney M

Title	Artist
Gotta Have Something In The Bank Frank	Frankie Vaughan & The Kaye Sisters
Gotta Pull Myself Together	Nolans
Govinda	Kula Shaker
Granada	Frankie Laine
Granada	Frank Sinatra
Grand Coolie Dam	Lonnie Donegan
Grand Piano	Mixmaster
Grandad	Clive Dunn
Grandma's Party	Paul Nicholas
Grease	Frankie Valli
The Grease Megamix	John Travolta /Olivia Newton-John
Greased Lightning	John Travolta
Great Balls Of Fire	Jerry Lee Lewis
The Great Pretender	Freddie Mercury
The Great Pretender	Jimmy Parkinson
The Great Pretender	Platters
Greatest Love Of All	Whitney Houston
Green Door	Shakin' Stevens
Green Door	Frankie Vaughan
The Green Door	Jim Lowe
Green Green Grass Of Home	Tom Jones
The Green Leaves Of Summer	Kenny Ball
The Green Manalishi	Fleetwood Mac
Green Onions	Booker T. & The M.G.'s
Green Tambourine	Lemon Pipers
Grey Day	Madness
The Groove	Rodney Franklin
Groove Is In The Heart	Deee-Lite
The Groove Line	Heatwave
The Groover	T. Rex
Groovin'	Young Rascals
Groovin' With Mr. Bloe	Mr. Bloe
A Groovy Kind Of Love	Mindbenders
Groovy Kind Of Love	Phil Collins
Groovy Train	Farm
Guaglione	Perez 'Prez' Prado
Guantanamera	Sandpipers
Gudbuy T'Jane	Slade
Guilty	Pearls
Guitar Boogie Shuffle	Bert Weedon
Guitar Tango	Shadows
Gurney Slade	Max Harris
Gypsy Woman (La Da Dee)	Crystal Waters
Gypsys Tramps & Thieves	Cher
Ha Ha Said The Clown	Manfred Mann
Halfway Down The Stairs	Muppets
Halfway To Paradise	Billy Fury
Hallelujah	Milk & Honey
Hallelujah Freedom	Junior Campbell
Hand On Your Heart	Kylie Minogue
Handful Of Songs	Tommy Steele
Hands Off-She's Mine	Beat
Hands To Heaven	Breathe
Hands Up (Give Me Your Heart)	Ottawan
Handy Man	Jimmy Jones
Hang On In There Baby	Johnny Bristol
Hang On In There Baby	Curiosity
Hang On Now	Kajagoogoo
Hang On Sloopy	McCoys
Hang On To Your Love	Jason Donovan
Hangin' Tough	New Kids On The Block
Hanging On The Telephone	Blondie
Hanky Panky	Madonna
Happenin' All Over Again	Lonnie Gordon
The Happening	Supremes
Happy	MN8
Happy Birthday	Altered Images
Happy Birthday	Stevie Wonder

Title	Artist
Happy Birthday, Sweet Sixteen	Neil Sedaka
Happy Days And Lonely Nights	Ruby Murray
Happy Days And Lonely Nights	Frankie Vaughan
Happy Hour	Housemartins
Happy Jack	Who
H.A.P.P.Y Radio	Edwin Starr
Happy Talk	Captain Sensible
Happy To Be On An Island In The Sun	Demis Roussos
Happy Together	Jason Donovan
Happy Together	Turtles
Happy Wanderer	Obernkirchen Children's Choir
Happy Wanderer	Stargazers
The Happy Wanderer	Frank Weir
The Happy Whistler	Don Robertson
Happy Xmas (War Is Over)	John And Yoko Plastic Ono Band
Harbour Lights	Platters
A Hard Day's Night	Beatles
A Hard Day's Night	Peter Sellers
Hard Habit To Break	Chicago
Hard Headed Woman	Elvis Presley
A Hard Rain's Gonna Fall	Bryan Ferry
Hard To Handle	Otis Redding
Hard To Say I'm Sorry	Az Yet
Hard To Say I'm Sorry	Chicago
Hardcore Uproar	Together
The Harder I Try	Brother Beyond
Hare Krishna	Radha Krishna Temple
Harlem Shuffle	Bob & Earl
Harper Valley P.T.A.	Jeannie C. Riley
Harvest For The World	Christians
Harvest For The World	Isley Brothers
Hats Off To Larry	Del Shannon
Have A Drink On Me	Lonnie Donegan
Have I The Right?	Dead End Kids
Have I The Right?	Honeycombs
Have I Told You Lately	Rod Stewart
Have You Ever Been In Love	Leo Sayer
Have You Ever Really Loved A Woman?	Bryan Adams
Have You Seen Her	Chi-Lites
Have You Seen Her	M.C. Hammer
Have You Seen Your Mother, Baby, Standing In The Shadow	Rolling Stones
Hawkeye	Frankie Laine
Hazard	Richard Marx
Hazy Shade Of Winter	Bangles
He Ain't Heavy, He's My Brother	Hollies
He Ain't No Competiiton	Brother Beyond
He'll Have To Go	Jim Reeves
He's Gonna Step On You Again	John Kongos
He's Got No Love	Searchers
He's Got The Whole World In His Hands	Laurie London
He's In Town	Rockin' Berries
He's Misstra Know It All	Stevie Wonder
He's On The Phone	Saint Etienne
He's So Fine	Chiffons
He's The Greatest Dancer	Sister Sledge
Head Over Heels	Tears For Fears
Headline News	Edwin Starr
Heal The World	Michael Jackson
Healing Hands	Elton John
Healing Hands	Elton John
Hear The Drummer (Get Wicked)	Chad Jackson
Heart	Max Bygraves

Title	Artist
Heart	Pet Shop Boys
Heart And Soul	T'Pau
Heart Full Of Soul	Yardbirds
The Heart Of A Man	Frankie Vaughan
Heart Of A Teenage Girl	Craig Douglas
Heart Of Glass	Blondie
Heart Of Gold	Neil Young
Heart Of My Heart	Max Bygraves
Heart Of Stone	Kenny
Heart On My Sleeve	Gallagher & Lyle
Heart-Shaped Box	Nirvana
Heartache	Pepsi & Shirlie
Heartache Avenue	Maisonettes
Heartaches By The Number	Guy Mitchell
Heartbeat	Nick Berry
Heartbeat	Ruby Murray
Heartbeat	Showaddywaddy
Heartbreak Hotel	Elvis Presley
Heartbreaker	Dionne Warwick
Heartless	Frankie Vaughan
The Heat Is On	Glenn Frey
Heatseeker	AC/DC
Heaven For Everyone	Queen
Heaven Is A Place On Earth	Belinda Carlisle
Heaven Knows I'm Miserable Now	Smiths
Heaven Must Be Missing An Angel	Tavares
Heaven Must Have Sent You	Elgins
Helen Wheels	Paul McCartney
Hell Raiser	Sweet
Hello	Lionel Richie
Hello, Dolly!	Louis Armstrong
Hello Goodbye	Beatles
Hello Happiness	Drifters
Hello Hello I'm Back Again	Gary Glitter
Hello Hurray	Alice Cooper
Hello, I Love You	Doors
Hello Little Girl	Fourmost
Hello Mary Lou	Ricky Nelson
Hello Susie	Amen Corner
Hello This Is Joannie (The Telephone Answering Machine Song)	Paul Evans
Help	Bananarama
Help!	Beatles
Help Me Girl	Eric Burdon & The Animals
Help Me Make It Through The Night	John Holt
Help Me Make It Through The Night	Gladys Knight & The Pips
Help Yourself	Tom Jones
Helule Helule	Tremeloes
Here Come The Nice	Small Faces
Here Comes My Baby	Tremeloes
Here Comes Summer	Jerry Keller
Here Comes That Feeling	Brenda Lee
Here Comes The Hotstepper	Ini Kamoze
Here Comes The Night	Them
Here Comes The Rain Again	Eurythmics
Here Comes The Sun	Steve Harley
Here I Go Again	Archie Bell & The Drells
Here I Go Again	Hollies
Here I Go Again	Whitesnake
Here I Stand	Bitty McLean
Here It Comes Again	Fortunes
Here We Go	Stakka Bo
Here We Go Round The Mulberry Bush	Traffic
Here's Where The Story Ends	Tin Tin Out Featuring Shelley Nelson
Hernando's Hideaway	Johnston Brothers

Title	Artist
Hernando's Hideaway	Johnnie Ray
Hero	Mariah Carey
Heroes And Villains	Beach Boys
Hersham Boys	Sham 69
Hey! Baby	Bruce Channel
Hey Child	East 17
Hey D.J. I Can't Dance To...	Beatmasters Featuring Betty Boo
Hey Dude	Kula Shaker
Hey Girl	Small Faces
Hey Girl Don't Bother Me	Tams
Hey Joe	Jimi Hendrix Experience
Hey Jude	Beatles
Hey Little Girl	Del Shannon
Hey Lover	LL Cool J
Hey Music Lover	S'Express
Hey Now (Girls Just Want To Have Fun)	Cyndi Lauper
Hey Paula	Paul & Paula
Hey Rock And Roll	Showaddywaddy
Hey There	Rosemary Clooney
Hey There	Johnnie Ray
(Hey There) Lonely Girl	Eddie Holman
(Hey You) The Rocksteady Crew	Rocksteady Crew
Hi-Fidelity	Kids From 'Fame'
Hi Hi Hi	Paul McCartney
Hi Ho Silver	Jim Diamond
Hi-Ho Silver Lining	Jeff Beck
Hi-Lili-Hi-Lo	Alan Price Set
Hi Tension	Hi Tension
Hide And Seek	Howard Jones
Hideaway	De'lacy
Hideaway	Dave Dee, Dozy, Beaky, Mick & Tich
High	Lighthouse Family
High Class Baby	Cliff Richard
High Energy	Evelyn Thomas
High Hopes	Frank Sinatra
High In The Sky	Amen Corner
High Life	Modern Romance
High School Confidential	Jerry Lee Lewis
High Time	Paul Jones
Higher Ground	UB40
Higher Love	Steve Winwood
Higher State Of Consciousness	Josh Wink
Higher State Of Consciousness '96	Wink
Hillbilly Rock Hillbilly Roll	Woolpackers
Hippy Hippy Shake	Swinging Blue Jeans
Hippychick	Soho
History	Michael Jackson
History	Mai Tai
Hit 'em High (The Monstars' Anthem)	B Real/Busta Rhymes/Coolio/LL Cool J/Method Man
Hit Me With Your Rhythm Stick	Ian Dury & The Blockheads
Hit That Perfect Beat	Bronski Beat
Hit The Road Jack	Ray Charles
Hold Back The Night	Trammps
Hold Me	P.J. Proby
Hold Me	B.A. Robertson
Hold Me Close	David Essex
Hold Me In Your Arms	Rick Astley
Hold Me Now	Johnny Logan
Hold Me Now	Thompson Twins
Hold Me Tight	Johnny Nash
Hold Me, Thrill Me, Kiss Me	Gloria Estefan
Hold Me, Thrill Me, Kiss Me, Kill Me	U2
Hold My Hand	Don Cornell
Hold On	En Vogue
Hold On	Wilson Phillips

Title	Artist
Hold On Tight	Electric Light Orchestra
Hold On To My Love	Jimmy Ruffin
Hold Tight	Dave Dee, Dozy, Beaky, Mick & Tich
Hold Your Head Up	Argent
Holding Back The Years	Simply Red
Holding Out For A Hero	Bonnie Tyler
Hole In My Shoe	neil
Hole In My Shoe	Traffic
Hole In The Ground	Bernard Cribbins
Holiday	Madonna
Holiday Rap	M.C. Miker 'G' & Deejay Sven
Holidays In The Sun	Sex Pistols
Holy Cow	Lee Dorsey
Holy Smoke	Iron Maiden
Homburg	Procol Harum
Home Lovin' Man	Andy Williams
Homely Girl	Chi-Lites
Homely Girl	UB40
Homeward Bound	Simon & Garfunkel
Honaloochie Boogie	Mott The Hoople
Honey	Mariah Carey
Honey	Bobby Goldsboro
Honey Come Back	Glen Campbell
Honey Honey	Sweet Dreams
Honey I Need	Pretty Things
Hong Kong Garden	Siouxsie & The Banshees
Honky Tonk Women	Rolling Stones
Hooked On Classics	Royal Philharmonic Orchestra
Hooray Hooray It's A Holi-Holiday	Boney M
Hoots Mon	Lord Rockingham's XI
Hopelessly Devoted To You	Olivia Newton-John
Horny	Mark Morrison
Horse With No Name	America
Hot Diggity	Michael Holliday
Hot Diggity	Perry Como
Hot In The City	Billy Idol
Hot Love	T. Rex
Hot Stuff	Donna Summer
Hot Track E.P. (Love Hurts Etc.)	Nazareth
Hotel California	Eagles
Hotlegs	Rod Stewart
Hound Dog	Elvis Presley
House Arrest	Krush
House Nation	House Master Boyz & The Rude Boy Of House
House Of Fun	Madness
House Of Love	East 17
House Of The Rising Sun	Animals
House Of The Rising Sun	Frijid Pink
The House That Jack Built	Alan Price Set
The House That Jack Built	Tracie
A House With Love In It	Vera Lynn
Housecall	Shabba Ranks Featuring Maxi Priest
How 'Bout Us	Champaign
How About That	Adam Faith
How Am I Supposed To Live Without You	Michael Bolton
How Bizarre	OMC
How Can I Be Sure	David Cassidy
How Can I Love You More?	M People
How Can We Be Lovers	Michael Bolton
How Come	Ronnie Lane
How Deep Is Your Love	Bee Gees
How Deep Is Your Love	Take That
How Do I Live	Leann Rimes
How Do You Do It?	Gerry & The Pacemakers
How Do You Do!	Roxette

Title	Artist
I Missed Again	Phil Collins
I Must Be Seeing Things	Gene Pitney
I Need Love	L.L. Cool J
I Need You	3T
I Need You	B.V.S.M.P.
I Need You Now	Eddie Fisher
I Need Your Love Tonight	Elvis Presley
I Need Your Lovin'	Alyson Williams
I Only Have Eyes For You	Art Garfunkel
I Only Wanna Be With You	Bay City Rollers
I Only Want To Be With You	Dusty Springfield
I Only Want To Be With You	Tourists
I Owe You Nothing	Bros
I Pretend	Des O'Connor
I Put A Spell On You	Alan Price Set
I Quit	Bros
I Remember Elvis Presley (The King Is Dead)	Danny Mirror
I Remember Yesterday	Donna Summer
I Remember You	Frank Ifield
I Saw Her Again	Mamas & The Papas
I Saw Him Standing There	Tiffany
I Saw Mommy Kissing Santa Claus	Beverley Sisters
I Saw Mommy Kissing Santa Claus	Jimmy Boyd
I Say A Little Prayer	Aretha Franklin
I Second That Emotion	Japan
I See A Star	Mouth & McNeal
I See The Moon	Stargazers
I Shot The Sheriff	Eric Clapton
I Shot The Sheriff	Warren G
I Should Be So Lucky	Kylie Minogue
I Should Have Known Better	Jim Diamond
I Shoulda Loved Ya	Narada Michael Walden
I Still Believe	Ronnie Hilton
I Still Believe In You	Cliff Richard
I Still Haven't Found What I'm Looking For	Chimes
I Still Haven't Found What I'm Looking For	U2
I Surrender	Rainbow
I Swear	All-4-One
I Think It's Going To Rain	UB40
I Think Of You	Perry Como
I Think Of You	Merseybeats
I Think We're Alone Now	Tiffany
I Touch Myself	Divinyls
I Understand	Freddie & The Dreamers
I Wanna Be A Hippy	Technohead
I Wanna Be The Only One	Eternal Featuring Bebe Winans
I Wanna Be Your Man	Rolling Stones
I Wanna Dance Wit Choo'	Disco Tex & The Sex-O-Lettes
I Wanna Dance With Somebody (Who Loves Me)	Whitney Houston
I Wanna Do It With You	Barry Manilow
(I Wanna Give You) Devotion	Nomad Featuring MC Mikee Freedom
I Wanna Go Home	Lonnie Donegan
I Wanna Love You	Jade
I Wanna Sex You Up	Color Me Badd
I Wanna Stay With You	Gallagher & Lyle
I Want Candy	Bow Wow Wow
I Want It All	Queen
I Want That Man	Deborah Harry
(I Want To Be) Elected	Mr. Bean & Smear Campaign
I Want To Be Free	Toyah
I Want To Break Free	Queen
I Want To Hold Your Hand	Beatles
I Want To Know What Love Is	Foreigner
I Want To Stay Here	Steve Lawrence & Eydie Gorme
I Want To Wake Up With You	Boris Gardiner
I Want You	Bob Dylan
I Want You I Need You I Love You	Elvis Presley
I Want You Back	Bananarama
I Want You Back	Jackson Five
I Want You Back '88	Michael Jackson With The Jackson Five
I Want Your Love	Chic
I Want Your Love	Transvision Vamp
I Want Your Lovin' (Just A Little Bit)	Curtis Hairston
I Want Your Sex	George Michael
I Was Born To Love You	Freddie Mercury
I Was Kaiser Bill's Batman	Whistling Jack Smith
I Was Made For Dancin'	Leif Garrett
I Was Made To Love Her	Stevie Wonder
I Was Only Joking	Rod Stewart
I (Who Have Nothing)	Shirley Bassey
I Will	Billy Fury
I Will	Ruby Winters
I Will Always Love You	Whitney Houston
I Will Always Love You	Sarah Washington
I Will Come To You	Hanson
I Will Return	Springwater
I Will Survive	Gloria Gaynor
I Wish	Skee-Lo
I Wish	Stevie Wonder
I Wish It Could Be Christmas Everyday	Wizzard
I Wish It Would Rain	Faces
I Wish It Would Rain Down	Phil Collins
I Won't Come In While He's There	Jim Reeves
I Won't Forget You	Jim Reeves
I Won't Last A Day Without You	Carpenters
I Won't Let The Sun Go Down On Me	Nik Kershaw
I Won't Let You Down	PHD
I Won't Run Away	Alvin Stardust
I Wonder	Dickie Valentine
I Wonder Why	Showaddywaddy
I Wonder Why	Curtis Stigers
I Wouldn't Normally Do This Kind O f Thing	Pet Shop Boys
I Wouldn't Trade You For The World	Bachelors
I'd Lie For You (And That's The Truth)	Meat Loaf
I'd Like To Teach The World To Sing	New Seekers
I'd Love You To Want Me	Lobo
I'd Never Find Another You	Billy Fury
I'd Rather Go Blind	Chicken Shack
I'd Rather Jack	Reynolds Girls
I'll Be	Foxy Brown Featuring Jay Z
I'll Be Back	Arnee & The Terminators
I'll Be Home	Pat Boone
I'll Be Loving You (Forever)	New Kids On The Block
I'll Be Missing You	Puff Daddy & Faith Evans
I'll Be Satisfied	Shakin' Stevens
I'll Be There	Mariah Carey
I'll Be There	Gerry & The Pacemakers
I'll Be There	Jackson Five
I'll Be There For You	Rembrandts
I'll Be Your Baby Tonight	Robert Palmer And UB40
I'll Come When You Call	Ruby Murray
I'll Do Anything For Love (But I Won't Do That)	Meat Loaf
I'll Find My Way Home	Jon & Vangelis
I'll Fly For You	Spandau Ballet
I'll Get By	Shirley Bassey
I'll Keep You Satisfied	Billy J. Kramer & The Dakotas
I'll Make Love To You	Boyz II Men
I'll Meet You At Midnight	Smokie
I'll Never Break Your Heart	Backstreet Boys
I'll Never Fall In Love Again	Bobbie Gentry
I'll Never Fall In Love Again	Tom Jones
I'll Never Find Another You	Seekers
I'll Never Get Over You	Johnny Kidd & The Pirates
I'll Pick A Rose For My Rose	Marv Johnson
I'll Put You Together Again	Hot Chocolate
I'll Remember	Madonna
I'll Say Forever My Love	Jimmy Ruffin
I'll Stand By You	Pretenders
I'll Stop At Nothing	Sandie Shaw
I'll Take You Home Again Kathleen	Slim Whitman
I'm A Believer	EMF/Reeves And Mortimer
I'm A Believer	Monkees
I'm A Better Man	Engelbert Humperdinck
I'm A Boy	Who
I'm A Clown	David Cassidy
I'm A Man	Chicago
I'm A Man	Spencer Davis Group
I'm A Man Not A Boy	North & South
(I'm A) Road Runner	Jr. Walker & The All Stars
I'm A Tiger	Lulu
I'm A Wonderful Thing (Baby)	Kid Creole & The Coconuts
I'm Alive	Hollies
I'm Alive	Stretch & Vern Present Maddog
(I'm Always Touched By Your) Presence Dear	Blondie
I'm Comin' Home	Tom Jones
I'm Crying	Animals
I'm Doing Fine Now	Pasadenas
I'm Easy	Faith No More
I'm Every Woman	Whitney Houston
I'm Every Woman	Chaka Khan
I'm Falling	Bluebells
I'm Free	Soup Dragons
I'm Gonna Be	Proclaimers
I'm Gonna Be Strong	Gene Pitney
I'm Gonna Get Me A Gun	Cat Stevens
I'm Gonna Get You	Bizarre Inc
I'm Gonna Knock On Your Door	Little Jimmy Osmond
I'm Gonna Make You Love Me	Diana Ross & The Supremes & The Temptations
I'm Gonna Make You Mine	Lou Christie
I'm Gonna Run Away From You	Tami Lynn
I'm Gonna Tear Your Playhouse Down	Paul Young
I'm In Love Again	Fats Domino
I'm In The Mood For Dancing	Nolans
I'm Into Something Good	Herman's Hermits

Title	Artist	Title	Artist	Title	Artist
It Ain't What You Do It's The Way That You Do It	Fun Boy Three & Bananarama	It's No Good	Depeche Mode	Jig A Jig	East Of Eden
		It's Not Unusual	Tom Jones	Jilted John	Jilted John
It Didn't Matter	Style Council	It's Now Or Never	Elvis Presley	Jingle Bell Rock	Max Bygraves
It Doesn't Have To Be Me	Erasure	It's Oh So Quiet	Bjork	Jive Talkin'	Bee Gees
It Doesn't Have To Be That Way	Blow Monkeys	It's One Of Those Nights (Yes Love)	Partridge Family	Jive Talkin'	Boogie Box High
It Doesn't Matter Anymore	Buddy Holly	It's Only Love	Elvis Presley	Joan Of Arc	Orchestral Manoeuvres In The Dark
It Don't Come Easy	Ringo Starr	It's Only Love	Simply Red	Joanna	Kool & The Gang
It Hurts So Much	Jim Reeves	It's Only Make Believe	Glen Campbell	Joanna	Scott Walker
It Is Time To Get Funky	D. Mob Featuring LRS	It's Only Make Believe	Child	Joe Le Taxi	Vanessa Paradis
		It's Only Make Believe	Billy Fury	John And Julie	Eddie Calvert
It Keeps Rainin' (Tears From My Eyes)	Bitty McLean	It's Only Make Believe	Conway Twitty	John I'm Only Dancing	David Bowie
		It's Only Rock 'n Roll (But I Like It)	Rolling Stones	John I'm Only Dancing (Again)	David Bowie
It May Be Winter Outside (But In My Heart It's Spring)	Love Unlimited	It's Over	Funk Masters	John Wayne Is Big Leggy	Haysi Fantayzee
It Mek	Desmond Dekker & The Aces	It's Over	Level 42		
		It's Over	Roy Orbison	Johnny Come Home	Fine Young Cannibals
It Might As Well Rain Until September	Carole King	It's Raining	Darts		
		It's Raining	Shakin' Stevens	Johnny Reggae	Piglets
It Must Be Him	Vikki Carr	It's Raining Men	Weather Girls	Johnny Remember Me	John Leyton
It Must Be Love	Madness	It's So Easy	Andy Williams	Johnny Will	Pat Boone
It Must Be Love	Labi Siffre	It's Still Rock And Roll To Me	Billy Joel	Join Together	Who
It Must Have Been Love	Roxette	It's Time For Love	Chi-Lites	The Joker	Steve Miller Band
It Only Takes A Minute	One Hundred Ton & A Feather	It's Too Late	Carole King	Jolene	Dolly Parton
		It's Too Late	Quartz Introducing Dina Carroll	The Journey	911
It Only Takes A Minute	Take That			Joy	Soul II Soul
It Only Took A Minute	Joe Brown & The Bruvvers	It's Too Soon To Know	Pat Boone	Joybringer	Manfred Mann's Earth Band
		It's Too Soon To Know	Pat Boone	Joy Ride	Roxette
It Should Have Been Me	Yvonne Fair	It's Wonderful	Jimmy Ruffin	Judy In Disguise (With Glasses)	John Fred & His Playboy Band
It Started With A Kiss	Hot Chocolate	It's You	Freddie Starr		
It Sure Brings Out The Love In Your Eyes	David Soul	It's Your Life	Smokie	Judy Teen	Cockney Rebel
		Itchycoo Park	Small Faces	Juke Box Jive	Rubettes
It Takes Two	Rod Stewart & Tina Turner	Itsy Bitsy Teenie Weenie Yellow Polka Dot Bikini	Brian Hyland	Julia Says	Wet Wet Wet
It'll Be Me	Cliff Richard			Julie Ann	Kenny
It's A Fine Day	Opus Iii	Itsy Bitsy Teeny Weeny Yellow Polka Dot Bikini	Bombalurina	Julie, Do Ya Love Me	White Plains
It's A Hard Life	Queen			Juliet	Four Pennies
It's A Heartache	Bonnie Tyler	Ja-Da	Johnny & The Hurricanes	Jump	Kris Kross
It's A Love Thing	Whispers	Jack And Jill	Raydio	Jump	Van Halen
It's A Miracle	Culture Club	Jack In The Box	Moments	Jump Around	House Of Pain
It's A Shame (My Sister)	Monie Love Featuring True Image	Jack In The Box	Clodagh Rodgers	Jump (For My Love)	Pointer Sisters
		Jack Mix II	Mirage	Jump They Say	David Bowie
It's A Sin	Pet Shop Boys	Jack Mix IV	Mirage	Jump To The Beat	Stacy Lattisaw
It's A Sin To Tell A Lie	Gerry Monroe	Jack O' Diamonds	Lonnie Donegan	Jump To The Beat	Dannii Minogue
It's All Coming Back To Me Now	Celine Dion	The Jack That House Built	Jack 'n' Chill	Jumping Jack Flash	Rolling Stones
		Jack Your Body	Steve 'Silk' Hurley	Jungle Rock	Hank Mizell
It's All In The Game	Tommy Edwards	Jackie Wilson Said	Dexy's Midnight Runners	Just A Feeling	Bad Manners
It's All In The Game	Four Tops			Just A Girl	No Doubt
It's All In The Game	Cliff Richard	Jailhouse Rock	Elvis Presley	Just A Little Bit Better	Herman's Hermits
It's All Over	Cliff Richard	Jam	Michael Jackson	Just A Little Too Much	Ricky Nelson
It's All Over Now	Rolling Stones	Jambalaya	Carpenters	Just A Step From Heaven	Eternal
It's Almost Tomorrow	Dream Weavers	James Bond Theme	Moby	Just An Illusion	Imagination
It's Almost Tomorrow	Mark Wynter	Jamming	Bob Marley & The Wailers	Just Another Day	Jon Secada
It's Alright	East 17	January	Pilot	Just Can't Get Enough	Depeche Mode
It's Alright	Pet Shop Boys	January February	Barbara Dickson	Just Don't Want To Be Lonely	Freddie McGregor
It's Alright (Baby's Coming Back)	Eurythmics	Japanese Boy	Aneka		
		Jarrow Song	Alan Price	Just For You	Glitter Band
It's Been So Long	George McCrae	Jaws	Lalo Schifrin	Just For You	M People
It's Different For Girls	Joe Jackson	Jazz It Up	Reel 2 Real	Just Got Lucky	Joboxers
It's For You	Cilla Black	Je Ne Sais Pas Pourquoi	Kylie Minogue	Just Keep Rockin'	Double Trouble & Rebel M.C.
It's Four In The Morning	Faron Young	Je T'Aime (Moi Non Plus)	Judge Dread		
It's Getting Better	Mama Cass	Je T'Aime...Moi Non Plus	Jane Birkin & Serge Gainsbourg	Just Like A Woman	Manfred Mann
It's Gonna Be A Cold Cold Christmas	Dana			Just Like Eddie	Heinz
		Jealous Guy	Roxy Music	Just Like Jesse James	Cher
It's Good News Week	Hedgehoppers Anonymous	Jealous Mind	Alvin Stardust	(Just Like) Starting Over	John Lennon
		Jealousy	Billy Fury	Just Loving You	Anita Harris
It's Impossible	Perry Como	The Jean Genie	David Bowie	Just My Imagination (Runnin' Away With Me)	Temptations
It's In His Kiss	Linda Lewis	Jeans On	David Dundas		
It's Late	Ricky Nelson	Jeepster	T. Rex	Just One Look	Hollies
It's Late	Shakin' Stevens	Jennifer Eccles	Hollies	Just One More Night	Yellow Dog
It's Like That	Run-DMC Vs Jason Nevins	Jennifer Juniper	Donovan	Just One Smile	Gene Pitney
It's My Life	Animals	Jenny, Jenny	Little Richard	Just Say No	Grange Hill Cast
It's My Life	Dr. Alban	Jericho	Prodigy	Just The Way You Are	Barry White
It's My Party	Lesley Gore	Jesamine	Casuals	Just This Side Of Love	Malandra Burrows
It's My Party	Dave Stewart & Barbara Gaskin	Jesus To A Child	George Michael	Just Walkin' In The Rain	Johnnie Ray
		Jet	Paul McCartney	Just What I Always Wanted	Mari Wilson

Listing by title: Just When I Needed You Most to Let's Have A Ball

Title	Artist
Just When I Needed You Most	Randy Vanwarmer
Just Who Is The Five O'Clock Hero	Jam
Justified And Ancient	KLF
Justify My Love	Madonna
Karma Chameleon	Culture Club
Karma Police	Radiohead
Kate Bush On Stage E.P.	Kate Bush
Kayleigh	Marillion
(Keep Feeling) Fascination	Human League
Keep On	Bruce Channel
Keep On Dancin'	Gary's Gang
Keep On Dancing	Bay City Rollers
Keep On Jumpin'	Lisa Marie Experience
Keep On Jumpin'	Todd Terry Featuring Martha Wash & Jocelyn Brown
Keep On Loving You	REO Speedwagon
Keep On Movin'	Soul II Soul
Keep On Runnin'	Spencer Davis Group
Keep On Walkin'	Ce Ce Peniston
Keep Pushin'	Clock
Keep Searchin'(We'll Follow The Sun)	Del Shannon
Keep The Faith	Bon Jovi
Keeping The Dream Alive	Freiheit
Kevin Carter	Manic Street Preachers
Kewpie Doll	Perry Como
Kewpie Doll	Frankie Vaughan
The Key The Secret	Urban Cookie Collective
Key To My Life	Boyzone
Kid Galahad E.P.	Elvis Presley
The Kid's Last Fight	Frankie Laine
Kids In America	Kim Wilde
Killer	Adamski
Killer (EP)	Seal
Killer On The Loose	Thin Lizzy
Killer Queen	Queen
Killing Me Softly	Fugees
Killing Me Softly With His Song	Roberta Flack
The Killing Moon	Echo & The Bunnymen
The Killing Of Georgie	Rod Stewart
A Kind Of Magic	Queen
King	UB40
King Creole	Elvis Presley
The King Of Rock 'n' Roll	Prefab Sprout
King Of The Cops	Billy Howard
King Of The Road	Roger Miller
King Of The Road	Proclaimers
King Rocker	Generation X
Kings Of The Wild Frontier	Adam & The Ants
Kingston Town	UB40
Kinky Afro	Happy Mondays
Kinky Boots	Patrick MacNee & Honor Blackman
Kiss	Art Of Noise & Tom Jones
Kiss	Prince & The Revolution
Kiss And Say Goodbye	Manhattans
Kiss Me	Stephen 'Tin Tin' Duffy
Kiss Me Honey Honey Kiss Me	Shirley Bassey
Kiss Me Quick	Elvis Presley
Kiss The Rain	Billie Myers
Kiss You All Over	Exile
Kisses Sweeter Than Wine	Jimmie Rodgers
Kisses Sweeter Than Wine	Frankie Vaughan
Kissin' Cousins	Elvis Presley
Kissin' In The Back Row Of The Movies	Drifters
Kites	Simon Dupree & The Big Sound
Klubbhopping	Klubbheads
Knee Deep In The Blues	Guy Mitchell
Knock Knock Who's There	Mary Hopkin
Knock On Wood	David Bowie
Knock On Wood	Amii Stewart
Knock Three Times	Dawn
Knocked It Off	B.A. Robertson
Knockin' On Heaven's Door	Dunblane
Knockin' On Heaven's Door	Guns N' Roses
Knowing Me Knowing You	Abba
Kommotion	Duane Eddy
Kon-Tiki	Shadows
Kung Fu Fighting	Carl Douglas
Kung-Fu	187 Lockdown
Kyrie	Mr. Mister
La Bamba	Los Lobos
La Dee Dah	Jackie Dennis
La Isla Bonita	Madonna
La La La Hey Hey	Outhere Brothers
La Primavera	Sash!
La Vie En Rose	Grace Jones
Labelled With Love	Squeeze
Labour Of Love	Hue & Cry
Ladies Night	Kool & The Gang
Lady	Kenny Rogers
Lady Barbara	Herman's Hermits
Lady D'Arbanville	Cat Stevens
Lady Eleanor	Lindisfarne
The Lady In Red	Chris De Burgh
Lady Love Me (One More Time)	George Benson
Lady Lynda	Beach Boys
Lady Madonna	Beatles
Lady Rose	Mungo Jerry
Lady Willpower	Gary Puckett & The Union Gap
Lambada	Kaoma
Lamplight	David Essex
Lana	Roy Orbison
Land Of Confusion	Genesis
Land Of Make Believe	Bucks Fizz
Language Of Love	John D. Loudermilk
Last Christmas	Wham!
The Last Farewell	Roger Whittaker
The Last Kiss	David Cassidy
Last Night A D.J. Saved My Life	Indeep
Last Night In Soho	Dave, Dee, Dozy, Beaky, Mick & Tich
Last Night Was Made For Love	Billy Fury
Last Of The Famous International Playboys	Morrissey
The Last Time	Rolling Stones
Last Train To London	Electric Light Orchestra
Last Train To San Fernando	Johnny Duncan & The Blue Grass Boys
Last Train To Trancentral	KLF
The Last Waltz	Engelbert Humperdinck
Lately	Stevie Wonder
Laugh At Me	Sonny
The Laughing Gnome	David Bowie
Lavender	Marillion
Lay All Your Love On Me	Abba
Lay Back In The Arms Of Someone	Smokie
Lay Down	Strawbs
Lay Down Your Arms	Anne Shelton
Lay Lady Lay	Bob Dylan
Lay Your Love On Me	Racey
Layla	Derek & The Dominoes
Lazy Days	Robbie Williams
Lazy River	Bobby Darin
Lazy Sunday	Small Faces
Le Freak	Chic
Leader Of The Pack	Shangri-Las
Lean On Me	Club Nouveau
Lean On Me	Mud
Lean On Me (Ah-Li-Ayo)	Red Box
Leap Up And Down (Wave Your Knickers In The Air)	St. Cecilia
Learnin' The Blues	Frank Sinatra
Leave A Light On	Belinda Carlisle
Leave A Little Love	Lulu
Leave Me Alone	Michael Jackson
Leavin' On A Jet Plane	Peter, Paul & Mary
The Lebanon	Human League
Leeds United	Leeds United F.C.
Left Bank	Winifred Atwell
Left To My Own Devices	Pet Shop Boys
Legend Of Xanadu	Dave, Dee, Dozy, Beaky, Mick & Tich
Les Bicyclettes De Belsize	Engelbert Humperdinck
Lessons In Love	Level 42
Let 'Em In	Paul McCartney
Let A Boy Cry	Gala
Let It Be	Beatles
Let It Be	Ferry Aid
Let It Rain	East 17
Let Me Be The One	Shadows
Let Me Be Your Fantasy	Baby D
Let Me Cry On Your Shoulder	Ken Dodd
Let Me Entertain You	Robbie Williams
Let Me Go, Lover	Teresa Brewer
Let Me Go, Lover	Kathy Kirby
Let Me Go, Lover	Dean Martin
Let Me Go, Lover	Ruby Murray
Let Me In	Osmonds
Let Me Show You	Camisra
Let Me Try Again	Tammy Jones
Let The Beat Control Your Body	2 Unlimited
Let The Heartaches Begin	Long John Baldry
Let The Little Girl Dance	Billy Bland
Let The Music Play	Barry White
Let The Sunshine In	Fifth Dimension
Let There Be Drums	Sandy Nelson
Let There Be Love	Nat 'King' Cole
Let There Be Love	Simple Minds
Let Your Love Flow	Bellamy Brothers
Let Your Yeah Be Yeah	Pioneers
Let's All Chant	Mick And Pat
Let's All Chant	Michael Zager Band
Let's Dance	David Bowie
Let's Dance	Chris Montez
Let's Dance	Chris Rea
Let's Get It Up	AC/DC
Let's Get Ready To Rumble	PJ And Duncan
Let's Get Rocked	Def Leppard
Let's Get Serious	Jermaine Jackson
Let's Get Together	Hayley Mills
Let's Get Together Again	Glitter Band
Let's Get Together No. 1	Big Ben Banjo Band
Let's Go All The Way	Sly Fox
Let's Go Crazy	Prince & The Revolution
Let's Go Round Again Pt. 1	Average White Band
Let's Go To San Francisco	Flowerpot Men
Let's Groove	Earth, Wind & Fire
Let's Hang On	Darts
Let's Hang On!	Four Seasons
Let's Have A Ball	Winifred Atwell

335

Title	Artist
Let's Have A Ding Dong	Winifred Atwell
Let's Have A Party	Winifred Atwell
Let's Have A Quiet Night In	David Soul
Let's Have Another Party	Winifred Atwell
Let's Hear It For The Boy	Deniece Williams
Let's Jump The Broomstick	Brenda Lee
Let's Party	Jive Bunny & The Mastermixers
Let's Pretend	Lulu
Let's Put It All Together	Stylistics
Let's Spend The Night Together	Rolling Stones
Let's Stay Together	Al Green
Let's Stay Together	Tina Turner
Let's Stick Together	Bryan Ferry
Let's Talk About Love	Helen Shapiro
Let's Talk About Sex	Salt-N-Pepa
Let's Think About Living	Bob Luman
Let's Try Again	New Kids On The Block
Let's Turkey Trot	Little Eva
Let's Twist Again	Chubby Checker
Let's Wait Awhile	Janet Jackson
Let's Work Together	Canned Heat
The Letter	Box Tops
Letter From America	Proclaimers
A Letter To You	Shakin' Stevens
LFO	LFO
Licence To Kill	Gladys Knight
Lido Shuffle	Boz Scaggs
Lie To Me	Bon Jovi
Lies	Status Quo
Life	Haddaway
Life Is A Long Song	Jethro Tull
Life Is A Minestone	10cc
Life Is Too Short Girl	Sheer Elegance
Life On Mars	David Bowie
Lifeline	Spandau Ballet
Lifted	Lighthouse Family
Light My Fire	Clubhouse Featuring Carl
Light My Fire	Doors
Light My Fire	Jose Feliciano
(Light Of Experience) Doina De Jale	Georghe Zamfir
Light Of My Life	Louise
Lightnin' Strikes	Lou Christie
Lights Of Cincinati	Scott Walker
Massachusetts	Bee Gees
Like A Baby	Len Barry
Like A Prayer	Madonna
Like A Rolling Stone	Bob Dylan
Like A Virgin	Madonna
Like Clockwork	Boomtown Rats
Like I Do	Maureen Evans
Like I've Never Been Gone	Billy Fury
Like Sister And Brother	Drifters
Like To Get To Know You Well	Howard Jones
Lil' Devil	Cult
Lily The Pink	Scaffold
Lily Was Here	David A. Stewart Introd. Candy Dulfer
The Lion Sleeps Tonight	Tight Fit
The Lion Sleeps Tonight	Tokens
Lip Up Fatty	Bad Manners
Lipstick On Your Collar	Connie Francis
Liquidator	Harry J. & The All Stars
Listen To Me	Hollies
Listen To What The Man Said	Paul McCartney
Listen To Your Heart	Roxette
Listen To Your Heart	Sonia
Little Arrows	Leapy Lee
Little Bird	Annie Lennox
A Little Bit Me, A Little Bit You	Monkees
A Little Bit More	Dr. Hook
A Little Bit Of Soap	Showaddywaddy
Little Bit Of Love	Free
A Little Bitty Tear	Burl Ives
A Little Boogie Woogie (In The Back Of My Mind)	Shakin' Stevens
Little Brown Jug	Glenn Miller
Little Children	Billy J. Kramer & The Dakotas
Little Darlin'	Diamonds
Little Devil	Neil Sedaka
Little Does She Know	Kursaal Flyers
Little Donkey	Beverley Sisters
Little Donkey	Nina & Frederick
Little Drummer Boy	David Bowie
Little Drummer Boy	Royal Scots Dragoon Guards
Little Drummer Boy	Harry Simeone Chorale
The Little Drummer Boy	Beverley Sisters
Little Fluffy Clouds	Orb
Little Lies	Fleetwood Mac
A Little Love, A Little Kiss	Karl Denver
A Little Love And Understanding	Gilbert Becaud
A Little Loving	Fourmost
Little Man	Sonny & Cher
Little Miss Lonely	Helen Shapiro
A Little More Love	Olivia Newton-John
A Little Peace	Nicole
Little Red Corvette	Prince & The Revolution
Little Red Rooster	Rolling Stones
A Little Respect	Erasure
The Little Shoemaker	Petula Clark
The Little Shoemaker	Frank Weir
Little Things	Dave Berry
Little Things Mean A Lot	Alma Cogan
Little Things Mean A Lot	Kitty Kallen
Little Things Mean A Lot	Jimmy Young
A Little Time	Beautiful South
Little Town Flirt	Del Shannon
Little White Bull	Tommy Steele
Little Willie	Sweet
Live And Let Die	Guns N' Roses
Live And Let Die	Paul McCartney
Live Forever	Oasis
Live In Trouble	Barron Knights
Live Is Life	Opus
Live It Up	Mental As Anything
Live The Dream	Cast
Live To Tell	Madonna
Live Together	Lisa Stansfield
Live Your Life Be Free	Belinda Carlisle
Lively	Lonnie Donegan
Liverpool Lou	Scaffold
Livin' On A Prayer	Bon Jovi
Livin' Thing	Electric Light Orchestra
Living After Midnight	Judas Priest
Living By Numbers	New Muzik
The Living Daylights	A-Ha
Living Doll	Cliff Richard
Living Doll	Cliff Richard & The Young Ones
Living In A Box	Living In A Box
Living In America	James Brown
Living In Harmony	Cliff Richard
Living In The Past	Jethro Tull
Living Next Door To Alice	Smokie
Living On My Own	Freddie Mercury
Living On The Ceiling	Blancmange
Living On The Front Line	Eddy Grant
Living On Video	Trans-X
The Living Years	Mike + The Mechanics
L-L-Lucy	Mud
Loadsamoney (Doin' Up The House)	Harry Enfield
Loco In Acapulco	Four Tops
The Loco-Motion	Little Eva
The Loco-Motion	Kylie Minogue
Locomotion	Orchestral Manoeuvres In The Dark
The Logical Song	Supertramp
Lola	Kinks
Lollipop	Chordettes
Lollipop	Mudlarks
London Calling	Clash
London Nights	London Boys
The Lone Ranger	Quantum Jump
Lonely	Peter Andre
Lonely	Acker Bilk
Lonely Boy	Paul Anka
Lonely Boy	Andrew Gold
Lonely Pup (In A Christmas Shop)	Adam Faith
Lonely This Christmas	Mud
Lonesome	Adam Faith
Long Haired Lover From Liverpool	Little Jimmy Osmond
Long Hot Summer	Style Council
Long Legged Woman Dressed In Black	Mungo Jerry
Long Live Love	Olivia Newton-John
Long Live Love	Sandie Shaw
Long Tall Glasses	Leo Sayer
Long Tall Sally	Little Richard
Long Train Runnin'	Doobie Brothers
The Look	Roxette
Look Around	Vince Hill
Look Away	Big Country
Look For A Star	Garry Mills
Look Homeward Angel	Johnnie Ray
The Look Of Love	Madonna
The Look Of Love (Part 1)	ABC
Look Through Any Window	Hollies
Look Wot You Dun	Slade
Lookin' Through The Eyes Of Love	Partridge Family
Lookin' Through The Windows	Jackson Five
Looking After Number One	Boomtown Rats
Looking For A New Love	Jody Watley
Looking Through Patient Eyes	P.M. Dawn
Looking Through The Eyes Of Love	Gene Pitney
Looking Up	Michelle Gayle
Loop De Loop	Frankie Vaughan
Loop Di Love	Shag
Loser	Beck
Losing My Mind	Liza Minnelli
Losing You	Brenda Lee
Losing You	Dusty Springfield
Lost In France	Bonnie Tyler
Lost John	Lonnie Donegan
Louise	Human League
Loungin'	LL Cool J
Love Action (I Believe In Love)	Human League
Love Ain't Here Anymore	Take That
Love And Affection	Joan Armatrading
Love & Kisses	Dannii Minogue
Love And Marriage	Frank Sinatra
Love & Pride	King
Love And Understanding	Cher
Love Bites	Def Leppard

Title	Artist
Love Can Build A Bridge	Cher, Chrissie Hynde & Neneh Cherry With Eric Clapton
Love Can't Turn Around	Farley 'Jackmaster' Funk
The Love Cats	Cure
Love Changes (Everything)	Climie Fisher
Love Changes Everything	Michael Ball
Love Child	Diana Ross & The Supremes
Love City Groove	Love City Groove
Love Come Down	Evelyn 'Champagne' King
Love Don't Live Here Anymore	Jimmy Nail
Love Don't Live Here Anymore	Rose Royce
Love Games	Belle & The Devotions
Love Grows (Where My Rosemary Goes)	Edison Lighthouse
Love Guaranteed	Damage
Love Hangover	Diana Ross
Love Hit Me	Maxine Nightingale
Love Hurts	Jim Capaldi
The Love I Lost	West End Featuring Sybil
Love In The First Degree	Bananarama
Love In The Sun	Glitter Band
Love Is A Many Splendoured Thing	Four Aces
Love Is A Stranger	Eurythmics
Love Is All	Malcolm Roberts
Love Is All Around	Troggs
Love Is All Around	Wet Wet Wet
Love Is Blue (L'Amour Est Bleu)	Paul Mauriat
Love Is Contagious	Taja Sevelle
Love Is In The Air	John Paul Young
Love Is Life	Hot Chocolate
Love Is Like A Violin	Ken Dodd
Love Is Like Oxygen	Sweet
Love Is Strange	Everly Brothers
Love Is The Drug	Roxy Music
Love Is The Law	Seahorses
Love Kills	Freddie Mercury
Love Letters	Ketty Lester
Love Letters	Alison Moyet
Love Letters	Elvis Presley
Love Letters In The Sand	Pat Boone
Love Like A Man	Ten Years After
Love Machine	Miracles
Love Makes The World Go Round	Perry Como
Love Me	Yvonne Elliman
Love Me As If There Were No Tomorrow	Nat 'King' Cole
Love Me Do	Beatles
Love Me For A Reason	Boyzone
Love Me For A Reason	Osmonds
Love Me Forever	Marion Ryan
Love Me Like I Love You	Bay City Rollers
Love Me Love My Dog	Peter Shelley
Love Me Or Leave Me	Sammy Davis Jr.
Love Me Tender	Elvis Presley
Love Me Tonight	Tom Jones
Love Missile F1-11	Sigue Sigue Sputnik
Love Of My Life	Dooleys
Love Of The Common People	Nicky Thomas
Love Of The Common People	Paul Young
Love On A Mountain Top	Robert Knight
Love On Your Side	Thompson Twins
Love Plus One	Haircut 100
Love Really Hurts Without You	Billy Ocean
Love Rears It's Ugly Head	Living Colour
Love Resurrection	Alison Moyet
Love Rollercoaster	Red Hot Chili Peppers
Love Shack	B-52's
Love Shine A Light	Katrina & The Waves
Love Song For A Vampire	Annie Lennox
Love Spreads	Stone Roses
Love Theme From 'The Thorn Birds'	Juan Martin
Love...Thy Will Be Done	Martika
Love To Hate You	Erasure
Love To Love You Baby	Donna Summer
Love Town	Booker Newberry III
Love Train	Holly Johnson
Love Train	O'Jays
Love Will Save The Day	Whitney Houston
Love Will Tear Us Apart	Joy Division
Love Won't Wait	Gary Barlow
A Love Worth Waiting For	Shakin' Stevens
Love You Inside Out	Bee Gees
The Love You Save	Jackson Five
Love's Been Good To Me	Frank Sinatra
Love's Gotta Hold On Me	Dollar
Love's Great Adventure	Ultravox
Love's Just A Broken Heart	Cilla Black
Love's Theme	Love Unlimited Orchestra
Love's Unkind	Donna Summer
Lovefool	Cardigans
Lovely Day	Bill Withers
Lover Come Back To Me	Dead Or Alive
A Lover's Concerto	Toys
Loverboy	Billy Ocean
Lovers Of The World Unite	David & Jonathan
Lovesick Blues	Frank Ifield
Lovin' Things	Marmalade
Loving You	Minnie Riperton
Loving And Free	Kiki Dee
Low Rider	War
L.S.I.	Shamen
Lucille	Little Richard
Lucille	Kenny Rogers
Lucky Five	Russ Conway
Lucky Lips	Cliff Richard
Lucky Man	Verve
Lucky Number	Lene Lovich
Lucky Stars	Dean Friedman
Lucy In The Sky With Diamonds	Elton John
Lullaby	Cure
Luv 4 Luv	Robin S.
Ma Baker	Boney M
Ma He's Making Eyes At Me	Johnny Otis Show
Ma He's Making Eyes At Me	Lena Zavaroni
Macarena (Bayside Boys Mix)	Los Del Rio
MacArthur Park	Richard Harris
MacArthur Park	Donna Summer
MacDonald's Cave	Piltdown Men
Mack The Knife	Bobby Darin
Mad About You	Bruce Ruffin
Mad Passionate Love	Bernard Bresslaw
Mad World	Tears For Fears
Madame Butterfly	Malcolm McLaren
Made You	Adam Faith
Madness (Is All In The Mind)	Madness
Maggie May	Rod Stewart
Maggie's Farm	Specials
Magic	Pilot
Magic Fly	Space
Magic Friend	2 Unlimited
Magic Moments	Perry Como
Magic Moments	Perry Como
The Magic Number	De La Soul
Magic Roundabout	Jasper Carrott
Magical Mystery Tour (Double E.P.)	Beatles
Mah Na Mah Na	Piero Umiliani
Maid Of Orleans (The Waltz Joan Of Arc)	Orchestral Manoeuvres In The Dark
The Main Attraction	Pat Boone
Main Title Theme From 'Man With The Golden Arm'	Jet Harris
Main Title Theme From The Man With The Golden Arm	Billy May
Mais Qui	King Brothers
Majorca	Petula Clark
Make It A Party	Winifred Atwell
Make It Easy On Yourself	Walker Brothers
Make It With You	Bread
Make It With You	Let Loose
Make Love To Me!	Jo Stafford
Make Me An Island	Joe Dolan
Make Me Smile (Come Up And See Me)	Steve Harley & Cockney Rebel
Make The World Go Away	Eddy Arnold
Makin' Love	Floyd Robinson
Making Up Again	Goldie
Making Your Mind Up	Bucks Fizz
Male Stripper	Man 2 Man Meet Man Parrish
Malt And Barley Blues	McGuinness Flint
Mama	Dave Berry
Mama	Connie Francis
Mama	Genesis
Mama	Spice Girls
Mama	David Whitfield
Mama Told Me (Not To Come)	Three Dog Night
Mama Used To Say	Junior
Mama Weer All Crazee Now	Slade
Mambo Italiano	Rosemary Clooney
Mambo Italiano	Dean Martin
Mamma Gave Birth To The Soul Children	Queen Latifah & De La Soul
Mamma Mia	Abba
The Man From Laramie	Jimmy Young
Man Of Mystery	Shadows
Man Of The World	Fleetwood Mac
Man On Fire	Frankie Vaughan
Man On The Edge	Iron Maiden
Man To Man	Hot Chocolate
The Man Who Sold The World	Lulu
Man With The Child In His Eyes	Kate Bush
A Man Without Love	Engelbert Humperdinck
Manchild	Neneh Cherry
Mandolins In The Moonlight	Perry Como
Mandy	Eddie Calvert
Mandy	Barry Manilow
Maneater	Daryl Hall & John Oates
Manic Monday	Bangles
Many Tears Ago	Connie Francis
Marblehead Johnson	Bluetones
March Of The Siamese Children	Kenny Ball
Marcheta	Karl Denver
Marguerita Time	Status Quo

Title	Artist
Maria	P.J. Proby
Maria Elena	Los Indios Tabajaras
Mariana	Gibson Brothers
Marie	Bachelors
His Latest Flame	Elvis Presley
Martha's Harbour	All About Eve
Mary Had A Little Boy	Snap
Mary Had A Little Lamb	Paul McCartney
Mary Of The Fourth Form	Boomtown Rats
Mary's Boy Child	Harry Belafonte
Mary's Boy Child-Oh My Lord	Boney M
Mary's Prayer	Danny Wilson
Masquerade	Skids
Master And Servant	Depeche Mode
Master Blaster (Jammin')	Stevie Wonder
Matchstalk Men And Matchstalk Cats And Dogs	Brian & Michael
Material Girl	Madonna
Matthew And Son	Cat Stevens
May I Have The Next Dream With You	Malcolm Roberts
May You Always	McGuire Sisters
May You Always	Joan Regan
Maybe	Thom Pace
Maybe Baby	Crickets
Me And Mrs Jones	Billy Paul
Me And My Life	Tremeloes
Me And You And A Dog Named Boo	Lobo
Me And You Versus The World	Space
Me The Peaceful Heart	Lulu
Mean Streak	Cliff Richard
Meet Me On The Corner	Max Bygraves
Meet Me On The Corner	Lindisfarne
(Meet) The Flintstones	BC-52s
Megablast	Bomb The Bass
Megamix	Technotronic
Mellow Yellow	Donovan
Melody Of Love	Ink Spots
Melting Pot	Blue Mink
Memories Are Made Of This	Val Doonican
Memories Are Made Of This	Dave King
Memories Are Made Of This	Dean Martin
Memory	Elaine Paige
Memphis Tennessee	Chuck Berry
Men In Black	Will Smith
Mercy Mercy Me - I Want You	Robert Palmer
Merrie Gentle Pops	Barron Knights
Merry Christmas Everyone	Shakin' Stevens
Merry Xmas Everybody	Slade
A Mess Of Blues	Elvis Presley
The Message	Grandmaster Flash, Melle Mel & The Furio
Message In A Bottle	Police
Message Of Love	Pretenders
Message To Martha (Kentucky Bluebird)	Adam Faith
A Message To You Rudy	Specials
Message Understood	Sandie Shaw
Messages	Orchestral Manoeuvres In The Dark
Metal Guru	T. Rex
Mexicali Rose	Karl Denver
Mexico	Long John Baldry
Miami Hit Mix	Gloria Estefan
Miami Vice Theme	Jan Hammer
Michael	Highwaymen
Michael Caine	Madness
Michael Row The Boat	Lonnie Donegan
Michelle	David & Jonathan

Title	Artist
Michelle	Overlanders
Mickey	Toni Basil
Midas Touch	Midnight Star
Midlife Crisis	Faith No More
Midnight	Eddie Calvert
Midnight At The Oasis	Brand New Heavies
Midnight In Cheisea	Jon Bon Jovi
Midnight In Moscow	Kenny Ball
Midnight Rider	Paul Davidson
Midnight Train To Georgia	Gladys Knight & The Pips
Midnite Dynamos	Matchbox
Mighty Quinn	Manfred Mann
Milk And Alcohol	Dr. Feelgood
A Million Love Songs (EP)	Take That
Mind Blowing Decision	Heatwave
Mind Blowing Decisions	Heatwave
Mind Of A Toy	Visage
A Minute Of Your Time	Tom Jones
The Minute You're Gone	Cliff Richard
Mirror In The Bathroom	Beat
Mirror Man	Human League
Mirror Mirror	Pinkerton's Assorted Colours
Mirror Mirror (Mon Amour)	Dollar
Mis-Shapes	Pulp
Misfit	Curiosity Killed The Cat
Miss Sarajevo	Passengers
Miss You	Rolling Stones
Miss You Like Crazy	Natalie Cole
Miss You Nights	Cliff Richard
Mrs. Robinson (E.P.)	Simon & Garfunkel
Mrs. Robinson	Simon & Garfunkel
Missing	Everything But The Girl
Missing You	Chris De Burgh
Missing You	John Waite
Mississippi	Pussycat
Mistletoe And Wine	Cliff Richard
Misty	Johnny Mathis
Misty	Ray Stevens
Misty Blue	Dorothy Moore
Mmm Mmm Mmm Mmm	Crash Test Dummies
Mmmbop	Hanson
Mo Money Mo Problems	Notorious B.I.G. Featuring Puff Daddy & Mase
Mobile	Ray Burns
Mockingbird Hill	Migil Five
The Model	Kraftwerk
Modern Girl	Sheena Easton
Modern Love	David Bowie
Moments In Soul	JT And The Big Family
Mona	Craig McLachlan & Check 1-2
Mona Lisa	Conway Twitty
Monday Monday	Mamas & The Papas
Money	Flying Lizards
Money For Nothing	Dire Straits
Money Go Round (Pt.1)	Style Council
Money Honey	Bay City Rollers
Money Money Money	Abba
Money's Too Tight (To Mention)	Simply Red
Monkey Spanner	Dave & Ansil Collins
Monsieur Dupont	Sandie Shaw
Montego Bay	Amazulu
Montego Bay	Bobby Bloom
Montreux EP	Simply Red
Mony Mony	Billy Idol
Mony Mony	Tommy James & The Shondells
Moody Blue	Elvis Presley
Moody River	Pat Boone
Moon River	Greyhound
Moon River	Danny Williams

Title	Artist
Moonglow/Theme From 'Picnic'	Morris Stoloff
Moonlight Gambler	Frankie Laine
Moonlight Serenade	Glenn Miller
Moonlight Shadow	Mike Oldfield
Moonlighting	Leo Sayer
Moonlighting ('Theme')	Al Jarreau
Moonshine Sally	Mud
More	Perry Como
More	Jimmy Young
More And More Party Pops	Russ Conway
The More I See You	Chris Montez
More Like The Movies	Dr. Hook
More, More, More	Andrea True Connection
More Party Pops	Russ Conway
More Than A Woman	Tavares
More Than Ever (Come Prima)	Malcolm Vaughan
More Than I Can Say	Leo Sayer
More Than I Can Say	Bobby Vee
More Than In Love	Kate Robbins
More Than This	Roxy Music
More Than Words	Extreme
More To This World	Bad Boys Inc
The More You Ignore Me, The Closer I Get	Morrissey
Theme From 'The Three Penny Opera'	Dick Hyman
Morning	Val Doonican
Morning Has Broken	Cat Stevens
Morning Side Of The Mountain	Donny & Marie Osmond
9 to 5 (a.k.a. Morning Train)	Sheena Easton
Morningtown Ride	Seekers
The Most Beautiful Girl	Charlie Rich
The Most Beautiful Girl In The World	Prince
Mother & Child Reunion	Paul Simon
Mother Of Mine	Neil Reid
Motor Biking	Chris Spedding
Motorhead Live	Motorhead
The Motown Song	Rod Stewart
Mouldy Old Dough	Lieutenant Pigeon
Mountain Greenery	Mel Torme
Move Any Mountain	Shamen
Move Away	Culture Club
Move Closer	Phyllis Nelson
Move It	Cliff Richard
Move Move Move (The Red Tribe)	Manchester United FA Cup Squad
Move On Baby	Cappella
Move Over Darling	Doris Day
Move Over Darling	Tracey Ullman
Move That Body	Technotronic Featuring Reggie
Move Your Body (Elevation)	Xpansions
Moving On Up	M People
Mozart Symphony No. 40 In G Minor	Waldo De Los Rios
Mr. Blobby	Mr. Blobby
Mr. Blue	Mike Preston
Mr. Blue Sky	Electric Light Orchestra
Mr. Custer	Charlie Drake
Mr. Loverman	Shabba Ranks
Mr. Sandman	Chordettes
Mr. Sandman	Four Aces
Mr. Sandman	Dickie Valentine
Mr. Sleaze	Bananarama
Mr. Soft	Cockney Rebel
Mr. Tambourine Man	Byrds
Mr. Vain	Culture Beat
Mr. Wendal	Arrested Development

Title	Artist
Mr. Wonderful	Peggy Lee
Ms Grace	Tymes
Mulder And Scully	Catatonia
Multiplication	Bobby Darin
Musclebound	Spandau Ballet
Music	John Miles
Music And Lights	Imagination
The Music Of The Night	Michael Crawford/Sarah Brightman
The Music Of Torvill & Dean EP	Richard Hartley/Michael Reed Orchestra
Musique	Daft Punk
A Must To Avoid	Herman's Hermits
My Arms Keep Missing You	Rick Astley
My Baby Just Cares For Me	Nina Simone
My Baby Loves Lovin'	White Plains
My Best Friend's Girl	Cars
My Boomerang Won't Come Back	Charlie Drake
My Boy	Elvis Presley
My Boy Lollipop	Millie Small
My Brother Jake	Free
My Camera Never Lies	Bucks Fizz
My Cherie Amour	Stevie Wonder
My Coo-Ca-Choo	Alvin Stardust
My Destiny	Lionel Richie
My Ding-A-Ling	Chuck Berry
My Dixie Darling	Lonnie Donegan
My Ever Changing Mood	Style Council
My Eyes Adored You	Frankie Valli
My Favourite Waste Of Time	Owen Paul
My Friend	Frankie Laine
My Friend Stan	Slade
My Friend The Sea	Petula Clark
My Generation	Who
My Girl	Madness
My Girl	Otis Redding
My Girl	Temptations
My Girl Lollipop (My Boy Lollipop)	Bad Manners
My Guy	Mary Wells
My Happiness	Connie Francis
My Heart Has A Mind Of Its Own	Connie Francis
My Heart Will Go On	Celine Dion
My Hometown	Bruce Springsteen
My Kind Of Girl	Matt Monro
My Life	Billy Joel
My Little Lady	Tremeloes
My Love	Petula Clark
My Love	Julio Iglesias (featuring Stevie Wonder)
My Love	Paul McCartney
My Love For You	Johnny Mathis
My Lovin'	En Vogue
My Mind's Eye	Small Faces
My Name Is Jack	Manfred Mann
My Name Is Prince	Prince & The New Power Generation
My Oh My	Slade
My Old Man's A Dustman	Lonnie Donegan
My Old Piano	Diana Ross
My One Temptation	Mica Paris
My Perfect Cousin	Undertones
My Prayer	Gerry Monroe
My Prayer	Platters
My Prerogative	Bobby Brown
My Pretty One	Cliff Richard
My Resistance Is Low	Robin Sarstedt
My Sentimental Friend	Herman's Hermits
My September Love	David Whitfield
My Sharona	Knack
My Ship Is Coming In	Walker Brothers
My Simple Heart	Three Degrees

Title	Artist
My Son My Son	Vera Lynn
My Special Angel	Malcolm Vaughan
My Star	Ian Brown
My Sweet Lord	George Harrison
My Toot Toot	Denise La Salle
My True Love	Jack Scott
My Way	Elvis Presley
My Way	Sex Pistols
My Way	Frank Sinatra
My Way Of Thinking	UB40
Mysterious Girl	Peter Andre Feat Bubbler Ranx
Mystery Song	Status Quo
Na Na Hey Hey Kiss Him Goodbye	Bananarama
Na Na Hey Hey Kiss Him Goodbye	Steam
Na Na Is The Saddest Word	Stylistics
Na Na Na	Cozy Powell
Nairobi	Tommy Steele
Naked	Louise
Naked In The Rain	Blue Pearl
Name And Number	Curiosity Killed The Cat
The Name Of The Game	Abba
Nancy Boy	Placebo
Nathan Jones	Supremes
Native New Yorker	Odyssey
Natural	Peter Andre
Natural Born Bugie	Humble Pie
Natural Sinner	Fair Weather
Naughty Lady Of Shady Lane	Dean Martin
The Naughty Lady Of Shady Lane	Ames Brothers
Neanderthal Man	Hotlegs
Need You Tonight	Inxs
Needles And Pins	Searchers
Needles And Pins	Smokie
Volare	Domenico Modugno
Nellie The Elephant	Toy Dolls
Nelson Mandela	Special AKA
Nessun Dorma	Luciano Pavarotti
Never	Heart
Never Can Say Goodbye	Communards
Never Can Say Goodbye	Gloria Gaynor
Never Do A Tango With An Eskimo	Alma Cogan
Never Ending Song Of Love	New Seekers
Never Ending Story	Limahl
Never Ever	All Saints
Never Forget	Take That
Never Gonna Give You Up	Rick Astley
Never Gonna Give You Up	Musical Youth
Never Gonna Let You Go	Tina Moore
Never Goodbye	Karl Denver
Never Had A Dream Come True	Stevie Wonder
Never Knew Love Like This Before	Stephanie Mills
Never Let Her Slip Away	Andrew Gold
Never Let Her Slip Away	Undercover
Never Never	Assembly
Never, Never Gonna Give Ya Up	Barry White
Never Never Land	Frank Weir
Never Never Never	Shirley Bassey
Never Too Late	Kylie Minogue
Never Too Much (89 Remix)	Luther Vandross
Never Trust A Stranger	Kim Wilde
Never Turn Your Back On Mother	

Title	Artist
Earth	Sparks
New Beginning (Mamba Sayra)	Bucks Fizz
A New England	Kirsty MacColl
New Life	Depeche Mode
New Moon On Monday	Duran Duran
New Song	Howard Jones
New Year's Day	U2
New York Groove	Hello
New York Mining Disaster 1941	Bee Gees
The Next Time	Cliff Richard
The Night	Frankie Valli & Four Seasons
Night Birds	Shakatak
The Night Chicago Died	Paper Lace
Night Fever	Bee Gees
Night Games	Graham Bonnett
The Night Has A Thousand Eyes	Bobby Vee
Night Of Fear	Move
Night Owl	Gerry Rafferty
The Night They Drove Old Dixie Down	Joan Baez
A Night To Remember	Shalamar
Night Train	Visage
Nights On Broadway	Candi Staton
Nightshift	Commodores
Nikita	Elton John
Nine Times Out Of Ten	Cliff Richard
19	Paul Hardcastle
1999	Prince & The Revolution
1979	Smashing Pumpkins
19th Nervous Breakdown	Rolling Stones
99 Red Balloons	Nena
Ninety-Nine Ways	Tab Hunter
Nite Klub	Specials
No Arms Could Ever Hold You	Bachelors
No Charge	J.J. Barrie
No Diggity	Blackstreet Featuring Dr Dre
No Doubt About It	Hot Chocolate
No Fronts - The Remixes	Dog Eat Dog
No Good (Start The Dance)	Prodigy
No Honestly	Lynsey De Paul
No Limit	2 Unlimited
No Matter How I Try	Gilbert O'Sullivan
No Matter What	Badfinger
No Milk Today	Herman's Hermits
No More 'I Love Yous'	Annie Lennox
No More (I Can't Stand It)	Maxx
No More Heroes	Stranglers
No More Lonely Nights (Ballad)	Paul McCartney
No More Mr. Nice Guy	Alice Cooper
No More Tears (Enough Is Enough)	Kym Mazelle & Jocelyn Brown
No More Tears (Enough Is Enough)	Barbra Streisand
No More The Fool	Elkie Brooks
No One But You	Billy Eckstine
No One Can Make My Sunshine Smile	Everly Brothers
No One Is Innocent	Sex Pistols
No Other Love	Ronnie Hilton
No Particular Place To Go	Chuck Berry
No Regrets	Midge Ure
No Regrets	Walker Brothers
No Sleep Till Brooklyn	Beastie Boys
No Son Of Mine	Genesis
No Surprises	Radiohead
No Woman No Cry	Fugees
No Woman No Cry	Bob Marley & The Wailers
No, No, No	Destiny's Child
Nobody Does It Better	Carly Simon
Nobody I Know	Peter & Gordon

Title	Artist
The Other Side Of Love	Yazoo
Our Favourite Melodies	Craig Douglas
Our House	Madness
Our Lips Are Sealed	Fun Boy Three
Out In The Fields	Gary Moore & Phil Lynott
Out Of Space	Prodigy
Out Of Time	Chris Farlowe
Over My Shoulder	Mike + The Mechanics
Over Under Sideways Down	Yardbirds
Over You	Freddie & The Dreamers
Over You	Roxy Music
Oxygene Part IV	Jean-Michel Jarre
Pacific	808 State
Paint It Black	Rolling Stones
Painter Man	Boney M
Pale Shelter	Tears For Fears
Paloma Blanca	George Baker Selection
Pamela Pamela	Wayne Fontana
Pandora's Box	OMD
Panic	Smiths
Papa Don't Preach	Madonna
Papa Was A Rolling Stone	Was (Not Was)
Papa's Got A Brand New Pigbag	Pigbag
Paper Plane	Status Quo
Paper Roses	Kaye Sisters
Paper Roses	Marie Osmond
Paper Sun	Traffic
Paperback Writer	Beatles
Paradise City	Guns N' Roses
Paralysed	Elvis Presley
Paranoid	Black Sabbath
Paranoid Android	Radiohead
Paranoimia	Art Of Noise
Parisienne Walkways	Gary Moore
Parklife	Blur
Part Of The Union	Strawbs
Part Time Lover	Stevie Wonder
Party	Elvis Presley
Party Fears Two	Associates
Party People...Friday Night	911
The Party's Over	Lonnie Donegan
Pasadena	Temperance Seven
Pass & Move (It's The Liverpool Groove)	Liverpool FC & The Boot Room Boys
Pass The Dutchie	Musical Youth
Passengers	Elton John
Passion	Gat Decor
Patches	Clarence Carter
Patience	Guns N' Roses
Patricia	Perez Prado
Peace	Sabrina Johnson
Peace In Our Time	Cliff Richard
Peace On Earth	Hi Tension
Peaches	Presidents Of The United States
Peaches	Stranglers
Peacock Suite	Paul Weller
Pearl In The Shell	Howard Jones
Pearl's A Singer	Elkie Brooks
Peek-A-Boo	New Vaudeville Band
Peggy Sue	Buddy Holly
Peggy Sue Got Married	Buddy Holly
Penny Lane	Beatles
People Are People	Depeche Mode
People Everyday	Arrested Development
People Get Ready	Bob Marley & The Wailers
People Hold On	Coldcut Featuring Lisa Stansfield
People Hold On (The Bootleg Mixes)	Lisa Stansfield Vs The Dirty Rotten Scoundrels
People Like You And People Like Me	Glitter Band
Pepe	Duane Eddy

Title	Artist
Pepper Box	Peppers
Peppermint Twist	Joey Dee & The Starliters
Perfect	Fairground Attraction
Perfect Day	Various
The Perfect Year	Dina Carroll
Perfidia	Ventures
Perseverance	Terrorvision
Personal Jesus	Depeche Mode
Personality	Anthony Newley
Personality	Lloyd Price
Peter Gunn	Art Of Noise & Duane Eddy
Peter Gunn Theme	Duane Eddy
Petite Fleur	Chris Barber Jazz Band
The Phantom Of The Opera	Sarah Brightman
Philadelphia Freedom	Elton John
Phorever People	Shamen
Photograph	Ringo Starr
Physical	Olivia Newton-John
Piano Party	Winifred Atwell
Pick A Bale Of Cotton	Lonnie Donegan
Pick Up The Pieces	Average White Band
Pick Up The Pieces	Hudson-Ford
Pickin' A Chicken	Eve Boswell
A Picture Of You	Joe Brown & The Bruvvers
Picture Of You	Boyzone
Picture This	Blondie
Pictures Of Lily	Who
Pictures Of Matchstick Men	Status Quo
Pie Jesu	Sarah Brightman
Piece Of My Heart	Shaggy Featuring Marsha
Piece Of The Action	Bucks Fizz
Pied Piper	Crispian St. Peters
Pied Piper	Bob & Marcia
Pinball Wizard	Elton John
Pinball Wizard	Who
Pink Cadillac	Natalie Cole
Pipes Of Peace	Paul McCartney
Place Your Hands	Reef
Play Dead	Bjork & David Arnold
Play Me Like You Play Your Guitar	Duane Eddy & Rebelettes
Play That Funky Music	Vanilla Ice
Play That Funky Music	Wild Cherry
Playing With Knives	Bizarre Inc
Pleasant Valley Sunday	Monkees
Please	U2
Please Come Home For Christmas	Bon Jovi
Please Don't Fall In Love	Cliff Richard
Please Don't Go	KC & The Sunshine Band
Please Don't Go	K.W.S.
Please Don't Go	No Mercy
Please Don't Go	Donald Peers
Please Don't Make Me Cry	UB40
Please Don't Tease	Cliff Richard
Please Forgive Me	Bryan Adams
Please Help Me, I'm Falling	Hank Locklin
Please Mr. Postman	Carpenters
Please Please Me	Beatles
Please Tell Him I Said Hello	Dana
Poetry In Motion	Johnny Tillotson
Poison	Alice Cooper
Poison Arrow	ABC
Poison Ivy	Lambrettas
Police Officer	Smiley Culture
Pool Hall Richard	Faces
Poor Jenny	Everly Brothers
Poor Little Fool	Ricky Nelson
Poor Man's Son	Rockin' Berries
Poor Me	Adam Faith

Title	Artist
Poor People Of Paris	Winifred Atwell
Pop Go The Workers	Barron Knights
Pop Goes The Weasel	Anthony Newley
Pop Muzik	M
Popcorn	Hot Butter
Poppa Joe	Sweet
Poppa Piccolino	Diana Decker
Portrait Of My Love	Matt Monro
Portsmouth	Mike Oldfield
Positively 4th Street	Bob Dylan
The Power	Snap
Power Of A Woman	Eternal
The Power Of Love	Celine Dion
The Power Of Love	Frankie Goes To Hollywood
The Power Of Love	Huey Lewis & The News
The Power Of Love	Jennifer Rush
Power Rangers	Mighty Morph'n Power Rangers
Power To All Our Friends	Cliff Richard
Power To The People	John Lennon/Plastic Ono Band
Pray	M.C. Hammer
Pray	Take That
Praying For Time	George Michael
Precious	Jam
Pretend	Alvin Stardust
Pretty Blue Eyes	Craig Douglas
Pretty Flamingo	Manfred Mann
Pretty Good Year	Tori Amos
Pretty Little Angel Eyes	Showaddywaddy
Pretty Paper	Roy Orbison
Pretty Vacant	Sex Pistols
The Price Of Love	Everly Brothers
Pride (In The Name Of Love)	U2
Prince Charming	Adam & The Ants
Princess In Rags	Gene Pitney
Private Investigations	Dire Straits
Private Number	Judy Clay & William Bell
Prize Of Gold	Joan Regan
Problems	Everly Brothers
Professional Widow (It's Got To Be Big)	Tori Amos
Promise Me	Beverley Craven
Promised Land	Elvis Presley
Promises	Ken Dodd
Proud Mary	Creedence Clearwater Revival
The Proud One	Osmonds
Prove Your Love	Taylor Dayne
A Pub With No Beer	Slim Dusty
Public Image	Public Image Ltd.
Pull Up To The Bumper	Grace Jones
Pump Up The Bitter	Star Turn On 45 Pints
Pump Up The Jam	Technotronic Featuring Felly
Pump Up The Volume	M/A/R/R/S
Punky Reggae Party	Bob Marley & The Wailers
Puppet On A String	Sandie Shaw
Puppy Love	Donny Osmond
The Puppy Song	David Cassidy
Purely By Coincidence	Sweet Sensation
Purple Haze	Jimi Hendrix Experience
The Purple People Eater	Sheb Wooley
Purple Rain	Prince & The Revolution
Push It	Salt 'n' Pepa
Push The Feeling On	Nightcrawlers
The Pushbike Song	Mixtures
Puss 'n Boots	Adam Ant
Put Your Hands Together	D. Mob Featuring Nuff Juice

Title	Artist
Set Me Free	Kinks
Set You Free	N-Trance
Setting Sun	Chemical Brothers
Seven Days And One Week	BBE
Seven Drunken Nights	Dubliners
747 (Strangers In The Night)	Saxon
Seven Little Girls Sitting In The Back Seat	Avons
Seven Rooms Of Gloom	Four Tops
Seven Seas Of Rhye	Queen
7 Seconds	Youssou N'dour
Seven Tears	Goombay Dance Band
7 Ways To Love	Cola Boy
7 Teen	Regents
Seventeen	Let Loose
Sexcrime (Nineteen Eighty Four)	Eurythmics
(Sexual) Healing	Marvin Gaye
Sexy Eyes	Dr. Hook
Sexy MF	Prince
Sh-Boom	Crew-Cuts
Sh-Boom	Stan Freberg
Sha La La	Manfred Mann
Sha La La La Lee	Small Faces
Shaddup You Face	Joe Dolce
Shadow Waltz	Mantovani
Shake It Down	Mud
Shake, Rattle And Roll	Bill Haley & His Comets
Shake You Down	Gregory Abbott
Shake Your Body (Down To The Ground)	Jacksons
Shake Your Head	Was (Not Was)
Shake Your Love	Debbie Gibson
Shakermaker	Oasis
Shakin' All Over	Johnny Kidd & The Pirates
The Shakin' Stevens E.P.	Shakin' Stevens
Shame, Shame, Shame	Shirley And Company
Shang-A-Lang	Bay City Rollers
Shapes Of Things	Yardbirds
Shattered Dreams	Johnny Hates Jazz
Shazam	Duane Eddy
She	Charles Aznavour
She Ain't Worth It	Glenn Medeiros Featuring Bobby Brown
She Don't Let Nobody	Chaka Demus & Pliers
She Drives Me Crazy	Fine Young Cannibals
She Loves You	Beatles
She Makes My Day	Robert Palmer
She Means Nothing To Me	Phil Everly & Cliff Richard
She Wants To Dance With Me	Rick Astley
She Wears My Ring	Solomon King
She'd Rather Be With Me	Turtles
She's A Lady	Tom Jones
She's A River	Simple Minds
She's Got Claws	Gary Numan
She's Got That Vibe	R. Kelly
She's In Love With You	Suzi Quatro
She's Leaving Home	Billy Bragg
She's Not There	Santana
She's Not There	Zombies
She's Not You	Elvis Presley
She's On It	Beastie Boys
She's Out Of My Life	Michael Jackson
She's So Modern	Boomtown Rats
Sheffield Grinder	Tony Capstick
Sheila	Tommy Roe
Sherry	Adrian Baker
Sherry	Four Seasons

Title	Artist
Shindig	Shadows
Shine	Aswad
Shine A Little Love	Electric Light Orchestra
Shine On	Degrees Of Motion
Shiny Happy People	R.E.M.
Ship Of Fools	Erasure
Shiralee	Tommy Steele
Shirley	Shakin' Stevens
Shocked	Kylie Minogue
The Shoop Shoop Song (It's In His Kiss)	Cher
Shoot Me With Your Love	D:ream
Shooting Star	Boyzone
Shoplifters Of The World Unite	Smiths
Short Short Man	20 Fingers
Shortsharpshock (EP)	Therapy?
Shotgun Wedding	Roy 'C'
Shout	Louchie Lou & Michie One
Shout	Lulu
Shout	Tears For Fears
Shout To The Top	Style Council
The Show	Doug E. Fresh & The Get Fresh Crew
Show Me Heaven	Maria McKee
Show Me Love	Robin S.
Show Me Love	Robyn
Show Me The Way	Peter Frampton
Show Me You're A Woman	Mud
The Show Must Go On	Leo Sayer
Show You The Way To Go	Jacksons
Showdown	Electric Light Orchestra
Showing Out	Mel & Kim
The Shuffle	Van McCoy
Shut Up	Madness
Shy Boy	Bananarama
Shy Guys	Diana King
Sick Man Blues	Goodies
Side Saddle	Russ Conway
Side Show	Barry Biggs
Sight For Sore Eyes	M People
The Sign	Ace Of Base
Sign O' The Times	Prince
Sign O' The Times	Belle Stars
Sign Your Name	Terence Trent D'Arby
Signed, Sealed, Delivered I'm Yours	Stevie Wonder
Silence Is Golden	Tremeloes
Silent Night	Bros
Silhouettes	Herman's Hermits
Silhouettes	Cliff Richard
Silly Games	Janet Kay
Silly Love Songs	Paul McCartney
Silly Thing	Sex Pistols
Silver Dream Machine (Pt. 1)	David Essex
Silver Lady	David Soul
Silver Machine	Hawkwind
Silver Star	Four Seasons
Simon Says	1910 Fruitgum Co.
Simon Smith & His Amazing Dancing Bear	Alan Price Set
Simon Templar	Splodgenessabounds
Simple Game	Four Tops
Since I Don't Have You	Guns N' Roses
Since Yesterday	Strawberry Switchblade
Since You've Been Gone	Rainbow
Sincerely	McGuire Sisters
Sing A Song Of Freedom	Cliff Richard
Sing Baby Sing	Stylistics
Sing It With Joe	Joe 'Mr. Piano' Henderson
Sing Little Birdie	Pearl Carr & Teddy Johnson
Sing Me	Brothers

Title	Artist
Sing Our Own Song	UB40
Sing Up For The Champions	Reds United
Singin' In The Rain (Pt. 1)	Sheila B. Devotion
The Singing Dogs (Medley)	Singing Dogs
Singing The Blues	Guy Mitchell
Singing The Blues	Tommy Steele
Single Life	Cameo
Sippin' Soda	Guy Mitchell
Sir Duke	Stevie Wonder
Sister	Bros
Sister Jane	New World
Sister Of Mercy	Thompson Twins
Sisters Are Doin' It For Themselves	Eurythmics & Aretha Franklin
Sit Down	James
Sittin' In The Park	Georgie Fame
(Sittin' On) The Dock Of The Bay	Otis Redding
The Six Teens	Sweet
16 Bars	Stylistics
Sixteen Reasons	Connie Stevens
Sixteen Tons	Tennessee Ernie Ford
Sixteen Tons	Frankie Laine
The Size Of A Cow	Wonder Stuff
Ska Train	Beatmasters
Skiing In The Snow	Wigan's Ovation
Skin Deep	Duke Ellington
Skin Deep	Ted Heath
Skweeze Me Pleeze Me	Slade
Sky High	Jigsaw
The Skye Boat Song	Roger Whittaker & Des O'Connor
Slam Dunk (Da Funk)	5
Slam Jam	WWF Superstars
Slave To Love	Bryan Ferry
Slave To The Rhythm	Grace Jones
Slave To The Vibe	Aftershock
Sledgehammer	Peter Gabriel
Sleeping Satellite	Tasmin Archer
Sleepy Joe	Herman's Hermits
Sleepy Shores	Johnny Pearson Orchestra
Slight Return	Bluetones
The Slightest Touch	Five Star
Slip Your Disc To This	Heatwave
Sloop John B	Beach Boys
Slow Down	John Miles
Slow Hand	Pointer Sisters
Slow It Down	East 17
Smalltown Boy	Bronski Beat
Smarty Pants	First Choice
Smells Like Teen Spirit	Nirvana
Smile	Nat 'King' Cole
Smoke Gets In Your Eyes	Platters
Smooth Criminal	Michael Jackson
The Smurf Song	Father Abraham & The Smurfs
Snap Mega Mix	Snap
Snooker Loopy	Matchroom Mob With Chas & Dave
Snoopy Vs The Red Baron	Royal Guardsmen
Snoopy Vs. The Red Baron	Hotshots
Snot Rap	Kenny Everett
Snow Coach	Russ Conway
So Cold The Night	Communards
So Do I	Kenny Ball
So Emotional	Whitney Houston
So Good	Boyzone
So Good	Eternal
So Good To Be Back Home Again	Tourists
So Hard	Pet Shop Boys

Title	Artist
Stop Her On Sight (SOS)	Edwin Starr
Stop Me (If You've Heard It All Before)	
	Billy Ocean
Stop Stop Stop	Hollies
Stop The Cavalry	Jona Lewie
Stop! In The Name Of Love	Supremes
Storm In A Teacup	Fortunes
Story Of My Life	Gary Miller
The Story Of My Life	Michael Holliday
The Story Of The Blues	Wah!
The Story Of Three Loves	
	Winifred Atwell
Story Of Tina	Ronnie Harris
The Story Of Tina	Al Martino
Stowaway	Barbara Lyon
Straight Up	Paula Abdul
Straighten Out	Stranglers
Strange Band	Family
Strange Kind Of Woman	Deep Purple
Strange Lady In Town	Frankie Laine
Strange Little Girl	Stranglers
The Stranger	Shadows
Stranger In Moscow	Michael Jackson
Stranger In Paradise	Tony Bennett
Stranger In Paradise	Eddie Calvert
Stranger In Paradise	Four Aces
Stranger In Paradise	Tony Martin
Stranger On The Shore	Acker Bilk
Strangers In The Night	Frank Sinatra
The Strangest Thing '97	George Michael
Strawberry Fair	Anthony Newley
Strawberry Fields Forever	Beatles
Strawberry Fields Forever	Candy Flip
Stray Cat Strut	Stray Cats
The Streak	Ray Stevens
Street Dance	Break Machine
Street Life	Crusaders
Street Life	Roxy Music
Street Spirit (Fade Out)	Radiohead
Street Tuff	Rebel MC/Double Trouble
Streets Of London	Ralph McTell
Streets Of Philadelphia	
	Bruce Springsteen
Strollin'	Prince
Strut Your Funky Stuff	Frantique
Stuck In The Middle With You	
	Stealer's Wheel
Stuck On You	Elvis Presley
Stuck On You	Lionel Richie
Stuck On You	Trevor Walters
Stuck With You	Huey Lewis & The News
Stupid Cupid	Connie Francis
Stupid Girl	Garbage
Stutter Rap (No Sleep 'til Bedtime)	
	Morris Minor & The Majors
Substitute	Clout
Substitute	Liquid Gold
Substitute	Who
Subterranean Homesick Blues	Bob Dylan
Suburbia	Pet Shop Boys
Success	Dannii Minogue
Such A Feeling	Bizarre Inc
Such A Night	Elvis Presley
Such A Night	Johnnie Ray
Sucu-Sucu	Laurie Johnson
Suddenly	Angry Anderson
Suddenly	Billy Ocean
Suddenly There's A Valley	Petula Clark
Suddenly There's A Valley	Lee Lawrence
Suddenly There's A Valley	Jo Stafford
Suddenly You Love Me	Tremeloes
Suedehead	Morrissey
Sugar And Spice	Searchers
Sugar Baby Love	Rubettes

Title	Artist
Sugar Candy Kisses	Mac & Katie Kissoon
Sugar Me	Lynsey De Paul
Sugar Moon	Pat Boone
Sugar Sugar	Archies
Sugar Sugar	Sakkarin
Sugar Town	Nancy Sinatra
Sugartime	McGuire Sisters
Sukiyaki	Kenny Ball
Sukiyaki	Kyu Sakamoto
Sultana	Titanic
Sultans Of Swing	Dire Straits
Summer Holiday	Cliff Richard
Summer In The City	Lovin' Spoonful
Summer Night City	Abba
Summer Nights	Marianne Faithfull
Summer Nights	John Travolta & Olivia Newton-John
Summer Of My Life	Simon May
Summer Set	Acker Bilk
Summer (The First Time)	Bobby Goldsboro
Summerlove Sensation	Bay City Rollers
Summertime	D.J. Jazzy Jeff & The Fresh Prince
Summertime City	Mike Batt
The Sun Ain't Gonna Shine (Anymore)	Walker Brothers
The Sun Always Shines On T.V.	A-Ha
The Sun And The Rain	Madness
Sun Arise	Rolf Harris
The Sun Goes Down (Living It Up)	Level 42
Sunchyme	Dario G
Sunday Girl	Blondie
Sunny	Boney M
Sunny	Georgie Fame
Sunny	Bobby Hebb
Sunny Afternoon	Kinks
The Sunshine After The Rain	Elkie Brooks
The Sunshine After The Rain	Berri
Sunshine Girl	Herman's Hermits
Sunshine Of Your Smile	Mike Berry
Sunshine On A Rainy Day	Zoe
Sunshine Superman	Donovan
Super Trouper	Abba
Superfly Guy	S'Express
Superman (Gioca Jouer)	Black Lace
Supermarioland	Ambassadors Of Funk/MC Mario
Supernature	Cerrone
Superstition	Stevie Wonder
Superwoman	Karyn White
Sure	Take That
Surrender	Elvis Presley
Surrender	Diana Ross
Surrender	Swing Out Sister
Surrender Your Love	Nightcrawlers Featuring John Reid
Surround Yourself With Sorrow	Cilla Black
Suspicion	Elvis Presley
Suspicious Minds	Fine Young Cannibals
Suspicious Minds	Elvis Presley
Sussudio	Phil Collins
Suzanne Beware Of The Devil	Dandy Livingstone
Swallowed	Bush
Swamp Thing	Grid
Sway	Dean Martin
Sway	Bobby Rydell
Sweat (A La La La La Long)	Inner Circle
Swedish Rhapsody	Mantovani
Swedish Rhapsody	Ray Martin

Title	Artist
Sweet Caroline	Neil Diamond
Sweet Child O' Mine	Guns N' Roses
Sweet Dream	Jethro Tull
Sweet Dreams (Are Made Of This)	
	Eurythmics
Sweet Freedom	Michael McDonald
Sweet Harmony	Beloved
Sweet Inspiration	Johnny Johnson & The Bandwagon
Sweet Little Mystery	Wet Wet Wet
Sweet Lullaby	Deep Forest
Sweet Nothin's	Brenda Lee
Sweet Old-Fashioned Girl	Teresa Brewer
Sweet Soul Music	Arthur Conley
Sweet Surrender	Wet Wet Wet
Sweet Talkin' Guy	Chiffons
Sweet Talkin' Woman	Electric Light Orchestra
Sweetest Smile	Black
Sweetness	Michelle Gayle
Sweets For My Sweet	CJ Lewis
Sweets For My Sweet	Searchers
Swing The Mood	Jive Bunny & The Mastermixers
Swing Your Daddy	Jim Gilstrap
Swingin' Shepherd Blues	Ted Heath
Swinging On A Star	Big Dee Irwin
Swiss Maid	Del Shannon
Swords Of A Thousand Men	Ten Pole Tudor
Sylvia	Focus
Sylvia's Mother	Dr. Hook
Sympathy For The Devil	Guns N' Roses
System Addict	Five Star
Tahiti (From Mutiny On The Bounty)	
	David Essex
Tainted Love	Soft Cell
Take A Bow	Madonna
Take A Chance On Me	Abba
(Take A Little) Piece Of My Heart	
	Erma Franklin
Take A Look Around	Temptations
Take Five	Dave Brubeck Quartet
Take Good Care Of My Baby	Bobby Vee
Take Good Care Of Yourself	
	Three Degrees
Take Me Bak 'Ome	Slade
Take Me To The Mardi Gras	Paul Simon
Take Me To Your Heart	Rick Astley
Take Me With You	Prince & The Revolution
Take My Advice	Kym Sims
Take My Breath Away	Berlin
Take On Me	A-Ha
Take That Look Of Your Face	Marti Webb
Take That Situation	Nick Heyward
Take These Chains From My Heart	
	Ray Charles
Take This Heart	Richard Marx
Take Your Time	Mantronix Featuring Wondress
Talk Of The Town	Pretenders
Talking In Your Sleep	Crystal Gayle
Talking Loud And Clear	Orchestral Manoeuvres In The Dark
Tallahassee Lassie	Tommy Steele
Tammy	Debbie Reynolds
Tap Turns On The Water	C.C.S.
Tarzan Boy	Baltimora
A Taste Of Aggro	Barron Knights
The Taste Of Your Tears	King
Tattva	Kula Shaker
Tea For Two Cha Cha	Tommy Dorsey Orchestra

Title	Artist
Teacher	Jethro Tull
A Tear Fell	Teresa Brewer
Teardrops	Shakin' Stevens
Teardrops	Womack & Womack
Tears	Ken Dodd
The Tears I Cried	Glitter Band
Tears In Heaven	Eric Clapton
Tears Of A Clown	Beat
The Tears Of A Clown	Smokey Robinson & The Miracles
Tears On My Pillow	Kylie Minogue
Tears On My Pillow	Johnny Nash
Tease Me	Chaka Demus & Pliers
Teddy Bear	Elvis Presley
Teddy Bear	Red Sovine
Teen Beat	Sandy Nelson
Teenage Dream	Marc Bolan & T. Rex
Teenage Lament '74	Alice Cooper
Teenage Rampage	Sweet
A Teenager In Love	Craig Douglas
A Teenager In Love	Marty Wilde
Telegram Sam	T. Rex
Telephone Line	Electric Light Orchestra
Telephone Man	Meri Wilson
Teletubbies Say Eh-Oh!	Teletubbies
Tell Her About It	Billy Joel
Tell Him	Billie Davis
Tell Him	Hello
Tell Him	Barbra Streisand & Celine Dion
Tell It To My Heart	Taylor Dayne
Tell Laura I Love Her	Ricky Valance
Tell Me What He Said	Helen Shapiro
Tell Me When	Applejacks
Tell Me When	Human League
Tell Me Why	Elvis Presley
Telstar	Tornados
Temma Harbour	Mary Hopkin
Temple Of Love (1992)	Sisters Of Mercy
Temptation	Everly Brothers
Temptation	Heaven 17
The Tender Trap	Frank Sinatra
Tenderly	Nat 'King' Cole
Tennessee Wig Walk	Bonnie Lou
Tequila	Champs
Terry	Twinkle
Tetris	Doctor Spin
Tha Crossroads	Bone Thugs N Harmony
Thank U Very Much	Scaffold
Thanks For The Memory (Wham Bam Thank You Mam)	Slade
That Girl Belongs To Yesterday	Gene Pitney
That Look In Your Eye	Ali Campbell
That Ole Devil Called Love	Alison Moyet
That Same Old Feeling	Pickettywitch
That Sounds Good To Me	Jive Bunny & The Mastermixers
That'll Be The Day	Crickets
That's All!	Genesis
That's Amore	Dean Martin
That's How A Love Song Was Born	Ray Burns
That's Living (Alright)	Joe Fagin
That's My Home	Acker Bilk
That's The Way	Honeycombs
That's The Way (I Like It)	KC & The Sunshine Band
That's The Way God Planned It	Billy Preston
That's The Way It Is	Mel & Kim
That's The Way Love Goes	Janet Jackson
That's The Way Love Is	Ten City
That's What Friends Are For	Deniece Williams

Title	Artist
That's What I Like	Jive Bunny & The Mastermixers
That's What Love Will Do	Joe Brown & The Bruvvers
Them Girls Them Girls	Zig And Zag
Theme For A Dream	Cliff Richard
Theme For Young Lovers	Shadows
Theme From 'Mission:Impossible'	Adam Clayton & Larry Mullen
Theme From 'A Summer Place'	Percy Faith
Theme From Dixie	Duane Eddy
Theme From Dr. Kildare (Three Stars Will Shine Tonight)	Richard Chamberlain
Theme From Harry's Game	Clannad
Theme From M.A.S.H.	Manic Street Preachers
Theme From M*A*S*H* (Suicide Is Painless)	Mash
Theme From Mahogany (Do You Know Where You're Going To)	Diana Ross
Theme From New York New York	Frank Sinatra
Theme From 'Shaft'	Isaac Hayes
Theme From S'Express	S'Express
Theme From 'The Legion's Last Patrol'	Ken Thorne & His Orchestra
Theme From 'The Threepenny Opera'	Billy Vaughn
Theme From The Deer Hunter (Cavatina)	Shadows
Theme From The Threepenny Opera	Louis Armstrong
Then He Kissed Me	Crystals
Then I Kissed Her	Beach Boys
There Are More Questions Than Answers	Johnny Nash
There But For Fortune	Joan Baez
There Goes My Everything	Engelbert Humperdinck
There Goes My Everything	Elvis Presley
There Goes My First Love	Drifters
There Is A Mountain	Donovan
There It Is	Shalamar
There Must Be A Reason	Frankie Laine
There Must Be A Way	Frankie Vaughan
There Must Be An Angel(Playing With My Heart)	Eurythmics
There There My Dear	Dexy's Midnight Runners
There Won't Be Many Coming Home	Roy Orbison
There's A Ghost In My House	R. Dean Taylor
There's A Gold Mine In The Sky	Pat Boone
There's A Heartache Following Me	Jim Reeves
There's A Kind Of Hush	Herman's Hermits
There's A Whole Lot Of Loving	Guys & Dolls
(There's) Always Something There To Remind Me	Sandie Shaw
There's No One Quite Like Grandma	St. Winifred's School
There's No Other Way	Blur
There's Nothing I Won't Do	JX
These Boots Are Made For Walkin'	Nancy Sinatra
These Days	Bon Jovi
These Dreams	Heart
They Don't Care About Us	Michael Jackson
They Don't Know	Tracey Ullman

Title	Artist
(They Long To Be) Close To You	Carpenters
They'll Be Sad Songs (To Make You Cry)	Billy Ocean
They're Coming To Take Me Away Ha-Haaa!	Napoleon XIV
Thieves In The Temple	Prince
The Thin Wall	Ultravox
A Thing Called Love	Johnny Cash
Things	Bobby Darin
Things Can Only Get Better	D:ream
Things Can Only Get Better	Howard Jones
Things That Make You Go Hmmmm....	C&C Music Factory Feat. Freedom Williams
Things We Do For Love	10cc
Think It Over	Crickets
Think Of You	Whigfield
Think Twice	Celine Dion
Thinking About Your Love	Kenny Thomas
Thinking Of You	Colour Field
Thinking Of You	Maureen
Thinking Of You	Sister Sledge
This Ain't A Love Song	Bon Jovi
This Beat Is Technotronic	Technotronic Featuring MC Eric
This Corrosion	Sisters Of Mercy
This D.J.	Warren G
This Flight Tonight	Nazareth
This Golden Ring	Fortunes
This Guy's In Love With You	Herb Alpert
This Is A Call	Foo Fighters
This Is How We Do It	Montell Jordan
This Is It	Adam Faith
This Is It	Dannii Minogue
This Is It	Melba Moore
This Is My Song	Petula Clark
This Is My Song	Harry Secombe
This Is Not A Love Song	Pil
This Is Tomorrow	Bryan Ferry
This Little Bird	Marianne Faithfull
This Old Heart Of Mine	Isley Brothers
This Old Heart Of Mine	Rod Stewart
This Old House	Billie Anthony
This Ole House	Rosemary Clooney
This Ole House	Shakin' Stevens
This One's For The Children	New Kids On The Block
This Time I Know It's For Real	Donna Summer
This Time (We'll Get It Right)	England World Cup Squad
This Town Ain't Big Enough For The Both Of Us	Sparks
This Used To Be My Playground	Madonna
This Wheel's On Fire	Julie Driscoll, Brian Auger & The Trinity
Thorn In My Side	Eurythmics
Those Were The Days	Mary Hopkin
Thought I'd Died And Gone To Heaven	Bryan Adams
3 A.M. Eternal	KLF
The Three Bells	Browns
Three Coins In The Fountain	Tony Brent
Three Coins In The Fountain	Four Aces
Three Coins In The Fountain	Frank Sinatra
3 Is Family	Dana Dawson
Three Lions (The Official Song Of The England Football Team)	Baddiel & Skinner & Lightning Seeds
Three Little Pigs	Green Jelly

Title	Artist
Two Can Play That Game	Bobby Brown
Two Different Worlds	Ronnie Hilton
2-4-6-8 Motorway	Tom Robinson Band
Two Hearts	Phil Collins
Two Kinds Of Teardrops	Del Shannon
Two Little Boys	Rolf Harris
Two Pints Of Lager And A Packet Of Crisps Please	Splodgenessabounds
Two Princes	Spin Doctors
Two Tribes	Frankie Goes To Hollywood
U & Me	Cappella
U Can't Touch This	M.C. Hammer
U Got The Look	Prince
U Got 2 Know	Cappella
U Got 2 Let The Music	Cappella
U R The Best Thing	D:ream
U Sexy Thing	Clock
U Sure Do	Strike
The Ugly Duckling	Mike Reid
Uh La La La	Alexia
Um Um Um Um Um Um	Wayne Fontana & The Mindbenders
Un Banc, Un Abre, Une Rue	Severine
(Un, Dos, Tres) Maria	Ricky Martin
Un-Break My Heart	Toni Braxton
Una Paloma Blanca	Jonathan King
Unbelievable	EMF
Unchained Melody	Les Baxter
Unchained Melody	Robson Green & Jerome Flynn
Unchained Melody	Al Hibbler
Unchained Melody	Righteous Brothers
Unchained Melody	Jimmy Young
Unconditional Love	Donna Summer
Under Pressure	Queen & David Bowie
Under The Boardwalk	Bruce Willis
Under The Bridge	Red Hot Chili Peppers
Under The Bridges Of Paris	Eartha Kitt
Under The Bridges Of Paris	Dean Martin
Under The Moon Of Love	Showaddywaddy
Under Your Thumb	Godley & Creme
Undercover Of The Night	Rolling Stones
Underwater Love	Smoke City
Undivided Love	Louise
The Unforgettable Fire	U2
Union City Blue	Blondie
Union Of The Snake	Duran Duran
United We Stand	Brotherhood Of Man
The Universal	Blur
Until It Sleeps	Metallica
Until It's Time For You To Go	Elvis Presley
Up Around The Bend	Creedence Clearwater Revival
Up On The Roof	Robson Green & Jerome Flynn
Up On The Roof	Kenny Lynch
Up The Junction	Squeeze
Up The Ladder To The Roof	Supremes
Up The Pool	Jethro Tull
Up Up And Away	Johnny Mann Singers
Up Where We Belong	Joe Cocker & Jennifer Warnes
Upside Down	Diana Ross
Uptown Girl	Billy Joel
Uptown Top Ranking	Althia And Donna
Use It Up And Wear It Out	Odyssey
Used Ta Be My Girl	O'Jays
Vacation	Connie Francis
Valentine	T'Pau
Valleri	Monkees
Veni Vidi Vici	Ronnie Hilton
Venus	Bananarama
Venus	Don Pablo's Animals

Title	Artist
Venus	Shocking Blue
Venus In Blue Jeans	Mark Wynter
Victim Of Love	Erasure
Victims	Culture Club
Video Killed The Radio Star	Buggles
Vienna	Ultravox
Vienna Calling	Falco
A View To Kill	Duran Duran
Vincent	Don McLean
Virginia Plain	Roxy Music
Virtual Insanity	Jamiroquai
Vision Of Love	Mariah Carey
Visions	Cliff Richard
Viva Bobbie Joe	Equals
Viva Las Vegas	Elvis Presley
Viva Las Vegas	ZZ Top
Vogue	Madonna
Voice In The Wilderness	Cliff Richard
Volare	Marino Marini
Volare	Dean Martin
Voodoo Chile	Jimi Hendrix Experience
Voodoo Ray (E.P.)	A Guy Called Gerald
Voulez Vous	Abba
Voyage Voyage	Desireless
Wait	Robert Howard & Kym Mazelle
Wait For Me	Malcolm Vaughan
Waiting For A Girl Like You	Foreigner
Waiting For A Star To Fall	Boy Meets Girl
Waiting For A Train	Flash And The Pan
Waiting For An Alibi	Thin Lizzy
Wake Me Up Before You Go Go	Wham!
Wake Up Boo!	Boo Radleys
Wake Up Little Susie	Everly Brothers
Walk Away	Matt Monro
Walk Away From Love	David Ruffin
Walk Away Renee	Four Tops
Walk Don't Run	John Barry Seven
Walk Hand In Hand	Ronnie Carroll
Walk Hand In Hand	Tony Martin
A Walk In The Black Forest	Horst Jankowski
Walk Like A Man	Four Seasons
Walk Like An Egyptian	Bangles
Walk Of Life	Dire Straits
Walk On By	Gabrielle
Walk On By	Sybil
Walk On By	Leroy Van Dyke
Walk On By	Dionne Warwick
Walk On The Wild Side	Lou Reed
Walk Right Back	Everly Brothers
Walk Right In	Rooftop Singers
Walk Right Now	Jacksons
Walk Tall	Val Doonican
Walk The Dinosaur	Was (Not Was)
Walk This Way	Run D.M.C.
Walk With Me	Seekers
Walk-Don't Run	Ventures
Walkin'	C.C.S.
Walkin' Back To Happiness	Helen Shapiro
Walkin' In The Rain With The One I Love	Love Unlimited
Walkin' In The Sunshine	Bad Manners
A Walkin' Miracle	Limmie & The Family Cookin'
Walking In Memphis	Cher
Walking In The Air	Aled Jones
Walking In The Rain	Modern Romance
Walking In The Rain	Partridge Family
Walking On Broken Glass	Annie Lennox
Walking On Sunshine	Katrina & The Waves
Walking On Sunshine	Rocker's Revenge

Title	Artist
Walking On The Moon	Police
Walking Wounded	Everything But The Girl
Wall Street Shuffle	10cc
Walls Come Tumbling Down!	Style Council
Wand'rin' Star	Lee Marvin
The Wanderer	Dion
The Wanderer	Status Quo
Wanderin' Eyes	Charlie Gracie
Wanderin' Eyes	Frankie Vaughan
Wanna Be Startin' Something	Michael Jackson
Wannabe	Spice Girls
Wanted	Perry Como
Wanted	Dooleys
Wanted	Al Martino
Wanted Dead Or Alive	Bon Jovi
Wap Bam Boogie	Matt Bianco
War	Edwin Starr
War Baby	Tom Robinson
The War Song	Culture Club
Warpaint	Brook Brothers
Watchin' The Detectives	Elvis Costello
Watching You Watching Me	David Grant
Water On Glass	Kim Wilde
Water Water	Tommy Steele
Waterfalls	Paul McCartney
Waterfalls	TLC
Waterloo	Abba
Waterloo Sunset	Kinks
Way Down	Elvis Presley
Way Down Yonder In New Orleans	Freddy Cannon
Way In My Brain	SL2
The Way It Used To Be	Engelbert Humperdinck
Way Of Life	Family Dogg
The Way You Make Me Feel	Michael Jackson
The Wayward Wind	Gogi Grant
Wayward Wind	Frank Ifield
Wayward Wind	Tex Ritter
We All Stand Together	Paul McCartney
We Are Detective	Thompson Twins
We Are Family	Sister Sledge
We Are Glass	Gary Numan
We Are In Love	Adam Faith
We Are The Champions	Queen
We Are The World	USA For Africa
We Built This City	Starship
We Call It Acieed	D. Mob Featuring Gary Haisman
We Can Work It Out	Beatles
We Close Our Eyes	Go West
We Didn't Start The Fire	Billy Joel
We Do It	R & J Stone
We Don't Have To ...	Jermaine Stewart
We Don't Need Another Hero (Thunderdome)	Tina Turner
We Don't Talk Anymore	Cliff Richard
We Got A Love Thang	Ce Ce Peniston
We Gotta Get Out Of This Place	Animals
We Have A Dream	Scotland World Cup Squad
We Have All The Time In The World	Louis Armstrong
We Love You	Rolling Stones
We Should Be Together	Cliff Richard
We Take Mystery (To Bed)	Gary Numan
(We Want) The Same Thing	Belinda Carlisle
We Will Make Love	Russ Hamilton
We'll Bring The House Down	Slade

Title	Artist
We're All Alone	Rita Coolidge
We're Gonna Do It Again	Manchester United 1995 Football Squad Feat Stryker
We're Not Alone	Frankie Vaughan
We're Through	Hollies
We've Got It Goin' On	Backstreet Boys
Weak In The Presence Of Beauty	Alison Moyet
Wear My Ring Around Your Neck	Elvis Presley
Weather With You	Crowded House
The Wedding	Julie Rogers
Wedding Bells	Eddie Fisher
Wedding Bells	Godley & Creme
Wee Rule	Wee Papa Girl Rappers
Weekend	Eddie Cochran
Welcome Home	Peters & Lee
Welcome To My World	Jim Reeves
Welcome To The Cheap Seats (EP)	Wonder Stuff
Welcome To The Pleasure Dome	Frankie Goes To Hollywood
Welcome To Tomorrow	Snap Featuring Summer
Well I Ask You	Eden Kane
West End Girls	Pet Shop Boys
West Of Zanzibar	Anthony Steel & The Radio Revellers
Western Movies	Olympics
Wet Dream	Max Romeo
Wham Rap	Wham!
What	Soft Cell
What A Diff'rence A Day Makes	Esther Phillips
What A Mouth	Tommy Steele
What A Waste	Ian Dury & The Blockheads
What A Wonderful World	Louis Armstrong
What Am I Gonna Do	Rod Stewart
What Am I Gonna Do With You	Barry White
What Are You Doing Sunday	Dawn
What Becomes Of The Broken Hearted	Robson Green & Jerome Flynn
What Becomes Of The Broken Hearted	Jimmy Ruffin
What Becomes Of The Broken Hearted	Dave Stewart & Colin Blunstone
What Can I Say	Boz Scaggs
What Can You Do For Me	Utah Saints
What Cha Gonna Do About It	Small Faces
What Difference Does It Make	Smiths
What Do I Do	Phil Fearon & Galaxy
What Do I Have To Do	Kylie Minogue
What Do You Want	Adam Faith
What Do You Want To Make Those Eyes At Me For	Emile Ford & The Checkmates
What Do You Want To Make Those Eyes At Me For	Shakin' Stevens
What Does It Take To Win Your Love	Jr. Walker & The All Stars
What Have I Done To Deserve This	Pet Shop Boys & Dusty Springfield
What Have They Done To The Rain	Searchers
What Have You Done For Me Lately	Janet Jackson
What I've Got In Mind	Billie Jo Spears
What In The World's Come Over You	Jack Scott
What Is Love	Haddaway
What Is Love	Howard Jones

Title	Artist
What Kinda Boy You Looking For (Girl)	Hot Chocolate
What Made Milwaukee Famous	Rod Stewart
What Now My Love	Shirley Bassey
What Now My Love	Sonny & Cher
What The World Is Waiting For	Stone Roses
What Time Is Love	KLF/Children Of The Revolution
What Would I Be	Val Doonican
What You're Proposing	Status Quo
What'd I Say	Jerry Lee Lewis
What'll I Do	Janet Jackson
What's Another Year	Johnny Logan
What's Love Got To Do With It	Warren G Featuring Adina Howard
What's Love Got To Do With It	Tina Turner
What's New Pussycat?	Tom Jones
What's The Colour Of Money ?	Hollywood Beyond
What's The Frequency, Kenneth?	REM
What's Up	DJ Miko
What's Up	4 Non Blondes
Whatever	Oasis
Whatever I Do (Wherever I Go)	Hazell Dean
Whatever Will Be Will Be	Doris Day
Whatever You Want	Status Quo
Whatta Man	Salt-N-Pepa Featuring En Vogue
Wheels	String-A-Longs
When	Kalin Twins
When	Showaddywaddy
When A Child Is Born (Soleado)	Johnny Mathis
When A Man Loves A Woman	Michael Bolton
When A Man Loves A Woman	Percy Sledge
When Doves Cry	Prince & The Revolution
When Forever Has Gone	Demis Roussos
When I Come Home	Spencer Davis Group
When I Fall In Love	Rick Astley
When I Fall In Love	Nat 'King' Cole
When I Fall In Love	Donny Osmond
When I Need You	Will Mellor
When I Need You	Leo Sayer
When I Think Of You	Janet Jackson
When I'm Dead And Gone	McGuinness Flint
When I'm Good And Ready	Sybil
When Johnny Comes Marching Home	Adam Faith
When Julie Comes Around	Cuff Links
When Love & Hate Collide	Def Leppard
When Love Comes To Town	U2 With B.B. King
When Mexico Gave Up The Rumba	Mitchell Torok
When My Little Girl Is Smiling	Craig Douglas
When My Little Girl Is Smiling	Jimmy Justice
When She Was My Girl	Four Tops
When Smokey Sings	ABC
When The Girl In Your Arms Is The Girl In Your Heart	Cliff Richard
When The Going Gets Tough, The Tough Get Going	Billy Ocean
When The Lights Go Out	5
When We Dance	Sting
When We Were Young	Bucks Fizz

Title	Artist
When Will I Be Famous	Bros
When Will I Be Loved	Everly Brothers
When Will I See You Again	Three Degrees
When Will The Good Apples Fall	Seekers
When Will You Say I Love You	Billy Fury
When You Are A King	White Plains
When You Ask About Love	Matchbox
When You Come Back To Me	Jason Donovan
When You Lose The One You Love	David Whitfield
(When You Say You Love Somebody) In The Heart	Kool & The Gang
When You Tell Me That You Love Me	Diana Ross
When You Walk In The Room	Searchers
When You Were Sweet Sixteen	Fureys & Davie Arthur
When You're In Love With A Beautiful Woman	Dr. Hook
When You're Young And In Love	Flying Pickets
Whenever You Need Somebody	Rick Astley
Where Are You Baby?	Betty Boo
Where Are You Now (My Love)	Jackie Trent
Where Did Our Love Go	Donnie Elbert
Where Did Our Love Go	Supremes
Where Did Your Heart Go	Wham!
(Where Do I Begin) Love Story	Andy Williams
Where Do You Go	No Mercy
Where Do You Go To My Lovely	Peter Sarstedt
Where Has All The Love Gone	Yazz
Where Love Lies	Alison Limerick
Where The Boys Are	Connie Francis
Where The Streets Have No Name	U2
Where Will The Baby's Dimple Be	Rosemary Clooney
Where's The Love	Hanson
Wherever I Lay My Hat (That's My Home)	Paul Young
Which Way You Goin' Billy	Poppy Family
Whisky In The Jar	Thin Lizzy
Whispering Grass	Windsor Davies & Don Estelle
Whistle Down The Wind	Nick Heyward
White Christmas	Bing Crosby
White Cliffs Of Dover	Robson Green & Jerome Flynn
White Horses	Jacky
White Lines	Grandmaster Flash, Melle Mel & The Furio
A White Sport Coat	King Brothers
White Wedding	Billy Idol
A Whiter Shade Of Pale	Procol Harum
Who Am I	Adam Faith
Who Are We	Ronnie Hilton
Who Could Be Bluer	Jerry Lordan
Who Do You Think You Are	Spice Girls
Who Found Who	Jellybean Featuring Elisa Fiorillo
Who Is It	Michael Jackson
Who Killed Bambi	Sex Pistols
Who Loves You	Four Seasons
Who Needs Love (Like That)	Erasure
Who Pays The Ferryman	Yannis Markopoulos
Who Put The Lights Out	Dana
Who The F**k is Alice?	Smokie Featuring Roy Chubby Brown

Title	Artist
You Are The Sunshine Of My Life	Stevie Wonder
You Better You Bet	Who
You Came	Kim Wilde
You Can Call Me Al	Paul Simon
You Can Do Magic	Limmie & The Family Cookin'
You Can Get It If You Really Want	Desmond Dekker
You Can Make Me Dance Sing Or Anything	Rod Stewart & The Faces
You Can Never Stop Me Loving You	Kenny Lynch
You Can't Be True To Two	Dave King
You Can't Hurry Love	Phil Collins
You Can't Hurry Love	Supremes
You Could Be Mine	Guns N' Roses
You Don't Bring Me Flowers	Barbra & Neil
You Don't Have To Be A Baby To Cry	Caravelles
You Don't Have To Be A Star (To Be In My Show)	Marilyn McCoo & Billy Davis Jr
You Don't Have To Be In The Army To Fight In The War	Mungo Jerry
You Don't Have To Go	Chi-Lites
You Don't Have To Say You Love Me	Guys & Dolls
You Don't Have To Say You Love Me	Elvis Presley
You Don't Have To Say You Love Me	Dusty Springfield
You Don't Know	Helen Shapiro
You Don't Know Me	Ray Charles
You Don't Love Me (No, No, No)	Dawn Penn
You Don't Owe Me A Thing	Johnnie Ray
You Drive Me Crazy	Shakin' Stevens
You Gave Me Love	Crown Heights Affair
You Give Love A Bad Name	Bon Jovi
You Got It	Roy Orbison
You Got It (The Right Stuff)	New Kids On The Block
You Got Soul	Johnny Nash
You Got The Love	Source Featuring Candi Staton
You Got What It Takes	Marv Johnson
You Got What It Takes	Showaddywaddy
(You Gotta) Fight For Your Right (To Party)	Beastie Boys
You Have Been Loved	George Michael
You Just Might See Me Cry	Our Kid
You Keep It All In	Beautiful South
You Keep Me Hangin' On	Supremes
You Keep Me Hangin' On	Kim Wilde
You Little Thief	Feargal Sharkey
You Make Me Feel (Mighty Real)	Jimmy Somerville
You Make Me Feel (Mighty Real)	Sylvester
You Make Me Feel Brand New	Stylistics
You Make Me Feel Like Dancing	Leo Sayer
You Make Me Wanna	Usher
You Might Need Somebody	Shola Ama
You Might Need Somebody	Randy Crawford
You Must Have Been A Beautiful Baby	Bobby Darin
You My Love	Frank Sinatra
You Need Hands	Max Bygraves
You Only Live Twice	Nancy Sinatra

Title	Artist
You Really Got Me	Kinks
You See The Trouble With Me	Barry White
You Sexy Thing	Hot Chocolate
You Should Be Dancing	Bee Gees
You Spin Me Round (Like A Record)	Dead Or Alive
You Take Me Up	Thompson Twins
You To Me Are Everything	Real Thing
You Wear It Well	Rod Stewart
You Were Made For Me	Freddie & The Dreamers
You Were On My Mind	Crispian St. Peters
You Win Again	Bee Gees
You Won't Find Another Fool Like Me	New Seekers
You You You	Alvin Stardust
You'll Answer To Me	Cleo Laine
You'll Never Find Another Love Like Mine	Lou Rawls
You'll Never Know	Shirley Bassey
You'll Never Stop Me From Loving You	Sonia
You'll Never Walk Alone	The Crowd
You'll Never Walk Alone	Gerry & The Pacemakers
You'll See	Madonna
You're A Lady	Peter Skellern
You're All That Matters To Me	Curtis Stigers
You're Breakin' My Heart	Keely Smith
You're Driving Me Crazy	Temperance Seven
You're Gonna Get Next To Me	Bo Kirkland & Ruth Davis
You're Gorgeous	Baby Bird
(You're) Having My Baby	Paul Anka with Odia Coates
You're History	Shakespear's Sister
You're In A Bad Way	Saint Etienne
You're In My Heart	Rod Stewart
You're Makin' Me High	Toni Braxton
You're More Than A Number In My Little Red Book	Drifters
You're Moving Out Today	Carole Bayer Sager
You're My Best Friend	Queen
You're My World	Cilla Black
You're No Good	Swinging Blue Jeans
You're Ready Now	Frankie Valli
You're Sixteen	Johnny Burnette
You're Sixteen	Ringo Starr
You're So Vain	Carly Simon
You're Still The One	Shania Twain
You're Such A Good Looking Woman	Joe Dolan
Devil In Disguise	Elvis Presley
You're The First, The Last, My Everything	Barry White
You're The One I Love	Shola Ama
You're The One That I Want	John Travolta & Olivia Newton-John
You're The Voice	John Farnham
You've Got A Friend	Brand New Heavies
You've Got A Friend	James Taylor
You've Got It Bad	Ocean Colour Scene
You've Got Me Dangling On A String	Chairmen Of The Board
You've Got Your Troubles	Fortunes
You've Lost That Lovin' Feelin'	Cilla Black
You've Lost That Lovin' Feelin'	Righteous Brothers

Title	Artist
You've Never Been In Love Like This Before	Unit 4 Plus 2
Young And Foolish	Edmund Hockridge
Young At Heart	Bluebells
Young Gifted And Black	Bob & Marcia
Young Girl	Union Gap Featuring Gary Puckett
Young Guns (Go For It)	Wham!
Young Hearts Run Free	Candi Staton
Young Love	Tab Hunter
Young Love	Sonny James
Young Love	Donny Osmond
Young Lovers	Paul & Paula
The Young New Mexican Puppeteer	Tom Jones
The Young Ones	Cliff Richard
Young Parisians	Adam & The Ants
Young Turks	Rod Stewart
Young-At-Heart	Frank Sinatra
Your Body's Callin'	R. Kelly
Your Cheatin' Heart	Ray Charles
Your Christmas Wish	Smurfs
Your Love Is King	Sade
Your Loving Arms	Billie Ray Martin
Your Mama Don't Dance	Poison
Your Song	Elton John
Your Woman	White Town
Yummy Yummy Yummy	Ohio Express
Zabadak	Dave Dee, Dozy, Beaky, Mick & Tich
Zambesi	Lou Busch
Zambesi	Eddie Calvert
Zoom	Fat Larry's Band
Zorba's Dance	Marcello Minerbi